Sustainable Measures

Evaluation and Reporting of
Environmental and Social Performance

Edited by Martin Bennett and Peter James

with Leon Klinkers

Sustainable Measures

EVALUATION AND REPORTING OF ENVIRONMENTAL AND SOCIAL PERFORMANCE

EDITED BY
MARTIN BENNETT AND PETER JAMES
WITH LEON KLINKERS

Greenleaf **Publishing** 1999

For Rosalie, Lorna and Geoff

For Sue, Helen and Nicholas

© 1999 Greenleaf Publishing Limited unless otherwise stated.

Published by Greenleaf Publishing Limited
Aizlewood Business Centre
Aizlewood's Mill
Nursery Street
Sheffield S3 8GG
UK

Typeset by Greenleaf Publishing Limited and printed on environmentally friendly, acid-free paper from managed forests by Bookcraft, Midsomer Norton, UK.

British Library Cataloguing in Publication Data:
    Sustainable measures : evaluation and reporting of
    1. Environmental protection 2. Environmental policy 3. Social
    policy
    I. Bennett, Martin II. James, Peter, 1953– III. Klinkers, Leon
    333.7

ISBN 1874719160

Contents

Foreword

Klaus Töpfer, United Nations Environment Programme

WITH GLOBALISATION, trade liberalisation and the increasing role of the private sector in global governance, many stakeholders are demanding greater responsibility and accountability of the private sector, in particular multinational corporations. This call is coming from a variety of stakeholders—witness Kofi Anan's recent statement at the World Economic Forum in Davos: 'We need to initiate a global compact of shared values and principles, which will give a human face to the global market.' The private sector is thus increasingly being held accountable to manage its operations in a manner that will enhance economic development, ensure environmental protection, and promote social justice.

But will business and industry undertake the process of change and perform the task quickly enough and adequately? Can it be blindly trusted? Awareness has been growing everywhere about local and global environmental issues, child labour and corruption. 'Trust Me' does not work anymore, and society wants to know what is going on and wants to be sure that the proper choice is made.

How will the enterprise and its stakeholders—investors, customers, environmentalists, employees—know when a company is moving its policies, plans, products and processes in a direction that supports the three dimensions of sustainable development: economic, environmental and social? Public reporting is an increasingly important means to determine if and how a company is seriously engaged in the sustainability transition.

In 1993, the United Nations Environment Programme (UNEP) joined forces with SustainAbility Ltd and a number of other partners to develop the *Engaging Stakeholders* programme, and I am happy that this work has inspired the authors of *Sustainable Measures*.

Since this work on environmental reporting began, UNEP has produced three benchmark surveys which have shown a steady increase in the number of environmental reports: in particular those prepared by multinationals in the natural resources and manufacturing sectors. UNEP's work on voluntary initiatives in sectors such as mining, oil and gas, as well as the manufacturing and service sectors, in particular tourism, banking and insurance, has also encouraged the publication of environmental reports. We certainly hope that this trend will continue, and hope to see all industrial sectors and companies of all sizes reporting publicly on their environmental and social performance.

It is clear that more work is needed to respond fully to the questions raised by environmental, social and sustainability performance evaluation and reporting (ESSPER). Indicators need to be developed, similar to the CO_2 indicator to link corporate carbon dioxide emissions with national reduction targets under the Kyoto Protocol, which UNEP has developed with other partners. We are hopeful that the Global Reporting Initiative, which UNEP and many other stakeholders support, will help to overcome the lack of consistency and comparability in current reports. In addition, the verification of reports is also a key issue where UNEP intends to build further dialogue.

UNEP welcomes the publication of *Sustainable Measures*. It is an excellent overview of state-of-the-art developments in this field and should be of considerable use to organisations seeking to respond to increasing stakeholder pressures for greater transparency and comparability in the reporting of environmental and social performance.

Klaus Töpfer

Klaus Töpfer is United Nations Under-Secretary-General, Executive Director of the United Nations Environment Programme and Director-General of the United Nations Office at Nairobi. He was formerly German Federal Minister for the Environment, Nature Conservation and Nuclear Safety.

Foreword

Jonathan Lash, World Resources Institute

AMARTYA SEN, the Nobel Prize-winning economist, observed that 'One of the remarkable facts in the terrible history of famine is that no substantial famine has ever occurred in a country with a democratic form of government and a relatively free press.' When information is widely available and discussed, government policies and individuals' behaviours tend to be more realistic, and the problems that do occur are harder to ignore.

The same applies to the environment. The more that we develop, disseminate and discuss accurate, credible and understandable information about environmental and social conditions and institutional performance, the more likely we are to improve them. The World Resource Institute tries to support this by building bridges between ideas and action, meshing the insights of scientific research, economic and institutional analyses, and practical experience, with the need for open and participatory decision-making. One recent initiative we are especially proud of is Global Forest Watch, which uses real-time satellite data and a geographic information system to provide instant information on the state of forests around the world. At present, it shows that their extent and health continues to decline—but I am sure that access to this kind of data by governments, NGOs and others will result in greater action to reverse it.

The greater availability and use of information by NGOs and the media has already exposed and helped to correct environmental problems caused by individual companies, and has enabled consumers to choose to buy from companies with excellent performance. Indeed, disclosure of environmental information provides a complementary driver of improvement to traditional command-and-control legislation which some governments have added to their policy toolbox. But all of these uses are dependent on information that is available in a comparable transparent format. This is why the World Resources Institute supports initiatives such as the Global Reporting Initiative, which seeks to standardise measurement and reporting of the linked aspects of sustainability. Ultimately, it will be in the interests of firms and others alike to converge on a standardised framework, because without this there will be no consistent standards of accountability for business, or practical means for companies and others to gauge and communicate progress toward sustainability.

This very useful book collects ideas and examples from around the world: using the Internet to create a step change in the availability of environmental performance information; the potential for—and value of—greater standardisation of environmental indicators; the need to extend environmental performance measurement and reporting into the economic and social dimensions of sustainability; the importance of helping developing countries to implement their own approaches to the subject; and the need for constructive dialogue and partnership between business, NGOs, governments and others in taking the subject forward. It should add considerably to the understanding and further development of social and environmental performance evaluation and reporting.

Jonathan Lash

Jonathan Lash is President of the World Resources Institute, the Washington, DC-based environmental research and policy centre, and co-chairman of the President's Council on Sustainable Development.

Foreword

Lise Kingo, Novo Nordisk

NOVO NORDISK wants to achieve—and report—good performance in all areas of the 'triple bottom line' (economic, environmental and social). All our stakeholders—including financial—are pushing for more information on environmental and social issues, and our experience of environmental and bioethics programmes over the last decade has shown us that a triple-bottom-line approach is good for business. It helps to attract, retain and motivate the best employees and, by building trust with stakeholders, it gives us freedom to operate and innovate.

To be credible in this area, companies have to demonstrate that they are 'walking the talk'. Our first steps were taken in the environmental area, where we soon discovered the value of measuring performance and setting targets. Understanding energy and waste flows, for example, has allowed us to reduce significantly the amounts we use per unit of final product. We produced our first environmental report in 1993 and soon learned that good reporting is not telling people what you think they want to know but listening to what they want and then trying to provide it.

In recent years, this dialogue with stakeholders has shown us that we need an integrated approach to sustainable development, and to spend more time understanding and communicating about social issues such as community relations and human rights.

We have responded to this by trying to integrate triple-bottom-line practice and stakeholder orientation right into the heart of our business, and have developed a corporate balanced business scorecard of 16 measurement areas, which are a mix of traditional business focuses combined with much more values-oriented issues. Five of these—company reputation, triple-bottom-line activities, stakeholder relationships, attracting and retaining talented people, and dialogue between staff and management—are directly related to our environmental and social performance, and most of the others are indirectly affected.

Our next challenges are therefore to produce and implement some very concrete plans to embed the scorecard—and the activities that drive its measures—into the heart of the company and to produce a social, and perhaps eventually an integrated sustainability, report. I am therefore especially interested in the final section of this book, which addresses these issues. I am also pleased that it contains contributions from developing countries—whose needs are so often ignored—as well as a chapter from my native Denmark! I am sure that the wide spread of authors and subjects collected here will be essential reading for anyone interested in the past, present and future of environmental and social performance measurement and reporting.

Lise Kingo

Lise Kingo is Vice-President, Stakeholder Relations, at Novo Nordisk, a $2.8-billion-turnover Danish-based producer of pharmaceuticals and industrial enzymes. She and her team have been responsible for producing all the company's environmental reports, the 1995, 1996 and 1997 editions of which won the European Environmental Reporting Award for those years.

Foreword

María Emilia Correa, Colombian Business Council
for Sustainable Development (CECODES)

THE MISSION of the Colombian BCSD is to lead the way towards sustainable development in Colombia. It has an unusual importance as a message of hope and confidence in the future, in a country that is richer but perhaps has greater social problems than many developing countries. Fortunately, the leaders of organisations such as the Business Council are personally committed to improve conditions in Colombia, convinced that there can be no healthy business in a sick society.

Doing business in Colombia makes it essential to address the social as well as environmental dimensions of sustainable development. I am therefore pleased that this book covers both these topics, from the perspective of developing as well as developed countries. Its emphasis on the value of measurement and reporting also parallels our own experience.

The Colombian BCSD has encouraged a culture of measurement and transparency by developing a framework of sustainability indicators, which has been adopted by many of its members. We promote core indicators that:

- Are useful and relevant for companies to monitor their sustainable use of natural resources and their proper social and environmental management

- Allow for comparison over time and between very different firms;

- Report physical and financial figures in a standard way for very diverse companies

- Promote continuous improvement as a long-term deliberate process. Our system has allowed for the collection and processing of information since 1990, so that companies can evaluate trends over time rather than just compare results against the previous year.

- Can be published and are meaningful for external stakeholders.

CECODES's core indicators cover economic, social and eco-efficiency performance. We measure **economic** performance as the value added by each member company to the country's Gross Domestic Product. **Social** performance is measured by considerations such as company investment per employee above legal requirements for salaries and compensation, and the frequency and severity of job-related disabling illness. Our core indicators for **eco-efficiency** cover the use of water and energy per unit of product and per value added, the generation of waste per unit of product, and efficiency in the use of raw materials per unit of product.

One example of what can be achieved is Asocolflores, the Colombian Flower Growers' Association. Flowers account for more than 6% of Colombia's total exports, and Asocolflores members represent more than 80% of cultivated area in the country. They have been members of CECODES since 1994, and they are implementing an environmental management system called *Florverde* (Green Flower), which includes a registration system to evaluate the results of the member companies, with a great emphasis on the development of employees and neighbouring communities. After implementing and monitoring a pilot plan which covered around 56% of the total cultivated area, they have been able to show results on:

▼ Optimisation of watering systems

▼ Identification of energy losses and increased energy efficiency

▼ Optimisation of the use of soil and fertilisers

▼ Reduction in the use of agrochemicals, favouring biological and less toxic products

▼ Reduction of waste, improvement of disposal systems, and active research on sustainable disposal systems

▼ Reforestation with native species and planting of live fences to improve the landscape and promote biological control

▼ Increased labour stability, less absenteeism and rotation, higher investment in employees, and increased training programmes

Asocolflores now expects to extend this system to all its members, thus promoting responsible production as a source of competitive advantage for exporters in Colombia.

All efforts by the private sector to improve and innovate would clearly be encouraged by institutional frameworks that reward long-term responsible behaviour and establish a common ground for business. Our next steps in Colombia are therefore to consolidate our relationship with environmental authorities through joint efforts to improve information management systems and the implementation of an Environmental Leadership Programme.

Initiatives such as CECODES allow us to remember that there are many honest, hard-working people in Colombia, who still believe that we can lead our country along a better road. We are convinced that our commitment and our joint efforts with other social partners will help change course in Colombia. And, in making this journey, we will certainly be taking on board many of the ideas and lessons contained within this book.

María Emilia Correa

María Emilia Correa is Executive Director of the Colombian Business Council for Sustainable Development, CECODES. The Council was created in late 1993 and has a current membership of 35 large companies and two trade associations. Its members represent more than 4% of Colombia's Gross Domestic Product (GDP), are responsible for more than 450,000 direct and indirect jobs, and represent more than US$1.6 million/year in exports.

Introduction

Martin Bennett, Peter James and Leon Klinkers

THIS BOOK spans a number of interrelated topics. These include:

- **Performance evaluation:** the process of informing a company's managers and stakeholders on its performance by selecting indicators, collecting and analysing data, assessing information against performance criteria, reporting and communicating, and periodically reviewing and improving the process[1]

- **Environmental performance:** the results of the interaction of an organisation's activities, products or services with the natural environment (for example, emissions of carbon dioxide which create global warming).

- **Social performance:** the results of the interactions of an organisation's activities, products or services with the social environment (including social perceptions of environmental performance) and relevant stakeholders within it

- **Sustainability:** economic, environmental and social performance that is in conformance with the requirements of sustainable development

- **Disclosure:** release of information to external stakeholders

- **External reporting:** disclosure to external stakeholders in the form of an integrated report, typically covering the activities, products or services of an entire organisation or a division or site within it

---

[1] This definition is based on that for environmental performance evaluation by ISO (1998b). Strictly speaking, we would ourselves define environmental performance measurement as the sub-set of environmental performance evaluation that is concerned with collecting, analysing and disseminating data. However, although we have endeavoured to maintain this distinction in our own contributions to this book, we have not tried to impose it on other contributors, so the terms are used interchangeably in some chapters.

▼ **Accountability:** the ability of an organisation to provide an account of its activities, both as an explicit record of them and as an acceptance of responsibility for them[2]

As later chapters discuss, there is a rapidly developing body of experience and theory around each of these topics. This is due to growing public interest in, and concern over, levels of corporate environmental and social performance. The result is growing demands for better information, more action and greater transparency by business.

In the case of environment, these concerns are related to growing human impacts on the planet and its natural systems. It now appears, for example, that global warming is occurring as a result of past and current emissions of carbon dioxide and other greenhouse gases, with profound implications for economic, political and social life in the next millennium. As a result of these growing impacts, there are stronger and more extensive pressures on business to improve the environmental performance of its processes, products and services. Regulation is becoming more demanding, and more incentive-based measures, which reward good performance and penalise bad performance, are being introduced.

Another new weapon in the regulator's arsenal is compulsory disclosure of environmental information, in the hope that this will shame poor performers into taking greater action. This also provides useful raw material for environmental and other pressure group campaigns directed either at business in general or at specific sectors and companies. One example is the disclosure of specified environmental data, as with the Toxic Release Inventory (TRI) in the USA.

Good management of environmental issues by business is therefore vital. It enables companies to gain the advantages of good performance, avoid the disadvantages of bad performance and—for the minority who adopt such strategies—to take control of their destiny by adopting long-term strategic responses to environmental concerns. Environmental performance evaluation is an important aspect of all these responses. So, too, is environmental reporting, which can publicise achievements, put into context less positive aspects, and raise awareness among, and underpin a dialogue with, key stakeholders.

The same applies to social performance. The relentless globalisation of economic activity weakens the bonds between companies and local communities, and allows them to switch their activities quickly from one part of the world to another. This, and intense competition, makes employment less secure and society more suspicious of a company's actions and intentions. It also directs attention to labour conditions in developing countries, particularly the level of their wage rates and their use of child workers. These are of concern—for ethical reasons as well as pragmatic concerns about job preservation—to a growing number of Western activists and consumers, who have mounted successful campaigns against companies such as Nike to change their practices. Similar campaigns have been mounted against companies such as Shell for alleged neglect of local communities and violation of human rights in some of their developing-world activities.

---

2   This definition is that developed by the New Economics Foundation (Gonella *et al.* 1998).

Companies' activities in the marketplace are also under growing scrutiny. Ethical, human rights and other groups are keenly interested in any or all of a company's involvement in businesses such as pornography and weapons, its use of controversial technologies such as genetic modification, or its activities in countries that they consider have oppressive regimes. And consumer groups are increasingly interested in these issues as well as their more traditional concerns with the price, quality and similar attributes of goods and services.

NGOs and other stakeholders target companies on such issues, in part because of the absence of international governmental structures and the diminished power of national governments and/or their unwillingness to take action. As the imbalance between government and large multinationals is increasing rather than diminishing—as with the ongoing consolidation of the oil and vehicles industries into a few global corporations—this trend is likely to continue.

Dealing with these issues is also made more difficult by the increased extent and speed of information flows around the world. This results from cheaper and faster computers and telecommunications; the information structuring and accessibility created by the World Wide Web; and the increasing global reach of media and NGOs. All these combine to create a 'CNN world' in which anything that happens in remote parts of the planet can be known by billions the next day. Being credible in this challenging, information-rich, business environment requires more measurement of areas of concern—such as the use of child labour, and investment in local communities—and greater dialogue with stakeholders, through preparation of social reports and other means.

Until recently, environmental and social performance evaluation and reporting have usually been separate activities. Many now see these as two interconnected elements in the business response to the concept of sustainable development. This also brings a third element into the equation, which is the sustainability of a company's economic activities. This is difficult to assess, since sustainability is a system property rather than an attribute of an individual company. Nonetheless, there is growing attention being paid to the evaluation and reporting of sustainable economic performance by individual companies.

All of these issues are discussed in the next 550 or so pages. They bring together contributions from many of the leading scholars, consultants and practitioners in the field from both developed and developing countries. They also combine a variety of disciplinary and professional approaches, including financial accounting, management accounting, corporate governance, environmental management and social auditing.

Most chapters came in response to a call for papers in the journal *Greener Management International*, with additional papers invited from selected experts. They are loosely organised into three sections, although any grouping can be only approximate: many papers would easily fit into two or even all three sections. The overall range reflects the fact that most research and practice to date has focused on the topic of environmental performance evaluation (the theme of Section 1) and environmental reporting (the theme of Section 2). However, the chapters in Section 3 on social and sustainability measurement and reporting demonstrate that this imbalance is likely to be remedied in coming years as more companies gain experience.

The following section provides short summaries of each of these contributions, with a final section identifying some of the key themes and questions that emerge from them.

◢ The Chapters

The book begins with an overview of the current literature by Martin Bennett and Peter James, in Chapter 1. They first describe a number of different approaches, and then analyse the development of and key issues in the evaluation of environmental and social performance and sustainability. After a similar discussion of environmental, social and sustainability reporting, they consider generic issues such as verification, standardisation and implementation. A final section examines parallels between financial performance evaluation and reporting, and environmental, social and sustainability evaluation and reporting, and discusses some possible future developments in the field.

Chapter 2, also by Martin Bennett and Peter James, describes and critiques ISO 14031, the guidelines on environmental performance evaluation that are being developed by the International Organization for Standardisation (ISO). After outlining the main features, the authors appraise the strengths and weaknesses of the guidelines. They conclude that they represent a valuable contribution to progress in this area but neglect some important issues which should be addressed in future revisions. They position ISO 14031 as covering the first and second stages of a three-generation model of the development of environmental performance evaluation, but argue that more will need to be done to encompass the third stage, too. They also develop a 'diamond' model of the main types of measure that are required in such a third-generation approach. An appendix to the chapter provides examples of each of these types.

In Chapter 3, William Young and Richard Welford describe an environmental performance evaluation framework that has been developed in the UK. After testing, the framework comprises three main areas: environmental policy; environmental management systems; and processes, products and services. The pre-testing framework had also contained 'state-of the-environment' indicators that sought to assess the organisation's overall impact, but these were found to be too difficult to develop in practice. The authors then discuss the main categories of indicator within the framework, and also describe and classify the main environmental benchmarking initiatives that have been developed in recent years.

Chapter 4, by Allen White and Diana Zinkl, argues the case from a US perspective for greater standardisation of environmental performance indicators. They note the wide variety that are in use, the limited extent of standardisation to date, and the resulting difficulties in trying to make comparisons. They provide a practical illustration of this by comparing data from Dow's and Monsanto's environmental reports. The main part of the chapter then describes a survey of participants at two US industry-focused conferences on pollution prevention and environmental accounting. The respondents considered that the most important issues for EPIs were comparability over time and the use of verified data. Over half thought that more standardisation would be useful, although there was also considerable concern over possible requirements for reporting of standardised data on chemicals inputs and usage to complement current requirements for output data. The authors conclude that there is a strong case for standardisation and that the new Global Reporting Initiative (which they have been involved in developing) could provide a framework for this.[3]

In Chapter 5, Pall Rikhardsson focuses on the environmental information systems that underpin environmental performance evaluation. He identifies five key dimensions to be considered within such systems: production processes; the product or service; environmental management; environmental impact; and financial impact. A survey of information software used by companies for some or all of these areas identified eight main categories: mass-flow accounting software, life-cycle assessment software, environmental cost assessment software, modelling software, health and safety software, EMS-support software, knowledge databases, and integrated module software. He then provides a case study of development of an integrated information system at a large Danish company. This added environment onto existing financial reporting software, with the advantages that mass and financial inputs and outputs could be compared, and the budgetary component used to track performance against environmental as well as financial targets. The author concludes that such systems can be a valuable tool for environmental management and performance measurement but that they need to be shaped by clear objectives and sensible cost–benefit analysis. He includes a checklist to help organisations to analyse these questions.

Chapter 6, by Christine Jasch, gives the first of two perspectives on ecobalancing, which she defines as a detailed input–output analysis of energy, materials, water and other physical flows through a site or component of a site. She provides a detailed discussion of the application of ecobalancing to the brewing and wood products sectors, and companies within them, in Austria. One important theme is the difficulty of defining system boundaries and collecting all necessary data. However, the author concludes that the effort can be worthwhile and can create both environmental and financial benefit. She also notes that the approach is shedding some of its 'Germanic' cultural associations and—if seen as a type of environmental input–output analysis— is becoming a universally applicable tool that can underpin ISO and other management system and performance evaluation initiatives.

Chapter 7, by Rainer Rauberger and Bernd Wagner, focuses on the process of ecobalancing, using the example of the German textiles company, Kunert. This was the first company to produce an ecobalance and is still the company most closely associated with its use. The authors identify and discuss four main stages in ecobalancing: data collection, data analysis, setting priorities and improvement goals, and reviewing. They argue that the approach has achieved considerable financial benefit for Kunert, with an average €300,000 per annum in savings outweighing costs of €60,000–120,000 a year (with the level of costs falling as greater use has been made of computerised data collection), and also considerable reputational benefits. The authors conclude that the value of ecobalancing can lie as much in creating dialogue

---

3   Chapter 23 reproduces the draft Global Reporting Initiative.

and building a consensus about opportunities and actions within different functions of the company as in the actual generation of data, important as that is.

Chapter 8 provides an account of Indonesia's Programme for Pollution Control, Evaluation and Reporting (PROPER), by Shakeb Afsah and Damayanti Ratunanda. This brings together two important topics: eco-rating, and environmental performance evaluation in developing countries. PROPER rates the performance of facilities into five categories, primarily on the basis of water pollution. To enhance communication, these are colour-coded, with gold representing best practice and black, worst. The authors explain that the scheme was developed in order to compensate for a relatively weak regulatory system, and describe the various options that were considered in constructing the ratings. They then outline the operational details of the scheme and present evidence that it has been extremely successful in reducing levels of water pollution. Although, as they note, the economic crisis that has engulfed Indonesia in recent years has impeded further progress there, a number of other developing countries have been sufficiently impressed by the scheme to introduce similar models themselves.

One of these is India, and Chapter 9 by Vandana Bhatnagar describes the development there of an eco-rating scheme that has been influenced by PROPER. She notes that India has a considerable amount of legislation requiring evaluation and disclosure but that, as in Indonesia, implementation and enforcement is often weak. As a result, there is an information gap which is causing considerable frustration to the growing number of NGOs, communities and other stakeholders with environmental concerns. She suggests that conditions in India—and, by extension, probably in other developing countries too—require simple evaluation tools and describes one such tool, the facility eco-rating scheme developed by the Tata Energy Research Institute. This provides both generic and sector-specific templates, and uses both management and operational performance indicators to produce an overall rating. It has been adopted by a number of Indian cement companies and is now being extended to other sectors.

Chapter 10 provides a case study of the US electric utility, Niagara Mohawk, by a member of its management team, Joseph Miakisz. Niagara Mohawk established a reputation as one of the most innovative US companies in the field of environmental performance evaluation through the development of its environmental performance index. This aggregates 20 parameters, in three basic categories, into a single composite index. The company has not only tracked performance on both the overall index and its sub-categories since 1991, but has also created linkages between outcomes and its business and personal performance appraisal processes. Although the index was designed, and has mainly been used, for internal management purposes, it has also been utilised by the New York State Public Service Commission as an indicator to track the company's environmental performance. The author also describes Niagara Mohawk's subsequent development, in connection with Research Triangle Institute, of an annual environmental benchmarking programme of North American utilities. The programme involves standardised measurement of many of the parameters within the company's index, with results fed back to participating companies on an anonymised basis.

Chapter 11, by Willem van der Werf, also discusses the development of an aggregate environmental performance index, in this case by the Dutch food producer, Unox (a subsidiary of Unilever). This differs from the Niagara Mohawk index in being based on a 'distance-to-target' methodology. The targets in this case are those established for 2000 by the Dutch National Environmental Plan in the eight significant environmental theme areas that it identifies. The index is being used at both corporate and site level to monitor and to drive environmental improvement.

Chapter 12, by Martin Bennett and Peter James, provides a case study of environmental performance evaluation and reporting at the US healthcare products corporation, Baxter. The chapter begins by describing the context and evolution of Baxter's activities. These include the establishment of 'state-of-the-art' standards for environmental management as the basis for target-setting, the development of an 'environmental financial statement' to assess the costs and benefits of environmental actions, and the introduction of an Intranet-based environmental information system. The authors then summarise the different types of indicator being used within Baxter, paying particular attention to their use of relative indicators and methods of adjustment for acquisitions and disposals. They also describe the implementation of measures within the business, the processes of data collection, and the corporation's future plans. They conclude that Baxter's experience demonstrates the importance of effective processes, data integrity, and the relating of environmental activities to business objectives, and the complementarity of internal performance evaluation and external reporting.

Chapter 13, by Martin Bennett, Andrew Hughes and Peter James, provides worked examples of three environmental performance evaluation tools for products: eco-points, eco-compass and eco-costing. The tools are used to assess an existing product and its possible replacement by a manufacturer of telephone-based security alarms. The authors begin by identifying four reasons to use such tools: identifying areas for attention in the product design and development process; making choices between different products or different designs of the same product; ensuring that products meet specified criteria and/or create no great environmental problems; and communicating environmental effects to customers and other interested parties. They then describe the tools chosen (the Eco-Scan eco-points package, the Dow eco-compass, and a generic costing model) and assess their strengths and weaknesses in terms of six criteria: precision, reliability, comprehensiveness, comprehensibility, credibility and convenience. They conclude that each method has its own balance of strengths and weaknesses and that all can be valuable at different points in a structured product development process. An appendix outlines a 'meta-approach' to product environmental evaluation which can incorporate the three tools and also take into account other factors such as risk and social impacts.

Chapter 14, by Roger Adams, Martin Houldin and Saskia Slomp, summarises a report on standardisation of environmental reporting by the European Federation of Accountants' Environmental Task Force (of which all three were members). The authors first discuss the variety of reporting practice and the value of greater standardisation. They then identify two conceptual models of reporting: an accountability model ('what users should know about', even if they may not realise it at present) and a 'user needs' model ('what users want to know about'). They adopt the latter perspective and discuss the needs of seven user groups: investors, employees, lenders, suppliers and other trade creditors, customers, governments and their agencies, and the public. They then identify 'underlying assumptions' that should inform environmental reporting, and highlight the importance of six qualitative characteristics. These are relevance, reliability, comprehensibility, comparability, timeliness and verifiability. They conclude that there is an urgent need to improve the conceptual underpinning and thus the quality of environmental reporting.

Chapter 15, by John Elkington, Niklas Kreander and Helen Stibbard, summarises the results of a 1997 benchmarking exercise on environmental reports by the values consultancy, SustainAbility, and UNEP. This was the third such exercise, which examined 100 CERs. The reports were scored on 50 criteria, grouped into five main areas: management policy and systems; input–output inventory; finance; stakeholder relations and partnerships; and sustainable development. They were then classified into a five-stage typology, with only one company, The Body Shop, being classified as reaching the highest stage, of full sustainability reporting. The authors draw five main recommendations from their analysis. One is to account for the triple bottom line (i.e. the economic, environmental and social dimensions of sustainable development). A second is to spotlight the real issues, impacts and priorities rather than trying to conceal them. A third is to develop, report and verify SMART (specific, measurable, attainable, relevant and trackable) targets. A fourth is to focus on financial users, and finally to link CERs with annual financial reports.

In Chapter 16, Pall Rikhardsson examines the compulsory environmental reporting scheme that was introduced to Denmark in 1996. The scheme requires preparation of reports for all major sites at approximately 1,300 companies in designated sectors or using designated processes. The reports are required to contain three sections: company information, specified environmental data (on energy, materials and water consumption, and pollutants used in production and/or outputted in emissions, wastes or products) and a management report on the relevance and significance of the environmental data and year-on-year trends. There is no requirement that the accounts be verified, but they can be rejected as grossly misleading by the Danish Environmental Protection Agency. The author summarises both his own and other researchers' examination of the first three years of the scheme and concludes that, although it has greatly increased the availability of information, more needs to be done to achieve reliability and relevance to external stakeholders.

Chapter 17, by Jan Biekart and Karin Ree, provides an NGO perspective on environmental reporting in the Netherlands. They note that, as in other countries, Dutch reporting has been patchy to date but that new legislation will require around 330 of the largest companies in most economic sectors to report annually, beginning in 2000. The legislation is closely linked to the Dutch practice of covenants—binding targets between the government and industry-sector associations for long-term environmental improvement—that are at the heart of the country's ambitious environmental policies. Detailed environmental data is required to monitor implementation of these covenants. The legislation therefore requires two reports: the first, in a specified format, to the regulatory authorities, and the second to the general public. Biekart and Ree note that there are few specific requirements for the latter, and describe an initiative by Dutch industrial bodies and environmental NGOs to work together to develop agreed guidelines to amplify the basic requirements as defined in the legislation. These were published in 1998 and should influence the first round of compulsory reporting in 2000.

Chapter 18, by Takehiko Murayama, analyses environmental performance evaluation and reporting in Japan. He first describes several surveys on reporting that have been undertaken. His broad conclusion is that there is considerable activity but that, as in the West, this varies according to sector, size of company and other factors. He also reviews the position in the electrical appliance industry, which has been at the forefront, and notes that the environmental report and performance record of an industry leader such as NEC seems broadly similar to those of its Western counterparts. He then assesses two factors that could influence the Japanese situation: the adoption of ISO 14001 by many companies and the introduction of a Pollutant Release and Transfer Register. He concludes that the former will raise the general levels of environmental management and performance evaluation activity but is unlikely to stimulate greater reporting activity. And, although the impending Pollutant Release and Transfer Register has some positive features compared to European and US equivalents, it is unlikely to require mandatory reporting. Hence, the immediate future is one of incremental changes to the current position.

Chapter 19, by Charl de Villiers, examines the status of environmental reporting in South Africa. The challenge of reporting there is to communicate with both a social élite whose lifestyles and interests approximate to those of European and North American countries, and also a majority group that has more in common with developing countries. The author's conclusion is that reporting is developing to meet the needs of the first audience—albeit lagging that of more developed economies—but that there is little effective communication with the latter. He notes that this is typically justified on the grounds that the economic and social, rather than environmental, dimensions of sustainable development are of the greatest concern to this group. He concludes that stakeholder pressures will require more environmental performance measurement and disclosure in future.

Chapter 20, by Peter Hopkinson and Michael Whitaker, considers the relationship between real and reported environmental performance through a review of measurement and reporting experience in the UK water industry. This is unusual in being dominated by ten broadly comparable companies and—as a result of regulatory initiatives—in already producing a large amount of standardised data. The starting point of the authors' analysis is an assessment of the ten CERs against the SustainAbility/UNEP framework for benchmarking reports. They conclude that there are some weaknesses in the framework, and that there is no inevitable relationship between a good score for the quality of a report and the quality of the underlying environmental performance. To substantiate this, they examine the use of standardised performance data within the CERs of all companies in the industry, and examine in detail a particular company, Yorkshire Water, as a representative example. They find that much of the publicly available standardised data that was potentially also available for the CERs has not been included, even for topics that have been highlighted by regulators as especially important. They conclude that the availability of standardised data does not necessarily always result in its actual use in practice, and that the best means of achieving this may be the development of such indicators through a broadly based sectoral process involving the companies themselves (which is now occurring in the UK water industry).

Use of the Internet by companies as a medium for their reporting has expanded rapidly in the last two or three years and continues to be topical. Chapter 21, by Kathryn Jones and Julia Walton, examines this subject. They report that not only are more companies now making their reports available in this way as an additional channel to the traditional paper form, but also that a small but growing number now use this as their sole medium for reporting. The authors point out that such Internet reporting can not only make reports more easily available to a wider range of people but can also create opportunities to add new features that are impossible in paper format. This includes opportunities to search, to insert linkages to other internal or external documents and sites, to create interaction with users, to gather feedback, and to create environmental discussion forums. The chapter concludes by setting out a number of criteria for good design of reporting websites.

Chapter 22, by Riva Krut and Ken Munis, describes a report benchmarking scheme that is an alternative, or complementary, to that of SustainAbility and UNEP. This was developed for the US Environment Protection Agency and draws on the work of the US President's Council on Sustainable Development. They first identify four main areas of focus: environmentally sound products, processes and services; integration of sustainable development and economic growth; reducing risks and hazards to human health and the ecosystem; and community/stakeholder participation in sustainable development. They then evaluate the reports of 16 companies in the electronics and photographic sectors. They conclude that there are still many weaknesses in reports—notably with regard to the social dimensions of sustainable development—and call for greater standardisation.

Chapter 23 reproduces the draft Global Reporting Initiative guidelines on sustainability reporting which are being reviewed and piloted during 1999–2000. As one of the chapter's appendices demonstrates, the guidelines have been developed by an international process involving many stakeholders from business, NGOs and others. The preamble to the guidelines sets out its aims and discusses general reporting principles and specific issues to be considered. The guidelines themselves have nine sections: CEO statement; key indicators; profile of reporting entity; policies, organisation and management system; stakeholder relationships; management performance; operational performance; product performance; sustainability overview. An appendix provides additional information on many of these points.

Chapter 24, by Janet Ranganathan, provides an overview of the current status of sustainability evaluation and reporting, with its three elements of economic, environmental and social performance evaluation and reporting. She believes that the key tasks of environmental performance evaluation are to achieve comparability, completeness and credibility. Underpinning all of these is the need for greater standardisation of measures. Based on an earlier World Resources Institute study, she argues that these should be materials use, energy consumption, non-product output and pollutant releases. In contrast, the author believes that the development of standardised social performance measures is at least a decade behind that of environmental performance. Nonetheless, she considers that standardisation will eventually be achieved, especially on core issues such as employment rights, community relations, ethical sourcing and social impacts of products. She also concludes that the Global Reporting Initiative (which she was involved in developing) will provide a considerable impetus to further standardisation. The chapter ends with an appendix summarising a number of current leading initiatives.

Chapter 25, by John Elkington and Franceska van Dijk, summarises the current status of social reporting. They note the burgeoning interest in the topic and a shift in its centre of gravity from 'values-led' organisations such as The Body Shop and Traidcraft to large multinationals such as BP, Novo Nordisk and Shell. The reasons for this (which are not mutually exclusive) include a desire to explain and/or ameliorate controversial issues (as with Shell and the Brent Spar and Nigerian human rights controversies), to establish a dialogue with stakeholders, and to report on all the dimensions of sustainable development. They also note four areas of diversity within the field. One is between companies who treat the issues as a philanthropic 'add-on' to their normal activities, and those who see it as a key strategic issue. A second is between a focus on internal ethics and values, and a broader approach that focuses on stakeholder dialogue. A third is whether the appropriate model is one in which (as in conventional accounting) the company is the main focus, or a more externally focused framework that is concerned with listening and responding to the 'voices' of stakeholders. A fourth is whether or not reports are verified externally and independently. The authors conclude with six recommendations for organisations interested in social reporting: build the business case; spotlight financial risks and opportunities; understand the changing role of government; focus on benchmarkability; don't fall into the global–local divide (but cover both); and fasten your safety belt for a challenging ride! An appendix examines the needs of five core stakeholder groups—employees, communities, suppliers, clients/customers and investors—and provides examples of how these are met at present.

Chapter 26, by Andrew Wilson, also considers social reporting. The first section develops a classification of four different approaches, based on their degree of comprehensiveness and whether they are internally or externally focused. The following sections then provide a detailed examination of three of the earliest and best-known social reports—by Ben & Jerry's, The Body Shop and the Co-operative (a UK retailer)—and demonstrate that there are considerable differences between them. The author concludes that there are three levels to social performance measurement and reporting: the first being concerned with performance against stated objectives, the second with dialogue with stakeholders, and the third with actual social impacts. He also provides a checklist for effective social reporting.

Chapter 27, by Maria Sillanpää, also examines The Body Shop (where she previously worked), but with a focus on its internal processes for social accounting. She begins by identifying different approaches to ecological and social issues and stresses the need for a holistic approach. She then outlines three principles that underlie The Body Shop's activities: compliance; accountability and transparency;

and active engagement and dialogue. She then outlines the development and main processes of social auditing within the company, including the agreement of key performance indicators and important external stakeholders. The final sections consider the future of social auditing and provide conclusions.

◢ Key Issues

As these summaries indicate, there are a number of underlying themes in environmental and social performance evaluation and reporting. These include:

- How can different aspects of environmental and social performance be compared?
- What limits (if any) should there be on the disclosure of environmental and social performance data?
- Do the benefits of environmental, social and/or sustainability reporting outweigh its costs?
- Should environmental reporting (and, perhaps in due course, social reporting also) be made mandatory?
- What kinds of system are required to collect environmental and social performance data?
- How useful is it to measure stakeholder and other perceptions of environmental and social performance?
- Is it desirable and/or feasible to measure the ultimate impacts of a company on the environment and/or to assess whether these are sustainable? If not, how can these be approximated?
- Is it desirable and/or feasible to measure the life-cycle impacts of products and services and, if not, how can these be approximated?
- What is the relationship between environmental and social performance and financial performance and how can this be measured?
- Are their trade-offs between environmental, health and safety and social performance?
- Should different standards be applied when evaluating environmental and social performance in developed and/or developing countries?
- Is more standardisation desirable and/or feasible?
- How significant are international differences in approaches, and will these widen or narrow in future?
- How does sustainability measurement and reporting differ from that of environmental and/or social measurement and reporting?

The following chapter surveys the literature on these and other topics, and considers what actions companies are already adopting—and need to adopt in future—in order to be taking truly sustainable measures.

Key Themes in Environmental, Social and Sustainability Performance Evaluation and Reporting

Martin Bennett and Peter James

ENVIRONMENTAL, social and sustainability performance evaluation and reporting (ESSPER) is an exciting topic. Only a minority of companies are doing it to any substantial degree, but practitioners in those that are can enjoy the satisfaction of helping their companies to adapt to new ways of doing business that help them to prosper while also contributing to the general good. Through this, they are making things happen that have previously only been dreamed of by academics and theorists. At the beginning of the decade, few would have imagined that large companies, to take just a few of the examples discussed in this book, would be:

- Implementing balanced performance scorecards with a substantial sustainability component

- Experimenting with ways of valuing natural and social capital

- Using their own reports and websites to publicise the views of their critics

The speed of change is such that it is difficult to keep track of everything that is happening, let alone to develop a coherent intellectual analysis of the field. Fortunately, however, it is relatively straightforward—if slightly simplistic—to group much of the writing on the topic into six bodies of work, which are summarised in Section 1. The next three sections then discuss, in turn, environmental, social and sustainability performance evaluation. Section 5 considers developments and issues in reporting, Section 6 the topics of comparability, standardisation and benchmarking; Section 7 analyses issues of implementation and Section 8 examines links between environmental, social and sustainability performance and financial performance. A concluding section provides some thoughts on the current situation and future directions of development.

1. *Approaches*

It is always difficult—and, to those being classified, sometimes irritating—to group the work of different individuals into a limited number of categories. In addition, of course, there are always individuals who defy classification. However, the volume of writing on the topic makes this essential. We distinguish five reasonably cohesive bodies of work that address ESSPER in an integrated way. (There is of course, a considerable practitioner and academic literature on discrete areas such as environmental performance evaluation.) They are:

- Accountability/social responsibility

- Business viability

- Management accounting/performance measurement

- Organisational change

- Contrarian

Each of these has different strands within it, usually including a mainstream and a radical variant.

◁ *Accountability/Social Responsibility*

The central argument of this body of work is that environmental and social challenges can be met only by creating a better-informed and more empowered civil society. This requires a broadening of the scope of accountability from its traditional—and legally defined—focus on financial stakeholders to an accountability to external stakeholders generally and society as a whole. Until recently, much of the work within this school was undertaken from an accounting perspective (Freedman 1993; Gray *et al.* 1993; Gray *et al.* 1996). Its advocates have pointed out that accountants and the accounting profession have much to contribute in this respect. Their experience is, or could be, valuable in the generation, collection and analysis of data on resources consumed and other aspects of performance, much of which will already be held within accounting records and systems (ICAA 1998). They also have expertise in verification of data collection and analysis methods and in reporting and communication of quantitative data.

These arguments have helped to create several initiatives by professional accounting bodies. These include reporting award schemes (see below), research on the topic (for example, Bennett and James 1998a; CICA 1993; Gonella *et al.* 1998), and developing guidance for their members. Chapter 14 by Adams *et al.* provides a summary of one such initiative, the Discussion Paper published by the European Federation of Accountants (FEE), which proposes a conceptual framework for environmental reporting.

In recent years, another strand—of social and ethical auditing—has become more prominent within the accountability school. This has stressed the qualitative, process, dimension of accountability as a continuous dialogue between an organisation and its stakeholders (Gonella *et al.* 1998). Conversely, there has also been a concern over an excessive emphasis on measurement and verification in other approaches, especially as these have become operationalised through mainstream accountancy and consultancy firms (Power 1997).

◻ *Business Viability*

The ultimate purpose of this body of work is to support the traditional 'customers' of shareholders and lenders through better information and more effective corporate decision-making. However, much of the analysis overlaps with the accountability school by arguing that good linkages with social stakeholders are important elements in business viability (Plender 1997).

One area of focus has been highlighting the financial risks associated with poor environmental and social performance. These risks—for example, liabilities associated with a need to clean up contaminated land—can be considerable, especially in the USA. There have been several reports on this by financial regulators such as the Securities and Exchange Commission, and the accountancy profession, on both sides of the Atlantic (FEE 1996) (although an argument has been made that the standards themselves are adequate provided that they are properly followed and enforced [ICAEW 1996]).

In recent years, environmental and social issues have also featured in the debate on reform of financial reporting (Centre for Tomorrow's Company 1998; ICAEW 1998). One reason for this suggestion is that they constitute an important aspect of the 'forward-looking information' of relevance to long-term shareholder value which regulatory authorities are seeking to encourage (FASB 1998).

A third, closely related, strand is that of corporate governance (Charkham 1994). There has been a long tradition of interest in worker representation, especially the German supervisory board model. This has translated into considerable activity on employee indicators and, in many cases, reports. More recently, several studies have suggested that successful business is increasingly about managing external relationships—primarily within the supply chain but also including other stakeholders (for example, RSA 1996). However, they have argued that the senior leadership of many companies is too narrow in its background and concerns to be successful in this. They believe that boards, and other leadership structures, require greater representation of, and should be more able to maintain a dialogue with, the needs of external stakeholders—including environmental and social ones. This requires more emphasis on the measurement and reporting of the information in which they are interested.

◻ *Management Accounting/Performance Measurement*

This approach builds on the generic work of individuals such as Eccles (1991), Geanuracos (1997), Kaplan and Norton (1996a, 1996b), Johnson and Kaplan (1987) and Neely (1999). They have argued that business needs to pay greater attention to measuring and improving its non-financial performance if it is to meet its long-term financial objectives.

One theme in this school has been the generation and use of data to support internal environmental decision-making (Bartolomeo *et al.* 1999). Although not opposed to external reporting, much of the work notes the findings of conventional management accounting research that external reporting can compromise the collection and use of data for internal decision-making (Eccles 1991; Johnson and Kaplan, 1987; Kaplan and Norton 1996a). A second theme has been the need for ESSPER to focus within a 'balanced scorecard' of key performance measures (Kaplan and Norton 1996b). Bennett and James (1998a) have also pointed out some of the potential disadvantages of total disclosure and questioned whether financial accounting models for data disclosure through annual reporting are entirely appropriate when applied to environmental management. A more business-oriented approach might be based on detailed materials and waste accounting, which draws on traditional management accounting skills (Birkin and Woodward 1997). A related theme within this is an interest in developing a better understanding of environment-related (and, in principle, social-related) financial costs and benefits. Much work on this topic has been done by the US Environmental Protection Agency and others (Bennett and James 1998b).

◻ **Organisational Values**

This body of work stresses the importance of organisational values in driving environmental and social performance.

One strand is that of total quality management (TQM). This began as a means of achieving continuous improvement by, in part, generating quantitative data on product defects and their causes, and is often operationalised in conservative and incremental ways. However, it is in essence a philosophy of management that stresses the importance of motivating employees through a sense of higher purpose, which is helping society by providing customers with better goods and services (Binney and Williams 1992; Grant *et al.* 1994). This is partially achieved through greater attention to, and measurement of, non-financial factors. Environmental and social performance have been explicitly linked to quality by the European Foundation for Quality Management (EFQM). This has developed a quality template against which companies can be assessed with the highest-scoring company each year winning the European Quality Award (EQA). The template contains a section on 'Impact on Society', dealing with environmental and social performance, which accounts for 6% of overall marks. A later section provides discusses the detailed implications of TQM for environmental performance measurement and reporting.

Another body of work on business ethics also argues that organisational values are the drivers of behaviour, including environmental and social behaviour (Newall 1996). Advocates of this view, such as Sheila Carmichael, argue that, if internal ethics are right, then appropriate performance and reporting will follow (SustainAbility/ UNEP 1999a).

◻ **Contrarian**

This body of work challenges many of the assumptions that have been made about ESSPER. Its advocates believe that a company's primary duty is to its shareholders and that, beyond compliance with the law, demands for corporate responsibility are asking them to do what they cannot and/or should not (Barry 1998; Friedman 1962; Rappaport 1998). Distracting from this duty serves only to create economic inefficiency. As wealth—and the new technologies it creates and investment it allows in innovation—is the ultimate solution to environmental and social problems, the end-result is to impede these solutions and thereby actually worsen rather than improve environmental and social conditions (Simon 1996, 1997).

A second argument is that much environmental data—and inferences drawn from it—are inaccurate and that many environmental problems are less serious than tends to be suggested by some environmentalists (Eberstadt 1996; Morris 1998; Simon 1997). Some also argue that the general public is less concerned about business environmental practices than environmentalists suggest—with a lack of public interest in environmental reports being cited as evidence (see below).

A third strand is that the environmental movement has no interest in changing this situation because its aims are political rather than environmental. Environmental problems are essentially a big stick with which to beat business and forward a political—many in this camp would say socialist—agenda. The composite result of these arguments is that companies should stop seeking dialogue with such groups—and certainly feel no imperative to prepare reports for them—and focus instead on environmental activities that are necessary to comply with (sensible) regulations and customer requirements.

◻ The Relationship between Environmental and Social Issues, and Performance Evaluation and Reporting

As the preceding discussion demonstrates, one area of debate is over the:

▼ Distinctiveness of environmental issues *vis-à-vis* social and/or economic ones

▼ Extent to which performance evaluation should be focused on internal management needs, as distinct from reporting to an external audience

There are two main arguments for not separating the environmental from the social, but instead trying to deal with them in an integrated fashion:

▼ That—together with the third area, economic development—they form closely interlinked components of a broader whole, which is sustainable development. The interlinkages are such that it could be distorting and misleading to analyse them separately.

▼ Sceptics argue that a cynical business might perceive that it has an interest in such a separation. It could make it easier to focus the company's efforts on the less threatening topic of environmental performance evaluation and reporting, and to marginalise the more contentious issues involved in social performance evaluation and reporting. Environment is said to be more acceptable because it can presented as an operational business issue which can be addressed by conventional managerial and technological approaches. Social issues, on the other hand, are said to be more challenging because they raise fundamental questions about business purpose and activities, particularly the question of the extent to which a business has moral obligations beyond maximising its value and profitability for the sole benefit of shareholders.

The arguments for keeping the areas separate for the purposes of both intellectual analysis and, in some cases, practical action, are:

▼ There are qualitative differences in the kind of information handled in the two areas. Environmental information potentially has a more fixed, scientifically based and universal quality than social information (which is not to say, of course, that environmental information cannot be subjective in its development and interpretation).

▼ In organisational terms, the areas have to be separated at some point in the chain of action (e.g. plant maintenance is always likely to be heavily environmentally focused, with much less scope to influence social parameters). The question of where integration is appropriate therefore becomes a decision variable, rather than an end in itself. Most organisations appear to be concluding that this is at the level of corporate or divisional units that co-ordinate or influence the work of more focused units or individuals, rather than at lower levels in the organisation.

▼ Pragmatically, the two areas have had different histories (which continue to influence their practice and development) and continue to have substantially separate communities of practitioners and, to a lesser degree, academics. Although this may change in future, at present communication and discussion is likely to be more effective if it respects these distinctions.

Much of the literature on performance evaluation and reporting assumes, either explicitly or implicitly, that these are tightly integrated activities. The Institute of Social and Ethical Accountability (ISEA), for example, has coined the term 'social and ethical accounting, auditing and reporting' (SEAAR) to describe a fairly seamless integration of performance evaluation and reporting. In the environmental area, the well-known discussions of environmental reporting by the SustainAbility/UNEP research partnership (see below) take a similar perspective.

The arguments for such integration are:

▼ Performance evaluation is not an end in itself: it is concerned with providing relevant and useful information to stakeholders. In the case of environmental and social issues, these stakeholders are external to the company so that there should be complete transparency between what is measured and what is reported.

▼ Some would see the central issue of social performance evaluation as being the content and process of interactions with external stakeholders.

▼ Companies have a bias towards concealing potentially embarrassing infor-mation—another reason for complete transparency between what is measured and what is reported.

▼ Pragmatically, much performance measurement in companies has been driven by initial commitments to report and the subsequent pressure that this has then created to maintain the standard of reports. Hence, there is an integral operational relationship between them.

The arguments against this are:

▼ As noted above, business performance evaluation is often explicitly posi-tioned as a management accounting activity, which is defined as distinct from financial accounting since it is seen as having different purposes and practices.

▼ Companies have legitimate reasons—for example, commercial sensitivity or a desire to put their own house in order before 'washing dirty linen' in public—to avoid disclosure of some environmental and social information, and therefore to maintain a distinction between their performance evalua-tion and reporting activities.

▼ Quite apart from any consideration of legitimacy, many companies do in fact undertake considerable environmental and social performance measure-ment without reporting on it: Chapter 18 by Murayama suggests that this is true of many companies in Japan, for example.

▼ As with performance evaluation reporting is not an end in itself but a means to an end—that of informing stakeholders about company activities. As discussed below, it may be that the conventional model of reporting (a single corporate environmental report produced annually) is fragmenting into a wider variety of forms of disclosure, which will bear different relationships with underlying performance evaluation activities (e.g. the fundamental difference in type between real-time data made available through the Web, as compared to periodic product stewardship reports). A clear intellectual distinction between the two entities is therefore required in order to understand this relationship.

On balance, we find the arguments for separating these topics more compelling at present, and therefore do so in the following pages.

2. Environmental Performance Evaluation

Environmental performance evaluation has had a longer history, and been subject to more discussion and research, than has social and sustainability performance evaluation. The first sub-section describes its evolution and subsequent sub-sections discuss environmental performance indicators and frameworks and some issues in using and selecting indicators.

⌂ *Evolution*

The history of environmental performance evaluation is one of great diversity, with many different strands developing in isolation from each other and only now becoming fully integrated. These strands include:

- Energy and materials accounting
- Health and safety measurement and management
- Environmental impact assessment
- Product evaluation
- Externality assessment
- Environmental auditing
- Measurement and reporting of toxic emissions
- Incentive-based regulation
- Total quality management
- External rating
- Strategic integration

The following sub-sections discuss each of these in turn.

Energy and materials accounting. Engineers and managers have always sought more efficient usage of energy and materials for obvious conventional business reasons. A key step forward occurred in the middle years of the century with the introduction of 'mass balances' (detailed input–output inventories) in the chemicals, nuclear and other industries. However, these usually focused on only the most economically important materials, and ignored trace substances that were unimportant in economic terms but could have potentially significant environmental effects. This was the focus of the ecobalancing that developed during the 1980s. As Chapter 6 by Jasch and Chapter 7 by Rauberger and Wagner describe, this aims to map all flows of energy and physical substances both into and out of an entity (typically a facility or a sub-process within it). This began as, and largely remains, a technique used in German-speaking countries but, as Jasch discusses in Chapter 6, may now be spreading elsewhere.

Health and safety measurement and management. Many see this as an important aspect of ESSPER in its own right. It is also relevant, as Bennett and James describe in Chapter 12 on Baxter International, because it can be a useful source of new ideas. This is particularly true, of course, when it is integrated into a common EHS function.

The basis of health and safety legislation is the recording of incidents and their notification to relevant authorities, and the requirements for this have considerably increased in most developing countries in recent decades. The costs and adverse publicity attached to industrial accidents have also created increased internal pressures for better health and safety management and measurement. For example, a series of well-publicised accidents in the inter-war years led the US chemicals company DuPont to start an initiative in the field which developed considerably in post-war decades. One result of the early development of both statutory requirements and corporate programmes has been standardisation of measures, particularly with regard to reportable injuries and deaths and the 'lost time' that they create.

Environmental impact assessment. Environmental impact assessment is concerned with mapping the total impact of defined business activities. The approach developed in the 1960s as a means of assessing the overall costs and benefits of individual industrial projects such as nuclear power stations. Since then, the technique has been developed in two different directions. The first is environmental 'footprinting', which attempts to map the aggregate impacts of a variety of economic activities ranging from those arising from prawn production to those involved in running major cities. In the second, it has developed into the mapping of product chains through life-cycle assessment techniques (see below). All these initiatives tend to be 'one-off' activities that can do much to raise awareness but can be difficult to routinise within day-to-day performance evaluation and reporting activities.

Product evaluation. There is a growing need for the environmental evaluation of products (Wenzel *et al.* 1997). The starting point for most approaches is life-cycle assessment (LCA), which aims to map the environmental footprint of a product from its 'cradle' (the original production, or extraction through mining, of its raw materials) to its 'grave' (final disposal). The first LCAs were undertaken in the 1960s in the energy sector, and since then there has been a growing use and a number of initiatives for standardisation. The latest comes from the International Organization for Standardisation, which is developing five guidelines on different aspects (ISO 14040, 14041, 14042, 14043 and 14048).

LCAs have provoked considerable controversy because of the assumptions that need to be made on, for example, how product life-cycles should be bounded; how environmental overheads should be allocated between products; and how contentious issues (such as the merits and demerits of chlorine-based chemicals) should be handled (Gameson 1998). This controversy has been exacerbated by the partisan use that has sometimes been made of them (for example, by a company that is defensive about one of its products and seeks to use a LCA to justify it). These uses have often led to competing LCAs drawing completely different conclusions on the environmental impacts of the same types of product, undermining their credibility.

LCA has proved less controversial when used as a tool to aid 'eco-design' by highlighting the significant environmental impacts over the entire life-cycle of a product. However, it is both complex and time-consuming, and this has led to the development of more simplified product evaluation tools (Gameson 1998; Simon *et al.* 1998). Chapter 13 by Bennett *et al.* describes and assesses two of the most common of these: eco-compass and eco-point techniques.

A related area of work has been the evaluation of products for the purposes of eco-labelling. There are now a number of national schemes, a European Union scheme and several ISO draft guidelines (ISO 14021, 14024 and 14025). Although the end-result of an eco-labelling exercise is usually a simple 'pass-or-fail' evaluation, they typically require measurement of several individual parameters. For example, Volvo's environmental product declaration for its S80 2.9 model—which conformed to the requirements of the draft ISO 14025—involved assessing 12 indicators in four categories: environmental management, manufacturing, vehicle operations and recycling (Birchard 1999).

Externality assessment. Where the activities of companies have effects on the wider environment and society for which they are not themselves financially responsible, a range of techniques is available to assign a monetary value to them. These include the costs of restoring environmental damage and imputed prices for use of unpriced natural resources. Using such techniques, Costanza *et al.* (1997) calculated an aggregate figure of $33 trillion per year as the total value of ecosystem services used by business.

One company that has used such an approach is the Swedish power utility Sydkraft. It has also calculated its environmental debt, which it defines as 'the costs of restoration of the environmental damages that are caused by the company's activities, and that are technically restorable, as well as the capital required for recurring the restoration measures and the compensation that has to be paid to other parties' (Görtz 1998). It found that this totalled 1,041 million Swedish kröner in 1997, half of which was attributable to carbon dioxide emissions. This constituted about 2% of its total assets.

The Dutch computer services company BSO/Origin (now part of Philips) also calculated the environmental costs of its emissions during the early 1990s, based on Dutch national figures.

However, as Bennett *et al.* note in Chapter 13, all such estimates are inevitably approximate and dependent on some degree of subjective judgement, and are therefore often controversial.

Environmental auditing. Environmental auditing developed in the US during the 1970s as a means of ensuring compliance with corporate policies and regulations (Friedman 1992). It was therefore concerned with assessing and encouraging environmental performance measurement, and has also been a source of measures in its own right (for example, the number of facilities audited, or number of audit recommendations still outstanding). It continues to be a key element in implementing environmental performance evaluation.

Measurement and reporting of toxic emissions. A major influence on environmental performance evaluation has been the US Toxic Release Inventory (TRI) legislation, which requires public reporting of emissions of specified toxic chemicals to air, land and water from large industrial sites. This has not only given US companies a useful means of measuring environmental progress—year-by-year reduction in TRI emissions—but has also facilitated at least limited comparisons between sites and companies (ENDS 1993, 1997c). As discussed below, it was also perhaps the main spur to the development of environmental reporting. In recent years, the TRI has formed the basis for development of a North American Pollutant Release Inventory which will standardise practices in Canada, Mexico and the USA. Similar schemes have been developed in Europe—although without having quite the impact of TRI—and, as Murayama describes in Chapter 18, in Japan.

Incentive-based regulation. Several countries, notably the USA, moved towards 'incentive-based' regulatory systems during the 1990s. One aspect of this is voluntary programmes to reduce energy consumption and specified emissions (with the incentive being public recognition, as well as potential cost savings). Another is government policy to create 'tradable pollution rights' so that companies that reduce their emissions by more than a specified amount can sell the rights to others, allowing the latter to exceed their own quota. This system has now been extended to the international stage, through the emissions trading element of the Kyoto Protocol on greenhouse gas emissions. In late 1998, for example, Suncor Energy of Canada purchased the rights to 100,000 tonnes of carbon dioxide emissions from Niagara Mohawk (Griss 1999). Schemes such as these clearly depend on considerable care and accuracy in the measurement of emissions and related parameters.

Total quality management. The *quality* approach to environment—sometimes termed 'total quality environmental management' (TQEM)—stresses that environmental actions are taken for the benefit of 'customers' and seeks to achieve a continuous improvement in performance (James 1994b; President's Commission on Environmental Quality 1993). The customers are both external (paying customers, regulators, the environmental movement, the neighbourhood or the ecosystem) and internal (line managers as customers of environmental specialists). Measuring their satisfaction is an important part of a TQM approach and some companies have sought to do this with environmental and social stakeholders.

Another important theme within TQM is the 'cost of quality', that is, the total costs of actions taken to ensure product quality and to deal with any failures to achieve it. TQM holds that, in most instances, the costs of prevention are likely to be far lower in the long term than costs incurred at later stages in the process. The parallel in an environmental context would be between pollution prevention at source through clean technology and/or product design, rather than leaving it to 'end-of-pipe' technology to deal with emissions, effluents and wastes only after they have been generated.

Chapter 12 by Bennett and James provides further details of TQEM initiatives at one company, Baxter.

External rating. This involves an aggregate rating of companies by some external body, based on a number of different parameters (Skillius and Wennberg 1998). It has become increasingly important at both corporate and site level and is undertaken for two main purposes. The first is to provide public information about good and poor performers. The second is to provide information to insurers, investors, lenders and other financial stakeholders that will help them to assess environment-related financial risks.

One group aiming to provide public information is NGOs, as with Canada's EthicsWatch or the US Council of Economic Priorities scheme for rating companies

(Gonella *et al.* 1998). Another is business associations such as the UK's Business in the Environment (1998), which rates the environmental management activities of the top 100 UK-based companies. Several business publications and business research bodies also produce ratings, such as that of *Fortune 500* companies by *Fortune* magazine (Rice 1993) and regular ratings of Japanese companies by the Nikkei Research Institute.

All the previous activities are undertaken at company level, but several developing countries are developing site-based rating schemes. Chapter 8 by Afsah and Ratunanda and Chapter 9 by Bhatnagar provide more details of such schemes in Indonesia and India.

Rating schemes for financial stakeholders are more focused on business risks and are less likely to be published. One exception—as described by Bennett and James in the appendix to Chapter 2—is the Moody's-style scheme developed by the Centre for the Study of Financial Innovation and applied to the UK power companies, Eastern Electricity and Scottish Nuclear. The level of knowledge about, and interest in, such schemes is likely to rise considerably when leading stock market index companies such as Dow Jones develop 'sustainability indexes' that include only companies deemed to be taking sufficient action to be sustainable.

Strategic integration. During the 1990s, these strands have increasingly been drawn together into an integrated approach to the topic (e.g. Bennett and James 1998a; Epstein 1996; European Green Table 1997; IIIEE and VTT 1997; Schaltegger *et al.* 1997; Skillius and Wennberg 1998; Tulenheimo *et al.* 1996; Tyteca 1996; Young 1996). The next sub-section discusses some of the key points that have emerged from this literature.

◻ *Environmental Indicators*

The Global Reporting Initiative guidelines on sustainability reporting (reproduced in Chapter 23) distinguish a hierarchy of environmental and social performance information:

- ▼ **Category:** general class or grouping of issues of concern to stakeholders (e.g. air, energy, labour practices, local economic impacts)

- ▼ **Aspect:** specific issue about which information is to be reported (e.g. smog precursors, corporate giving to local communities)

- ▼ **Indicator:** the most precise (and usually quantitative) measures of performance during a report period (e.g. metric tons of emissions, monetary contributions per year to local communities)

An important element in performance evaluation—required, for example, in the ISO 14001 standard for environmental management systems—is establishing the most significant categories and aspects for an organisation. Evaluation of these will often require clusters of indicators addressing different elements within them (Skillius and Wennberg 1998; WICE 1994).

An OECD report has elaborated on the nature of environmental (and, by extension, social) performance indicators by stating that:

In a very general way, an indicator can be defined as a parameter or a value derived from parameters which provides information about a phenomenon. The indicator has significance that extends beyond the properties directly associated with the parameter value. Indicators possess a synthetic meaning and are developed for a specific purpose. This points to two major functions of indicators:

1) they reduce the number of measurements and parameters which normally would be required to give an 'exact' presentation of a situation. As a consequence, the size of a set of indicators and the amount of detail contained in the set need to be limited. A set with a large number of indicators will tend to clutter the overview it is meant to provide. Too few or even a single indicator, on the other hand, may be insufficient to provide all the necessary relevant information. In addition, methodological problems related to weighting tend to become greater with an increasing level of aggregation;

2) they simplify the communication process by which the results of measurement are provided to the user. Due to this simplification and adaptation to user needs, indicators may not always meet strict scientific demands to demonstrate causal chains. Indicators should therefore be regarded as an expression of 'the best knowledge available' . . .

There are several frameworks around which indicators can be developed and organised. There is no unique framework that generates sets of indicators for every purpose. Also, a framework may change over time as scientific understanding of environmental problems increases, and as societal values evolve (OECD 1993: 5).

One important issue, as Jasch discusses in Chapter 6, is the bounding of the areas to be covered by indicators—for example, facilities, processes within them or an entire organisation. Generally speaking, as Rauberger and Wagner note in Chapter 7, the narrower the boundaries, the more reliable the indicator is likely to be.

◻ *Environmental Performance Frameworks and ISO 14031*

There has been a number of attempts to develop generic categories of environmental performance indicators (for example, Bragg *et al.* 1993; Business in the Environment 1992; European Green Table 1997). Young and Welford, in Chapter 3, describe the next step of testing one such framework in practice. Their model is partly based on that of Azzone and Manzini (1994), and partly on ISO 14031, a guidance document on environmental performance evaluation (ISO 1998b; Kuhre 1998) which is likely to become the standard framework in future.

The central feature of ISO 14031 is a definition and detailed discussion of three basic types of indicator that can be used for environmental management. It firstly distinguishes between 'environmental condition indicators' (ECIs) and 'environmental performance indicators' (EPIs), and then subdivides the latter between operational performance indicators (OPIs) and management performance indicators (MPIs), resulting in three broad types:

- Environmental condition indicators (ECIs)

- Operational performance indicators (OPIs)

- Management performance indicators (MPIs)

ISO 14031 defines environmental condition indicators (ECIs) as a specific expression that provides information about the local, regional, national or global condition of the environment. Chapter 3 also notes how difficult it is to develop such indicators in practice.

ISO 14031 defines operational performance indicators (OPIs) as EPIs that provide information about the environmental performance of an organisation's operations. ISO 14031 identifies five OPI sub-categories: inputs of materials, energy and services; the supply of inputs; the design, installation, operation and maintenance of the physical facilities and equipment; outputs of products, services, wastes and emissions; and the delivery of outputs.

Finally, a management performance indicator (MPI) is an EPI that provides information about management's efforts to influence an organisation's environmental performance. This can include the policies, people, planning activities, practices and procedures at all levels of the organisation, as well as the decisions and actions associated with the organisation's environmental aspects. ISO 14031 distinguishes four main sub-categories of MPI: implementation of policies and programmes; conformance; financial performance; and community relations.

The guidelines additionally identify five types of quantitative measure, defined in terms of the basis (and degree of complexity) of their calculation, which can form the basis of environmental indicators: direct, relative, indexed, aggregated and weighted.

The three categories of ECIs, OPIs and MPIs can be seen as a pressure–state–response model of business's impacts on the environment (which is itself an adaptation of the basic generic input–process–output model). **Pressures** on the environment are created by the operations of the business, which affect its **state** or **condition**, leading (hopefully) to a **response** through action by management to address the problem. By including indicators in all three of these categories, the ISO 14031 framework can be seen as ensuring a good balance of coverage.

ISO 14031 also represents a blend of different national or regional approaches. As Jasch notes in Chapter 6, its input–output-based classification of EPIs reflects the ecobalancing approach that has been developed in Germanic-speaking countries. It also assimilates US experience that using output-based indicators—such as emissions and wastes—alone can create a bias towards 'end-of-pipe' rather than pollution prevention solutions (Aucott 1995). Conversely, the emphasis on MPIs reflects the influence of the North American/UK/Japanese process/system approaches arising from total quality management. The use of financial indicators also reflects North American/UK interests in linking environment with mainstream business objectives such as cost reduction and shareholder value (see below).

Chapter 2 by Bennett and James provides a fuller discussion of the ISO 14031 framework.

◻ *Selecting and Using Environmental Performance Indicators*

ISO 14031 (ISO 1998b) identifies seven criteria for assessing indicators: whether they are representative, responsive to change, helpful to prediction, relevant, cost-effective, target-related and comparable. A guide by the German government (Federal Environment Ministry 1997) and Wehrmeyer (1995) also have good discussions of this topic.

All these sources note that the value of high-quality indicators has to be weighed against the cost of producing them, which can be considerable. Certainly, in the early stages, most research suggests that it is better to begin with simple, readily understood measures and to develop these over time (Bennett and James 1998a). This was certainly the case with Niagara Mohawk and Baxter, whose respective experiences are detailed in Chapter 10 by Miakisz and Chapter 12 by Bennett and James.

The relevance of indicators is obviously related to the objectives to be achieved. Examples of a variety of objectives can be found in the chapters in this book:

- ▼ Communicating successful performance (or at least evidence of commitment to improve future performance) to external stakeholders

- ▼ Ensuring that senior management is promptly informed of potential problems, usually related to compliance or public reputation

- ▼ Providing senior management with the information necessary to exert control over those at more junior levels whose actions influence the overall environmental performance of the company as a whole

- ▼ Informing planning for the future in business decisions such as new product development, and the acquisition of new capital equipment

- ▼ Providing internal recognition within an organisation of good performance and thereby motivating further efforts

- ▼ Helping to establish environmental management within the organisation as a recognised area of management

Different indicators will be more or less appropriate to each of these objectives.

Bennett and James (1998a) have also distinguished between four different kinds of indicator, depending on whether they are intended (a) to police or to drive improvement, or (b) to provide a continuous stream of information or to provide information geared to supporting point decisions (see Fig. 1). These are monitoring; verification; awareness/opportunity; and tracking.[1]

Monitoring indicators provide regular—and often continuous or near-continuous—streams of information about areas where deviation from pre-set standards has high costs. Examples are compliance with regulations about air and water emissions or with important corporate targets. Immediate corrective action and investigation is likely when monitoring indicators suggest deviation from the standard. This strong policing element means that staff are often unenthusiastic about these indicators and can create a risk of manipulation.

---

1   See also Chapter 7 by Rauberger and Wagner for a discussion of the differences between regularly and periodically collected data.

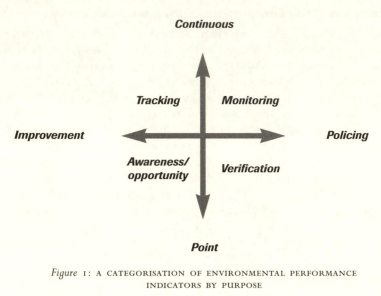

Continuous

Tracking   *Monitoring*

Improvement   **Policing**

Awareness/   *Verification*
opportunity

Point

Figure 1: A CATEGORISATION OF ENVIRONMENTAL PERFORMANCE
INDICATORS BY PURPOSE

Source: Bennett and James 1998a: 55

Verification indicators are also concerned with policing—and can therefore encounter the same resistance—but focus on actions that are being taken at particular points in time. As with compliance auditing, they often focus on processes and implementation of environmental policy, and indicators are often expressed as absolute or percentage non-conformances with a standard.

Awareness or **opportunity** indicators are concerned with providing greater information about specific areas in order to provide a better characterisation of problems and to identify opportunities for improvement. One area of use is to provide data about emerging environmental problems in case action is needed in future: some companies are beginning to track carbon dioxide emissions for this reason. They are also developed to aid point decisions—such as choices between product alternatives or capital investment decisions—or to provide base information for environmental policy-making. Examples are life-cycle assessment (LCA), eco-point schemes and mass balances.

Tracking indicators provide regular information about areas where constant compliance is not essential but where there is a need or strong potential for improvement. They are used to track progress towards corporate environmental targets where short-term deviation does not have high costs and also to identify and provide better understanding of areas for possible future action. Examples often include indicators of resource consumption and waste generation and incident indicators. See also Chapter 12 for a discussion of tracking management performance indicators at Baxter International.

Of course, many indicators are not clear-cut and contain, for example, elements of both improvement and policing. Tracking indicators can also become monitoring indicators as the areas that they address become embedded in policies and systems. However, it is difficult in practice to reconcile these elements, and having a clear conception of the primary purpose of an indicator is helpful in achieving successful implementation.

As ISO 14031 demonstrates, it is also important to have a variety of input, process and output indicators. And leading indicators that give some insight into future circumstances are needed to complement current or lagging indicators.

Many of these points, of course, apply to all areas of evaluation, including social performance and sustainability performance, the two topics to which we now turn.

3. *Social Performance Evaluation*

There is a long history of interest in this topic (summarised, for example, in Zadek *et al.* 1997). Indeed, the first use of the term 'social audit' was in the 1940s, when it was coined by Theodore Kreps. There was an upsurge of interest in the 1970s and again in the 1990s. In both cases, this interest was focused on performance evaluation primarily in order to disclose information to external stakeholders (see Section 5).

In general, there has been much less discussion of social than of environmental performance measurement. Ranganathan argues in Chapter 24 that the former is at least a decade behind the latter in terms of its overall development. David Wheeler, the former head of ethical audit at The Body Shop, puts the gap at five to six years and believes that this is mainly due to the fact that 'the social side is more complex, because you're dealing with perception indicators rather than hard indicators' (*Business and the Environment* 1999).

Spencer-Cooke (1998) has summarised the main categories of social performance for which indicators can, at least in principle, be developed as:

- Human rights
- Labour conditions (including forced and child labour, collective bargaining, etc.)
- Supply chain and overseas suppliers (including fair trade and factory monitoring, etc.)
- Consumer products (including safety and quality, etc.)
- Technology transfer and investment in emerging economies
- Trade with oppressive regimes
- Defence and weapons
- Alcohol, tobacco, gambling and pornography
- Animal testing
- Philanthropy and volunteerism
- Community development

▼ Downsizing and restructuring

▼ Employment policies and empowerment (including affirmative action and sexual harassment, etc.)

▼ Stakeholder relations and accountability

Chapter 23, on the Global Reporting Initiative, and Chapter 24 by Ranganathan provide further summaries, as do Gonella *et al.* (1998).

An opinion survey by the Future Foundation (Grimshaw *et al.* 1998), on behalf of BT, gives some interesting insights into the views of the UK public on corporate responsibility for such issues. They asked respondents which categories on an extensive list of social issues they considered that companies have responsibility for—and, by implication, should evaluate and perhaps report on. Contrarians might observe that only three issues—training the workforce (63%), protecting the environment (51%) and work discrimination (51%)—were seen as a company responsibility by more than half the respondents—and that two of those are only just above this level. On the other hand, many will be surprised by the relatively high scores for topics that are often seen as minority concerns of 'bleeding-heart liberals'—discrimination at work (51%), fair trade (48%) and human rights (45%). And, from a practical viewpoint, many of those concerned about such issues are politically and socially influential.

There have been only a few discussions of all the dimensions of social performance evaluation (Business in the Community 1998; SustainAbility/UNEP 1999a; Gonella *et al.* 1998; Zadek *et al.* 1997). However, there has been considerable discussion of some specific topics. This is particularly true for employee conditions, and it is therefore unsurprising that employment-related indicators is the most well-developed area. As Elkington and van Dijk note in Chapter 25, the Renault *Bilan Social* covers a number of detailed issues, including gender/age profiles, levels of remuneration, hygiene and security, hours of work, noise, staff development and training and employee satisfaction.

One interesting issue in social performance evaluation is that of compliance with regulations. At a global level, there are a number of international conventions that have been signed by most countries. These include the United Nations Universal Declaration of Human Rights, the OECD's Guidelines for Multinational Enterprises, and a number of examples from the International Labour Organisation. However, these are often too general to form the basis of a detailed measurement system in themselves. Their practical interpretation can also fall foul of cultural differences: for example, while many Westerners might see child labour as a violation of human rights, it is both legal and socially acceptable in some countries.

Nonetheless, the various conventions have formed the basis of SA 8000, a social accountability code of conduct launched by the Council on Economic Priorities' Accreditation Agency (CEPAA) in 1997 (Marlin 1998). The standard is awarded at site level and cannot be attached to products. It focuses on the primarily employment-related aspects of child labour, forced labour, health and safety, freedom of association and right to collective bargaining, discrimination, disciplinary practices, working hours, compensation and management systems. The first company, Avon Cosmetics, was certified in 1998. Fair trade organisations will also have additional criteria and, as with the UK organisation Traidcraft, might be concerned to measure the extent and effectiveness of the help that they themselves are providing to suppliers.

Another well-developed area for indicators is that of corporate community involvement (CCI). Most companies report at least some of their expenditures in annual financial reports and, in a few cases, stand-alone reports on the topic. One of the more interesting examples of this is the British financial services company, Allied Dunbar, whose 1996 *Stakeholder Accountability* report not only detailed its activities but also the views of relevant external stakeholders. The London Benchmarking Group of a number of leading UK companies has also begun to develop a performance evaluation framework for the area (LBG 1997).

Several reports have also highlighted the importance of measuring the health of key business relationships, which includes those with important social stakeholders (Centre for Tomorrow's Company 1998; ICAEW 1998). As De Villiers observes in Chapter 19, the South African King Committee represents an interesting initiative in a developing country to address these issues (IOD 1994).

As with environmental performance evaluation, an area of rapidly growing importance is that of financial indicators related to social performance. The Prince of Wales Business Leaders Forum, in collaboration with the World Bank and UN Development Programme has, for example, developed the concept of 'social value added' as an equivalent of shareholder value added (Nelson 1998). Others are also seeking to operationalise the concept of 'social capital' developed by Fukuyama (1995) and others.

4. Sustainability Performance Evaluation

Many companies, at least in the UK, have still to assimilate the concept of sustainable development (Bebbington and Thompson 1996). Nonetheless, there has been considerable discussion in recent years of how this can be applied to business (Arnold and Day 1998; Elkington 1997; Frankel 1998; Fussler with James 1996; Roome 1998; Wheeler and Sillanpää 1997; Willums 1998). The emerging view, as Ranganathan describes in Chapter 24, is that it requires an extension of existing measurement and reporting activities to encompass all the three elements of sustainable development—economic, environmental and social—and the interactions between them. As she and others (for example, Morris *et al.* 1998) have noted, this requires a variety of indicators. Developing these has proved relatively straightforward for product evaluation but is much more difficult for overall corporate activities.

One cause of this difficulty is the need to choose between 'weak' and 'strong' definitions of sustainability—with the key distinction being the willingness in the first approach to make trade-offs between economic growth and environmental and social harm, at least in principle. To a considerable degree, this maps onto another distinction made in a Web-published SustainAbility briefing paper for Shell:

> A key question which will face any company deciding how to respond to the sustainability agenda focuses on which of the two following options to adopt:
>
> • a social accountability process largely driven by stakeholder-defined targets and indicators of performance; or
>
> • a triple bottom line process focusing on targets and indicators relevant to each Shell business—and specifically designed to build competitive advantage and long-term shareholder value.
>
> This is probably going to be a case of both/and, rather than either/or, but the emphasis chosen will be crucial (Shell 1998b: 1).

The authors assumed that Shell would take the latter route (see below).

This has certainly been true of most companies' attempts to address the topic at a corporate level to date. Many have focused their attention on the concept of eco-efficiency (DeSimone and Popoff 1997; Müller *et al.* 1996; OECD 1998; WBCSD 1998). This means creating greater economic value from activities that also minimise environmental impacts, or at worst maintain them at no more than their current level. Both these parameters can be measured and several initiatives have sought to develop standardised eco-efficiency indicators (Canadian National Round Table 1997; WBCSD 1999). However, some of these attempts—and particularly those associated with the World Business Council for Sustainable Development, a business association that brings together many leading multinationals—have been criticised by some sceptics. They argue that this is a narrow interpretation of sustainability which tries to distract attention from issues of eco-justice and/or leads in practice to a focus on incremental improvement rather than radical innovation (Gray *et al.* 1996; Welford 1996a).

Certainly, leading-edge environmental thinkers—and a growing number of policy-makers—believe that sustainable development will require a 'factor 4' improvement in the environmental performance of goods and services, i.e. reducing the amounts of resources needed, and pollution generated to deliver goods and services to consumers, by at least 300% over the next 20–30 years (von Weizsäcker *et al.* 1997). One implication of this is that a true marriage of sustainable development and eco-efficiency requires measures that compare actual with theoretically possible performance.

However, a small number of companies have been trying to develop a 'balanced scorecard' of sustainability indicators that encompass all the different dimensions.

One approach is to replicate as many as possible of the macro-level sustainability indicators that have been developed by governments and other agencies (DETR 1998b; Hammond *et al.* 1995; NEF 1997; President's Council on Sustainable Development 1996). One example of this is the UK's 'quality-of-life barometer' which tracks 13 indicators: level of GDP; level of social investment (e.g. in health and transport); expected years of healthy life; homes unfit for habitation; number of days of moderate or worse air pollution; number of rivers of better than fair quality; new homes built on 'brownfield' sites; people of working age in employment; proportion of people aged 19 with designated qualifications; emissions of greenhouse gases; level of traffic; level of wild bird populations; and net waste generation (McCarthy 1998). Although companies will find it difficult to develop equivalent measures for some of these categories, their completeness should mean that they do not miss any key parameters.

Few companies have yet adopted a complete sustainability template of this kind. However, a number have based their environmental performance evaluation activities on national indicators. Much Dutch work, for example, has used the key environmental themes identified in the country's National Environmental Policy Plans (NEPP) as the starting point for their work on EPE. This was the case with Unox's development of a weighted environmental index, as described by van der Werf in Chapter 11. Such close linkages between micro and macro indicators also have the potential advantage of allowing the latter to be generated from aggregation of the former, rather than by estimation, as is often the case at present (Seifert 1996). Material flow-based indicators appear particularly appropriate for this purpose (Spannenberg 1998).

A complementary approach is to develop 'bottom-up' indicator frameworks based on some concept of what sustainable business is. Sillanpää provides, in Chapter 27, some insights into the process of doing this at The Body Shop. One interesting insight into the kinds of areas that need to be addressed within such frameworks—even if not always capable of being measured—has been provided by van Riemsdijk in the form of a self-assessment checklist. She has summarised this as (in slightly abbreviated form):

> An organisation's 'reason for being': what core values underlie the organisation's practices? What contributions are made in daily operations to sustainable innovation and restorative activities? How is public trust and credibility in the organisation's work established and maintained? Does it practise what it preaches?
>
> The Environmental: What is the policy on material use, energy, water consumption, life cycle design, packaging, product stewardship etc.?
>
> The Social: How are the health and safety, and the learning and development, of employees ensured? How are customer needs defined and their satisfaction measured? Are suppliers involved in partnerships etc.? Does the organisation apply human rights and fair trade principles in its business practices? Does it pursue animal protection or minority group advancement? How does it realise community involvement etc.?
>
> The Economic: What financial/environmental/social indicators are in place? Does annual reporting include internalised environmental and social costs including taxes? Are there employee ownership programmes in place? What percentage of profit is related to support sustainable projects etc.? . . .
>
> Stakeholders: Does the organisation understand the different needs of its stakeholders? How does the organisation involve its stakeholders—by passive communication or through an active dialogue? Does the organisation set the agenda or are the boundaries set by mutual agreement? How open, verified or standardised is the reporting? And how useful is it for setting targets? Can the organisation's performance be benchmarked? Is the engagement of stakeholders ad hoc or an integral part of business planning and decision making and therefore a long term process? (van Riemsdijk 1997: 3).

Old measures	New measures
Volume intensity	Knowledge intensity
Volume output	Value per volume output
Capital investment	Value per unit of capital invested
Material throughput	Material per customer served
Virgin material and energy	Recovered material and energy
Focus on product	Focus on function

Table 1: CHANGING MEASURES OF RESOURCE PRODUCTIVITY

Source: Arnold and Day 1998: 9

The previous sections have discussed the range of environmental and social indicators that can be applied, so the following discussion focuses on van Riemsdijk's categories of value and economic sustainability indicators.

Measuring values is important but difficult, since it can easily become a relatively superficial opinion-survey exercise (Zadek *et al.* 1997). However, several more rigorous approaches have been developed and tested (for example, Barrett 1998; van Luijk *et al.* 1995; Zadek *et al.* 1997). Barrett's approach has been used within the values consultancy, SustainAbility (1999). It involves individuals choosing from a list of values those that most represent their personal views, those that best describe how they feel their organisation should operate, and those that best describe how it actually operates. The degree of alignment between the three areas can then be identified and the results plotted onto a model of value development and a 'Balanced Needs Scorecard'. The Scorecard has six categories, of 'Survival' (profitability and shareholder value), 'Fitness' (productivity, efficiency and quality), 'Customer and Supplier Relations', 'Evolution' (innovation, products and services), 'Culture' (trust, creativity and employee fulfilment) and 'Society and Community Contribution'.

The incremental way into economic sustainability indicators is to adapt existing business performance measurement activities to take account of sustainable development. Table 1 gives one view of the new, sustainability-based, measures that can be introduced to replace existing ones. The developers of this framework argue that:

> The new, value-related measures will lead a company away from commodity products and toward a search for ways to differentiate products through branding, upgrading function, or building with services. These measures reward delivery of value to the customer—translated into sales or value added—and the simultaneous reduction in environmental footprints. The older measures, in contrast, reward increases in throughput, capital investment, and production (Arnold and Day 1998: 9).

Of their six new measures, knowledge intensity and focus on function are the most challenging. The first is related to the question of measuring intellectual capital, which is attracting growing interest in conventional business performance measurement circles. The best-known example is that of the Swedish insurance company, Skandia (1994), which has put a financial value on it in recent financial reports. Focus on function is concerned with attempts to build a greater service component into sales. However, although there is a growing literature on the topic (Hockerts 1999), there are few indications at present on how it can be measured.

A more radical approach to measuring sustainability is to place a financial value on an organisation's consumption or enhancement of natural and/or social capital. This is the approach being adopted by Shell, which is working with SustainAbility and Arthur D. Little to develop 'triple-bottom-line accounting' (Shell 1998b). The main argument for such an approach is that it provides information that is readily understandable by management and financial stakeholders and which can easily be compared with economic value added.

However, attempts to create such valuations are always controversial. One critic has argued that

> The concept misleads companies into thinking that by somehow aggregating economic, social and environmental 'value-added', they can claim both responsibility and sustainability.
>
> The delusion is that they compensate for the 'value' they are subtracting from one bottom line—the environmental, say—by 'adding value' to another 'bottom line'—for example the economic—even though the two forms of value are of a very different nature . . .
>
> The problem with such technocracy is that it obfuscates rather than clarifies. The metrics may provide some semblance of rationality to empower corporate decision-making in the short term, but it is likely to alienate rather than include many stakeholders. This approach will therefore do little to bring about a more consensual way of working or to minimise risk (Mayhew 1998: 10).

5. Reporting

Much performance evaluation has occurred as part of a process of reporting to external stakeholders. The first sub-section examines the pressures for such reporting, the next three examine environmental, social and sustainability reporting respectively, while a final sub-section examines some generic issues within all forms of reporting.

☐ The Pressures for Reporting

Reporting is the meeting point of two powerful forces. On the one hand, there are growing pressures for greater disclosure of environmental, social and other information by companies. On the other, there is business's increased sensitivity to these issues (Financial Times Management 1998).

The pressures for disclosure include:

- Concern that an organisation's activities can damage the health of individuals around its facilities or affected by its products, with resulting demands for more information about risks and safeguards

- Demands from governments, NGOs, the media and others for more information on where organisations stand, and what they are doing about, major environmental and social issues

- A growing desire for more information from customers and other business partners, who realise that their own reputations and operations can be put at risk by environmental or social problems among their suppliers or partners

As Elkington and van Dijk note in Chapter 25, the changes have been summarised by Shell as a move from a 'Trust Me' culture (where companies can rely on society's broad acceptance that they act in good faith), through a 'Tell Me' culture (where society wants to be told what is going on) to a 'Show Me' culture (in which companies have to demonstrate their serious intent to change for the better).

At the same time, companies have become much more sensitive to such pressures. The reasons for this include:

- The growing economic value of a good corporate reputation and a strong, positively regarded, brand—both of which can be put at risk by adverse criticism of environmental and social performance (Fomburn 1996)

- The growing numbers of customers who are taking environmental and social criteria into account in their purchasing decisions

- The increased flow of information within a 'CNN world' which heightens the visibility of all aspects of a company's activities

- The growing dependence on 'intellectual capital', in the form of highly educated and motivated workforces who frequently tend to have higher levels of interest in environmental and social issues than do their less educated peers

Gonella *et al.* (1998) have also noted the emergence of what they term 'value-shift' companies that have an interest in disclosure as part of a new, more socially connected, way of doing business. They see The Body Shop, Tata and VanCity as examples of such companies (although noting that a company's positioning can change with time). This contrasts with 'managerialist' companies who disclose for utilitarian business reasons such as to maintain their licence to operate, and 'public interest' companies who disclose because it is required by governments or irresistible stakeholder demand. The authors see BT, Sbn Bank and Skandia as examples of the former and Nike and Shell as examples of the latter.

The response to these pressures and sensitivities has been a steadily increasing supply of corporate environmental reports. Social reports and sustainability reports are still only a trickle but they too seem likely to increase in coming years. The next three sub-sections examine each of these topics in turn.

⃞ *Environmental Reporting*

The first environmental reports by business were published during the late 1980s and early 1990s. These were prepared for a variety of reasons but perhaps the main driver, especially for US companies, was the requirement to disclose toxic emissions data. Initially, reports were helpful in putting into context apparently high levels of emissions—and in drawing attention to environmental achievements in other areas. Later, they became useful vehicles for reporting the reductions that were stimulated by the requirement to disclose.

These early reports—and the majority of current reports—summarise the overall results for a single organisation, and are generally known as a corporate environmental report (CER). Most of the remainder are site-level reports on individual facilities. There are also a small but growing number of reports on other topics such as aggregate sectoral impacts and products (for example, American Petroleum Institute 1998; Mining Association of Canada 1998). In addition, some companies have included short summaries of environmental performance in financial reports. According to one estimate, 7,000–10,000 environmental reports of one kind or another are now being published around the world (Rikhardsson 1998). As Chapter 16 by Rikhardsson describes, around 1,300 of these are site reports by Danish companies under the terms of that country's mandatory environmental reporting law. The numbers will be further swelled in 2000 when, as Biekart and Ree note in Chapter 17, the first compulsory corporate reports are produced by the 330 Dutch companies affected by an equivalent law in the Netherlands (although some of these are already reporting at present in any case). A number of other countries seem set to follow in coming years.

The pressures for voluntary environmental reporting are also increasing. Many governments are encouraging it, either directly, or indirectly by requiring increased disclosure of environmental information. For example, the UK government has adopted a tactic of 'naming and shaming' prominent companies who have not produced a CER and has also announced its intention of requiring more disclosure of data on carbon dioxide emissions. NGOs and other stakeholders also continue to press for more reporting. Positive inducement is also provided by the growing number of reporting awards. Several national accounting bodies such as the Canadian Institute of Chartered Accountants (CICA) and the UK Association of Chartered Certified Accountants (ACCA) run environmental reporting award schemes, and provide commentary both on individual reports and on the general state of the art of reporting and measurement. Danish, Dutch and UK accounting bodies have also launched a European Environmental Reporting Award, won in 1999 (as in the previous two years) by Novo Nordisk. A number of countries also have similar initiatives, including several in Japan (see Chapter 18 by Murayama; and Kokubu *et al.* 1998).

The evolution of environmental reporting has been tracked in a sequence of reports produced by the *Engaging Stakeholders* research partnership between the United Nations Environmental Programme (UNEP) Industry and Environment initiative and the values consultancy, SustainAbility. Their first three reports (UNEP 1994a; Sustain-

Ability/UNEP 1996a, 1997) surveyed leading CERs and developed a five-stage classification model that can be used to benchmark them. This collaboration was preceded
by a survey undertaken by SustainAbility, Deloitte Touche Tohmatsu International
and the International Institute for Sustainable Development (SustainAbility *et al.*
1993). Chapter 15 by Elkington *et al.* summarises the findings of the 1997 SustainAbility/
UNEP survey, while Chapter 20 by Hopkinson and Whitaker discusses the relevance
of the SustainAbility/UNEP criteria to the UK water industry. Krut and Munis, in
Chapter 22, also provide an alternative and simpler report benchmarking model which
they have developed for the US Environmental Protection Agency.

Other studies or guidance documents on the topic have been published by ACCA
(1997b), Brophy and Starkey (1996), the Canadian Institute of Chartered Accountants
(CICA 1994), Clausen and Fichter (1998), Company Reporting (1996, 1997), Deloitte
& Touche Miljo (1997), the Fondazione ENI Enrico Mattei (1995), the Global Environ-
mental Management Initiative (GEMI) (1994b), Hibbitt and Blokdijk (1997), KPMG
(1997), Lober *et al.* (1997), and Owen (1992). The UK government's Advisory
Committee on Business and the Environment (ACBE 1996), the Institute of Chartered
Accountants in England and Wales (ICAEW 1996), the European Federation of Financial
Analysts' Societies (Müller *et al.* 1994) and the German standards body, NAGUS
(*Environmental Accounting* 1997) have also provided guidance on reporting from the
perspective of financial stakeholders. Finally, the UK's Centre for Sustainable Design
has produced a manual (Centre for Sustainable Design 1998) and video (Centre for
Sustainable Design 1997) on designing an environmental report.

A general point that emerges from many of these publications is that corporate
environmental reporting remains an unsystematic activity, with a wide variation
between the leaders and the rest (*Environmental Accounting* 1998c; Owen *et al.* 1997).
A number of studies (for example, Deegan and Gordon 1996; Gamble *et al.* 1995; Gray
et al. 1995a; Robertson and Nicholson 1996; WBCSD 1998) have also shown that it is
influenced by variables such as company size, sector, capital intensity and national
base.

As yet there has been less analysis of site environmental reports, the numbers of
which have been growing in recent years. However, Grafe-Buckens (1998), Marsanich
(1997) and Miljoeko (1997) are some of those who have conducted surveys of site
environmental statements required under the European Union's Eco-Management
and Auditing Scheme (EMAS) for verifying environmental management systems.
They all found a wide variation in both the content and format of the publications,
which makes it as difficult to use them for comparative purposes as is the case with
corporate reports. Rikhardsson reaches a similar conclusion in Chapter 16, where he
surveys the site reports being produced under Danish mandatory reporting legislation. Nonetheless, some studies (for example, Bennett and James 1998a) have found
that site reports are often valued more highly than corporate by some stakeholders.

A final point is that, even though the amount of reporting is increasing, it continues
to be only a small proportion of total companies and is likely to be confined to larger
organisations as long as it remains voluntary. A survey of 696 UK companies in five
sectors, for example, found that one-third were already disclosing environmental data
and that half were likely to be doing so within the next couple of years (Stray 1998).

However, only half of these did so through an environmental report. She concludes that, in the UK at least, disclosure is unlikely to increase substantially as long as reporting is voluntary.

A SustainAbility/UNEP (1998b) study of reasons for non-reporting was slightly more optimistic—perhaps because its sample consisted of larger companies in a number of countries—but also concluded that the majority of companies do not feel pressure to report and that many will not do so until required by legislation. They found that the main reasons for not reporting were doubts about the advantages and cost. These doubts were heightened by the lack of any standardisation.

⌐ *Social Reporting*

The first substantial activity in this area occurred in the 1970s (Epstein 1996; Zadek *et al.* 1997). One aspect of this was an upsurge in mandatory or voluntary employment reporting. France, for example, made it compulsory for larger companies to produce an employee report (*Bilan Social*) for its staff and many companies in other countries produced an employee and/or full social report voluntarily. Several organisations, such as the UK's Social Audit, were also established to produce independent external reports. A few companies also produced more comprehensive social reports focusing on corporate citizenship as well as employment. Interestingly, as Elkington and van Dijk note in Chapter 25, one of these occurred in India, with a report by the Tata group of companies.

However, the initiatives made then failed to persist because, in the analysis of a leading proponent at the time:

> Corporate social accounting did not survive the 1970s in good health. It had been used too extensively as a public relations tool and not extensively enough as a way to make fundamental changes in corporate culture . . . more permanent changes could be achieved only by incorporating social accounting into the internal accounting systems of these organisations . . . Neither the executives or their accountants, however, were interested in a significant permanent change in corporate culture and the implementation of corporate social accounting (Epstein 1996: 12).

Although several academics kept the issue alive, the topic had little further impact on the business or political mainstream for a decade. A second stage began in the early 1990s when a number of organisations then started to produce a variety of disclosure formats to discuss issues of social performance. Table 2 reproduces a classification of these made by Gonella *et al.* in 1998. As can be seen, some of these were as much focused on disclosing records of social performance processes as actual information. Indeed, one of the first full social reports, by Traidcraft, a UK fair trade organisation, was accompanied by an account of the process of generating it (Zadek and Evans 1993). The reports of three of the 'values-driven' organisations—Ben & Jerry's, The Body Shop and the Co-operative (a UK retailer)—which were prominent in this second stage of social reporting are profiled by Wilson in Chapter 26.

A third stage began in the late 1990s when mainstream companies began to issue social reports. Some common threads are large companies that have operations in

Stated or 'named' approach	Examples of organisations using these approaches	Description
Capital valuation	Skandia	Regularly disclosed process to understand, measure, report on and manage various forms of capital (which could include intellectual, human, social, environmental, organisational, structural and financial capital)
Corporate community involvement reporting	Diageo (Grand Met), BP	Description, illustration and measurement of community involvement policies and activities through occasional reports. This approach may also include benchmarking against other company performances.
Ethical accounting	Sbn Bank, Scandinavian public sector	Regularly disclosed process, based on shared values that stakeholders develop through ongoing dialogue, aimed at designing future actions
Ethical auditing	The Body Shop International	Regular, externally verified process to understand, measure, report on and improve on an organisation's social, environmental and animal testing performance through stakeholder dialogue. The resulting report incorporates three separate social (see 'social auditing' below), environmental and animal testing issues.
Social auditing	VanCity Credit Union, Black Country Housing Association, Co-op Bank	Regular, externally verified process to understand, measure, report on and improve on an organisation's social performance through stakeholder dialogue
Social balance	Coop Italia, UNIPOL	A regular reconstruction and aggregation of financial data across stakeholder groups which specifies financial costs associated with 'social activities'
Statement of principles and values	Shell International	Statement that develops, evolves and describes an organisation's principles in meeting its financial, social and environmental responsibilities
'Sustainability' reporting	Interface	Evolving report process that identifies ways forward and reports on progress against sustainability principles

Table 2: APPROACHES TO SOCIAL ACCOUNTABILITY

Source: Gonella *et al.* 1998: iv

potentially controversial industries, and/or a significant impact on social life in particular countries or regions, and/or traditions of consumer feedback.

Although there have not yet been sufficient social reports produced to allow the same level of analysis and partial standardisation that has happened with environmental reports, this is likely to occur. The New Economics Foundation, for example, has built on the SustainAbility/UNEP environmental benchmarking scheme and developed a 'Five-Stage Ladder' of social reporting based on scoring 56 different elements (Gonella *et al.* 1998).

◰ *Sustainability Reporting*

The logic of companies committing to sustainable development is that they should create sustainability reports that integrate all the 'triple-bottom-line' issues of economics, environment and society into a holistic view of their progress towards sustainability. In fact, a number of companies have issued reports with the word 'sustainable'—or some derivation of it—in their title, but many of these focus largely on environmental and health and safety issues (*Environmental Accounting* 1998a; WBCSD 1998). Conversely, some others deal with all the three elements but do not term themselves 'sustainability reports'. This was the case with the 1998 publication that helped to bring the issue of sustainability reporting into the mainstream, Shell International's *Profits and Principles* report (Shell 1998a) (which was soon followed by a similar report from Shell UK).

The Shell report was positively received by many because it appeared to move beyond separate sections on environmental and social, spliced into a common report, and to exemplify some key elements of a sustainability report. These features included:

▼ A 'humble' tone which signalled a recognition that stakeholders had legitimate concerns which Shell needed to address

▼ A focus on explaining and auditing overall corporate values and business principles as the underpinning of discussions of more detailed topics

▼ An honest and open-minded discussion of sensitive issues such as corruption, human rights, the role of multinationals and operating in politically sensitive countries

▼ Inclusion of sensitive data such as the number of bribery investigations within the Shell group (23 in 1996)

▼ Inclusion of an external viewpoint, by John Elkington

Of course, not everyone who admires the report and the intentions behind it is convinced that it will create changes in Shell's practices (*Environmental Accounting* 1998a). One observer, for example, commented that:

> It is clear that Shell is serious about responding to the increasing demand for greater corporate accountability . . . However, one is tempted to ask whether all this work represents an especially sophisticated way for Shell

Components of value added and distributed	
Cash generated	**Stakeholders**
Sale of products	Customers/consumers
Payment for supplies and services	Suppliers
CASH VALUE ADDED	
Cash utilised	
Remuneration	Employees
State taxes	Government
Social investment	Community/environment
Interest/finance costs	Lenders
Dividends	Shareholders
CASH DISBURSED	
Cash retained	
Funding of growth and replacement	Management

Table 3: SOUTH AFRICAN BREWERIES' VALUE ADDED STATEMENT

> to repair its battered corporate reputation, justify the continuation of its
> core business-as-usual, and renew its 'licence to operate'. Shell's problem
> is that it has not yet managed to set up a rigorous process by which it can
> claim to be interacting meaningfully with its stakeholders. The suspicion
> lingers that it is more interested in using stakeholder consultation for 'issue
> management' purposes than for genuinely understanding the impact of
> its activities and perhaps changing its priorities (Mayhew 1998: 10).

One cause of this suspicion was an aspect of the report that others might perhaps
see as quite radical: the attempts to account for environmental and social value (see
Section 4).

An alternative way of relating environmental and social to financial performance
has been developed by South African Breweries. Its 1998 *Corporate Citizenship Review*
identifies the key stakeholders for each element of its value-added statement (see
Table 3). The thematic discussion suggested by the Global Reporting Initiative (see
Chapter 23) is a similarly qualitative approach.

Arguably, another important attribute of a sustainability report is explicit recognition of future generations as a stakeholder in the business. This was only implicit
in Shell's report—and those of most other organisations—but was highlighted in
another innovative example, the Co-operative Bank's 1997 *Partnership Report*. Indeed,
that extended the temporal boundaries to include also the past generations who
contributed to the development of the bank to its current position.

⌑ *Generic Issues in Reporting*

Verification. As Elkington and van Dijk note in Chapter 25, a growing number of external stakeholders are putting pressure on companies to have their reports verified[2] by a third party. (Interestingly, they note that this desire appears to be somewhat less in Scandinavia, a 'high-trust' society where individuals are more inclined to believe in the honesty of companies.)

At first sight, the purpose of verifying a report is the same as that of auditing a financial report: i.e. to provide reassurance to its users that the information contained within it is accurate. Proponents of verification argue that this is essential if the information is to be credible to stakeholders (Elkington and Fennell 1996; van Dalen 1997) and their arguments have been heeded to some degree. Verification is required in one of the countries where environmental reporting is mandatory, the Netherlands (see Chapter 17 by Biekart and Ree), by the European Union's EMAS, and by most voluntary guidelines such as the Green Reporting Initiative. (However, as Rikhardsson discusses in Chapter 16, it is not required in the country with another large-scale mandatory reporting scheme, Denmark.) It is also becoming more common in voluntary reporting: Toyota, for example, introduced the practice to Japan when it became the first Japanese company to have its report verified in late 1998.

Seeing verification as analogous to auditing a financial report naturally suggests that the accountants who do the latter are also the best qualified to verify environmental and/or social reports. Certainly, the large accounting firms would claim that their professional integrity, public credibility and skills in assessing the reliability of data, understanding internal accounting and information systems and handling the internal complexities of large organisations make them the most appropriate organisations to undertake the task. These arguments have certainly convinced a large number—probably a majority—of companies to entrust their verification to the major accounting firms such as Arthur Andersen, Deloitte Touche, KPMG, Ernst & Young, and PricewaterhouseCoopers. The concentration of the profession has also made it easier to develop *de facto* standards for the activity (*Environmental Accounting* 1998b).

The other main group of verifiers consists of environmental consultancies. Their contrary argument is that it requires environmental expertise to understand and validate environmental data. In private moments, they might also echo the criticisms of verification by accountants that have been made by many environmentalists. One such criticism is that the business orientation of accounting firms does not equip them to understand the needs of external stakeholders such as communities and NGOs. Another is that recent, well-publicised, scandals about the quality of financial audit and the scope for 'creative accounting' mean that the credibility of the

2   This is analogous to the audits that are required by law of companies' annual financial reports. However, the term 'verification' is more usual in the environmental context since the term 'audit' is used specifically in financial auditing to refer exclusively to the independent attestation of the reliability and accuracy of a set of information. In environmental management, the term 'audit' is frequently used more loosely to cover, for example, reviews of past and current activities, risk assessments, investigations into operations, evaluations of management systems, etc.

accountants is not as high as they might like to imagine. (The accountants can, of course, counter that the relatively small size of most environmental consultancies makes them far more susceptible to pressure from the organisation than themselves.)

Verification by either of these groups—but perhaps especially environmental consultancies—can potentially create an additional benefit of advice on the company's reporting processes and environmental management generally. According to one source, such advice tends to be absent from published verification statements by accountancy firms but a central feature of those by consultancies (although it may well, of course, be delivered in private) (*Environmental Accounting* 1998b). On the other hand, it could be considered that this is inconsistent with the purpose of verification by appearing to compromise the independence of the verifier. A report attesting to the accuracy of the information in a CER, or to a company's environmental programme generally, might be perceived as less credible if the verifier had also been involved in helping to prepare the report or advising the company on its environmental programme.[3]

Other alternative sources of verification that have been explored are by attorneys (as with Baxter), by business schools (as with the forthcoming BT social report) and by NGOs (as with the 1995 Body Shop *Values Report*, which was verified by the New Economics Foundation). Some companies have also included a section by a well-known environmentalist, either as an alternative to verification or as a complement to it.

The two latter options represent not just a different choice of verifier but also a different model of verification. This model is concerned not just with validation of data but also with its interpretation. It provides an opportunity for an external party to assess the organisation's performance. This assessment might, for example, include comparison with others on what is possible and involve qualitative as well as quantitative considerations. It is obviously a higher-risk option for a company. But it does respond to the desire of many external stakeholders to make reporting a process that is less under the control of the company and more attuned to their desire for unvarnished information about actual environmental and social performance.

Such measures may be needed to reduce the dangers of what Kamp-Roelands (1999) has termed an 'expectation gap' between what verifiers are providing and what stakeholders want. Her study found a lack of uniformity in verification assignments, report wording and work undertaken. Other studies (for example, FEE 1996; IRRC 1996) have reached similar conclusions. Power (1997) has also warned of the dangers of overestimating what can be achieved by measurement and verification.

A final criticism that is often made of conventional verification procedures is that they address the information that is contained within the report but do not really consider the information that is not there but perhaps should be. Hopkinson and Whitaker's study of the UK water industry in Chapter 20 demonstrates that, even

---

3   This is not unique to environmental management: a similar debate has persisted for several years in respect of financial audits. Purists have clashed with pragmatists over whether auditors should also be permitted also to provide further services such as management consultancy and taxation advice and planning.

when standardised data is available, it is not always fully reported by companies. Interestingly, this appears to be true even for the company that won the 1998 ACCA Reporting award, Anglian Water.

Greater variety of disclosure. Another issue is a move towards a greater variety of disclosure. This will be driven partially by differing user requirements (Green Alliance 1996; SustainAbility/UNEP 1996a, 1996b)[4] and partially by new technological opportunities. Simon Zadek has argued, for example (and in words that apply equally to environmental reporting), that:

> In ten years, we won't have social reports—we're going to move towards not simply web-delivered reports but also to real-time reporting. Audiences will become users of information, rather than just receivers. Software will enable each user to access and assemble customised information from the original accounts (quoted in SustainAbility/UNEP 1999a: 6).

Jones and Walton provide further discussion of Internet-based reporting in Chapter 21, as do a number of other authors (for example, Axelrod 1998; SustainAbility/UNEP 1999b).

This vision appears less futuristic when one considers that conventional financial reporting may be moving in a similar direction. According to one expert, for example, 'constantly updated internal information, standardised internal systems and continuous auditing create the possibility of more frequent release of audited information to shareholders . . . with monthly frequency a realistic target' (Martin 1999).

However, while using the Internet can bring more up-to-date information to more people more easily, there are some potential disadvantages. One is that the majority of the public in many countries do not have access to information technology. Another is that of ensuring that information communicated through this service does not bypass established quality control procedures, whether accidentally or by design.

Additionally, annual financial reports summarising a whole year's trading are likely to remain important—if not quite so central—for the foreseeable future. These contain a surprising amount of 'silent reporting' of social and, to a lesser extent, environmental information (Gray 1997; Adams *et al.* 1995). However, with some exceptions, this is usually not presented in an integrated or strategic fashion (Foundation for Performance Measurement 1998). The question is whether it should be in future, either voluntarily or as a result of requirements by reporting authorities. Research to date has suggested that, while many users see environmental and

---

4   One area of difference is the degree of expertise of different users and therefore the appropriate level of detail in information provided. In financial reporting in the UK, it was traditionally required that the same full-length Annual Report had to be provided—at significant expense—to all shareholders, whether analysts working on behalf of major financial investing institutions or a layperson with only a small shareholding. However, it is now acceptable for a simplified and shortened report to be provided to those shareholders who do not require a full-length version. A similar consideration of differing levels of expertise applies with readers of CERs, with additional variety since different readers may be interested in different aspects of performance. For example, communities living close to major airports will have a different interest in an airline's CER than will those more concerned with its effects on eco-tourism or its contribution to global warming.

social data as material, in practice they do not pay it great attention in their analysis (Business in the Environment 1994; Deegan and Rankin 1997; UNDP 1997). While one reason for this is lack of strategic priority, another is a feeling that the information is too complex or unreliable—aspects that could potentially be resolved through greater standardisation (see below).

It may also be that qualitative schemes—with quantitative underpinnings—will be most appropriate for the needs of users who need simple go–no go or good–bad measures. Chapter 8 by Afsah and Ratunanda and Chapter 13 by Bennett *et al.* provide examples of two such schemes.

Costs and benefits of reporting. Reporting can be expensive, and research has shown that this is a major reason for many companies not to undertake it (SustainAbility/UNEP 1998b). For environmental reporting, Rikhardsson notes in Chapter 16 that preparation of the relatively straightforward site statements required by Danish legislation cost €10,000–100,000. Corporate reports are obviously much more expensive: one UK survey quoted figures of up to £118,000 (ENDS 1998b). For social reporting, Elkington and van Dijk quote figures in Chapter 25 of $100,000 for preparing the VanCity social report, $750,000 for The Body Shop and 'significantly greater' amounts for large multinational companies such as Shell.

Does reporting create benefits that outweigh such costs? A considerable amount of research has been undertaken on the benefits and costs of environmental reporting. A survey of 47 reporting companies by EAG Environ in the UK, for example, found that most felt that they had gained improved stakeholder relations and improvements in management strategy (ENDS 1998b; EAG Environ 1998). A number of SustainAbility/UNEP publications have also presented evidence that the benefits can be considerable.

However, there is some disquiet among both companies and stakeholders about the degree of benefit (ACBE 1996; Gonella *et al.* 1998). Some practitioners express concern that few people other than academics, students and consultants, actually read environmental reports. Rikhardsson, for example, notes in Chapter 16 that this has been the case for Danish reporting to date. And some stakeholders are sceptical about the reliability and/or comparability of much of the data within environmental reports, even when these are verified (Carter 1997; Gonella *et al.* 1998; IRRC 1996; Kelly 1996). One reason for this is concern about the relationship between reports and actual performance. Hopkinson and Whitaker suggest, in Chapter 20, that much relevant data is not disclosed by the water industry in England and Wales, for example. An ENDS (1998a) comparison of the ratings of ten company CERs by SustainAbility/UNEP (1997) and the ratings of environmental management by Business in the Environment (1998) also found a major discrepancy in five cases.

On the other hand, many stakeholders can also feel overwhelmed by the amount of data presented. For example, a European Green Table study of the implementation of environmental performance indicators at 12 Norwegian and Swedish companies found that:

> few environmental stakeholders (except for environmental groups and authorities) were able to express specific needs or requirements for environmental information (European Green Table 1997: 21).

Other studies have made the same point about financial stakeholders. For many, the actual data is important as a sign that management is in control but is too detailed and complex for the aggregate judgements they need to make about a company's performance. In such cases, simple, qualitative, indicators of the kind discussed above can be highly useful.

Overall, therefore, it seems that environmental reporting at least will have to become both more standardised and more differentiated if the benefit–cost ratio is to be unequivocally positive.

There has been less analysis to date of the benefits from social or sustainability reporting, but Elkington and van Dijk argue in Chapter 25 that these can be considerable. However, some of the same debates as with environmental reporting are likely to recur as the field develops.

Developing countries. As several authors note, reporting in developing countries is increasing but faces particular challenges. While there are often high levels of environmental knowledge and sophistication among some sections of the population, others might be illiterate and/or have poor knowledge of international business languages such as English. Clearly, alternatives or complements to conventional CERs need to be found in such circumstances—though, to date, have not yet been found in South Africa. Fortunately, a number of contributions—for example, the Foreword by María Emilia Correa, Chapter 8 by Afsah and Ratunanda on Indonesia, and Chapter 9 by Bhatnagar on India—demonstrate that there are many interesting innovations occurring in the developing world.

Correa and De Villiers note the much greater relative importance of economic development in poorer countries and the implications that this has for what is measured and reported.

6. *Comparability, Standardisation and Benchmarking*

One issue that is generic to both reporting and performance evaluation is comparability. Many writers on ESSPER have seen this as one of the core principles of good practice (for example, Adams *et al.* in Chapter 14, Ranganathan in Chapter 24; and Gonella *et al.* 1998).

◻ *Types of Comparability*

Performance indicators do not generally have intrinsic meaning: they have to be put into context by comparison against an appropriate and relevant point of reference. Three broad types of comparator can be identified:

- ▼ Over time, against earlier indicators in the same organisation
- ▼ Against some other standard: an example in the environmental area is the 'distance-to-target' bases sometimes used to evaluate performance (where the targets are based, at least in principle, on an estimate of what would be needed across the whole of a nation to achieve sustainability)

▼ Over space, against indicators of the same attribute in other organisations

Comparisons over time measure the rate of improvement, but do not themselves indicate whether performance is satisfactory: an improvement may have been merely from 'very poor' to 'poor'. However, they should not usually be difficult to under-take, provided that the data-collection systems and accounting policies have not changed. Comparisons against standards are potentially the most useful, as they provide unambiguous evidence on what needs to be achieved. However, establishing the most important standard—what needs to be achieved for a company to be considered sustainable—has proved difficult to date. Comparisons against other organisations provide useful guidance on 'distance to best practice'. However, there are problems of obtaining access in the first place, and then of being confident that it is genuinely comparable; are there, for example, hidden differences in data definitions or methods of data capture? In reality, as White and Zinkl note in Chapter 4, there is a wide variation between organisations (and their sub-units) in *what* is measured and reported, *how*, and for what *purpose*.

◁ *Standardisation*

These difficulties of comparison have been one reason for a growing demand for standardisation (for example, ACBE 1996; Ditz and Ranganathan 1997; Owen *et al.* 1997). Other reasons include concern that companies will use the flexibility offered by non-standardisation to provide misleading information and a desire to avoid the costs of each company having to develop its own approach independently.

Many investors, insurers and others value such indicators both as a means of reducing financial risks from poor environmental performance and as a more general indicator of a company's quality of management. However, many financial stake-holders complain that the current generation of environmental reports is too unreliable and partial to meet their needs, and call for more standardised reporting formats (Elkington and Spencer-Cooke 1997). In the UK, the Advisory Committee on Business and the Environment (ACBE) has suggested general guidelines to achieve this, while the Association of Chartered Certified Accountants (ACCA 1997b) has provided specific advice on energy.

Many environmentalists and regulators also believe that publication of standard-ised data—such as that required under the US TRI—provides, through both negative and positive publicity, an effective means of penalising those who perform poorly and rewarding those who perform well (Unison 1995). Policy-makers also find such data useful, as do a number of companies that use them as a basis for benchmarking and continuous improvement. These demands are echoed by many of the authors in this volume: for example, by Krut and Munis in Chapter 22 and by Ranganathan in Chapter 24.

A number of different initiatives are now seeking to achieve such standardisation in three main ways:

▼ Standardisation of processes

▼ Standardisation of measurement and reporting frameworks

▼ Standardisation of individual indicators[5]

In the environmental area, discussion of process standardisation has focused on verification procedures although, as previously discussed, little progress has been made. In the social area, the focus is more on the process of informing and undertaking dialogue with external stakeholders. However, it is not entirely clear that standardisation of these and other processes is desirable. One view is that differences are entirely acceptable as they reflect varied needs for which different approaches are required. It is 'possible to envisage a situation in which each organisation has its own unique "methodology" or approach' (Gonella *et al.* 1998: 4). However, the same authors do also develop eight criteria by which to assess the effectiveness of social auditing processes.

A number of standardised frameworks for environment reporting have been developed in recent years (SustainAbility/UNEP 1996a, 1996b, 1997). The most recent of these is the Global Reporting Initiative, which takes the broader issues of sustainability into account and is reproduced in Chapter 23. As previously noted, the draft ISO 14031 has also developed a standardised framework for environmental performance indicators. To date, there have been fewer initiatives that have attempted standardisation of social performance measurement and reporting.

Bennett and James (1998a) have termed generic frameworks of this kind a 'light bulb' approach: illuminating a wide area at varying degrees of intensity, depending on the commitment of the measuring and/or reporting organisation. Together with others (notably Ditz and Ranganathan 1997 and Ranganathan in Chapter 24) they have contrasted this with a 'laser' approach, which would illuminate a smaller area more intensively through the use of standardised data on specific key aspects—for example, energy, materials and water inputs and outputs, emissions, waste outputs—and have suggested that the latter might be a more effective driver of improvement. These areas have also been the focus of mandatory environmental reporting in Denmark, as Rikhardsson discusses in Chapter 16, although he notes that the country is still a long way from standardisation of individual indicators and offering stakeholders a reliable basis for comparisons.

The best-known example of standardisation of indicators is the US Toxic Releases Inventory, which is often used for comparison (Ditz and Ranganathan 1997; Unison 1995). However, even this well-established initiative has a number of limitations for comparability (Aucott 1995; Freeman *et al.* 1992). There can be problems of comparability of data even within the same industry, and considerable attention needs to be paid to issues such as definition and measurement protocols (Irwin *et al.* 1995). The same will be true of other standardised indicators that are now being developed, notably for emissions of carbon dioxide and other gases that contribute to global warming (ENDS 1998c).

---

5   We are grateful to Allen White for raising this point during the March 1999 conference on the Global Reporting Initiative.

The presentation of environmental indicators and other data in reports is also an area of great variability and potentially misleading practice (Carter 1997). Although complete standardisation of presentation is impossible and probably undesirable, there is much that can be done to achieve greater consistency between environmental reports.

Standardisation is even more difficult with social reporting, where different societies have differing attitudes towards many of the most central issues. It may also be much more difficult to report on, and even to measure, social performance in some societies. Elkington and van Dijk note, in Chapter 25, that examples include countries with gross abuses of human rights, civil insecurity, high levels of corruption or where transparency is seen as a negative rather than positive virtue. They provide Japan as an example of the latter—a point confirmed in Chapter 18 by Murayama who cites this as one reason for the relatively low pace of environmental reporting in Japan. For these reasons, Ranganathan argues in Chapter 24 that there is less pressure for standardisation of social than of environmental performance evaluation and reporting. However, she does foresee a *de facto* focus on four main areas of evaluation: employment practices, community relations, ethical sourcing and social impact of product.

In practice, the rate and extent of standardisation will be influenced by a number of contingent factors, such as the nature of the issue, the range and nature of stakeholder interest and, perhaps most crucially, the willingness and capability of sectoral bodies to take action. The latter is especially important because, as Jasch suggests in Chapter 6, the industry sector is perhaps the most appropriate unit for comparative analysis (see Chapter 20 by Hopkinson and Whitaker for a discussion of this issue in the UK water industry). Sectoral bodies therefore have a dual role both in adapting broad standards or criteria for environmental and social performance measurement to individual sectors, and also ensuring consistency within them. However, successful initiatives must be transparent and consensual to overcome external suspicion. Chapter 17 by Biekart and Ree provides an example of how this was achieved in the Netherlands. Given the conservatism and 'convoy' tendencies (travelling at the pace of the slowest member) of many trade associations, this may mean that the chances of success are highest when they are led by ad-hoc groupings of more progressive enterprises.

◁ *Benchmarking*

Once achieved, standardisation should facilitate much greater use of benchmarking. In Chapter 3, Young and Welford classify benchmarking initiatives into four categories: regulatory, market-sector (for example, by industry associations), business service (for example, offered by consultancies), and public benchmarking (undertaken by outside parties). Until now, most such exercises have overcome the difficulties of achieving strict comparability by focusing on management performance indicators (MPIs) and/or accepting that the process will be as much about qualitative as quantitative comparisons (see, for example, BTI 1997; Business Roundtable 1993; CBI 1996; GEMI 1994a; James 1994c; Klafter 1992; Levinson 1997, 1998; Szekely *et al.* 1997). However, Chapter 10 by Miakisz provides details of one successful scheme in the US power industry which is using OPIs as well as MPIs. A German benchmarking initiative in the banking sector also experienced considerable success in gathering quantitative data (Rauberger 1998), as did a project in the Italian ceramics industry (Bartolomeo and Ranghieri 1998).

There have been fewer benchmarking initiatives in social performance, although an exception is the London Benchmarking Club, for corporate community involvement.

7. Implementation of Performance Measurement and Reporting

There is now a growing literature on implementation and how to overcome the numerous barriers to effective performance evaluation and reporting, especially in the environmental area (Bragg *et al.* 1993; European Green Table 1997; Larson and Brown 1997; van Epps and Walters 1996; Wehrmeyer 1995). The study by the European Green Table (1997) is especially interesting, being based on pilot implementation of indicators at 12 Norwegian and Swedish companies. Chapter 3, by Young and Welford, provides details of a similar exercise in the UK.

Some key implementation themes that emerge from the contributions to this book are:

- ▼ The importance of seeing performance evaluation and reporting as a process
- ▼ The value of balanced scorecards
- ▼ The value of business-focused indicators
- ▼ The need for data integrity and robust data-collection systems

The case study of Baxter by Bennett and James in Chapter 12 provides one illustration of the importance of process. The company has identified that a key aim in its environmental performance measurement and reporting is to create a dialogue between the environmental function and other parts of the organisation, with the aim of educating and building support among the latter over time. Rauberger also stresses, in Chapter 7, the fact that ecobalancing is—like the many waste minimisation exercises in the UK and USA—as much a process as a one-off point exercise mapping inputs and outputs. And Sillanpää, in Chapter 27, stresses the importance of process to social performance evaluation and reporting.

In any performance measurement and reporting system, there is a risk that attention can become focused on only a few indicators at the cost of paying inadequate attention to others. A frequent criticism of most conventional business performance measurement systems is that financial indicators such as profitability and liquidity come to take precedence, and other indicators of strategic and operational success—such as customer satisfaction—become under-regarded (Eccles 1991; Johnson and Kaplan 1987; Geanuracos 1997). Kaplan and Norton (1992a, 1992b, 1996a, 1996b), Doyle (1994) and others have therefore advocated the need for a 'balanced scorecard' of financial and non-financial indicators.

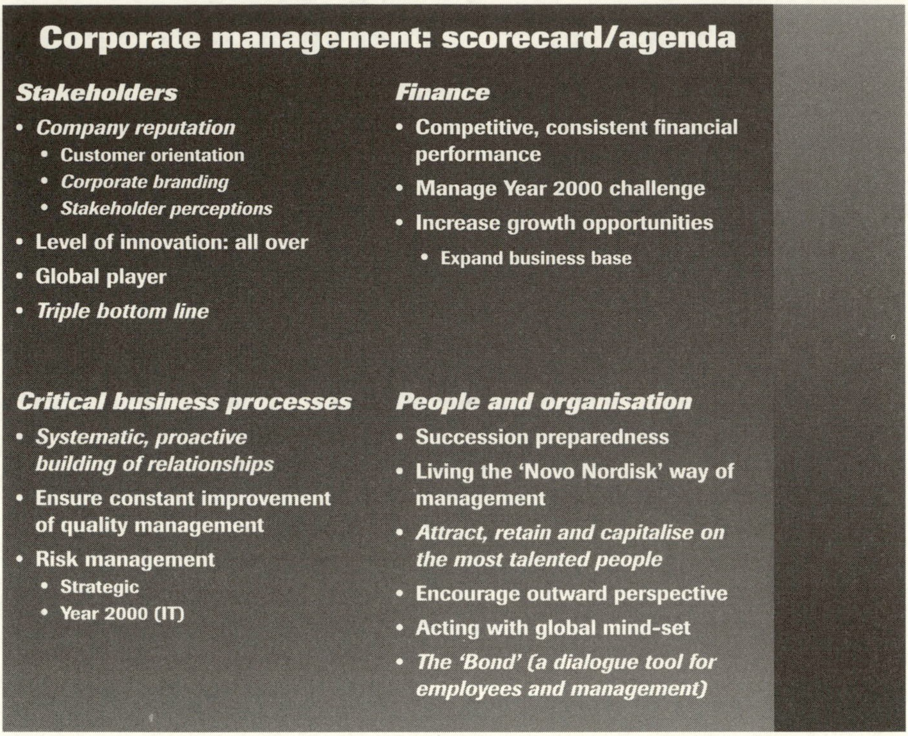

Corporate management: scorecard/agenda

Stakeholders

- *Company reputation*
  - *Customer orientation*
  - *Corporate branding*
  - *Stakeholder perceptions*
- Level of innovation: all over
- Global player
- *Triple bottom line*

Finance

- Competitive, consistent financial performance
- Manage Year 2000 challenge
- Increase growth opportunities
  - Expand business base

Critical business processes

- *Systematic, proactive building of relationships*
- Ensure constant improvement of quality management
- Risk management
  - Strategic
  - Year 2000 (IT)

People and organisation

- Succession preparedness
- Living the 'Novo Nordisk' way of management
- *Attract, retain and capitalise on the most talented people*
- Encourage outward perspective
- Acting with global mind-set
- *The 'Bond' (a dialogue tool for employees and management)*

Figure 2: THE NOVO NORDISK CORPORATE MANAGEMENT SCORECARD

The implications for ESSPER are twofold:

- First, that environmental and social indicators need to be part of an overall corporate balanced scorecard

- Second, that there needs to be a balanced scorecard for the environmental and social areas to highlight priorities and ensure that important areas are not neglected

As the Foreword by Lise Kingo indicates, Novo Nordisk provides one of the most interesting examples of a company trying to include sustainability issues within a corporate balanced scorecard. Figure 2 shows the individual components of this scorecard. According to the company, sustainability is being introduced both directly—through the 'triple-bottom-line' element—and indirectly through incorporation into many of the other elements: for example, 'company reputation' and 'the Bond' (Kingo 1999).

Balanced scorecards are important within the environmental and social areas because of the range of issues that need to be considered and the risks of distortion if only a few indicators are used. For example:

- ▼ Indicators of emissions or wastes may not be taken seriously in the long term if there is no connection with other business indicators such as profitability.

- ▼ Indicators of customer or stakeholder satisfaction can bias action towards what is popular and/or desired by an élite rather than what is scientifically or socially justified.

One particularly important aspect of a balanced scorecard in respect of implementation is the inclusion of indicators that relate to strategic priorities, such as reducing costs. For example, one study of the implementation of a system for measuring the use of chemicals at Polaroid has noted that the system:

> is relatively complex and prescriptive. It introduced significant new burdens for engineers and workers, through its new data-reporting requirements for materials use. Building more user friendliness into the system might have avoided some of the organisational resistance Polaroid faced during implementation. In addition, had Polaroid linked its material use reductions to cost savings directly, the program might have lessened the perceived burden of new duties on employees. Linking toxic reduction and divisional cost reduction, through materials purchasing and disposal, for example, might have helped workers to see stronger rewards in their new labours (Maxwell *et al.* 1997: 125).

Conversely, Chapter 7 by Rauberger and Wagner and Chapter 12 by Bennett and James on Baxter demonstrate that attempts to highlight such financial opportunities through environmental performance evaluation can deliver real savings.

A final implementation theme that emerges from many of the chapters is the need to ensure both data integrity and also cost-effective data collection (Brown and Larson 1997; Fitzgerald 1995, 1997; Orlin *et al.* 1993). The best solution is usually to make maximum use of existing business information systems, which contain a surprising amount of environmental data (Bartolomeo *et al.* 1999; Fitzgerald 1997). Several chapters—for example, Chapter 12 by Bennett and James and Chapter 5 by Rikhardsson—provide further discussion of this topic.

8. *The Relationship between Environmental, Social and Sustainability Performance and Business Performance*

As has been noted, many writers on ESSPER—including ourselves—argue that virtue will be rewarded, and that companies that achieve high levels of environmental, social and sustainability performance will gain business benefits and increased shareholder value (Bennett and James 1998c; Blum *et al.* 1998; DeSimone and Popoff 1997; Johnson 1996). An increasing amount of work is now being directed at substantiating these claims with regard to environmental performance, which has been surveyed by Adams (1997) and Day (1998).

To date, only one individual company—the US-based healthcare products company, Baxter—has attempted to measure the full financial effects of environment on its finances (Bennett and James 1998b; see also Chapter 12). Their *Environmental Financial Statement* estimates the net benefit realised in 1997 at over $100 million.

The main focus of academic research has been on the links between environmental and stock market performance. Day (1998) has identified four types of study:

- Event studies
- Regression studies
- Screening studies
- Valuation models

Event studies compare a company's share price relative to the market following environment-related announcements. These have demonstrated that such announcements can influence share prices in the short term if they do not address long-term relationships between share price and financial performance. Regression studies examine statistical correlations between one or more measures of environmental performance (typically TRI emissions or fines and penalties) and share price performance. Screening studies use similar environmental performance data to create portfolios of good and bad environmental performers and then compare the performance of these with the market average. Day (1998: 4) notes that 'a number of these studies have found that environmentally screened portfolios actually outperformed unscreened ones, with varying degrees of statistical certainty'. These findings have important practical implications in that they suggest that green investment funds can produce above-average market returns. The final category— which, according to Day, has only one application, a study by ICF Kaiser (Feldman and Soyka 1997)—introduces environment into an existing valuation model to see whether it influences stock values.

Day notes that all the studies are hampered by inadequate data on environmental performance and, in most cases, fail to take into account sectoral differences with regard to environmental risk. He also argues that they do not take account of perhaps the most important factor of a company's capacity for good environmental performance in the future, by developing green products and services. He concludes that there appears to be a moderate positive relationship between environmental and financial performance but also offers three cautionary observations:

> First, mainstream investors and most of the finance people within corporations are well behind their corporate strategy counterparts in understanding the connection between environmental and financial performance. Second, virtually all of the current corporate sustainable development activity focuses on environmental and not social issues. The final observation is that the field is nascent and subject to occasional exaggeration. Skepticism would well serve those who are following this topic (Day 1998: 1).

Adams, too, is cautious. He concludes that:

> The overall results DO NOT seem to lend support to the hypothesis that improved environmental performance leads to improved financial perfor-

mance in terms of improved (or outstanding) share price performance. What the papers DO seem to suggest is that improved financial performance does not appear to act as a brake on profitability or share price performance as compared with non (or less)—environmentally conscious companies. Thus, investors who make a deliberate choice to single out environmentally (or ethically) commendable companies will no longer feel that they have to pay a financial penalty for doing so (Adams 1997: 7).

The difficulties of measuring social and sustainability performance has meant that no such statistical studies have been conducted for them. However, more qualitative research (for example, by Collins and Porras 1995) has suggested a relationship between a long-term orientation, socially responsible performance and good treatment of employees and financial performance (Centre for Tomorrow's Company 1997).

One issue raised by these studies is that of causality. Does good environmental performance create business benefits that flow though to share price performance or do the latter attributes create resources and support for environmental action? Or could both environmental and financial performance be linked variables, both of which are driven by good management and/or other factors such as national circumstances? James *et al.* (1997), for example, have suggested that a number of factors need to be taken into account when considering differences in environmental performance between British and German companies.

9. *Conclusions*

Many of the discussions in this volume and other publications draw analogies between ESSPER and financial performance evaluation and reporting (FPER).[6] How accurate are these?

One point often made is that FPER at the turn of the century was equally as hampered by lack of standardisation and consensus as ESSPER is today. Only decades of analysis and action have allowed questions such as for whom to measure and report, what to measure, how to measure, when to measure and report, and in what form to report, to be answered satisfactorily.

One implication is that, although it may be a slow process, such questions will eventually be answered for ESSPER. If it tracks FPER, this process will involve a mix of ad-hoc action to achieve commonality by companies and ESSPER 'consumers'; action by professional bodies; and legislation. Standardisation within FPER began with private initiatives, particularly the demands of users such as investors and lenders who would refuse to provide finance unless there was at least a minimum standard of common formats and contents of information. However, this still left too high a degree of variability and too limited a total body of information for the adequate functioning of the economic systems that rely on this. Hence, in all advanced

---

6   See also Gonella *et al.* 1998 for a discussion of the relationship of social and ethical auditing, accounting and accounting to the FPER.

countries there is now a substantial (and continually increasing) body of law and quasi-legal standards-setting processes by professional associations that govern financial reporting. Hence, the implication for ESSPER is that initiatives such as GRI are complementary rather than alternatives to legislation and/or voluntary actions by companies and business associations.

Even after a century, there are still considerable differences between countries with regard to FPER. National differences in ESSPER are therefore likely to persist for some time. One such difference is between Germanic countries, which have tended to focus on comprehensive ecobalancing approaches, and the US and UK, which have tended to be driven by management considerations such as usability and simplicity of concept. Another is the differences between the UK (and the rest of Europe) and the USA, concerning the disclosure of environmental information. The USA has more statutory requirements for disclosure, as with the TRI requirements. On the other hand many US companies are often said to be reluctant to disclose—or even to collect—some data voluntarily, for fear that it could be used as evidence in litigation in the more legalistic climate of that country. Such fears appear to form the basis of some of the weaknesses in ISO 14031.

A related lesson from accounting history which seems relevant to ESSPER is the importance of detailed attention to issues such as data definitions, data-collection protocols and adjustment procedures, for example, in response to acquisitions and disposals. Financial standards-setters have also developed a detailed and analytic set of qualitative characteristics for good information. As Chapter 14 by Adams *et al.* and Chapter 24 by Ranganathan discuss, the need to apply these to the environmental area is obvious when even different units within the same company can be taking different approaches to these issues.

Some of these difficulties may be solved through greater integration of ESSPER information systems with mainstream systems. These are becoming more complex and seeking to integrate all business information, notably through enterprise resource planning (ERP) software. It is relatively straightforward to attach new, environment-focused modules, to such systems and this is likely to become much more common in future.

One area where parallels can be misleading is that between environmental and financial reporting. There has been a tension in accounting over the primary purpose of financial reports. Should this be simply to discharge the obligation of accountability/stewardship, which implies a backward-looking (historic) perspective and a report where reliability takes precedence, or should they aim rather to provide information that is useful to the users in forming decisions on the basis of it? Decision-useful information implies a future-oriented rather than a historic perspective, and would necessarily mean a need for estimation, forecasts and judgement and a decrease in reliability. In practice, financial reporting has evolved for reasons of accountability/stewardship rather than decision-usefulness, and financial analysts and others seeking information to support decisions such as whether to invest or disinvest in a company need to seek the main part of their information from elsewhere.

To some degree, this is also true of environmental reports, which in some respects fall between two stools. By following an accountability model they can be seen as irrelevant by forward-looking analysts (primarily financial but also others). However, the accountability itself is incomplete because they are mistrusted by some important stakeholders.

A similar point applies to auditing and verification. A core activity of the accountancy profession is the independent audit of company financial reports, resulting in an audit report attesting to the reliability and accuracy of the information reported and its compliance with legal requirements and generally accepted practice. This has provided a model for the present trend towards verification[7] of corporate environmental reports. However, these tend to be, at least at present, both looser and broader than would be appropriate for an audit in the usual financial use of the term, in the strict (and restricted) sense of solely independent attestation of information. At present, they also lack what has been one of the important elements in financial audit, which is (occasionally misplaced) trust in the results by all the main stakeholders. Many are seeking a dialogue about the meaning of information presented rather than the closure of a professional opinion, of which they are automatically suspicious.

This reflects another important difference between FPER and ESSPER: the fact that the latter is much more a process of discovery rather than the routine application of standards and procedures. No one really knows what a sustainable company is and what are acceptable levels of environmental and social performance. In this situation, performance evaluation is as much a process of mutual education and of building shared views as to what is important and why.

However, this may change in the medium term, for one final difference between FPER and ESSPER is the former's lack of a clear conceptual framework to provide a guide in developing practice. Financial reporting standards largely reflect an *ex-post* rationalisation of practice; most build on existing generally accepted accounting practice, and aim to make this best practice common across companies as a whole. On occasions where radical innovations have been attempted, such as with proposals for inflation-adjusted accounting in the UK in the 1970s, these have often attracted strong opposition and—as with inflation accounting—have been ultimately unsuccessful. This reflects a continuing lack of clarity over the fundamental purpose of financial reports.

However, a conceptual framework does exist for environmental performance. Environmental sustainability largely depends in principle on matters that are open to science, even though the level of scientific understanding at present is still too limited for connections to be universally accepted. If a definition can be produced of what level of development is environmentally sustainable, this could provide a framework within which the contributions of individual companies can then be evaluated.

What is less clear is whether it will also require valuation of the economic and social impacts of business. As discussed, there is a growing level of interest in trying to do this as the ultimate means of integrating economic and social with economic

---

7   As noted earlier, the term 'verification' or 'expert statement' tends to be used in the context of environmental reports rather than 'audit'.

concerns. However, equally, there is considerable opposition. The precedents are not auspicious, in that most of the companies that have begun to move along this route—for example, BSO, Dow and Ontario Hydro—have, for various reasons, not proceeded. On the other hand, there is a first time for everything.

It also appears that there is no similar framework that is even potentially available in respect of the social aspects of sustainability. What constitutes good practice is likely to be more inherently based on values that will be specific to different cultures. Its evolution is therefore likely to be much more ad hoc than with environment.

A final way in which the analogy breaks down is with regard to the relationship between FPER, ESSPER and the existing economic and social order. Neely (1999), for example, has argued that business performance measurement has three distinctive roles:

- To ensure compliance with crucial minimum standards

- To check how well organisations are doing

- To test strategic assumptions.

This book provides many examples of all these areas. Much of the initial activity within the area of environmental and, to a lesser degree, social performance measurement was either directly or indirectly driven by compliance with legislation, regulations or standards. Over time, the focus has shifted more to measurement connected with voluntary activities, and concerned with tracking progress over time or in relation to external benchmarks. And, in many respects, almost every aspect of an advanced ESSPER programme can be seen as challenging the assumptions of most organisations that these areas are not strategically important. It is therefore inherently more radical than FPER, at least for the present. Rather than supporting existing ways of doing business, it requires new, truly sustainable, measures.

1 EVALUATING ENVIRONMENTAL PERFORMANCE

2
ISO 14031 and the Future of Environmental Performance Evaluation

Martin Bennett and Peter James

THE INTERNATIONAL Organisation for Standardisation (ISO) is currently supplementing ISO 14001, the standard on environmental management systems, with a number of guidance documents. These are collectively known as the ISO 14000 series and cover different aspects of system design, implementation and auditing. Two of these deal with environmental performance evaluation (EPE). The main one of these is ISO 14031, which provides detailed guidelines on the topic (ISO 1998b). The second is ISO 14032, a supporting technical report which will provide case studies from a number of sectors. Both should be officially published by the end of 1999.[1] They will be an important element in the ISO 14000 series, since the selection and use of appropriate indicators will enable businesses (and their outside stakeholders) to ascertain the effectiveness of their environmental management systems in generating genuine improvements in environmental performance.

This chapter analyses the ISO 14031 guidelines and how far they reflect the issues discussed in other parts of the book. Section 1 provides a description of the guidelines. Section 2 compares them with current practice, as revealed by a recent research study. Section 3 examines their strengths and weaknesses. Section 4 positions them in terms of a three-generational model of EPE and Section 5 develops a 'diamond' model to position different types of 'third-generation' indicator. An appendix provides examples of each of the individual indicators.

---

1   At the time of writing, ISO 14031 is expected to be issued in late 1999. This chapter is based on the current draft version, issued in 1998 for discussion and comment in 1999 (ISO/TC/SC4 N279).

1. *ISO 14031*

The central feature of ISO 14031 is a definition and detailed discussion of three basic types of indicator that can be used to support environmental management. It first distinguishes between 'environmental condition indicators' (ECIs) and 'environmental performance indicators' (EPIs), and then subdivides the latter between operational performance indicators (OPIs) and management performance indicators (MPIs), resulting in three broad types:

- Environmental condition indicators (ECIs)

- Operational performance indicators (OPIs)

- Management performance indicators (MPIs)

ISO 14031 defines environmental condition indicators (ECIs) as

> a specific expression that provides information about the local, regional, national or global condition of the environment.

It does not identify any sub-categories of ECI.

It defines operational performance indicators (OPIs) as

> an EPI that provides information about the environmental performance of an organisation's operations.

ISO 14031 identifies five OPI sub-categories: inputs of materials, energy and services; the supply of inputs; the design, installation, operation and maintenance of the physical facilities and equipment; outputs of products, services, wastes and emissions; and the delivery of outputs.

Finally, a management performance indicator (MPI) is

> an EPI that provides information about the management efforts to influence an organisation's environmental performance.

ISO 14031 distinguishes four main sub-categories of MPI: implementation of policies and programmes; conformance; financial performance; and community relations.

ISO 14031 additionally identifies five types of quantitative measure, defined in terms of the basis (and degree of complexity) of their calculation, which can form the basis of EPE indicators: direct, relative, indexed, aggregated and weighted. (Earlier drafts also mentioned a sixth category, of qualitative measures, though this was defined only as 'data which cannot be quantified'.)

ISO defines **direct** (i.e. absolute) measures as 'basic data or information, such as tonnes of contaminant emitted'. This is the primary form of data for all EPIs and the one in which most, in practice, are expressed. Data from direct measures can then be manipulated in different ways to create the four more complex forms of data. ISO 14031 defines them thus:

- **Relative** measures are 'data or information compared to or in relation to another parameter' (e.g. tonnes of contaminant emitted per tonne of product manufactured).

▼ **Indexed** data or information is 'data or information converted to units or to a form which relates the information to a given standard or baseline, such as contaminant emissions in the current year expressed as a percentage of those emissions in a baseline year'.

▼ **Aggregated** data or information is 'data or information of the same type, but from different sources, collected and expressed as a combined value', e.g. total tonnes of sulphur dioxide from all facilities in a given year.

▼ **Weighted** data is 'data or information modified by applying a factor relating to its significance' (ISO 1998b).

ISO's terminology differs in several respects from much of the previous literature on the topic. For example, its category of 'weighted' data is what would perhaps more often be termed an 'index', i.e. a single cardinal measure of no intrinsic significance that reflects a variety of different components, such as an index of retail prices or share prices (or, in this context, of a range of different aspects of a business's environmental performance). ISO, on the other hand, uses the term 'indexed' to define measures that are tracked over time, in trend analysis. Others have used the term 'normalised' to describe measures for which ISO uses 'relative'. ISO's 'aggregated' data, i.e. summing site-level quantities of data or information of the same type across the whole of an organisation, is equivalent to the financial accounting process of preparing 'consolidated' accounts. Care is needed to ensure that, in any particular application, terminology is being used consistently in order to avoid confusion.

2. Current Practice in EPE

A recent study for the Association of Chartered Certified Accountants (ACCA) (Bennett and James 1998a) provides some indication of the relationship between the ISO 14031 model and current practice. The study involved a survey of the top 100 UK companies and interviews with 54 environmental managers and others. The survey examined the use of different categories of indicator, using terms that were broadly comparable to those adopted by ISO.

Only a small majority of respondents or interviewees used any kind of environmental condition indicator (ECI), the most frequent being biological oxygen demand (BOD) and chemical oxygen demand (COD) indicators of the impacts of effluents into watercourses. However, many—particularly those considering progressing to sustainability reporting—considered that they would need to extend their use in future. A large majority—more than 80% of participants—were also using risk indicators (for example, of environmental 'incidents') which can sometimes be proxies for ECIs.

Three kinds of OPIs—solid wastes, resources and effluents to water—were also used to at least some degree by over 80% of respondents. Solid wastes and resources were both the most prevalent and those where respondents generally considered that they have the most comprehensive range of indicators.

Although most companies who responded to the survey were using indicators of emissions to air and water, it is notable that only a minority felt that they had a comprehensive set of indicators in place, suggesting that most may be primarily responding to regulatory requirements. This is understandable for air emissions, which can be dispersed and difficult to measure, but is more surprising for water, where there tend to be fewer waste-streams.

It was also striking that very few companies were measuring their emissions of another substance that is of increasing importance in the environmental agenda, carbon dioxide, even though it is relatively easy to make approximate calculations of its emissions. Indeed, one company had gone backwards in its ability to do this, having consolidated several previously separate cost codes for different forms of energy into a single code.

Given the potential cost savings attached to waste reduction, it is perhaps surprising that, although a majority of companies were using waste indicators, only a minority considered that these were comprehensive.

Almost all the survey respondents were using resource consumption indicators such as energy, material and water, and these were the only type where a near-majority felt that they had comprehensive indicators in place. This is unsurprising, as consumption of resources tends to be both visible and costly, and—since they are usually purchased and therefore invoiced—relatively easy to calculate. Fewer respondents were measuring the efficiency of energy, materials or water usage.

The survey and accompanying interviews found that the use of management performance indicators (MPIs) was less developed than that of OPIs. The questionnaire combined ISO's categories of implementation and conformance indicators into a single category of input/process indicators. These were generally given a low ranking—surprisingly, given the weight put on these in the performance measurement literature as leading indicators of future results—though some companies did place high emphasis on them.

A number of the companies interviewed were tracking—and achieving—financial gains from environmental actions. However, this generally applied only to a limited range of areas such as energy or waste. This is corroborated by the results from a parallel study across several European countries, by a European Union research team of which the authors of this chapter were members (Bartolomeo *et al.* 1999).[2]

Although most interviewees identified financial indicators as an area that they intended to develop further, one environmental manager argued against them on the grounds that such measures are inherently backward-looking, and incapable of capturing changes in any aspect of performance that does not result in an immediate monetary saving (or other benefit) or cost.

Only 45% of the survey respondents reported that they were using relative indicators (in the ISO use of the term), though a large majority of the companies who were interviewed were using them in some form. Many were experiencing difficulties in determining the best way in which to calculate the indicator—i.e. the most

---

2   Further details of the project—and of the associated international Environmental Management Accounting Network—can be obtained from the project co-ordinator Teun Wolters at *two@eim.nl*; tel: +31 79 341 36 35; fax: +31 79 341 50 24.

appropriate measure of business volume to include as the denominator, in a ratio in which the direct environmental measure is the numerator.[3]

Relative indicators are useful for management but can be misleading if too much emphasis is placed on them. Although—in our opinion—one environmental manager may have exaggerated the point, there was some food for thought in his assertion that they 'are a second-order consideration. What primarily matters is the absolute amount, since improvements in eco-efficiency per individual unit can be more than offset by increases in volume.' Several others held a similar view, i.e. that their real targets are absolute quantities, and that the role of relative measures is to provide a means of steering towards these.

One-fifth of the companies surveyed were using what the ISO terms 'weighted' indicators (or 'indices', in more usual terminology). Most of these were companies belonging to the Chemical Industries Association, since this is a requirement of their Responsible Care programme. However, weighted indicators are remote from the original data and are therefore not transparent (although the formulae by which they are calculated can be), and many environmental managers are unenthusiastic about them for this reason.

The use of weighted indicators in evaluating products appears to engender far less scepticism than their use in measuring overall corporate performance (see Gameson 1998 and Chapter 13 for more discussion of this point). Possible reasons include the relatively bounded world of product development which makes any fundamental challenge less likely, and the time constraints on the process which introduce a bias towards 'good enough' rather than theoretically optimal outcomes. However, their use at a corporate level may become more prevalent as the indicators become more widely used and environmentalists, governments and others take more interest in them.

In summary, it is clear that most EPE activity is still focused on operational performance indicators (OPIs), and particularly resource, emissions and wastes indicators. Although no area of EPE is easy, these are perhaps the most straightforward, since the aspects that they measure are highly visible and the necessary data is usually already being captured and is therefore available from the relevant part of the organisation. They are also required in order to demonstrate compliance with legislation and to monitor business efficiency.

In fact, this narrow focus is not unique to the UK: a joint study of the use of indicators in the USA by Tellus Institute and the World Resources Institute has drawn similar conclusions (Ditz and Ranganathan 1997; White and Zinkl 1997).

3. Strengths and Weaknesses of ISO 14031

These findings suggest that there is a need to extend the horizons of companies, auditors and others in respect of the aspects of their environmental performance that they

---

3   See Chapter 12 for a review of the various types of normalising base used by Baxter International.

should be measuring. ISO 14031 could therefore be an excellent means of achieving this. It provides a clear, logical structure for an environmental version of the 'balanced scorecard' (see Chapter 1) and directs particular attention to the value and feasibility of ECIs and MPIs. It also provides useful checklists for guiding the process of developing measures, and suggests a large number of different possible indicators that could be relevant for companies with differing environmental issues. These outputs are of course exceptionally useful and credible because they systematise the experience and views of the large number of organisations and individual experts who are involved in the ISO process. Hence, ISO 14031 is a welcome and potentially extremely valuable complement to current EPE practice.

However, we believe that the current draft ISO 14031 also has a number of gaps, which we would summarise as:

- Limited emphasis on standardisation

- Incomplete discussion of implementation

- Excessive complexity

- No requirement for external disclosure

- Limited linkage with the broader issues of sustainable development

As Chapter 1 has discussed, the ability to make comparisons between sites, organisations and industries, which standardised performance data permits, can be an important stimulus of performance improvement. However, ISO 14031 does not really address the two central issues of standardisation: the scope of what is to be standardised and, once this is determined, definitions and measurement protocols. Rather, it prefers to leave companies to make their own choices. The point has been made by Janet Ranganathan of the World Resources Institute who argues that

> ISO 14031, as written, is not strong enough to lend the necessary credibility to the flagship 14001. There's too much choice and freedom—there should have been at least some recommendations about firms needing to adopt a basic set of key measures. Essentially firms can pick and choose their indicators.[4]

The draft guidelines have a number of useful 'Practical Help' boxes—and the case studies in ISO 14032 should provide further insight into implementation—but more could still be said about some important aspects of establishing EPE within companies and the trade-offs between different objectives that this involves. For example, the guidelines do not address issues such as the basis on which standards should be set (for example, whether as realistic expectations or incorporating a 'stretch target' element); how far the emphasis is to be on providing senior management with the means of organisational control rather than on stimulating and supporting continuous improvement; and the trade-off between, on the one hand, the value of having data that is relevant and reliable, and, on the other hand, the need to limit the cost of obtaining that data.

---

4   Personal communication.

ISO 14031 provides many examples (over 100) of different indicators from which each company can make its own selection. Reasonably, it recognises that, because of the diversity of organisations and their policies, objectives and structures, it is not possible to be prescriptive on a single set of measures that would be universally relevant. However, it does not provide any clear guidance or criteria by which each organisation should make its own selection, other than to 'select indicators for EPE that it recognises as important to achieving its environmental performance criteria'. In practice, some measures will have greater importance than others because, for example, they have major strategic significance or are based on standardised data. One finding of the ACCA project reviewed in Section 2 is that the approach that is most likely to be successful is in the early stages to develop simple, readily understood measures that reflect environmental priorities, make maximum use of existing data sources, and speak to non-environmental staff in the company by addressing mainstream business concerns. Hence, the sophisticated framework of ISO 14031 may be inappropriate for beginners or smaller companies.

The draft ISO 14031 discusses the issue of reporting environmental performance data but does not recommend it or discuss its advantages. This position is of course consistent with ISO 14001 itself which—unlike the European Eco-Management and Auditing (EMAS) scheme—has no requirement for public reporting of data used within or produced by the environmental management system. However, it does diminish the document's credibility for many external stakeholders.

The same is true of ISO 14031's limited reference to the links between environmental performance and other dimensions of sustainable development, which have been stressed by many mainstream publications (for example, President's Council on Sustainable Development 1996). While most (including ourselves) would accept that it is reasonable to define tightly and focus any detailed discussions of performance measurement on environment alone, the opportunity at least to raise awareness of the topic among companies around the world has not been taken.

Of course, these points have to be considered in the light of ISO realities. The organisation is seeking to achieve an international consensus on a complex and controversial topic, so compromise is inevitable (ENDS 1999a). But some environmentalists and others believe that these compromises are overly weighted towards the interests of large multinational companies (Benchmark 1995; ENDS 1996; WWF 1996).

4. Three Generations of Environmental Performance Measurement

Our own view is that ISO 14031 is a valuable first step towards defining and standardising EPE, but one that will need further development over the next decade. This development will probably reflect the experience of the second and third generations of measurement which are identified in the ACCA study (see Table 1). These three generations are intended as broad indications of type rather than strictly defined, and are not necessarily strictly evolutionary, though it does represent a logical

	First generation	Second generation	Third generation
Drivers	External pressures for compliance	Stakeholder management	Stakeholder dialogue/partnership
	Costs	TQM	Sustainable development
		Pollution prevention	Life-cycle management
Measurement objectives	Risk management	Inform environmental stakeholders	Strategic effectiveness through a balanced scorecard and data re-purposing
		Communicate targets and progress internally/externally	Data credibility
		Drive continuous improvement	Support debate
		Resource productivity	Assess business sustainability
			Drive discontinuous improvement
			Assess strategic business impacts
Primary audiences	Senior management	Mass media	Employees
	Environmental staff	Environmental stakeholders	Product chain members
		Line management	Financial stakeholders
		Sites/communities	Functional management
Key indicators	Business process	Energy and materials usage/efficiency	Balanced scorecard
	Regulated emissions and wastes	Significant emissions and wastes	Relative (comparative)
	Costly resources	Financial	Eco-efficiency
	Compliance	Implementation	Stakeholders
			Environmental condition
			Products
Data collection	Ad hoc	Required monitoring	Integrated environmental information system
		Questionnaire	
		Simple mass balance	Ecobalancing

Table 1: THREE GENERATIONS OF ENVIRONMENTAL PERFORMANCE EVALUATION

Source: Bennett and James 1998a

and common direction in which to progress. They are also cumulative, with a supplementation rather than replacement of the activities of previous stages. The ISO 14031 guidelines can be seen as reflecting the experience of first-generation and, to some degree, second-generation approaches.

The first generation of EPE comprises companies whose environmental policies are mainly reactive. The ACCA research suggests that these are a substantial proportion even of the large companies who formed the sample, and probably a majority of medium-sized ones. It may be that moving this mass of companies towards the second generation—which ISO 14031 might help to achieve—would actually deliver greater environmental improvements than further progress by an élite towards third-generation EPE.

The first generation of EPE is largely about risk management and dealing with obvious environment-related costs, such as high energy consumption, high wastage rates or emissions that require expensive pollution control measures. The risks to be managed are those of non-compliance with legislation and of financial liability, primarily from contaminated land. The environmental performance data that is available is used largely for internal purposes. This is typically the monitoring of audit results by environmental managers and their senior managers, and the raising of awareness through the identification of energy costs (supplemented in some cases by their allocation to individual budgets). External publications are rare and, if they exist, are typically short and glossy with little quantitative data.

Stakeholder management is a key part of the framework for second-generation EPE. Hence, most companies moving into this stage focus on corporate and/or site reporting, and some gear all their activities to this. Even for companies that do not publish environmental reports, data about emissions, hazardous wastes, management systems and other areas can be important in order to make a positive impression on— and to achieve specific objectives with regard to—external stakeholders such as regulators, bankers and insurers.

Second-generation EPE is also influenced by total quality management (TQM) (see Chapter 1). Key aims of quality measurement are to stimulate and support continuous improvement, particularly through awareness and tracking measures, and to provide data that is usable by line managers and staff generally, and these are central to this stage.

So too is a pollution prevention approach, which tries to solve problems at source rather than to rely on end-of-pipe solutions. This requires much more detailed data on inputs, throughputs and outputs of energy, materials and water—although the emphasis in this stage is more on 'good enough' data from simple mass balances rather than on introducing more comprehensive and sophisticated approaches such as ecobalances (see Chapters 6 and 7).

Energy, materials and waste data is also crucial to another key element of second-generation EPE, which is to increase resource productivity through waste minimisation and other initiatives. This tends to be the focus of eco-efficiency actions with, conversely, much less attention being given to other aspects such as product development where environmental screening and other relatively simple techniques remain the norm.

The second generation is also associated with the introduction of environmental management systems and a growing emphasis on implementation and other management performance indicators. However, although data collection systems become more sophisticated, they are seldom fully integrated or standardised and often remain reliant on estimates rather than on direct measurement.

All of these remain important in the third stage of EPE, but the small number of companies that are moving towards this are also responding to new or changing drivers with revised objectives, additional target audiences, and new or modified indicators.

The new or changing drivers include:

▼ Stakeholders' growing expectations of a dialogue with companies—often based on partnership—about contentious issues which goes well beyond the one-way communication implied by stakeholder management (see Loughran 1998 for an example of this at Novo Nordisk).

▼ The need to respond to pressure from environmentalists, policy-makers and others to relate business activities to the concept of sustainable development. This includes the social as well as environmental dimensions of sustainability.

▼ The need to take measurement across the life-cycle to provide more holistic analyses and to take account of specific pressures, such as those for product take-back or elimination of substances from components

▼ More general linkages between environment and strategic business performance, particularly with regard to corporate and brand reputations and revenue opportunities from eco-efficient products

The overall objective of third-generation EPE is to achieve strategic effectiveness, so that an increasingly integrated body of data is shaped to meet specific objectives, and reprocessed into multiple outputs for various audiences. The overall objective of measurement at this stage therefore becomes a balanced scorecard that covers both significant environmental issues and business-related parameters. Specific objectives that are added or adapted in response to this include:

▼ Strengthening the credibility of data

▼ Supporting debate

▼ Providing a balanced scorecard of business sustainability

▼ Driving discontinuous improvement

▼ Assessing strategic business impacts

Achieving data credibility extends well beyond post-hoc external verification of reports and/or data collection procedures (and, indeed, in some respects, potentially reduces the importance of this). It includes much more detailed attention to data collection protocols, the maximisation of direct measures, incorporation of stakeholder inputs into the framing and implementation of measurement systems and individual indicators, and obtaining stakeholder interpretations and feedback on the results.

Public policy debates are greatly aided by credible business-level data. Relevant data will often be business-specific but will increasingly be about the 'space' between individual sites and organisations, i.e. life-cycle impacts, overall patterns of consumption and production and interactions between different organisations. Hence, company evaluation activities will increasingly need to address such issues. Whatever the area of measurement, there will be growing pressure to provide more objective and less self-serving data about business-specific issues than has perhaps been the case in the past.

Providing an overall assessment of business sustainability—including social dimensions—becomes an increasingly important objective in this stage. However, as Chapter 1 discussed, there will be different approaches to such assessment for the foreseeable future. Interpretations of sustainability that focus on eco-efficiency and ignore the social and political dimensions of sustainable development will also become increasingly untenable.

One aspect of discontinuous improvement is that 'unintentional environment'— that is, the improvements in performance that result from non-environmental drivers of action such as investment in new equipment, or cost reduction programmes— can be the most important cause of environmental improvement in many industries (James *et al.* 1997). Hence, it is vital that measurement activities be extended into those areas, such as research and development, new product development and capital budgeting, that influence—whether intentionally or unintentionally—the eco-efficiency of future processes and products, so that improvement opportunities can be maximised.

The second-generation focus on resource productivity associated with waste minimisation also extends to cover the broader costs of inefficiency as well as development of eco-efficient products to provide potential revenue streams (Bennett and James 1998b).

Two audiences that become increasingly important during this third stage are functional management—particularly in forward-looking areas such as product development and research and development—and, from a growing emphasis on life-cycle management, product chain members. Product reports or summary life-cycle assessments are one means of communicating with this audience. Financial stakeholders are also seen as more important—even though the evidence on the present level of their interest is rather mixed—and initiatives are taken in environmental accounting.

As noted, this is accompanied by a shift in emphasis from individual indicators to the development of balanced scorecards. Within this, relative indicators become more important for comparative analyses while financial performance and environmental condition indicators are developed for the strategic reasons discussed above.

5. Towards a Next-Generation ISO 14031

Figure 1 presents a model for EPE that is in broad conformance with the current ISO 14031 but which is also intended to address some of the points identified above. The model is formed in the shape of a diamond because this conveys three important facets of EPE:

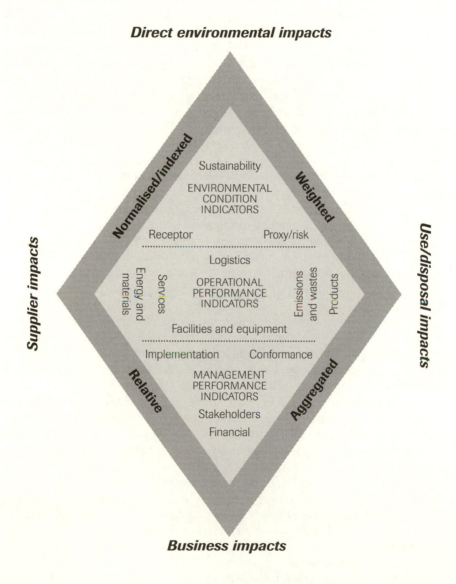

Figure 1: THE ENVIRONMENTAL PERFORMANCE EVALUATION DIAMOND

Source: Bennett and James 1998a

▾ Most companies have, to date, used only a limited range of indicators.

▾ A life-cycle perspective is vital.

▾ The ultimate objectives are to assess both environmental and business impacts.

The first facet reflects the fact that the bulk of measurement activities tend to be in the area of OPIs, and in particular those dealing with energy, materials, emissions and wastes. This explains the greater breadth of the diamond in its middle than at either extremity. The second facet is a west–east axis which cuts across the organisation, i.e. the product chain which includes the environmental impacts of upstream (suppliers) and downstream activities. As Ranganathan notes in Chapter 24, these are an increasingly important aspect of EPE. The diamond's north–south axis (the third facet) also indicates that EPM ultimately has two objectives. One is to assess the direct environmental impacts and the sustainability (including social sustainability) of an organisation's activities. The other is to assess the business implications (for profits, market share, customer satisfaction, etc.) of its environmental actions.

In line with this, we introduce three new sub-categories of ECI. These are **receptor** indicators (an organisation's absolute impacts on receptor media or objects such as air, water, flora and fauna, people, and buildings), **sustainability** indicators (the relationship between an actual and a sustainable level of impacts) and **proxy/risk** indicators (likelihood of causing environmental damage). We also extend the MPI sub-category of community relations into a broader category of **stakeholder** indicators to indicate that a wide range of business and non-business stakeholders are of significance to the organisation. The other nine sub-categories are the same as in the current draft ISO 14031.

Each indicator within these 13 sub-categories can be calculated in any of the five ways defined by ISO 14031—either as a simple, direct indicator, or as one of the four more complex types (relative, indexed, aggregated, weighted) that are shown at the edges of the diamond. The appendix provides more discussion, and examples, of each of these types of indicator.

As with ISO 14031, the diamond implies that the more indicator categories that are covered in an environmental 'balanced scorecard', the more effective an organisation is likely to be at EPE. However, the use of indicators will also vary according to an organisation's sophistication and its particular drivers of environmental management, which will evolve over time.

The setting for the diamond is greater standardisation of data. Current approaches represent a 'light bulb' approach to performance—illuminating a wide area at varying degrees of intensity, depending on the commitment of the reporting organisation. A 'laser' approach, which illuminates a smaller area more intensively through use of standardised data—for example, on energy, materials and water inputs and outputs of product, emissions and waste—might be a more effective driver of improvement.

Of course, standardisation of measurement is difficult or impossible for individual companies to achieve. Action by groups of companies and, still more, sectoral associations will be vital. The industry sector is usually the most appropriate unit for comparative analysis, and industry-sector associations therefore have a dual role both in adapting broad standards and criteria for EPE to individual sectors, and also in ensuring consistency within them. However, successful initiatives must be transparent and consensual to overcome external suspicion. A next-generation ISO 14031 that clearly signals priority indicators and makes suggestions on how they might be measured would provide a valuable external foundation for this, as well as sending clear signals to companies about the best approach to EPE.

◢ *Appendix: Examples of Environmental Performance Indicators*

This appendix provides a brief discussion, and examples, of each of the types of indicator identified in the environmental performance diamond (for a fuller discussion, see Bennett and James 1998a). These are grouped in the three ISO 14031 categories of ECIs, OPIs and MPIs. A fourth section discusses relative, normalised, aggregated and weighted indicators. Chapter 12 also provides a discussion of the use of all these types of indicator at Baxter International.

1. *Environmental Condition Indicators (ECIs)*

Receptor indicators. Most environmental condition indicators focus on impacts on a receptor medium: air, water and soil. The most commonly used indicator is probably that of the biological oxygen demand (BOD) of effluents. The ecotoxicity indicators which are attracting interest from regulators provide another example.

One of the few attempts to consider impacts on flora and fauna has been made by the Swedish power producer and distributor Vattenfall. It assesses the proportion of the threatened animal and plant species in Sweden to which its own activities are part of the threat scenario. Its calculations suggest that the main impact is from its hydro dams, which are part of the threat for 6% of threatened animal species and 4% of threatened plant species.

Sustainability indicators. For the environmental dimension of sustainability, the ideal approach would be to compare actual performance with some benchmark of sustainable performance, such as emissions of a substance per unit of value added, or per volume of production, etc., which are deemed by experts, stakeholders, etc. to be compatible with sustainable development. As no such targets exist at present, the best that can presently be done is either for a company to set its own independent sustainability target or to develop relative sustainability measures. The limited activity in this area has focused on the latter. Several companies (for example, British Telecom) compare their percentage of total national emissions with their percentage of national economic activity.

Proxy environmental condition indicators. One way of responding to the difficulty of developing receptor or sustainability indicators is at least to express emissions and waste data in terms of their capacity to cause environmental damage. This is the approach chosen by the British chemicals producer, ICI (see below).

Risk indicators focus on the likelihood and consequences of environmentally harmful events. They can therefore be a near proxy for actual measurements of impact and a useful means of identifying opportunities for risk reduction and deciding between alternative options. One means is through ecological risk assessments (Brown *et al.* 1996). The Norwegian oil company Statoil provides an example of this approach (Klovning and Nilsen 1996).

Another common risk measure is incidents—an upward trend in these is interpreted as signalling a fundamental problem in a company's activities and systems that might ultimately result in a serious impact. A key indicator for BP, for example, is the number of oil spills that they experience.

2. *Operational Performance Indicators (OPIs)*

The draft ISO 14031 distinguishes nine sub-categories of OPI:

▼ Inputs of **materials**, **energy** and **services**

▼ The operation of **facilities and equipment** and **logistics**

▼ Outputs of **products**, **services**, **wastes** and **emissions**.

Materials indicators. The extraction and processing of materials creates major environmental impacts. Reducing their consumption is therefore environmentally positive, and also creates economic benefits. For this reason, indicators of material consumption pre-date environmental concern and many companies have simply used these existing production measures for environmental purposes.

One company that has moved beyond this and developed a sophisticated materials accounting system is Polaroid. The company was embarrassed by its high levels of TRI emissions in the 1980s and set ambitious targets for reductions in toxic chemical emissions. To support this, and drive long-term pollution prevention, it developed an Environmental Accounting and Reporting System (EARS). EARS classifies almost all of 1,400 materials used in the business into five basic categories (Nash *et al.* 1992). Materials are classified on the basis of their ability to do environmental harm, with toxicity regarded as the most important indicator of this. The company's long-term goal is to minimise use of the most hazardous materials. Consumption of hazardous materials is monitored and measures are taken to reduce this over time. However, the system has been criticised for being over-complicated (Maxwell *et al.* 1997) and now appears to be given less emphasis within Polaroid.

Another materials indicator in widespread use is the usage of recycled materials. By avoiding the impacts associated with production of virgin materials, recycling can potentially reduce environmental impacts. Whether this actually happens in practice depends on the impacts that are associated with recycling itself, which can—as when cars are used to ferry small amounts of paper to recycling points—exceed the impacts avoided.

Electrolux deals with this objection by using what it terms a 'recycling index' which relates the financial value of raw materials going into a product with the anticipated financial value of disassembled components and materials at the end of its life. The higher the recycling value, the more likely it is that end-of-life disassembly for recycling or re-use will be economically feasible. The indicator therefore highlights the importance of considering the end-of-life of products during the design stage.

Energy indicators. As with materials, energy production and consumption both have major environmental impacts and represent a significant business expense. For this reason, companies with energy-intensive processes will usually have long-standing energy indicators, and these are an early priority for others who are starting to measure their environment-related performance. Thanks to various government initiatives and a well-developed network of energy managers, this is also the area where most comparable data is available.

Dow Chemical is one company that makes extensive use of energy indicators. Its basic indicator is energy consumption per pound (weight) of chemical production. This declined by over 35% between 1980 and 1995 and the company's long-term target is to achieve a further 20% reduction between 1996 and 2005.

Input service indicators. Service inputs to many activities can often be as or more environmentally significant than material or energy inputs. This the case for airports, which create considerable indirect environmental impacts through transport of passengers and staff to and from their site. As a result, one of the key EPIs for London's Heathrow Airport is the percentage of non-connecting passengers using public transport to reach the airport. This stood at 34% in 1995, and the airport has a long-term objective of increasing this to 50% and a medium-target target of achieving 40% by 31 March 2000. It hopes that this will be achieved through investment in new rail and bus services.

Facilities and equipment indicators. Many aspects of facilities and equipment affect environmental performance: for example, modern versions tend to perform better than old, and emissions can often be dramatically reduced through effective maintenance.

The noise emanating from aircraft and ground-level facilities and equipment is the most significant local impact of airports so it is important to have good indicators of performance. Heathrow Airport therefore has a number of indicators relating to noise generation from both its own facilities and equipment and those operated by airport users. One source of noise is the operation of diesel generators or other mobile ground supply units to aircraft parked on stand at terminals. This can be prevented by installing and using fixed electrical ground power (FEGP) systems. One key indicator is therefore the number of passenger-related stands having FEGP available. A second is the serviceability and availability of FEGPs. Chapter 20 provides a discussion of a key facilities indicator for water companies: the levels of leakage from their system.

Logistics indicators. The movement of materials, components, products, etc. both within companies, and between them and their suppliers and customers, has major environmental impacts. Common indicators of this include vehicle fuel efficiencies and consumption—either as a direct (absolute) indicator, or related to tonnes carried or kilometres travelled. Xerox also measures the proportion of vehicles used for its logistics that carry goods on return trips.

An especially interesting transport indicator is that developed by the Swedish pulp and paper producer, Stora. It has developed a 'transport chain assessment' which calculates significant emissions and energy consumption for each type of transport that it uses. They are then expressed as a relative measure, i.e. per tonne of product transported (ENDS 1997d).

Product indicators. There are a number of different kinds of product indicator (Hauschild and Wenzel 1998; Wenzel *et al.* 1997). One distinction is between indicators that focus on corporate product design processes (which many would regard as being a form of MPI) and those that focus on the performance of specific products or product lines. The latter are especially important for eco-design purposes (Fiksel *et al.* 1998; Conway-Schempf and Lave 1996).

Sweden has been a leader in this area and provides several interesting examples. One is the environmental product profile developed by Volvo which was first applied in 1998 to its S80 2.9 passenger car. The profile assesses 12 parameters in four categories (ENDS 1999b). Each parameter has a total score of 100 and the overall profile was certified by Lloyd's Register.

The Swedish-based domestic appliance manufacturer Electrolux also uses two innovative product indicators—its 'fleet average' and the size of its 'green range'. The 'fleet average' is the average performance of all units sold in respect of key parameters such as energy consumption, water consumption and noise levels. This is calculated both for its own product range and for those of competitors, both on an aggregate basis and disaggregated to individual product segments. The company can then track improvements over time and how these compare with those of rivals.

The 'green range' is the proportion of Electrolux's products meeting specified—and exacting—environmental criteria. The criteria are largely based on 'best-practice' performance and eco-labelling requirements. Electrolux then tracks the green range's percentage of its sales by volume and value, and of its gross profit. The indicator has already revealed that the range is one of the more profitable of Electrolux's lines (although this may be because the better environmental performers are generally also the most advanced and expensive products).

Output service indicators. The output of an increasing number of organisations in today's service-intense economies is a service, either to other businesses or to final consumers. These services can often be of great environmental benefit: for example, by substituting for material artefacts (as when video-by-wire replaces cassettes) or by allowing them to be used more intensively.

Thames Water provides an example of an output service indicator. The company supplies water in one of the driest areas in the UK and therefore has strong business and public pressures to minimise usage. Although many business users have to pay according to consumption, and therefore have a financial incentive to use less, residential consumers have a choice of basis of payment—by consumption, or at a fixed rate based on property value. However, providing them with knowledge of their consumption through water metering can have some effect on their level of usage. Hence, Thames and some other water companies offer a free water-metering service—involving installation of a meter and free subsequent reading—to provide this knowledge. The company has a target of installing 300,000 free meters by 2000, some of which will be in premises charged by consumption but others of which will be in homes that can continue to pay a standard fee.

Emissions and waste indicators. Emissions and wastes indicators are ubiquitous because they are often required by regulators and deal with what are usually highly visible phenomena. For these reasons, and also because targets can easily be set and understood, they can be powerful drivers for improvement. One example of a forward-looking emissions indicator is that of Tokyo Electric (TEPCO). The company measures its carbon dioxide emissions and set a target of 24 million tonnes for 1997 (which it narrowly exceeded) and 31 million tonnes for 2007. The latter allows for load growth (see below for further discussion).

One well-developed waste indicator is that used by 3M, which has developed a uniform methodology for comparing material inputs with valueless waste outputs. All 3M facilities report on a uniform basis their waste generation, and this is the primary EPI throughout the company. Wastes are measured prior to treatment or recycling so that the success of pollution prevention indicators can be estimated. Waste figures are also normalised to levels of production so that judgements about pollution prevention are not influenced by business fluctuations.

Emissions indicators can also be made more sophisticated by expressing them in terms of their environmental impact. A review of ICI's performance in the early 1990s commented that:

> the traditional way of reporting on a company's environmental performance treats all wastes in the same way. It does not help in the understanding of how certain wastes, even in small quantities, cause more damage than others. In our new measuring approach, we focus on those wastes which impose a greater burden on the environment and their reduction is given a high priority. This will help us pinpoint areas where we can make the most effective progress in our environmental programme (ICI 1996: 19).

This new approach involves assessing the environmental burden of ICI's emissions to air and water in terms of seven parameters (ICI 1997; Wright *et al.* 1998):

▼ Acidity—both of direct emissions to water and the acidification potential of gases released to atmosphere

- Global warming
- Human health effects
- Ozone depletion
- Photochemical ozone (smog) creation
- Aquatic oxygen demand
- Ecotoxicity to aquatic life

Each individual emission is assigned a factor reflecting the potency of its impact on relevant parameters. ICI's environmental burden for each of these parameters is then calculated by multiplying, for each emission, the weight emitted by the potency factor. This aggregate number has no meaning in its own right but does allow trends to be tracked over time.

The technique has been widely acknowledged as a serious and innovative attempt to move towards consideration of the environmental impacts of activities, albeit with some debates about the details of its calculation and implementation. Unfortunately, its credibility—as with all of ICI's environmental activities—has often been damaged by the continuing poor publicity that ICI regularly attracts when it experiences environmental problems.

3. *Management Performance Indicators (MPIs)*

ISO 14031 identifies four sub-categories of MPI:

- **Implementation of policies and programmes**
- **Conformance** of organisational actions with requirements or expectations
- Community relations—although this is rather narrow, and we therefore substitute a broader category of **stakeholder** indicators
- Environment-related **financial performance**

Implementation and conformance indicators. A company's environmental performance is determined by the extent to which environment—or environment-related parameters such as energy and materials efficiency—is an important consideration in its internal business processes (Greenberg and Unger 1992). If processes are guided by environmental objectives, and function as intended, then emissions and impacts should be minimised not only now but also in the future. Ensuring that environmental processes are thorough and effective is also a key objective of ISO 14001 and EMAS. A number of chemical companies, for example, measure their performance against the process-focused codes of conduct that form part of the Responsible Care programme. The UK organisation Business in the Environment (1998) also ranks Britain's top 100 companies on a combination of implementation, conformance and other MPIs, based on their responses to its questionnaire.

Specific processes can also be measured. The Swedish power company, Vattenfall, tracks the percentage of its staff receiving environmental training as an indicator. Volvo measures and sets targets for its use of life-cycle assessments.

Stakeholder indicators. The quality movement has extended the definition of 'customer' from its original meaning of buyers of goods and services to include any user of business processes or outputs. The intention is to increase both efficiency and effectiveness by making all business activities responsive to their users, rather than being protected by many intermediate stages from the pressures of ultimate purchasers. The usual way of doing this is to measure customer satisfaction. The Total Quality Environmental Management (TQEM) movement has added a further refinement by considering regulators, communities, environmental groups and other external stakeholders to be important customers for business environmental management activities. Hence, it is equally logical to see indicators of their satisfaction or other attributes as an important area of EPE (Wells *et al.* 1993).

This is the case at Volvo, which includes a question in its employee satisfaction survey on whether respondents are 'satisfied with the manner in which Volvo is managing its environmental responsibilities'. The company then sets a target percentage which it aims to achieve.

Several companies have also measured customer and other stakeholder views as part of the process of preparing their environmental reports: for example, IBM UK (IBM 1995; ten Brink *et al.* 1996) and Glaxo Wellcome (1996).

Financial indicators. Financial data is the language of business. For these reasons, there is growing interest in converting environmental data into, or relating it to, financial parameters (Bennett and James 1998b; Schaltegger *et al.* 1996; Tuppen 1996). Some of this interest is in order to gain better information for making 'point' decisions, such as:

- Guiding product pricing, mix and development decisions
- Future-proofing investment and other decisions with long-term consequences
- Prioritising between specific environmental actions.

In other cases it is more concerned with developing an overview through ongoing monitoring, for example by:

- Identifying total expenses for environmental protection
- Demonstrating the income statement (i.e. profit and loss account) and/or balance sheet impact of environment-related activities
- Identifying cost reduction and other improvement opportunities
- Assessing the eco-efficiency and/or sustainability of a company's activities.

Two of the best-known examples of financial indicator are those used by 3M and Baxter. 3M tracks the net avoided costs and benefits created by measures undertaken as part of its Pollution Prevention Pays (3P) programme. The aggregate first-year benefits of measures introduced between 1975 and 1995 totalled over $750 million—a figure that would have been even higher if second-year and subsequent savings were also counted. This is the practice at the healthcare company, Baxter International, which produces an *Environmental Financial Statement* to assess its environmental costs and benefits (see Chapter 12).

4. *Relative, Normalised, Aggregated and Weighted Indicators*

The previous sections have already provided a number of examples of these four 'complex' EPIs. However, their importance is such that they merit separate discussion (see also Chapter 3).

Relative indicators. These relate data in different units to each other (for example, emissions per million dollars of turnover, or wastes per unit of production). The most common form of relative measure is one that relates an environmental measure such as emissions, wastes, or energy and material consumption, to a measure of business activity such as production or sales revenues. The value of relative indicators is that they screen out macro fluctuations, such as variations in volumes of output over time, and allow critical operational relationships to be identified and managed. However, finding the most appropriate business indicator to which to relate environmental data can be difficult (Shapiro *et al.* 1995). Behmanesh *et al.* (1993) concluded that the precise choice of business activity indicator does not significantly alter industry rankings of environmental performance (although more work is needed to test the validity of this proposition). Greiner (1995) and Shapiro *et al.* (1995) provide practical assistance in selecting business activity indicators. Chapter 12 also discusses the use of relative indicators at Baxter International.

Perhaps the most advanced corporate use of relative indicators is by Roche, the Swiss-based producer of pharmaceuticals, vitamins and fine chemicals, diagnostics, fragrances and flavours (Bennett and James 1998a; Gameson 1998). It has a long-standing commitment to high environmental standards, which are implemented and audited in a similar way in all its worldwide operations. To support this, the company has developed four relative indicators:

▼ The Roche Energy Rate (RER), which is a standardised measure of energy consumption at site level

▼ The Roche Environmental Impact Figures (REIF), which measure raw material consumption per unit of end-product for sites and for individual products

▼ The Roche Eco-Efficiency Rate (EER), a measure of overall environmental impact per million Swiss francs of turnover

▼ The specific contribution to global warming, which calculates the company's emissions of greenhouse gases per million Swiss francs of turnover

Another innovative relative measure is that used by Royal Mail. Its main environmental impacts are emissions from and fuel used by lorries and vans, and energy consumption in sorting offices and other buildings. One measure that can be used in both these areas is emissions of carbon dioxide, which—as a contributor to global warming—is important both in its own right and also as a proxy for related emissions from energy production and consumption. Royal Mail therefore calculates an aggregate indicator of its annual carbon dioxide production, based on its electricity and fuel consumption.

This figure is made more useful by relating it to a unit of business activity, which for Royal Mail is one thousand letters delivered. The result is a measure of 'real unit environmental cost' (RUEC), expressed as grams of carbon dioxide per thousand letters. This can be calculated for a variety of levels, from individual sorting and delivery offices, to regions and Royal Mail nationally. It can therefore be used both for year-on-year and for intra-organisational comparisons. It can also be influenced both by environmental activities—such as energy efficiency campaigns—and by mainstream business activities such as investment in more modern (and generally more fuel-efficient) vehicles. Over recent years, Royal Mail has reduced the RUEC considerably, demonstrating that it is—literally—delivering more to customers with less environmental impact.

TEPCO also uses a relative measure of carbon dioxide emissions per kilowatt-hour of electricity generated. Its calculations indicate that it has lower emissions than an average utility in most other developed countries. However, its report also shows that its target for this measure in 2007 was the same as was achieved in 1997. As it expects load growth to increase its absolute carbon dioxide emissions by almost a third over the this period, this is perhaps unfortunate.

Indexed/normalised indicators. Indexed/normalised indicators (in ISO 14031 terminology) relate a direct or relative measure to a defined baseline. This is most commonly done in the area of emissions, with a given year being designated as the base and subsequent years' outcomes expressed as a proportion of this. The description of Niagara Mohawk in Chapter 10 provides an example of this approach being used for a weighted index.

Aggregate indicators. Aggregate indicators are commonly used to provide data about the company's overall environmental effects: for example, total emissions to air of specified substances, or total volume of wastes. They have limited information value for most managers within the business at operational levels, whose individual responsibilities and performance will be subsumed within a larger total, but reflect progress over time at the level of the corporation as a whole, and (as would be expected) usually represent the main type of quantitative indicator included in corporate environmental reports. General Motors' calculation of the total carbon dioxide emissions generated by its cars in the US each year provides an interesting example of such an indicator.

Weighted indicators. Often termed 'indices', these take the form of dimensionless numbers calculated from a number of weighted individual parameters. The key design issues are therefore which parameters should be included and how they should be weighted (Gameson 1998). A major issue with weighting is whether it is based on quasi-scientific analysis of environmental impacts or whether it is also influenced by other factors such as public perception or business significance. Achieving consensus on either of these can be difficult, especially when external stakeholders are included in the process. Nonetheless, weighted indicators are valuable because some internal and external users of environment-related performance information want its complexity to be reduced to a single number that can be used as a basis for comparison or motivation. The process of discussing weightings can also increase awareness of the relative importance of environmental issues and help to build bridges between individuals, departments and organisations. Chapters 7, 8, 10 and 11 provide practical examples of the development of weighted indicators.

Several public interest bodies have developed weighted indicators of overall corporate environmental performance. The US Council on Economic Priorities, for example, did this in collaboration with *Fortune* magazine to assess the 130 leading US corporations (Rice 1993). This gave marks for performance in 20 areas (of different weighting) and identified 20 leaders, ten most improved, and ten laggards. Business in the Environment (1998) has also published an Index of Corporate Environmental Engagement, based on an assessment of a number of environmental management areas using data supplied in questionnaire responses.

Some companies have undertaken similar exercises for themselves, for example, Nortel (1997) and the US utility Georgia Power (Metcalf *et al.*). The Nortel index is based on 25 indicators covering emissions, compliance, resources and remediation, which are weighted according to criteria such as environmental impact and degree of risk (Nortel 1997). Overall, emissions account for 50% of the index, compliance for 25% and resources and remediation for 12.5% each. The scores for individual indicators are based on performance relative to targets and to the preceding year. The overall index was set at 100 for the base year, 1993, and has a maximum level of 175. The 1996 score was 142, a significant improvement since 1993 but only marginally better than the 140 of 1995.

A number of companies have also developed weighted product indicators that can be used to guide new product development and to compare products with each other. These involve assigning points to key environmental features of the product—e.g. materials composition and methods of disposal—and summing these to produce an aggregate score. A number of such 'eco-point' schemes have been developed, of which the best known are those developed by Philips (now available as a commercial software package, Eco-Scan) and Volvo, in collaboration with other Swedish organisations (Tulenheimo *et al.* 1996).[5] The schemes are similar in that they cover all life-cycle stages: production, distribution, use and end-of-life. For each stage, the user selects appropriate materials, processes, usage and transportation details from the

---

5 Eco-Scan software can be obtained from Turtle Bay, PO Box 84, 3000 AB Rotterdam, Netherlands; details from *info@ turtlebay.nl* or +33 102651178.

options provided in the software. The package then calculates an 'eco-score' for each of these elements, based on a number of points for a given quantity or usage. Chapter 13 provides more information on this.

Another major area of application for weighted indicators is that of environmental risk rating (Skillius and Wennberg 1998). This is intended to measure the degree of risk attached to an organisation and its activities. Risk can be assessed through a qualitative integration of a wide variety of individual measures. Alternately, a single measure or a small number can be used as a proxy: for example, the existence (or otherwise) of an environmental management system to give an indication of the company's degree of preparedness. In practice, most financial stakeholders appear to seek an integrated approach.

One of the more sophisticated risk rating methodologies is that developed by the Centre for the Study of Financial Innovation. This was first applied to Scottish Nuclear, an operator of nuclear power plants (and now part of British Energy) (Centre for the Study of Financial Innovation 1995). It focused on a number of elements, including: regulation; safety/environment record and actions; short-term and long-term liabilities; legal disputes; suppliers; wastes; public/political perceptions; quality of management; financial condition; business prospects; and environmental benefit created by the company's activities. The output is expressed in the same format as that adopted by the financial rating agency Moody's, i.e. a three-letter grade, with AAA as the highest. In the event, Scottish Nuclear gained a relatively high rating, reflecting what was perceived to be its impressive management approach and extensive safety measures. The approach has since been applied to another UK utility, Eastern (Centre for the Study of Financial Innovation 1998).

3

An Environmental Performance Measurement Framework for Business

C. William Young and Richard J. Welford

ENVIRONMENTAL management systems have been one of the routes followed by many organisations in the United States and Europe to improve their impact on the environment (Roberts 1994). Welford (1996b) describes the workings of environmental management systems (EMSs) and associated standards, where 'continual improvement' of the organisation's environmental performance is a requirement (ISO 1996). Continual improvement can be tracked using environmental performance indicators (ISO 1998b). Epstein expands:

> 5 or 10 years ago, most corporations did not seriously consider their environmental liabilities in either internal decision making or external reporting. The rapid increase in environmental costs now has caused companies to begin to integrate these considerations into management decisions at all levels . . . measuring and reporting corporate environmental performance is still in its infancy but significant developments are occurring. Companies are beginning to recognise that they need to be proactive rather than reactive and that planning orientation rather than a compliance orientation pays off in both reduced environmental impacts and increased long-term corporate profitability (Epstein 1996: xxix).

SustainAbility and UNEP (1996a) stress the urgency in developing environmental performance indicators by charting the development and implementation of environmental management tools by the business community (see Table 1). Environmental indicators, as suggested by Epstein (1996), have been one of the last environmental management tools to be developed, but should, in fact, be one of the first to be used by the business community, according to SustainAbility and UNEP (1996a, 1997) (see Table 1). Companies should first track their environmental performance and use this

Actual chronology	Ideal chronology
Environmental auditing	Environmental/full-cost accounting
Environmental reporting	Environmental indicators
Environmental management system	Environmental management system
Verification	Environmental auditing
Environmental benchmarking	Environmental reporting
Environmental indicators	Verification
Environmental/full-cost accounting	Environmental benchmarking

Table 1: ENVIRONMENTAL INDICATORS IN RELATION TO THE
OTHER ENVIRONMENTAL MANAGEMENT TOOLS

Source: SustainAbility/UNEP 1996a: 8

information to manage, audit, report, verify and benchmark their environmental performance (Epstein 1996).

Bartolomeo describes environmental performance indicators as having:

> the aim of evaluating company efficiency (economic and environmental) and effectiveness in achieving environmental objectives and allow:
>
> - the adoption of the most appropriate measures of environmental protection in terms of effectiveness and efficiency;
>
> - the empowerment of environmental policy by a better definition and monitoring of environmental objectives;
>
> - an effective definition of responsibilities and an aid for the implementation of the environmental management system; and,
>
> - the improvement of external and internal communication on environmental achievements and programmes' (Bartolomeo 1995: 22).

A further reason for measuring corporate performance is to allow for benchmarking between companies in the same market sectors (WBCSD 1996). Eccles (1991) points out that, just as quality-related measures have made the performance measurement revolution more real, so has the development of competitive benchmarking. Benchmarking gives managers a methodology that can be applied to any measure, financial or non-financial, but non-financial measures should be emphasised. Benchmarking has a transforming effect on managerial mind-sets and perspectives. In the case of environmental measures, this is a priority if companies are to move towards sustainability and to cause the organisational culture to change (Jones 1996).

The term 'environmental performance indicators' (EPIs) is defined by Tyteca as 'tools that allow the analysis of the improvement (or deterioration) of a given firm's environmental performance' (Tyteca 1994a: 3). This environmental performance can be compared over time, or between various plants within a firm, or between various firms in an industry, or between the industrial sectors. Ashford and Meima (1993) explain that the environmental performance of the firm is the extent and effectiveness of actions that the firm takes to mitigate its environmental consequences. The European Green Table suggests that 'environmental performance indicators are measures of company proficiency in protecting the environment' (1993: 4). Hence carbon dioxide and methane emissions, for example, could be indicators of an organisation's effect on global climate change.

The ISO 14031 guidelines on Environmental Performance Evaluation are also being developed, with an initial definition of it as:

> [A] process to facilitate management decisions regarding an organisation's environmental performance by selecting indicators, collecting and analysing data, assessing information against environmental performance criteria, reporting and communicating, and periodic review and improvement of this process' (ISO 1998b: 5).

◢ *Background*

Apart from other environmental management system tools described by Welford (1996b), there are four environmental performance measurement methods:

1. Frameworks to select indicators

2. Different types of indicators

3. Performance measurement frameworks

4. Mathematical measurement models

Young (1996) reviews the corporate environmental performance measurement field.

The first methodology is described by James and Bennett (1994) and ISO 14031 Environmental Performance Evaluation guidelines (ISO 1998b). This methodology selects indicators to monitor directly the company's significant aspects. The advantage of this method is that the indicators selected relate to the company's individual environmental aspects. The disadvantage is that each company applies resources and time into selecting indicators, and significant aspects may change over time or may be incorrect. The second methodology selects indicators according to its type, i.e. physical measures of mass and volume; efficiency measures; customer measures; and so on. The different types of environmental performance indicator are discussed later in this chapter and in Young and Rikhardsson (1996). Callens and Tyteca (1995), James (1993), Welford and Gouldson (1993), Wells *et al.* (1993) and Wolfe and Howes (1993) suggest differing types of indicator that can be used in conjunction with the implementation frameworks (methodology 1 above) to monitor a company's significant aspects. ISO 14031 also does this by applying different types of indicators—i.e. direct, aggregated, relative, indexed and weighted—to a company's significant aspects (see Chapter 2).

Research process

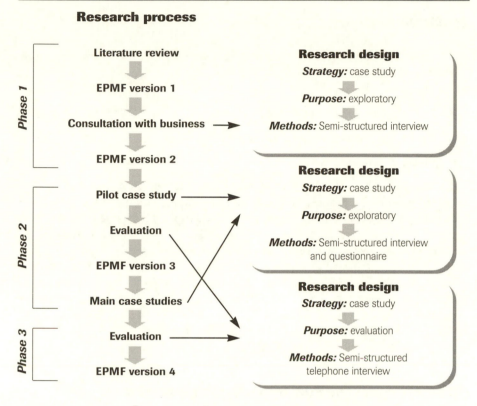

Figure 1: THE PhD METHODOLOGY IN PRACTICE

The third methodology presents a measurement framework that encompasses all of the company's activities. Bartolomeo (1995), BMU and UBA (1997), CICA (1994), European Green Table (1993, 1997), Hanssen (1996), Lober (1996) and VfU (Rauberger and Wagner 1996) all suggest frameworks that contain different types of indicators. The advantage of a framework is that the company does not spend resources and time selecting indicators and, further, the framework should be comprehensive enough to cover all the company's operations and activities. The disadvantage in using a framework is that significant aspects of the company may not be measured.

The final methodology is for the company's environmental performance to be measured using mathematical models. Tyteca (1994b) and Wehrmeyer (1993) both suggest mathematical models but both may be difficult to implement for managers and the results may be complicated to communicate. Thus the two mathematical models may be better utilised as external assessment tools.

This chapter will describe the results of the development of an internal assessment tool. It is based on the third measurement methodology described above, i.e. encompassing all of the company's activities, as well as elements of the first two measurement methodologies.

◢ *Methodology*

An Environmental Performance Measurement Framework (EPMF) was developed during the course of the research period. The research project was divided into three major phases (see Fig. 1):

- ▼ **Phase 1:** theoretical framework development and consultation with industry
- ▼ **Phase 2:** testing with case study companies
- ▼ **Phase 3:** evaluation and refinement of EPMF

At the start of the research project, a theoretical EPMF was formed from current literature (especially Azzone *et al.* 1996), and the integrated opinions and experience from the business community, consultants and academia. This framework was then put to the test first by piloting it and then through further trials with eight UK-based companies with business in aggregates, pharmaceuticals, hotels and plastics. Once the case studies had provided information for the framework, a single report on the environmental performance of each of the companies being researched was compiled for the case studies to critique. Following the environmental performance report, an evaluation interview was conducted with the case studies to gain feedback on the report, the framework and the data collection methodology.

◢ *Environmental Performance Measurement Framework (EPMF)*

The original theoretical EPMF described in Azzone *et al.* (1996) had four measurement areas:

1. Environmental policy

2. Environmental management system

3. Processes, products and services

4. State of the environment

These measurement areas are now assessed as to how they fit into the post-field-trials EPMF.

◻ *Environmental Policy Measurement Area*

The original environmental policy measurement area first presented the organisation's environmental policy and, second, compared the organisation's environmental policy to an environmental policy statement survey (Brophy 1995) and the International Chamber of Commerce (ICC) Business Charter for Sustainable Development. The evaluations with the case studies found that the presentation of their company's

Organisation's target (1995)	Indicator (1997)
By 2000 to reduce energy usage by 20%	Energy reduction 10%

Table 2: EXAMPLE OF COMPARING THE ORGANISATION'S ENVIRONMENTAL
TARGETS TO CURRENT PERFORMANCE

environmental policy within an internal measurement tool was unhelpful. The policy was already known to the company and its inclusion in an environmental perfor-mance report did not aid the reader in assessing the company's environmental performance.

The comparison of the company's environmental policy to the ICC/WBO charter was found useful by the case studies as a comparison. It is, of course, a matter of debate whether such a comparison is relevant in an internal measurement tool. Arguably, an environmental measurement tool should be used over time to produce trends using indicators (European Green Table 1997). Benchmarking the company's environmental policy to an external business charter will not produce an indicator that can be used over time. An organisation should, of course, periodically review its environmental policy to see whether it needs to be updated (ISO 1996). So it would be argued that the assessment of the appropriateness of an organisation's environ-mental policy does not fit within the scope of an internal measurement tool.

An organisation should ideally set objectives and targets in line with its environ-mental policy to provide goals for improvement (European Commission 1993; ISO 1996, 1998b). The original theoretical EPMF (Azzone *et al.* 1996) aimed to make comparisons between an organisation's current and actual environmental perfor-mance with its set objectives and targets (see Table 2). Unfortunately, the evalua-tion found that none of the case studies participating in this research had set any objectives and targets against which to measure performance. But it is important that this element remains in the refined EPMF because not only is this part of ISO 14031 (ISO 1998b), but it also monitors whether the company is achieving (or maintaining) the objectives and targets it has set itself.

◁ *Environmental Management System Measurement Area*

In Azzone *et al.* (1996), the original theoretical environmental management measure-ment area first compared the organisation's environmental management with set environmental management system standards. Second, it identified both descriptive and quantitative, financial and non-financial indicators in three areas, namely: compliance, commitment and stakeholders.

The organisation's environmental management system (EMS) was compared to the EMS standards the Eco-Management and Auditing Scheme (EMAS) (European Commission 1993) and BS 7750 (BSI 1994) (which was succeeded by ISO 14001 [ISO

1996]). The original EPMF used BS 7750 because ISO 14001 was published only after this research started in 1994.

This type of comparison was well received by the case studies, as it benchmarked their progress in developing an EMS. This type of methodology is used by other organisations such as the consultancy DNV to rate a company's environmental performance (Jebsen and Schlumberger 1997). Thus this type of comparison can chart companies' progress over time to achieve an EMS. In Table 3 the improved EPMF uses ISO 14001 because BS 7750 technically does not exist now that the new international standard has been published. The two standards are similar and the EPMF comparison is only an indication of the completeness of an organisation's EMS, not conformance to the standard. This comparison demonstrates to what extent an organisation has implemented (formally or informally) an EMS. An indication of implementation of an EMS component does not necessarily mean that it conforms to either of the standards.

From the evaluations, an improved set of indicators has been produced which portray the organisation's performance in three sub-sections, namely: compliance (see Table 4), commitment (see Table 5) and stakeholders (see Table 6). In each of these sub-sections, the indicators are grouped into qualitative, quantitative economic, and quantitative non-economic indicators. The compliance indicators relate to the organisation's compliance to environmental legislation as well as its environmental liabilities. The commitment indicators deal with the organisation's commitment to

Company EMS	ISO 14001	EMAS	System component
	✓	✓	**1.** Company policy
	✓	✓	**2.** Senior management involvement
	✓	✓	**3.** Review of impacts
	✓		**4.** Register of regulations
	✓	✓	**5.** Register of impacts
	✓	✓	**6.** Allocated responsibilities
	✓	✓	**7.** Objectives and targets
	✓	✓	**8.** Management programme
	✓	✓	**9.** Manual
	✓	✓	**10.** Operational control
	✓	✓	**11.** Records
	✓	✓	**12.** Training
	✓	✓	**13.** Audits (internal)
		✓	**14.** Public statement/reporting
	✓	✓	**15.** System verification
		✓	**16.** Statement/report verification
	✓	✓	**17.** Commitment to continuous improvement of system

Table 3: COMPARISONS OF ENVIRONMENTAL MANAGEMENT SYSTEM STANDARDS
ISO 14001 AND EMAS

Qualitative indicators
Compliance to a listing of relevant environmental legislation, authorisations and regulations over last three years

Quantitative economic indicators	
Amount of environmental fines	
Costs related to environmental incidents	
Environmental liabilities	
Annual cost of environmental insurance	

Quantitative non-economic indicators	
Number of formal legal warnings over last three years	
Number of prosecutions over last three years	
Number of environmental incidents	
Number of working days lost due to environmental incidents or lack of compliance	

Table 4: INDICATORS FOR COMPLIANCE

Qualitative indicators
Tangible evidence of explicit commitment of top management
Description of the roles and functions of departments dedicated to the environment
Description of the professional profiles of people partly or fully employed or otherwise dedicated to the environment
Description of specific activities related to the environment
Description of environmental management tools used by the organisation, e.g. EMS and LCA
Description of technologies used to control and monitor the organisation's environmental impact

Quantitative economic indicators	
Budget of departments dedicated to the environment and percentage of turnover	
Amount of reactive environmental costs, e.g. resource use and waste disposal	
Amount of proactive environmental costs, e.g. employee training and energy efficiency equipment	

Quantitative non-economic indicators	
Number of people partly or fully dedicated to functions or activities	
Number and frequency of environmental audits	
Number and frequency of published environmental reports	

Table 5: INDICATORS OF COMMITMENT

Qualitative indicators
Define and list the organisation's stakeholders
Description of collaborations with suppliers, customers, same-market-sector organisations and local economic or geographical regions to reduce environmental impacts
Description of projects with non-business stakeholders

Quantitative economic indicators	
Amount of charity donations and percentage of turnover	
Costs of collaborations and projects with stakeholders	
Quantitative non-economic indicators	
Number of positive and negative enquires from stakeholders	
Percentage of suppliers with certified or verified EMS	
Percentage of inputs where the environmental quality is controlled	

Table 6: INDICATORS OF STAKEHOLDERS

reducing its environmental impact through financial and personnel resources and projects. The indicators for stakeholders deal with the organisation's interaction with its stakeholders through complaints as well as proactive projects. These environmental management indicators are directed at summarising the organisation's efforts (or lack thereof) to reduce its environmental impact.

◁ Processes, Products and Services Measurement Area

During the field trials, the processes, products and services measurement area used the ecobalance analysis (see Rubik and Baumgartner 1992; White and Wagner 1994; and Chapters 6 and 7 for details), detailing the energy and material flows through the organisation to collect data for the relative indicators (see Table 7). Relative indicators describe the key areas of the organisation's resource use, emissions and wastes, either relative to a kilogram of its product (or, for example, customer per night in the case of a hotel) or as a quota. A quota is where the energy or waste product is shown as a percentage of the total amount of energy or waste. These relative performance indicators highlight the efficiency of a company in producing a product or providing a service over time. Relative indicators can also be used for an organisation's internal use or for industry benchmarking.

The main field trials introduced aggregated indicators which served as a summary of the organisation's process, products and service measurement area. These indicators are a summary of the ecobalance analysis which set out the organisation's energy

Production- or service-specific ratios	
1. Water consumption (l per kg product or customer)	
2. Energy consumption (kWh per kg product or customer)	
3. Emissions (total kg per kg product or customer)	
• NO_X emissions (kg per kg product or customer)	
• SO_2 emissions (kg per kg product or customer)	
• CO_2 emissions (kg per kg product or customer)	
4. Waste (total kg per kg product or customer)	
• Hazardous waste (kg per kg product or customer)	
• Residual waste (kg per kg product or customer)	
• Recyclables (kg per kg product or customer)	
Energy and water quotas	
1. Energy quotas %	
• Gas	
• Electricity	
• Oil	
• Combined heat and power	
• Fuel	
• Renewable, e.g. solar and wind	
2. Waste quotas %	
• Hazardous waste	
• Recyclables	
• Residual waste	
Material ratios	
1. Packaging (kg per kg product or customer)	
Emissions quotas	
1. CO_2 (kg per kWh of energy use)	
2. NO_X (kg per kWh of energy use)	
3. SO_2 (kg per kWh of energy use)	

Table 7: RELATIVE INDICATORS FOR PROCESSES, PRODUCTS AND SERVICES

and material flows. These aggregated performance indicators provide an overview of the organisation's total resource use, emissions and waste without being relative to production.

The evaluation suggested that the relative and aggregated indicators were of use to the companies researched, but needed to be used over time to produce trends. These trends could then be used in conjunction with setting targets. Thus, in the improved EPMF, the processes, products and services measurement area continues to use the ecobalance to collect data for relative indicators in Table 7 and aggregated indicators shown in Table 8. The relative indicators have changed slightly from the original theoretical set (Azzone *et al.* 1996) to include summed totals, renewable energy sources such as wind and solar energy and are applicable to manufacture or service industry companies.

◁ State-of-the-Environment Measurement Area

The original theoretical state-of-the-environment measurement area (Azzone *et al.* 1996) attempted to calculate the organisation's contribution to environmental impacts, such as global climate change. But from the evaluation it was concluded that this methodology was complicated and statistically unsound. For the main case studies, the environmental performance index was developed to compare the key areas of the organisation's energy and material flows to the UK national total. This attempted to show the organisation's potential contribution to national environ-

Description	Total annual inputs	Total annual stock	Total annual output
1. Total land (m²)			
2. Total plant and equipment (pieces)			
3. Total product/service-related goods (kg)			
3.1 Total raw materials (kg)			
3.2 Total semi-finished and finished goods (kg)			
3.3 Total auxiliary goods (kg)			
3.4 Total ancillary goods (kg)			
3.5 Total products/services marketed (kg/rooms)			
3.6 Total by-products (kg)			
3.7 Total waste (kg)			
4. Total energy (kWh)			
5. Total water (m³)			
6. Total air emissions (kg)			

Table 8: AGGREGATED INDICATORS FROM THE ECOBALANCE ANALYSIS

mental impacts and also illustrated how the organisation's figures fared in comparison to the UK total. The index was calculated by producing a ratio between the UK figures and GDP, and the organisation's figures and turnover. The organisation's ratio is calculated as a percentage of the UK ratio producing the index. Thus the index aimed to show how the organisation's emissions per £ of turnover fared against the national total.

Unfortunately, this second methodology was found to be unsatisfactory by the main case studies who wanted (rightly) to be benchmarked to companies in the same market sector and not to the whole of the UK. The state-of-the-environment index may also be impractical as part of an internal management tool because a company would have to find relevant up-to-date national figures. This may be too time-consuming to justify when external benchmarking schemes could be more effective (WBCSD 1996). The issue of benchmarking is discussed further later in this chapter. Thus the state-of-the-environment measurement area is not included in the improved EPMF.

◢ Resulting Environmental Performance Measurement Framework

The revised EPMF that was formulated following field trials, evaluation, benchmarking, amendments and improvements is presented in Table 9. The EPMF contains three measurement areas: environmental policy; EMSs; and processes, products and services. The environmental policy measurement area forms indicators by comparing the

Measurement area	Indicators		Refer to
1. Environmental policy	**1.1**	Performance against set objectives and targets	Table 2
2. Environmental management system	**2.1**	Comparison of EMS to ISO 14001 and EMAS	Table 3
	2.2	Management performance indicators:	
	2.2.1	Indicators of compliance	Table 4
	2.2.2	Indicators of commitment	Table 5
	2.2.3	Indicators for stakeholders	Table 6
3. Processes, products and services	**3.1**	Relative performance indicators	Table 7
	3.2	Aggregated performance indicators	Table 8

Table 9: THE RESULTING EPMF

company's performance to its set objectives and targets. The EMS measurement area contains three sets of indicators: compliance; commitment; and stakeholders. Each of these sets of indicators contains qualitative, quantitative economic and qualitative non-economic indicators. The processes, products and services measurement area contains two types of indicator: relative and aggregated.

The aim of this research project was to develop a theoretical EPMF, then to field-trial the framework in a range of business organisations, and finally to evaluate and refine it. Different-market-sector organisations participated in the field trials enabling the framework to be developed for applicability as both an internal and a generic tool. The generic indicators and indices described above have been developed because organisations need a methodology for monitoring their environmental performance (SustainAbility/UNEP 1996a, 1997). This is due to increasing pressure from the government, trade organisations, proactive companies and other stakeholders for information on organisations' environmental performance (James 1994a; Ashford and Meima 1993; Fiksel 1994). This generic framework will also facilitate external reporting to stakeholders using standard indicators which may lead to benchmarking either within sites in organisations or between organisations.

◤ *EPMF Strengths and Weaknesses*

This study has developed an EPMF, trialled it, evaluated and altered it, and proposed an improved version. According to Metcalf *et al.*, benefits should be provided to a company using an environmental performance indicator that:

- Tracks progress towards corporate goals.
- Adds definition and support to corporate environmental policy.
- Highlights areas of excellence.
- Demonstrates continuous improvement.
- Identifies weak spots in environmental management systems.
- Allows for more efficient distribution of resources.
- Provides a communication tool focusing on stakeholders.
- Provides a mechanism for establishing accountability for environmental results' (Metcalf *et al.* 1996: 8).

Bearing these in mind, this section summarises the strengths and weaknesses of the post-field-trials EPMF.

◁ *EPMF Strengths*

1. The EPMF is generic, providing a set of indicators that could be used by many UK business organisations.

2. The EPMF is an internal management tool that a company's management can use independently of external organisations or data.

3. The EPMF contains a comprehensive range of indicators:
   - ▼ Economic quantitative, non-economic quantitative and qualitative
   - ▼ Absolute, aggregated and relative

4. The EPMF covers most business activities, products or services that interact with the environment in three measurement areas:
   - ▼ Environmental policy
   - ▼ Environmental management system
   - ▼ Processes, products and services

5. The EPMF could provide evaluation information by:
   - ▼ Comparing the company's performance against its set targets in the environmental policy measurement area
   - ▼ Comparing the company's performance over time producing trends

◁ EPMF Weaknesses

1. The EPMF does not address the specific impacts each company may have on the environment, i.e. does not select significant aspects and measure these aspects, such as James and Bennett (1994) and ISO 14031 (ISO 1998b).

2. The EPMF has only been trialled in four UK companies and may only be applicable to some UK companies in some market sectors.

3. It does not externally benchmark the company to other companies in the same market sector or other industries.

4. If a company wished to progress towards sustainable development and measure this, the EPMF measures only environmental performance and not the other areas of sustainable development, specifically intra- and inter-generational equity.

◢ Working with Environmental Performance Indicators

There are four types of environmental performance indicator (Business in the Environment 1992; ISO 1998b): absolute, aggregated, relative and index/ weighted. Of course, environmental performance indicators can also be presented in quantitative or descriptive formats (Davis 1994).

Absolute indicators measure basic data (Fiksel 1994). An example of an EPMF absolute indicator from the ecobalance analysis is: 'carbon dioxide emissions (kg)'. While absolute indicators provide useful information, care must be taken not to draw false conclusions from the information they provide. The fact that carbon dioxide emissions in, for example, Year 2 have fallen when compared to the emissions in Year

1 does not necessarily mean that company's efficiency has improved, i.e. carbon dioxide emissions per unit of output have fallen. The fall in emissions may simply be due to a downturn in business, i.e. the company is operating at the same level of efficiency but producing less output. If carbon dioxide emissions have dropped because of an increase in efficiency, the company could reasonably claim that environmental performance had improved. But, if efficiency had remained the same and output had merely fallen, such a claim would not be justified.

A solution may be to use relative indicators that compare absolute consumption or emission figures with meaningful reference data, such as units of production (ISO 1998b). As shown by the processes, products and services measurement area, relative indicators can be separated into efficiency ratios and quotas, where:

- Efficiency ratios describe the use of resources or the amount of emissions in relation to production inputs or production outputs, e.g. carbon dioxide emissions per unit of output, or ratio of waste per unit of input material.
- Quotas describe the sub-section of a measure in relation to the whole measure, e.g. the proportion of the company's energy sourced from gas in relation to the company's total energy consumption.

A problem occurs with relative indicators in, for example, large organisations. Relative indicators may show for a particular company an increase in efficiency of carbon dioxide emissions per unit of production. But this may hide the total amount of carbon dioxide produced in absolute terms, which could be significant if benchmarking a large company to a smaller one.

Aggregated indicators bring together data from a number of separate categories into a more general category (James 1993). An example of an aggregated indicator from the processes, products and services measurement area is 'annual waste disposal'. Annual waste disposal is a general category and consists of the sum of all the separate waste streams. Aggregated indicators are useful as they can bring together a large amount of data and express it as a single value, thereby providing an overview of a particular area. However, because aggregated indicators paint a broad picture, there is a limit to how much detail they can show. If annual waste disposal stays constant from one year to the next, then, without a further breakdown of the figures, it would not be known that, whereas paper (non-hazardous waste) disposal had gone down, organic solvents (hazardous waste) disposal had increased by the same amount. This can be solved to a certain extent by weightings that increase or decrease the importance of certain components within the aggregated indicator. So, while useful, aggregated indicators should be used to complement absolute indicators and not as an alternative.

Index indicators are comparisons of a piece of data to another baseline piece of data (Business in the Environment 1992). The evaluation found that indexing is difficult, can be statistically uncertain and hides detail. Weighting environmental aspects is also to some extent subjective and judgements relating to the significance of environmental aspects will vary from firm to firm (Wehrmeyer 1995).

Thus, as presented in the post-field-trials EPMF, absolute, relative and aggregated indicators should all be used in conjunction with each other to produce an overall picture of the company's environmental performance. Index indicators with or without weightings should be avoided in an internal management tool.

Hammond *et al.* (1995: 1) presented an information pyramid that illustrated the different information formats for measuring environmental performance. From the experiences of developing, trialling and evaluating the EPMF, this information pyramid can be adapted.

The *y*-axis label has been changed from 'complexity of indicators' to 'complexity of information'. This reflects more accurately the process of collecting primary or raw data and converting them into indicators. The Hammond *et al.* information pyramid was split into four areas: primary data, analysed data, indicators, and indices. The experience of using indices in the EPMF was that they were complex and unreliable. Thus the altered triangle in Figure 2 illustrates the three stages that, this study has concluded, should be used to measure a company's environmental performance, from the perspective of an internal management tool. At the base of the triangle, large quantities of relatively simple data are collected to be summarised in more complex indicators (Wehrmeyer 1995). These indicators are then evaluated (European Green Table 1993) by comparisons over time to produce trends (Tyteca 1994a), comparisons to the company's set targets (ISO 1997) or benchmarking to other companies or industries (WBCSD 1996). As previously discussed, the EPMF as an internal management tool was unsuccessful at benchmarking and concluded that this aspect of evaluation should be conducted externally to the organisation. The next section discusses the issue of benchmarking further.

◢ *Benchmarking*

Benchmarking enables comparisons to be made between sites within a company (internal benchmarking) and between companies in the same industry (external benchmarking). Benchmarking as part of the EPMF was not feasible because of its subjectivity and difficulty in operationalising as part of an internal management tool. It was suggested that benchmarking may be more appropriate as part of an external assessment conducted by a third party. This section will briefly discuss the possibilities.

The WBCSD (1996) suggests that benchmarking should be conducted between companies in the same sectors or between industries. In order to benchmark the environmental performance of companies within a specific sector, the issues that could be considered are:

1. Market sectors would need to be clearly defined.

2. A set of sector-specific environmental performance indicators would need to be developed.

3. Information about the environmental performance of the industry sector as a whole in relation to these indicators would need to be collected so that a company could be benchmarked against the industry average.

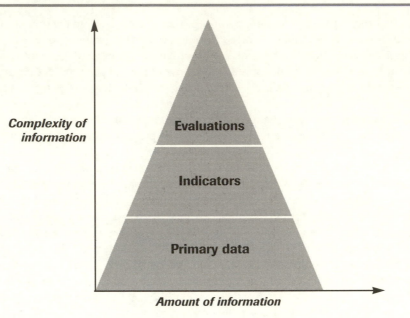

Figure 2: THE ENVIRONMENTAL PERFORMANCE MEASUREMENT INFORMATION PYRAMID

Source: Adapted from Hammond *et al.* 1995: 1

In the UK, defining sectors and developing relevant indicators would be challenging. It is difficult to see how sector-wide information could be obtained on environmental performance so as to determine an industry average against which to benchmark. The situation is different in the United States where the regulatory system requires companies to disclose large amounts of information (EPA 1997b). Using this disclosed information, for example, the US EPA is setting up a benchmarking-type scheme known as the 'sector facility indexing project' (SFIP) (EPA 1997b). In the UK, the Environment Agency's Operator and Pollution Risk Appraisal (OPRA) scheme will also be used as a benchmarking tool, but only for regulatory assessment. According to Her Majesty's Inspectorate of Pollution (HMIP)'s 1995 consultation document: 'OPRA will provide information on indicators such as . . . performance differences between similar authorised processes, e.g. within a multi-site company group or within an industry sector' (HMIP 1995: 6).

Environmental performance indicators developed for specific market sectors include the Canadian Institute of Chartered Accountants (CICA 1994) and the European Green Table (1993). The UK chemical industry's 'Responsible Care Programme' involves the use of set indicators designed for the chemical industry (CIA 1996). The German Association of Environmental Management in Banks, Savings Banks and Insurance (VfU) has developed a set of environmental indicators to assure the comparability of environmental data presented in company reports (Rauberger and Wagner 1996).

Benchmarking schemes by external organisations across market sectors include the Safety, Health and Environment intra-industry Benchmarking Association (SHEiiBA), which was formed in the UK in 1996 and is running a benchmarking scheme involving 112 companies (ENDS 1997a). Another SHE benchmarking project, 'Contest', was carried out on a pilot basis by the CBI, also in 1996 (ENDS 1997b). The Investor Responsibility Research Centre (IRRC) also provides a benchmarking service for companies in the US (Naimon 1994).

There are benchmarking schemes that are conducted externally by third parties which compare major companies across market sectors. These are used to publicise the progress, or lack thereof, that companies are making in improving their environmental performance against each other. These include the journal *Fortune* (Rice 1993) which in the US compared the environmental performance of a range of companies using selected measures. More recently, Business in the Environment (1996) in the UK compared the FTSE 100 companies using an 'index of corporate environmental engagement'.

In conclusion, at present, environmental performance benchmarking seems to be split into four categories depending on their purposes:

1. Regulatory benchmarking by government agencies to assess conformance to legislation and regulations, e.g. EPA (1997b) and HMIP (1995).

2. Market-sector benchmarking, where sector-specific indicators are used by that sector's companies, who then compare themselves to the industry averages, e.g. CICA (1994), CIA (1996); European Green Table (1993, 1997) and VfU (Rauberger and Wagner 1996).

3. Business service benchmarking, whereby a company can be confidentially benchmarked against other companies, e.g. CBI (ENDS 1997b), IRRC (Naimon 1994) and SHEiiBA (ENDS 1997a).

4. Public benchmarking, where companies are benchmarked against other companies and the information made public, e.g. Business in the Environment (1996) and *Fortune* (Rice 1993).

Obviously, companies will prefer option 3, where all information remains confidential. Option 2 may also be attractive to companies because benchmarking can remain confidential, by the company comparing its own data against industry data (from publicly available sources or confidential clearing-house services). But before companies commit resources to such services, issues such as methodology and data quality should be investigated.

◢ *Conclusions*

In conclusion, this study has attempted to develop an internal management tool that companies can implement to measure their environmental performance. The theoretical Environmental Performance Measurement Framework (EPMF) developed in Azzone *et al.* (1996) was trialled before being evaluated. Benchmarking was experimented with by using the case studies to form an environmental performance index. A new EPMF was described after the field trials.

Essentially, measuring environmental performance in business comprises summarising all of a company's activities using environmental performance indicators. These indicators can then be used to evaluate the company's environmental performance for decision-making in three ways:

1. Comparison of the indicators over time to produce trends

2. Comparison of the indicators to the company's set objectives and targets to assess if they have been met

3. Using the indicators for benchmarking the company against other companies in its market sector

The EPMF developed environmental performance indicators and incorporated the first two of the above evaluation methods. Benchmarking was deemed to be inappropriate as part of an internal management tool.

This study took the approach of action research (Robson 1994). It was the decision of the authors that, at the very least, this study should contribute to developing the participating case study companies' environmental management practices. These environmental management practices would then (in theory) help to reduce the case study companies' potential environmental impacts.

4

Standardisation

The Next Chapter in Corporate Environmental Performance Evaluation and Reporting*

Allen L. White and Diana Zinkl

AS RECENTLY AS 1990, a mere handful of North American and European companies produced corporate environmental reports (CERs), or included environmental information in their annual reports. Most simply did not see the value in communicating their environmental performance to stakeholders. For many, in fact, the inclination was exactly the opposite: to avoid the risk of adverse public reaction by keeping environmental information out of the public eye. These early reports often consisted of self-congratulatory anecdotes and lists of environmentally oriented charitable contributions. Quantitative, self-critical information was decidedly scant.

Today, at least 1,000 companies worldwide produce stand-alone environmental reports and many more include environmental information in their annual reports. CERs have emerged as the public expression of the burgeoning field of environment-related management accounting (Bennett and James 1997, 1998b). Their evolution from the early years of 'green glossies' to the present era of more balanced and candid CERs containing hard data and mixed news has been driven by a gradual recognition that forthright reporting is not only expected, but respected, by various stakeholders. Anecdotes alone are simply inadequate to meet the expectations of increasingly sophisticated readers (SustainAbility/UNEP 1996a).

Clearly the idea of standards for CERs has arrived. But what is the advantage for those companies that would use such standards (White and Zinkl 1998a)? Externally, CERs can improve communication with stakeholder groups, including investors, environmentalists, consumers and host communities. For investors, an informative,

---

* We gratefully acknowledge the many valuable comments of the co-editors of this volume on earlier drafts of this chapter. Any remaining errors, of course, are the sole responsibility of the authors.

transparent CER provides a glimpse into the company's management quality as well as its environmental liabilities. As evidence mounts that environmental performance correlates closely with financial performance, providing reliable environmental information to investors will be an advantage for proactive, environmentally aware companies. For environmentalists, CERs provide essential benchmarking information on company performance. For consumers and host communities, CERs can provide information on the types of materials used to make products, the type and amount of wastes generated while making products, and the disposal of waste materials.

Central to the evolution of CERs are environmental performance indicators (EPIs). EPIs are environmental information directly linked to environmental performance and used on a continuing basis to measure such performance (Ditz and Ranganathan 1997). Like financial performance indicators that communicate a firm's financial condition to government, shareholders, employees and other stakeholders, EPIs provide a means by which environmental performance may be tracked and reported for both internal and external audiences. Thus, EPIs quantify resource use such as energy and water, and environmental releases such as air pollutants, waste-water and solid wastes. Tracking standardised EPIs over time allows a comparison of a company's current performance with its earlier performance, with other firms in the same sector, or with industry overall.

Some standardised EPIs are required by law. The best-known example is the US government requirement that some facilities report their total emissions of over 600 chemicals to the Toxics Release Inventory (TRI). Approximately 21,000 facilities now report based on the threshold criteria of manufacturing or processing 25,000 lb, or otherwise using 10,000 lb, of a listed chemical. Data gathered by the government informs citizens about chemicals used and released, and the treatment and disposal of toxic substances in their communities. US companies subject to these regulations usually include these data in their CER, if they produce one.

While most data reported to governments is publicly available, there is no requirement that companies include it in their CER. Other information, such as chemical use, which a company may track for internal purposes, may also fail to appear in a CER. In an informal review of corporate EPIs currently in use in the annual environmental reports of 30 companies in the US, Canada and Europe, we found that: (1) there are dozens of EPIs in use; (2) firms use a variety of units—pounds, tons or percentages—to report indicators, making comparisons difficult; (3) different industries use different indicators; and (4) a range of normalisation techniques are currently practised. Without normalisation, of course, meaningful comparisons of EPIs over time within the same company or between companies are difficult, if not impossible. Our assessment found over 100 EPIs in use, from 'Number of compliance citations' to 'Amount of packaging waste produced/unit of product'. Approximately 40% of the EPIs were normalised by some method, a figure considerably higher than the 20% (normalised by production or sales) for CERs published up to autumn 1995 found in an earlier study (Lober *et al.* 1997).

This wide array of EPIs attests to the shortcomings of current practices. In the sample of 30 firms, as expected, the most commonly reported EPIs were data collected under regulatory mandates, such as TRI, workplace safety and hazardous waste

Typical EPIs	Dow	Monsanto
Toxics Release Inventory (TRI) emissions	6,200 tons*	49 million lb
Energy used in manufacture	296,000,000 million BTUs*	n/a
Capital environmental expenditures	$120,000,000†	$47,000,000

1 ton = 2,000 lb
* 1994 data
† Includes health and safety capital expenditures

Table 1: DOW AND MONSANTO: TYPICAL ENVIRONMENTAL PERFORMANCE INDICATORS
Sources: Dow Chemical 1996; Monsanto 1996

generation for US companies, and National Pollutant Release Inventory (NPRI) data for Canadian companies. However, most firms included a few EPIs of their own creation, and this is the source of most inconsistency. Some stem from the simple reality that not all EPIs are relevant to all sectors. For instance, the number of oil spills per year is applicable to the petroleum production and refining industry, but has little relevance to the textile industry. Alternately, some EPIs might have geographic importance: firms or facilities located in arid regions or near wetlands are more concerned about water use and effluents. While there will always be a need for different companies and industries to report specialised indicators, ample opportunity exists for standardising both what information companies include in their CERs and how it is reported.

The Standardisation Imperative

Why, again, is standardisation of CERs so compelling? As a simple illustration, consider the case of an investor seeking to compare the performance of two chemical companies, Dow and Monsanto, using the three recently reported EPIs in Table 1.

Which company is the best environmental performer? The first three EPIs are typical, appearing in most CERs. Also typical, unfortunately, are different and inconsistent units of measurement and types of information provided. Monsanto's emissions exceed Dow's by a factor of four.[1] However, both companies include only releases and off-site transfers when tallying their TRI emissions and exclude on-site treatment and disposal, and wastes burned for energy recovery. Monsanto, often viewed as an environmental leader, does not report energy use data, so it is impossible to compare the two companies in this essential aspect of environmental performance. In environmental expenditures, Dow exceeds Monsanto by $73 million, but this

---

1   6,200 tons = 12,400,000 lb.

Next-generation EPIs	Company 1 (46,300 million lbs product)	Company 2 (60,000 million lbs product)
Total emissions/unit of product	0.22 lbs emissions/ lb product	0.19 lbs emissions/ lb product
Total energy used/unit of product	2,822 BTU/lb product	2,700 BTU/lb product
Total emissions/total raw materials used	0.06 lb. emissions/ lb raw materials	0.05 lb. emissions/ lb raw materials

Table 2: NEXT-GENERATION ENVIRONMENTAL PERFORMANCE INDICATORS
USING HYPOTHETICAL FIGURES

Source: White and Zinkl 1998b

comparison is misleading, since Dow groups environmental health and safety capital expenditures together. In other words, the two companies are using different definitions of environmental expenditures, thereby prohibiting a fair comparison across firms on this common (though flawed) EPI. Of course, even if the two firms used the same definition, interpreting different levels of environmental expenditure is problematic. A higher figure may signify either high remediation costs or, alternatively, investment in new, cleaner technologies. The latter, of course, probably reflects astute management; the former, in contrast, is a non-value-adding activity reflecting past mismanagement.

Even if definitions were consistent, what would these EPIs tell us? With no adjustment for scale of operations, it is impossible to make fair comparisons. Dow's TRI emissions are four times less than Monsanto's, but what if Monsanto is producing 20 times more product than Dow? Neither company provides information on the magnitude of their operations (e.g. total pounds of product, gross revenues), so there is no way for our perplexed investor easily to normalise these figures. With no universal protocol for estimating emissions, energy use or environmental expenditures, and no normalisation of data, any CER user may well be left more confused than illuminated when comparing performance. These inconsistencies are compounded for companies located in different countries, with different regulatory regimes, units of measurement and currency. For instance, Dow Europe does not report TRI emissions; the Dow Europe and Monsanto reports share no common emissions data.

Now consider the potential next generation of EPIs (Table 2) using hypothetical figures. Our investor now sees that Company 2 produces fewer emissions per pound of product, uses less energy per pound of product, and demonstrates a slightly higher efficiency in its use of raw materials. On this basis, a CER reader may conclude with some degree of confidence that Company 2 is performing better environmentally, and more efficiently, than Company 1. Of course, there is no information about the life-cycle impacts of the product: are Company 1's products environmentally friendlier? And are its management practices superior? And are the physical measures themselves the best approach to normalisation in light of the product mixes and degree of vertical integration in each firm? Whatever the answer to these questions, we can say with some assurance that the second set of indicators provides more useful information than the first.

◢ *Proliferating Guidelines*

To advance the quality of CERs, at least 30 organisations worldwide have developed guidelines for companies producing CERs. Most offer only loose guidelines; only nine organisations, to our knowledge, have developed specific standards or metrics (see White and Zinkl 1998b for a compendium of initiatives and full citations). These include, for example:

▼ The Association for Environmental Management in Banks, Savings Banks, and Insurance Companies (VfU), founded in 1994, develops sector-specific strategies and tools for environmental management in the banking and insurance industries. VfU produces a detailed guidance document for environmental reporting in the banking and insurance industry, including recommended quantitative indicators.

▼ The Coalition for Environmentally Responsible Economies (CERES) offers a detailed, comprehensive reporting form that includes both qualitative and quantitative information. The form, either in standard or short version, is currently used by more than 50 firms, primarily in the United States. CERES also offers, or will soon offer, customised forms for the health services, electric and gas, and financial services sectors.

▼ Since 1996, the Danish government has required companies in certain industry sectors to produce facility-level annual environmental reports called 'Green Accounts'. The reporting requirements include both qualitative and quantitative information, some of which is publicly available (see Chapter 16 for more discussion of this).

▼ The European Chemical Industry Council (CEFIC) has guidelines for corporate reports and site-specific reports, a standard emissions inventory, and a list of 'dos and don'ts' of environmental reporting for the chemical industry. In 1998, the CEFIC guidelines were revised and now include 16 types of indicator.

▼ The Investor Responsibility Research Center (IRRC) compiles and disseminates information on corporate environmental performance, primarily as a service to the financial and social investment community. Data includes both government mandated quantitative information and qualitative information, plus selected performance ratios for benchmarking.

▼ The United Nations Environment Programme and SustainAbility, a London-based consulting firm, developed a system for ranking CERs according to 50 'reporting ingredients'. In 1994, 1996 and 1997, SustainAbility applied its ranking system to 100 CERs (see Chapter 15).

▼ The World Business Council for Sustainable Development (WBCSD), through its Eco-Efficiency Working Group, is developing a set of internal indicators for tracking eco-efficiency performance. Some of these may also serve external reporting purposes.

▼ The World Resources Institute (WRI) in its *Measuring Up* study (Ditz and Ranganathan 1997), recommends four categories of EPI: materials use, energy consumption, non-product output, and pollutant releases.

▼ The Global Reporting Initiative (GRI), convened by CERES in 1997, is a multi-stakeholder effort with the explicit goal of producing standardised corporate sustainability reporting guidelines for worldwide application (see Chapter 23).

While these programmes are a mix of sector-specific, country-specific and generic, some common elements exist. For instance, there is virtual consensus that companies should report information on chemical releases, energy use, water use and hazardous and non-hazardous waste management. In other ways, however, reporting elements vary widely. The CERES reporting forms, for example, contain dozens of questions on the qualitative aspects of a firm's operation, while at present the Danish and WBCSD approaches contain none. GRI, in turn, seeks to reconcile all these approaches into a single format comprising both qualitative and quantitative information.

◢ The Manager's Perspective

To understand better the prospects for standardised reporting, WRI recently commissioned Tellus Institute to perform a survey of how managers perceive and use EPIs (White and Zinkl 1997). Our survey focused on three key areas: who uses EPIs and how; the current status of EPI use and development within corporations; and future trends in the development of EPIs. The survey had three purposes: (1) to inform WRI's *Measuring Up* report; (2) to provide a baseline to track future progress in EPI applications; and (3) to help advance the quality and utility of EPIs within the business community.

WRI and Tellus collaborated on the design of the survey which was distributed at two conferences: *Putting Pollution Prevention into Action*, Washington, DC, in September 1996; and an environmental accounting seminar in Whistler, British Columbia, Canada, in October 1996. The first conference focused on pollution prevention issues; participants comprised delegates from companies participating in US EPA voluntary programmes, government and academia. The second conference focused on advanced environmental accounting topics for managers in the resource and energy sectors.

Of 58 industry participants from the Washington conference, 22 responded to our survey, for a response rate of 38%. Eleven out of 23 industry participants from the second conference responded to our survey, for a response rate of 49%. The overall response rate was 41% of industry attendees at both conferences.

◻ *Respondent Profile*

Respondents represented 14 different industry sectors; however, two industries, chemicals and allied products, and electric, gas and sanitary services, dominate the field with 33% and 27% of respondents, respectively. This principally reflects the make-up of the two forums: the Washington conference was weighted toward chemical industry participants, while the Whistler meeting targeted the energy sector.

A majority of respondents work for larger companies, with 52% working for companies with gross revenues greater than $1 billion. Industry participants from the Washington conference included only companies that report to the Toxics Release Inventory (TRI), thereby screening out smaller firms which are exempt from TRI reporting requirements. Participants in the Whistler conference all work in the energy sector which, by and large, comprises large enterprises, e.g. oil and gas exploration, transmission and power generation.

Sixty-one per cent of respondents described their principal function as environmental health and safety (EHS); 18% described their function as regulatory; 6% as finance and accounting; and 3% each described their principal function as operations, marketing, economics or process engineering. Seventy-six per cent of respondents function at the corporate level in their company; 15% at the division level; and 6% work at the plant level. In sum, the typical profile of our respondents is a corporate EHS staff person in a large energy or chemical firm. This undoubtedly colours our findings, since EHS staff are more likely both to value and to use EHS information than are senior corporate managers and line managers who, of course, make most of the principal strategic and operational decisions within the firm.

◻ *Current Uses and Views of EPIs*

Ninety-one per cent of participants report that they use EPIs to support day-to-day decisions (Table 3). Most participants, 67%, also report that environmental criteria are an important consideration in decision-making. However, the responses to questions 2, 3 and 6 show that, while EPIs and environmental criteria play an important part in decision-making, usable EPIs are not always available, and developing them can be resource-intensive. In other words, the information systems necessary for developing and communicating crucial EPIs do not always exist in these companies.

◻ *What Makes a Useful EPI?*

EPIs continue to evolve to serve the needs of stakeholders within and outside the firm. These needs are linked to a wide range of decisions which require EPIs to deliver

Questions	Response (%)		
	Almost always	Sometimes	Rarely
I use EPIs to support day-to-day decisions	36	55	9
Adequate EPIs are available to evaluate firms	24	52	24
Adequate EPIs are available to evaluate products or processes	9	52	39
EPIs enhance resource productivity	24	67	6
Environmental criteria are a relatively important consideration in my decision- making process	67	27	6
Resources required to gather, report and maintain EPIs equal or exceed their value	18	55	24

Table 3: CURRENT USES AND VIEWS OF ENVIRONMENTAL PERFORMANCE INDICATORS

information that is timely, rigorous and comparable. What, then, are the specific characteristics that will allow EPIs to meet these objectives?

Respondents to our survey see the single most important characteristic of an EPI as comparability over time (Fig. 1). Eighty-five per cent think this is essential; an additional 15% think it is helpful. Of course, comparability over time is a prerequisite to charting progress of programmes internally and externally. In addition, comparability across products and within a company scores high marks as well. Clearly, companies use indicators internally to compare the performance of different product lines, facilities and divisions.

Second to comparability over time is verifiability, which 73% view as essential. Verifiability may take many forms, from internal audit to external, third-party verification. While the latter is still dominated by compliance (as distinct from performance) auditing, industry is moving slowly in the direction of more comprehensive coverage by external auditors. In any case, verifiability is the cornerstone of credibility regardless of whether upper management or community stakeholders are the EPI users in question. Normalisation also received high marks, with 36% of respondents viewing normalisation as essential and 51% as helpful.[2]

What about external uses and comparisons of EPIs? Respondents did not view comparability across companies within industries, across industries and across countries to be as vital as comparability over time and verifiability. Together, these results show that EPIs are currently used primarily for internal decision-making and benchmarking, and not for external comparisons. However, external comparisons

---

2 This would be *relative* measures in ISO 14031 terminology.

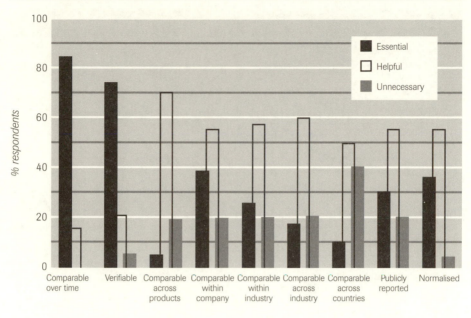

Figure 1: IMPORTANCE OF CHARACTERISTICS OF ENVIRONMENTAL PERFORMANCE INDICATORS

Source: White and Zinkl 1997

are an important, secondary role for EPIs, but still well short of their internal value in the view of our respondents.

Whether for internal or external purposes, standardised EPIs would benefit decision-makers by making EPIs more comparable. By adopting specific EPIs for use at all facilities, standardisation would smooth internal comparisons and aid the development of corporate-wide indicators. Externally, this would enable business decision-makers to make inter-company comparisons, though this benchmarking function has yet to achieve the standing that is accorded to internal uses of EPIs.

Table 4 summarises the same questions, but only for respondents who regularly use EPIs. Clearly, for the regular users, all comparability attributes are significant. The only characteristic that regular users of EPIs view as less important is comparability across countries: only 16% of regular users of EPIs found it essential and 40% found it helpful. This may reflect an overall domestic focus on environmental issues within the companies represented in the survey. Alternately, it may result from a disinclination to make such transnational comparisons since so many other variables (e.g. regulations, cost, production requirements) may render such comparisons uninterpretable. Nonetheless, it may be that a movement toward global environmental standards will change this perspective. International comparisons aside, it is clear

Characteristic	Respondents (%)
Comparable over time	100
Verifiable	93
Comparable across products	77
Comparable across facilities within company	93
Comparable across companies	80
Comparable across industry sectors	80
Comparable across countries	56
Publicly reported	87
Normalised	90

Table 4: REGULAR USERS OF ENVIRONMENTAL PERFORMANCE INDICATORS
WHO FOUND CHARACTERISTICS OF EPIs ESSENTIAL OR HELPFUL

Source: White and Zinkl 1997

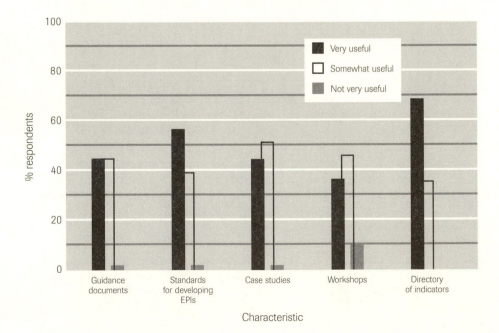

Figure 2: UTILITY OF TOOLS TO ENHANCE THE USE OF
ENVIRONMENTAL PERFORMANCE INDICATORS

Source: White and Zinkl 1997

that comparability is of critical importance to regular users of EPIs. And, again, standardised, publicly available EPIs will make this possible.

⬜ *Approaches to Enhancing EPIs*

Though interest in EPIs is keen, up to this point progress toward refining and institutionalising them has been uneven. What initiatives by government, non-governmental organisations and business might serve to advance the science and practice of EPIs?

Many respondents would value outside guidance on the use and development of EPIs (Fig. 2). Two-thirds think a directory of current EPIs would be very useful, and nearly half think that guidance documents would be very useful. Over half think that standards for developing EPIs would be very useful. This latter point is a strong signal that standardisation is ripe for business support. Finally, case studies and workshops garnered a substantial positive response.

Beyond the approaches listed in the survey, respondents made several suggestions to strengthen EPI practices: a network of companies using indicators; mutual assistance between companies and entities outside the company who use EPIs; and a coalition of firms willing to share data for benchmarking. Again, reporting standards would be a major contribution in the success of such initiatives.

⬜ *Plans for Advancing EPIs*

To assess what concrete EPI actions are under way in corporations, we asked respondents to characterise activities their firms have initiated (Table 5). Nearly all respondents report some kind of activity in their firms. Two-thirds report that corporate guidelines have been or are being developed, an impressive figure which speaks both to interest and to action in developing EPIs. Over half are developing EPIs at the facility level, as well as benchmarking their choice of EPIs against other firms.

	Respondents (%)
Corporate guidelines have been or are being developed	76
One or more facilities are developing EPIs	61
Benchmarking EPIs against other firms	52
Seeking input on EPIs from external stakeholders	27
No future plans for EPIs	6

Table 5: CORPORATE PLANS FOR DEVELOPING ENVIRONMENTAL PERFORMANCE INDICATORS

Source: White and Zinkl 1997

◻ *The Public and EPIs*

Use and public disclosure of EPIs are not one and the same. A firm may well be inclined to sharpen its use of EPIs to support internal decisions, while at the same time resist public disclosure of those same EPIs, especially at a disaggregated (i.e. process) level. The degree of public disclosure is actually a continuum of options. That is, a company may report to government with a prior confidentiality agreement; report to government for permitting/compliance purposes with limited circulation allowed or anticipated; report to government with the knowledge and expectation that data will be widely available and easily accessible; or develop a corporate environmental report using its own or a third-party format with the explicit purpose of informing a broad array of stakeholders.

Each of these presents its own set of perceived and actual costs and benefits. Some firms believe that it is possible that publicly reported environmental information, e.g. chemical use, can be used to reverse-engineer patented products, or provide competitors with sensitive information on production volume (White *et al.* 1997). On the other hand, some community and environmental stakeholders believe that making such information available to the public is critical to understanding the nature of local environmental risks, most notably the transport and storage of hazardous materials. They further contend that public reporting is beneficial to companies in the long run, despite concerns about proprietary information, citing the benefits of TRI as both an internal decision-support tool and an external communications vehicle.

A strong majority of respondents to our survey strongly support public reporting of three EPIs: chemical releases, regulatory compliance and greenhouse gas emissions (Table 6). Of course, to a great extent, release and compliance information in the US

Indicator	Respondents (%)
Chemical releases	73
Water use	48
Regulatory compliance	67
Chemical inputs or use	30
Energy use	36
Environmental expenditures	5
Efficiency of chemical use	18
Greenhouse gases	57

Table 6: RESPONDENTS FAVOURING PUBLIC REPORTING BY
ENVIRONMENTAL PERFORMANCE INDICATOR

Source: White and Zinkl 1997

and Canada is already in the public domain, so it is not surprising that respondents favour public reporting of these EPIs. Though TRI initially met with resistance from the industrial community, today there is little sentiment in US industry to eliminate such programmes.

In contrast to release and compliance information, however, respondents do not favour public reporting of efficiency of chemical use information or chemical inputs information. Currently, this is the subject of considerable debate in the United States, with the business community citing proprietary, competitiveness, resource and redundancy concerns as reasons for opposing the expansion of the TRI programme to include such information (EPA 1997a; Hearne 1996).

◢ Conclusions

EPIs are on the agenda of large North American corporations. Our survey findings suggest that they are regularly used by management in the energy and chemical sectors. In addition, public reporting of environmental requirements is gaining acceptance as a standard business practice, driven by a combination of regulatory requirements, internal business benefits and rising public expectation for corporate accountability.

Notwithstanding these trends, it is clear that there is ample room for improving the scope and utility of EPIs. EPIs are often viewed as difficult and costly to develop and maintain. Some are publicly reported, and some stakeholders would like to see more public reporting. However, industry concerns with regulatory burdens and confidentiality persist. Further, there remains the question of what types of indicator should be placed in the public domain. Particularly controversial is public reporting of EPIs related to product inputs, such as chemical use and chemical efficiency information.

Standardised environmental reporting, and its companion, sustainability reporting, promises to address many of these challenges:

▼ Expanded usability of CERs through standardised formats, indicators and metrics

▼ Simplification of EPI development and the public reporting process for companies

▼ Enhanced value of reported information for both internal and external uses

▼ Quick and reliable benchmarking of company, facility and, depending on report content, product and process performance

The barriers to achieving standardised environmental reporting are formidable. Sceptics rightly point to the considerable differences across industry sectors in terms of environmental impacts of processes and products. From an environmental perspective, do auto, chemical and forest products industries share enough in common to make standardised reporting an achievable, and desirable, vision? Further, can manufacturing firms be evaluated using the same metrics as service industries such as financial services and telecommunications? In the broadest sense, can environmental performance be measured comparably and consistently when, unlike financial reporting, it does not enjoy the luxury of a neat and universally recognised denomination, namely, dollars and cents?

What is clear is this: standardised reporting is at a crossroads. In one direction lies a future in which companies react on an ad-hoc basis to stakeholder demands for usable information, with the publication of CERs containing data compiled and reported according to unique formats, metrics and protocols. If the last five years is a guide, we can reasonably expect this pathway to lead to increasing volumes of information in the public domain, but little or no gain in the *value* of such information to investors, environmentalists, communities and consumers. This scenario depicts a future wherein CERs fall well short of their potential as a market-based instrument capable of driving firms toward continuous improvement. While information volume grows, information value will not. The opposite, in fact, is more likely: larger quantities may well lead to disillusionment among both the report generators and the report users as CERs fail to meet the need for consistent, comparable and timely information.

The alternative future is starkly different. Working within the constraints of diverse industry sectors, the dozens of disparate reporting initiatives worldwide blend into an organised movement that co-ordinates and optimises the considerable resources now expended to produce and disseminate CERs. This scenario paints a future wherein standardised environmental reporting takes its place alongside financial reporting as a tool for investors, communities and consumers in making choices ranging from investments and purchasing to setting priorities for facility–neighbour dialogues. This is a scenario wherein environmental information is routinely reported in a timely, comparable, consistent format in much the same way that financial information appears today. Key environmental indices, built on a core for all firms and supplemented by customised information for each industry sector, become a universal tool for company performance evaluation.

It is precisely this vision that underlies the Global Reporting Initiative (GRI), whose guidelines are reproduced in Chapter 23. Convened in late 1997 by the Coalition of Environmentally Responsible Economies (CERES), a Boston-based NGO, GRI seeks to bring uniform, generally accepted guidelines to corporate sustainability reporting worldwide (White and Zinkl 1998c; Adams and Willis 1998). Governed by a Steering Committee comprising North American, European, Asian and Latin American business, NGO and accounting society representatives, GRI released a pilot test version of its guidelines in March 1999. At least a dozen companies worldwide will test these guidelines and provide feedback in preparation for release of a first version in early 2000. The process is under way to locate GRI in a permanent institutional home to continue its work of refining, disseminating and supporting the use and verification of corporate sustainability reports.

Developing EPIs that are useful to business and the public, and are relatively easy to maintain, will be a challenge for many years to come. Many of the characteristics of EPIs that respondents see as essential or helpful are not yet integrated into common reporting practices. Normalisation, a key step in developing EPIs that are comparable across facilities, companies, industries and countries, weighs heavily among these characteristics. Finally, a variety of external EPI-supporting products—guidance documents, standards and directories—will reinforce the substantial internal efforts which respondents to our survey report already are under way.

5
Information Systems for Corporate Environmental Management Accounting and Performance Measurement

Pall M. Rikhardsson*

AS ENVIRONMENTAL MANAGEMENT tasks develop, different systems emerge to deal with those tasks. One such function is environmental management accounting (Bennett and James 1998b). This function can be defined as 'the process of identifying, measuring, accumulating, analysing, preparing, interpreting, and communicating financial and non-financial environmental information that helps managers fulfil corporate environmental objectives'.[1]

In order to evaluate alternatives, to decide on a course of action or to communicate with internal and external stakeholders, environmental managers need information about corporate environmental performance. This chapter proposes a concept of corporate environmental performance that combines the financial and non-financial elements of the concept. It discusses and describes various types of environmental information system that might be used in managing environmental performance information. Furthermore, it identifies possible strategies for a company when designing an environmental performance information system and touches on several important implementation issues. Finally, it discusses experience of designing such a system from the perspective of a large Danish production company and the possibilities of using the system for achieving an integration of the financial and non-financial elements of corporate environmental performance.

---

* The views expressed in this chapter are the author's own and should not necessarily be associated with the institutions he represents.
1 Based on the definition of management accounting by Horngren and Sundem 1993: 3.

1. *Corporate Environmental Performance Measurement*

Environmental performance, as defined by the impending ISO 14031, is the company's achievement in managing any interaction between the company's activities, products or services and the environment (ISO 1998b). Improvement of environmental performance thus implies that the company has minimised the relative environmental impact of its activities, products or services.

Based on the use of performance measurement in traditional management accounting, environmental performance measures can be (Horngren and Sundem 1993):

- ▼ Attention-directing, where they point to problems and indicate which problems are to be given priority

- ▼ Used in problem-solving, where they (should) enable environmental managers to choose between possible solutions and evaluate possible outcomes

- ▼ Used in keeping track of activities and results—i.e. scorecard-keeping

A survey of environmental managers (Rikhardsson 1998), as well as other sources (Schaltegger *et al.* 1996; Epstein 1996; Welford and Starkey 1996; Young and Rikhardsson 1996; ISO 1997; Loeber 1996; Deloitte & Touche 1996; Ulhøi and Rikhardsson 1997; James and Bennett 1994) indicates that corporate environmental performance as a concept has at least five dimensions, as shown in Figure 1.

The operations of the company include the production processes that generate the physical product or service offered by the company. In practice, this means

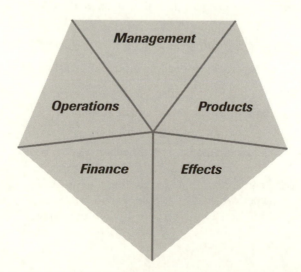

Figure 1: THE CORPORATE ENVIRONMENTAL PERFORMANCE PENTAGON

performance measurement that focuses on the environmental efficiency and effectiveness of the production processes. The second dimension is the product(s) or service(s) itself. This includes the measurement of environmental aspects of the product itself (in most ecobalance methodologies called the 'product balance' [Kunert AG 1996]) or the product life-cycle (in most product life-cycle assessment methodologies called the 'inventory stage' [SETAC 1992]). The third performance dimension is how environmental issues are addressed by management. This often includes the results of implementing the environmental policy and the performance of the environmental management system, as well as how well the environmental objectives of the company have been reached, including regulatory compliance objectives. The fourth, and perhaps the most difficult area to measure, covers the environmental impact of a company's operations as well as the use of its products. At a process level, this could be the contribution of the company's heavy metal emissions to concentrations in the local aquatic environment, as measured by some biological indicators. From a product perspective, it might include the energy consumption of the product during its lifetime and the resulting contribution to the greenhouse effect. The fifth and final environmental performance dimension is the financial one. As the company is an economic entity, many managers (and stakeholders) see the need for linking environmental performance and financial performance (see e.g. Bouma 1996; Bennett and James 1998b). This includes defining and allocating environmental costs, investments and liabilities.

Environmental performance measurement as part of environmental management accounting is therefore broadly focused and covers both non-financial and financial information. Not many companies consider all of the above dimensions at the same time. However, the benefits of keeping these five areas in mind when designing environmental performance measurement systems are the same as in designing a balanced scorecard in other contexts (Kaplan and Norton 1992a). Measuring and reporting performance in only one dimension (such as solely focusing on operations) involves a risk of:

- Drawing attention to wrong or insignificant problems
- Supplying inadequate or misleading information for problem-solving
- Keeping a score that is useless at best and misleading at worst
- Misleading communications with stakeholders

As studies show, most companies focus on non-financial information in environmental performance measurement (see e.g. Loeber 1996 or Deloitte & Touche 1996). However, the link to financial measures is fast becoming important as financial stakeholders request information about the links between environmental performance and financial performance. The case described in Section 4 shows a possible system for integrating these two aspects in a practical context.

2. Environmental Information Systems

Eccles emphasises the role of information technology in performance measurement. He states that:

> Thanks to dramatically improved price–performance ratios in hardware and breakthroughs in software and database technology, organisations can generate, disseminate, analyse and store more information from more sources, for more people, more quickly and cheaply than was conceivable even a few years back (Eccles 1991: 133).

Corporate information systems are the combination of hardware, software, people, procedures and tasks that manage information and support managers in attaining corporate objectives (based on Long 1989). Accordingly, environmental information systems are the combination of hardware, software, people, procedures and tasks that manage environmental information and support (environmental) managers in reaching the environmental objectives of the company.

But which attributes should the ideal information system for supporting environmental performance measurement have (Siegenthaler *et al.* 1995; Donley Technology 1996)? Based on the environmental performance pentagon, an ideal environmental information system supporting environmental performance measurement would focus on the collection, processing, storage and reporting of the data and information shown in Table 1.

When designing an environmental information system, a company basically has two alternatives. One is to buy a software package. Such packages come in three types: (1) a complete-solution package requiring no changes in set-up; (2) a parameter-selection package which requires selection of various parameters; and (3) a skeleton package which is fully configurable. The other alternative is to develop custom software either from scratch or based on existing company software.

In a survey of environmental managers and the information systems used for environmental purposes, several combinations were reported (Rikhardsson 1998). Most of the managers used spreadsheets to some extent, while two had implemented standardised information-collection procedures and interfaces between systems. Only a single manager had invested in specific software for environmental information management, and few had even considered using other company information systems in environmental management. Another survey of 5,000 environmental managers found that only 11% had attempted to build integrated environmental information systems.[2]

When buying a standard environmental information system package, the purchaser is faced with several alternatives. A survey of approximately 100 suppliers carried out by this author in early 1997 showed that environmental information system packages for management purposes generally fall into eight categories, as shown in Table 2.

---

2   BTI Consulting Group quoted in *EMIS Tech* 1.1 (July 1997): 2.

Performance area	Information on
Operations	Input and output such as: • Significant raw material consumption • Use of chemical substances • Water consumption • Energy consumption • Emission to air • Emission to water • Solid waste • Noise • Odour
Products	Product input and output based on: • Each product line • Stages of the life-cycle
Management	Environmental management initiatives such as: • Environmental management system implementation • Performance of the environmental management system • Environmental management audits and reviews
Financial issues	Environmentally related: • Costs • Revenues • Investments • Liabilities
Environmental impact	The environmental impact of the company in either a process or product perspective

Table I: THE FUNCTIONS OF AN IDEAL ENVIRONMENTAL INFORMATION SYSTEM

An interesting difference emerged between the software sold in the US and Europe. The software sold in the US is more often sold under the banner of being tools for complying with environmental laws and regulation. Consequently, many software products focus on heavily regulated areas such as emission to air and hazardous waste. In addition, there are several software products designed to help managers in estimating costs of various environmental initiatives including compliance. The European focus, on the other hand, seems to be on constructing some sort of a mass balance for use in determining areas for improvement. The compliance aspect is not as apparent, although it is an underlying aspect. Furthermore, software for assessing the financial aspects of environmental management is virtually unknown in the European market.

It is also interesting to note that some suppliers of large business information systems, often called 'Enterprise Resource Planning Systems', such as SAP and Oracle, have introduced modules for environmental information management compatible with the modules of their other products.

3. *Implementing Environmental Information Systems: A Methodology*

The Corporate Accountability Services of PricewaterhouseCoopers Denmark has developed a methodology for implementing environmental information systems called

Type	Description
Mass-flow accounting software	Includes software enabling the construction of full mass-flow input and output at different company levels. Also includes software with a more limited focus on partial mass flows mostly focusing on heavily regulated areas such as flows of dangerous substances, or emissions to air or water.
Life-cycle assessment software	Some of these packages contain facilities for constructing and maintaining records for mass flows but go one step further to allow for the linking of environmental interaction to environmental impact and assess these aspects for the whole product life-cycle.
Environmental cost assessment software	For use in identifying and assessing costs associated with e.g. clean-up, remediation and process changes due to environmental considerations.
Modelling software	Enables the user to construct models of processes and sites. Some of the packages use Geographical Information Systems (GIS) technology.
Health and safety software	Focuses on government health and safety regulations, workplace assessments, health and safety project management, illness records and injury statistics.
EMS support software	These packages contain tools for facilitating the implementation of an environmental management system. Some also contain the full text of standards such as ISO 14001 and directives such as the European Union EMAS. Many packages are designed to be integrated within the company's own intranet
Knowledge databases	Include legal databases for use in monitoring compliance with government environmental limits containing the full text of environmental laws and regulations, sometimes with comments. Also databases containing knowledge of chemical substance characteristics and international standards for hazard labelling, etc.
Integrated modular software	These combine two or more of the types mentioned above in one software package. Either module-based or part of an ERP (Enterprise Resource Planning) solution.

Table 2: TYPES OF STANDARD ENVIRONMENTAL INFORMATION SYSTEM PACKAGE

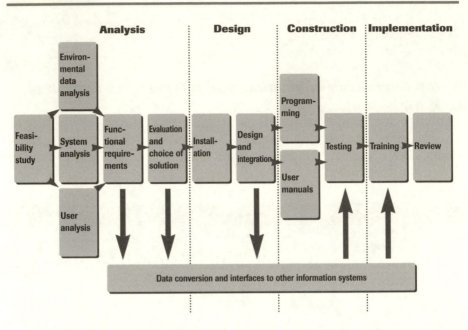

Figure 2: PRICEWATERHOUSECOOPERS CAS DENMARK EMIS-IM©

the Environmental Management Information System—Implementation Method-ology© or EMIS-IM© for short. EMIS-IM© can be used in the implementation of environmental information package software or custom-made software. Being a standardised method, EMIS-IM© has the advantages of having been refined in a variety of contexts and applicable to a wide range of projects. Figure 2 shows the main elements of EMIS-IM©.

The PricewaterhouseCoopers EMIS-IM© is based on analysing the requirements of the client, selecting the software solution based on these requirements and then designing, constructing and implementing the solution to fit the requirements.

Before deciding to buy or customise a system for environmental information management, the company may wish to get a clearer picture of the required functionality of the solution needed, regarding both general environmental manage-ment issues and specific system issues. A checklist for this purpose is presented in the appendix to this chapter. After going through the checklist, the company will have a clearer idea of what to look for in the standard packages available or which parameters the customisation project ought to focus on.

An example of an EMIS-IM© for mass-flow accounting software (see Table 2) is shown in Table 3. The steps in Table 3 include specific tasks which are not shown here. As much of the difference encountered in implementing an environmental management information system, as compared to, say, an accounting system, lies in the analysis and design phases, the case study in the next section is used to illustrate these phases. It should be kept in mind, however, that the system and technological changes are just one type of change entailed by a standard system implementation project. The other change types are organisational change, business process change and cultural change. These issues have to be addressed as well if the implementation project is to be a success (Price Waterhouse 1995a).

Phases	Steps
Analysis	1. Conduct a feasibility study for the entire project.
	2. Assess current collection of environmental data, focusing on, e.g., types, formats, procedures, etc..
	3. Build an overview of the information technology available to and used by environmental management.
	4. Identify and prioritise user requirements and expectations of the system.
	5. Construct the functional requirements of the system, including environmental data registration, data processing and reporting. Also start work on data conversions and interfaces to other information systems.
	6. Based on steps 1–5, select solution type (standard or custom development) and select between different vendors of possible packages fulfilling the functional requirements and company criteria for e.g. vendor characteristics, competences and package price. Specify what additional modifications are needed.
	7. Start analysis of data conversions and the development of interfaces to other information systems, as these activities often take more time than originally estimated.
Design	8. Software installation on environmental department hardware and initial training sessions.
	9. Develop a workbook for the environmental management information system using the selected system solution, including, e.g., modifications specifications, plan for integration into company IT architecture, business processes, organisation and culture.
Construction	10. System parameter construction, modification programming, interface programming, data converters programming, etc.
	11. Writing of process descriptions, user manuals, system descriptions, etc.
	12. System test, including operations tests and functionality tests.
Implementation	13. Training of employees who are to use the environmental information system.
	14. Post-implementation review to assess system compliance, effectiveness and acceptance. The evaluation might include drawing on open standards such as COBIT (see e.g. *http://208.240.90.17/exec13.htm*).

Table 3: AN EXAMPLE OF AN IMPLEMENTATION PROCESS FOR
MASS-FLOW ACCOUNTING SOFTWARE

4. Designing an Environmental Performance Information System: A Case Study

The Case Company Background

The case company is a large production company, founded in 1933 and specialising in mechanical monitoring, measuring and controlling equipment. The largest product groups include refrigeration control devices, heat and water control devices, and motion control devices, primarily sold on business-to-business markets. The company has approximately 17,000 employees worldwide, and in 1996 it recorded a worldwide turnover of more than £1.2 billion.

As the company already had an environmental management system in place, it had defined its significant environmental performance areas, which at the time included only operations. Furthermore, it had already published two environmental reports and, therefore, environmental data collection was an important environmental management activity.

The aim is to have all of the company's European sites registered to EMAS (the European Union Eco-Management and Audit Scheme) before 2000. This implies that each site will publish public environmental statements according to the EMAS requirements. However, this raised some issues which the environmental manager wanted to explore regarding the possibilities of developing an information system that:

- Enables the consolidation of environmental performance information from the European sites.
- Allows site as well as corporate managers access to a central database in which information on environmental performance is stored.
- Saves time and money in collecting, processing and reporting environmental data and performance.

Input	Output
• Raw materials consumption • Water consumption • Energy consumption • Use of dangerous substances	• Solid waste • Waste-water • Heavy metals emissions • Substances causing eutrophication • Emission of volatile organic compounds (VOCs) • Emission of CO_2, NO_X and SO_2
Other categories	
• Health and safety • Compliance • Data for calculating the environmental indices	

Table 4: ENVIRONMENTAL DATA CATEGORIES

The company defines environmental performance in terms of the environmental aspects of the operating process. The product element is, however, entering through a life-cycle assessment project, but this is still at an early stage. The company currently sees no need to link environmental performance to financial performance.

Defining Environmental Data Categories, Types and Information System Use

Through interviews with the environmental department as an element of the analysis phase of the EMIS-IM© implementation procedure, the environmental management information requirements took shape, as did a number of environmental data types that the system would have to include (see Table 4).[3] Although based on an input–output framework, this it not intended to be a full ecobalance as used by, say, Kunert AG (Rauberger 1996; see also Chapter 7) or the Danish Steelworks (Danish Steelworks 1996).

The next step according to the implementation procedure was to determine where the environmental data were currently collected, what information technology was used and how the data were transferred to the environmental department. Some of the results are shown in Table 5. As is evident, the environmental data are obtained from different sources and are collected in different information systems, and different methods are used to transfer the data to the environmental department. This required considerable time and effort for the environmental department and was one of the issues that a new environmental management information system was intended to simplify.

Selecting a Solution

The next step was to develop a concept for an environmental performance information system, based on the general parameters identified and described, and within the context of specific software. As described in Section 2, many environmental software packages exist. However, before evaluating these, it was decided to explore the possibility of customising existing software.

A specific type of accounting information system is the so-called financial reporting system such as 'Hyperion Enterprise' or 'Solver'. Such systems are not transaction systems *per se*, but use data from accounting transaction systems to provide managers with information without having to drill through layers of accounting data. In short, these systems are a level 'above' transaction-based accounting systems and capture data from these systems to enable more efficient reporting of financial information. In the context of the case company, this was seen as similar to the role performed by an environmental information system. Environmental data are already being collected by various functions and departments in many different systems and it would be too costly to register them again for environmental management purposes.

---

3   The categories of environmental data were 'input data', 'output data' and 'other data', and environmental data types within those categories are shown in Table 4.

Environmental data category	Data collection responsibility	Main use of information technology	Transfer to the environmental department
Input			
Raw materials	Purchasing department	SAP R/2 environmental raw materials classification module developed	Hard copy
Energy	Building maintenance	Excel spreadsheet	Electronic via e-mail
Water	Building maintenance	Excel spreadsheet	Electronic via e-mail
Dangerous substances	Purchasing department	From purchasing control systems in • SAP R/2 and R/3 • An old company-developed database • Excel	Some electronically and some in hard copy
Output			
Solid waste	Waste treatment facility	A waste database constructed in Access	Hard copy
Waste-water	Water treatment facilities	Excel	Electronically
Emission of heavy metals	The environmental laboratory	• An old company database • Excel	Electronically
Substances causing eutrophication	The environmental laboratory	An old company database	Electronically
VOC emissions	Environmental department	• Excel • An old company database	Calculated based on consumption of products containing VOCs
CO_2, SO_2, NO_x	Environmental department	Excel	Calculations in Excel based on energy consumption
Other data			
Health and safety	Health and safety department	Paradox database	Hard copy
Compliance	Environmental department and environmental laboratory	• Excel • An old company database	Electronically
Data for use in calculating the environmental performance indices	All of the above as well as the accounting department. Calculations made by the environmental department.	All of the above	Hard copy and electronically

Table 5: IT AND ENVIRONMENTAL DATA: AN OVERVIEW

The company had already invested in the financial reporting system 'Hyperion Enterprise'. As this system was being implemented in the company, the environmental manager was interested in establishing whether the software could be used as a basis for an environmental performance information system. The benefits would include:

- The company would not have to invest in new environmental software.

- The in-house expertise existed regarding both software functions and implementation.

- Hyperion Enterprise is a corporate-wide system, meaning that all the company's sites in all the countries in which it operates will be using it. This offers a number of possibilities of collecting environmental information at a site level and consolidating it to a corporate level.

Previous work in co-operation between PricewaterhouseCoopers and Hyperion Software Denmark had shown that the software itself was flexible enough to accommodate non-financial data and would not require any programme changes. The design of the environmental measurement system for the case study was therefore performed within the framework of Hyperion Enterprise.

◻ Designing the Environmental Data Structure and Chart of Accounts

Although it is not possible to describe the entire environmental information system concept developed in Hyperion Enterprise, two of the more important tasks within the design phase of the EMIS-IM© procedure presented in Figure 2 were designing (1) the environmental data structure; and (2) the chart of environmental accounts.

The environmental data structure basically defines the levels at which the data are to be collected (such as site or corporate), the scope of the performance entity (say, division or process line), as well as the path for the consolidation of environmental data to a corporate level. Based on the international nature of the business, a four-tier structure was determined, which is shown in Figure 3.

Although the four tiers would be considered the corporate standard, the relative flexibility of Hyperion Enterprise allows local managers to create their own structures as needed without affecting the corporate standard. An example would be a manager in the UK interested in reviewing performance only for the sites in England and Wales, who could create a separate data structure to obtain this information.

If the environmental data structure is the 'body' of the environmental application in Hyperion Enterprise, then the chart of environmental accounts is the 'heart'. As with traditional financial accounts, these show the category (e.g. input), the type (e.g. energy consumption), and the quantity of environmental data. Additionally, the environmental accounts also show the data unit since the unit will vary, which is of course not the case in financial reporting. Here a relative strength of financial software emerges. The debit–credit structure on which financial accounting systems are necessarily based enables the creation of mass flows using the input–output structure with relative ease. For the case company, an initial draft chart of the environmental accounts is shown in Table 6.

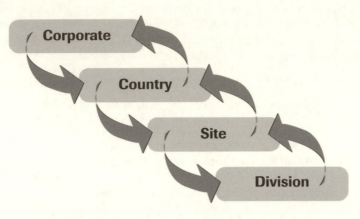

Figure 3: THE ENVIRONMENTAL DATA STRUCTURE

◻ *Possibilities and Pitfalls*

An interesting feature of using financial information systems as a platform for environmental performance reporting is the possibility of combining non-financial environmental performance and financially related environmental performance. The non-financial accounts shown in Table 6 could be paired with 'mirror' accounts in monetary terms. This could be based on links to the financial reporting structure already in use by the company (made easier as both are based on the same software) or it could be based on specific formulae calculating the input into the financial environmental accounts based on the non-financial accounts. Although the case company does not in fact use this approach, examples of the financial environmental accounts mirroring the non-financial accounts are shown in Table 7.

One benefit of this is that the company can view changes in environmental performance in both non-monetary and monetary terms. Savings in, say, energy consumption are reflected both in the measurement unit for energy and in money terms. And less waste is reflected in lower waste disposal costs. As the financial environmental accounts are in this context based on the environmental aspects of operations, they reflect only environmental operating costs. Other types of financial account could potentially be added, such as investments in air emission treatment facilities, and liabilities due to old waste deposits. These are not, however, included in this example.

Yet another benefit of integrating financial and non-financial performance measures appears when using the budgeting function in the Hyperion Enterprise system. Budgeting is a well-established tradition within accounting and may be compared to the establishment of environmental targets in the context of environmental management. A feature of most financial reporting software is the possibility of viewing performance compared to budgeted figures. In the case of the environmental application, this could be used both in comparing non-financial performance to

Category	Main account	Sub-account(s)
Input	Raw materials consumption	Sub-accounts (21 in total) for different types of raw materials classified according to their environmental relevance.
	Water consumption	None
	Energy consumption	Electricity consumption Heat consumption Natural gas consumption Waste oil consumption Gas oil consumption
	Use of toxic or dangerous substances	12 sub-accounts for various classes of substance
Output	Solid waste	**Oil and chemical waste** Waste treated at own facilities Waste sent to municipal facilities Waste sent to other disposal facilities **Metal waste** Metal waste groups **Other** Paper and cartons for re-use Industrial waste for incineration Industrial waste for landfill Industrial waste for re-use
	Waste-water	Emission of industrial waste-water Emission of waste-water containing organic materials
	Heavy metal emissions	Copper emissions Zinc emissions Chrome emissions Nickel emissions Lead emissions Silver emissions
	Substances causing eutrophication	Phosphates Nitrogen
	CO_2 emissions	CO_2 emissions from natural gas CO_2 emissions from gas oil CO_2 emissions from burning waste oil
	SO_2 emissions	SO_2 emissions from natural gas SO_2 emissions from gas oil SO_2 emissions from burning waste oil
	NO_x emissions	NO_x from natural gas NO_x emissions from gas oil NO_x emissions from burning waste oil
	VOCs	None
Other	Working environment statistics	Total number of accidents Total number of work-related illness reports Accident frequency Work-related illness frequency
	Compliance	Transgression of consent limits
	Environmental performance indices	Sub-accounts for indices

Table 6: THE CHART OF ACCOUNTS FOR THE ENVIRONMENTAL MANAGEMENT INFORMATION SYSTEM CONCEPT

environmental targets and in comparing financial performance to the financial budget.

There are certain issues of which companies developing an environmental performance information system by using financial reporting software should be aware. One is that environmental performance properties are measured in differing units. This may create problems if the software is not flexible enough by, for example, not allowing different units to be added together, not allowing data input in different units, or not enabling the user to construct mathematical rules for converting between units (e.g. converting energy consumption in kWh and Nm^3 into Joules). Another issue that may prove problematic is the variation between the periods in which environmental data are 'born'. Some data may be collected on a daily or a weekly basis, while others are collected less frequently. The software structure would have to accommodate this by allowing selection between different registration frequencies.

Category	Non-financial	Linked financial accounts
Input	Raw materials consumption	Procurement costs of raw materials
	Water consumption	Costs of water consumption
	Energy consumption	Costs of different types of energy
	Use of toxic or dangerous substances	Procurement costs of toxic or dangerous substances
Output	Solid waste	Waste treatment costs Waste disposal costs Waste transport costs
	Waste-water	Operating costs of water-treatment facilities
	Heavy metal emissions	Costs of heavy metals discharged with waste-water
	Substances causing eutrophication	Operating costs of specific effluent treatment
	CO_2 emissions	Amount paid in CO_2 emissions-related eco-taxes
	SO_2 emissions	Amount paid in SO_2 emissions-related eco-taxes
	NO_x emissions	Amount paid in NO_x emissions-related eco-taxes
	VOCs	Cost of products containing VOCs
Other	Working environment statistics	Cost of days lost due to injury
	Compliance	Cost of environmental laboratory for monitoring consent limits

Table 7: INTEGRATING NON-FINANCIAL AND FINANCIAL ENVIRONMENTAL PERFORMANCE

◢ Summary and Conclusions

In summary, this chapter has focused on defining environmental performance as a multi-dimensional concept that will in the future need balanced scorecard thinking if it is to reflect the success or failure of the corporate environmental strategy. An overview of different environmental software packages was given and certain types of software were described. A methodology for implementing environmental information systems was presented, and a case study reported to illustrate some of the steps of the implementation process.

The main conclusions are:

▼ Company environmental performance is a multi-dimensional issue that includes physical as well as financial data.

▼ There are numerous environmental software packages on the market addressing different aspects of environmental management and environmental performance.

▼ Information technology is important in capturing, processing and reporting information on environmental performance and can be used to integrate the different dimensions of environmental performance.

▼ A company wanting to build an environmental performance measurement system must use an implementation method to ensure that the objectives of the project will be reached.

Finally, a word of warning. Information technology is a tool. Nothing more, nothing less. It is important not to focus on the 'bells and whistles' of information technology but carefully evaluate what needs IT has to fulfil and what costs and benefits are associated with implementing it in the organisation. This, of course, goes for environmental information systems as well.

◢ Appendix: A Checklist for the Required Functionality of an Environmental Performance Information System [4]

Company environmental management issues
1. What is the primary role of the environmental performance information system?
    1.1. Data support to environmental managers
    1.2. Internal performance reporting
    1.3. External environmental reporting
    1.4. Support the implementation of ISO 14001 or other environmental management standards
    1.5. Other

---

4 This checklist also includes elements from the EHSSDG 'Functional Requirements Outline' (EHSSDG 1996).

2. What is the scope of the environmental performance information system?
   2.1.   One site
   2.2.   National sites
   2.3.   European sites
   2.4.   International sites
   2.5.   Global

3. What environmental management functions are to be included in the system?
   3.1.   Organisational responsibility delegation
   3.2.   Document management and control
   3.3.   Electronic access to international standards such as ISO 14001 and EMAS
   3.4.   Electronic access to relevant national and international legislation
   3.5.   Sampling and analysis
   3.6.   External inspections
   3.7.   Compliance monitoring
           3.7.1.   Legislation
           3.7.2.   International standards
           3.7.3.   Own targets
   3.8.   Audit management
           3.8.1.   By company audit teams
           3.8.2.   By independent third parties
   3.9.   Project management
   3.10. Environmental training needs management
   3.11. Other

4. What environmental data are to be registered in the system?
   4.1.   Use of raw materials
   4.2.   Energy consumption
   4.3.   Water consumption
   4.4.   Use of materials considered hazardous
   4.5.   Air emissions
   4.6.   Water emissions
   4.7.   Solid waste
   4.8.   Noise data
   4.9.   Odour
   4.10. Remediation data
   4.11. Others

5. Is the system to include life-cycle data?
   5.1.   Inventory data
   5.2.   Impacts data
   5.3.   Assessment data
   5.4.   Improvement data

6. Is the system to include financial environmental data?
   6.1.   Environmentally related operating costs
   6.2.   Environmentally related investments
   6.3.   Environmental liabilities
   6.4.   Environmentally related benefits

7. Is the system to include measures of environmental impact?
   7.1.   Concentration levels
   7.2.   Toxicity levels
   7.3.   Biological damage
   7.4.   Health effects
   7.5.   Other

Required environmental software characteristics

1. What type of solution is desired?

    1.1.   A complete environmental software package solution implemented without changes in the package?

    1.2.   An environmental software package implemented with minimal change in the package parameters?

    1.3.   A skeleton environmental software package implemented with full customisation of all package parameters?

    1.4.   A modification of an existing information system?

2. What hardware is the system required to run on?

3. Is the system to be a client–server system?

4. Is the system to be groupware-enabled?

5. Is the system to be connected to the Internet?

6. What security arrangements are required?

7. What language(s) is the system to be in?

8. Who is going to be responsible for the new system?
    8.1.   Individual sites
    8.2.   National headquarters
    8.3.   Corporate level

9. Who is going to be responsible for the day-to-day operations of the system?

10. What help functions are required?

11. Required import/export of data to/from other company information systems?
    11.1.   Materials management systems
    11.2.   Production management systems
    11.3.   Accounting systems
    11.4.   Human resources systems
    11.5.   Spreadsheet tools
    11.6.   Word-processing software
    11.7.   Quality management systems
    11.8.   Other

12. What are the number and complexity of required interfaces?

13. What databases are required?
    13.1.   Chemical lists databases
    13.2.   Databases for legal requirements
    13.3.   Substance databases
    13.4.   Environmental impact databases
    13.5.   Environmental management standards
    13.6.   Employee environmental training databases
    13.7.   Product life-cycle databases
    13.8.   Other

14. Is a geographic information function required?

15. Is a process modelling function required?

16. What are the report writer flexibility requirements?

17. Is system reporting to be
    17.1.   Electronic?
    17.2.   Paper reporting?
    17.3.   Both?

18. Is the system to provide company managers with performance reports?
    18.1.   Process management
    18.2.   Site management
    18.3.   Regional management
    18.4.   Corporate management
    18.5.   Other

19. Is the system to provide interested parties with environmental performance reports?
    19.1. Local authorities
    19.2. Regional authorities
    19.3. National authorities
    19.4. Shareholders
    19.5. Investors
    19.6. Employees
    19.7. Others
20. What consolidation requirements are made?
    20.1. Number of sites
    20.2. Ownership of subsidiaries
    20.3. Elimination of internal transactions
    20.4. Unit conversions
    20.5. Reporting across the organisation
    20.6. Other

Software implementation issues

1. What data conversion requirements are made?

2. What are the estimated training needs?

3. Potential impacts on job descriptions?

4. Potential organisational changes?

5. Cultural issues?

6. Will there be any changes in corporate power structures?

7. Are there any employee acceptance issues?
   7.1. Preparation of change
   7.2. Change integration

8. What system testing strategies are to be adopted?
   8.1. By the company
   8.2. By an independent third party

9. What user procedures are to be written?

10. Are there any post-implementation reviews to be carried out?
    10.1. What control standards are to be used?
    10.2. What evaluation criteria are to be used?
    10.3. Who is going to do the evaluation?

6

Ecobalancing in Austria

Its Use in SMEs and for Benchmarking

Christine Jasch

MUCH OF THE PRACTICAL WORK on environmental performance evaluation (EPE) in German-speaking countries such as Austria and Germany has been based
on ecobalancing. Since its first application by the Institute for Environmental
Economics and Management (IÖW) in Germany in the mid-1980s, it has been adopted
by a large number of companies, who consider that the detailed and quantitative
information that it provides on inputs, outputs and process flows is essential for
successful environmental management.

This chapter is based on over a decade's experience of ecobalancing and EPE at the
Austrian IÖW, and focuses on two neglected areas: its use in SMEs, and the
opportunities and feasibility of making comparisons on the basis of sector-specific
input–output frameworks. The chapter's structure is as follows: Section 1 provides
a brief description of what ecobalancing is; Section 2 describes the use of EPE in the
Austrian brewing industry; Section 3 describes the use of EPE in the Austrian wood-
processing industry; Section 4 considers the relationship between ecobalancing and
benchmarking; and Section 5 provides conclusions.

1. *Ecobalancing in Context*

Ecobalancing is based on an input–output analysis of materials flows, but includes
the separate step of aggregating, evaluating and interpreting the results. Its primary
focus is the flow of energy, materials and water associated with a company, site,
process or product. An important principle of successful ecobalancing is that physical
flows within a company represent money flows, and can therefore be traced back

using the accounting system. Most waste and emissions are materials that have been purchased but not transformed into profitable products.

The term 'ecobalancing' has been used in a variety of ways in Germanic countries. However, ISO has standardised the terminology. The term 'product ecobalance' is now used for life-cycle assessment (LCA), as in the ISO 14040 guidance document on *Life Cycle Assessment: Principles and Framework* (ISO 1998a). Input–output (I/O) materials flow analysis at a corporate, site or process level, and the related operational performance indicators, are highlighted by ISO 14031, the guidance document on Environmental Performance Evaluation (ISO 1998b), but are no longer referred to as 'ecobalances'. A site I/O analysis also provides most of the data that is required for Eco-Management and Auditing Scheme (EMAS) site statements.

In the 1980s, IÖW (1989) produced a systematic approach to defining the system boundaries of an ecobalance, which distinguished four segments:

- ▼ Input–output analysis for the company

- ▼ Input–output analysis for production processes

- ▼ Input–output balance for individual products

- ▼ Site assessment

For all segments, the evaluation and interpretation of the data inventory (I/O analysis) is performed as a distinctly separate step, and only then is the term 'ecobalance' used.

The fourth segment, the site assessment, has its theoretical background in the structure of financial book-keeping. While I/O analysis relates to profit and loss accounts and can be derived therefrom, the site assessment was an attempt to mirror the balance sheet of assets and liabilities at a fixed date in environmental terms. However, due to severe methodological evaluation problems, it has never gained much popularity.

◻ Input–Output Balance at a Corporate Level

The mass balance of materials flows is the starting point for an environmental information system, and gives an overview of the mass flows of materials and energy used in a company over a period of time, such as a year. Even if a company has no technical and emission monitoring, which is often the case for SMEs, there will still be a book-keeping system to provide information on materials flows and basic environmental costs.

This level is especially useful for controllers, accountants and the purchasing department, as it allows for a general overview of materials flows and consistency checks. The top-down approach from the book-keeping system can later be cross-checked with bottom-up data from the technical and cost calculation information systems, which tend to be operated within narrower system boundaries and are therefore often blind to the overall system. The corporate or site level is used to derive indicators and to set quantitative targets. In many companies, the materials balance is calculated monthly, together with the production planning, storage and purchase system and cost calculation system, and provides a powerful controlling tool. It should record the amounts in kilograms, units and values, and the corresponding account, materials number and cost centres. The corporate balance is crucial for controlling waste and emission streams, as many flows are monitored only on an annual basis and are not process-specific.

In the first stage of the corporate materials flow analysis, the quantities of materials purchased and used for production are compared to the output of products that are produced within a defined time—usually the fiscal year—and the resulting emissions. The qualitative characteristics of materials and emissions will be evaluated only at a second stage. Thus the degree of detail in the data survey is dependent on the goal of the investigation and its ecological relevance. A rough pre-survey may be sufficient for the first weak-point analysis. The scope of a detailed process review can already be defined at this point.

The items of the I/O analysis are derived from the profit and loss account, since this is the only means of determining the full total of a company's purchases of materials (although only in terms of monetary value). For some accounts, especially for supporting and operational materials such as chemicals, paints and cleaning materials, a more detailed listing (such as an account page) can be set up. To the degree that a company works with materials classification numbers, the amounts purchased can be derived comparatively easily from the storage system.

It is essential for the balancing exercise that quantity units are defined in, or recalculated into, units of mass (kg). The recording of units of the used materials is useful only if there is a software programme for production planning that relates the processed units to the resulting products. A weight balance (kg) of materials purchased and processed, and the resulting products and waste, would be preferable. It has been found helpful to quote the relevant kilodata immediately when defining the materials number for a specific material within the storage system.

The exercise starts from the materials purchased, and the materials used in the production of goods, within an accounting period. The amount of sales need be considered only when actual production data is not known. Ideally, an I/O comparison should be carried out on materials actually used for production (processed), and compared against the actual amounts produced. However, this is possible only with a well-developed production planning system, in which supporting and operating materials are also considered. The difference between (1) the materials used and (2) the standard materials content of the actual output, based on pre-set production standards, reflects the actual waste and scrap that has been generated during the production process. This survey is distorted if, because of deficiencies in the internal corporate data system, the quantities of materials purchased have to be compared against total sales. There will usually be inventory differences between the quantities of materials purchased and those actually processed, due to stock-keeping; and differences can also arise between the quantities produced and quantities sold due to internal needs (for example, presentation pieces for trade fairs). Further, the time-lag between the purchase of raw materials and the sale of the finished products can be substantial in the case of special manufacturing with long production cycles. These inventory gaps should be calculated, as they have to be adjusted for in different ways.

To check the consistency of the materials balance, an adjustment with the materials supply from stock-keeping, sales information and production lists is attempted as far as is possible. In the areas of supporting and raw materials, packaging materials and finished products, this task can to a large degree be solved by adjusting the existing computer software so that there is relatively little work involved.

It becomes more complicated, however, if the majority of the environmentally relevant operational materials—such as chemicals, paints and lacquers, cleaning materials, workshop requirements, etc. that are subject to emissions and proper disposal procedures—cannot be extracted by reference to materials numbers, so that the amounts used cannot be traced back. There is then a large number of environmentally relevant accounts and expenditure items that 'vanish' in the total costs and can be directly related neither to the storage book-keeping nor to the bill of costs.

In many companies, when tracking the variable costs and general costs to different cost objects, the variable costs include only the raw materials and part of the packaging materials, whereas the supportive and operational materials, as well as the costs of proper disposal, are not included. Therefore, numerous stimuli in terms of the arrangement of accounts, the classification criteria between material numbers, and the classification of accounts and costs, occur while checking consistency.

In order to use information efficiently (and not, as is necessary in some companies, to have to return to information from original bills), an agreement between the departments involved, concerning the organisation of records, should be undertaken. The departments responsible for purchasing and for materials management, respectively, will thus become more important in the context of the environmentally relevant inventories and the corresponding recording obligations.

Process Flow Charts

A subdivision of the company balance statement into individual procedural steps leads to process balances. The process flow charts give insights into company-specific processes, and allow the determination of leakages and waste-streams at source. This requires a detailed examination of individual steps of production—again in the form of an I/O analysis (see Fig. 1). The process flow charts combine technical information with cost calculation data. They are carried out not on an annual basis, but rather for a specified production line. In total, they should aggregate to the annual amount. This level of materials flow analysis will usually be the responsibility of technicians, but the data gathered should be cross-checked and consistent with the cost calculation system and with the annual input and output amounts.

Splitting up the corporate flows into cost centres, or even down to specific items of plant and machinery, allows for more detailed investigation into technical improvement options, and also for tracing the sources of costs. Special attention has to be paid to the quantitative recording of the materials on a consistent kilogram basis. The key questions are:

- What amounts of materials have actually been used for production?
- What cost centres have processed how much of the materials, and can it be further distinguished between production lines and machinery?

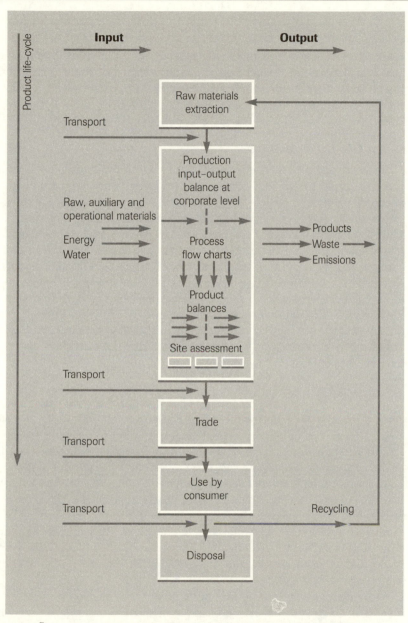

Figure 1: RELATION OF INTERNAL AND EXTERNAL SYSTEM BOUNDARIES
FOR INPUT—OUTPUT ANALYSIS

▼ How large were the resulting emissions, scrap and waste, preferably recorded separately for each cost centre?

The process level is the main area for pollution prevention projects. Data at process level is also a necessity for further distinction between products. It is crucial that the system boundaries for financial calculation of cost centres and for technical monitoring can be related to each other.

◿ *Product Life-Cycle Analysis*

The I/O analysis can be further subdivided, from the company and process level to products. The product assessment comprises two levels. 'Company internal' is the subdivision of the process data to the manufactured products (such as raw materials, water and energy input per product, for each product category). The other level of product assessment leaves the company and follows the product throughout its life-cycle by adding upstream and downstream life-cycle stages. This type of analysis serves to evaluate the environmental impacts of raw materials, various production stages, transport, consumption and disposal of a product. Product life-cycle assessment (LCA) can be defined as the sum of all process flow charts related to a product's entire life-cycle. Due to data problems, they are mostly performed through a more qualitative screening approach. This level of materials flow assessment is used to evaluate the environmental profile not only of products, but also of the purchased materials.

2. Environmental Performance Evaluation in Breweries

There is much to be said for using a standardised framework for I/O analysis within a single industry sector. This means that no relevant entry (inputs and outputs) can be left out; the scope can be limited to relevant materials; and it allows for aggregation and comparison with other sites and firms. For SMEs in particular, a full recording of materials flows often exceeds the capacity of their information systems. While maintaining the overall structure of the operational system, the sector-specific entries can be varied and modified to accommodate purpose and ecological relevance. Annual monitoring allows for the evaluation of improvements and achievements of environmental targets.

The I/O framework for brewing shown in Table 1 was developed by Jasch and Rauberger (1998) as part of the pilot project for the Austrian manual on EPE which was developed for the Austrian Ministry of Environment. This sector is relatively straightforward in that most sites essentially produce a single product from a limited number of raw materials (water, hops and malt). Consequently, breweries are at the forefront of benchmarking practices, and have generally produced quite explicit environmental reports. The reference unit of their indicator systems is almost exclusively hectolitres of product (beer), a single common reference unit which is harder to identify in other industry sectors.

Input	Output
Raw materials	**Product**
Barley	Bottled beer
Wheat	Cask beer
Other additives	Canned beer
Malt	Alcohol-free drinks
Hops	**By-products**
Lemonade elements	Malt
Brewing water	Malt dust
Auxiliary materials	Hops
Additives (beer)	Barley waste
Additives (lemonade)	Used grains
Laboratory materials	Silicic acid
Packaging	**Waste**
Crates (new)	Glass
Bottles	Metal
Cans	Labels
Kegs	Plastics
Palettes	Paper, cardboard
Labels	Municipal waste
Foils	**Hazardous waste**
Corks	Fluorescent tubes
Screw tops	Refrigerators
Operational materials	Oils
Cleaning materials	Oil-contaminated materials
Disinfecting materials	Used colours
Neutralisers	Chemical remnants
Filters	Electrical scrap
Oils/grease	**Waste-water**
Salts	Quantity in m^3
Cooling materials	Chemical oxygen demand (COD)
Repair and maintenance materials	Biological oxygen demand (BOD)
Workshop	Phosphates
Canteen	Nitrogen
Office	Ammonium
Energy	Biogas
Electricity	**Air emissions**
Heating	CO
Gas	CO_2
Oil	SO_2
Diesel	NO_X
Petrol	**Noise**
Water	Noise at night
Municipal water	Noise on-site
Fountain water	
CO_2 cleaned internal	

Table 1: INPUT—OUTPUT FRAMEWORK OF ACCOUNTS FOR BREWERIES

Of course, the choice and calculation of reference unit is of pivotal importance to the interpretation of the data, and this should be clearly explained and laid down in writing, especially when making comparisons between sites. Even minor differences in the calculation of the number of employees (whether by head count or 'full-time equivalents', by the number employed on a specific date or the average number throughout the year as a whole), for example, can lead to significant distortions when comparing data.

The Austrian Brewery Union has used indicators for several years to compare production data between sites, applying indicators that evaluate costs as well as weight. Significant deviations from the mean can also be attributed to historical differences in site structures (some production sites date back to the Middle Ages) and to differing production cycles. Consequently, despite the relatively homogeneous production processes, plans are under way to implement a system of indicators at process and production line level.

Data comparison at site level allows for benchmarking in relation to the company's average and best figures and, as the data is monitored on a monthly basis, to quickly trace unusual developments. When interpreting the data, management is aware of the unequal site structure, but, when trying to assess technical improvement options, data at a process level is crucial. When deviations from best practice become too costly, some companies have decided to convert some of their old brewery buildings into museums or restaurants.

For detailed data assessment there can be significant differences in terms of whether, for example, a malting house is a component of the brewery at a site, or whether the brewery acquires its malt from external sources. Similarly, it is important, in order to be able to make valid comparisons of water and energy data, to know whether bottling occurs on all or only certain sites. In Austria, most breweries also produce lemonade in order to be able to provide non-alcoholic drinks as well. Additionally, analysis can focus on the heat, energy and water requirements of different production stages. So, eventually, energy and water is monitored for each important single step in the process, and materials input is directly attributed via the storage cost calculation system to each cost unit, the information system thereby being refined every year.

Beer production generally involves the following stages:

- Malt delivery to brewing house
- Brewing house
- Fermentation and storage
- Bottling
- Casking
- Administration
- Delivery

Table 2 shows the production flow of a brewery. For a valid comparison with other sites, it is essential that the corresponding stages are clearly defined. An in-house

Input	Process	Side process	Output
Malt Energy	Grinding		Dust
Brewing water Detergent Energy	Mashing		Heat
Water Energy	Purification		Used grain Heat Waste-water
Hops Energy	Preparation of wort		Heat
Water Energy	Removal of hop waste		Hop waste
Water Energy Detergent Refrigerant	Cooling of wort		Warm water
Yeast Sterile air Water Energy Refrigerant	Fermentation		Yeast Wasted beer Carbonic acid Waste-water
Water Energy Refrigerant Disinfectant	Storage		Storage dust Waste-water Wasted beer CO_2
Water Energy Carbonic acid Detergent Disinfectant Auxiliary materials	Filtration		Waste-water Filtrate Auxiliary materials
Water Energy Refrigerant Detergent Disinfectant Carbonic Acid	Pressure tank		Waste-water CO_2
Water Energy Detergent Disinfectant Bottling		Bottle and cask cleaning	Waste-water Waste paper Waste glass Sludge Heat
Lemonade raw materials Sugar		Lemonade production	
Water Energy Carbonic acid Packaging	Bottling, casking		Bottled wasted beer Casks, boxes Packaging waste Waste glass Rinsing water Residue Waste-water
Department-specific inputs		Workshop, canteen, administration	Department-specific outputs
Fuel oil Water		Steam/heat production	Air emissions
Petrol	Transport and delivery		Air emissions

Table 2: PRODUCTION FLOW OF BREWERIES

malting house, lemonade production on-site, or a self-owned delivery fleet, can all distort production data. The production plan should be compatible with the structure of the firm's accounting systems, so that data can be collected directly from the firm's book-keeping system. The possibility of aggregation according to the classification given above allows for benchmarking across the entire industry sector.

One example of a company that covers many of these parameters is the Obermurtaler Brewery Ltd, which has committed itself to using only organically grown raw materials, and which was the first Austrian site to be EMAS-verified in December 1995. It uses quantitative environmental targets that aim to reduce its specific uses of resources, despite strongly increasing volumes of production. As stated, the indicators are quite detailed and have been monitored over several years (see Table 3).

3. *Ecobalancing in the Wood-Processing Industry*

Another sector where a sectoral I/O framework has been established is wood processing (see Table 4). I/O analysis is frequently used in this sector to investigate

Indicator	1996	Unit
Input		
Freshwater	6.73	hl/hl drink
Electricity	11.86	kWh/hl drink
Fuel oil (steam)	2.85	hl/hl drink
Fuel oil (heat)	0.57	l/hl drink
Diesel	26.17	l/100 km
Filter materials	0.15	kg/hl beer
Oils/lubricants	0.005	kg/hl drink
Etiquette glue	0.037	kg/hl drink
Neutralisers	0.62	kg/m³ waste water
Detergents	0.59	kg/hl drink
Output		
Used grain	19.01	kg/hl beer
Yeast waste	0.34	kg/hl drink
Municipal waste	0.1	kg/hl drink
Filtrate	0.35	kg/hl beer
Broken glass	0.34	kg/hl drink
Waste labels	0.45	kg/hl drink
Paper/cardboard	0.24	kg/hl drink
Plastics	0.09	kg/hl drink
Oils/oil-contaminated materials	0.006	kg/hl drink
Precipitation waste	0.016	kg/hl drink
Waste-water	5.4	kg/hl drink

Table 3: INDICATOR SYSTEM OF THE OBERMURTALER BREWERY

Source: Obermurtaler Brauereigenossenschaft 1996

Input	Output
Raw materials Wood Metals Synthetics Textiles Glass and stone	**Products** Products in tonnes or m^3 Product packaging
Half-products (components) (Springs, hinges, fittings, wheels, etc.)	**Merchandise**
Merchandise	**Waste** Wood Metals Textile and leather Synthetics Paper/cardboard Municipal waste
Auxiliary materials Varnishes Solvents Stains and impregnations Waxes Fillers and surfacers Glue Adhesives Chemicals Salts	**Hazardous waste** Oils Oil-contaminated materials Sludges Varnish and glue wastes Workshop wastes Chemicals Electrical scrap Fluorescent tubes Incinerary residue
Packaging Product packaging Transport packaging	**Waste-water** Production water Cooling water Sanitary water Rain water
Operational materials Detergents Lubricants Safety materials Repair and maintenance materials Workshop materials Canteen requirements Office materials	**Air emissions** CO CO_2 SO_2 NO_X Hydrocarbons Dust Solvent emissions
Energy Electricity Waste wood District heating Gas Heating oil Diesel Petrol	**Noise** Noise at night Operational noise
Water Municipal water Spring water	

Table 4: INPUT–OUTPUT FRAMEWORK OF ACCOUNTS FOR THE WOOD-PROCESSING INDUSTRY

materials flows, especially for wood and surface treatment materials, in order to calculate the scrap percentage and losses in process.

Apart from absolute data from the I/O analysis and time-series comparisons, the formation of relative indicators is hindered in this industry sector (unlike brewing) by the problems of defining reference units. End-products include such dissimilar items as tables, office and conference furniture, cupboards, chests of drawers, chairs, custom-made fittings, interior furnishings and many others. Many firms, therefore, know their revenues but cannot express them in terms of kg, m^3 or other comparable units.

Although data collection remains transparent for a small firm, it becomes an almost insoluble problem for the wood-processing industry as a whole, due to the wide variety of processes and products. Unlike breweries, where most of the data could be referenced to output, serious technical problems are encountered when trying to define a reference unit for the wood-processing industry. Often, furniture includes metal and other components, so the product is not homogenous. Also, not all raw materials are processed on-site, so some components are delivered to the site as semi-finished products, and some process steps are undertaken externally. Thus, comparison between sites on the basis of environmental reports becomes impossible.

By using an environmental indicator matrix, however, inputs can be ascribed to certain cost centres, machines, production processes, etc., and thus, for internal use, can be expressed in a more comprehensive way. So, even if there is no homogenous output, the different inputs can be related to production hours, square metres or other reasonable reference units. An example of such a matrix which has been developed together with environmental managers from the wood-processing industry is shown in Table 5 (Jasch and Rauberger 1998). A company's overall output can be quoted only in terms of total sales revenues, but several relevant input items and other indicators can instead be related to the output of significant cost centres, working hours, number of employees, etc.

Some companies take a more detailed approach. The wood-processing industry became the focus of public attention for its environmental impacts in the early 1990s. The main items were tropical rainforest depletion and forestry management, but also carcinogenic dust at the workplace and the use of lacquers and paint. Consequently, some of the first ecobalances were started in this sector. One of the first Austrian companies to do this was Wiesner & Hager Möbel GmbH, a company with a total sales revenue of approximately €44 million, 500 employees and a market share in Austria of about 30% (Jasch 1997).

Their goals for the ecobalance were to:

- Systematically assess environmental performance
- Assure legal compliance
- Install closed loops for materials management
- Market environmentally sound products
- Motivate employees
- Identify improvement options

	Production line	Cost centre	Machine	Materials use	Energy use	Employees	Working days	Shifts/ Working hours	Site area	Revenue	Production costs
Materials inputs	✓	✓	✓					✓		✓	✓
Packaging											✓
Energy use	✓	✓	✓				✓				
Water use	✓		✓			✓	✓				
Detergents	✓	✓	✓			✓			✓		
Waste	✓	✓		✓		✓		✓			
Waste-water		✓			✓	✓					
Emissions	✓	✓	✓			✓					
Traffic						✓	✓				
Accidents						✓		✓			
Complaints							✓	✓			
Environmental training							✓				
Environmental costs										✓	✓

Table 5: REFERENCE UNIT MATRIX FOR THE WOOD-PROCESSING INDUSTRY

The project, in collaboration with the IÖW, began in 1990. The main focus was the installation of an environmental information system combined with the existing production planning tool. As expected, the first round of data-gathering for the mass balance was not easy. Monetary values were available from the financial accounting systems, but the related mass balance data often had to be calculated or estimated. So, even in the first phase of the project, defining the improvement needs for the computer-aided materials management system was a major task. The existing production calculation programme, which contained more than 5,600 separate single materials, was improved so that the moment a material was ordered, put into storage or taken from storage into the production process, the related amount was also listed and conversion factors were installed to calculate directly the relevant quantity in kilograms.

The company's production planning system allowed for a comparison and consistency check of materials purchased against production output. The procedure applied for this is shown in Figure 2. In the first year of the mass balance, about 70%

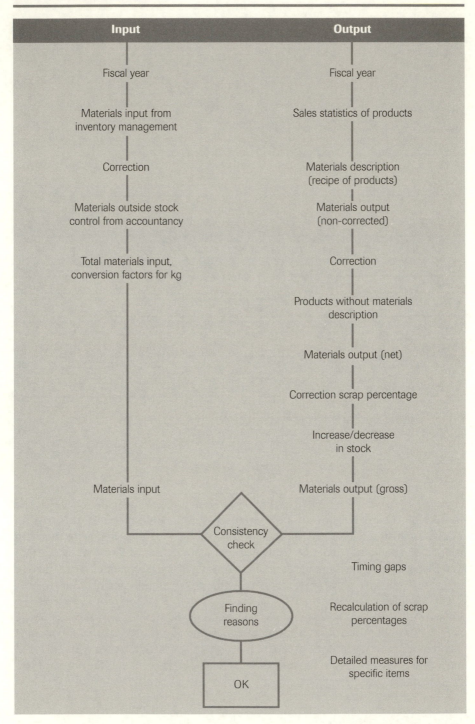

Figure 2: CONSISTENCY CHECK WITH THE PRODUCTION PLANNING SYSTEM,
WIESNER & HAGER MÖBEL GmbH

of all materials were traced back and accounted for. One of the first results was to adjust the percentages used to calculate scrap generated during the cutting of raw materials, and to install computer-aided design and cutting machinery and thereby significantly increase profit. In the following two years, consistency improved, reaching 97% of all materials purchased of the company; and even office equipment materials were eventually monitored within the materials storage system.

Problems were encountered, however, and these related to:

▪ The amount of information and data to be managed, which could be handled only by adjusting the production planning system

▪ Limited willingness of suppliers to submit specific environmental data—in many cases because they did not have this data themselves

▪ The production planning system was originally used only for standard production units, but about 15% of total sales were attributable to specially customer-designed products, such as concert halls. Eventually, these too were integrated into the materials monitoring system.

▪ In 1990, wastes were not regularly monitored. In the following years, a waste-monitoring system was installed not only for the company as a whole, but also on a cost centre-specific level, so that the relevant amounts could be directly allocated to specific production lines.

▪ There are significant time-intervals between the purchase of materials, their use in production, the finished product being put into store, and final delivery and invoicing to the customer. In times of changing production patterns, the related emissions might occur in significantly different time-periods than do the materials inputs and product outputs. As in subsequent years, the mass balance was calculated from the point of materials input into production rather than from their purchase, and correspondingly product output was based on the time of production of the product rather than on its sale, so that these time distortions could be limited.

▪ Treatment of changes in stock levels for both materials input and product outputs: there were significant losses of materials and products from stock, which were also accounted for separately in order to add them into the input–output materials balance.

With the constant refinement of the materials balance at the corporate level, which is undertaken on a monthly basis together with the financial accounting data, Wiesner & Hager GmbH has a very powerful controlling tool. Also, several pollution prevention projects have been performed over the years and the company was one of the first sites to be registered under EMAS.

A further example—derived from the Austrian Ministry of Environment's EPE manual—is the environmental indicator system of a small carpentry business (see Table 6). The firm employs ten employees in production and administration, with

Environmental indicators	Unit	1993	1994	1995
1. Electricity	kWh	n/a	16,997	15,813
2. Water	m³	345	698	367
3. Wood content	%	85	70	80
4. Varnish and Priming	kg	610	435	270
5. Surface area waxed/oiled	%	3	22	31
6. Solvent/thinner	litres	125	110	90
7. Municipal waste	kg	1450	1740	1490
8. Charges for waste and waste-water	ATS	n/a	3,990	4,750

n/a = data not available
ATS = Austrian schillings

Table 6: INDICATOR SYSTEM OF A CARPENTRY BUSINESS

a total sales revenue of just under €500,000 (ATS 7 million). The company has traditionally placed a high emphasis on the environmental and health implications of its products and aims to meet the market demand for ecological products, in particular through the production of pure wood furniture and the use of natural oils and waxes for their treatment.

The emphasis of its environmental indicator system, therefore, is on the percentage wood content of its products as opposed to multi-material products (Indicator 3), the use of varnishes and primings (Indicator 4), the percentage of surface area treated with waxes and oils rather than with lacquers (Indicator 5), and the use of solvents (Indicator 6). Additionally, special attention was paid to the optimisation of electricity and water usage (Indicators 1 and 2), as well as to indicators for waste production and waste disposal costs (Indicators 7 and 8). Indicators were developed to document not only resource use optimisation, but also the use of more environmentally friendly inputs and treatment methods, and to convey these to environmentally aware consumers through an environmental brochure.

4. The Relationship between Ecobalancing and Benchmarking

Several other sector-specific mass balance projects have been conducted in Austria. One of the first with a benchmarking objective was carried out in 1991 by the IÖW on behalf of the food industry association of Austria (Jasch 1992). The project was funded by the Research Fund for Industry (FFF), together with four Austrian providers of canned food and an Austrian producer of cans. The I/O analysis was undertaken for all companies and for the canning production processes, and a screening life-cycle analysis on canned goulash soup was added in. Waste prevention plans and environmental performance indicators were provided for all companies. The project was the first approach to industry sector-specific benchmarking, and struggled with the lack of comparability of data between the companies.

In order to obtain comparable data, the analysis had to go down to process level and distinguish between the various production lines. Some of the companies also had production lines for frozen food and other methods of manufacturing. Therefore, the process flow charts for the canning manufacturing process had to be separated from both a technical and from an accounting and cost calculation perspective. This was achieved quite easily for energy consumption, but for detailed materials input and waste output it proved to be more difficult, as the data assessment methodologies with regard to cost calculation and accounting, as well as for waste and emissions monitoring, had to be improved significantly. For the definition of system boundaries, it was also important to define which products were manufactured on-site as opposed to those provided by suppliers, since this aspect was not uniform across the participating companies.

Another project, on behalf of the Austrian association for the building materials and ceramics industry, provided a manual for a sector-specific inventory model for all member companies, which provides the inventory framework for mass balancing within this sector and can also be used to apply different evaluation methodologies for ecobalances and LCAs (Bruck *et al.* 1996).

Despite these initiatives, a survey—undertaken by the IÖW in autumn 1998 (Jasch and Gyallay-Pap 1998)—of environmental performance indicators for the electricity, pulp and paper and printing industries, as published in environmental statements in Austria and Germany, showed that it was still very difficult to make valid comparisons, because of the very uneven structure of production and reporting formats. EMAS statements are site-specific, but most companies are not single-site. Some companies publish a description of the organisation's management system and then add site-specific data sheets for materials flows and performance indicators.

In general, most reports provide detailed figures on raw materials use, energy and water use. Figures on auxiliary materials are mostly given for the printing industry, which reflects their relative importance in production; when these are a significant cost factor, they tend to be monitored via the storage system and therefore their amounts are also available. In the paper and electricity industry, however, only half the reports include this information.

Production figures are published in almost all statements except in the printing sector, where there are major methodological difficulties in defining a unit of production output. Relative indicators for production are not yet common. If used, they are usually presented in time series. Sometimes reference units other than production are encountered: for example, primary energy efficiency degree, or energy use per m^2 production area. The most frequent use of relative indicators occurs in the paper industry, in respect of waste-water emissions.

Wastes are frequently reported as an aggregate amount which includes several types of dissimilar waste materials, or else are subdivided between wastes for disposal and wastes for re-use. This form of presentation is most common in the paper industry, whereas the printing industry generally provides more specific details of its waste production.

Air emissions data is well documented by the electricity industry, with the paper industry coming second, as these have to be monitored by law. In this category, one can find the most diverse forms of presentation, ranging from absolute values to emissions as a percentage of legal boundaries.

Waste-water data is published most frequently by the paper industry, closely followed by the electricity industry (about 70%). Due to the relatively low water requirements in the printing industry, waste-water data is given by only about 30% of firms in this sector.

Some of the lessons from these experiences are now being incorporated into a European research project, Measuring Environmental Performance Evaluation (MEPI). This focuses on quantitative indicators of environmental performance at process and firm level for the textile, pulp and paper, printing, fertiliser, computer manufacture and energy supply sectors of European industry.[1]

The project has three main objectives (Jasch 1998):

▼ To develop quantitative indicators for the environmental performance of manufacturing firms

▼ To apply these indicators in deepening the understanding of the causes of changes in industrial environmental performance

▼ To assess the effectiveness of different policy instruments in improving firms' overall environmental performance

The approach adopted is to develop environmental performance indicators (EPIs) appropriate to manufacturing firms in six industrial sectors, and to collect relevant quantitative data on a large sample of firms, where possible at process level. Environmental performance of firms will be analysed using sector-specific physical, economic and sustainability indicators.

Table 7 summarises indicators that have been identified as being specific to sectors, while energy and water consumption, and total waste, are treated as generic.

5. *Conclusions*

There is a worldwide trend in environmental reporting away from purely qualitative descriptions of environmental practices towards a more comprehensive, quantitative depiction of environmental performance through the use of input–output materials flow analysis and the use of environmental indicators. However, for this data to be useful, there must be a consistent definition of system boundaries and reference units. This is best done by developing standardised input–output frameworks for individual sectors.

---

1 The MEPI project is funded under the Fourth Framework Programme (Environment and Climate) of DGXII of the European Commission, and runs from April 1998 until May 2000.

Sectors	NACE code	Functional unit of product	Selected sector-specific physical indicators (emissions, eco-efficiencies)
Electricity production	40	kWh	NO_X, SO_2, thermal efficiency, production bottom ash, spent nuclear fuel
Fertiliser	24.15	kg P and kg N	NO_X, SO_2, waste gypsum, cadmium, airborne fluoride
Computer industry	30.02	number of units	Volatile organic compounds (VOCs) in manufacturing, energy consumption of products, recyclability of products
Pulp and paper industry	21	tonnes	COD/BOD, AOX in waste-water, water consumption, hazardous waste, recycled fibre
Printing	22.1 22.2	impressions $\times$ m^2	Ink consumption, VOC emissions, hazardous waste
Textile finishing	17.11 17.21 17.31	tonnes processed	COD, BOD, AOX in waste-water, hazardous waste, % of heavy metal-free dyes, heavy metals input in dyes, VOC emissions

Table 7: SECTOR-SPECIFIC PHYSICAL INDICATORS

At company level, the goals of ecobalances until recently were mainly to compare companies and products and to use relative advantages for marketing purposes. However, with the development of environmental management methodologies, this goal has shifted towards finding internal improvement options. One reason for this is that the extension of ecobalancing into full LCA, which was necessary for the former objectives, proved to be extremely difficult and time-consuming in its preparation, and the final results were too complex to be easily communicated to the customer. On the other hand, the controlling system of combined materials and cash flow management at production process and cost centre level has proved to be a very powerful tool for internal cost management and performance improvements.

The standardisation of measurement created by sectoral input–output frameworks also makes it possible to use key indicators for benchmarking purposes, allowing participating companies to ascertain where they stand in relation to the average and best performers, respectively, in their sector. By moving in this direction, ecobalancing is shedding some of its Germanic origins and becoming—as environmental input–output analysis—a more universal approach which can form the foundation of any environmental performance evaluation activity, and which is fully compatible with new frameworks such as ISO 14031.

7
Ecobalance Analysis as a Managerial Tool at Kunert AG

Rainer Rauberger and Bernd Wagner*

IN GERMANY, companies are under strong societal as well as market-led pressure to assess, control and reduce their impact on the environment (Wagner and White 1994). Many German firms have responded to this challenge with a new managerial tool: **ecobalance analysis**. This chapter provides a case study of one of the pioneers of ecobalancing: the textile producer Kunert. It is structured as follows: Section 1 provides a short overview of ecobalancing; Section 2 discusses the application of ecobalancing at Kunert; Section 3 describes the links between ecobalancing and cost management at Kunert; and Section 4 provides conclusions.

1. *Ecobalancing: An Overview*

◺ *Historical Background*

The early roots of ecobalance analysis can be traced to the concept of 'ecological accounting' developed in the 1970s by Müller-Wenk (1978), which is based on the notion that products whose manufacture entails higher environmental costs should carry higher prices. Although difficult to implement in practice, Müller-Wenk's concept did stimulate European researchers to develop other methods for evaluating a firm's environmental performance.

One line of inquiry focused on assessing the impact of different materials and resources used in a product's manufacture. Swiss researchers developed a method

---

* Section 1 is based on previous work with Mark White, University of Virginia, to whom the authors express their thanks.

for comparing the effects of competing packaging materials based on 'critical thresholds' for environmental damage. Results were expressed as 'eco-profiles': bar charts illustrating the product's environmental performance regarding the four dimensions of energy use, air emissions, water discharge and solid waste. This system has since then been refined by combining all of a product's environmental impact into a single indicator: the so-called 'eco-points' system (BUWAL 1991). There are now several similar eco-points systems in use, and other product-based instruments such as product-line analysis and life-cycle assessments have emerged and flourished during the last decade, bringing into account a wide range of environmental impacts from a cradle-to-grave perspective.

A broader-based project designed to measure environmental impacts on a 'whole-firm' basis was started in the late 1980s at the Institut für ökologische Wirtschaftsforschung (IÖW) in Berlin. There, researchers developed an ecobalance concept to analyse and measure the environmental impact of industrial activities, processes and products (IÖW 1989). German firms were among the first to pioneer the ecobalance concept, with Kunert AG being the first company to make its ecobalance analysis publicly available. Today, many European firms—including Siemens, Volkswagen, Allianz Versicherung, Sanyo, Novartis and Swissair—are using ecobalances for controlling purposes.

The Concept

Ecobalances can be defined as a structured method for measuring, analysing and reporting physical inflows and outflows of resources, raw materials, energy, products and wastes occurring in a particular organisation over a specified period of time. In an ecobalance, data are collected in a number of physical units such as kilograms, square metres and kilowatt-hours. Preparation of an ecobalance assists a firm in identifying opportunities for pollution prevention and cost savings, prioritising these opportunities for subsequent implementation, and measuring the performance of its environmental management efforts.

According to the boundaries of the analysis, three subsets of ecobalances can be distinguished: the company or site balance, the process balance and the product balance (see Fig. 1). The **company** or **site balance** encompasses all of the energy and materials entering and leaving the entire company (or site) over the course of a year. The **process balance** provides an overview of resource and energy use in specific production processes. **Product balances** are prepared in order to assist management in determining the environmental impact of particular products or product groups. Product balances limit their scope to the material streams that are handled within the 'company gates'. They constitute the starting point for evaluations over the whole life-span of a product (i.e. life-cycle assessment). For all three subsets of an ecobalance, the main structure is identical: the major input accounts are materials, energy, water and air. Corresponding output accounts are products, solid waste, energy emissions, waste-water and air emissions.

Preparing an ecobalance involves posing questions rarely asked before. And, often, expressing data in physical units generates new insights for management: the very

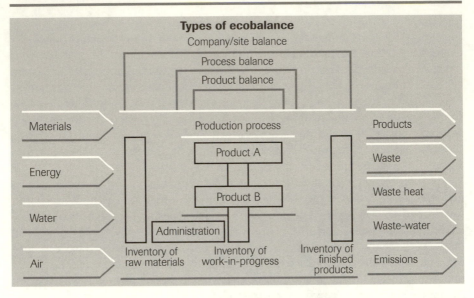

Figure 1: TYPES OF ECOBALANCE WITH SYSTEM BOUNDARIES

complex flow of materials and energy through the company and its production processes becomes transparent and assessable. Through the holistic approach of scrutinising all inputs and outputs, the company can ensure that no potentially relevant aspect is missed or omitted in the first place. Also, by comparing differences between inputs and outputs, inconsistencies of data can be checked and eliminated.

◻ **The Balance Equilibrium**

According to the laws of thermodynamics, material and energy cannot be destroyed but only transformed from one form to another. Based on this principle, ecobalance accounts should correspond regarding the inputs and the outputs entering and leaving the company. The balance equilibrium can be calculated for material flows (in kg) and energy flows (in kWh). Other units of measurement (i.e. megajoules, litres, units) should be translated into kg or kWh, either by using conversion tables (e.g. for the heating equivalent of different fuels) or by weighting exercises.

However, at the level of the company as a whole, this is valid only over longer periods of time, since in practice it is usually not possible to take all incoming, process and outgoing quantities into account, or indeed all variations in stocks and work in process. The main strength of the ecobalance, therefore, is that it is a structured and consistent account of potential environmental impacts through resource use, product output and waste-streams and emissions.

The principle of ecobalance analysis can be explained using the example of Kunert AG (see Fig. 2). In the knitting workshop, it was known that 2,000 litres of knitting

Figure 2: BALANCE EQUILIBRIUM IN A PRODUCTION PROCESS AT KUNERT AG

oil were used annually, on average. However, only 700 litres of used knitting oil were sent for incineration annually. The previously 'unknown' remainder (1,300 litres) evaporates into the air (and then settles in the structure of the building), leaves through diffuse air emissions, and (this accounts for the majority) remains on the semi-finished product. This caused considerable problems relating to the quality of the subsequent dyeing process and emissions into water (since the oil is washed out during the wet-dyeing process). Thus, for single materials, and for limited sets of material flows, 'mini-ecobalances' can be prepared, which are in perfect equilibrium. On a large scale, for whole companies and including all energy and material flows, this is not practicable. In principle, ecobalances are therefore very similar to detailed mass balances. The main difference, however, is that ecobalances include the assessment of energy use and heat emissions. Expressed in kWh, this allows comparisons of energy consumption between different energy sources and estimations of releases of energy into the natural environment.

◻ *The Process*

The first issue to be resolved concerns the intended audience and/or purpose of the ecobalance analysis. Is it primarily for internal use, as a management tool, or will it also be used to provide information for outside parties, or perhaps in marketing efforts? If the study is for internal use, technical details and confidential commercial data are likely to be included without aggregation. If the ecobalance is to be disseminated outside the company, special care should be taken to avoid misunderstandings and to mask commercial confidentialities.

The actual process of performing an ecobalance analysis consists of the following steps: planning, data collection, data analysis, priority-setting and improvement goals, and reviewing. It is a reiterative process, which is carried out—in general—annually. The next section describes how each of these steps were conducted at Kunert.

2. The Ecobalance Experience of Kunert AG

Kunert AG is Europe's largest manufacturer of socks and nylon stockings. With approximately 4,000 employees, the company has a consolidated sales revenue of about DM 450 million (Kunert AG 1996). The group operates nine production sites in Germany, southern Europe and northern Africa. Due to the general downswing in the textiles industry in Germany, the group suffered considerable restructuring losses from 1994 to 1996 though has now reached an economic turnaround. During this period, five production sites have been closed—mainly in Germany—with production being transferred to countries with lower labour costs.

As regards environmental management, the Kunert group has had a strong record since the end of the 1980s and represents one of the environmental pioneers in Germany (Schulz and Schulz 1995). The company has received at least ten environmental awards for its environmental management achievements based on ecobalances, and its environmental report was ranked in the top five by an independent study carried out in 1993 on behalf of the United Nations Environmental Programme (UNEP 1994b). However, against a background of an unfavourable economic situation for the industry and the general unwillingness of consumers to pay higher prices for environmentally sound products, Kunert AG needed to find 'win–win' situations, both economic and environmental. It achieved this through ecobalancing.

◁ The Process of Preparing the Ecobalance

Data collection. The first step in preparing any ecobalance, including Kunert's, is to set up organisation-wide 'accounts' for the areas to be analysed. Starting from the general categories of inputs and outputs that apply to all companies (cf. Fig. 1), for each category either a single account or a set of main accounts and underlying sub-accounts have to be created. The higher the complexity of materials flows and their environmental relevance, the deeper the system of sub-accounts will go. It is inevitable that organisations conducting an ecobalance analysis for the first time will experience difficulties in determining what items should be included, to what degree of detail, and how these items can be measured or estimated. In all probability, it will prove impossible to measure data directly for all accounts. However, it is possible to calculate output values based on the known inputs—e.g. the amount of energy used times conversion factors for emissions into air—or by estimating the missing value by differences between inputs and outputs.

If no reliable estimate for a particular measure is available, that account should be left blank until it is judged to be of sufficient importance to invest resources in obtaining reliable and meaningful figures. Thus, their presence on the balance sheet serves as a useful reminder of areas for improvement. At Kunert AG, the system of accounts for the ecobalance developed over time, both to cover a greater variety of inputs and outputs in a degree of detail that could not be estimated or measured in the first place, and to achieve a greater level of data accuracy with more sophisticated data collection methods. The summary data sheet for 1995/96 is shown in Figure 3.

Input	1995	1996	Output	1995	1996
Raw material (kg)	3,157,519	2,992,878	Hosiery (kg)	5,062,271	4,432,403
			Outer wear (kg)	266,506	339,823
Semi and finished goods (kg)	2,669,921	1,954,433			
			Transport packaging (kg)	809,112	735,196
			Product packaging (kg)	2,111,362	1,808,171
Dyes (kg)	73,050	60,310			
Chemicals (kg)	1,295,357	1,071,012	Special waste (kg)	72,926	83,687
Product packaging (kg)	2,544,073	1,824,532	Waste for recycling (kg)	1,753,807	1,472,896
Product applications (kg)	117,845	85,553	Waste for disposal (kg)	290,833	171,040
Ancillary material (kg)	1,652,541	1,325,893	Waste heat (MWh)	not recorded	
Energy (MWh)	110,009	101,635	Waste-water (m³)	294,936	284,662
			Heavy metals (kg)	43	30
Water (m³)	377,845	373,620			
			NO_X (kg)	54,428	52,159
			SO_X (kg)	188,607	192,029
Air (m³)	not recorded		CO_2 (kg)	32,339,933	30,837,598

Figure 3: ECOBALANCE SUMMARY SHEET FOR THE KUNERT GROUP OF COMPANIES 1995/96

Source: Kunert AG 1997

By comparing the data from successive years, ecobalances demonstrate trends regarding the consumption of resources and the emissions side of production. They provide information about the nature and amount of materials and energy input and relate this to the nature and amount of product and emission output. As explained above, due to the large scale of an ecobalancing exercise at a company level (nine sites), and, since some categories are not recorded (i.e. air), the sum of inputs as presented in Figure 3 does not equal the sum of outputs.

All materials, water and energy streams are based either on measurements, on ongoing accounting systems or on external data such as invoices for electricity or fuel bills for company vehicles. Data for air emissions and for heavy metals in waste-water are estimated based on specific energy conversion factors and detailed analyses of dyeing formulas and process data. For the estimated values, data accuracy can roughly be estimated to be between 80% and 95%.

Data analysis. On the basis of the summary balance sheet for the inputs and outputs, first conclusions can be drawn on increases or decreases in resource use and pollutant emissions. However, comparison over time and with other subsidiaries or competitors remains difficult if only absolute data is used, since it is not adjusted for differences in the size of the company or for changes in production output. Thus, in order to measure production efficiency, changes in production levels have to be taken into account using environmental ratios for a more comprehensive assessment of environmental performance.

Taking the absolute performance indicators of the ecobalance data, environmental ratios and quotas (*relative* performance indicators) can be derived to provide management with data that is adjusted for changes in production. Thus, data becomes assessable over time and between production sites, regardless of the actual level of output. Table 1 gives a detailed overview and definition of the environmental ratios used by Kunert. The appendix contains an example of Kunert's environmental performance indicators, 1995/96.

Production-specific ratios were chosen to monitor development towards an efficient use of the main environmentally relevant resources (energy, water, auxiliary materials, dyes) and towards the minimisation of waste and emission streams in production. The materials, waste and energy quotas were selected to follow up the shift to less harmful substances or materials (i.e. the proportion of heavy metal-free dyes versus conventional dyes; the proportion of low-emission fuels such as gas versus the use of electricity or fuel oil) and the recycling of resources (proportion of waste for recycling versus waste for disposal). The emission quotas finally describe how energy systems were optimised following Kunert's energy efficiency and emissions reduction policy.

In selecting 'unit of output' as reference data for specific consumption and emission ratios, care has to be taken regarding its definition. At Kunert AG, the level of sales

---

Production efficiency ratios

Specific energy consumption = energy consumption per unit output (in kWh/kg)
Specific water consumption = water consumption per unit output (in l/kg)
Specific dyestuff consumption = dyes per unit output (g/kg)
Specific auxiliary materials consumption = auxiliary material per unit output (g/kg)
Specific amount of waste = waste per unit output (in g/kg)
Specific emissions = emissions per unit input (in g/kWh)

Materials quotas

Proportion of heavy metal-free dyes = heavy metal-free dyes per total dyes (in %)
Average heavy metal content in dyes = heavy metal content in g per total dyes in kg
Packaging efficiency = packaging per unit of product sold (in %)

Emissions quotas

CO_2 efficiency = CO_2 emission per unit of energy use (g/kWh)
NO_X efficiency = NO_X emissions per unit of energy use (g/kWh)
SO_X efficiency = SO_2 emissions per unit of energy use (g/kWh)

Waste and energy quotas

Energy quotas = proportion of energy sources (i.e. gas, fuel, etc.) in total energy use
Waste quotas = proportion of individual waste-streams in total amount of waste

Table 1: ENVIRONMENTAL RATIOS AND QUOTAS OF KUNERT AG

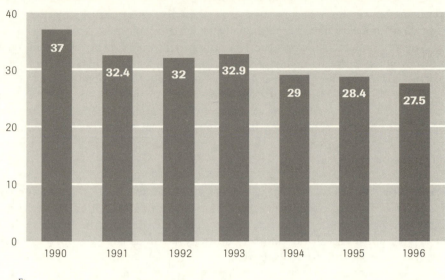

Figure 4: EXEMPLARY PERFORMANCE INDICATOR AND TARGET: PACKAGING EFFICIENCY

Source: Kunert AG 1997

may differ heavily from the production output. The reason for this is that finished goods are also bought from other producers and then sold under Kunert's brand name. Also, fluctuations in stocks of semi-finished and finished products may influence production output in one period, while emissions and resource consumptions occur in other periods. Therefore, reference data for production efficiency ratios had to be adjusted in order to remain in line with the base values being assessed. 'Unit output' has been defined as the average throughput in kilograms of the most environmentally relevant production processes, i.e. knitting and dyeing. Together, they account for more than 70% of water consumption and over 80% of energy consumption and emissions.

Setting priorities and improvement goals. Based on the results of the ecobalance analysis, the company's priorities were set and improvement goals were defined for the most important areas. In the past, priority areas for improvement at Kunert were increasing materials efficiency (waste avoidance), reducing packaging volume, increasing the proportion of recyclable waste-streams, and shifting to heavy metal-free dyes. The reason for prioritising these areas lies in their economic relevance (waste avoidance and reclamation) together with ecological and eco-toxicological optimisations of products (environmental and health aspects). For example, the considerable improvement in packaging proportion per unit of product sold (see Fig. 4) went hand in hand with major economic savings.

The reason for the decrease in the average proportion of packaging per unit of product sold (from 37.0 % in 1990 to 27.5 % in 1996) is to be found in a series of optimisations in the packaging area. First, the cover sheet and the plastic foil in pantyhose products have been gradually reduced in thickness, from 135 g/m² to 115 g/m² for the cardboard cover sheet and from 50 μ to 35 μ for the plastic foil. With a sales volume of 80–100 million units of pantyhose per year, this leads to annual reductions in cover sheet material of 150 tons and in plastic foil of about 120 tons. In monetary terms, it resulted in savings of approximately DM 650,000 per year. Furthermore, sealing and pricing stickers on the packaging have been replaced by direct printing and adhesion sealing, resulting in another materials saving of approximately 25,000 kg and DM 400,000 per year (initial capital outlay for the modified packaging machines was DM 700,000).

Reviewing. Periodically, the achievement of defined improvement goals and the suitability of the chosen ecobalance accounts and performance indicators is reviewed. If target achievement is not satisfactory, corrective action is taken. In cases where objectives prove unrealistic, target values may be adjusted. Following technical reviews of the adequacy of collected data, a whole series of improvements have been undertaken since the start of the ecobalance project in 1990.

For example, whereas in the first 1990 ecobalance only the absolute amount of dyes could be retrieved from the company's information systems, from 1991 onwards the dyes used could be classified according to their use and suitability for different product groups and processes (i.e. reactive dyes for wool, disperse dyes). Since 1993, each dye can be classified according to a set of ecological criteria (e.g. content of heavy metals by percentage, eco-toxicity, etc.). For the first time, the classification allowed for a comprehensive assessment of the ecological harmfulness of dyes and the subsequent development of reduction programmes. Other improvements to the ecobalance and performance evaluation processes relate to enhanced data retrieval systems, i.e. the direct linkage of financial or production data with corresponding ecobalance accounts, leading to increased data consistency, greater reliability and reduced effort in preparing the annual balance.

◁ Levels of Environmental Performance Measurement

Depending on the focus of the analysis, ecobalances can be applied at all levels of the organisation: from fully aggregated figures at company level, through plant or site indicators, down to parameters for processes and machinery, and also for products. The more aggregated the level of performance measurement (company level, site level), the more that ecobalances are appropriate for use as global information instruments for management or for the general public (i.e. in public environmental statements). The lower the level of aggregation, the more the figures lend themselves to detection of weaknesses and definition of specific improvement targets (Rauberger 1995).

For example, at a group level, the summary ecobalance data is mainly produced for environmental reporting purposes. At individual production sites, data from site balances is used for participation in the Eco-Management and Auditing Scheme (EMAS) and/or in support of ISO 14001. At process level, environmental performance indicators are derived on a monthly or quarterly basis for management control of key processes such as knitting, dyeing or packaging. At Kunert, process performance indicators were used from the beginning of the ecobalance analysis for comparisons between the dyeing departments of various sites (e.g. cost per kilogram of dyed product, water and energy consumption per kilogram, etc.).

In summary, an eco-efficiency comparison is of higher validity at lower levels of aggregation. Highly aggregated environmental ratios at company level can be used as general information instruments showing broad trends, whereas operational control mechanisms using environmental ratios perform best at lower levels of aggregation, i.e. at process or machinery level.

◁ The Implementation of Ecobalancing at Kunert AG

The full ecobalancing system at Kunert AG was developed over a period of about three years until the final accounting structure and data could be fully determined. The first ecobalances were prepared in 1991 for the years 1989 and 1990. Including the drafting of environmental objectives and targets, and the editing of an environmental report to explain the findings, it took about nine months to broadly implement the system and generate the first results. The initial work was undertaken by a working group, co-ordinated by an environmental officer and advised by an external (process) consultant. The working group contained representatives from key functional areas.

Due to the incremental implementation of the ecobalancing system, it is not possible to assess the exact cost of the initial implementation. However, it is possible to provide an estimate of the staff cost involved in preparing the balances, including target-setting, report-writing and their internal and external communication (cf. Rauberger 1994). From 1993 to 1996, the average annual cost (for the whole group of companies, including 12 production sites) could be approximated at 50% of the group environmental officers' hours (approximately US$40,000), 5% of 12 site environmental officers' hours (approximately US$40,000), and various team meetings including consultancy fees of about US$40,000. This leads to an average annual running cost of about $120,000 (DM 200,000) for the ecobalancing system including improvement analysis and reporting. Due to more elaborate data collection systems and their link to standardised accounting procedures, the current total cost could today be reduced to about half of this amount, i.e. US$60,000 (DM 100,000) per year. Proof that the ecobalancing exercise was worthwhile for Kunert AG is in the annual cost savings, which comfortably outweigh the average capital spending and operating costs of the system (cf. Section 3). From a marketing perspective also, environmentally aware buying behaviour by consumers rewards firms that manufacture their products in a socially and environmentally friendly manner and reduce health risks for customers. Or, as Rainer Michel, former CEO of the company, puts it, 'protecting the environment according to economic principles makes sense for businesses' (Kunert AG 1997: 5).

3. Environmental Cost Management

Ecobalances constitute an important planning, control and information instrument for management. However, in order to be most effective, they should not aim to replace conventional business planning and control processes. One way of achieving this is to integrate the financial perspective of environmentally relevant aspects into production planning and controlling. This led Kunert AG to a more systematic assessment of environmental cost saving potentials.

Kunert AG's experience with ecobalances from 1990 to 1994 has shown that higher transparency and improved materials and energy control mechanisms have led to a number of environmental improvement projects which have also reduced costs. From an analysis of 20 environmental projects (Rauberger 1994), the following conclusions can be drawn. Over the five-year span, average investment and operating costs for preparing the ecobalances and resulting improvement measures amounted to approximately US$550,000 (DM 900,000). About one-quarter of that amount relates to personnel costs (i.e. preparing the ecobalance, target-setting and report-writing), and three-quarters represents capital investment, mostly in integrated environmental technology and cleaner production techniques. On the other side of the equation, the average cost reductions amounted to US$1.55 million (DM 2.6 million). Thirteen of the 20 projects have been realised by organisational improvements, without any capital outlay (Wucherer *et al.* 1997).

These insights formed the starting point for a three-year pilot project (1994–96) on environmental cost management at the Mindelheim site, with subsequent roll-out of the results to the group's other sites. The aim of the project was to systematically develop new methods of linking environmental and business data, going beyond the pragmatic approaches previously adopted. These new methods would:

- Further reduce solid waste, waste-water and energy consumption through integrated environmental protection, and reduce cost. The main focus here was on optimising the flows of energy and materials, based on the ecobalance results, from input through all production stages to output.

- Set up an environmental information system in the group, which would allow significant opportunities for environmental protection and cost reductions to be systematically registered and exploited, and to continue this in the future.

On the basis of the site ecobalance, input, output and throughput costs have been systematically allocated to all ecobalance categories. In the reference year, the total costs were in the order of DM 68 million. Of that, DM 4.9 million was related to non-value-adding waste-streams (solid waste, waste-water, air emissions). For the purpose of comparison, the site ecobalance analysis yielded related results on materials efficiency: only 47% of all input materials go into the product, whereas 35% are used for packaging (i.e. turn into consumer waste at first use of the product) and 18% leave the site directly as solid, liquid or gaseous waste (see Fig. 5). These percentages were

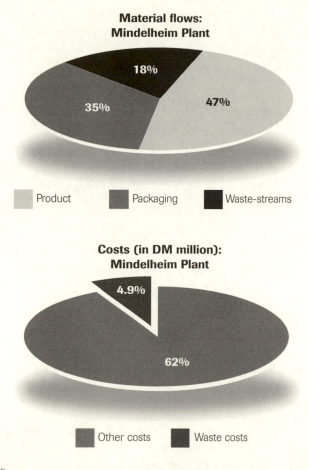

Figure 5: MATERIALS FLOWS AND COSTS AT THE MINDELHEIM PLANT

Source: Kunert AG 1996

calculated using a limited mass balance approach, taking only solid materials and waste-streams into account (i.e. without water, air and emissions throughput).

The result of the cost analysis (see Fig. 6) was that actual disposal costs accounted for only a small part (15%) of total environmental costs. The dominant factor is not the fees paid for disposal, but the original purchase cost of the wasted materials (59%). About a quarter of the total cost (26%) relates to throughput costs, i.e. labour and depreciation of machinery. This means that the economic viability of waste-avoidance projects is unlikely to be significantly influenced by possible future changes in waste disposal and effluent fees within a normal range (Wucherer *et al.* 1997).

By the end of the project, a programme with a further total cost saving potential of DM 800,000 was developed and partially implemented at the Mindelheim site.

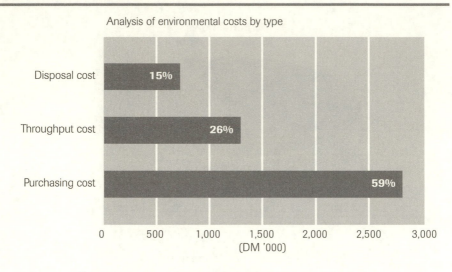

Figure 6: ENVIRONMENTAL COST SAVING POTENTIALS BY TYPE

4. Conclusions

Ecobalancing can be regarded as a materials- and energy-oriented approach to good environmental management. Through its continual improvement approach based on continuing cycles of data collection, assessment, target-setting and reviewing, it can even be seen as a specialised environmental management system. However, it differs from an environmental management system in being concerned solely with a subset of operational performance indicators, i.e. flows of energy, materials and wastes. It also differs from the mass balancing and waste minimisation exercises that are often carried out in American or British companies in its comprehensiveness and level of detail.

The main strength of ecobalances in relation to other means of environmental performance measurement (e.g. benchmarking, environmental ratios, etc.) is their holistic approach. On a company level, as well as on a process or product level, it ensures that all opportunities for optimisation are evaluated at first sight, i.e. nothing less obvious is missed, so that it is not only the 'low-hanging' environmental impacts that are considered for action. Also, plausibility checks can be conducted by comparing corresponding input and output streams. At a process level, it is also possible to estimate quantities of 'missing' material flows (i.e. fugitives).

However, ecobalancing does share one important attribute with waste minimisation exercises, in that it provides a cross-functional forum for discussing opportunities for improving environmental performance and reducing costs. This makes it easier to build awareness and commitment in non-environmental functions.

Of course, performing a complete ecobalance exercise is costly, particularly in terms of work involved. This establishes ecobalances as the basis for regular internal controlling processes, which are then conducted based on the most relevant environmental indicators (i.e. on a weekly or monthly basis). Full ecobalances create longer-term and more global demands, and can be seen rather as 'point exercises' over longer intervals (i.e. yearly).

The Kunert example demonstrates that these costs are often outweighed by benefits. Even during the economically difficult situation that the whole sector faced in the mid-1990s, the improved transparency, identification of environmental and business 'weak points', and the improved materials control mechanisms that ecobalancing generated in the company, led to a number of highly profitable environmental projects. This specific example therefore suggests that ecobalancing analysis can be expected to produce both environmental and business benefits in many companies and sectors.

◢ *Appendix:*
Kunert's Environmental Indicators 1995/96

No.	Indicator		1995	1996	+/– (%)
A	**Production efficiency ratios***				
1	Water consumption per kg product	(l/kg)	174.1	189.4	+9
2	Energy consumption per kg product	(kWh/kg)	50.7	51.5	+1
3	Emissions per kg product				
3.1	NO_x emissions	(g/kg)	25.08	26.44	–5
3.2	SO_2 emissions	(g/kg)	86.9	97.36	–11
3.3	CO_2 emissions	(kg/kg)	14,9	15.63	+5
4	Waste per kg product	(g/kg)	975.9	875.7	–10
4.1	Special waste	(g/kg)	33.6	42.2	+26
4.2	Waste for disposal	(g/kg)	134.0	86.7	–35
4.3	Waste for recycling	(g/kg)	762.0	746.6	–9
5	Auxiliary materials per kg product				
5.1	Dye consumption	(g/kg)	33.7	30.6	–9
5.2	Dye consumption containing heavy metals	(g/kg)	10.7	8.3	–22
5.3	Chemicals consumption	(g/kg)	597.6	543.3	–9
B	**Energy and waste quotas**				
6	Energy quotas				
6.1	Gas	%	15.4	13.7	–11
6.2.	Electricity	%	26.1	26.4	+1
6.3	Fuel oil	%	37.3	37.7	+1
6.4	Distance heating	%	6.1	7.8	+28
6.5	Vehicle fuel	%	15.1	14.4	–5
7	Waste quota				
7.1	Special waste	%	3.4	4.8	+41
7.2	Waste for recycling	%	77.6	85.3	+10
7.3	Waste for disposal	%	14.1	9.9	–30
C	**Materials quotas**				
8	Proportion of heavy metal-free dyes	%	68.1	72.8	+ 7
9	Average content of heavy metal per kg dyestuff	(g/kg)	5.3	4.3	–19
10	Average proportion of packaging per kg product	%	28.4	27.5	–3
D	**Emission quotas[†]**				
11	CO_2 emissions	(g/kWh)	346.5	303.4	–12
12	NO_x emissions	(g/kWh)	0.58	0.51	–12
13	SO_2 emissions	(g/kWh)	2.02	1.89	–6

* Calculated on the basis of all input and output streams, not only for production but also including inputs and
  outputs for administration, warehousing, logistics, etc.
† Including all emissions for which Kunert is directly accountable, on-site or off-site
  (i.e. including external emissions of power generation and district heating plants).

Source: Kunert AG 1997

Environmental Performance Evaluation and Reporting in Developing Countries

The Case of Indonesia's Programme for Pollution Control, Evaluation and Rating (PROPER)

Shakeb Afsah and Damayanti Ratunanda

IN JUNE 1995 Indonesia became the first developing country to introduce a public environmental reporting initiative, the 'Programme for Pollution Control, Evaluation and Rating' (PROPER). Under PROPER, industrial enterprises[1] are evaluated by the Environmental Impact and Management Agency (BAPEDAL), Government of Indonesia, for their environmental performance, and the results, in the form of a five-colour rating scheme, are reported to the public through press conferences[2] and the Internet.[3] The five colours—gold, green, blue, red and black—reflect performance ranging from excellent to poor. This kind of colour-coding provides a simple but effective format for communicating environmental information to the public. Early results suggest that the programme has already been very effective in improving environmental performance and, by providing better information for policy-makers, NGOs and the public, it is creating pressure for further change. It is therefore a major argument against the assumption that concern with economic development prevents real improvements in environmental performance in poorer countries.

---

1   An industrial enterprise refers to an individual production unit, facility, factory or plant. Thus, several enterprises within a single company could be rated in PROPER. However, ratings are assigned only to enterprises and not to the company.
2   Examples of PROPER's press coverage is available at *http://www.kompas.com/9601/03/H03/proper.htm*
3   *http://www.bapedal.go.id/info/proper/merah97.html*

The origins of PROPER lie in the desire of Indonesian regulators, particularly Nabiel Makarim, then Deputy for Pollution Control at BAPEDAL, to reinforce the existing command-and-control system, which had failed to reduce pollution largely due to problems of enforcement. Indonesia is known for a weak regulatory system, and, even when regulations exist on paper, actual implementation remains extremely limited. PROPER was conceived by Mr Makarim as a way of creating an incentive for compliance by exploiting the ideas of honour and shame, which are powerful motivators in many Asian societies.

Since its introduction in 1995, PROPER has received considerable attention from international agencies such as USAID and The World Bank. The latter has published several reports[4] and a case study[5] on PROPER, and its *World Development Report* for 1998 cited it as a model for a modern knowledge-based policy instrument.[6]

Because much time has been spent in tailoring the scheme to the needs of a developing country, the initiative has considerable international relevance. Indeed, it is already being emulated by other countries. The Philippines government introduced a similar programme called EcoWatch[7] in 1997, and in 1998 publicly disclosed the ratings of around 50 enterprises using PROPER-type colour codes. Thailand, India (see Chapter 8) and Colombia are also planning to introduce schemes that are based on or influenced by PROPER. As noted, one generic advantage of such schemes is that they complement and reinforce 'command-and-control' approaches, which are difficult to enforce in many developing countries.

PROPER also satisfies another key need for reporting in developing countries, which is the ability to communicate with audiences that have no familiarity with mainstream business language or may even be illiterate. As the likelihood is that most companies will be relatively poor performers, it is also important to avoid simple polarised 'go/no-go' assessments. Discriminating between various states of 'poorness', for example, helps to prioritise attention and also provides an incentive for improvement for companies who have many demands on their attention.

This chapter begins by describing PROPER in more detail, followed by a discussion of the conceptual issues involved in developing composite indicators. The third section describes the specific approach adopted by PROPER, while a fourth section examines its real impact in Indonesia. The final section presents some thoughts on what can be learned from the PROPER experience.

---

4   *http://www.worldbank.org/nipr/comrole.htm*
5   *http://www.worldbank.org/nipr/work_paper/vincent/index.htm*
6   *http://www.worldbank.org/NIPR/wdr99.htm*
7   Shakeb Afsah served as advisor for EcoWatch during 1996–97 in the Department of Environment and Natural Resources, Government of the Philippines. Some of the press coverage of EcoWatch is available at *http://www.denr.gov.ph/070998.htm*, *http://www.worldbank.org/nipr/ecowatch/ecowatch2.htm*, and *http://www.worldbank.org/nipr/ecowatch/ecowatch1.htm*

◀ *The PROPER Programme: Key Features*[8]

Since public disclosure and environmental ratings were novel ideas for the Indonesian public, BAPEDAL's strategy focused on the social marketing of these concepts. Also, BAPEDAL was aware that effectiveness of PROPER ratings would be determined by whether or not the public considered the ratings credible. A careful analysis of the credibility issue led to two key elements: technical and institutional credibility. Technical credibility was necessary to ensure that ratings accurately convey the idea of relative performance. Similarly, institutional credibility was necessary to ensure that the ratings were free from corruption or other distorting influences. Accordingly, an incremental approach was devised to ensure a high level of accuracy and consistency in the first few years of implementation. Also, a strict rating and review process was adopted, which included an advisory committee consisting of members of other government agencies, NGOs and well-known public figures. These features are described in the following.

◻ *Incremental Approach*

It was important to initiate PROPER on a small scale but with a high level of accuracy. Accordingly, in the first phase, the focus of environmental performance was on water pollution, to be gradually expanded to include hazardous waste and air pollution. Water pollution regulations in Indonesia were introduced in the late 1980s, and BAPEDAL therefore had considerable experience of managing industrial water pollution. In contrast, hazardous waste and air pollution regulations were introduced only in 1994 and 1995 respectively. Also, through one of its programmes, the Clean River Management Programme (PROKASIH), it was possible for BAPEDAL to identify the main industrial water-polluting sources in Indonesia. Thus, in 1995, BAPEDAL was best positioned to implement the ratings programme for industrial waste-water.

In addition to the factories included in the PROKASIH programme, there were two other categories of participant. First, BAPEDAL invited factories to participate voluntarily in PROPER, and, second, BAPEDAL reserved the authority to enforce participation by factories that were considered to be significant polluters. Thus, overall, PROPER has both regulatory and voluntary features—and can perhaps be best described as a semi-voluntary programme. When it was first introduced in June 1995, there were 187 factories covering 14 industrial sectors from all Indonesia.

◻ *Coverage of Pollutants and Indicators*

For three categories of performance—average, bad and very bad—the pollutants covered in the programme are governed primarily by the water regulations. The total number of water pollution parameters includes more than 40 types of waste, including organic, hazardous, toxic, nutrients, metals and others. However, for

---

8 Complementary (though now slightly outdated) information on PROPER is available at *http://www.worldbank.org/nipr/work_paper/propwhat/index.htm* (1996).

performance categories that are very good and excellent, the coverage of pollutants and indicators is wider.

◻ *The Rating Process*

The rating process was an important part of the overall strategy to ensure political acceptance of the programme and to ensure high quality and accuracy in ratings. As shown in Figure 1, the rating process involves extensive data collection, verification and analysis components. Second, there is an advisory committee to ensure external stakeholders' participation in the process. And, finally, the ratings are evaluated by the Minister of Environment; when PROPER was first launched, the programme was cleared at presidential level. Such a high level of political acceptance was essential in order to signal government commitment and seriousness to industry.

◻ *Multi-Media-Based Environmental Performance: Conceptual Issues*

The basic framework for multi-media-based environmental performance analysis is shown in Figure 2. Plants produce a wide range of pollutants that are released as air and water pollution and as hazardous wastes. It is often observed that, at plant level,

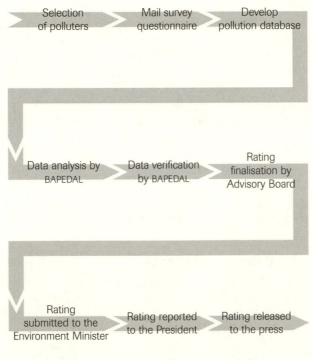

Figure 1: PERFORMANCE RATING PROCESS

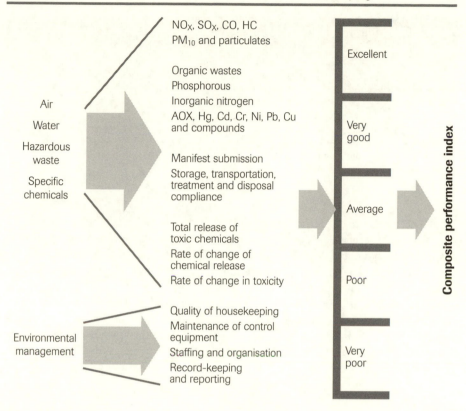

NO$_X$, SO$_X$, CO, HC
PM$_{10}$ and particulates

Organic wastes
Phosphorous
Inorganic nitrogen
AOX, Hg, Cd, Cr, Ni, Pb, Cu
and compounds

Manifest submission
Storage, transportation,
treatment and disposal
compliance

Total release of
toxic chemicals
Rate of change of
chemical release
Rate of change in toxicity

Quality of housekeeping
Maintenance of control
equipment
Staffing and organisation
Record-keeping
and reporting

Air
Water
Hazardous
waste
Specific
chemicals

Environmental
management

Excellent

Very
good

Average

Poor

Very
poor

Composite performance index

Figure 2: FRAMEWORK FOR A MULTI-MEDIA-BASED ENVIRONMENTAL PERFORMANCE ANALYSIS

there is considerable variation in the extent of pollution control across air, water and toxic waste pollution. Industrial enterprises also consume resources such as water, energy and materials, and this consumption may have its own detrimental impact. Within this framework, a multi-media-based facility-level performance analysis system consists of four main components: the development of a rule for aggregating across pollutants; determination of appropriate performance categories; resolving the issue of continuous versus category-based rating; and determination and selection of pollutant-specific benchmarks.

◻ *Development of Composite Index*

Aggregating across multiple indicators is not easy, and there are few models available. One of the main issues in developing a composite index is whether or not it is desirable to allow poor performance in one pollutant type to be compensated for by good performance in another. In theory, this would be a desirable approach, but information on the elasticity of substitution across pollutants would be essential.

Aggregation approaches	Advantages	Disadvantages
Min–min rule	Easy to communicate and conservative	Too much weight on the worst-performing indicator
Average	Simple to compute	Can be misleading
Numerical index	Easy to communicate	Hard to interpret

Table 1: THREE APPROACHES FOR AGGREGATING ACROSS MULTIPLE INDICATORS

However, in practice, the information that would enable such trade-offs is not usually available, and therefore developing a composite index could require several arbitrary assumptions that could ultimately undermine the usefulness of this approach. Some of the options available for aggregation are shown in Table 1.[9] Clearly, there is no single approach that is perfect.

In the case of Indonesia's PROPER, it was decided to adopt the min–min rule, as a conservative and transparent approach was preferred. Driven by practical considerations, it was desirable to start with a conservative approach where a composite index reflects the worst performances in each of the pollutant groups. Such an index can be expressed as:

Composite index (I) = *Worst*[Air, Water, Hazardous waste, Specific chemicals]

This index will create incentives for some minimum performance level for all pollutants, which may or may not be desirable. However, without information on benefits and costs associated with each of the pollutants, it was not possible to assess the extent of distortion that this index may create. In the first phase, it was considered desirable to adopt this approach in order to minimise the risk of large grading errors, but to allow the possibility of adjusting the performance analysis scheme as the programme evolves and more experience and better data is accumulated.

◁ Performance Categories

In general, 'excellent', 'average' and 'bad' are three simple and easy-to-understand categories of performance, though limiting the number of categories to only three could prove too restrictive. This is a problem that is common to measuring

---

9   The three concepts in Table 1 are illustrated by a simple example. Let the values of three environmental indicators be 10, 20 and 30, such that the higher the value, the worse for the environment. Under the min–min approach, the final value will be the worst of the three, or 30. If the average is used, the composite value will be $\frac{10 + 20 + 30}{3}$ = 20. Finally, if there is an index based on the assumption that higher values have more weight, then an example of a possible composite index is $\sqrt{10^2 + 20^2 + 30^2}$ = 37.5.

performance in all areas: for example, in grading systems in educational assessment or in the corporate credit ratings undertaken by services such as Moody's and Standard & Poor's, where the number of categories into which performance is grouped and reported is typically much higher. In this case, it would be possible to introduce a fourth category, 'very good', between 'excellent' and 'average', and a fifth, 'very bad', as the worst category of polluters and hence priorities for pollution control measures.

There are potentially several different ways of representing these five groups in communicating the final results of the evaluation; this could be based on, for example:

- Colour-coding, on a 'traffic-light' model (which was the method finally decided on for PROPER)

- Numerical scores (such as Mexico City's air quality index)

- Alphabetical rating (such as the Moody's and Standard & Poor's bond rating systems)

The choice of method should be governed by ease of communication, and the ability to reflect performance level accurately.

Continuous Numerical Rating versus Category Rating Scheme

The difference between 'continuous numerical' and 'categorical rating' can best be illustrated by an example. We are all familiar with the most commonly used indicator of national income, the GNP. If we express every country's income by its GNP, then this is a case of continuous numerical rating. However, we can also group countries by income levels; such a grouping leads to a categorical rating. In the case of national income, we often group countries in of terms of high income, middle income or low income. Category rating schemes, an ordinal type of measure, have the advantage of simplicity, and the implication of any specific category is easy to understand and communicate.

However, environmental performance may require quantitative as well as qualitative information in order to form a comprehensive assessment, which would imply a continuous numerical rating scheme (a cardinal measure). If this were intended to cover a broad range of different aspects of performance, the evaluation of at least some elements would inevitably require some degree of subjective judgement by the evaluators in assigning a numeric score to qualitative information. It was considered that this would be inherently inconsistent with the concept of numerical rating, so a category grading approach was therefore preferred.

Determination of Pollutant-Specific Benchmark

To implement any grading scheme, a benchmark, or point of reference, is essential. For environmental performance analysis, there are three potential options. Depending on the pollutant, it can be expressed relative to:

Rating	Performance level	Definition
Gold	Excellent	All requirements of Green, plus similar levels of pollution control for air and hazardous waste. Polluter reaches high international standards by making extensive use of clean technology, waste minimisation, pollution prevention, recycling, etc.
Green	Good	Pollution level is lower than the discharge standards by at least 50%. Polluter also ensures proper disposal of sludge; good housekeeping; accurate pollution records; and reasonable maintenance of the waste-water treatment system.
Blue	Adequate	Polluter only applies effort sufficient to meet the standard.
Red	Poor	Polluter makes some effort to control pollution, but not sufficiently to achieve compliance.
Black	Very poor	Polluter makes no effort to control pollution, or causes serious environmental damage.

Table 2: THE FIVE COLOUR CODES

- ◗ Compliance requirements
- ◗ Best possible performance with regard to pollution and resource intensities
- ◗ Rate of change over time of pollution releases and resource intensities

The choice of reference point will depend on the availability of the relevant data, which will vary: for example, in some areas of environmental performance there may not currently be any regulations set by government against which to monitor compliance. In these cases, the alternatives of best possible performance in pollution and resource intensities could be used. In a situation where compliance is not well defined and pollution and resource intensity data are not available, the best available option is to use the rate of change as the indicator of improvement.

◢ *Indonesia's Five-Colour Rating Scheme*

PROPER is expected to serve three environmental objectives:

- ◗ Promote compliance with existing regulations
- ◗ Reward firms whose performance exceeds regulatory standards
- ◗ Create incentives for clean technology adoption

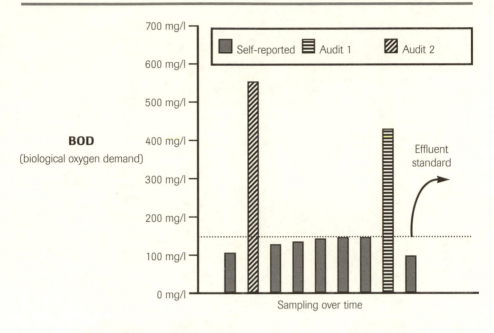

Figure 3: DATA QUALITY PROBLEM

Based on these objectives, a five-colour rating scheme was developed. In the Indonesian context, a well-defined system of regulatory compliance requirements was available to form the basis around which the first three categories of performance were developed. The further two categories covered performance that exceeded compliance and represented clean production. The basic definitions of the five colour codes are shown in Table 2.

For practical purposes, Indonesia focused on water pollution in the first phase of the programme. However, plants that were likely candidates for Green and Gold ratings were also assessed for compliance with other environmental regulations. An important factor in this decision was that the implementing agency had access and authority to collect self-reported as well as inspection data.[10] Inspection data are crucial for verification and accurate assessment of environmental performance. Figure 3 illustrates the issue of data quality; the chart in this figure is based on the actual data from a factory that participates in PROPER. It is observed that the data collected by the environmental agency through two different programmes show that the pollution level for BOD (biological oxygen demand), a common indicator of organic waste in industrial waste-water, is considerably higher than the factory has reported

---

10   Inspection data refers to effluent sampling and testing by the government agencies. In the case of Indonesia, the environmental agencies can sample and test effluent quality through several programmes. Under PROPER, data collected through multiple programmes are processed through a common database and a computer model, which facilitates the detection of anomalies.

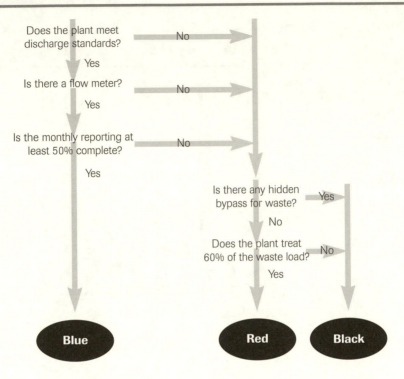

Figure 4: RATING FLOWCHART: BLUE / RED / BLACK

in its self-monitoring reports. Since two government sources found a similar result, it is probable that the factory has deliberately attempted to misrepresent its true pollution levels. In the absence of an arrangement to combine data from different sources, accuracy of the results could be adversely affected.

The ranking methodology based on the water pollution control regulation in Indonesia is illustrated in Figures 4, 5 and 6. All waste-water discharges are expected to meet effluent standards, to install flow meters, and to take sampling and flow rate measurements on a regular basis. While most weight is given to meeting the discharge standards and installation of flow meters, even a partial fulfilment of reporting requirements may be sufficient for an average rating. A Black rating is assigned to blatant violators who make no effort at all to control pollution, while polluters who undertake only a partial treatment are given a Red rating.

The next step is to assess which of the Blue plants could achieve a Green rating. Performance requirements for Green significantly exceed regulations, and include assessment of the quality of housekeeping, maintenance of pollution control equipment, and compliance with other environmental regulations, as shown in Figure 5. Clearly, criteria for Green are based on broader environmental management concepts. Indonesia is also evaluating the possibility of setting the criteria for Green to be same as the requirements for ISO 14001 certification.

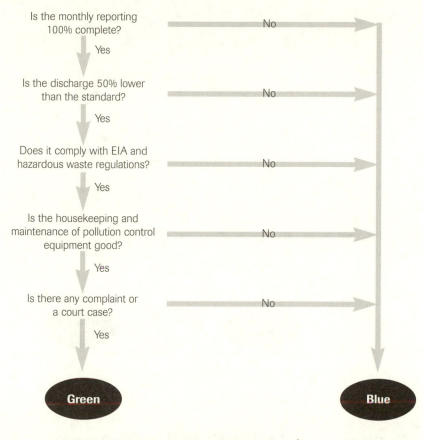

Figure 5: RATING FLOWCHART: GREEN/BLUE

The final step involves the selection of Gold from the Green. Here the criteria are based on clean technology principles, as shown in Figure 6. Clean technology refers to a production process that is inherently cleaner compared to other processes in the same sector. For example, for production of chlor-alkali, a diaphragm cell process is cleaner than a mercury cell process. Similarly, in the pulp and paper sector, a totally chlorine-free process represents clean technology.

At this stage, the plants that are likely candidates for Gold are audited to assess the extent of clean production concepts in use. Expert auditors check for innovations at the process and production levels, the extent of recycling and resource conservation, and the use of clean raw materials. It is possible that, in some sectors, adequate technological developments in clean production methods are not fully established. For such sectors, the benchmark is based on the best available technology. Currently, the quantitative indicators of clean production are under development. So far, no company has received a Gold rating.

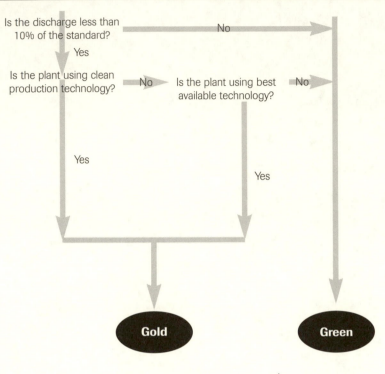

Figure 6: RATING FLOWCHART: GREEN/GOLD

◢ *Effectiveness of PROPER's Rating Methodology*

One way of testing the effectiveness of PROPER's performance evaluation methodology is to see whether or not the rating system has produced the expected results.
The first indicator here is the rate of improvement in the industrial enterprises that
get Blue or better ratings. As shown in Figure 7, based on the data on 173 factories,
the number of facilities with Blue and Green ratings improved from 32% and 2% to
47% and 4% respectively between June 1995 and December 1996. Since there was no
other environmental initiative during this period, it is reasonable to attribute this
improvement to the PROPER programme.

A fairly significant improvement in ratings was also observed in the Philippines,
which introduced a PROPER-based EcoWatch programme in June 1997.[11] Between 1997
and 1998, the number of companies with Blue ratings improved from 4 to 26.[12]

The second indicator of PROPER's effectiveness is the impact on compliance levels.

---

11 *http://www.worldbank.org/nipr/ecowatch/ecowatch2.htm* and *http://www.worldbank.org/nipr/ecowatch/
    ecowatch1.htm*
12 *http://www.worldbank.org/nipr/ecowatch/ecov2rate.htm* and *http://www.worldbank.org/nipr/ecowatch/
    manstand1.htm*

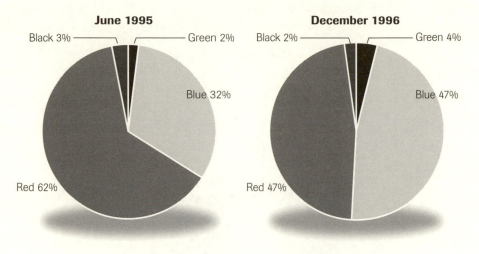

June 1995

Black 3% ——— Green 2%

Blue 32%

Red 62%

December 1996

Black 2% ——— Green 4%

Blue 47%

Red 47%

Figure 7: RATINGS IMPROVEMENT

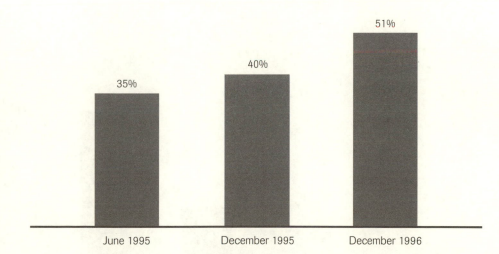

35%

40%

51%

June 1995

December 1995

December 1996

Figure 8: IMPACT OF PROPER ON COMPLIANCE LEVELS

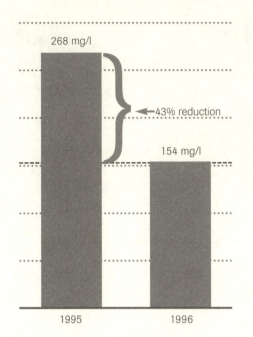

Average BOD concentration at source

Based on June 1995 list of factories

268 mg/l

←43% reduction

154 mg/l

1995   1996

Figure 9: IMPACT OF PROPER ON POLLUTION LEVELS

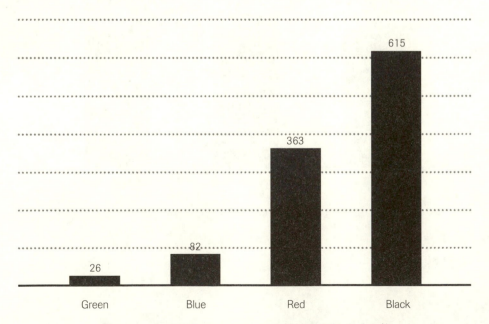

615

363

82

26

Green   Blue   Red   Black

Figure 10: AVERAGE BOD CONCENTRATION BY RATING (mg/l)

Here we observe that the level of compliance with regulations, as shown in Figure 8, has also improved from 35% in 1995 to 51% by 1996. However, these two indicators by themselves do not provide definitive information about direct environmental impacts. One way of testing for this is to analyse the changes in average enterprise-level pollution during the two years of implementation of PROPER. Here, using the average BOD concentration as an indicator, we find (see Fig. 9) that there has been a 43% reduction between 1995 and 1996. Finally, there is a check to ascertain whether or not the differences in colour-code are consistent with pollution levels observed in each category. As shown in Figure 10, factories that are Green have the lowest average pollution level and factories that achieve Black have the highest. These numbers are consistent with the basic definitions of the ratings, and therefore validate the underlying concept and environmental indicators applied in PROPER programme.

◢ A Case Study

To highlight the impact of PROPER at the factory level, there now follows a brief case study of a rayon-producing facility. This facility had a history of non-compliance, with complaints from communities in its neighbourhood. The environment agency had been trying to enforce environmental regulations for more than two years, but the factory had failed to respond to the regulatory pressure. While the exact reason for the failure of enforcement is not well understood, it is evident that regulatory requirements were insufficient to motivate compliance.

In June 1995, this factory was included in the PROPER programme and received a Black rating—the worst possible. Reasons for the rating included persistent compliance failure and high pollution levels. The factory was given six months to improve its rating before a planned disclosure in December 1995. The mere threat of disclosure was enough to stimulate improvement in performance. As shown in Figure 11, there was a significant drop in BOD concentration to a level well within effluent standards. Also, it can be seen that this factory has maintained a compliance level for BOD concentration until the most recently collected data in 1999. A similar profile of improvement is observed for other pollutants as well. As a result, the factory is now rated Blue.

◢ PROPER and the Financial Crisis in Indonesia

Indonesia's financial crisis began around July 1997 and it adversely affected the activities of most public agencies and private organisations. With regard to the environmental sector, and PROPER in particular, the financial crisis affected the performance of the programme through three channels. First, the government budget on environment was reduced, and consequently the PROPER programme suffered a reduced operational budget for conducting inspections. In 1996 and 1997, the PROPER programme conducted more than 250 inspections but in 1998 only around 100. There

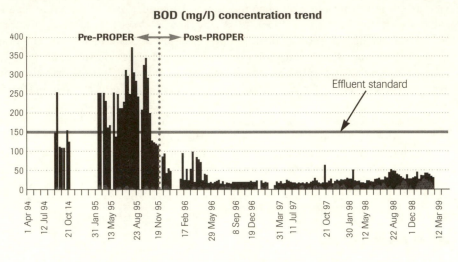

Figure 11: AN EXAMPLE OF FACTORY-LEVEL IMPACT OF PROPER

are potentially two negative effects on the PROPER programme of reduced inspections. First, the factories that have improved their performance due to increased regulatory vigilance created by the high probability of inspection may become non-compliant. And, second, some of the factories that tend to under-report their data on pollution level are less likely to be detected. These two effects combined may reduce the number of firms with Blue or better ratings and also increase the likelihood of error. To minimise the effects of these factors, a fairly sophisticated computerised data quality-control system has been developed that enables BAPEDAL to identify factories that are likely to under-report. These factories then become the priority for inspections.

The second adverse effect caused by the crisis is simply the increased cost of pollution control. Most of the factories require imported raw material and working capital to run their pollution-control equipment. Due to the crisis, the Indonesian currency has devalued considerably and the interest rate has also increased. These direct effects on input costs of pollution abatement, coupled with the overall decline in revenue due to lower demand and higher production costs, will compel many producers to cut down on the level of pollution control. This will also tend to increase pollution levels[13] and reduce the overall effect of PROPER.

The third potentially important factor is the role of the community and the press. Due to the crisis, communities tend to focus more on basic needs rather than pollution issues. In some cases, communities may be willing to tolerate pollution if

---

13   'Impact of Financial Crisis on Industrial Growth and Environmental Performance in Indonesia'
      by Afsah (1998) can be downloaded from *http://www.worldbank.org/nipr/work_paper/shakeb/index.htm*

it ensures employment and income. Similarly, most newspapers are more interested in other political issues and unwilling to make a list of environmental ratings front-page news. Thus, the incentive for improvement in environmental behaviour for firms, created by the threat of disclosure, has probably been weakened by the crisis.

It is hard to predict the future of PROPER. However, the press, NGOs and the general public are strong supporters, and so there is considerable political force to demand its continuation in some form or other. Nevertheless, how effective an environmental management tool it will be if the current situation of economic and political crisis persists is difficult to predict.

◢ Concluding Remarks

Environmental performance evaluation is a relatively new area of environmental management. There are many concepts and indicators currently in use at corporate level and by public agencies and NGOs. The PROPER programme demonstrates that a performance evaluation system that is conceptually well constructed and implemented can work in a developing-country setting. We also believe there are many novel ideas underlying PROPER's methodology that are applicable to ongoing developments in this topic in OECD countries, particularly the concept of rating rather than disclosing the raw data on pollution.

9
Evaluating Corporate Environmental Performance in Developing Countries

TERI's Eco-Rating System*

Vandana Bhatnagar

IF INDIVIDUALS IN INDIA wish to know the level of emissions from a factory located in their neighbourhood, they have two choices. First, they can ask the local pollution control board office for emissions data reported by the facility. In all probability, they would be informed that the file is not available. Even if it were available, the data would offer little comfort in the way of reliability or adequacy. The second option is to approach the factory manager himself. Needless to say, neither option seems particularly effective. A case exists for the introduction of tools to provide better information to the Indian public. Such tools need to be designed with the realities of the Indian situation in mind.

---

* TERI (the Tata Energy Research Institute, New Delhi) is an autonomous, not-for-profit research institute established in 1974. Starting with an initial focus on documentation and information dissemination activities, it later moved into research in the fields of energy, environment, biotechnology, forestry and the whole range of sustainable development issues. Over 400 professionals, drawn from a wide range of disciplines, work at TERI's headquarters in New Delhi, as well as at its regional centres and field sites in India and overseas.

The Institute is engaged in a wide range of activities. Those relating to the industrial sector are: energy audits; environmental impact assessments and management planning; health exposure studies; technology (energy- and environment-related) development and adaptation; information dissemination; and training.

TERI's advisors include leading members of both government and industry, and several senior TERI staff members are associated with various government and industry bodies, as well as individual companies. The Institute is financially independent, raising resources primarily through project activity.

What characterises Indian industry is its diversity—in scale, age and technology. Such diversity can be witnessed on the environmental front as well. India has some of the worst instances of industrial pollution and environmental degradation, but also examples of novel, proactive initiatives aimed at improving environmental performance. As regards environmental performance evaluation and reporting (EPER), however, the trend is fairly uniform: namely, aiming simply to meet legal reporting requirements.

By law, all potentially polluting facilities are required to report emissions data on a monthly basis, and to submit annual environmental statements to the regulatory authorities. The environmental statements must be audited, though not necessarily by third-party auditors. Instances of EPER going beyond these requirements do exist, but are rare. Reports published for external audiences by the more visible corporations take the form of 'green glossies' (as identified in SustainAbility's five-point scale [SustainAbility *et al.* 1993]). Recent initiatives such as ISO 14001 and Responsible Care, however, do encourage facilities to go beyond mere compliance in tracking and managing environmental issues, but to what extent they succeed in this endeavour in India is, however, as yet unclear.

◢ Pressures for Change

Despite the uninspiring status of EPER in Indian industry, there is a gradual yet perceptible improvement. The reason for this is changing attitudes towards the environment.

Several research studies have indicated the seriousness of environmental degradation in India; one recent study estimates the cost of degradation to be roughly 10% of GDP (Pachauri and Sridharan 1998). The bulk of the Indian populace—and not just isolated, backward communities—is experiencing these impacts, resulting in a heightened awareness and sensitivity to environmental concerns. Several other key factors have also come into play in the last 10–15 years.

▼ Growing environmental activism. There are currently over 10,000 environmental and development-oriented NGOs, citizen groups and pressure groups in India (roughly 20 times the figure in 1985 [Confederation of Indian Industry 1995]). With a view to further strengthening the environmental movement in the country, the MoEF (Ministry of Environment and Forests) established an NGO cell in 1992.

The frequency of public interest litigation (PIL) has also risen considerably. Changes in environmental legislation have given individuals, even if unaffected, the power to file legal complaints with relative ease. PIL has effectively spotlighted the link between environmental and business risks.

▼ Regulatory trends indicate a gradual tightening of emission norms[1] and heightening of corporate accountability for environmental problems. Recent

---

1   Emission norms (CO + HC + NO$_x$) for petrol cars were lowered from 16.3–30.0 g/km (1991) to 11.68–16.76 g/km (1996), and will be further reduced to 3.69 g/km (2000). A similar drop has occurred in other vehicle categories.

examples have included the inclusion of public hearings in the environ-mental impact assessment (EIA) process, the Public Liability Insurance Act (1991) for damages caused by accidents involving hazardous substances, and reporting of energy consumption data in annual balance sheets. Enforce-ment, however, remains slow and weak (based on unofficial figures, the Confederation of Indian Industry estimates the compliance level at approx-imately 45% for all large, medium and small industrial sectors).

▼ Globalisation is exposing an increasing number of companies to the more stringent environmental standards of the West: e.g. green criteria for products; ISO 14001 certification.

▼ Shortage of resources such as water, energy and forests is not only impacting ordinary citizens but is also constraining industrial activity, hence the increasing importance being placed on resource conservation measures.

▼ The size of Indian businesses has been growing rapidly, and so too has the number of associated stakeholders/shareholders. For instance, the share of public (versus private) limited companies in total paid-up capital moved from 40% in 1987/88 to 50% in 1990/91, and to 70% by 1995/96. This shift has resulted in a broadening of the investor/lender base, which in turn has created pressures for greater corporate accountability and transparency. Hence the rise of standardised accounting/disclosure norms, financial ratings, codes of corporate governance—and now, hopefully, environmen-tal performance reporting.

◢ The Key Problem Being Addressed

Despite the concern over environmental problems, considerable ambiguity prevails on the subject. Conflicting perspectives are provided by various stakeholder groups, such as NGOs, local community representatives, industry associations and govern-ment bodies. The lack or poor quality of information further compounds the confusion. Enforcement agencies do not enjoy public credibility, nor have the requisite capability/resources to play the role of 'referee'. The fact that the subject is a technical one further discourages the layperson from seeking out information and arriving at independent conclusions.

As a result, the environmental debate has become a matter of opinions rather than hard facts. People appreciate the significance of the problem, but view it as too subjective or controversial a topic to be incorporated into mainstream decision-making. A need exists for a tool—an objective and credible performance evaluation system—to address this information gap. Various evaluation schemes have been introduced internationally; however, due to the existence of one or more of the following features, these systems have been considered unsuitable in an Indian context:

- Focus on management systems, not end-performance aspects

- Systems based on self-assessments rather than on third-party evaluations

- Use of publicly accessible data for evaluation

- High level of complexity of assessment framework

- Industry-specific framework (as in the case of companies' internal rating programmes)[2]

Consequently, the need has been felt for an indigenous rating system that takes account of local conditions and stakeholder requirements in its design and implementation.

◢ *About Eco-Rating*

Recognising this information gap, which was further ratified by informal views expressed by some external stakeholders, TERI developed the **Eco-Rating System** (ERS): a framework for evaluating the environmental performance and risk of facilities against generally accepted benchmarks.

The ERS is intended to achieve the following objectives:

- Provide an evaluation of corporate environmental performance

- Present the evaluation in layperson's terms (in contrast to technical/ scientific analyses)

- Make environmental performance measurable and comparable

The ultimate aim of the above is to improve information sharing and the quality of decision-making with respect to the environment. Some of the key features of the system are:

- Facility-based evaluation, i.e. not a product life-cycle analysis or corporate evaluation

- Use of a combination of (in ISO 14031 terminology) operational, management and environmental condition indicators—the emphasis being on the first two

- A two-tiered rating framework consisting of a generic template applicable across all industries, and sector-specific indicators/benchmarks feeding into the generic template

- Use of primary and secondary [3] data (collected as part of a facility visit) in the assessment process

- A completely voluntary scheme: i.e. the rating is performed and made public only with the consent of the facility

---

2   The relevance of these factors is explained in greater detail below.
3   Primary data would include sample monitoring data and visual observations at the facility. Secondary data would include reported/recorded information.

Systems factors >	Risk factor >	Intermediate > impact	Final impact
(ISO standards)	(Legal standards)		(EIAs)
e.g. Air pollution	Emission	Ambient air quality	Health of local population, natural habitat
• Production systems			
• Raw material/fuel used	• Mix		
	• Concentration		
• Control equipment	• Load		
• Operational and managerial aspects			
• Material storage/handling			

Table 1: RISK CHAIN

◿ *Significance of the Rating*

What the rating actually represents can be discerned using the schematic in Table 1. The ERS focuses on indicators relating to the **systems** and **risk factors**. **Intermediate impact indicators** are also used selectively to ratify the assessment. This combination of parameters makes the rating assessment a two-fold one:

a   An assessment of environmental performance in terms of the risk factors, based on primary and reported/recorded data

b   An assessment of the 'confidence' associated with the performance evaluation reached through process (a) above (i.e. the extent to which it is representative of ongoing performance) is arrived at using the systems and intermediate impact indicators.

To illustrate this, using air pollution in the cement industry as an example, the rating would assess not only emission levels (point [a]), but also confidence factors (point [b]), such as the frequency of ESP (electro-static precipitator) tripping, maintenance of pollution control systems, monitoring facilities, and ambient air quality. Therefore, even if two facilities have similar emission levels, the overall rating may still differ if confidence factors differ significantly.

◿ *Rating Categories*

Rating categories have been developed using the above rationale, and are also derived from the PROPER rating system being used in Indonesia (see Chapter 8). Rating

Eco-Rating	PROPER
A World-class performance on environment, health and safety (EHS)	World-class performance on EHS
B Pollution control and housekeeping significantly exceed compliance.	Emissions control and housekeeping significantly exceed compliance.
C Compliance assured	Compliance with regulations
D Compliance—with risk of non-compliance	Some pollution control, but short of compliance
E Unsatisfactory	Non-compliance with no effort to control pollution

Table 2: RATING CATEGORY DESCRIPTIONS

categories used in the two systems are described in Table 2. While the similarities between the two schemes are strong, there are differences as well. For instance, the single category for 'compliance', under Proper, has been split into two in the case of ERS. The rationale behind this is to distinguish facilities suspected of erratic operation of pollution control systems[4] (rating 'D') from those having the requisite monitoring and control systems for ensuring compliance on an ongoing basis (rating 'C').

◁ Scope: Indicators/Performance Standards

Aspects addressed as part of the rating are:

- ▼ **Pollution/ecological impacts.** Air, water, solid wastes, hazardous materials/wastes, etc.

- ▼ **Resource intensity.** Energy, water, materials use.

- ▼ **Work environment.** In-plant pollution/exposure.

- ▼ **Contingency management systems.** Safety systems, contingency plans, functionality.

- ▼ **Environmental management systems.** Extent of development and efficacy.

Certain components of various frameworks were selected for the development of indicators under the ERS construct, after testing for their relevance in an Indian context. Some of these frameworks (apart from PROPER) include the ISO 14000 series,

---

4   Even Indian government documents use the phrase 'Having adequate facilities to comply with standards', as opposed to an unambiguous 'In compliance'.

Rating	Profile condition
A	More than 50% of parameters to be rated 'A', and none rated 'C' or below
B	More than 50% of parameters to be rated 'A' or 'B', and none rated 'D' or below
C	More than 50% of parameters to be rated 'A', 'B' or 'C', and none rated 'E'
D	Any other combination, but no parameter rated 'E'
E	Any parameter rated 'E'.

Table 3: PERFORMANCE PROFILING

the European Green Table (European Green Table 1997), the Environmental Self-Assessment Programme (ESAP) of the Global Environmental Management Initiative (GEMI 1992) and Total Quality Environment Management (TQEM) (President's Commission 1993). In addition, systems used by large multinationals such as Allied Signal, Nortel, DuPont and Union Carbide were also studied while developing the system.

Performance standards for the indicators have been defined bearing in mind the rating category descriptions. For instance, to arrive at world-class performance benchmarks, the legal standards of developed countries (e.g. Germany, Japan and the US) were reviewed, as were international industry benchmarks (where available) and norms stipulated by international agencies such as the World Bank or the Asian Development Bank. These standards are now being reviewed periodically, in order to take account of ongoing advances in technological and operating systems.

◻ *Collation*

Various options were available for collation of scores across the rating parameters. Weighted averaging, the most commonly used technique, was discarded in view of the widely disparate criteria being collated and multiple levels of aggregation. Instead, a logic framework was used, incorporating a combination of performance profiling (see Table 3) and maxima/minima conditions.[5] Performance profiling indicates a general performance level, subject to a minimum parameter level rating. For instance, a 'B' rating would indicate that most parameters are well above compliance ('B'), with none representing risk of non-compliance ('D'). In addition to profiling, maxima/minima conditions have been used selectively to emphasise performance in critical rating parameters. Unlike the weighted average approach, this collation technique minimises the likelihood of poor performance on one set of parameters being offset by good performance on another.

---

5   A similar methodology has been used by Union Carbide in their internal rating programme.

| Stack | Stack emission (SPM [mg/Nm³]) | | | | | | Rating* |
	Legal limits	Data points[†]	Mean	Min	Max	Median	
1 Unit-I Kiln	250	15	169	65	244	159	C
2 Unit-II Kiln	250	16	137	81	203	135	C
3 Unit-III Kiln	250	16	89	41	139	90	B
4 Unit-I Coal mill	150	15	85	27	172	73	B
5 Unit-II Coal mill	150	16	88	56	144	85	C

Section stacks	Rating
Kiln + raw mill	C
Coal mill	C
Cooler	D
Cement mill	C

Stack emission
C

* Arrived at after evaluating mean, median, etc. against predefined benchmarks
† Number of emission readings used for each stack

Table 4: COLLATION FOR STACK EMISSION PARAMETER

Using the example of stack emissions, Table 4 illustrates how the above methodology enables collation of assessments across various levels of parameters. In most rating schemes, the collation logic would begin at the stack emission level, rather than the detailed observations listed in the first part of Table 4 (usually incorporated in audit protocols). The aim here is to provide for integration of data/observations across a wide range of parameters, in as systematic and objective a manner as possible.

◢ Reasons for an Indigenous Model

Several contextual factors need to be taken into account in developing an assessment framework, some of which are:

▼ **Quality and availability of information for use in assessments.** Both of these are typically poor in developing countries, relative to developed countries.

▼ **Systems orientation of business.** This is far greater in developed countries. Credibility associated with systems evaluations is correspondingly higher as well.

▼ **Emphasis on compliance issues.** Given low levels of compliance in developing countries, performance evaluations need to take account of this aspect to a greater extent.

▼ **Stakeholder pressures.** In developing countries, while awareness and sensitivity to environmental issues might exist, these might not be translated into stakeholder pressures since the affected populace typically belongs to the economically and politically weaker sections of society.

The Indian situation is in many ways distinct from that of any other country, but some aspects are generic to all other developing countries (at least those in Asia). Specific differentiating factors (with their impact on the development of the rating model, in brackets) are discussed below.

Lack of reliable public information on pollution (third-party assessment; facility visit; voluntary participation). Regulatory reporting—*viz.* the monthly report and annual environmental statement—has little credibility. To quote the (open) minutes of a MoEF meeting, 'quality and reliability of data generated is considered secondary by facilities, and some routinely rely on engineered[6] data for compliance purposes.' Apart from the data being of poor quality, it is fairly inaccessible. The environmental statement is supposed to be publicly accessible at the local regulatory offices, but in reality this is rarely the case. Consequently, an assessment system based on publicly available reported data—e.g. the kinds used by the Investor Responsibility Research Centre (IRRC) or the Council of Economic Priorities (CEP)—was not considered appropriate. Instead, the assessment had to be based on data obtained from the facility itself for it to be credible. Consequently, the rating had to be voluntary in order to allow for collection of data from the facility.

Absence of reliable historical performance data also precludes the possibility of using relative benchmarks, e.g. indices using a base year performance: hence the use of absolute performance standards for evaluating performance.

Erratic compliance (use of system factors). A common problem relates to facilities' non-compliance despite their having the ability to comply. Investments in pollution control systems are often considered a waste of money, and the tendency is to minimise operating costs by not running the equipment. Moreover, since Indian emission standards are generally concentration-based rather than load-based,[7] little data is available on pollution loads over a period of time.

---

6 Data generated without actual monitoring being performed, or modified with the prime motive of indicating compliance.

7 Standards for quantities of pollutant releases can be set per unit volume of emission/effluent released (concentration-based) or per unit of production (load-based).

Taken together, these two factors imply that point-in-time data by itself is inadequate, since it is not representative of ongoing performance. Use of 'confidence' factors is warranted to assess the reliability of point-in-time performance data. As mentioned above, the compliance level has been split into ratings 'C' and 'D' (see Table 2) primarily to take account of this factor.

Diversity of industrial profiles (need for rating, as opposed to certification). As mentioned at the beginning of this chapter, the Indian industrial landscape is characterised by a wide range of industry types and environmental performance levels. Certification programmes such as ISO 14001 can encourage a reasonably good facility to make an incremental effort to achieving the standard. However, facilities at the lower end of the spectrum have little motivation to make the huge transition in operating systems, and consequently are omitted from the scope of such programmes. However, a rating programme, by offering a gradient, incorporates all levels of performance and recognises incremental progress. It thus encourages facilities of all kinds to step into the system and to initiate the process of evaluation and improvement.

Scepticism associated with management systems programmes (measurable environmental performance indicators). India's experience with management systems standards is distilled in the implementation of the ISO 9001 quality management standard. Launched with much fanfare, this gradually lost its credibility as it became widely perceived that certifications were being awarded to manufacturers with widely varying levels of performance. Greater care and precaution is being taken in the implementation of the ISO 14001 programme in order to prevent it from suffering the same fate. Nevertheless, in the eyes of the ordinary public, the scepticism remains. Reward-seeking behaviour—e.g. better market (export) positioning, fiscal incentives—leads to surface adoption of the standard, as against a genuine desire to improve performance (Wiebke 1998). The system thus gets reduced to mere paper procedures. An additional problem is the pronounced hierarchical structure of most Indian (possibly most Asian) organisations, which hinders employee participation—a prerequisite for successful implementation of a systems-based standard.

Therefore, instead of pure management systems frameworks such as ISO 14001, TQEM, ESAP and Responsible Care, ERS uses operational environmental performance indicators (EPIs) and benchmarks—which are tangible and measurable—along with management systems criteria.

Limited knowledge of environmental technicalities (simplicity of rating structure). Several complex risk indices (e.g. the Safety and Environmental Risk Management Rating, Centre for the Study of Financial Innovation, Loss Prevention Council) have been developed keeping specific users in mind, e.g. lenders or insurers (Costaras 1996). In an Indian context, such indices were perceived to be premature. The aim was first to provide a rule-of-thumb (heuristic) indicator that could introduce the concept of measurability with respect to environment and serve a cross-section of users. Later, this could be followed up by more refined assessment tools. The use of a discrete rating scale, as opposed to a continuous rating function (e.g. similar to Nortel's) was also chosen keeping the 'simplicity' criterion in mind.

◢ ERS in Relation to Other International Schemes

While the relatively unique Indian circumstances warranted an indigenous evaluation framework, features of various international schemes/frameworks were also emulated while developing the model. The matrix in Table 5 shows the positioning of ERS in relation to other evaluation programmes.

◁ ERS in relation to ISO 14001

ERS is designed to be distinct from, yet complementary to, the ISO programme. It differs from ISO 14001 in the following ways:

▼ ERS focuses on physical performance indicators for assessment, while also incorporating environmental management system (EMS)-related aspects.

▼ It uses a gradient of performance levels, which recognises several stages in the 'green' evolution of a company (in contrast to a 'yes/no' certification), and, consequently,

   – facilitates participation by a wider cross-section of companies, including lower-end performers

   – enables the tool to serve as a trend indicator.

The complementarity between ERS and the ISO 14001 programmes is twofold:

▼ Companies that have not acquired an ISO certification can use the ERS to work towards achieving this.

Types of indicator and benchmark	Self-assessment	Third-party assessment	
		Voluntary	Not voluntary
Management EPIs	TQEM,* Responsible Care, ESAP*	ISO 14001, EMAS	
Management and operational EPIs	Union Carbide	ERS	PROPER, Eco-Watch, IRRC
Operational EPIs	Nortel*		Council of Economic Priorities

The above include both facility assessments and corporate assessments. Responsible Care is predominantly a corporate-level assessment, though the option to participate at a facility level also exists. Programmes marked with an asterisk use a continuous rating scale. The others may entail certifications, discrete rating scales or other forms of performance evaluation (e.g. IRRC).

Table 5: COMPARISON OF EPE FRAMEWORKS

▼ On the other hand, companies that have been certified can use it to compare performance across facilities, or against benchmarks. Once a certification is obtained, a common sentiment is, 'What next?' The benchmarking incorporated in the rating model offers a useful follow-through to a certification exercise, and can help to keep the performance graph pointing upwards.

Cross-facility/company comparisons can even be used in industrial complexes where common facilities (common effluent treatment plants, emergency services) are used. Greater transparency and performance monitoring could increase accountability (thereby addressing the 'free-rider' problem[8]) and improve co-ordination activities.

The applicability of ISO 14001 to small and medium-sized enterprises (SMEs) has prompted some debate. Some of the problems in the adoption of ISO 14001 by SMEs are as follows (Wiebke 1998):

▼ The time perspective of SMEs is typically limited. In contrast, establishment of an EMS for certification is a relatively time-consuming process. Moreover, the benefits of such a system are likely to materialise only over the long term.

▼ Detailed and continuous documentation required under ISO 14001 can be too intensive in time, personnel and knowledge, all of which are scarce resources in SMEs.

▼ Lack of systems orientation, and strictly hierarchical structures, characterise most SMEs—features that can hinder the proper understanding and implementation of an EMS.

Some of the suggested ways of avoiding these constraints include:

▼ Group-centred approaches that focus on collaboration among SMEs, where ERS can help to migrate best practices and facilitate the use of common resources for monitoring, auditing, etc.

▼ Emphasis on day-to-day operations, as opposed to strategic environmental planning systems incorporated in the ISO framework—an objective that ERS can once again help to achieve.

◢ *Development and Implementation*

Cement manufacturing was identified as the starting point for development of the rating model. Pilot-study rating exercises were conducted at two live cement

---

8   Usually observed in CETP (common effluent treatment plant) operations, where some facilities release effluents with higher pollution loads than the designed capacity of the plant. This may be offset by better-quality effluent released by other more responsible facilities sharing the same CETP. The first set of facilities thus become 'free-riders'.

manufacturing facilities, in November 1997 and May 1998. In keeping with the completely voluntary nature of ERS, consents were obtained from the companies prior to performing the test ratings, and at their request the ratings were kept confidential. Participation of the companies was driven partly by their self-perception of being responsible and proactive industry leaders, and partly by a curiosity to know where they stood under the rating system. The fact that TERI had prior working relationships with them helped to secure their involvement.

The ratings involved a two-stage process: a facility visit of approximately four days, followed by assessment (about two weeks). Details about the facility were obtained prior to the visit, using a standard questionnaire format. Information collected as part of the visit was processed using the rating model to arrive at a rating. This assessment was subsequently ratified by a group of experts (the Review Committee). Summary results of the two exercises are provided in Table 6. A further breakdown of ratings can be obtained in order to isolate critical success factors.

As well as the ratings, the facilities were also provided with detailed reports presenting the rationale behind the ratings. Despite the relatively adverse or mediocre ratings assigned, the facilities accepted the assessments as fair and objective. Several of the observations (specifically weaknesses) were known to facility staff, but had not been addressed as they had not been given priority.[9] The rating exercises helped to spotlight some of these, identify means of improvement—e.g. acquisition of additional monitoring equipment, maintenance of monitoring points, monitoring of in-plant environment—and secure the co-operation of operational management.

Some of the constraints faced in the rating process are listed below:

▼ Consent (regulatory approval) conditions—e.g. monitoring frequencies, emission limits—were found to vary across the facilities, which complicated the assessment process. However, these variations were attributable to technological factors such as differing ages and scales of plant and equipment.

▼ Where certain production processes had been outsourced, or were being performed at other locations, some ambiguity arose about the definition of a 'facility'. For the purpose of the rating, however, the term 'facility' was (and is being) interpreted to represent one integrated operation at a particular geographic location.

At a system level, some of the constraints faced by ERS are:

▼ Use of industry-specific EPIs and benchmarks makes implementation of the system correspondingly more complex. However, it is this feature that lends objectivity and transparency to the system—an important consideration given industry's suspicions on the subject of environment.

---

9 Environmental staff reported to the facility's operational management. The environment function's issues therefore tended to get overshadowed by mainstream production concerns. Such a situation increased the environmental staff's reluctance to make a nuisance of themselves by pushing hard for changes.

Parameters	Facility 1	Facility 2*
Pollution	D	C
Pollution: air	D	C
Stack emission	D	C
Stack heights	D	B
Confidence factors (operating systems, pollution control systems,monitoring systems, ambient air quality)	D	C
Pollution: other (noise, water, solid waste)	D	C
Resource intensity	C	C
Energy	C	C
Raw materials (fly ash use)	B	C
Work environment	D	C
In-plant environment	D	B
Confidence factors (H&S systems, medical infrastructure)	C	C
Contingency management systems	B	B
Environmental management systems	C	B
Overall rating	D	C

NB: The framework encompasses only manufacturing operations, and not mining.

* Facility 2 was on the verge of being certified under ISO 14001 at the time the rating was performed.

Table 6: SUMMARY RESULTS OF TEST RATING EXERCISES

* Practical considerations relating to measurability and availability of data to some extent influenced the choice of operational EPIs. For instance, in the case of emissions, while it would have been more appropriate to use load-based EPIs, absence of data mandated the use of concentration-based EPIs instead. However, such constraints were recognised at the development stage itself, and minimised in the design of the model.

* Use of compliance as a basis for defining rating categories implies that the system automatically internalises some of the inconsistencies associated with regulatory standards, e.g. absence of load-based standards. However, this is offset by two important advantages, namely:

   a For all their limitations, regulatory standards are a universally accepted baseline—a tangible, unambiguous baseline that ordinary people can relate to. Accusations of biases or prejudices and the probability of misinterpretations are thus minimised by the use of compliance as a norm.

   b Regulatory standards constitute an important common denominator that translates environmental risk into business risk (*viz.* legal prosecution, fines and public interest litigation). Inclusion of these in the construct is therefore vital if the rating is to be of any relevance to mainstream categories such as financiers, investors and business partners.

▼ Standards used can vary across regions and over time. The same rating can thus imply differing performance in absolute terms. ERS, however, aims to profile performance using readily understood—even if moving—benchmarks (*viz.* legal standards, industry best-in-class and international standards). If compliance levels vary across time and regions, these reflect the changing technological and environmental contexts in which the facility operates, and against which the facility's performance would be evaluated.

Subsequent to successful completion of the test ratings, ERS was launched for the cement sector in September 1998; a dissemination programme was simultaneously undertaken in co-ordination with the Cement Manufacturers' Association. TERI has taken on the task of performing ratings (on a chargeable basis) at least in the initial stages. The terms associated with a rating are as follows:

▼ The rating is valid for one year, subject to no major changes in the production facility.

▼ The rating agency (i.e. TERI) is free to visit the facility during the validity period, to assess interim performance.

▼ Public disclosure of the rating is subject to the facility's approval.

▼ Outputs of the rating exercise include a facility-level overall rating, a summary rating profile (similar to the illustration in Table 6) and a detailed assessment report.

Given the novelty of the concept, it is important that the scheme be perceived as credible. TERI's image as an objective and neutral applied research entity is well suited for performing this role. Later, once the system gains wider acceptance, other agencies may be brought in to perform the ratings.

The rating framework is currently being extended across other sectors such as sugar, iron and steel, petroleum (pipelines, storage and refining), chemicals and power.

◢ *System Impact/Utility*

The impact of ERS may be observed at two levels: in a company's internal decision-making and in stakeholder decision-making in relation to a company. As regards the former, ERS evaluations would help in the following ways:

a. Make environmental assessments more accessible to senior and middle management. Current environmental assessments such as EIAs or environmental audit reports tend to be voluminous and technical: one of the many deterrents to the integration of environmental concerns in mainstream business decision-making.

ERS addresses this problem by providing an environmental assessment in layperson's terms, which staff outside the environmental function can also relate to.

Senior and middle management could also use Eco-Ratings to confirm facilities' compliance status. Currently, most facilities operate with a 'minimal compliance' mind-set, i.e. compliance with regulatory requirements by recourse to least-cost strategies, including engineered data and reports, or 'managing' the enforcement agencies. While generally this may be a reflection of senior management attitudes, there are several instances where this might not be the case. Senior managers and function heads located at head office presume compliance based on the availability of regulatory consents, unaware of the ambiguous status of this kind of compliance. In such cases, ERS could help to confirm compliance and identify corrective action where necessary.

b. Facilitate a monitoring and benchmarking process. The rating construct helps to compare performance across facilities, and also against benchmarks. By doing so, it helps catalyse a process of target-setting in line with industry and international benchmarks. For instance, when the framework was shared with the head of environment at one of the leading cement companies, he was surprised to see the industry benchmark for frequency of employee health check-ups and in-plant air quality monitoring, and decided to incorporate these in facility-level environment management plans. Such initiatives can be further aided by using ERS for tracking progress over a period of time.

ERS could also help external stakeholder decision-making in the following ways.

a. Transparency, objectivity, simplicity of evaluation. The ERS framework is primarily aimed at addressing the problem of ambiguity and lack of transparency in environmental issues (see 'The Key Problem Being Addressed', above). By providing objective and credible environmental performance evaluations in layperson's terms, ERS fosters stakeholder interest in the subject, and also corporate ability to share factual environmental information—both of which help facilitate exchange of information on the subject.

b. Environmental risk evaluation. The rating system not only profiles environmental performance, but also serves as an indicator of business risk associated with this performance. For instance, a facility rated 'D' or 'E' indicates that there is a risk of the facility facing legal or public action. A rating exercise could thus be valuable for financial stakeholders, who might incorporate such a due diligence process as part of routine lending. Requisite loan caveats could then be incorporated for identified risk issues. If necessary, ERS could be accompanied by a more detailed risk analysis for further quantification of risks.

It must be mentioned here that external stakeholders can use the rating only if it is made public by the company. The ERS implementation programme therefore also aims to create pressures for disclosure by fostering a demand for the rating among external stakeholders. In the initial stages, the focus is on specific user categories (not necessarily warranting user-specific tools) such as financiers, insurance companies and banks. Simultaneously, an awareness campaign is being undertaken which is likely to yield results only in the long term. Table 7 summarises the functions performed by the rating.

◻ *Applicability to Other Countries*

While the system has been designed to suit the Indian situation, several of its features make it amenable to being used in other developing countries as well. Some of these are:

- Use of operational (industry-specific) EPIs

- A system design that takes account of low quality and availability of data

- Use of compliance in the definition of rating categories ('B', 'C' and 'D' and 'E')

The resemblance of ERS to the PROPER (Indonesia) and Eco-Watch (Philippines) programmes to some extent reaffirms the commonality of contexts prevailing in most Asian developing countries. Unlike these two programmes, however, ERS is not a government-backed initiative (and can therefore be expected to take longer to yield results). It may accordingly be considered for adoption in other countries where government agencies are unable to undertake such initiatives.

Roles/functions	Outcomes
Publicity tool. It provides a means of recognising good environmental performance, as well as improvements in performance.	• Creation of incentives/pressures for companies to improve performance • Fostering of information sharing by companies.
Risk indicator. ERS enables external stakeholders to incorporate environmental risk considerations in their decision-making processes.	• Heightening of stakeholder sensitivity to environmental risk considerations. • Increasing stakeholder pressure for company information-sharing.
Feedback mechanism. The system helps companies benchmark their performance against competitors and international standards, and hence work towards continuous improvement.	• Facilitation of benchmarking/target-setting by companies. • Quicker migration of best practice.

Table 7: ERS: ROLES AND IMPACTS

◢ Going Forward

While the initiative is not government-run, efforts are nevertheless under way to seek regulatory support for it, the programme being complementary to enforcement efforts. Some of the support measures that could be considered are:

Incentives

- ▼ Consent fee waivers for facilities with disclosed ratings
- ▼ Relaxed reporting requirements for facilities with disclosed ratings

Mandates

- ▼ Eco-Rating to be made a requirement for loan approvals[10]
- ▼ Disclosure of Eco-Rating in company balance sheets
- ▼ Disclosure of Eco-Rating made compulsory for public equity/bond issues

◻ Project Extensions

- ▼ Ratings performed over a period of time would generate an **analytical database** which could aid understanding of key performance drivers for environment, and identification of suitable interventions. Such an analysis is already being undertaken as part of the Indonesian programme for improving enforcement efforts.

- ▼ The concept of ERS can also be used to develop risk assessment tools for the **EIA stage**—for which considerable interest exists (especially among financiers), as revealed in informal discussions. Eco-Ratings could also be used to track implementation of the environmental management plan, and help address lapses during the project phase itself.

- ▼ ERS could be extended to develop an **environmental reporting** format for companies to adopt on a voluntary basis. A two-tiered format could be considered, using generic and sector-specific performance indicators.

◢ Conclusion

In conclusion, ERS is a novel initiative—its uniqueness being that it:

- ▼ Is the first such system to be introduced in India
- ▼ Covers the three critical aspects: management systems, compliance and operational issues

---

10   Banks and financial institutions are also being targeted for this purpose.

▼ Complements the ISO 14001 programme, thereby minimising multiplicity of standards

▼ Has a sector-specific component capable of providing technical inputs and feedback to the assessee

▼ Has a flexible, yet transparent and mature framework logic, which allows for modifications and improvements to be incorporated with relative ease

Preliminary experience indicates that ERS is a tool with the potential to improve the quality of decision-making and also encourage information-sharing in the area of corporate environmental performance.

10

Measuring and Benchmarking Environmental Performance in the Electric Utility Sector

The Experience of Niagara Mohawk

Joseph A. Miakisz

NIAGARA Mohawk Power Corporation (NMPC) is an investor-owned electric and gas utility, providing energy services to the largest customer service area in New York State. Based in Syracuse, NY, NMPC serves over 1.5 million residential, commercial and industrial customers and over 500,000 gas customers. The company's electric generation is supplied by hydroelectric (8%), coal (16%), oil and natural gas (17%) and nuclear (13%) generating units currently owned by the company, as well as through purchase contracts with other utilities and independent power producers (46%). NMPC is the 24th-largest US electric and gas utility company. With sales of $3.96 billion in 1997, it ranked as the 372nd-largest US corporation (Environmental Information Services, Inc. 1998).

NMPC is recognised as a pioneer in the US electric utility industry in respect of several of its environmental management system initiatives. One area in which the company has received considerable recognition, both within the US and abroad, is in relation to the development of environmental performance measures and environmental benchmarking. In 1991, NMPC developed a then unique and innovative Environmental Performance Index (EP Index) designed to measure and communicate its environmental performance. A year later, in 1992, it acted as a catalyst for the development and implementation of a comprehensive annual Environmental Benchmarking Programme (EBP) within the electric utility industry which compares the performance of the participants on a wide range of environmental performance measures.

◢ *NMPC's Environmental Performance Index*

In 1991, NMPC's senior management unveiled a new Corporate Policy on Protection of the Environment. This new policy reflected a recognition that environmental protection and stewardship are compatible with sound business practices. It also expressed the company's desire to be recognised not just as an environmentally compliant business but as a leader in addressing environmental issues. One of the keys to NMPC's success in achieving its environmental policy objectives over the subsequent eight years was the recognition by NMPC's environmental management leadership team at that time that, without a sound means of measuring and demonstrating progress in achieving environmental goals that were established, the new environmental policy would probably serve as nothing more than a mere trophy. This recognition has led to the development of a set of environmental performance measures (the EP Index) that could be used as a tool in gauging whether the company's environmental programme was moving forward or backward. As it turned out, the EP Index has proven to be not only a useful tool for measuring the company's environmental performance, but also for communicating its performance to its internal and external stakeholders.

NMPC's EP Index was developed by in-house technical personnel; however, valuable input was received from a team of external experts who reviewed and critiqued NMPC's work. A set of criteria was developed at the outset, against which various options for establishing environmental performance indicators (EPIs) would be evaluated. Among the criteria developed were the following:

1. The indicators should accurately and consistently measure the company's environmental performance over time.

2. Measurable performance data for the indicators must be currently available or reasonably attainable.

3. The indicators should explicitly address compliance with applicable environmental laws, regulations and policies.

4. The indicators should be relatively easy to understand and interpret.

5. The cost of start-up and of operating and maintaining the indicators should be a factor, although not an overriding factor, in the evaluation of alternatives.

6. The indicators should be able to measure progress in achieving the company's Corporate Policy on Protection of the Environment.

7. The indicators should be designed to balance long-term versus short-term goals and objectives.

8. The indicators should be sensitive to factors within the company's control and insensitive to factors outside the company's control.

Several different approaches for monitoring environmental performance were evaluated by NMPC, ranging from a limited set of key environmental performance indicators (e.g. air emission indicators) that would be measured and tracked discretely to a rolled-up, multi-category index that would incorporate a broad array of indicators considered to have a significant bearing on environmental performance. A decision analysis exercise was performed to evaluate these options, reflecting the criteria outlined above. The selected approach was a single composite EP Index that utilises a weight and rating scheme to reflect environmental performance in three categories: emissions/wastes, regulatory compliance and environmental enhancements. These three categories were derived as a means of grouping a list of indicators that were considered to be important in terms of demonstrating environmental performance (NMPC 1991).

A fundamental decision in the adoption of EPIs is whether or not to aggregate the indicators and, if so, how to aggregate and to what extent to aggregate. At one extreme, EPIs may be identified and tracked discretely with no aggregation at all. At the other extreme, which is similar to NMPC's approach, all of the indicators may be aggregated and weighted in a single composite index. An intermediate approach may be to attempt to aggregate only similar 'thematic' indicators such as air emissions. There are certain advantages and disadvantages to each of these approaches.

Relying on a discrete set of EPIs with no attempt at aggregation avoids the problem of combining and weighting fundamentally different aspects on a common scale (i.e. the 'apples and oranges' problem) and provides transparency in terms of the indicators selected to reflect environmental performance. On the negative side, overall interpretation of performance is much more difficult with a discrete set of indicators, in that mixed signals may be presented where strengths are evident with respect to some indicators and weaknesses with respect to others.

With total aggregation of EPIs in an index, one is faced squarely with the problem of combining indicators on a common scale that may be fundamentally different in nature (e.g. air emissions and fisheries effects). Weighting schemes often accompany aggregation of indicators in an index in order to reflect considerations of relative importance, and this introduces another layer of subjectivity into the performance measure. The accuracy and credibility of the measurement tool remains a lingering question, in that the aggregation and weighting system can skew the results in one direction or another. On the other hand, the intended audience is not burdened with the problem of evaluating a set of individual measures and formulating overall conclusions on performance. While the construction and calculation of a single, composite index may be more complex than relying on discrete indicators, the measure it provides is easy to understand and interpret. The intended audience has a single index value that can be compared over time as a measure of a company's overall environmental performance.

NMPC chose the single, composite index, approach to its EP Index for several reasons. First and foremost, the EP Index was primarily intended to provide the company's senior management and a major stakeholder—the New York State Public Service Commission (the state agency that regulates the company's activities)—with a tool for gauging progress in achieving the goals and objectives set forth in its Corporate Policy on Protection of the Environment. These target audiences voiced a strong preference for a single, composite, EP Index. Second, the potential problems associated with aggregation of indicators were not viewed as a fatal flaw by NMPC because the EP Index was intended to measure improvement in its own performance over time. It was not envisaged that NMPC's EP Index would be compared to other companies, so the absolute value of the index number was not considered especially important. What *was* important was that the EP Index be implemented consistently over time such that *relative* changes in performance could be detected. Finally, NMPC was convinced that it had captured in its EP Index all of the essential environmental performance factors associated with its operations and that the scoring system developed would perform a good job in reflecting overall performance, at least on a qualitative basis (i.e. it was believed that significant increases in the composite EP Index value over time would equate to improvements in performance).

The emissions/wastes category is the heart of NMPC's EP Index. This quantifies the air emissions, waste-water discharges and waste generation/disposal from company operations. A set of compliance factors was incorporated into the index because compliance with all applicable environmental regulatory requirements is an objective of the Corporate Policy on Protection of the Environment and is considered by NMPC to be the 'minimum point' for an environmental leadership programme. An environmental enhancement category was added to the EP Index in order to capture other initiatives that the company considers to be important in assessing its environmental performance, such as investments in fish and wildlife habitat improvement projects, outdoor recreational facilities and waste site clean-up.

One may cynically view the inclusion of environmental enhancement initiatives in an EP Index as a way for companies with inherently 'dirty' (or highly polluting) operations to artificially make themselves look good from an environmental performance standpoint. Viewed in isolation, it is theoretically true that companies with inherently highly polluting operations (and perhaps higher profit margins that may result from any competitive advantage associated with their highly polluting operations) can afford to make capital investments in environmental enhancement initiatives as a way of making themselves appear better environmental performers than they really are. However, if companies are measuring both the burden of their operations on the environment (e.g. air emissions, waste-water discharges, etc.) *and* their investments in environmental enhancement initiatives, this should not be so much of a concern. What should be of concern is that companies improve their environmental performance on an *overall* basis. As long as companies are attempting to reflect all the factors that bear on their environmental performance in their measurement system (or at least a majority of the important factors), there is no reason that credit should not be taken for responsible actions taken to enhance the environment.

Benchmarks, or baselines, for the emissions/wastes and compliance categories of environmental performance indicators incorporated into NMPC's EP Index were established in most cases based on the company's average annual performance over the three-year period 1989–91 (see Tables 1 and 2). This period was chosen because it was the most recent period at the time the EP Index was being developed and was considered a good reference point for gauging future progress. In a few cases (e.g. solid waste disposal), alternative baseline periods are used, either because an indicator

Parameter	Weight	Benchmark	Units	Benchmark years	% reduction	% increase	Multiplier	Score
SO₂	17	13.2	lbs/MWh	1989–91			20	
NOₓ	36	3.79	lbs/MWh	1989–91			20	
CO₂	7	1,239	lbs/MWh	1989–91			20	
Solid (non-hazardous) wastes disposed of	10	4,131	tons	1997			20	
Combustion wastes beneficially re-used	10	0	percent	3-year rolling average[2]			20	
Hazardous wastes[3] disposed of (non-PCB)	12	150,889	kilograms	1989–91			20	
Herbicide use impacts on rights-of-way	tbd[4]	tbd[4]	tbd[4]	tbd[4]			20	
Heavy metals discharged in waste-water discharges at steam stations	4	3,371 (fossil)	lbs	1990–91			20	
	4	6,842 (nuclear)	lbs	1990–91			20	
Total of weights						**Total weighted average score**		

1. Percentage increase/reduction expressed as decimals, e.g. 10% = 0.1.
2. No combustion waste was beneficially re-used in 1989–91. Performance will be measured by the percentage of waste beneficially re-used. Future quantities of waste marketed for beneficial re-use (in tons) will be divided by a rolling three-year average quantity of combustion waste generated.
3. Quantities exclude PCB wastes, waste materials generated from a clean-up of a spill/waste site, sandblast waste and waste materials that are beneficially recycled.
4. To be determined.

Table 1: ENVIRONMENTAL PERFORMANCE INDEX: EMISSIONS / WASTES CATEGORY

Parameter	Weight	Benchmark[1]	Units	-2	-1	0	1	2	Total
Notices of violation received	12	4	Number	>7	6-7	3-5	1-2	0	
Fines paid	12	281	$ × 100	>360	310-360	250-310	200-250	<200	
Non-conforming opacity emissions	4	3	Percent1	>4.6	3.25-4.6	2.75-3.25	1.4-2.75	0-1.4	
Opacity monitor downtime[2]	4	2.17	Percent	>6	5-6	4-5	2-4	<2	
Non-conforming water discharges	5	39	Number	>59	44-59	35-43	20-34	0-19	
Reportable oil spills to surface waters[3]	4	2	Number	>3	3	2	1	0	
PCB spills[3]	4	1	Number	>1	–	1	–	0	
Reportable chemical releases	5.0	2	Number	>3	3	2	1	0	
Total weighted average score (maximum = 100)									

1. Benchmark established based on annual average data for each parameter over period 1 January 1989–31 December 1991, with exception of non-conforming opacity emissions which are based on 1990 opacity data for Oswego 5 and 6, and 1991 data for Albany 1–4 opacity monitor downtime which is based on 1997 data, and reportable chemical releases which are based on 1991 data.

2. Includes start-up and shutdown exceedances.

3. Only spills that reflect performance (i.e. were preventable) are reflected in this category. Examples include spills resulting from overfilling equipment, material handling activities, valving errors, lack of or improper maintenance of equipment, etc. Excluded are spills caused by unavoidable equipment failure, explosions, storms and other acts of God.

Table 2: ENVIRONMENTAL PERFORMANCE INDEX: COMPLIANCE CATEGORY

was added to the EP Index at a later date or because 1989–91 data were not available for the indicator.

Performance associated with the third category of environmental performance indicator, environmental enhancements, is simply determined as a function of the annual dollar investment made in these enhancements (described in more detail below).

◢ The EP Index Scoring System

NMPC's EP Index is calculated in the following manner. For each indicator contained in the emissions/wastes category, annual reductions or increases in pollutants are calculated relative to the benchmark. This value (in decimal form) is multiplied by the pre-assigned weight for that indicator and then by a multiplier of 20. This multiplier was incorporated for the purpose of aligning the relative weight of the emissions/wastes category scoring system with the scoring system established for the compliance and environmental enhancements categories (this issue is addressed further below) (Miakisz 1994).

For example (see Table 3), projected NO_x emissions for NMPC's fossil fuel generating units in 1998 were 31% lower than 1989–91 benchmark emissions of 3.79 lbs/MWh, based on actual emissions data through the first six months of 1998. The corresponding score for NO_x emissions in the EP Index is 223 (0.31 × weighting factor of 36 × multiplier of 20 = 223). Scores for the remaining indicators in the emissions/wastes category are calculated in the same manner, and then the weighted scores are summed to arrive at a total score for this category.

The weights for the indicators within the emissions/wastes category were established based on a combination of environmental externalities work conducted in New York State and on some subjective judgements. First, air emissions effects were viewed as the major environmental impacts associated with NMPC's operations, and a weight of 60% was subjectively assigned to air emissions relative to the remaining indicators in the emissions/wastes category. Then, with respect to the air emissions indicators (SO_2, NO_x and CO_2), the results of pioneering assessments conducted by the New York State Public Service Commission in the late 1980s on environmental externality costs associated with fossil fuel-fired generating facilities was used to apportion weights among the three air pollutants (PACE University Center for Environmental Legal Studies 1990). Finally, subjective judgements on the relative importance of the non-air emission indicators in the emissions/wastes category (i.e. solid/hazardous waste disposal and waste-water discharges) were made to apportion the remaining 40% of the total weighting scheme for this category.

Performance for each compliance category indicator (see Table 2) is rated on a point scale ranging from −2 to +2. The scale was developed so that an assignment of zero points represents no change in performance relative to the 1989–91 benchmark performance. Scores of +1 and +2 represent improved performance relative to the benchmark. Again, weights were pre-assigned for each compliance indicator and these weights are multiplied by the raw score earned to arrive at a weighted score. The

Parameter	Weight	Benchmark	Units	Targeted % reduction/increase	Targeted score	Projected % reduction/increase	Projected score	Business group contribution
SO$_2$	17	13.2	lbs/MWh	0	0	−11	−37	Fossil/hydro/nuclear
NO$_X$	36	3.79	lbs/MWh	39	281	31	223	Fossil/hydro/nuclear
CO$_2$	7	1,239	lbs/MWh	19	27	−4	−6	Fossil/hydro/nuclear
Solid (non-hazardous) wastes disposed of	8	4,131	tons	0	0	6	10	All
Ash utilisation	11	0	%	50	110	57	125	Fossil/hydro
Hazardous wastes disposed of	13	150,889	kg	63	164	76	198	Fossil/hydro/nuclear/ energy delivery
Heavy metals								
Fossil	4.0	3,371	lbs	0	0	72	58	Fossil/hydro
Nuclear	4.0	6,842	lbs	56	45	30	24	Nuclear
				Total	**627**	**Total**	**595**	

Table 3: EMISSIONS / WASTES CATEGORY

weighted score for each indicator is then summed to determine a total weighted score for the compliance category (Miakisz 1994).

Table 4 demonstrates how the scoring system for the compliance category of the EP Index category is employed. For example, based on actual data for the first six months of 1998, the number of notices of violation that the company anticipated receiving for the year as a whole was six. Referring back to the design of the compliance category scoring system (see Table 2), this level of performance earns a score of −1 for that indicator; −1 × weight for the notice of violation indicator (12) = −12. Scores for each indicator in the compliance category are calculated in the same manner and then the weighted scores are summed to arrive at a total score for this category.

Weights for the compliance category were established based on subjective judgements of the relative importance of each indicator, with relatively high weights

Parameter	Weight	Benchmark	Units	Targeted performance	Targeted score	YTD performance	Projected performance	Projected score	Business group contribution
Notices of violation	12.0	4	#	0	24	3	6	−12	Energy delivery/ fossil/hydro
Fines	12.0	281	$×1,000	<200	24	0.7	2	24	Energy delivery/ fossil/hydro
Excess opacity	4.0	3	%	0–1.4	8	0.72	0.72	8	Fossil/hydro
Opacity monitor downtime	4.0	2.17	%	2–4	4	0.95	0.95	8	Fossil/hydro
SPDES* excursions	5.0	39	#	0–19	10	6	12	10	Nuclear/ fossil/hydro
Reportable oil spills	4.0	2	#	0	8	0	0	8	Energy delivery/ fossil/hydro
PCB† spills	4.0	1	#	0	8	0	0	8	
Chemical releases	5.0	2	#	0	10	0	0	10	
Total					96			64	

* State Pollutant Discharge Elimination Systems

† Polychlorinated biphenyls

Table 4: COMPLIANCE CATEGORY

assigned to major environmental infractions (i.e. cases where notices of violation and/or fines were assessed) and relatively lower weights for isolated environmental events such as small oil spills, minor exceedances of permit limitations, etc. The scoring system for the compliance category was purposely designed so that this category as a whole could make only a relatively small contribution to the overall index score (a maximum of 100 index points out of a total maximum potential EP Index score of 2,600). This was done because the company did not want to claim credit for substantial improvements in environmental performance merely by complying with environmental regulatory requirements. The drawback of this

Description	Targeted expenditures	Targeted points	Projected '98 expenditures	Projected '98 points	Business group contribution
Fossil/hydro	$4,996,500	24.9825	$4,989,500	25	Fossil/hydro
Waste site clean-up	$7,835,000	39.175	$7,835,000	39	Corporate
Environmental R&D					
Electric	$1,567,000	7.835	$1,102,000	6	Electric R&D
Gas	$38,000	0.19	$38,000		Gas R&D
Other	$30,000	0.15	$32,000		Corporate
Total	**$14,466,500**	**72**	**$13,996,500**	**70**	

Table 5: ENVIRONMENTAL ENHANCEMENT CATEGORY

Category	Target	Actual score
Emissions/wastes	627	595
Compliance	96	64
Enhancements	72	70
Composite	795	729

Table 6: ENVIRONMENTAL PERFORMANCE INDEX: SUMMARY

approach, however, is that relatively poor compliance with environmental regulatory requirements in a given year would not significantly influence the index score in a negative manner.

As indicated above, environmental enhancements are rated based on NMPC's dollar investment in enhancements in each calendar year. Examples of environmental enhancements include investments in outdoor recreational facilities, fish and wildlife habitat improvement projects, voluntary waste site clean-up, environmental education and environmental research. For each $200,000 of investment in an environmental enhancement initiative, one index point is earned.

The manner in which the scoring system for this category was derived was an attempt to provide some semblance of consistency between the scoring system for the environmental enhancement category and the emissions/wastes category, notwithstanding the problem of comparing apples and oranges. The approach used was to take the single highest weighted indicator in the emissions/wastes category (i.e NO_x emissions) and determine, on a cost-of-control basis, what an index point roughly equated to. At the time, NMPC was planning a major NO_x reduction programme for its fleet of fossil fuel generating units. Estimates were that a 35% reduction in NO_x emission rate, across the fleet, could be achieved by investing approximately $50 million in combustion control equipment (e.g. low NO_x burners). Using the scoring system already derived for the emissions/wastes category, a 35% reduction in NO_x emissions would equate to about 250 index points. Thus, using the $50 million estimate for achieving this 35% reduction in NO_x emissions, a cost-of-control-based equivalent value of $200,000 was derived for each index point in the environmental enhancement category.

A self-imposed limit of 500 index points is applied to the environmental enhancement category to prevent the company from focusing inordinate attention on improvements in this area. It also attempts to address at least the perception, if not the reality, that companies with inherently highly polluting operations can artificially inflate their environmental performance evaluation by using profits to buy into environmental improvement projects that may appear beneficial from a public relations standpoint but may not mean a lot substantively. Care is also taken not to double-count investments in environmental enhancements and performance reflected in the other two categories of the EP Index, such as emissions/wastes reductions.

A composite EP Index score is determined at the end of each calendar year by first calculating scores for each of the three categories and then adding them together. Tables 3, 4, 5 and 6 display actual environmental performance data for NMPC for the first six months of 1998, as measured by its EP Index. The index design allows for a maximum possible score of 2,000 index points for the emissions/wastes category (the heart of the index); 500 points for the environmental enhancements category; and 100 points for the compliance category (total maximum composite score of 2,600). The absolute composite index score in itself is meaningless, since it is based on subjective weights and scores calculated relative to a fixed baseline. By comparing the absolute index value with the maximum possible index value, NMPC's performance relative to a set of ideal goals could be measured (e.g. elimination of all pollution sources). However, the real value of the index is obtained from monitoring relative changes in the index value over time. If the index is consistently implemented, increases in the index over time will reflect improvements in environmental performance, while decreases over time will indicate degradation in environmental performance (Miakisz 1994).

◢ Environmental Performance Targets

NMPC implemented its EP Index beginning in 1992. At the beginning of each year since then, performance targets for each EP Index indicator have been established. Several of these targets have been incorporated into company business plans. At the end of each quarter, actual performance data are collected and 'year-to-date' and 'projected year-end' EP Index scores are calculated as a means of tracking progress. At the end of the year, an 'actual achieved' EP Index score is determined and a report is prepared which compares in detail the actual achieved results against the performance targets. Both the quarterly and annual EP Index status reports are provided to senior management as well as to managers responsible for environmental performance in NMPC's business groups. Senior management uses these reports to track performance in achieving business plan environmental performance targets. If progress lags expectations, mid-course corrections can be made and employees can be held accountable for performance deficiencies.

Figure 1 depicts NMPC's annual EP Index performance targets and actual results from 1992 to the present. While the index value has not increased every year (and is not

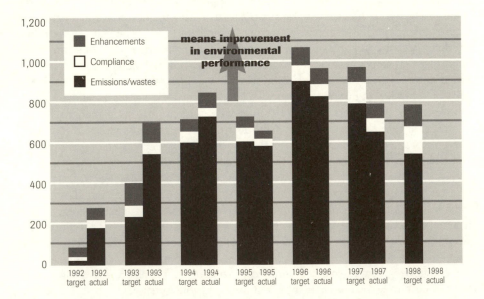

Figure 1: NIAGARA MOHAWK POWER CORPORATION
ANNUAL ENVIRONMENTAL PERFORMANCE INDEX SCORES

expected to do so), the trend is certainly in an upward direction, indicating continuing improvement in environmental performance.

The reason that NMPC's environmental performance has tailed off in the past few years can largely be attributed to the company's recent financial condition. Federal and state laws enacted in the early 1990s to encourage the development of independent power facilities (e.g. co-generation projects) forced NMPC to purchase a substantial amount of its generation from independent power producers, at prices significantly higher than the costs that it would otherwise have incurred for electricity from its own generating facilities. Primarily because the high oil prices forecast in the early 1990s failed to materialise, these laws resulted in enormous overpayments to the independent power producers and brought the company to the verge of bankruptcy in 1996 and 1997 (NMPC has not paid a dividend on its common stock since 1995). This situation has significantly limited its ability to invest in non-mandated pollution control facilities and environmental enhancement projects in recent years.

The laws requiring NMPC to purchase uneconomic independent power producer generation have since been rescinded, and in 1998 NMPC bought out the majority of these contracts at a cost exceeding $4 billion. This has resulted in greater reliance on the company's own fossil fuel generating facilities to serve its energy customer needs and relatively higher emissions of air pollutants from its own generating facilities. Now that the company has started to recover from its dire financial condition, it is anticipated that its environmental performance will rebound as well.

◀ Environmental Benchmarking Programme

While NMPC's EP Index provides a good measure of changes in the company's environmental performance over time, it does not provide information on how its environmental performance compares to other companies. Consequently, in late 1992, NMPC began to pursue development of an Environmental Benchmarking Programme (EBP). First, it began this process by enlisting a group of electric utilities operating in the north-eastern US (the Working Group) to explore the feasibility of an EBP. The Working Group established as its objective the development of an accurate and reliable method for comparing the environmental performance of one electric utility company against that of others (Miakisz and Miedema 1998).

Over a period of approximately a year, the Working Group discussed and attempted to resolve numerous issues surrounding the development of a set of environmental performance metrics. Two issues proved to be particularly thorny: (1) the basis of comparison for the indicators; and (2) the degree of aggregation of the results. In determining the basis of comparison for the indicators, the Working Group had to decide whether to compare each company's absolute level of environmental performance or changes in annual performance. It chose to use absolute levels because they were considered more appropriate for the programme's goal of external comparisons, whereas measuring annual changes was considered most appropriate for internal environmental measurement systems.

In determining whether and how results should be aggregated, the Working Group considered using a collection of operational performance indicators with no aggregation, versus an indexing approach derived by combining the individual indicators into a single composite value using numerical weights. The participants decided that separate indicators would be preferable, despite the simplicity of interpretation and communication associated with a single index. The choice of using discrete indicators for the EBP avoided a debate among the participants on the relative importance of each indicator, and would allow each company and its stakeholders to draw their own conclusions from the results. In addition, reporting individual indicators would reduce the potential concern about 'winners and losers'. Separate indicators would allow participants to determine those areas in which they are performing well and those that offered greater potential for improvement. A composite index could potentially mask this valuable information.

Once these important issues were resolved, the next step in the development of the EBP was to select the specific indicators for the programme. This process proved to be much easier than expected, primarily since all of the companies' operations, and their associated environmental impacts, were similar. Another factor working in the Group's favour was that all of the representatives of the participating companies were experienced environmental managers.

One concern of the Working Group was that all participants should measure exactly the same indicators. For example, the EBP would not accurately compare environmental performance if some participating companies excluded recycled portions of their waste-streams when calculating amounts of waste generated, while others included them. Similarly, an accurate comparison of air emissions could not be made if some companies reported continuous emission-monitoring data, while others reported emissions data based on published emission factors. To address this concern, the Group agreed that specific definitions for each indicator would have to be established and that the type of monitoring data reported for each indicator would have to be specified as well. Agreement on these definitions would take into account data accuracy considerations as well as existing data collection systems of the participants (in order to minimise the burden of developing new data collection systems).

A related problem would arise if the same waste-stream at different companies varied substantially in composition. For example, suppose one company discharged waste-water with twice the concentration of a particular heavy metal as that discharged by another company. If an EBP indicator focused solely on the volume of waste-water discharges, then both companies would appear to have the same environmental performance, even though one discharges twice as much of the heavy metal. In such a case, it was agreed by the Working Group participants that it would be better to focus on the mass of the metals discharged in waste-water rather than on the volume of waste-water discharged.

Since the intended use of the EBP was to compare the level of environmental performance of different companies, the Working Group also recognised that the EBP indicators needed to be adjusted for differences in the size of the participating companies. All of the EBP indicators were normalised in some manner, in the majority of cases by BTUs (British Thermal Units) of electricity and gas sold (i.e. the product delivered by the participating companies).[1] For air emissions such as SO_2 and NO_x, the amount of electricity generated in a year (MWh) was viewed as an appropriate 'normalising factor' for size, because a company that produces more electricity than another company would produce more air emissions, other things being equal. Thus, the Working Group suggested measuring air emissions as pounds of pollutant per MWh of electricity generated. Other normalising factors used were total utility operating revenues and total operating time.

Based on their assessment of the potential benefits and concerns associated with an EBP, the Working Group concluded that comparing one electric utility's environmental performance against another using a set of normalised environmental performance indicators (EPIs) was both feasible and desirable. The Group recommended implementing a pilot programme in 1994 with interested electric utilities in the north-east of America, and, if the pilot were successful, the programme would be broadened in 1995.

The pilot programme was successful and, in early 1995, participation in a formal EBP programme was solicited from all electric utilities operating in the US and Canada. Research Triangle Institute (RTI) was selected as an independent administrator for the EBP.

Thirty-three companies (32 from the US and one from Canada) committed to participate in the 1995 EBP programme. A total of 60 discrete environmental performance measures were included in the benchmarking programme. These measures were grouped into eight performance categories:

- Air emissions
- Other generated residuals
- Spills, releases, and applications of other regulated substances
- Fines and exceedances
- Environmental expenditures[2]
- Alternative fuel vehicles and demand-side energy savings
- Heat rates
- Combustion turbine environmental indicators

---

1 These would be *relative* indicators in ISO 14031 terminology.
2 Environmental expenditures are defined in the EBP as the sum of environmental investments and environmental expenses. Environmental investments are the capital costs spent on air and water pollution control facilities, solid waste management, noise abatement and aesthetics impact abatement. Environmental expenses include the costs of operating and maintaining pollution control facilities, costs associated with waste disposal and waste remediation and the costs of developing and maintaining a company's environmental management programme. Clearly, increases in environmental investments can be viewed as positive. Environmental expenses, on the other hand, include some aspects that may be viewed positively (e.g. implementation of an environmental management programme) and some aspects that may be viewed negatively (e.g. waste site remediation). This begs the question as to whether or not increases in total environmental expenses should be viewed as positive or negative. NMPC interprets its environmental expenses in conjunction with other environmental performance indicators. What the company strives for is excellent environmental performance at relatively

Indicator	Measures	Indicator
1	1–20	Air emissions
2	21–36	Other generated residuals
3	37–42	Oil spills and chemical releases
4	43–52	Fines and exceedances
5	53–66	Environmental expenditures and investments
6	67–76	Alternate fuel vehicles, demand-side management savings, renewable energy and heat rates
7	77–84	Combustion turbine environmental parameters

Table 7: ENVIRONMENTAL BENCHMARKING PROGRAMME:
ENVIRONMENTAL PERFORMANCE INDICATOR GROUPS

The final report for the 1995 EBP was distributed to the participants in February 1996 and, shortly after, all participants met to critique the programme. One of the important suggestions offered at this session was the need to conduct a survey of best practices to identify policies, programmes and methods associated with superior performance. The participants felt that it was insufficient to know how they stood on each EPI compared to the other companies: they also wanted to know what was responsible for the superior performer's success.

In response to this, RTI conducted a survey of best practices to identify those policies, programmes and practices that contributed to the success of the top performers participating in the 1995 EBP. RTI asked each participant to provide some insight about the specific practices or methods that they believe contributed most to their performance in the 1995 EBP. These responses were grouped by area of performance and summarised, and a confidential report was distributed to participants.

Since 1995, the EBP has been conducted on an annual basis, with the number of participating companies ranging from as few as 19 to as high as 33. Some companies have participated in the EBP on an annual basis since its inception, while others prefer to participate in the programme every other year or every three years. RTI continues to conduct and manage the EBP, with each subscriber paying a small fee (approximately $5,000) to RTI to cover the survey design, data collection, data analyses and reporting costs. As has been the case since the programme's inception, each company executes a confidentiality agreement with RTI to maintain data confidentiality: RTI assigns each company a randomly selected, confidential identity code used to identify company-specific data in the reports provided. These measures have been critical to the success of the programme because, without them, many companies would not be willing to share data that was not publicly available either because it was viewed as competitive information and/or out of fear that the data would be improperly used against the company.

RTI uses data from survey instruments completed by each participant to calculate environmental performance measures, typically ratios that relate some type of environmental performance outcome (e.g. emissions) to a 'normalising' variable (e.g. MWh). Eighty-four discrete environmental performance measures were calculated from the survey responses in the 1997 EBP and then grouped into seven performance groups (see Table 7). Table 8 lists the performance indicators examined in each of these groups. Changes made to the EBP indicators since 1994 primarily reflect a learning process among the participants on which indicators are the most relevant and useful. Data availability and quality considerations have also led to revisions in the list of indicators carried forward in the EBP.

In identifying appropriate EPIs for the EBP, an attempt was made to include alternative measures that could be used by the participants, recognising that 'perfect' measures do not exist and that each company (and their stakeholders) may have a different way of looking at performance. In some cases, three or four performance measures were derived from a single indicator. For example, with respect to environmental expenses, expenses for each company in 1997 were normalised by reference to two variables: BTUs of electricity and gas sold, and total operating

Air emissions	**Other generated residuals**
SO_2	Hazardous wastes
NO_x	Combustion waste from coal units
CO_2	Non-hazardous non-combustion solid waste
	Low-level radioactive waste
	PCB removal
Oil and chemical releases	**Fines and exceedances**
Reported oil spills to navigable waters	Notices of violation that reach final resolution
Oil spills to land	Non-compliance expenditures (e.g. fines)
Reported release of chemicals	Water discharge permit exceedances
	Opacity (air) exceedances
Environmental expenditures and investments	**Alternative fuel vehicles, demand-side management savings, renewable energy and heat rates**
Environmental investments (changes in book value)	Alternative-fuel vehicles
Non-capital expenses	Demand-side management energy savings
Hydroelectric expenditures	Renewable energy sources
	Heat rate efficiencies

* As indicated above, several different measures may have been developed for a given performance indicator. For example, while only three performance indicators are included in the air emissions group (SO_2, NO_x and CO_2), 20 distinct measures for these indicators are included in the programme.

Table 8: ENVIRONMENTAL BENCHMARKING PROGRAMME: ENVIRONMENTAL PERFORMANCE INDICATORS

revenues.[3] In addition, 1995–97 annual average expenses were normalised by reference to each variable. It is likely that, if this flexibility were not incorporated into the programme, few companies would participate (i.e. it would be virtually impossible to get 20–30 electric utility companies to agree on a finite list of environmental performance indicators) (Miakisz and Miedema 1998).

The results of the EBP are provided to each participant in both hard copy and electronic form by RTI, using three methods of data summarisation, each at increasing levels of detail (see Figs. 2, 3 and 4) (Engel and Miedema 1998).

◢ Benefits Derived from EP Index and EBP

Measuring environmental performance *per se* does not drive results. What drives performance is a company's environmental policy, strategies and objectives. Reductions in pollutants from a company's operations, for example, do not occur merely because a company has an EPI in place. What does drive performance of this nature (beyond regulatory requirements) is a commitment by a company's senior management to environmental leadership, and a desire to have its facilities operate in harmony with the environment. One factor that may motivate this type of thinking is a desire to be a good corporate citizen and to do the 'right thing'. Or it may be influenced by the desire of the company's various stakeholders who support this type of behaviour (for example, Toxic Release Inventory reporting requirements in the US have put high pressure on companies to reduce their reliance on toxic chemicals, from the communities surrounding their facilities). Or, as a lot of companies are coming to realise today, this type of thinking may be motivated by the belief that good environmental performance contributes to good financial performance and competitive advantage.

Companies that elect to employ environmental performance measurement as part of their environmental management system toolbox do so to help to ensure that their environmental policy objectives are achieved and as a means of communicating their performance to their stakeholders. EPIs provide visibility for environmental policy objectives and, if they are used effectively, can be a motivating factor in terms of fostering performance as well as a means of assigning accountability for demonstrating results.

Multiple benefits have been derived from NMPC's environmental performance measurement and environmental benchmarking initiatives. These benefits have convinced the company that there is a lot of truth behind the adage 'what gets measured, gets done' and that environmental performance measurement and

---

3   In about half the cases, use of total operating revenues as the normalising factor changed the participants' benchmarked position by at least one quartile, as compared to using BTUs of electricity and gas sold as the normalising factor. BTUs of electricity and gas sold was probably the better normalising factor in this case, since it is a uniform factor, whereas operating revenues are a function of the price charged for electricity and gas, which may vary widely from jurisdiction to jurisdiction.

Legend for symbols: ● = 1st group (top 25%); ◉ = 2nd group (26%–50%); ⊙ = 3rd group (51%–75%); ○ = 4th group (76%–100%); · = no value.

	Measures																			
	1	2	3	4	5	6	7	8	9	10a	10b	11	12	13	14	15	16	17	18	19
Utility 1	○	·	·	·	○	·	⊙	·	·	⊙	●	·	●	◉	·	⊙	·	·	○	⊙
Utility 2	⊙	○	⊙	○	⊙	●	●	●	⊙	⊙	⊙	⊙	⊙	·	·	○	⊙	●	⊙	○
Utility 3	⊙	●	⊙	⊙	⊙	·	·	·	○	○	●	○	●	·	·	·	·	·	·	·
Utility 4	●	·	●	●	●	·	⊙	●	⊙	·	●	·	·	⊙	·	●	·	·	·	·
Utility 5	○	⊙	○	⊙	●	●	●	●	●	●	●	·	●	·	●	●	○	●	●	●
Utility 6	○	●	○	○	○	○	○	○	○	○	⊙	⊙	·	·	○	⊙	○	○	·	·
Utility 7	⊙	⊙	○	⊙	●	●	●	○	●	●	⊙	●	●	·	·	⊙	●	⊙	⊙	⊙
Utility 8	·	·	·	·	·	·	·	·	·	·	·	·	·	·	·	·	·	·	·	·
Utility 9	●	◉	●	●	●	◉	○	○	○	●	●	·	●	·	·	●	●	●	⊙	○
Utility 10	●	●	●	●	●	●	●	●	●	●	●	·	●	·	·	⊙	○	●	●	●
Utility 11	●	○	○	●	●	⊙	⊙	●	·	○	⊙	●	⊙	⊙	·	⊙	○	·	⊙	●
Utility 12	·	●	●	●	●	·	●	●	●	●	●	·	·	·	·	●	○	○	●	●
Utility 13	·	⊙	●	●	●	·	●	●	●	●	●	·	·	·	·	●	●	●	●	⊙
Utility 14	●	○	○	⊙	●	●	○	○	·	·	·	●	○	○	⊙	·	●	○	·	·
Utility 15	●	⊙	●	⊙	●	●	●	●	●	●	●	·	·	·	·	●	●	●	●	⊙
Utility 16	⊙	·	⊙	○	⊙	·	●	⊙	⊙	⊙	○	●	●	·	●	·	⊙	⊙	⊙	·
Utility 17	○	●	○	○	○	○	⊙	⊙	○	○	○	○	·	·	●	⊙	●	●	⊙	·
Utility 18	●	·	●	○	●	·	⊙	⊙	○	·	●	·	·	○	·	⊙	○	○	·	·
Utility 19	●	●	○	●	○	●	●	⊙	●	·	⊙	○	·	●	●	○	●	●	·	·

● = 1st group (top 25%)

◉ = 2nd group (26%–50%)

⊙ = 3rd group (51%–75%)

○ = 4th group (76%–100%)

· = no value*

* A 'no value' designation in this table reflects inapplicability of the parameter to the respondent. For example, Utility 8 has no fossil fuel generating units, therefore does not emit air pollutants.

In other cases, a utility may not have a particular type of fossil fuel-fired generation (e.g. coal, oil, natural gas) that relates to a particular parameter.

Figure 2: ENVIRONMENTAL BENCHMARKING PROGRAMME: AIR EMISSIONS INDICATOR

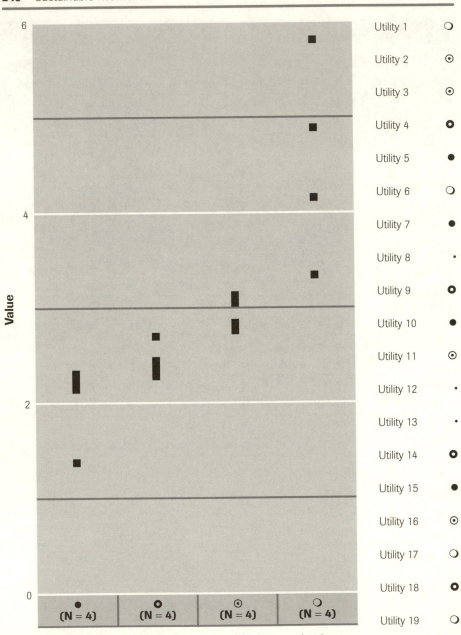

Coal units represented in this figure are coal-fired, steam electric
generating units

Figure 3: ENVIRONMENTAL BENCHMARKING PROGRAMME:
ENGLISH TONS OF NOₓ FROM COAL UNITS/MWh NET INTERNAL GENERATION FROM COAL UNITS (× 1,000)

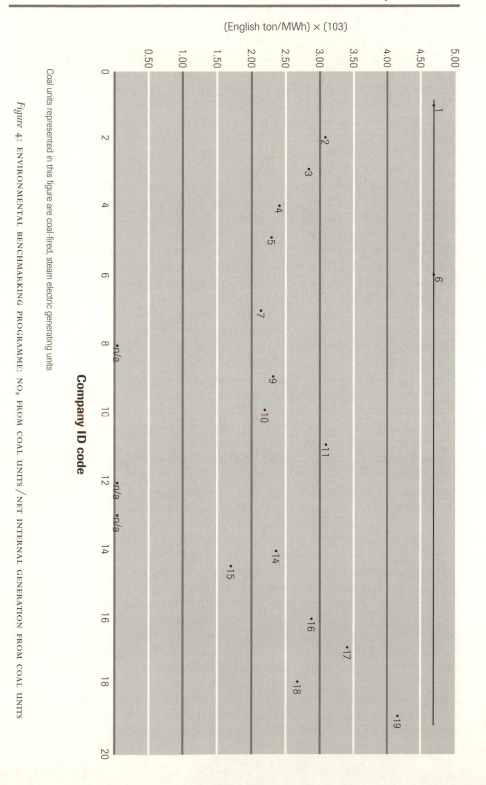

(English ton/MWh) × (10³)

Figure 4: ENVIRONMENTAL BENCHMARKING PROGRAMME: NOₓ FROM COAL UNITS / NET INTERNAL GENERATION FROM COAL UNITS

Coal units represented in this figure are coal-fired, steam electric generating units

evaluation must be an integral component of any company's environmental excellence programme.

At NMPC, environmental performance has been linked with the achievement of business plan objectives, with employee compensation programmes and with financial performance in general. A prerequisite for the establishment of these linkages was a strong commitment from upper management. Soon after the EP Index was launched in 1992, the CEO and president of the corporation sent a memo to all management personnel within the various business units directing them to incorporate EP Index goals into their business planning activities. The memo indicated that line management would be held accountable for the achievement of EP Index goals, which led to their inclusion in the company's management incentive compensation programme. The plant managers of the company's fossil fuel generating plants, for example, have environmental performance goals such as opacity targets (a reflection of air emissions), water discharge permit excursions and other environmental targets included in their performance reviews, along with such traditional goals as achievement of heat rate targets, budget targets and the like. The inclusion of EP Index goals in the performance reviews for these and other individuals has proven to be a powerful motivator. NMPC has evidenced marked reductions in pollutant discharges from those fossil fuel stations where reduction goals have been incorporated into individual performance evaluations and achievement of these goals is measured by the EP Index.

From 1991 to 1995, a portion of the return that NMPC was allowed to earn by the New York State Public Service Commission was incentive-based. Approximately $50 million in rate relief annually during this period was tied to the company's performance in various areas, including cost control, customer service, reliability and environmental performance. Over the five-year period, approximately $7.2 million in incentive rate relief was tied to NMPC's environmental performance, as measured by the EP Index. Of the $7.2 million maximum, approximately $6.6 million was actually earned.

Another benefit of the EP Index is that it has served as a catalyst for continuous improvement in environmental performance. Although NMPC's Corporate Environmental Policy states that it will strive for continuous improvement, without some type of measurement in place it is difficult to claim or demonstrate improvement beyond mere anecdotal evidence. It is also difficult to hold employees accountable for environmental performance if targets are not established and a measurement system is not in place for determining progress in achieving the targets. NMPC's EP Index provides a clear and visible yardstick for demonstrating achievement of environmental performance targets. As described earlier, this does not necessarily mean that an improvement in performance will be achieved each and every year. A host of factors may prevent this, including financial, operational and other constraints. However, over a several-year period, achievement of continuous improvement goals is not only practical but achievable.

An important benefit resulting from implementation of NMPC's EP Index that was not initially foreseen has been a substantial improvement in the company's environmental information system. Much of the data used in the EP Index to measure environmental performance was already being collected for regulatory reporting purposes or for other reasons. However, for several of the indicators deemed important to measure in the EP Index, NMPC had either a very rudimentary or no data collection process already in place.

For example, NMPC had a fairly sophisticated, automated system in place for tracking hazardous wastes generated at company facilities, in large part because hazardous wastes have been highly regulated in the US for quite some time. With respect to the company's non-hazardous solid waste-stream, on the other hand, no system was in place for quantifying the amounts and types of wastes being generated at virtually all of its generating stations, service centres, crew locations, substations and office complexes (which number in the thousands). Implementation of the EP Index provided the impetus for the development of an information system that could accurately track the amounts and types of solid wastes being generated at the company's facilities and how they were being disposed of. The benefit of this was not to provide data for the EP Index for the sake of measurement *per se*, but rather it provided the company the ability to manage this waste-stream effectively.

As indicated earlier, another important purpose that the EP Index serves is as a tool for communication with stakeholders. The EP Index is highly visible. As indicated earlier, EP Index results are reported to senior management and line managers on a quarterly basis. EP Index data has also been communicated to the company's employees, its stockholders, its regulators, the communities that it serves and other constituencies in various ways: for example, it is routinely reported in the company's employee newsletter. EP Index data has also been featured in environmental reports that the company has published in the past which are sent to all of its stakeholders, and has been periodically shared with the agencies that regulate the company's activities.

Like the EP Index, the EBP that NMPC initiated and in which it participates on an annual basis has yielded important benefits. First and foremost, NMPC firmly believes that, without the type of voluntary and confidentiality-protected programme that has been developed, it would be virtually impossible to have at its disposal the amount and breadth of environmental performance data that is obtained from this programme. External companies that conduct environmental benchmarking on private companies, such as the Council on Economic Priorities, the Investor Responsibility Research Center and Environmental Information Services, must necessarily rely primarily on publicly available information. This is because private companies are often reluctant to share environmental performance data with an external party who could use the data in a way that could compromise its competitive advantage, or in a way that could reflect negatively on the company (whether it may be warranted or not). The beauty of the EBP is that the participating companies feel free to share with one another all data deemed necessary to provide a good picture of a company's environmental performance. The upside of participating is that each company receives comprehensive data on all of the other participants (although the data is not matched to individual company names). At the same time, with the confidentiality agreement in place, the downside risk of the data that each participant provides being used in an inappropriate or unintended manner is minimised.

One of the tangible benefits of NMPC's participation in the EBP is that it has been able to get a good sense of its strengths and weaknesses in environmental performance relative to the other participants. Before its involvement in the programme, it would have been very difficult to identify these strengths and weaknesses. A good example is NMPC's track record in terms of compliance with its water discharge permit effluent limitation requirements at its steam electric generating stations. When the company's baseline for this indicator was determined back in 1992, it was determined that the average annual number of exceedances of effluent limits at its five steam electric generating stations for the period 1989–91 was 39. Considering that this was 39 exceedances out of over 4,000 indicator measurements per year, this performance was not viewed negatively.

However, when the benchmarking programme was started in 1995, NMPC found that it consistently ranked in the bottom quartile of performance for this indicator relative to the other participants. This finding led to a root-cause analysis of all of the company's exceedances of water discharge permits, which identified at least four distinct contributing factors. Three were determined to be technology-related and could be remedied by treatment system changes, and the fourth factor was administrative in nature. Some errors in the permits were identified and it was also determined that the company was failing to take full advantage of certain flexibility afforded in the regulations. This problem was remedied simply by sending a few letters to the New York State environmental regulatory agency and getting approval for certain modifications of the company's permits (though of course this, although beneficial for the company, improved only measured rather than actual performance). Nonetheless, the changes that have been implemented as a result of the EBP information and root-cause analysis of performance deficiencies have resulted in a substantial reduction in the number of annual water discharge permit exceedances that occur at NMPC's steam stations (11 in 1997) and have improved performance ratings for this indicator, relative to the other EBP participants.

Another benefit of NMPC's participation in the EBP is that the company has learned significantly from other participants in the programme about how they have achieved top-quartile performance with respect to certain environmental indicators. This benefit should not be overstated, because in reality some companies are reluctant to share best practice information that may be viewed as contributing to their competitive advantage. Nevertheless, some useful information has been obtained from participants who recognise the mutual benefit of sharing best practice information with each other. As an example, NMPC has shared information with the other EBP participants on how it has integrated its internal environmental performance measures with other business performance measures and the benefits it has derived from this process. Conversely, NMPC has learned from other EBP participants about successful methods that have been employed at fossil fuel generating stations to minimise oil spills. It has also gained valuable information from other companies on how to effectively minimise the generation (and disposal) of hazardous wastes by properly managing the chemicals that are procured for company activities.

Finally, the EBP provides participating companies with useful insight on their environmental leadership position. Many companies profess to be leaders in certain aspects of their business, but often the rhetoric is not backed up with substance. Data from the environmental benchmarking programme, while not a perfect gauge of a company's environmental leadership, certainly provides an objective measure of each participant's standing on a wide array of environmental performance measures.

◢ Concluding Remarks

NMPC's experience with environmental performance measurement and benchmarking has provided some insights that may be helpful to other companies interested in developing their own environmental performance metrics. First, the measures that are developed do not need to be 'perfect', only accurate enough to detect significant shifts in performance. Second, the measures developed should be designed with the company's major stakeholders in mind, whether they be senior management, employees, customers, regulators or others. Third, developing a good environmental performance measurement tool, in itself, is meaningless, unless the company has established a set of specific environmental performance targets. Ideally, these targets should be integrated into all levels of planning and operations from the company's strategic planning process to the employee performance evaluation process.

For Niagara Mohawk, the linkage of EP Index goals with other important company goals such as financial performance has produced positive, measurable improvement in environmental performance. The EP Index and EBG have heightened environmental performance awareness within the company, have instilled a focus on results, and have established a means of assigning accountability. These tools are considered essential elements in achieving its objective of continuous improvement in environmental performance.

11
A Weighted Environmental Indicator at Unox

An Advance towards Sustainable Development?

Willem N. van der Werf

UNOX is one of the six working companies of Van den Bergh Nederland, the largest food company in the Netherlands and a subsidiary of Unilever. Unox's production process is concentrated in three factories: the meat products (CFO, Conserven Fabriek Oss), soup and sauce operations.

- CFO produces packaged meat products and smoked sausages, which in 1997 amounted to 23 million kg. The collagen casing and the smoked flavour are produced by the Industrial Products section.

- The soup factory produces a variety of canned soups and sauces. In 1997 around 45 million litres of soup (85 million cans) were produced.

- The sauce factory produces heat-processed sauces in glass jars, including 'Raguletto' and 'Chicken Tonight'. The production of sauces is almost fully automated. In 1997 this factory produced almost 10 million kg of sauce (30 million jars).

◁ *Environmental Policy*

The environmental policy of Unox is summarised as follows:

> Unox aims to be one of the leading companies producing food for daily consumption. This necessitates working to high standards in the care of product and processes, and in the safety of the employees and the environment.

> In carrying out company activities, working conditions, care for the environment, continuity, quality and attention to costs and profits are an integral part of company policy. Unox is constantly working to improve quality of products and processes, with the additional purpose of improving and optimising working conditions, of creating minimal impact on the environment and guaranteeing safety and health in the vicinity of the company (Unox Sourcing Unit, 1997 Environmental Policy).

In addition, Unox must comply with the environmental policy both of the national government and of Unilever.

The environmental policy of the Dutch government is embodied in the National Environmental Policy Plans (NEPP) (NEPP 1989, 1990, 1994, 1998; RIVM 1997). The key principle of the NEPP is an environmental policy that aims for sustainable development.

Unilever's environmental policy endorses this complex and challenging concept. One stipulation of the policy is that every Unilever company must define a set of environmental parameters in relation to the target of sustainable development. Furthermore, a company must be able to demonstrate continual improvement against targets set.

◀ The Environmental Policy Indicator at Unox

To tackle environmental issues effectively, the Dutch government has chosen a thematic (category) approach. Environmental issues are divided into a finite number of categories and a quantitative target has been set for each. In the NEPP these categories are arranged according to five geographical levels: global, continental, fluvial, regional and local. For example, climate change is considered a global issue, whereas noise pollution is experienced locally. The Dutch government has set targets for 2000 ('NEPP2000') and these are considered to be a minimum for reaching sustainable levels in 2020. There are also attempts to define targets (for 2020) in relation to sustainable development.

Unox has developed a measurement tool to help demonstrate compliance with the environmental policies of both the Dutch government and Unilever, and also with ISO 14001. This tool is designed to demonstrate, with a single value, whether the company is complying with the environmental policy's quantitative targets (NEPP2000), and is known as the Environmental Policy Indicator. By comparing Environmental Policy Indicator scores from year to year, Unox can demonstrate continual improvement.

Indicators must lead to the quantification and simplification of environmental issues; they allow comparison between environmental categories and facilitate communication of environmental performance when used as an environmental management tool. A good set of indicators can also help with the prioritisation of environmental projects.

Environmental management at Unox is evolving in such a way that, by using the Environmental Policy Indicator tools, environmental problems are made clear to all employees, and each employee is aware of his/her responsibility. The indicators allow environmental problems to be presented in a clear, thematic and effective way.

The Environmental Policy Indicator is an empirical model developed by the Dutch Centre for Energy Conservation and Environmental Technology in Delft. It illustrates the distance between the current situation and the target situation. Indicators are defined on the basis of 'intra-weighting' and 'inter-weighting'.

▼ **Intra-weighting** is the weighting of environmental effects *within* a single category: 'the contribution of an emission or use of energy and water related to a reference value of an environmental category'.

▼ **Inter-weighting** is the weighting of the environmental effects of *different* categories: 'the contribution of a category to the total environmental score relative to the target of that category'.

◻ *Intra-Weighting*

The calculation of an Environmental Policy Indicator starts with the classification of a large number of environmental issues such as emissions, use of energy and raw materials, into a limited number of relevant environmental categories. These categories are also set out in the NEPP:

1. Global warming
2. Ozone depletion — Climate change
3. Acidification of the environment
4. Eutrophication of the environment
5. Dehydration of soils
6. Disposal of solid wastes
7. Disturbance of the local environment
8. Dispersion of solid waste

Using a classification factor, it can be calculated to what extent an environmental issue contributes to the category, in relation to a reference value for that category. The sum of these converted environmental issues is the environmental category score. Energy and water use, the company's emissions and, for example, transport can all be converted, via intra-weighting, into environmental category scores.

◻ *Inter-weighting*

A comparison between the different environmental category scores is possible using the **distance-to-target** method. The distance-to-target is the quotient of the environmental category score and a quantitative target. The Environmental Policy Indicator is the sum of the distance-to-target of all the categories and therefore a measure for the environmental score of a company or a project, and is, of course, dependent on the target set.

The Indicator can illustrate the development of environmental categories. For example, installation of a water purification plant may improve eutrophication, but will adversely affect global warming (energy), disturbance (noise, odour) and disposal (waste water sludge).

◢ Results

Ultimately, the Environmental Policy Indicator must be as low as possible, which would mean the highest possible environmental performance in relation to the chosen targets. The main benchmark for Unox is the NEPP2000 targets, the advantage of which is that they are also used by the authorities and therefore provide a common base from which to discuss performance. Sustainability targets are needed to measure performance to meet both Unilever policy and ISO standards (see Table 1).

The Environmental Policy Indicator score, based on NEPP2000 targets, is presented in Figures 1 and 2. The Environmental Policy Indicator score is calculated using the Dutch national targets, so the absolute number of the Indicator is very low. Therefore Figure 2 presents the absolute score of Unox related to the 1994 score, which was set at 100%, and Figure 3 presents the score per tonnes of production (i.e. in relative terms), the reference year still being 1994.

In 1995 the absolute Environmental Policy Indicator score was high in relation to 1994, due to a large amount of solid waste from site demolition activities. If the demolition activities were excluded, there would be an improvement in the 'disposal' score for the period 1994–97. There were problems with leakages of CFC-12 in 1996. Even small amounts of CFC-12 have large implications for the company's environmental performance, due to the very low target for the 'ozone depletion' category.

Category	NEPP2000	Sustainability	
Global warming	1.95E+11	1.00E+10	kg CO_2 equivalents
Acidification	3.20E+08	5.30E+06	Acidification equivalents (amount protons in equivalents)
Eutrophication	1.20E+08	8.60E+07	kg phosphorous equivalents
Dispersion	1.20E+19	1.20E+18	kg contaminated environment
Disposal	5.00E+09	3.00E+09	kg industrial waste equivalents
Disturbance	1.12E+06	8.00E+04	number of households affected
Ozone depletion	5.40E+04	2.50E+03	kg CFC-12 equivalents
Dehydration of soils	1.32E+09	1.00E+08	m^3 soil water equivalents

(The sustainability levels for the categories are still under discussion, but the targets for NEPP2000 are generally accepted.)

Table 1: QUANTITATIVE NATIONAL TARGETS FOR THE EIGHT CATEGORIES IN WHICH UNOX PRESENTS ITS ENVIRONMENTAL PERFORMANCE

Source: Adriaanse 1994

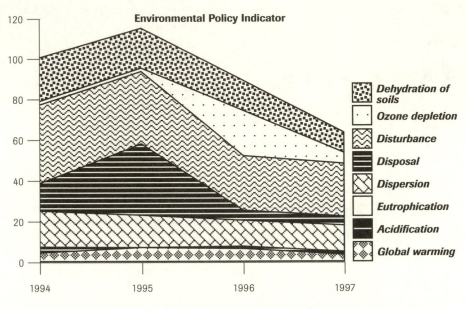

Figure 1: UNOX'S ABSOLUTE EPI SCORE 1994–97

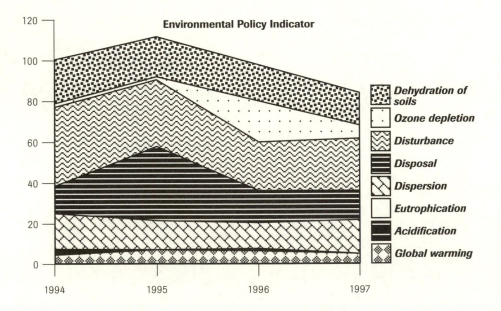

Figure 2: UNOX'S RELATIVE EPI SCORE PER TONNE OF PRODUCTION 1994–97

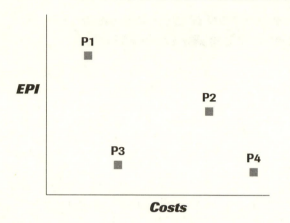

Figure 3: ENVIRONMENTAL POLICY INDICATOR SCORE VERSUS COSTS OF FOUR PROJECTS

When these two aspects (demolition, and leakage of CFC-12) are ignored, the absolute score of the ongoing production of Unox has improved since 1994. The main categories for continual improvement of Unox's environmental performance are 'disturbance of the local environment', 'eutrophication' and 'dehydration of soils'.

The relative measure of environmental performance per tonne of production also shows an improvement in the period 1994–97. However, the improvement is less than for the absolute measure, due to a combination of lower production volumes (1996–97) and an increased number of product change-overs and hence cleaning activities, etc.: after every product change-over the same rigorous cleaning procedure must be followed regardless of production volumes.

◢ Selecting Projects Using Environmental Policy Indicators

An Environmental Policy Indicator can be used to evaluate environmental performance, and can also be used in the decision phase as a tool for prioritisation of projects or environmental measures.

Since different environmental categories can be compared using inter-weighting, it is possible to demonstrate the effect of environmental damage per project. It is therefore possible to use the model as a tool for choosing between different environmental impact-reducing techniques.

By relating the score to the costs of a project (Fig. 3), the most effective option (that with the highest score relative to project cost) is identified. Project P1 has a high score and is also relatively cheap, whereas project P4 is expensive but still has only a low score.

◢ *The Environmental Policy Indicator Model in Practice: An Overview*

Unox has developed software for Environmental Policy Indicator calculation. Every three months, Unox factories are informed of their Environmental Policy Indicators and the results are discussed with factory managers and team leaders. The decision to replace CFC-12 with HCFC and other coolants was accelerated by the results of 1996. Since 1996, Environmental Policy Indicators have been taken into account in decision-making on various projects in relation to the 'disturbance of the local environment' category.

The system has now been in place for over two years. Unox also reports Environmental Policy Indicators annually (beginning in 1998) to the board of Van den Bergh Nederland to illustrate its factories' environmental performance. Environmental and financial target-setting by the board plays an important role here.

The results of the model depend on the target of the category, which is why it still cannot be used for compliance with local requirements, when emission levels have to be taken into account. There is current discussion on whether environmental permits should be issued on the basis of a business's performance against categories. The Environmental Policy Indicator model will certainly play an important role in this debate.

12

The Evolution of Integrated Environmental Performance Evaluation and Reporting at Baxter International

Martin Bennett and Peter James

THIS CHAPTER examines the development of environmental performance evaluation and reporting during the 1990s at an individual company, Baxter International. Baxter is widely recognised as one of the leading companies in the field because of the range and depth of its activities. Its published corporate environmental report (CER) was rated by the SustainAbility/UNEP *Engaging Stakeholders* survey (summarised in Chapter 15) in 1997 as second only to the atypical Body Shop. One reason for this and other accolades has been its innovative approach to developing and using financial indicators.[1] Baxter has also won several awards for the quality of its environmental performance and reporting and is a signatory to the CERES Principles, and its experience is therefore of wide interest.

This case has seven sections. Section 1 provides background business and environmental management information, and Section 2 provides a detailed description of the evolution of Baxter's environmental performance evaluation activities. Section 3 describes and discusses the types of measure used by Baxter, while Section 4 describes the process of performance evaluation and reporting within the company. Section 5 details the development of data collection practices and systems; Section 6 considers the company's future plans; and the final section provides conclusions.

---

1   A case study by the authors of this chapter on Baxter's use of financial indicators in its annual Environmental Financial Statement is included in Bennett and James 1998b: 294-309. An earlier, more detailed, version is included in Tuppen 1996: 53-71.

1. Background Information

Baxter International is a leading producer, developer and distributor of medical products and technologies. It operates in over 300 facilities around the world, 100 of which are manufacturing facilities, employs 42,000 staff worldwide, and had revenues of $6.6 billion in 1998 generated from several tens of thousands of different product lines.

Following a corporate reconstruction in 1996 which divested the US distribution, medical kits, gloves and surgical instruments businesses into a separate company, Allegiance Corporation, the post-spin-off Baxter has four production divisions, which enjoy considerable autonomy:

- Biotechnology, which develops therapies and products in transfusion medicine

- Cardiovascular medicine, which develops products and provides services to treat late-stage cardiovascular disease

- Renal, which develops products and services to improve therapies for patients with kidney disease

- Intravenous systems and medical products, which develops technologies and systems to improve intravenous medication delivery, and distributes medical products

Baxter's marketing and distribution is organised in four regional divisions, for America, Europe, Japan/China and the Rest of the World, respectively.

Baxter's most significant environmental impacts are emissions to air and water, use of energy and other natural resources, packaging, waste generation, and emissions of global-warming gases. Historically, it has also been a large user of ozone-depleting substances, but these have now been phased out from all production processes other than a few essential medical uses.

Up to 1996, Baxter's environmental activities were the responsibility at a corporate level of two functions: Corporate Environmental Affairs and Environmental Engineering. Corporate Health and Safety was separate, within Human Resources. Following the Allegiance Corporation 'spin-off' and a consequent corporate reconstruction, the three functions were merged into an integrated Environmental, Health and Safety function on a company-wide basis. This is led by Bill Blackburn, Vice-President and Chief Counsel, Corporate Environmental, Health and Safety (and previously Vice-President and Chief Counsel for Environment at the pre-spin-off Baxter). Each division also has an EHS function, and each facility has staff with responsibilities for environmental performance, for which they are accountable both to their local line managers and to the corporate EHS function. In total, environment-related activities occupy the equivalent of 77 full-time employees, of whom the majority (over 80%) are at facility level, with the remainder equally split between the divisions and the corporate centre. (There are also similar numbers engaged in each of Health and Safety and Occupational Health respectively.)

2. *The Evolution of Environmental Performance Evaluation and Reporting at Baxter*

Baxter's explicit attention to environmental management dates back to 1976 when a professional environmental attorney and an environmental engineer were recruited. During the period 1976–90, several initiatives were undertaken, starting with the development of the company's first environmental policy and environmental manual, establishment of a network of environmental managers at the manufacturing plants in North America, a programme of audits, and a series of regular company environmental conferences. Achievements during this period included an energy programme, led by a formal energy management group, which achieved an improvement in Baxter's overall energy efficiency by 50% over the period 1976–86; and a programme (1988–93) to remove all single-wall underground storage tanks worldwide and clean up any contamination that was found, which eliminated a potentially huge liability and made property sales easier.

A programme to reduce toxic air emissions was also introduced, and continued when Baxter made a step-change to upgrade its environmental management programme in 1990. This aimed to take a more proactive approach to environmental management and to demonstrate more visibly its relevance to the business (through, in particular, a more structured approach to performance evaluation and reporting and the introduction of the *Environmental Financial Statement* [EFS]; see below). In this year, a new environmental policy was introduced, and a vice-presidential position created for Corporate Environmental Affairs, with Bill Blackburn as the first appointee. As the new, stronger programme was being developed, its design was affected by two important factors. The first was the audits undertaken at both old and new sites, which highlighted the systems and practices that could produce superior environmental performance. The second was the total quality management (TQM) culture which had been established within the company in the 1980s.

According to Bill Blackburn,

> I was impressed at that time by the relevance of the ideas of total quality management to solving environmental problems. The goals of TQM are to clearly define requirements, and measure conformance to these requirements, in order to foster continuous improvement towards a target of zero defects—or in our case full compliance with internal and regulatory standards. The quality gurus preached that the best kind of continuous improvement was that which solved the root causes of problems rather than putting quick patches on their symptoms—in other words, pollution prevention rather than end-of-pipe solutions, and management standards rather than fire-fighting. They also said that total quality was driven by measurement, benchmarking and target-setting which, of course, are central to environmental improvement. Indeed, you don't even have to change the words of one of the most important quality tenets—measuring the total cost of waste—into environmental language. And when the quality gurus talked about the importance of recognising and responding to customers, both internal and external, it put NGOs and other environmental stakeholders into a different light. So my challenge was to develop a kind of total quality environmental management (TQEM) at Baxter.

The starting point for Baxter's TQEM programme was to use the detailed information available from the audits to benchmark their individual facilities and identify key influences on good and bad performance. One outcome was a realisation that the better-performing facilities tended also to be those with the more focused environmental staff with better training, good management support and a proactive TQM approach. The focus on TQM also led to the setting of medium-term stretch goals for a number of areas, including reduction of packaging, reduction of hazardous and non-hazardous waste, and removal of underground storage tanks.

A parallel initiative was to push or 'deploy' many environmental responsibilities that had previously been carried out at a corporate level (e.g. permitting) down to divisional and facility level. This was done by establishing part-time or full-time professional environmental co-ordinator posts. It had became apparent from rapidly changing distribution lists for corporate memos that these posts were often being used by some facilities as only very temporary postings—either as a final resting place for someone about to retire, or putting into the post a junior person on the promise that after a few months in the job (described by one person as an 'initial penance') they would be allowed to move on. This meant a loss of experience to environmental management, and reduced motivation. On the other hand, audits showed that successful facility programmes had more permanent dedicated personnel who were specifically trained for their roles. To address this, corporate staff established a temporary metric to track such staff turnover so that they could identify problem facilities and divisions and take action to deal with them—for example, by explaining to local management the qualifications needed, the time demands of the job, and the nature of local EHS jobs, and to help them in hiring future EHS managers. The job status was also increased by upgrading the position within the organisational structure, which also meant a change in title from 'Environmental Co-ordinator' to 'Environmental Manager', and interested qualified people were invited to fill the positions. Getting more dedicated people in the position resulted in improved performance and facility environmental results. As a result, staff turnover gradually decreased and the changes that did occur were more frequently for positive reasons such as promotions. The indicator, having served its specific problem-solving purpose of providing better information about the issue and helping to identify solutions, was then discontinued.

In 1991, Baxter commissioned Arthur D. Little to benchmark environmental leaders—initially in the US and, in a second stage, internationally—and to define 'state-of-the-art' (SOA) environmental management standards for corporate, divisional and facility levels. (These turned out to be very similar to ISO 14001, which was also in its early stages of development at that time.) Once identified, Baxter began to measure the degree of compliance with the SOA standard at all its worldwide facilities and divisions as well as corporate headquarters. It set targets of achieving 100% compliance in its North American activities by 1993 and in its worldwide activities by 1996, both of which were met ahead of time.

Bill Blackburn believes that this kind of measure—a management performance indicator, in ISO 14031 terminology (see Chapter 2)—is a good leading indicator of future environmental performance. Our experience is that a good SOA score for a facility means that the infrastructure for good environmental performance is solidly in place there, and it will eventually turn in good scores on operational performance measures such as emissions, NOVs [notices of violation], waste and compliance as well. With SOA being measured annually at each site, there was no place to hide.

To ensure senior management awareness, the results of these initiatives were summarised in a *State-of-the-Environmental, Health and Safety Program Report* (SOP). The first of these reported on performance in 1990, and was presented to the board and circulated within the corporation to other managers in 1991. In this and subsequent years, the fact that the Board was scrutinising facility and divisional results helped to give the EHS function the legitimacy they needed to collect data and improve performance elsewhere.

The first SOP was geared to internal management purposes, with a summary of goals and progress towards them and data on key management issues such as training. According to Verie Sandborg (Manager, Corporate Environmental Health and Safety), who is responsible for preparing Baxter's environmental report,

> there had always been an intention also to report externally but this was accelerated by pressure from a major church-based stockholder, the Christian Brothers. They were pressing all the companies in which they had invested to become a signatory to the Valdez Principles [now the CERES Principles].

Although Baxter did not wish to sign up at that time (they did eventually did so in 1997), on the grounds that this could reduce flexibility and distract from their own internal goals, they were happy to commit to report externally. Its first CER was published in 1993, on performance in 1992, after first being piloted in early 1993 through a brochure (a simple 'green glossy') which was issued to all employees. With no specific budget for publishing costs, this first report was a simple publication of effectively just the internal report that had already gone to Baxter's board, but restricted to information at the level of the corporation as a whole (i.e. without divisional details). In subsequent years, a specific budget was allocated to make the report more appealing to users in its presentation.

Over subsequent years, the CER has expanded to cover a wider range of topics and to provide divisional as well as corporate data (see below for a description of the current situation). It has remained based on the internal SOP, although the latter also contains comparative data on individual divisions and facilities, and qualitative comment on this, which is excluded from the final published report.

The 1996 corporate reorganisation and merger of the environmental function with the health and safety functions coincided with the achievement of Baxter's original SOA targets. As a result, a decision was made to develop new standards, to be known as the 'Baxter Environment, Health and Safety Standards' (BEHSt), initially for facilities and subsequently for divisional and corporate levels. Like the SOA standards, BEHSt is an internal, company-specific standard that focuses on management systems rather than on the details of compliance or topic-specific programmes. It is designed to be flexible and to accommodate the wide range of EHS issues and risks in Baxter's global operations, products and services. It draws on a variety of sources, including the original SOA standards, ISO 14001, and various health and safety standards, and includes 36 distinct elements. Their aim is to ensure a standard approach across the corporation but at the same time to provide maximum flexibility in how facilities or divisions achieve them. According to Baxter's 1998 environmental report, the standards

> go further than ISO 14001 by more explicitly addressing topics such as top management support, line responsibility and accountability, community relations, employee involvement and compliance results. By going above and beyond ISO 14001 (in respect of, for example, community outreach and waste-site evaluations for liability control), the BEHSt standard makes the ISO requirements more compatible with business and ensures that the equally important health and safety issues are fully addressed.

The BEHSt standard became effective in April 1998; Baxter's current policy is to require all its manufacturing facilities worldwide to reach this standard by 31 December 2000, and all other facilities by 31 December 2002. Targets will be set for divisions and corporate levels once their standards are finalised. Compliance with standards will be determined by an internal audit, based on a standard scoring system for the individual elements (with some elements being weighted more highly than others). Sites scoring more than 70% of the total points on the initial audit can achieve certification after demonstrating that they have dealt with identified areas of weakness. Sites scoring less than 70% will be re-audited before achieving certification.

One area of learning that emerged from the experience of the SOA standards of the early–mid 1990s was that a single focus on achieving or failing a standard gave little incentive for further improvement for those who did pass it. To provide such an incentive, the BEHSt standards will be reviewed every 18 months and the very best facilities will be given an additional commendation of having achieved 'excellence'.

Bill Blackburn considers that the correspondence between BEHSt and ISO 14001 is such that 'facilities wanting ISO certification should be able to get it without any further work—just incurring a few thousand dollars for certification fees. Whether they actually do so is up to them.' To date, nine facilities worldwide have obtained ISO certification, and a further 60 (over half of Baxter's facilities) have committed to achieve it. None have yet applied for EMAS (Eco-Management and Auditing Scheme) verification, although the company expects that this too would be achievable relatively easily.

1997 was also the year in which Baxter signed the CERES Principles. Generally, its existing reporting was in conformance with these principles. The only difficulty lay in some of the details—for example, CERES's requirement for detailed emissions data by substance rather than by broad classes of substance. Baxter considered that much of this information would be of significant interest only to the neighbouring communities living close to specific facilities, and that to include it in a corporate report would make this unwieldy and distract from the main information. A compromise has been reached whereby company-wide emissions information is provided both in Baxter's CER and also (in greater detail, broken down into more categories) in a separate return which they provide to CERES. Facility-specific information continues to be excluded but is made available to local parties on request.

The data also appears on Baxter's website, which—as with many companies (see Chapter 21)—is rapidly becoming a more important medium for reporting. One advantage that has already become apparent is that Internet access makes it easier for readers to e-mail the company to request further data or to offer feedback on the CER or the company's performance generally. The 1994 CER was the first to be put on the website, although in the first place simply by putting this into HTML language rather than by taking advantage of any specific Internet features. By 1996, this had evolved to putting only selected parts into HTML language, with users able to download the remainder as a PDF file if wanted. Current concerns are to increase the website's visibility to potential users through search engines, and more fundamentally to consider adapting the style of reporting to reflect more fully the different nature of Internet-based communications from those that adopt a traditional paper-based form.

The CER has evolved over time in response to a combination of a recognition of the need for programme improvement in new areas, the realisation that measurement and evaluation drive changes, and changing external pressures from stakeholders. The most recent (issued in 1998, covering performance in 1997) extends over 54 pages, including sections on:

- Programme overview
- Sustainable development
- Employees
- Compliance
- Business integration (including the *Environmental Financial Statement*)
- Customers
- Suppliers/contractors
- Community/government

The report combines factual quantitative data on performance and qualitative textual content; the latter discusses topical issues such as climate change, ozone depletion and social justice, explains for the benefit of readers the scientific and commercial implications, and sets out Baxter's policy on these issues and actions being taken and planned. There are reports of particularly creditable initiatives and achievements by Baxter facilities, to bring public attention to good and innovative practice.

One new feature in the 1997 report was a sub-section within the 'Business Integration' section on climate change, supported by a 'Chairman's Letter' by Vernon R. Loucks Jr, Chairman and CEO, stating Baxter's support as a corporation for greenhouse gas reduction and applauding the use of market-based instruments such as tax incentives to help to achieve the Kyoto objectives. The report also broadened its scope from environment alone to include health and safety data and discussion of Baxter's contribution to sustainable development. To date, this has been interpreted as a more holistic approach to environmental issues, with greater attention focused on topics such as eco-justice, eco-efficiency, product life-cycle issues and environmental impacts such as climate change. There has been no content on the social aspects of sustainable development other than the 'Community Outreach' section, although, as discussed below, this may change in future.

One other 'road not taken' to date has been inclusion of detailed environmental information in the annual financial report. This does contain a short 'Corporate Citizenship' section which includes some environmental information, as well as information on environmental liabilities which is required by the Securities and Exchange Commission (SEC). However, a divergence in reporting cycles (the financial report for the previous year having to be prepared by end-March, compared to end-June for the environmental report), as well as a feeling that this information is more adequately presented in the CER, has kept it at this level.

The 1997 report concludes with a statement of 'Affirmation of Process' by Bill Blackburn, and three separate auditors' letters attesting to the quality of Baxter's environmental management.

In the 1997 SustainAbility/UNEP *Engaging Stakeholders* survey, Baxter's CER was rated second only to The Body Shop. This reflected not only their predictable success in the 'Finance' category, where the EFS helped them to secure the highest score of all 100 reports rated, but also in the 'Stakeholder Relations and Partnership' category. The latter reflected their coverage of several stakeholder groups: customers (a group that SustainAbility advise is surprisingly often ignored both in CERs and in annual reports), suppliers and contractors, employees, local communities, and government. Other aspects of performance for which they were rated highly included waste minimisation and energy use.

After almost a decade's experience, Bill Blackburn's view on reporting is that

> Its main value is internal: it identifies opportunities for improvement, heightens the environmental awareness of managers and employees, and shows them that it's an important strategic issue which can actually be of net benefit to the company. The annual reporting cycle—and the need to publicly disclose our progress towards our environmental goals—also provides a strong pressure for positive environmental management within the company. The external picture is more patchy. We only have a relatively small number of response cards returned—although the comments on these are extremely valuable. Overall, the main feedback is from academics and NGOs. This is good in itself but we'd like more communication with business stakeholders. There has been mixed interest from stockholders: few specifically request the report but many investor groups—especially those who are also CERES members—have indicated that they consider our CER an important source of information in assessing the overall soundness of company management, which in turn affects the attractiveness of our stock. Furthermore, the report has been useful as a data source for the many questionnaires we receive from green funds. One unexpected and very positive aspect we'd like to build on is the way that our European

operations have used the report to build bridges with customers—especially those in Germany, who are very environmentally conscious.

Section 6 provides more details of how Baxter is planning to develop its reporting to address these points. First, however, the following sections describe the types of indicator used, their implementation within the company and the data collection procedures that underpin them.

3. *Environmental Indicators*

This section reviews four particular aspects of the particular indicators that Baxter uses:

- An analysis in terms of ISO 14031's typology of **categories** of indicator
- An analysis in terms of ISO 14031's typology of **types** of indicator
- Methods used by Baxter to calculate **relative** indicators, i.e. bases of normalisation
- Adjusting historic time-series data for **acquisitions** and **disposals** of businesses

◁ *Categories of Indicator*

ISO 14031 (the section of ISO 14000 that deals with environmental performance evaluation) distinguishes between three broad categories of indicator:

- Operational performance indicators (OPIs)
- Management performance indicators (MPIs)
- Environmental condition indicators (ECIs)

It goes on to identify several specific sub-categories within each category. In Chapter 2, a framework is proposed that positions these in terms of the respective relevance of each sub-category to environmental performance for its own sake, and to business performance in conventional terms. This is reproduced in Figure 1. The following paragraphs use the framework to position the various indicators used within Baxter.

Several types of OPI are reported in both the CER and the internal *SOP* (in greater detail in the latter, with quantities analysed by individual division and facility). On **outputs**, they report:

- **Emissions** to air in total volumes over time
- **Wastes**, distinguishing between hazardous/regulated and non-hazardous, and also reporting quantities recycled and revenues earned through this for each of eight different materials types
- Quantities of packaging and solution-containers, which are a significant component of final **product** in their business, and which in recent years have been the focus of intense activity to reduce quantities

Direct environmental impacts

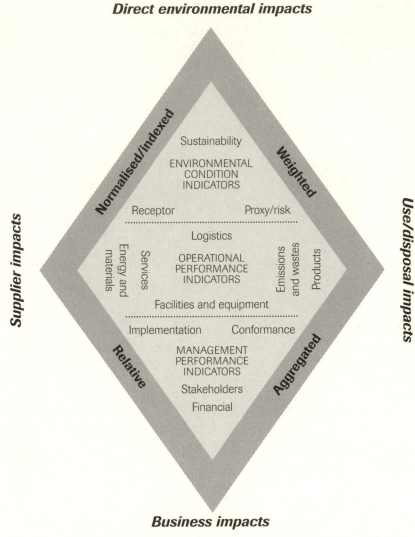

Supplier impacts

Use/disposal impacts

Business impacts

Figure 1: THE ENVIRONMENTAL PERFORMANCE EVALUATION DIAMOND

Source: Bennett and James 1998a

Inputs are reported of **energy**, analysed between different fuel sources (oil, natural gas, diesel, etc.) and including the fuel used in **logistics**; and of **water**.

There are several MPIs in each of the published CERs and the internal *SOP*, though as would be expected more in the latter. The CER reports **implementation indicators**, such as progress towards internal management standards, the number of facilities with ISO 14001 certification, and the outcomes of environmental audits including any deficiencies identified in the audits and the action then taken to address them. The internal *SOP* also has disclosures on real estate transactions where environmental assessments were carried out prior to transaction, and a detailed status report, division by division, on progress in dealing with audit items.

Conformity indicators are represented by frank disclosure of NOVs received, fines paid (no environmental fines, in the most recent report year), and potential Superfund exposure. **Stakeholder indicators** are mainly qualitative, with descriptive reports of Baxter facilities' local community outreach and employee wellness activities, contributions to events such as Earth Day, and the many awards won by facilities worldwide.

Baxter has put particular emphasis on **financial indicators** with its innovative annual *Environmental Financial Statement (EFS)*.[2] This is an annual statement of costs and benefits arising over the report year which can be attributed not only to the environmental programme itself but to any environmentally beneficial activities across the corporation. Its aim is to provide a focus within the corporation and attract attention to the environmental programme, stimulate discussion in internal meetings, and encourage motivation.

The effect of the *EFS* is to demonstrate that, contrary to some preconceptions, environment need not be a burden on business performance but can make a positive contribution. The 1997 *EFS* showed that the financial benefits arising in 1997 from projects that had been initiated in the same year exceeded the costs included in the statement as having been incurred in order to achieve them, as well as also producing the unquantifiable benefits of reduced liability exposure, enhanced corporate reputation, etc. If benefits arising in 1997 from initiatives taken in earlier years are also considered (on the premise that many changes will require only one-off costs to implement, but will then generate benefits over several subsequent years), the benefits exceed the costs by a factor of over seven.

Developing the *EFS* has required some ingenuity in devising appropriate methods of measuring and explaining costs and benefits, in particular the formula of 'cost avoidance' to measure continuing benefits over time which take into account underlying changes in the volume of the company's business, and price inflation in the markets in which they trade. Mary Marshall (Manager, Occupational Health) is currently investigating how to extend the principles of the company's *EFS* also to cover health and safety-related costs and benefits, using the experience gained in developing the *EFS* since 1992.

Baxter does not use any ECIs, since it considers that attempts to measure the proportionate effect of an individual company on global problems such as ozone or

---

2   See Note 1 on page 253.

global warming would not be meaningful, and it considers that a comprehensive and accurate reporting of emissions (an operational performance indicator) achieves the same purpose more informatively. However, with Baxter's aim of developing sustainability reporting (see Section 6), it may become appropriate to try to devise some relevant ECIs in future.

◻ *Types of Indicator*

In addition to its definition of **categories** of environmental indicator, ISO 14031 also identifies five **types** of quantitative indicator: direct, relative, normalised/indexed, aggregated, and weighted (see Chapter 2). Baxter's CER and internal *SOP* include examples of all of these. The main indicators of emissions and wastes can be found in both direct and relative forms. In the CER's 'Climate Change' section, emissions of greenhouse gases are reported in total quantities as a direct measure, without being related to production volumes, since it is the absolute amounts that are relevant to the condition of the environment. In contrast, solid wastes (hazardous and non-hazardous), reductions in packaging and solution-container materials, and energy consumption, are reported in both absolute and relative per-unit quantities, since it is considered that this more accurately reflects the success or otherwise of the business in improving underlying performance.

'Normalisation/indexation', in the ISO use of the term to mean trend analysis over time, is implicit throughout the CER and *SOP*. For all indicators where the data is available, comparative figures are given in respect both of the previous year (1996)

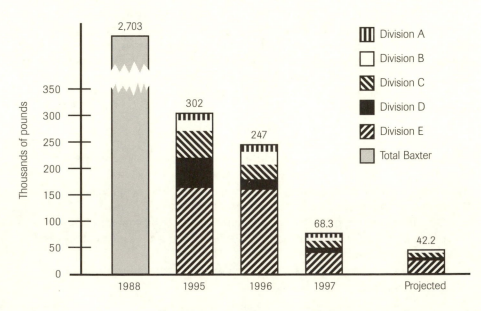

Figure 2: CFC EMISSIONS BY DIVISION

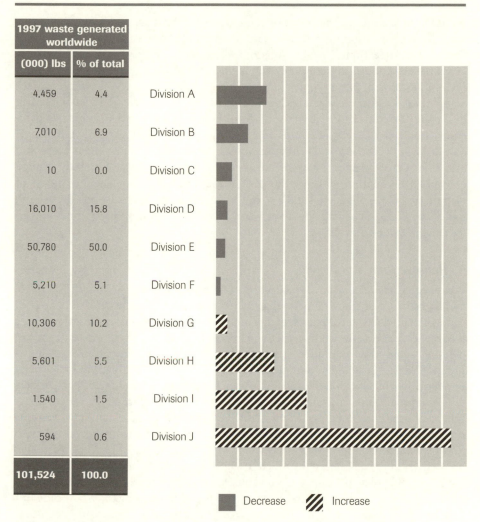

1997 waste generated worldwide				
(000) lbs	% of total			
4,459	4.4	Division A		
7,010	6.9	Division B		
10	0.0	Division C		
16,010	15.8	Division D		
50,780	50.0	Division E		
5,210	5.1	Division F		
10,306	10.2	Division G		
5,601	5.5	Division H		
1.540	1.5	Division I		
594	0.6	Division J		
101,524	**100.0**			

Decrease   Increase

Figure 3: PERCENT CHANGE IN NON-HAZARDOUS WASTE GENERATED—FROM 1996 LEVELS

and, where possible, of earlier years also, to show the extent of improvements over time (see Fig. 2 for an example taken from the 1997 *SOP*; the divisions' identities are concealed in this example but identified in the original). The *SOP* highlights this further by including charts that report not merely comparative figures, but also a division-by-division comparison of percentage changes over time in (for example) non-hazardous wastes generated (see Fig. 3, also from the 1997 *SOP*).

'Aggregation' (i.e. consolidation of similar figures across the corporation) is similarly implicit in all indicators reported at a corporate level—by definition, all must have been aggregated from the figures for individual facilities sent in through the divisions.

As noted in Section 5, ensuring consistency in definitions across all its facilities, so that this consolidation is valid, is a major concern of those responsible for environmental data collection.

Baxter has not attempted to develop a weighted index to represent its environmental performance as a whole along the lines of the Niagara Mohawk index (see Chapter 10), since it considers that this would not be meaningful for most of its users and could be confusing. However, it has developed weighted indices, based on conversion factors, for two groups of similar impacts. The CER's 'Climate Change' section reports both emissions of greenhouse gases for each source and process, and also their CO_2 equivalents, which are then summed to a total. Similarly, energy consumed is reported in terms both of the quantities of each source (kWh of electricity, gallons of oil, etc.) and also of the total British Thermal Units (BTUs) and joules consumed, when all sources are converted to a common basis and summed (see Fig. 4, taken from the 1997 CER).

△ **Relative Indicators**[3]

Baxter considers calculation of relative indicators to be essential in order to generate a valid measure of improvement that is genuine rather than attributable only to changes in production volumes, and meaningful to the operational staff whose efforts will be needed to make improvements. However, it has had to address problems in defining appropriate measures of volume to provide a denominator. At a single-product plant, this would be non-problematic—basing on units of output will usually be adequate—but it can be a problem to benchmark divisions or facilities that have different products or processes. With a high number of products in its range, this is the usual situation for Baxter, so proxies have to be devised. The two most suitable measures that are available within Baxter (since they have already been calculated for other purposes) are 'cost of goods sold' (COGS) and 'value of production' (VOP), both of which provide a basis on which to aggregate different products with differing manufacturing costs per unit. Sales revenue could in principle be another possibility, but is not used in Baxter since this could introduce a distorting factor where different products have differing profit margins. VOP (i.e. cost of manufacture), which is calculated by the company only at facility level (and is relevant for only some facilities) is used to calculate relative indicators at that level. To calculate overall relative indicators on a company-wide basis, an adjusted measure of COGS is used. The adjustment is in respect of any changes in inventory levels during the period, so that the adjusted measure of COGS reflects the volume of *production* rather than of *sales*. For non-production facilities, other relevant 'activity factors' are used—for example, warehouses base on the numbers of cases shipped.

In calculating relative indicators at a corporate level, the calculation is based on conservative (prudent) estimates of the overall underlying trends in production volumes (these are the same as are used to calculate 'cost avoidance' in the EFS), which

---

3   The term 'relative' is used here, for consistency with ISO 14031's terminology, although the term 'normalised' is the one usually used in Baxter in this context. As noted in Chapter 2, terminology varies and the definitions adopted in ISO 14031 are far from universal in practice.

Energy Use

Facilities

Energy source	Amount used			Billions of BTUs*		Cost of energy ($ million)	
	Units	1997	1996	1997	1996	1997	1996
Electricity	Million kilowatt hours	700	680	2,320	2,271	49.5	50
Natural gas	Million cubic feet	1,663	1,620	1,709	1,757	7.3	6.8
Fuel oil	Million gallons	6.0	5.8	870	838	4.1	3.9
Wood (scrap)	Million pounds	73	69	656	622	2.9	2.7
Propane	Million pounds	1.3	1.3	27	29	0.2	0.3
Total energy used by facilities				**5,582** **[5,883]***	**5,517** **[5,815]***	**64.0**	**63.7**

Aviation, Fleet and Trucks

Energy source	Amount used			Billions of BTUs*		Cost of energy ($ million)	
	Units	1997	1996	1997	1996	1997	1996
Aviation fuel	Thousand gallons	387	359	39	36	0.2	0.2
Gasoline	Thousand gallons	333	233	23	16	1.1	0.5
Diesel fuel	Thousand gallons	990	935	136	129	0.8	0.8
Total energy used by aviation, fleet and trucks				**198** **[208]***	**181** **[191]***	**2.1**	**1.5**

| **Total estimated energy used** | | | | **5,780** **[6,092]*** | **5,698** **[6,006]*** | **66.1** | **65.2** |

* British Thermal Units. Numbers in brackets show amounts in trillion joules.

Figure 4: ENERGY / USAGE

Source: 1997 CER, page 16

means that the calculations are capable of being independently verified. To enhance comparability over time, inventory-based COGS is used, which is inflation-adjusted using the average of three producer price indices, and the resulting figure then rounded down to the nearest whole number in order to be conservative. It is accepted that this is still only 'a rough cut'. Some might consider that similar adjustments should also be made for other potentially significant distorting factors such as changes in product mix. However, these are difficult in practice to adjust for, and in any case, Baxter considers, would be inappropriate. Its view is that changes in product mix can legitimately change the eco-efficiency of a company, and in any case will usually tend to be compensating distortions that cancel each other out.

◻ *Adjusting for Acquisitions and Disposals*

As noted under 'Categories of Indicator' above, Baxter reports indicators not only for the current year but also, for comparison, 'normalised/indexed' comparative figures for earlier years back to 1990. The calculation of 'Cost Avoidance in Report Year from Efforts Initiated in Prior Years back to 1990' in the EFS also requires historic data.

The problem is that a fast-changing corporation will alter in shape and size over time through acquisitions of new businesses and disposals and closures of existing businesses. The largest such change for Baxter in the 1990s has been the spin-off in 1996 of what became the new Allegiance Corporation, but there have been several large acquisitions in other years too. To maintain information integrity and valid comparability over time, the comparative figures have to be changed to reflect this. This is more straightforward for disposals and closures than for acquisitions, since the relevant data will be available in the usual Baxter format, so can be deducted from the previous years' database.

With acquisitions, this is unlikely. At best, some of the necessary data may be available, though may need revising to meet Baxter's own definitions and format. More often, if acquired facilities have not previously been collecting data in the same detail as Baxter, it will have to be estimated. Ron Meissen (Senior Director, Engineering, Corporate EHS) does this by, in the first place, assuming the same quantities in previous years as currently, then adjusting for any changes in production volumes and for major changes in plant design or product range. Sometimes proxies can be used to help in estimation—for example, costs paid to waste disposal contractors (which should be available from financial accounting records to estimate physical quantities of wastes). Sometimes, an initial approximate estimation at a corporate level has had the effect of prompting facilities subsequently to attempt again to make their own estimates, in some cases leading to the discovery of data of which they had not previously been aware.

4. Using Environmental Performance Evaluation in the Business

Baxter's annual performance evaluation and reporting cycle begins with data collection in December/January, compilation and analysis between then and April, and presentation of the internal SOP to the board in May, with publication of the external CER following in July/August. The SOP is presented in person by Bill Blackburn and his staff to the board. The latter's responses have included directions to put greater focus on a particular part of the programme (for example, last year on health promotion), and challenges on particular points such as the universality of common standards across all of Baxter's facilities worldwide.

The purpose of Baxter's system is not measurement for its own sake, but to stimulate improvement in performance. Goal-setting is central to this and has always been recognised as crucial, though there have been differences in approach over time in setting goals and targets. Ron Meissen believes that

> company-wide goals addressing a company's specific major aspects are extremely important—they help to focus on the desired reductions and improvements and achieve savings for the company. Without these goals neither the progress or savings would be achieved. Goals should be:
>
> - Specific (such as 'reduce hazardous waste generation by 20% by 2000 from 1998 levels')
>
> - Realistic, but at the same time challenging
>
> - Both long-term goals at a corporate level, which are periodically reviewed to see that they are still realistic, and shorter-term goals at the levels of facility and division
>
> - If possible, visionary: something catchy that the team can get excited about.

Baxter's goals for the early–mid 1990s were primarily set by the corporate centre on the basis of 'stretch' engineering estimates of what was possible—for example, the air emissions reduction target of 80% between 1988 and 1996. However, when these goals expired and the process of goal-setting began anew in the mid-1990s, Baxter had become much more decentralised as a corporation, so that there had to be more negotiation between the centre and divisions. According to Ron Meissen:

> we definitely wanted long-term goals: they're more dramatic, and there's more time for people to become familiar with them and take ownership for implementation. So we went for 2005 as the target year. But we had to recognise that there are differences in different divisions' and facilities' capabilities of achieving improvements. Those who've already taken all the low-hanging fruit found it harder to make big improvements than others who were not yet so advanced. So the divisional and facility sub-goals are now set as target rates of improvement over time.

The new goals are termed 'Collective Directional Goals' to indicate that:

▼ They are collective in that they were set with the involvement of all those who would be involved in achieving them, not merely handed down from the corporate centre, and that each division and facility would contribute to performance according to their own ability and opportunity.

▼ Although all divisions and facilities aim to move in the same direction, in terms of the same aspects of performance as defined by the centre, the rate of progress towards them could differ to reflect the fact that significant improvements may be more readily available to some units than to others.

▼ Goals would be periodically evaluated and adjusted upward if found to be too easy, or downward if progress was retarded by unforeseen factors such as new acquisitions.

The new goals were set to cover the nine-year period from 1996–2005, with reviews every three years. Within these three-year periods, it is up to divisions and facilities to set their own shorter-term goals in order to monitor progress towards these longer-term corporate goals.

One danger in this 'bottom-up' target-setting approach is that facilities/divisions may commit themselves only to what they know they can relatively easily achieve. But Ron Meissen believes that this is not a problem for well-established performance evaluation as

> there's lots of experience within and outside Baxter as to what can be achieved. The bigger difficulty is with new areas such as, for Baxter, energy conservation, which we began targeting at a corporate level only in 1996.[4] I think that facilities/divisions have tended to be less aggressive than they could have been in setting goals here—and will probably end up overachieving them. But this can be picked up in the regular reviews of the goals we'll be conducting every three years.

As discussed above, a core principle of Baxter's environmental management is to identify and draw attention to the financial implications of environmental actions, to continue to show that these can offer financial as well as environmental benefits. The CER therefore reports not only the areas of environmental performance for which goals are set and the amount of the goal for the corporation as a whole, but also the estimated savings and cost avoidance in the year 2005 (in millions of dollars) if the goal is achieved. These help both to determine which priorities to focus on (which led to a focus on energy and packaging) and engage the attention and commitment of others in the corporation. The financial targets are determined on the basis of estimates based on historical relationships between, for example, physical quantities of waste and the related costs, and for health and safety on benchmarked data from other companies which will be firmed up when Baxter's own H&S measurement

---

4   There had been an earlier successful company-wide energy efficiency programme between 1976 and 1986 which resulted in a 50% improvement in Baxter's overall energy efficiency over that period, but in 1986 the corporate group leading this was disbanded and responsibility delegated to the divisions.

system is in place. Progress will be monitored against both physical and financial targets.

Benchmarking is also an important element in Baxter's environmental performance evaluation process. As noted above, this began in the late 1980s when it compared the environmental performance of its facilities and found significant variations. It continued with regular benchmarking on achievement of SOA standards and corporate goals, and through the regular quality-controlling carried out on reported data, through comparing the data submitted by different facilities. There is also regular benchmarking, by reviewing and analysing other companies' CERs, in order to improve its own reporting.

Benchmark comparators are not generally so readily available for environmental indicators as for health and safety, where indicators such as injury statistics (per 100 full-time equivalent staff) are available from government, analysed by industry sectors, and can be used to identify and close gaps (though, even here, these tend to be 'lagging' rather than 'leading' indicators, which Baxter considers could provide a better barometer on the effectiveness of their health and safety programme). However, the results from benchmarking may need to be interpreted with caution. For example, when the volume of data collected on health and safety, and the incidence of auditing, were increased following the merger in 1996 with the environmental function, an initial effect was that reported injury and illness rates actually increased. This turned out to be because of better reporting—staff were now more likely to register on the system injuries or illnesses that might previously have gone unrecorded, as they now understood better what needed to be recorded and what did not. This had been a particular problem in countries where Baxter's information requirements differed from the legal reporting requirements of that particular country. However, this was only an initial effect, and the following year showed a substantial fall in the rate, as reported cases were analysed and proactive measure implemented.

5. Data Collection

The term 'garbage in; garbage out' (GIGO) has long been used in designing information technology (IT) systems to express that, however sophisticated the system may be in itself, the quality of its output is always dependent on the quality of its input: even the most sophisticated system cannot compensate for gaps in the data input into it. Baxter recognises that the GIGO principle applies equally to environmental performance measurement: however sophisticated the types of indicator used and the methods of reporting them may be, it is still critical to ensure the integrity of data on which these are based. It is therefore important, particularly in a widespread global corporation, to ensure that everyone is collecting and reporting data to common standards. A further consideration in a corporation with devolved responsibilities is that it is not practically possible, even if it were desirable, for a corporate staff function such as EHS to compel divisions and facilities, with their own business priorities, to report an indefinite volume of data.

Baxter has therefore aimed to make its data collection system as user-friendly as possible, while at the same time not postponing action until an advanced system could be available. Like the environmental performance evaluation and reporting system as a whole, the data collection system in Baxter has evolved over time—the principle has been that it is better to start with something simple and then improve it, rather than to be over-ambitious initially and run the risk of stalling. There have been three main phases:

▼ Phase 1, from 1990 to 1993, based on paper forms

▼ Phase 2, from 1994 to 1997, based on purpose-designed software applications distributed on floppy disk throughout the company, and with facilities submitting their data also on disk through divisions to the corporate centre. The software has been, successively, applications written in Excel and then Access, and finally a bespoke system written in Visual Basic.

▼ Phase 3, an Intranet-based system—the Environment, Health and Safety System Module (EHSSM), which was phased in during 1998–99

Phase 1 involved a paper form which the environmental manager (then the 'environmental co-ordinator') in each facility completed from the data available and then passed both to his/her own management and to the division. The divisions would then 'roll up' their facilities' data into a divisional report, which similarly would go to each of the divisions' management and to the corporate EHS function. They in turn would consolidate the divisional reports and report both to the board and externally. The system sufficed at the time, and in the absence of any alternative was an essential part of being able to measure and report environmental performance. However, it was time-consuming for both the inputters and the recipients of the data, and procedures such as data validation had to be carried out as a separate process, manually.

Phase 2 was a significant step forward, but was bedevilled by software incompatibility problems between the centre and divisions and facilities, which gradually improved but were never completely resolved. Some other fundamental problems in this phase were:

▼ Data entry was time-consuming for the facilities, with each report taking on average ten hours or more for each facility to complete.

▼ The exercise was perceived by facilities as being for the sole benefit of the corporate centre, to provide them (and, only incidentally, divisions) with data that they could then report to the board and externally in the CER.

▼ The facilities did not derive any direct benefit from their work in data collection and entry, not even a database that they could then use themselves; to obtain this would require them to re-input data into their own parallel local system. One facility environmental manager commented, 'We spend 15 hours collecting and entering the data, and then it all disappears.' Although this was an overstatement, since the facilities did also have their own reports on another disk, it indicated a widely shared perception at facility level.

▼ Data validation was a problem: the data entry exercise was undertaken by facilities only once each year, in a single major exercise at the year-end when divisional staffs were already busy. Although they were expected to quality-check the data before consolidating and passing it on to the corporate centre, the system was not conducive to this, which meant that this step was frequently omitted. This represented a major input of effort for a corporate team of four people for a significant proportion of their time over a period of up to ten weeks, in checking data and reverting to facilities when queries arose over its accuracy.

However, this phase did also provide an opportunity to improve the system by, for example, developing quality-checking techniques that could be built into the system, which were then carried over to Phase 3.

Bob Seguy (Manager, Industrial Hygiene and EHS Information Systems) was given the task of developing an Intranet-based system. One key asset was his experience in developing Health and Safety applications known within the company as 'BaxHealth'. Prior to the combining of the functions, he had worked in the Health and Safety function, which had a dedicated staff to manage the development of their applications. Baxter had begun to automate its H&S processes in 1994. Bob Seguy notes that

> BaxHealth was based on three technologies—Intelligent Fax, Client–Server and Intranet—each of which requires a different approach to developing systems. Early on in development we used a 'rapid development environment', which required a much closer working relationship between analysts/programmers and users. I required the analysts/programmers to spend time sitting alongside users, to experience at first hand the problems that they might meet in using the system.

Today, because Baxter has an integrated system, changes to the applications must be carefully thought through, so that a change in one part of the system does not adversely affect other applications. However, Bob Seguy feels that 'although we are not able to develop software so rapidly today, we are better able to leverage our existing technologies to meet the needs of our customers and the organisation.'

The introduction of BaxHealth meant that, for the first time, Baxter was recording all work-related injuries and incidents on a common platform, as well as employee chemical and physical exposure results. Additionally, Material Safety Data Sheets (MSDSs) could be maintained electronically and made available to the entire Baxter enterprise. Access to information was improved at all levels—facilities, divisions and corporate—which meant, among other things, that problems at facilities could sometimes be resolved from a distance rather than requiring a prolonged visit by a divisional or corporate specialist, reducing the need for expensive and time-consuming travel. One symptom of the effectiveness of the new system was its demand-driven expansion over time. Originally, in 1993, only four 'modules' had been planned:

MSDS, Occupational Incidents and Injuries, Industrial Hygiene and Occupational Health. Since then, demand from information customers for more information has stimulated the development of a further six modules, making ten in the system in total; and the rate of change in the company has meant that the system has been further upgraded in order to better handle changes in future.

The principle behind the Environment, Health and Safety System Module (EHSSM) is to move conceptually away from the earlier model of reporting environmental information upwards through the corporation to a model where facilities will track their environmental information on a real-time basis. By doing so, they would not duplicate the tracking or reporting of information that is requested by corporate EHS for the *SOP* and the CER.

The corporate *SOP* data collection system is now available via the corporation's Intranet, and 98% of the facilities can access the application. Provision has been made for the other 2% to access it indirectly, via their divisions. The system has built-in checks to ensure validity of the data at the point of entry, and can be checked periodically at divisional level, to compare the facility's performance against historical data, its goals or other criteria. The aim is that 95% of the information needed for the *SOP* should already be in the system before it is required for corporate-wide reporting, so that most of the report can be generated from the system at the click of a button. The remaining 5% would be text that would need to be added in order to explain performance.

The main benefits of the Intranet-based EHSSM compared to the previous system are:

- ◗ Steadier input of data through the year, avoiding a rush at the year-end

- ◗ Facilities can run off their own reports from the corporate system when they want, e.g. quarterly; and can avoid having to operate their own systems (i.e. Excel spreadsheets) in order to do this, in parallel to the corporate system, with the duplication of effort that this implies.

- ◗ It incorporates checking features to identify possible errors in data entry at source—if the data entered differs from the quantities recorded in the previous year by more than a pre-set percentage, the system will flag this and ask the inputter to confirm that the data which he/she has just input is in fact correct. This year, the task of verifying and validating data that remains to be done by the corporate team will be much reduced.

- ◗ The system will include a non-conformance log, to track internal audits and government inspections. This will record every occasion on which a government inspector gives a citation, identify the person responsible within Baxter, and notify the relevant corporate and division people within two hours of the original citation.

- ◗ The 'Assistant' module of the system enables users to specify which customised reports they want and how frequently; alternatively, a report can be automatically triggered by the occurrence of a specified incident. The aim is that data should be input only once, then the report writer can pull different reports from a single database.

▶ At present, audit findings are written up on paper and then typed into the database. The EHSSM can develop from this a scheduling tool to help to plan future audits and ensure that findings are followed up.

▶ EHSSM will track more in line with internal reporting requirements, to ensure that the system helps people throughout the entire organisation to meet company requirements. For example, there is a requirement that Corporate EHS is notified any time that there is a change at a facility such as the appointment of a new facility EHS manager or plant manager. The new system will allow the facility or division to make this change and corporate EHS will then automatically be notified, eliminating the step that previously required the facility or division to notify them. Similarly, the relevant divisional and corporate staff will also be automatically notified when additions or deletions of criteria or information in the system are made by the facility.

▶ The system will 'institutionalise the knowledge' by retaining knowledge within a system that will remain even if particular key individuals leave the corporation.

Bob Seguy summarises the progression as one that allows Baxter

> to leverage the information in the system and make it a management tool to help facility, division and CEHS managers to better manage and prioritise their EHS activities. The original concept was a database; now it is knowledge management: 'how can it help me to manage my business?'.

This has all been done within tight cost control. To demonstrate this, Bob Seguy carried out a benchmarking exercise with six other companies, from medical products, pharmaceuticals, aerospace and consumer products industry sectors. This asked the type of IT system used, and compared this against the cost of developing and running the system (see Table 1). The exercise was only approximate and relied on data provided by each of the participant companies, and it is always difficult to assure total consistency of data in these exercises. Nonetheless, it seems to demonstrate Baxter's success in achieving value-for-money in its environmental information systems.

It is essential in a widespread and devolved global corporation to ensure that data is being collected and reported consistently to the same corporate definitions and standards by all facilities. One lesson that Baxter has learned over the years has been the need to pay careful attention to standardising its definitions. For most employees, English is not their first language, so the corporate EHS function has to spell out in careful detail terms such as, for example, 'recycling off-site'—emphasising that, according to Baxter's definition, this term does not include anything that ultimately ends up in landfill. A further example is what counts as hazardous waste, since national definitions differ. A similar example from the health and safety area is that, in Switzerland, an employee's accident on his/her journey to work is legally defined as work-related, whereas in the US it is excluded. The data input screens therefore

Company	Global system	Total modules	Annual cost ($ million)	No. of people on project	Technology	Integrated*
Baxter	Yes	10	0.85†	4	Multi	Yes
Company A	No	6	0.40–0.60	Not known	Client–Server	No
Company B	No	5	0.25–0.40	7	Multi	No
Company C	No	3	0.25–0.40	Not known	Hybrid	No
Company D	No	0	1.0–1.25	7	Internet	No
Company E	Yes	7	1.0–1.25	Not known	Client–Server	Yes
Company F	No	2	0.60–0.80	4	Hybrid	No

* 'Integrated' means that different applications share information with each other or trigger another application. This means that, before considering any change to one element in the system, the potential effects on other elements should be considered.
† The system is operated for the benefit of both Baxter and another company, who share the total annual cost of $850,000 p.a.. approximately equally.

Note: The identities of the companies in the benchmarking exercise, other than Baxter, have been kept anonymous.

Table 1: COMPARATIVE COSTS OF ENVIRONMENTAL INFORMATION SYSTEMS

include extra fields to collect data that is 'country-related' as well as the core of 'company-related' data. This allows overseas facilities to use the same data set both to generate reports for their own governments (in their own native languages, where necessary) and also to report to Baxter's corporate centre.

To help local facility staff remain consistent with corporate policy, data definitions are now built into the EHSSM data collection system through brief informal explanations against each item. An example is 'non-hazardous wastes are those which are not regulated, and which are typically put into a dumpster/skip/etc.' (a range of different terms is used, to reflect usage in each country in which Baxter operates). A further principle that has been designed into EHSSM is to allow the computer to do as much of the computational work as possible. For example, data entry can be in metric, US or other measures, at the data inputter's preference, with the system making translations into a common unit.

6. *Plans for the Future*

These include:

- Development of sustainability reporting
- Further development of data collection within the corporation
- Extension of the EFS to facilities

◻ *Development of Sustainability Reporting*

Baxter's environmental performance evaluation and reporting since 1990 has been focused primarily on measuring achievement of its own goals. In future, the focus will become more external and ask how Baxter's environmental performance can be evaluated in terms of sustainability. This recognises the recent rapid increase of interest in sustainability generally,[5] and is also partly in response to demand from some of their own stakeholders—for example, some ethical funds are now starting to request social as well as traditional environmental information.

This will mean a need to consider and report on social as well as environmental aspects of performance, and therefore a challenge of first deciding what are the significant areas of performance, and then of defining appropriate indicators and obtaining the data needed to calculate them. According to Bill Blackburn, 'Research-ing this has shown us that there is little consensus of what or how to measure social performance at a corporate level—it's still all over the lot.' An intrinsic problem is whether it is appropriate to measure against a single set of standards socially, in the same way as Baxter does environmentally, where the same standards of performance are set, and measured against, worldwide. However, in the social context, it could be presumptuous to apply a single set of standards universally and it may be necessary to recognise that, unlike environmental indicators, some social indicators at least must be inherently local.

A practical problem that has been experienced in dealing with even the limited requests for social information that have been received from some ethical funds is obtaining the data internally. By its nature, social performance is not clearly the sole responsibility of the EHS or any other specific function, and, even if the desired data exists within the corporation in the first place, ownership is often diffused. Until it becomes recognised that a specific unit within the corporation has the responsibility of tracking and reporting on social performance for the organisation as a whole, obtaining data from other units can be problematic. EHS are therefore working with other functions such as Employee Relations, Business Practices and Community Relations (corporate communications) to brainstorm what aspects of performance are most relevant and decide how best to measure these. Although this process is far from complete, as Bill Blackburn comments, 'The process is important as much as the output: sitting down and talking has already helped us to clarify what we need to do and established that there is quite a lot of data already in the system—though there are also several gaps we need to fill.' He summarises the main stages in the process as:

- Identify who in the organisation are the relevant players and bring them together

- Brainstorm around the parameters

- Decide what it is reasonable to report on

---

5   See Chapters 23–27.

- Define a mechanism and a person to pull it all together
- Initiate reporting, evaluate it, and consider long-term direction for the initiative

One possibility that EHS is considering is to become involved in established corporate processes with a social responsibility dimension, such as working with the Business Practices group, which has developed a corporate ethics manual.

The move to sustainability reporting could also mean a shift in emphasis in environmental reporting too, with more emphasis on environmental condition indicators. Conversely, Bill Blackburn also wonders if

> the emphasis on triple-bottom-line reporting will dilute the importance of environmental performance. Also, how close are we getting to the financial element, as it is intended under sustainable development? I think back to some of the demands for information we experienced a few years ago during the NAFTA debate from Mexican community groups who requested such information as local wages paid, money invested in the local community, etc.

For the immediate initiative with the 1998 CER, Verie Sandborg does not anticipate a major change in content, though there will be some restructuring and redefinition of existing information to indicate how it relates to the concept of sustainability:

> in line with our evolutionary approach generally, we intend that taking this first step will provide the focus to stimulate the design and definition of a more extensive range of sustainability indicators in the future.

Further Development of Data Collection

The principal current development is the implementation of the EHSSM system. Beyond this, the EHS team would like to explore possibilities of integrating parts of the environmental data collection systems with other established similar systems, in particular the financial accounting systems. Some pilot studies are being explored, set up together with the Chief Financial Officer. It may also be possible to benefit from the experience gained from reporting environmental financial performance, applying a similar approach to measure costs and savings using the experience gained from initiatives already taken in the Health and Safety area. A template has already been developed to track the costs of work-related injuries and illnesses in the US, and is currently being globalised to make it applicable to Baxter's overseas facilities as well.

A further possibility could be to make further use of established Baxter processes such as the system of Value Improvement Programmes (VIPs) as a vehicle for environment-related proposals. VIPs are similar in principle to capital investment proposal appraisals, but broader in scope; they could include, for example, proposed changes in processes that do not involve any significant upfront investment, or product redesigns. Benefits that can be claimed for proposed VIPs include financial benefits such as cost savings which can be expected, and also less tangible benefits such as the extent to which a project contributes to corporate goals in areas such as customer service.

Examples of possible VIPs of an environment-related nature could include:

- Changing a process from using solvents for cleaning to an aqueous wash

- Switching from in-company production of components to an outside supplier who could promise clean methods of production. (An actual example is of one plant that was using a large quantity of freon for cleaning its products, who switched to a 'free moulding' process so that products were produced in a cleaner form in the first place and did not subsequently require the same extent of post-production cleaning.)

- Packaging reductions

Since the VIP process is already well established in Baxter, there could be advantages in using this procedure as a vehicle for proposing and advertising environmental improvements, since this would be in a form that others in the corporation would readily recognise. The environmental manager in one division took a proactive approach to this and asked all its facilities to identify projects that would help meet environmental goals (e.g. packaging, waste, etc.), to identify their likely costs and benefits, and to put these into the usual VIP format. When the facility plant managers saw the results, several expressed surprise, as they had not previously appreciated the potential of environment-inspired actions to deliver business benefits. One consequence was that the divisional management, which had not previously been monitoring any environmental data beyond what was necessary to comply with legal and corporate requirements, now required their own quarterly internal environmental performance report to track progress in implementing these projects and achieving the environmental and financial benefits that they offer.

◻ *Extension of the Corporate* EFS *to Facilities*

It has for several years been Bill Blackburn's aim to 'cascade' the preparation of *EFS*s down the organisation by encouraging facility-level and division-level environmental managers to draw up their own statements, to communicate and publicise the value of environmental initiatives more locally. Recently, the Irish Manufacturing Operations facility (IMO) has trialled this and in 1997 produced its own *EFS* for 1996, based on the methods and format of the corporate version.[6] The project demonstrated that this is possible at a level below that of the corporation as a whole, and it was found to be a valuable experience by the environmental people who were involved by providing a forum for them to work with financial and operational colleagues in a

---

6   A case study on the development of IMO's *Environmental Financial Statement*, in which the authors of this chapter were involved together with the environmental and financial staff of IMO, is available from Wolverhampton Business School (Working Paper WP 004/98, February 1998, ISSN 1363-6839).

situation that would otherwise not have been possible. A revision of the relevant parts of the data collection system will re-sort the information at facility level in order to provide a classification that will support the preparation of facility-level *EFS*s. It is hoped that, now that IMO has proved that this is possible, other facilities and divisions will also adopt the practice.

7. Conclusions

The lessons from Baxter's experience include:

- ▼ The evolutionary nature of EPER
- ▼ The need for data integrity
- ▼ The value of management performance indicators
- ▼ The complementarity of internal performance evaluation and reporting
- ▼ The need to relate environmental actions to business objectives

△ Evolution over Time

Baxter's EPER activities have continuously developed over the last decade in response both to changing external pressures and to internal factors such as organisational change and data availability.

The present performance evaluation and reporting system was not designed from the outset from a single clear concept of its function; rather, it has evolved over time. The joint determinants of what is reported have been the needs of the environmental programme, as new issues and projects have developed, and the availability of data. Given the cost of collecting data, and sensitivity in the divisions and facilities to information requirements imposed by the corporate centre, it is rarely possible to have the data easily available in an ideal form, and pragmatism has been needed. Estimation has been necessary when actual directly measured amounts were not available (or only at an unacceptable cost). However, efforts are made to restrict this to less material items, and to evolve over time from estimated to actual figures as data collection and reporting systems can be adapted. Since Baxter estimates that there has to be a two-year lead period between the company's environmental leaders deciding that an additional item of information is needed and facilities being able to set up systems to generate the data that can be reported, this is a gradual process.

This evolutionary consensual approach has some risks: for example, if the consequence were to lag behind other organisations who might be able to move more quickly. It could also potentially give a *de facto* veto on progress to less positive sections of the organisation (although this seems to have been avoided in Baxter to date). On the other hand, it makes it easier to learn from experience and to build trust and buy-in among operational levels. It also helps progress through what can be termed a 'ready, fire, aim' approach which tries to make things happen and learn by doing rather than waiting for perfect information. In order to minimise the load on those providing the data, Baxter has always been ready to look for short cuts and approximations until more formal systems could be established at reasonable cost.

◻ *Data Integrity*

Baxter recognises that the information reported is only as good as the data that is captured and collected through the organisation, and that the credibility of the environmental programme could be undermined if it were perceived to be based on inaccurate or over-optimistic data.

Where choices have had to be made between different possible definitions, these have usually been standardised on the more conservative basis, to maintain the credibility of the statement. Experience has shown the importance of keeping the figures 'clean and consistent'. At least up to a point, provided that the definition used is made clear, the actual choice of definition may be less important than users' ability to have confidence in the reliability of the figures.

It has also invested time in the unglamorous but essential process of developing its data collection system, while at the same time following an evolutionary approach and not allowing the absence of adequate systems in the early years to be a barrier. Since the company estimates that it can typically take two years from identification at a corporate level of what data is needed, to that data being generally available from all facilities, such a pragmatic attitude is necessary if reporting is to progress. However, this also means that, in the early stages, when estimates may be unavoidable in the absence of reliable direct measures, reporting has to be candid and disclose this estimation, at the same time as working to develop the system in order to improve this.

This principle is most obviously visible in the development of the data collection systems (firstly paper-based, then in successively more sophisticated IT systems) over time to include self-checking procedures and to make it more user-friendly for those at facility level on whom it depends for data. It is also evident in the attention paid to developing appropriate techniques for normalising data in order to calculate relative indicators, and in adjusting past time-series data in respect of corporate acquisitions and disposals. The latter in particular provides an example of an adjustment that is recognised as essential and taken for granted in financial accounting, but is not always followed in less well-developed areas of performance measurement—with, on occasion, unfortunate results for the credibility of some other companies who have been discovered to have been reporting over-flattering results.

◻ *The Value of Management Performance Indicators*

Baxter's experience with the SOA standards demonstrates how important management performance indicators can be during the early stages of environmental performance evaluation (see Chapter 2 for further discussion of this). Its EFS also shows the value of financial indicators in building organisational support for environmental action.

◻ *Complementarity of Internal Performance Evaluation and External Reporting*

Bill Blackburn has always been clear that his main aim is to exert an influence within Baxter. However, reporting externally is not only important for its own sake but also supports the internal programme by stimulating awareness. His experience has been that the need to disclose publicly annual progress towards environmental goals is also a strong stimulus for positive environmental management within the company. He is keen to experiment with sustainability reporting at an early stage for the same reason: 'When this goes into print, it will get even more attention from people in the company.'

◻ *The Need to Relate Environmental Actions to Business Objectives*

A key principle at Baxter has been to relate the environmental programme to the needs of the business as a whole, and avoid the environmental management function being perceived as no more than a hygiene factor on the fringe of the business. This is most evident in the EFS, which was designed primarily to draw the attention of managers throughout the organisation to the potential of good environmental management to contribute in conventional and measurable financial terms to profitability. It was also one reason behind building the process-based SOA approach in 1990 (and, currently, the BEHSt approach) on quality management principles, which were already well established in Baxter and part of the corporate language and culture. It is displayed too in the desire to develop so far as possible a broad scorecard of measures that reflect performance across the corporation and show that all in the organisation have the potential to make a contribution.

Ron Meissen sums up the attitude that the environmental management team has sought to encourage: 'Sometimes in the past individuals outside of Baxter have said to me, "How can Baxter afford to spend so much time and resources on environmental management?" My reply is, "We can't afford not to." ' Bill Blackburn concurs:

> We all saw in the 1980s how expensive it could be to get it wrong, with Superfund, the effect of real estate transactions, and fines; now we're showing that there are positive reasons too through opportunities for cost reductions. Either way, a strong proactive environmental programme is not only the right thing to have but makes good business sense.

▶ Baxter's Environmental Performance Report (CER) is available from their website at *www.baxter.com/EHS*, or from Verie Sandborg, Baxter International Inc., One Baxter Parkway, Deerfield, IL 60015, USA (tel. +1 847 948 4757).

13
Evaluating the Whole-Life Environmental Performance of Products

A Comparison of Eco-Points, Eco-Compass and Eco-Costing Approaches*

Martin Bennett, Andrew Hughes and Peter James

A NUMBER OF TOOLS are now available to evaluate the environmental performance of products (Simon *et al.* 1998). Two of the best known are eco-points schemes (which assign points to specific environmental dimensions and combine these into a single aggregate score) and eco-compass schemes (which score individual environmental dimensions and display them on a simulated compass or radar screen). A few organisations are also experimenting with life-cycle costing tools, which attempt to calculate the total internal and environmental costs of a product.

This chapter presents the results of an 'action research' project with a company, XYZ plc,[1] to evaluate the strengths and weaknesses of the approaches and select the most appropriate for aiding product designers and communicating environmental information to customers. XYZ is a large manufacturer of electronics-based business systems, in particular of property security systems such as intruder alarms. The aim of the project was to examine the potential offered by different methods to carry out environmental evaluations of XYZ products, both as a guide to product designers and potentially also as a marketing tactic for the benefit of customers for whom envi-

---

* This case study was prepared for the 'Eco-Management as a Tool of Environmental Management' (ECOMAC) Project, sponsored by the Commission of the European Union (DGXII, Environment and Climate; contract no. ENV4-CT96-0267).

1 'XYZ plc' is a fictitious name. For reasons of commercial confidentiality, the identity of the company and certain details of the project (including the recommendations arising from it) cannot be disclosed in this chapter.

ronmental performance is a criterion in purchasing decisions. It was set up as a limited-scale, low-cost pilot study based on a comparison of two of the company's products (an existing product, and its potential replacement).

One research aim was to assess the value of various tools in a situation faced in most product development processes, i.e. that the available life-cycle data is incomplete. The details of the calculations should therefore be seen as a 'worked exercise' used to illustrate general points rather than as a definitive assessment of the products.

Section 1 describes the two products that were used as the basis for evaluating the alternative techniques; Section 2 outlines the three methods of evaluation—eco-points, eco-compass and eco-costing; Sections 3, 4 and 5 provide details of the results obtained from their application and assess each on the basis of six criteria—precision; reliability; comprehensiveness; comprehensibility; credibility; and convenience; Section 6 draws conclusions from the exercise. An appendix then describes and explains a software package that is being developed by one of the authors (Peter James) to support evaluation of the sustainability of products.

1. *The Two Products*

Among other activities, XYZ manufactures and installs in customers' premises a range of intruder alarm systems, which are permanently on-line to a central control unit through a telecommunications infrastructure. One component in this is a device that interfaces between the physical system on the customer's premises and the national telecommunications system.

Two versions of this component (Products A and B) were used as the basis of this study. Product A is the component currently in use; Product B is a potential replacement which is currently in design. If successful, XYZ plans to replace all the Product As currently in use with Product Bs.

The physical design of both components is largely similar. The main difference is that a sub-component has been redesigned and offers substantially superior features and benefits, in particular:

- ▶ With Product B, faults will be diagnosed on-line from the central control unit and, in most cases, also repaired on-line; whereas with Product A this would require a visit by an XYZ maintenance engineer.

- ▶ There is a fast rate of product research and development in the industry. The Product B sub-component will enable a large proportion of potential future upgrades to be delivered on-line, rather than requiring (i) the manufacture of new components, and (ii) a visit by an engineer to install them.

The product evaluation is based on a 'quick and dirty' life-cycle assessment (LCA); the main flows and inventory for the two products are summarised below.

Production. Both products are composed mainly of PVC, but Product B differs from Product A in that it contains more electronic components, and therefore a larger quantity of metals such as silver and copper, and more non-PVC plastics. However, since full materials composition data was not available, the analysis assumed that both were composed of a given quantity of virgin PVC (the same quantity for each product). Based on a supplier's suggestion, some analysis was also undertaken of a variant made from the same quantity of an alternative material (ABS). It was also assumed that both products had identical production processes and transportation requirements in production.

Distribution. This was assumed to be identical for both products, with a figure calculated of 20 km travel in distribution per product. There was no data available on the packaging of components during distribution, but these are unlikely to be significant.

Use. For simplicity, the evaluation assumed only a five-year lifetime for the products. This is likely to discriminate against Product B in the analysis of environmental performance, since its remote diagnostics and ease of component replacement will probably mean a longer service life, and will also mean that dealing with faults will not require on-site diagnostics and maintenance visits. It was calculated that this translated into a significant saving of transport, expressed in average kilometres per product. On the other hand, remote diagnosis of Product B would require additional telecommunications infrastructure system energy.

End of life. When faulty, Product B can be repaired by replacing components, whereas Product A has to be disposed of. New components should also allow upgrading to provide new telecommunications services and therefore make Product B more durable over time. Also, the higher value and metals content of Product B may make re-use or recycling more economical at its ultimate end of life than is the case for Product A. However, since no detailed data was available on disposal routes, it was assumed that the two products would be dealt with in identical ways. Separate analyses were made of incineration, landfill and recycling options. Due to lack of data, no evaluation was made of the possible reconditioning and re-use of products, although discussions with recyclers suggested that this could be an option that might offer both economic and environmental benefits.

2. *The Three Methods of Evaluation*

Three possible tools of evaluation were examined: eco-points, eco-compass and eco-costing. These methods were selected for evaluation based on their potential relevance to the nature of XYZ's business, and their availability. These were applied, in turn, to evaluate Product B in comparison with Product A, with each tool being assessed against six criteria which were identified as desirable in management information generally:

- Precision
- Reliability

- Comprehensiveness
- Comprehensibility
- Credibility
- Convenience (i.e. feasibility in use)

These criteria were selected on the basis that the tools had not only to be accurate and reliable, but also useful in practice both for those applying them and for those receiving, interpreting and acting on the results.[2]

Based on this, their suitability was assessed for four main purposes that product environmental evaluation techniques can be required to serve:-

1. Identifying areas for attention in the product design and development process

2. Making choices between different products or different designs of the same product

3. Ensuring that products meet specified criteria and/or create no great environmental problems

4. Communicating environmental effects to customers and other interested parties.

2.1 *Eco-Points*

A number of eco-points schemes have been developed, of which the best known are those used by Philips and Volvo. They are similar in that they cover all life-cycle stages: production, distribution, use and end of life. For each stage, the user selects the appropriate materials, processes, usage and transportation details from the options provided in the software. The package then calculates an 'eco-score' for each of these elements, based on a number of points for a given quantity or usage.

This study evaluated the eco-points approach by testing the Eco-Scan software. This is based in part on the work of the Philips corporation and therefore has an industrial background, and is one of the most widely used of commercial packages.

Databases. Three separate databases of eco-points were provided with the Eco-Scan package, allowing users to select which they consider most appropriate. At the time of the study, these were:

- **Eco-Indicator** 95. This was developed in the Netherlands in 1995 by a multidisciplinary team of representatives from industry, science and government, and intended for use in Europe. It contains data on 120 materials, processes, etc.

---

2   The criteria are broadly similar in principle to those followed by the European Federation of Accountants (FEE) and described in Chapter 14. The FEE criteria were not available at the time of this study.

- **Idemat 96.** Idemat 96 is a materials and processes database developed by the Environmental Product Development section in the Industrial Design Engineering Faculty of Delft University of Technology, the Netherlands. It contains data for 290 parameters, including various modes of transportation, such as bus, rail, car, motorcycle and air. It also contains cost data for some of these (primarily materials).

- **Eco-Indicator 97.** This database contains around 280 eco-indicators which have been collated from public sources by environmental experts from Philips. The database has been tested in practice by both designers and engineers as well as by materials and processes experts, and is in use within Philips.

Users of Eco-Scan can also insert their own eco-points assumptions, if desired. The 'Eco-Indicator 97' database was selected for use in this exercise, on the basis of its industrial provenance.

Calculation of eco-points. Eco-points scores within Eco-Scan are based on a 'distance-to-target' methodology. The underlying premise is that there is a correlation between the seriousness of an effect, and the distance between the current level and the target level to achieve sustainability. Thus if, for example, acidification would have to be reduced by a factor of 10 in order to achieve a sustainable society, whereas smog levels would require reduction by a factor of only 5, then acidification is weighted in Eco-Scan as being twice as serious.

Some other eco-points systems define targets on the basis of government policies. However, the Eco-Indicator 97 database is based on the judgements of scientists from both inside and outside Philips. The main criteria used are:

- Human wellbeing: with a target of one fatality per million inhabitants per year, and minimal health effects

- Ecosystem degradation: targets have been chosen at which, over several decades, 'only' 5% degradation of the ecosystem will occur.

This results in the weights shown in Table 1, which reveals that high priority must be given to limiting the use of substances that cause damage to the ozone layer, and to the use of pesticides. Furthermore, serious consideration must be given to the diffusion of acidifying and carcinogenic substances.

A number of effects that some might regard as environmental problems have not been included for particular reasons, and these are:

- **Toxic substances** which are a problem only in the workplace. Many substances are harmful only if they occur above a certain concentration. Such harmful concentrations can occur relatively easily in the workplace, while the concentration in the outside atmosphere often still remains very low and well below the damage threshold. This is both because in the wider environment the substances are generally greatly diluted, and also because many substances disappear from the atmosphere due to natural decomposi-

Environmental effect	Weight	Criterion
Greenhouse effect	2.5	5% ecosystem degradation = 0.1°C rise every 10 years
Ozone layer depletion	100	Maximum probability of 1 fatality per year per million inhabitants
Acidification	10	5% ecosystem degradation
Eutrophication	5	5% ecosystem degradation
Summer smog	2.5	Minimal respiratory effects and maximum 5% ecosystem degradation
Winter smog	5	Minimal respiratory effects and maximum 5% ecosystem degradation
Pesticides	25	5% ecosystem degradation
Airborne heavy metals	5	Minimal health effects
Water-borne heavy metals	5	Minimal health effects
Carcinogenic substances	10	Maximum probability of 1 fatality per year per million people

Table 1: WEIGHTS OF ENVIRONMENTAL EFFECTS BASED ON ECO-SCAN ECO-POINTS SYSTEM

tion processes. Only substances that actually occur in harmful concentrations are included in the database. This means that a product with a low Eco-Indicator score can still potentially cause poor working conditions because substances are released that are harmful on a local scale.

▼ **Exhaustion (depletion) of raw materials.** Only emissions and other direct health and ecological impacts are considered; the database does not take into account issues of resource depletion.

▼ **Land requirements.** Space requirements for waste disposal and other land-using activities are not considered, on the grounds that they do not directly impact on human health and ecology (unlike emissions and water pollution resulting from land-using activities, which are included).

Eco-Indicator 97 also has a distinctive approach to end-of-life issues. Where they exist, the environmental benefits of recycling can be recognised in two alternative ways: eco-points can be credited either for the use of recycled materials in the manufacture of new products, or for the recycling of materials at the end of the life of the old product. The database developers argue that, even if a product is designed for recyclability, this does not guarantee that it will necessarily actually be recycled at the end of its life. Hence, Eco-Indicator 97 assigns eco-points instead to the use of recycled materials, in contrast with the Eco-Indicator 95 database which credits them to the end-of-life stage. The consequence of this is that the use of PVC within mixed recycled plastics is credited with 30% fewer eco-points, and the use of recycled PVC monomer with 90% fewer eco-points, than if virgin PVC were used. Clearly, the value of the Eco-Indicator 97 database, and of any other such database, is dependent on the credibility of these assumptions and the weightings that they generate.

2.2 Eco-Compass

The eco-compass has been developed by Dow Chemical to provide a simple, visual summary of LCA data (Fussler with James 1996). It is based on the indicators of eco-efficiency developed by the World Business Council for Sustainable Development (WBCSD), with some minor amendments (DeSimone and Popoff 1997). The eco-compass has six 'poles' or dimensions (see Fig. 1 in Section 4):

- Energy intensity
- Mass intensity
- Health and environmental potential risk
- Resource conservation
- Extent of revalorisation (re-use, remanufacturing and recycling)
- Service extension

The latter measures the ability to deliver greater service from given inputs, for example by improving durability.

Mass intensity. 'Mass intensity' refers to the physical mass of the materials that make up a product, plus the additional weight of materials displaced or consumed during its production and distribution (this additional element is described as the product's 'rucksack'). The measure used is 'material intensity per unit of service'.

Energy intensity. Energy inputs over the whole life-cycle are totalled and converted to 'energy intensity per unit of service'.

Health and environment potential risk. The following indicators are used, scored individually, then totalled:

Human health risks

1. Short-term acute human toxicity
2. Long-term carcinogenic, teratogenic and mutagenic effects
3. Potential danger of persistent toxins that bioaccumulate
4. Emissions to the atmosphere of organic substances
5. Potential for creating allergies and irritations
6. Accident risk

Environmental risks

1. Terrestrial eco-toxicity

2. Aquatic eco-toxicity

3. Acidification potential

4. Nitrification potential on biological oxygen demand (BOD)

5. Global warming potential

6. Ozone depletion potential

Revalorisation. All opportunities for use of materials at end of product life are accounted for. This can be in any of the following manifestations:

- Re-use
- Remanufacturing
- Recycling
- Incineration for energy recovery

Resource conservation. This focuses on the nature and renewability of energy and materials needed for a product or process. The exercise is not carried out in isolation: the effect of a particular material on biodiversity is also important. For example, a crop monoculture that can be grown year after year may be renewable, but, if it reduces the habitat of an endangered species, then it is not sustainable.

Service extension. Service can be extended through a variety of ways, including:

- Increased reliability
- Increased durability
- Reparability and upgradability
- Multifunctionality
- Shared use

Again, however, criteria should be looked at not in isolation but in unison; a multifunctional product is of limited extra value if any one of the functions is unreliable.

The scores. The scoring scale used for each dimension is 0–5, with 2 being the score allocated to the 'base case', i.e. the comparator, or reference point—usually an existing product. The performance of another product or product variant is then scored relative to this, on the scale shown in Table 2. A deliberate aim in defining bands of this width is to provide a 'stretch' scoring system which is deliberately biased against environmental improvements that are merely incremental, in order to encourage

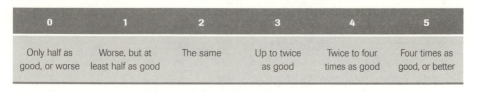

0	1	2	3	4	5
Only half as good, or worse	Worse, but at least half as good	The same	Up to twice as good	Twice to four times as good	Four times as good, or better

Table 2: ECO-COMPASS SCORING SCALE

industry to search for significant 'step' improvements, consistent with the 'Factor 4' and 'Factor 10' philosophy. This should make the method more credible to those environmental activists who have sometimes criticised industry for making only marginal improvements in environmental performance that are insufficient to be consistent with the demands of sustainability. The corresponding disadvantage of this feature is that an eco-compass score of 1 or 3 may have only limited significance, since this can be achieved through only marginal changes for better or worse, and the method would not distinguish between these and more substantial improvements (or deteriorations) by a factor of up to 2.

The eco-compass requires no data conversions or weightings, and is therefore more transparent than the eco-points method. However, it does depend on the availability of accurate life-cycle data for the key parameters, and the reasons for the six compass poles are not completely self-evident.

2.3 *Eco-Costing*

An eco-costing approach analyses the environment-related costs created by a product. Unlike the output from an eco-points or eco-compass analysis, the result is in a monetary form and is therefore expressed in the same unit of account as other primary corporate objectives such as profit and shareholder value. This has the attraction that it can be applied to a wide range of alternatives, not limited to those that are environment-related.

Two different aspects of eco-costing must be distinguished. A narrow interpretation focuses on those environment-related costs that are internal to the organisation; a broader approach considers the external costs to society, either alone or in conjunction with the internal costs.

Internal costs. There is no question that internal environment-related costs are relevant and should be included in any analysis; the issue is whether conventional accounting and project appraisal methods are always adequate to achieve it. There is considerable evidence that environment-related costs are either treated by conventional costing systems as overheads, or alternatively that they appear only after some time, so that environmentally positive actions (e.g. the introduction of clean technology) that are cost-effective may not immediately appear to be so.

One response to this is to introduce activity-based costing approaches which assign costs to the activities that generate them, so that environmental performance can be recognised as a significant 'cost driver'. Another response is to develop methods of life-cycle costing that bring into account the long-term as well as the immediate effects of current decisions (Brouwers and Stevels 1997).

External costs. The broader approach considers the external costs to society of the company's actions. It is not so obvious that this is relevant in business: a hard-nosed short-termist attitude might hold that, if these costs are in fact external and will therefore not impact the company's own financial performance, there is no reason to take them into account. The case for not only recognising an organisation's external environmental impacts but also calculating their monetised value depends on two conditions:

- The **principle**: that it is accepted to be appropriate that external effects should in fact be considered by the business, for whatever reason

- The **method**: that calculating a monetised value of external effects is judged to be the most appropriate method to measure these (rather than other methods, such as the eco-compass or eco-points)

On the first point, two reasons are advanced to justify taking externalities into account in business decisions:

- That enlightened organisations need to be aware of the external effects of their actions, both for corporate responsibility for its own sake and to protect the organisation's 'licence to operate' in the long term.

- As environmental factors become increasingly pressing both for business and for society generally, costs that are currently external may become actual and internal, either through market-based instruments of government policy (e.g. environmental taxes) or directly through market forces.

If the principle is accepted, the question becomes one of method: is the calculation of a monetised value of external effects the most appropriate approach? This is not obvious; although the principle and practice is well established in the public sector, it can be controversial even here, and it is unusual in the private sector. The technique inevitably rests on several assumptions, each of which can be challenged. They can be objected to not only because of the intrinsic difficulty of measuring the value (which would apply whichever unit of account were used), but also—since the technique necessarily involves assigning a monetary value to human mortality and morbidity, and to ecological damage—on principle by those who are uncomfortable with the concept of 'putting a price on a life' or on nature.

Advocates of the technique argue that monetisation does no more than make explicit what is in any case inescapable, if only implicitly, since any decision in which both mortality and costs differ between alternatives (and in which both have some influence on the final decision) must indirectly involve some trade-off. Even if this is not taken into account directly by the decision-takers, subsequent analysis of the decisions reached can deduce the effective 'shadow prices' that were used in reaching the decisions. The argument for making this explicit is that otherwise the shadow prices actually used may be arbitrary and inconsistent. One UK study (Moody 1977) analysed a number of safety regulations and other public expenditure decisions, and found implicit values which he estimated to range from £50 per life, implied by the decision not to spend on a particular medical screening programme, to £20,000,000 per life saved by a change in building regulations following the collapse of a block of flats caused by a gas explosion.

Economists have developed a number of techniques for costing environmental externalities. The **damage costs** method aims to assess the cost actually caused by the external impact, estimated through a variety of alternative techniques such as contingent valuation, hedonic pricing and travel cost methods. The **cost of control** approach is less ambitious. Instead of attempting directly to assign monetary values to non-monetary factors such as human lives, it takes as a basis a level of impact that is considered to be sustainable, and calculates the cost of moving from present performance to that level (analogous to the 'distance-to-target' philosophy of the Eco-Scan software discussed above). Estimates have been published for a number of environmental effects, particularly those related to road transport, though there is still considerable controversy over the validity of these figures.

Most of these studies have been carried out by economists primarily interested in the development of public policy rather than as a potential business tool; for example:

- To argue the case for, and estimate the appropriate levels of, market-based instruments of public policy such as environmental taxes (Maddison *et al.* 1996; Pearce *et al.* 1989; Pearce 1991; Pearce *et al.* 1993; Pearce and Barbier 1994)

- To offer an alternative to the conventional national income accounts, which would replace Gross Domestic Product with a broader measure of 'quality of life' (see Chapter 1)

The range of environmental impacts to which the technique has been applied has also been limited, with the main areas of interest being:

- Road transport (Maddison *et al.* 1996)

- Energy use (e.g. the European Commission's 'ExternE' study [European Commission 1995])

- Air quality (e.g. by Ontario Hydro [Tuppen 1996])

The use of externalities costing in the private sector is less common, though there are a number of reasons why organisations might wish to calculate, or take account of, the externalities created by their processes or products:

- To demonstrate to customers and others that a particular product, process or activity does not create major externalities, or that it creates fewer externalities than alternatives

- To inform decision-making by allowing comparisons between the externalities created by different options

▼ To highlight significant externalities in order to provide an impetus for organisational or governmental action to reduce them

Two examples of the use of externalities costing in business are BSO/Origin and Ontario Hydro (Tuppen 1996). BSO/Origin used a cost-of-control approach to produce an 'environmental value added' statement, which restates the conventional profit and loss account in value-added form, and brings in quantified values of the business's environmental impacts. The amounts are based on calculations of long-term costs of control in the Dutch National Environmental Protection Plan.

Ontario Hydro uses a damage costing approach, in a four-stage process, to calculate a single monetary amount to reflect environmental impacts arising from different sources of power generation (nuclear, fossil fuel and hydro) and from different generating stations. They found that the external costs could add up to 1.6¢ to the cost of a unit of electricity (compared with an average internal cost of 4¢), although, since this was based initially on only a limited range of impacts, a wider range might have produced higher figures.

3. *Eco-Points Evaluation*

Twelve options were identified for assessment—each possible combination of:

▼ Three product options: Product A; Product B, if made of PVC composition; and Product B, if made of ABS composition

▼ Four end-of-life options: landfill; municipal waste; recycling; and incineration

Eco-points scores were calculated for each of these combinations using the Philips Eco-Indicator 97 database. These showed that:

▼ On the available data, the energy consumption of both Products A and B over their life-cycles is dominated by the 'energy overhead' of the electronic communications made over the telecommunications infrastructure. This demonstrates that, as a general rule (though not necessarily relevant in this particular case), any changes in volume of usage that might result from a product change are likely to be one of the most important environmental issues.

▼ Conversely, the reduction in transport emissions from the remote diagnosis and repair which is possible with Product B (though not Product A) is insignificant in environmental terms over the first five years. (However, this conclusion might be changed by an analysis over a longer period, since the failure rates of Product A would probably increase in the long-term.)

▼ Eco-Scan assigns 1,225 eco-points to a kilogram of silver, compared to 9.38 for a kilogram of ABS and 4.24 for a kilogram of PVC. However, silver was excluded from the analysis in this exercise since data was not available on the quantities used in each product. If this data had in fact been available, this—and possibly other non-ferrous metals—might have emerged from an eco-points analysis as a major environmental issue associated with the product.

▼ The Eco-Scan software suggests that, overall, PVC is environmentally preferable to ABS, and that in either case landfill is a better environmental option at end of life than recycling.

The last result was an unexpected finding, though it was explicable, on investigation, by the judgement (described in Section 2.1) made by the Eco-Scan designers on the appropriate point at which to recognise the benefits of recycling. This demonstrates how the assumptions contained within such software drive their conclusions, and therefore how carefully they need to be examined.

⌐ *Assessing an Eco-Points Approach*

The eco-points approach was assessed against each of the criteria identified (as described in Section 2 above).

▼ **Precision.** The method produces results of high apparent precision, since its outputs are calculated and reported to several significant places.

▼ **Reliability.** The degree of perceived reliability depends on the user's faith in the judgements of the experts who designed the system (in this case, from Philips and Delft University). The results are very sensitive to the weighting and scoring mechanisms on which the particular eco-point scoring system has been based. The quantity of life-cycle data that is available is less critical, since this exercise demonstrated that meaningful conclusions can still be reached: the impacts of differing solutions can be compared even on the basis of only limited data, albeit rather in isolation from the full environmental picture.

▼ **Comprehensiveness.** In this project, the database covered all the materials and processes that were needed in the analysis, with one specific exception. A review of the full list of parameters included in the database suggests that it is likely to be adequate for most purposes—it is clearly satisfactory for Philips. The system also offers users the option of compiling their own bespoke database, which could also include further items, though this would then involve the difficulty of needing to reach decisions on weightings.

▼ **Comprehensibility.** The format and layout (which uses 'personal organiser'-type graphics) is straightforward to follow. The terms that are used are not technical or scientific, and descriptors are provided in everyday language. Designers should have no significant problems in understanding it.

▼ **Credibility.** The scoring and weighting criteria (see Section 2.1) are the main factors in determining which options are concluded to be preferable; however, these are not universally accepted. The preference shown by the system for landfill as the best end-of-life option, for example, may be inconsistent with current opinion in many countries. Also, as the Brent Spar incident demonstrates, it takes no account of possible public reaction if large quantities had to be disposed of at a single time in a manner that was generally perceived to be not environmentally responsible, such as by landfill.

▼ **Convenience.** The specifications for each product are recorded in the format of a computerised notebook or personal organiser, and options are offered to present the information in the form of graphs or tables. The tables are particularly useful since they enable the scores for the whole process to be compared between two different products. The 'wizards' provided for calculating energy usage over product life-span, and the provision of travel distances between various European locations in particular types of vehicle, also facilitate the user's task.

◻ *Eco-Points: Conclusions*

The value of eco-points schemes such as Eco-Scan is that they can provide quick analyses of the overall environmental effect of products and of how different elements of the design contribute to this. Their main disadvantage is that they are ultimately dependent on subjective weightings of different environmental effects and that, as with Eco-Scan's bias towards landfill rather than recycling, these are not always transparent to users. Hence, they are particularly well suited to identifying areas for attention and for exploring (rather than making) choices between different alternatives. They are less appropriate as a method of communication, since an eco-point score is meaningless in itself, and some users such as customers and other stakeholders may challenge the assumptions upon which it rests.

4. Eco-Compass Evaluation

Several composite eco-compasses were plotted in order to compare different alternatives. The eco-compass for the basic comparison between Product A and Product B is shown as Figure 1.

The analysis was limited by the data available in several ways:

Energy intensity. It was assumed that Products A and B comprised identical quantities of PVC, therefore requiring the same quantity of energy in production. No data was available on energy consumption in assembly, production or at end of life, so this was excluded. Energy used in transportation—which was assumed to differ only in the use stage, where Product B's remote diagnosis facility reduces its transport effects—was calculated to show a marginally lower quantity for Product B. This meant that in the eco-compass a score of 3 was assigned to Product B.

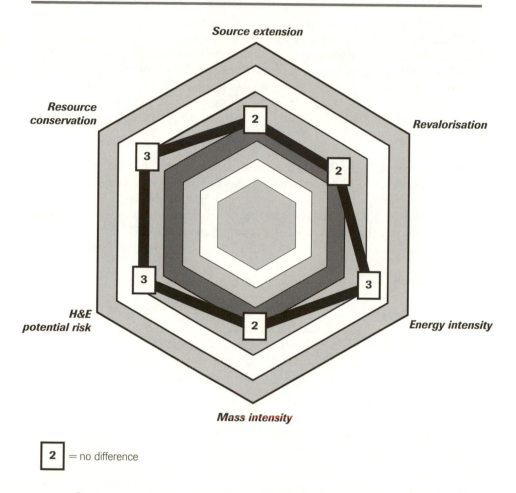

Source extension

Resource
conservation

Revalorisation

H&E
potential risk

Energy intensity

Mass intensity

2 = no difference

Figure 1: ECO-COMPASS, EVALUATING PRODUCT B RELATIVE TO PRODUCT A

Mass intensity. It was assumed that both products had the same mass, so that Product B scored 2 on this dimension.

Health and environmental potential risk. In the absence of detailed data on composition and production processes, the analysis was restricted to the impacts of transport. Externalities data—which is based on calculations of environmental impact—was used as a proxy for health and environmental potential risk. It was assumed that the cost of accidents was 2.3p per km and of emissions 4p per km (Maddison *et al.* 1996). This produced a marginally lower figure for Product B, which again resulted in a score of 3.

Resource conservation. There was no difference between the products in the quantity of fossil fuel that was required in the manufacture of the PVC (the main material in both). However, Product B required a marginally smaller quantity in use (a difference of approximately 1%—although over a high anticipated volume of production this would still have generated a significant total saving) and therefore scored 3.

By comparison, the ABS variant of Product B required significantly more fossil fuel in manufacture than when made from PVC—overall, around 50% worse. However, since this fell within the range ('up to twice as good') of a score of 3, the Product B/PVC option still scored only this same rating even when compared against Product B/ABS.

Service extension. In the absence of definite data, it was assumed that both Product A and Product B had identical patterns of use and therefore both scored 2. However, other features of the product (not considered in this exercise for reasons of confidentiality) could enhance both its functionality and its durability. If it were possible to measure these, it would probably score higher on this dimension—possibly a 4 or even a 5.

Revalorisation. No data was available on this, so both products were therefore scored as 2.

As with the Eco-Scan analysis, the limited availability of data meant that a full analysis could not be completed, so that the eco-compass profile (Fig. 1) appears to show the two products to be more similar than may actually be the case. Some points that might be expected to change in a fuller analysis are:

- A much higher ranking for service intensity, based on the ability of Product B to provide higher, and environmentally better, customer service through offering a wider range of options. Some of these could substitute for the purchase of other new physical products, each with their own environmental impacts.

- A more precise estimate of health and environmental risk. If 'precautionary' rather than consensus assumptions were made about the health effects of PVC—based on the recent EPA report on dioxin and on suggestive if inconclusive research on the possible health effects of some additives used in its manufacture—then the ABS alternative would probably be ranked much higher on environmental and health risk potential.

- A much higher ranking for an ABS-based Product B on the revalorisation axis. ABS is a high-value material which is both cost-effective and feasible to recycle, whereas this is not always the case with PVC.

◻ *Assessing an Eco-Compass Approach*

Precision. The deliberately wide ranges for each point (so that, for example, an improvement of 1% could produce the same rating as an improvement of 99%) mean that precision is low.

Reliability. Reliability is no more than reasonable, since the method requires considerable judgement and aggregation of different aspects within (though not across) the different dimensions.

Comprehensiveness. The six points of the compass cover all major environmental eventualities conceptually. However, the comprehensiveness of an eco-compass analysis largely depends on the data input. The more comprehensive the life-cycle data, the more complete will be the eco-compass picture. Clearly, if the picture is incomplete, it could be harmful to use the compass as a corporate communication tool. Also, since it adopts a holistic approach, a compass with limited data input would be of little value to, and could even mislead, a designer.

Comprehensibility. A major attraction of the eco-compass is its visual impact which enables findings to be understood immediately. Conceptually, it is very easy to grasp, though details of the scoring system can be obscure.

Credibility. The eco-compass requires no data conversions or weightings, and is therefore more transparent than the eco-points method. As a 'stretch' scoring system, it is also biased against merely incremental environmental improvements, which should make it credible to environmentalists. On the other hand, an eco-compass score of 1 or 3 may have only limited significance if it is based on only marginal changes for better or worse.

However, the method does depend on the availability of accurate life-cycle data for the key parameters, and the reasons for the six compass poles are not completely self-evident.

Convenience. The final stage of plotting positions on the compass from calculations is straightforward, but the two preceding stages can be time-consuming:

1. Identifying the relevant data in the first place from the life-cycle analysis

2. Making the calculations from the data

These activities are more time-consuming than for the eco-points calculation, since for the latter the software performs some of those calculations and data retrieval as part of the distribution of eco-points. Naturally, there will be a threshold beyond which it would be impractical to include more data for reasons of time and resources, but there will also be another lower threshold below which the outcome of the compass would be unreliable.

◻ *Eco-Compass: Conclusions*

The eco-compass provides a holistic, visual overview of products using dimensions that have been subject to considerable discussion and development by the international business community. It was considered to be helpful for Purpose 2, making choices between different products or different designs of the same product; and with some explanation, also for Purpose 4, the communication of environmental performance to customers and other interested parties. It can also, when used as part of a workshop process, contribute to Purpose 1, identifying areas for attention in the product design and development process. One problem is that it requires reasonably complete LCA data and also that scoring some of the dimensions can be difficult.

5. *Eco-Costing Evaluation*

Section 2.3 outlined the distinction between internal environment-related costs (those that are already being incurred by a company or its customers and suppliers) and external costs, which are borne by society and the natural environment. The latter are important for both their social implications and also since there is a trend for such external costs in the long term to be internalised through taxation and other means. A calculation of the external costs associated with a product therefore offers a means of measuring that part of its environmental performance that is not already reflected in the costs being currently incurred by the business.

◻ *Internal Costs*

As several studies have already been done on this topic (for example, Brouwers and Stevels 1997), a review of XYZ's internal product costings methods was not a part of this study, and in any case the data that would have been required was not fully available. However, it did become apparent as the exercise proceeded that there could be opportunities, by making changes at the design and introduction phase, to realise direct environment-related savings for Product B over the life of the project. This is consistent with experience with other companies, where typically whole-life costs are not always calculated in full.

Contact with manufacturers and disassemblers suggested that analysis of environment-related internal costs might reveal opportunities for savings, either for XYZ directly or elsewhere in the supply chain, for example:

- PVC moulding requires costly ventilation equipment which is not needed for ABS.

- Use of non-ferrous metals makes mechanical separation from plastics more difficult.

- If re-use or reconditioning is an option, screen-printed logos are easier to obliterate than are raised moulded logos.

However, lack of adequate cost data meant that these issues could not be explored further.

◻ *External Costs*

The calculation of external costs requires two elements of data, in sufficient detail and to an acceptable level of reliability:

Source	Air pollution	Climate change	Noise and vibration	Accidents and injuries	Congestion
Royal Commission (1994)	⟵ 4.6–12.9 (aggregate) ⟶			5.4	
Pearce *et al.* (1993)	⟵ 2.8 (aggregate) ⟶		0.6	4.7–7.5	13.5
European Federation for Transport and Environment (1993)	6.4	2.0	0.4	3.9	
Earth Resources Research (1993)	2.5	0.7	2.1	4.8	15.0
Maddison *et al.* (1996)	19.7	0.1	2.6–3.1	2.9–9.4	19.1

Table 3: ESTIMATES OF SOCIAL COSTS OF UK ROAD TRANSPORT SYSTEM IN £ BILLION PER ANNUM

▼ Life-cycle assessment data on the physical attributes of the product, process, etc.: e.g. the energy and raw materials required in production, the distances to be travelled in inbound and outbound logistics and after-sales, etc. (To make a difference in any particular analysis, it is also necessary that these should differ significantly as between the two [or more] alternatives being considered.)

▼ A figure for the external costs incurred for each impact, per unit of impact.

The availability of physical data is equally required by an eco-points analysis (though less so for the eco-compass), and this has already been covered in that section of this chapter.

The calculation of external costs per unit of impact is a major exercise, and this study did not attempt to carry out any such exercise but instead accessed the results of past externality costing studies which are already in the public domain. Despite the status of their authors and the rigour and depth of the studies, these results are often contentious and of dubious reliability. This is confirmed by the wide ranges of values produced for the same environmental impact by different studies, as shown in Tables 3 and 4. The differences are due to the different assumptions and methodologies adopted by different studies. Even the keenest supporters of this approach claim no more than approximate accuracy, though they argue that this is still more accurate than an analysis that does not take this step and which thereby effectively assigns an implicit value of zero.

There are three areas where the external costs of Product B could be of economic and social significance, and where internalisation might therefore occur in the medium to long term. These are:

▼ Acceptance of some of the more pessimistic assessments of the environmental impacts of PVC, particularly with regard to the effects of dioxins and hormone-mimicking chemicals. One scenario could be a ban on PVC, which would require the redesign of Product B. Another could be the classification of PVC as a hazardous material, which would create increased handling and disposal costs.

▼ More stringent regulations on the disposal of telecommunications equipment, requiring introduction of a take-back loop for Product B (and also for Product A).

▼ Increased transport costs due to fuel levies, carbon and other environmental taxes, and other measures to reduce the environmental impacts of road transport (which could work to the advantage of Product B).

Source	Air pollution	Climate change	Noise and vibration	Accidents and injuries	Congestion
Royal Commission (1994)	⟵ 8.26–23.16 (aggregate) ⟶			9.69	
Pearce *et al.* (1993)	⟵ 5.03 (aggregate) ⟶		1.08	8.44–13.46	24.24
European Federation for Transport and Environment (1993)	11.53	3.56	0.71	7.03	
Earth Resources Research (1993)	4.49	1.26	3.77	8.62	26.93
Maddison *et al.* (1996)	32.72	0.18	4.32–5.15	4.82–15.61	31.73

Table 4: ESTIMATES OF SOCIAL COSTS OF UK ROAD TRANSPORT SYSTEM IN £ PER 1,000 PASSENGER-KILOMETRES

Because of the insufficiency of data, it was not possible to calculate a full external cost for Product B as compared with Product A. The study therefore focused on the area where data is most readily available and where in this case there is also the clearest distinction between the two products—transport.

Their respective external costs for road transport were calculated and then summed. First, their road transport requirements, expressed as vehicle-kilometres per product, were calculated based on information and estimates provided by XYZ, for the relevant life-cycle stages:

- Transport of components, pre-manufacture
- Transport required in distribution
- Transport required during use, in servicing

These were then summed and monetised, expressed as pence per passenger-kilometre, based on the external costs associated with the main adverse environmental impacts of road transport calculated by Maddison *et al.* (1996):

- Air pollution
- Climate change
- Noise and vibration
- Accidents and injuries
- Congestion

This showed that, over the expected volumes of products, there would be a modest but significant reduction in the total external costs of Product B as compared with the comparable total for Product A. A more extensive calculation would require further data on both physical attributes, and external costs of a wider range of environmental impacts.

Assessing Eco-Costing

Precision. The total amounts of external costs could be calculated with a high level of apparent precision.

Reliability. The reliability of the results is modest, since—as for eco-points—the outcome depends on the assumptions and weightings, and involves loss of transparency. It also requires the additional—and equally controversial—process of monetising. There is considerable dispute about precise externality figures in almost every area, and the technique is therefore not reliable for detailed calculations or comparisons.

Comprehensiveness. This approach can be comprehensive in principle for internal costs, though in practice key data is often not available. For external costs, it is comprehensive only for limited areas of environmental impacts—in particular, for transport where several studies to calculate external costs have been conducted and the results published. However, data on external costs is sparse on other areas of impacts and organisations would need to make their own calculations if they wished to use the technique in these areas.

Comprehensibility. This is high in general, as the method makes use of the widely understood concept of monetary costs and benefits. However, the methodologies for calculating environment-related costs and benefits can be obscure.

Credibility. Credibility is potentially high internally since this method expresses the results in monetary terms, although there is room for debate about allocation procedures and other accounting activities. The broad concept of externalities is widely accepted and therefore has considerable credibility. However, the methods for calculating them are more contentious and so disagreements are to be expected on the validity of the actual numbers calculated.

Convenience. Convenience is high, as this technique can utilise eco-points software. For example, all materials, processes, etc. covered in Eco-Scan can be assigned a cost figure, and cost calculations made for products.

◻ Eco-Costing: Conclusions

Eco-costing approaches are potentially of great value. Internal costing can highlight short- to medium-term opportunities for financial savings. External costing can also highlight possible increases in cost—as a prelude to taking action to avoid them— as well as highlighting areas of negative social impact.

At present, external costing seems most practicable in the transport area. Data is available and it is relatively easy to calculate travel saved through use of telecommunications services. However, it is less practicable for other stages of the life-cycle where data is too sparse to allow meaningful calculation.

One caveat for eco-costing of products where environmental costs are either in the medium or long-term, and/or are not a high proportion of total costs, is that they may not appear significant when analysed through net present value models which apply high discount rates. The major cost issues might be those such as effects on image which can be financially significant but hard to quantify. It is important that these are not neglected in any analysis.

Costing approaches can identify the benefits to business and/or society from environmental actions in terms—i.e. money—that are readily understood. They were therefore considered to be especially valuable for Purpose 4, communicating environmental effects to customers and other interested parties. However, there is no consensus about the costs that should be attached to externalities, and there is also little readily usable data outside the area of transportation. The figures therefore need to be used with care. Their aggregate and non-consensual nature also means that they have little relevance to Purposes 1, identifying areas for attention in the product design and development process, and 3, ensuring that products meet specified criteria and/or create no great environmental problems.

6. Conclusions

The characteristics of each method, and their evaluation against the six criteria, are summarised in Table 5. As suggested in Section 2, product environmental evaluation techniques serve four main purposes:

1. Identifying areas for attention in the product design and development process

2. Making choices between different products or different designs of the same product

3. Ensuring that products meet specified criteria and/or create no great environmental problems

4. Communicating environmental effects to customers and other interested parties

This study suggests that each method has its own balance of strengths and weaknesses with regard to these purposes and therefore that the relative attractiveness of each depends on the relative importance, in any situation, of each of the criteria.

All of these techniques also depend on the availability of data on the key environmental effects. While this data does not have to be extremely detailed, it does need to cover all relevant areas. Therefore a prerequisite for successful product evaluation is cost-effective procedures to gather such data. The absence of such data severely constrained the analysis that could be undertaken here and, in the authors' experience, is a more general constraint on product evaluation. This experience reinforces the lessons that can be drawn from other areas of accounting and performance measurement, that an excessive focus on the development of intellectually fascinating analytic techniques may be of less practical value than more prosaic issues such as data collection procedures and the ability to make simple judgements about environmental attributes (see the appendix).

The eco-points and eco-compass calculations also demonstrate the importance of another central feature of accounting and performance measurement implementation: the allocation of costs or impacts between different cost or impact objects. One of the most significant factors in the eco-points scores was the use made of the telecommunications infrastructure, the figures on which are the outcome of a complex exercise to allocate the aggregate energy requirements of the overall system to different telecommunications activities. Different allocation principles might have produced very different results.

Another conclusion is that none of these techniques—nor any others of which the authors are aware—provides an unambiguous and unchallengeable approach to the environmental evaluation of products. The results of all methods require interpretation, and arguably they are the most effective when used in combination. Above all, they all need to be embedded in a product development process so that they can be used when most effective, and conversely ignored when other approaches would be more suitable.

	Eco-points	Eco-compass	Eco-costing
Characteristics	Assigns scores to individual impacts and aggregates these into an 'eco-score': a cardinal measure.	Scores products on a 0–5 (cardinal) scale on six key environmental parameters: a relative (ordinal) measure.	Calculates internal and/or external financial costs and benefits of a product's environmental impacts, giving a cardinal measure.
Precision	High	Low (wide ranges for each point)	High
Reliability	Reasonable—no more, since it requires considerable judgement and aggregation of different aspects within (though not across) the different dimensions.	Modest—not transparent and depends on assumptions and weightings.	Modest—as for eco-points, depends on assumptions and weightings, and involves loss of transparency. Also requires the additional and equally controversial process of monetising.
Comprehensiveness	Excellent as different databases can be used (including self-generated ones).	Six poles cover most, but not all, issues. Also deals with customer as well as environmental benefits.	Can be comprehensive in principle for internal costs but in practice key data are often not available. Comprehensive for external costs of transportation but not other areas.
Comprehensibility	Basic principles are clear and well explained in software. However, weighting methodologies can sometimes be obscure.	Aided by conceptual simplicity and clear visual display. However, details of scoring system can be obscure.	High in general as makes use of widely understood concept of costs and benefit. However, methodologies for calculating environment-related costs and benefits can be obscure.
Credibility	Rests on faith in experts' weighting of different environmental impacts —may be high internally but unlikely to persuade sceptics. One possible response is to use normal and worst-case weightings.	Increased by limited conversion of basic data and a 'stretch' scoring system which is improvement and will therefore please environmentalists. However, reasons for the six compass poles are not completely self-evident.	High internally in that it expresses findings in monetary terms—but assumptions, for internal and especially external costs, can be challenged by sceptics.
Convenience	Excellent—a user-friendly software package that most people can understand and use within hours.	Easy to calculate if data is present—but needs more data than eco-points.	Requires both environmental and financial data and therefore more time and resources for data collection.
Conclusions	Good for internal use— quick comparisons and highlighting key areas of impact. As results are easily challenged, less suitable for making choices or communicating to stakeholders.	Good for making comparisons and highlighting improvement opportunities, both internally and externally. However, too aggregated for detailed analysis.	Internal costings are managerially persuasive but can be time-consuming to generate and not impact budgets for many years. External costings are useful internally for broad understanding and communication of social benefits and potentially valuable to policy-makers. However, basis of calculations can easily be challenged and difficult to apply outside transportation

Table 5: STRENGTHS AND WEAKNESSES OF THREE PRODUCT EVALUATION METHODOLOGIES

In the case of an XYZ-type exercise, for example, eco-points software could be used—with health warnings about the assumptions being made—to quickly assess different product alternatives and highlight key environmental issues during the main decision stages and once designs are decided. The eco-compass could be used to compare design alternatives and to communicate environmental data to customers and other external stakeholders. Externalities costing could be used to highlight the benefits to society of substituting telecommunications for physical movement of people and goods.

A further conclusion is that no current, mainstream, product evaluation approach yet encompasses social issues as well as environmental. This is unfortunate, given the growing ability of such issues—for example, use of child labour during the manufacture of products—to create difficulties for companies. (See the appendix for one such attempt to integrate environmental and social issues into a single framework.)

A final conclusion is that all the three evaluation approaches—and most others within the field—can be termed 'number-forcing', i.e. they require users to assign cardinal or ordinal numbers to all the parameters under consideration. While this is useful, it has one fundamental problem, which is that of recognising and signalling uncertainty or disagreement: for example, about the environmental impacts of PVC. A related point is the value, at certain stages of environmental performance evaluation processes, of qualitative information. In the case of product evaluation, this is particularly important at the start of the process, when one key aim is to identify areas where information is lacking and will need to be obtained for a full assessment. Only then can a decision be made as to whether the benefits of a fully fledged life-cycle assessment are likely to outweigh the benefits. The appendix provides one example of a tool that has been developed to meet this need.

◢ Appendix: Evaluating the Sustainability of Products

This method makes use of the PEER (performance evaluation error reduction) software package that is being developed by one of the authors (see James 1997 for an earlier version of this approach). The software provides a visual and simple framework for quickly judging projects, performance over time and other business problems. It creates 'traffic light' assessments which present information in terms of a limited number of states, rather than in highly complex forms or in ways that involve summarising several different factors into a single number (see Chapter 8 for another example of such an approach). It also allows both quantitative and qualitative information to be taken into account and highlights the issues of risk and uncertainty which are often ignored but frequently cause a reversal of original judgements. It should be seen as a complement rather than an alternative to other evaluation tools such as those described in the chapter.

The approach has five stages.

Stage 1 is to identify the number of elements to be assessed (although it is easy to modify this at a later stage).

Stage 2 is to group the elements into one or more categories. For example, when assessing the sustainability of a product, three categories might be identified : economic, environmental and social.

Stage 3 is choosing the display form: for example, concentric rings in a circle (see Fig. 2).

Stage 4 is colouring each of the elements. The purpose of evaluation is then to colour-code each of the elements, based on a modified traffic light system. Four or five colours can be used:

- **White**: to denote an absence of information but no indications of serious problems

- **Red**: to indicate serious problems

- **Amber**: to denote question marks, caused by lack of crucial data and/or conflicting interpretations on significant questions

- **Green**: a positive assessment, i.e. a 'go-ahead' signal. (Light green and dark green can be used if more discrimination is required.)

Such a scoring scheme provides clear and readily understandable distinctions, even in the absence of full quantitative data. In particular, it quickly differentiates elements with major

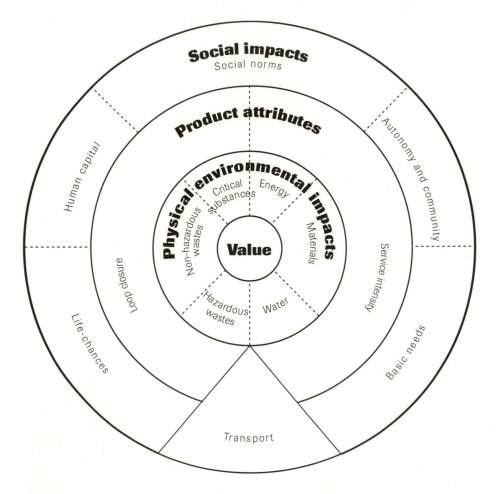

Figure 2: THE SUSTAINABILITY CIRCLE

problems or question marks (large arrays of red and amber)—on which more work needs to be done—from those without them, i.e. those that are mainly green. It also allows lack of consensus to be taken into account by assigning amber to elements where this applies.

Stage 5 is creating links from the elements to the material that has helped to inform the assessment. Users who wish can then 'drill down' to explore the reasons for the assessment provided, e.g. to documents, databases or websites. In the case of environmental performance evaluation, this can include data from life-cycle assessments, and eco-compass or eco-point analyses.

For product evaluation, the authors have found four groups of elements to be the most useful, covering:

- Customer value
- Physical environmental impacts
- Product attributes
- Social impacts

⌂ *Customer Value*

Customer value is at the centre of the circle as it is the central aim of all product development. Often, environmental product evaluation will take value creation as given and find ways of reducing the environmental impacts associated with an existing option. However, there are often opportunities to develop new sources of customer value through eco-innovation processes, and it is important to consider opportunities for new value-creating options when each of the elements of the wheel are being considered (Fussler with James 1996).

⌂ *Physical Environmental Impacts*

The second layer is that of primary or physical environmental impacts: i.e. those that can be quantified through the use of life-cycle assessment techniques. Three of these relate to inputs (energy, materials and water) and three to outputs (hazardous substances and radiation, non-hazardous wastes, and environmentally critical substances such as CFCs or carbon dioxide).

One option within this layer is to use eco-points to provide an aggregate measure of impacts. However, care must be taken that issues that are not addressed in many eco-points schemes—such as depletion of resources, or land-take—are not ignored.

⌂ *Product Attributes*

The third layer is attributes of products that are major determinants of the physical environmental impacts of the product itself and/or society as a whole. Although their effects will usually—although not inevitably—show up in other elements, their importance is such that they are worth considering in their own right.

Three broad kinds of product attribute can be identified:

- **Transport**: the total use of transportation over the life-cycle

- **Revalorisation**: the extent to which the product can itself be recycled, re-used or remanufactured, or can use inputs or components that have been recycled, re-used or remanufactured

- **Service intensity**: the provision of additional service to customers in ways that potentially reduce environmental impacts

Service intensity is an all-embracing category and there are in fact six significant ways of achieving it:

▼ **Product substitution**: e.g. 'video by wire', in which a provider of an entertainment service delivers films by wire to final consumers rather than through cassettes.

▼ **Use intensity**: increased use of a single product, as when two or more people share use of a single vehicle. This can be facilitated by introducing new features, such as meters that monitor levels of individual usage.

▼ **Life extension**: for example, by making artefacts more durable or of modular design so that key components can be replaced. This can facilitate leasing of products rather than their sale.

▼ **Product augmentation**: which involves addition of new features to facilitate a service. An example is installation of on-board computerised monitoring to vehicles to provide more data to providers of maintenance services.

▼ **Multi-functionality**, so that products meet several different needs simultaneously.

▼ **Product integration**: products meeting different functional needs can be integrated with each other to optimise their environmental and, sometimes, functional performance. In the case of buildings, for example, integration of heating, insulation, ventilation and other systems can reduce energy and materials consumption by avoiding oversizing of equipment or preventing conflict between them—as when heating systems are activated thermostatically because of excessive ventilation or air-conditioning.

However, none of these measures automatically generates net environmental improvement, so judgements need to be validated by some kind of life-cycle assessment. Extending the useful lives of road vehicles, for example, reduces the energy and material requirements that would be needed to build their replacements; however, it could also mean missing possible opportunities to take advantage of new technology that offers environmental improvements (such as cleaner engines).

◁ *Social Impacts*

The fourth layer is attributes of the product that have significant social impacts. As Chapter 1 notes, there is still much disagreement on what should be included here. It is also difficult to deal with social issues at the design level. There is often a lack of knowledge about social impacts, which will be complex and often occur only some time in the future. For this reason, quantified data may be difficult or impossible to obtain. In addition, products are designed for specific contexts and it may be inappropriate or futile to assess them against universal criteria. In many cases, assessment can only be about whether there are gross violations of the social conditions for sustainability. Finally, the social arena contains many different points of view and there will be seldom be consensus. This often means that there is no single 'right answer' and that the main objective is simply to recognise that there are different points of view and to violate as few as possible.

Nevertheless, in a brief exercise which is intended to generate only indicative and approximate conclusions, five elements should usually cover most product-related aspects:

▼ Life chances
▼ Basic needs
▼ Social norms

- ▼ Human capital
- ▼ Autonomy and community

As transport also has major social implications, this element is also incorporated into the fourth layer.

Basic needs. The people with the world's poorest life-chances are the one billion plus who have inadequate food, shelter and other bare necessities of life. Their situation is so critical—and so central to successful sustainable development—that it needs to be considered explicitly. The reality of product development—which is undertaken primarily in and for richer countries—means that little can be said in many cases. However, at the very least, gross problems can be identified and addressed.

Life-chances. Equality is one of the more controversial aspects of sustainable development. However, it is generally interpreted as focusing more on equality of opportunity than of outcome and the creation of a situation where the poorer have greater 'life-chances'—of employment, education, etc. The same argument also applies to other groups which some have felt are disadvantaged—such as women and minorities. There will seldom be consensus about this, but the minimum question is whether a product will accentuate existing disparities of life-chances and, if so, what is being done to address it.

Social norms. New products or product-related actions create emotional reactions and can acquire a 'symbolic loading' by providing a tangible manifestation of broad trends or debates in society that challenge or impinge upon established or majority norms. Hence, the disposal of Brent Spar resulted in a debate not only about the environmental impacts of the platform itself but also about the end-of-life of all oil facilities and the broader acceptability of any kind of marine waste disposal. Advance consideration of the ways in which products might challenge or change societal norms—particularly those relevant to sustainability—is therefore essential. Use of child labour or other forms of employment that might be considered exploitative in the developed world is one obvious example.

Human capital. One controversial attribute of many new products and processes is that they often require less human labour to operate than previous versions: i.e. they increase productivity. Although this, by definition, increases wealth per unit of human input, and could be claimed to be beneficial by increasing leisure time, an opposing view could be that, given the central and problematic nature of employment in most societies, this could be seen as socially negative. However, most economists would argue that the additional wealth created by this increase in efficiency would then, through the multiplier effect, go on to create employment elsewhere in the economy, and also that, in the medium to long term, new products can create new forms of employment to exploit and maintain them. Hence, while immediate labour effects are important, the key indicator is the overall effects of a product on knowledge, skills and other dimensions of human capital.

Autonomy and community. There is a widespread belief that many modern products and technologies threaten individual freedom and local community (which are themselves not always in harmony). As Brent Spar shows, these feelings are especially likely to crystallise around large multinational companies, which can often be perceived as antithetical to freedom and community. Hence, it is important to check the effects of products on this dimension. One example at an aggregate level is provided by British Telecom, who recognises that the national and global connections of telecommunications could potentially undermine community and therefore has a Community Networks section to identify ways in which this can be prevented.

2 REPORTING ENVIRONMENTAL PERFORMANCE

14
Towards a Generally Accepted Framework for Environmental Reporting*

Roger Adams, Martin Houldin and Saskia Slomp

THIS CHAPTER summarises the discussion paper 'Towards a Generally Accepted Framework for Environmental Reporting' prepared by the Environmental Task Force of the European Federation of Accountants (FEE). The discussion paper reflects the view that more attention needs to be paid to the various qualitative reporting characteristics that should underpin the practice of corporate environmental reporting, if that practice is eventually to achieve the same degree of public acceptance as financial reporting.

For the purpose of the discussion paper, 'environmental reporting' covers the preparation and provision of information, by management, for the use of multiple stakeholder groups (internal or external), on the environmental status and performance of their company or organisation. This information is most often provided in a separate environmental report, but it may (either as well or alternatively) be included within other forms of reporting (such as financial, and social/ethical reporting). Generally speaking, the location of the information should not significantly impact on its credibility. Financial information relating to the environment, if reported other than in the audited financial statements, should be consistent with any similar disclosures made through the audited accounts.

At the start of the 1990s, only a very few companies produced environmental reports—and these came mainly from the 'heavier polluting' industries. A number

---

* This chapter is an introduction to the main issues raised in the paper of the same name which was first presented as a discussion paper issued for comment by the Environmental Task Force of the European Federation of Accountants (FEE). It also constitutes Appendix A of the CERES Global Reporting Initiative (GRI) Guidelines (see Chapter 23).

of recent surveys, at national and international level, have identified growth not just in the number of companies reporting, but also in the sectoral coverage of such reporting. Based on the evidence of such surveys, it is the larger (usually multinational) companies that appear to have accepted environmental reporting most rapidly.

The growth in environmental reporting, however, has not been simply a matter of the development of a single type of reporting. A reference to an 'environmental report' means different things to different people. Some tend to think of separate (stand-alone) environmental reports which have been modelled on the financial statements (annual reports) of the enterprise; these are often referred to as corporate environmental reports (CERs). For others, the focus will be on the environmental content (if any) of the annual report itself.

In some parts of Europe, the term 'environmental report' may be interpreted as an environmental impact statement or ecobalance report. To a growing number of people (again, particularly in Europe) an 'environmental report' will mean the Environmental Statement required for registration to the EU's EMAS (Eco-Management and Auditing Scheme). In the United States, and other places, the term may mean the reporting of regulatory information for legal compliance purposes.

We have thus seen many different types of report emerge: reports that, by their nature and purpose, are all 'environmental', and which all have as a common feature the provision of environmental stewardship, compliance or performance data for stakeholder groups. However, with the exception of EMAS-based public environmental statements, these reports seem to have emerged through a series of random initiatives, rather than through any form of co-ordinated or coherent developmental process. It is our belief that corporate environmental reporting has now reached the stage where enterprises and users alike would benefit from greater structure and definition.

Preparers of environmental reports would like confirmation that their reports are effective, and users of such reports (in particular, an increasingly environmentally aware financial community) are demanding more consistency in the way(s) in which environmental issues and performance are measured and reported. A formal set of recognised reporting principles and a standardised reporting framework (not dissimilar in principle to those adopted in the EC 4th Directive on Company Law) should help overcome any perception that environmental reports lack credibility.[1]

◢ The Aim of the Paper

The aim of the discussion paper is to encourage discussion between accountancy professionals, providers of environmental information and stakeholder groups (all of whom we assume to have a better than general awareness of environmental

---

1 Such a framework is currently being constructed through the medium of the CERES Global Reporting Initiative (GRI), to which FEE is contributing (see Chapter 23).

reporting and related guidelines) regarding the introduction of a framework for qualitative characteristics in environmental reporting.

Experience with financial reporting, over more than 100 years, has shown that qualitative characteristics, such as relevance, comprehensibility, usefulness and comparability, are as important as the basic (performance-oriented) quantitative content in establishing the credibility of reported data. The general issue addressed by this discussion paper is the process via which similar qualitative principles and frameworks, as applied successfully to financial reporting, can be effectively applied to environmental reporting.

The focus of the discussion paper is therefore primarily on the separate external reporting of environmental issues and performance by enterprises, whether at corporate or site level. The inclusion of environmental information in financial reports and in internal management reporting is addressed, although we think it reasonable to assume that environmental information included within the audited section of the annual report is produced in accordance with relevant accounting standards. Financial statement auditors have a duty to ensure that data included elsewhere in the annual report package is not in conflict with the audited financial statements themselves. Because of timing, however, it is unlikely that financial statement auditors will be able to check for conflict with any free-standing environmental performance report (unless—as sometimes happens—the two types of report are issued simultaneously).

A number of environmental reporting guidelines are available to prospective (and actual) preparers of environmental reports. The focus of these guidelines is mostly on 'what' should be reported (for example, to include bad as well as good news; to report against objectives and targets; to include financial/economic data), rather than on those qualitative characteristics that would make the reports more useful (i.e. the 'how' of reporting).

The role of all conceptual frameworks is to standardise and underpin external corporate reporting, thus giving users greater confidence in the reporting process itself and the credibility of the information reported. The FEE Environmental Task Force believes that the practice of corporate environmental reporting will benefit from the development of an underpinning conceptual framework as much as has the practice of financial reporting.

A number of conceptual frameworks for financial reporting already exist and the FEE Environmental Task Force has looked to these to provide a suitable starting point. In particular, the International Accounting Standards Committee (IASC) framework for the Preparation and Presentation of Financial Statements ('Framework') has been adopted as a model for this paper because, in the view of the Task Force, it is the one conceptual framework to which the phrase 'generally accepted' can realistically be applied at the global level.

There are additional reasons for wishing to secure the conceptual foundations of this new discipline. On the practical side, demands for environmental reports to be externally verified can only realistically be met once such an underpinning guidance framework has been developed and operationalised. Also, environmental reporting, though itself only in its infancy, is already beginning to mutate into 'sustainability reporting', 'social reporting' and 'triple-bottom-line reporting'. We believe that, unless a generally applicable qualitative framework for non-financial reporting is developed, these extensions of corporate environmental reporting will fail to engender the support and credibility that their proponents apparently expect.

◢ The Objective of Environmental Reporting

In a world where the long-term environmental sustainability of the planet is increasingly in question, enterprises report on the environmental consequences of their activities, both beneficial and adverse, so that the results of management's stewardship of the environmental resources entrusted to it may be demonstrated. The FEE Environmental Task Force defines the objective of external environmental reporting as being

> the provision of information about the environmental impact and operational performance of an entity that is useful to relevant stakeholders in assessing their relationship with the reporting entity.

In many cases, users will wish to assess management's environmental stewardship or accountability so that opinions can be formed about environmental status, policies and performance in general terms. The consequences of this assessment will usually be one of a number of factors in influencing a user's opinion in regard to more specific decisions (such as the purchase of corporate assets). In the case of governmental organisations, the focus will usually be on management's accountability for use and management of 'public' environmental resources.

In financial reporting, there is a strong link with commercial or economic decisions, such as the purchase/sale of shares, lending or corporate acquisitions and mergers. In most cases, we think that environmental reporting will not be focused on purely economic decision-making, although we recognise that 'general purpose' environmental reports may often provide the only (partially reliable) source of published information.

At present, we believe that environmental reporting is used more to give a general understanding of environmental issues, and related risk, and as an indication of performance levels. It is reasonable, we believe, to expect that, as environmental reporting becomes more focused, and as practice with regard to reporting environmental impact and performance becomes more sophisticated (particularly on a sectoral basis), financial-sector users will find that such reporting becomes increasingly more important. This is where recognised qualitative characteristics have an important role to play in establishing the credibility of the reported data.

◢ Users and their Information Needs

There are two main conceptual models that can be applied when deciding on the content and presentation of any kind of corporate reporting:

1. The **Accountability Model** assumes that stakeholders are not always adequately qualified to determine their own needs and/or that their needs are (or may appear to be) difficult to define. In this case, financial and/or environmental reporting recommendations are based largely on a normative interpretation of 'what users *should* know about'.

2. The **Users' Needs Model** makes the opposite assumption: i.e. that, through a process of discussion and involvement, the information needs of a range of potential users can be identified adequately in advance of the reporting process, and can also be defined in terms of appropriate accounting disclosures (based on relevant recognition and measurement techniques).

In preparing this paper we have observed that, although both approaches can be identified in the past and current practice of environmental reporting, the current trend among more progressive companies is to seek to identify and involve stakeholders wherever possible. Thus this section is therefore written from a users' needs perspective.

The IASC conceptual framework differentiates between seven user groups. Although the IASC framework can be read as incorporating a general assumption that there are needs that are common to all users, it should be emphasised that it is based on a primary assumption that the needs of financial investors are pre-eminent, and that, if their needs are met, then the needs of most other users should be at least partially met. Such research as has been carried out into the needs of users of environmental reports (e.g. SustainAbility/UNEP 1996b) shows that the information needs of different environmental stakeholder groups can be substantially different. Insofar as these needs can be identified, they are set out in the rest of this section.

◻ *Investors*

Environmental performance is increasingly seen to have an influence (either directly or indirectly) over financial performance and financial risk assessment. Mainstream (or conventional) investors in risk capital should probably obtain most of the information they need from audited financial statements (e.g. on environmental provisions, liabilities, contingencies, expenditures, risk exposures and other financial implications). We suspect that, at present, they tend to make only general use of environmental reports.

For some other financial stakeholders (for example, the emerging groups of environmental and social/ethical investments funds), information needs go well beyond the narrowly financial, and could include information to help them make a judgement on the environmental and ethical probity and sustainability of the company. Non-financial environmental information may thus have a direct influence over their investment decision-making.

◻ *Employees*

Generally speaking, anything that can have an *economic* impact on their employers should be of interest to employees. However, with growing general/public environmental awareness, for example of the impact of business activities on non-renewable elements of the environment, employees may increasingly request information purely to help them understand the enterprise's environmental status. They may take an interest in whether their employer is seen by local community groups (and by wider stakeholder groups) as a responsible company. They will also need to see their employer's business as a going concern, recognising that environmental performance may have some influence on this.

◻ *Lenders*

The information needs of lenders may be even greater than those of investors. Environmental reports should be of particular interest to lenders if there are direct financial implications or risks associated with environmental issues. Lenders will need to understand, *inter alia*, about the quality of an entity's assets, its environmental management systems, its compliance record, its technological status and its marketplace positioning, as all of these may be influenced by environmental factors. We note that the Swiss Bankers Association (1997) has been extremely active in defining desirable environmental disclosures.

◻ *Suppliers and Other Trade Creditors*

The needs of suppliers and other trade creditors will often be the same as those outlined above for investors and lenders. Public environmental reports could help them understand the environmental issues of their major customers. Such an understanding may present them with a market opportunity to protect or to expand their business through product support and because of their own (superior) environmental performance.

◻ *Customers*

Where environmental liabilities and regulatory compliance issues are relevant, customers will have an interest in information concerning the going-concern status of a supplier. More commonly, however, customers are recognising the links with their suppliers in terms of the environmental life-cycle. Suppliers, through their use of certain substances and materials, may directly affect their customers' environmental performance. Some companies are already demanding that 'first-line' suppliers are accredited to a recognised environmental management system (e.g. EMAS or ISO 14001). An increasing number of companies are taking a positive interest in information that identifies and illustrates the quality of environmental practices in the supply chain.

◻ *Governments and their Agencies*

Government departments, with responsibility for environmental legislation, and the relevant regulatory/enforcement bodies, have an interest in information that gives an indication or assurance of good environmental management. This may help them in making regulatory decisions, which in turn may affect the level and cost of monitoring and inspection. For example, many governments collect data on environmental expenditures and regulatory (consent) compliance. Governments are also responsible for making the public policy decisions that reflect society's response to calls for more sustainable methods of managing our economies. Environmental reporting should reflect the response and pace of progress of entities operating at the micro level.

◁ *The Public*

Enterprises affect members of the public in a variety of ways: as members of the local community, as customers, as employees, or as shareholders. Increasingly, members of the public wish to see that enterprises are behaving as good neighbours in the local community, not just from a compliance perspective, but also in respect of longer-term sustainability. Credible, comprehensible environmental information will help them in their evaluation of this. Environmental performance may also affect an enterprise's longer-term viability, and in this respect members of the public will have an interest in information that shows that the enterprise is making a contribution to the local economy.

◢ The Underlying Assumptions of Environmental Reporting

The building blocks of the IASC conceptual framework include 'underlying assumptions' and 'qualitative characteristics'. Broadly speaking, the difference between an underlying assumption and a qualitative characteristic is that underlying assumptions have a more direct and significant effect on the absolute numbers reported. Qualitative characteristics are no less important for the overall credibility of reporting, but tend to address non-financial, evidential issues. This section considers the 'underlying assumptions' shown in Table 1, and the following section considers the 'qualitative characteristics'.

Reporting on the nature of environmental impacts means that, in order to make the processes of measurement and reporting feasible and credible, certain underlying assumptions may need to be made about either the reporting enterprise or the data being reported on. This is partly due to the fact that environmental impacts do not always naturally occur in the same time-period as the activity that has caused them. Similarly, impacts do not always occur within the physical boundaries of the reporting enterprise. More importantly, perhaps, there is a need to present data in as uniform a manner as possible if it is to be of any significant use to external stakeholders.

Underlying assumptions	Qualitative characteristics
The entity assumption	1. Relevance
The accruals basis of accounting	2. Reliability
The going-concern assumption	3. Comprehensibility
The precautionary principle	4. Neutrality
The concept of materiality or significance	5. Completeness
	6. Prudence
	7. Comparability
	8. Timeliness
	9. Verifiability

Table 1: UNDERLYING ASSUMPTIONS AND QUALITATIVE CHARACTERISTICS

The Entity Assumption

In any form of corporate reporting it is essential that the boundaries of the reporting entity are clearly defined by management and reported clearly and explicitly in any public statement. Financial accounting and reporting standards have been developed to deal with variations in the form through which corporate control is exercised (e.g. via joint ventures, associates or subsidiary operations).

In financial reporting, identification of the legal status and boundaries of the reporting unit is vital in determining accountability and in avoiding accusations of misleading financial reporting (e.g. by ignoring 'off-balance-sheet liabilities'). In the case of environmental reporting, it is similarly important to identify clearly the boundaries of the reporting entity and not to permit or encourage the originator of, or contributor to, environmental impacts to shelter within formal legal boundaries, as may be the case in the purchase of sensitive materials such as rainforest hardwood.

Further, where organisations form part of a supply chain, comprehensive accountability may require the total life-cycle impact of the product, from resource extraction to disposal, to be covered in some way. While it would be controversial (and possibly misleading) to require consolidated environmental reports that included separate legal entities along the entire supply chain, it might nevertheless be helpful to some users if environmental reports included reference to the more significant environmental impacts (such as from off-site waste disposal) upstream or downstream from the reporting entity. The traditional entity concept may therefore require modification for environmental reporting.

A minimum requirement for environmental reporting is therefore that the report itself (or any accompanying verification statement) clearly identifies the extent to which the entity (as defined for financial reporting purposes) is fully disclosing the significance and impact of its environmental activities. Environmental reporting standards—when developed—should contain provisions that stipulate disclosure relating to the legal (or administrative) scope of the reporting entity, and the completeness of disclosure *vis-à-vis* significant environmental aspects.

A related issue concerns the acquisition or disposal of significant elements of the operation and the need to adjust prior-year comparatives accordingly.[2]

◻ The Accruals Basis of Accounting

The practical application of the accruals basis of accounting requires that the results or impacts of activities should be disclosed in the period in which those activities occur. In financial reporting, for example, use of the accruals basis is driven by recognition of the 'critical event' (as occurring at the point of sale). There may, however, be variations on this central theme, including recognition of revenue and profit on a percentage-of-completion basis in the case of long-term contracts.

For environmental reporting, the need for prompt reporting probably means that full recognition of ultimate impacts will normally require an accruals approach based on the point of production, if not earlier. Examples may include remote impacts from air emissions (acid rain), land pollution (potential groundwater impacts), and raw material extraction (ecological disturbance). The inclusion of a 'year-end physical inventory' section in some recent 'ecobalance' statements (see, for example, the Kunert 1995/96 Environmental Report; Kunert AG 1997) illustrates the importance of adopting the accruals basis in environmental accounting and reporting. Environmental reporting standards—when developed—need to address the accruals (or matching concept) to ensure that production activities, emissions and waste are appropriately related from an activity perspective.

There is still some debate relating to the timing (and measurement) of provisions for environmental liabilities and remediation costs, in particular costs relating to the decommissioning of long-lived assets, such as oil rigs or nuclear plants. The new international standard IAS 37 indicates that, for financial reporting purposes, these liabilities will in future be provided for in full at current values at the time the environmental damage is caused, before being discounted at an appropriate rate (IASC 1998).

Despite the obvious potential applications of the accruals (or 'matching') concept, however, it is clear that, from an environmental reporting perspective, the link between *event* and *environmental impact* may not always be obvious. In some instances, an event (e.g. an accidental emission) may have no obvious environmental consequence until some years have elapsed. In other cases, an environmental impact or consequence may be identified (e.g. contaminated land) for which no causal event can ever be identified.

◻ The Going-Concern Assumption

An enterprise that is categorised as being a 'going concern' is generally expected to continue operations for the foreseeable future (note that 'foreseeable future' in financial auditing terms is rarely longer than 18 months after the balance sheet date).

---

2   See also Chapter 12.

This principle is adopted in financial reporting with the result that assets are conventionally carried at current or historical cost rather than at liquidation values.

Liabilities for environmental costs (such as land remediation) will need to be recognised in the financial statements under the going-concern concept, as long as there is either a legal or constructive obligation present (see IASC 1998 for more detail on these terms).

Since longer-term environmental impacts and prospective environmental legislation can be very important for the financial statements, it seems appropriate that environmental reporting standards—when developed—should include a requirement that, when potential environmental liabilities are significant, the environmental report should provide a clear indication of whether the enterprise is capable of funding necessary remediation/clean-up procedures. On a related point, it can also be argued that, while environmental liability provisions do serve to inhibit the ability of a company to make distributions to its shareholders, this does not at the same time guarantee the availability of cash resources to fund a necessary remediation process. In the event of a corporate failure, this may throw the cost burden onto the public purse. At a policy level there may be strong arguments for requiring companies operating in environmentally sensitive industries to ensure adequate provision of financial resources. In part, this may be handled through the conventional insurance framework—but for known long-term liabilities some form of 'environmental bonding' could serve to insure society should the organisation in question fail as a financial going concern.

Finally, it can be argued that, as some enterprises may adopt sustainable development as the guiding principle for reporting, this would represent an extended interpretation of the going-concern concept as conventionally used for financial reporting purposes. This, however, would seem to be an attempt to carry a good idea one step too far, since the concept of sustainable development involves a paradigm shift embracing financial, environmental and social issues not easily identifiable in current experiments in environmental reporting.

◁ *The 'Precautionary Principle'*

Understandably from almost all stakeholder perspectives, pollution *prevention* is always a preferred alternative to post-contamination *remediation* or clean-up. From this prudential perspective has developed the so-called 'precautionary principle'—a principle often cited by policy-makers and green lobby groups as a defence against the introduction of new technologies and procedures.

The operation of the 'precautionary principle' is illustrated in this short extract adapted from *Environmental Science for Environmental Management* by O'Riordan.

- there should be thoughtful action in advance of scientific proof of cause;
- decision-makers should leave ecological space as 'room for ignorance', or as a margin of error, because of lack of information or scientific evidence;
- there should be a reversal in the normal 'burden of proof', from affected party to the corporate decision-maker (O'Riordan 1995: 9).

We believe that environmental reporting policy disclosures—when developed—should include a requirement to inform users as to whether or not the precautionary principle is embedded in the environmental policies, programmes and decision-making processes of the reporting entity.

◻ *The Materiality Principle*

Materiality is a principle that is related to relevance and which is sometimes referred to as a 'threshold characteristic' (Accounting Standards Board 1996). The underlying assumption here is that information is relevant to a user only if it is material in financial terms—which means: Does its presence or absence influence the user's decision? For financial reporting purposes, materiality is usually assessed by preparers and auditors in strictly financial terms, as a (commonly accepted) percentage of some 'headline' accounting number—such as turnover, operating income, net assets employed, etc.

We believe, however, that the application of the materiality concept in environmental reporting situations is more complex than in financial reporting, and heavily dependent on the nature and circumstances of an item or event (as well as its scale). In particular, the carrying capacity of the receiving environment (such as availability of landfill capacity or background air pollution levels) is central to the issue of environmental materiality.

We suggest that environmental reporting standards—when developed—should address the issue of materiality from an empirically researched and scientifically supportable environmental impact/user-driven perspective.

◢ *The Importance of Qualitative Characteristics in Environmental Reporting*

In financial reporting, it is considered that qualitative characteristics are the attributes that make published information useful. At the highest level of conceptualisation, 'usefulness' is usually equated with 'relevance' on the basis that information will not be relevant unless it is useful for decision-making purposes. Similarly, something that is not relevant for decision-making is unlikely to be useful to the user (ICAEW 1992). We suggest that appropriately modified interpretations of the same characteristics will enhance the usefulness or relevance of environmental reporting.

◻ *Relevance*

To be useful, information must be relevant to the decision-making needs of user groups. In environmental reporting, it is likely that the predictive role of information may be less important than is the case in financial reporting. The most relevant information is likely to be useful for attention-directing, knowledge-building and opinion-forming rather than clear decision-making. In environmental reporting, the issue of what is or is not relevant may best be gauged as a result of surveys of stakeholder needs (such as those conducted by SustainAbility/UNEP, or at the corporate level by many companies including Glaxo Wellcome, BP and IBM).

◻ *Reliability*

Information has the quality of reliability when it is free from bias and material error. Users should be able to depend on the fact that the information is faithfully represented. A number of different interlinked attributes contribute to reliability:

Valid description. The way in which environmental aspects are described will be important for the users' understanding. This is of particular importance in environmental reporting where it is often the case that reports are technical in nature. The common characteristics that exist between generic types of air emissions, wastewater discharges and wastes should allow some guidance to be given on the types of description that might be considered to be valid. How 'waste' is described, or air emissions are referenced, could vary considerably between reports, and lead to confusion.

Substance. Presenting information in accordance with its environmental reality and substance, rather than in a strict legal form, is important. In environmental reporting, the data may often be accurate, but without context or benchmark may not be useful. For example, a furniture manufacturer that produces hardwood furniture may accurately present the quantity of wood procured, but it will require the 'substance' (i.e. the source of that timber) also to be disclosed to provide a valid context for that information.

Neutrality (freedom from bias). Environmental reports are not neutral if by selection/omission or presentation of information they influence a decision or judgement. The accidental or deliberate use of inappropriately constructed graphs, or the omission of controversial issues (such as frequent pollution incidents, or historical land contamination, or the storage of highly toxic/hazardous materials), may bias the judgements and opinions of the user groups. The absence of generally accepted environmental reporting standards currently leaves any report open to charges of deliberate selection.

Completeness. Making a report more complete in its coverage of environmental issues will help to make it neutral and reduce the risk of bias. All significant issues that may be considered to be material should be reported. Consideration should be given to the reporting of indirect, as well as direct, environmental effects. Once again, the absence of generally accepted environmental reporting standards means that reports are often criticised for being 'incomplete'.

Prudence. This is related to the precautionary principle. Uncertainty is a major factor in environmental reporting, particularly concerning the likely or potential consequences of environmental incidents and uncontrolled releases. The exercise of a proper degree of prudence in environmental reporting should serve to ensure that:

1. Adverse environmental impacts are not downplayed.

2. Uncertain environmental impacts are not reported prematurely.

3. Positive environmental progress is not misreported—for example, by claiming that the entity is 'sustainable' in some way or other.

As noted above, the qualitative characteristic of 'prudence' may be linked to the 'precautionary principle'—for example, the reporting entity may wish to demonstrate its prudent anticipation of ever more stringent environmental laws. By the same token, it may be imprudent to make claims of improvements, as yet unrealised, as a result of investments. For example, a statement that capital expenditure has been made to reduce discharges to a local river in order to reduce pollution levels should not lead people to believe that the quality of the river has already been improved.

⌀ *Comprehensibility*

Comprehensibility is an essential quality of any form of reporting. In financial reporting, however, a reasonable knowledge of business and economic activities and of accounting is assumed. Also in financial reporting, the basis for the IASC assumption is perhaps the general level of education and experience of the assumed 'primary' user group; in other words, investors. In environmental reporting, such knowledge may not be sufficient to enable the user to understand readily the information being presented, although a broad understanding of the problems facing an industrial sector should be assumed.

In environmental reporting, it is not at this stage valid to identify any single group as the 'primary' user group. Also, it is difficult to make general assumptions about the level of environmental education and experience of user groups. Consequently, technical and scientific terms should be used carefully and explained within the report. To make environmental reports more comprehensible, further research is required into the levels of technical information that can be presented while ensuring that the report will be readily understandable.

⌀ *Comparability*

Users of environmental information will want to monitor and compare the results of environmental performance over time in order to identify significant trends. Users will also wish to compare the results of different enterprises, particularly within industry sectors. Consistency in the recognition, measurement and presentation of environmental information is therefore essential. Consistency should initially be established internally, determined by the information needs of the enterprise's user groups. Caution is needed when seeking to benchmark between enterprises within the same sector, as even apparently minor differences in process, product or location can be significant in terms of environmental effect. As with financial reporting, it is important that corresponding information be reported for preceding periods on a comparable and consistent basis.

There is a considerable amount of effort currently being expended on the development of appropriate benchmarks and environmental performance indicators (for example, by the CERES GRI,[3] by the World Business Council for Sustainable Development [WBCSD] and by the UN ISAR group of experts). These initiatives range from the generic (e.g. the ISO 14031 environmental performance evaluation measures) to the specific (e.g. metrics appropriate to the water or telecommunications industries). In the longer term, we assume that the appropriateness of the metrics selected for publication will pass some 'generally accepted' test.

◻ *Timeliness*

This is not addressed by the IASC Framework, as the reporting periods for financial reporting are well defined, in many cases within company law. For environmental reporting, however, some guidance is required to set out how the frequency of reporting should be determined. One of the problems not yet directly addressed by preparers of environmental reports is that the ecological impact cycle of their operations may not easily lend itself to meaningful public reporting in that it may not be as predictably cyclical in nature as the financial cycle. An alternative formulation of this argument is to say that 'continuous improvement' may not be easily identifiable if the reporting cycle is too short. Schaltegger *et al.* (1996) identify the following timing possibilities:

1. A separate environmental report is published at the same time as the financial report.

2. A separate environmental report is published at a time other than the financial report.

3. The environmental report is integrated within the annual report and accounts package.

At this time, we do not seek to prescribe how and when environmental reports should be published. We recommend, however, that all environmental reports contain a clear indication of the reporting period covered and the reasoning behind the choice of reporting period and/or frequency of reporting.

Some reporters have chosen to issue full reports each year. Others have indicated that the 'pace of change' (or the ability to identify and clearly demonstrate continuous improvement) in systems, processes and results is relatively slow. Thus, in the view of this latter group, a full report may be necessary only every two or three years. Such reporters normally produce short-form interim reports dealing with key emissions/performance data. We suggest that, in the interests of standardisation and comparability, report issuers seek to synchronise their financial and environmental reporting period ends.

---

3   See Chapter 23.

▢ *Verifiability*

It is a *sine qua non* of external reporting that, for reports to be credible in the eyes of a user, then the report should be verified or attested to by an independent third party. It follows that the information contained within the report and which is the subject of the independent third party's opinion should possess the characteristic of verifiability.

Financial statement standard-setters have historically sought to keep the content of the audited accounts narrowly focused on financially quantified, objectively determined, data in the belief that such data is more verifiable than non-financial values-derived information. Environmental reporting techniques are now beginning to evolve towards a point where environmental management systems are providing increasing amounts of objective, verifiable physical data. It remains the case, however, that environmental reports typically also contain some information that is neither objectively determined nor physically quantified (discussions on environmental impact and long-term sustainability, for example). In our view, it is important that statements provided by independent verifiers clearly identify the scope of their examination, and the verification standards applied, in order that unsupported assertions or unverifiable data can be highlighted by the user.

◢ Recommendations and Conclusions

The work of the FEE Environmental Task Force sub-group on environmental reporting has led to the following conclusions and recommendations:

- ▶ Environmental reporting is now established as a mainstream element of corporate reporting, but there is an urgent need to improve the conceptual underpinning and thus the quality of external environmental reporting itself.

- ▶ Conceptual underpinning requires the development of a framework of general assumptions and qualitative characteristics. In this draft, we have explored the relevance of existing conceptual frameworks (particularly that developed by the International Accounting Standards Committee) to environmental reporting issues. We find that at the qualitative level of reporting the accounting framework is highly relevant.

- ▶ This paper has identified a range of such qualitative characteristics and has sought to establish their environmental relevance and context. Some, however, require further discussion and development.

- ▶ The framework of assumptions and qualitative characteristics set out in this draft is complementary to and supportive of the work being carried out by other groups on the issue of the content of/elements of environmental reports.

▶ FEE itself is preparing a discussion paper on the independent verification of environmental reports. This, together with the present paper on qualitative characteristics and the work still to be done on elements, are essential ingredients of a total package that defines the reporting standards to be applied.

15

A Survey of Company Environmental Reporting

The 1997 Third International Benchmark Survey

John Elkington, Niklas Kreander and Helen Stibbard

THE VALUES CONSULTANCY SustainAbility and the United Nations Environment Programme (UNEP) have a long-standing research partnership on environmental and sustainability reporting, called *Engaging Stakeholders*. This is based on the assumptions that markets work most efficiently and effectively when there is adequate information—and that, as a result, business must increasingly get used to operating in a global 'goldfish bowl'. The overall aims of the programme are to:

1. Promote wider and more honest reporting
2. Catalogue and analyse sectoral trends
3. Track and evaluate trends in the main world regions
4. Review and respond to the latest reports
5. Explore the links between current CERs and sustainable development reporting.

The partnership has produced a number of publications:

- A first, 1994, survey of corporate environmental reporting (UNEP 1994a)
- A second, 1996, survey of corporate environmental reporting (SustainAbility/ UNEP 1996a, 1996b)
- A third, 1997, survey of corporate environmental reporting (SustainAbility/ UNEP 1997)
- A report on board-level accountabilities and perspectives (with additional support from the Association of Chartered Certified Accountants [ACCA]

and the Prince of Wales Business Leaders Forum) (SustainAbility/UNEP 1998a)

▼ A survey of non-reporting companies and the reasons for this (SustainAbility/UNEP 1998b)

▼ A report on social reporting (with additional support from Shell) (Sustain-Ability/UNEP 1999a)

▼ A report on environmental and social reporting on the Internet (Sustain-Ability/UNEP 1999b)

This chapter summarises the results of the latest, 1997 survey, while Chapter 25 summarises the work on social reporting.

◢ The 1997 Benchmark Survey

The objectives of the 1997 *Benchmark Survey* were to: (1) update our 1994 and 1996 findings (SustainAbility/UNEP 1996a, 1996b) by ranking 100 of the latest CERs against the SustainAbility/UNEP 50 reporting criteria and revised five-stage model; (2) begin the regional and sectoral analysis of such reports; and (3) outline what will be expected from future CERs.

The survey was restricted to companies that produce stand-alone, printed environmental reports; therefore, disclosures in annual reports or other documents were not included. In addition, the survey scope was limited to 100 CERs, although this meant excluding many good reports. It was decided to include only one CER from each company, thus excluding some of the reports benchmarked in the 1996 survey. Some of the companies in the 1996 survey had not produced a new report during the benchmarking period. This meant that, out of the forty CERs in the 1996 survey, 24 were included in 1997.

The Body Shop	131
Baxter	102
Neste	98
Novo Nordisk	97
British Airways	96
Volvo	93
General Motors	92
Sun Company	92
Bristol Myers Squibb	90
Polaroid	90
Tokyo Electric Power	90

Table 1: THE TOP 11 CERs, 1997

Company and year of CERs	Move upwards	Why?
Norske Skog: 1994, 1996	33	Much wider coverage of management systems and policies, input–output data and stakeholder relations.
Landesgirokasse: 1994, 1996	27	Improved information on many topics, especially relating to input–output section.
ICI: 1994, 1996	23	Improvements in management systems and policies, stakeholder relations and sustainable development sections.
Danish Steel Works: 1994, 1996	14	Increased scope of reporting, plus inclusion of company information, environmental policy, goals and stakeholder relationships.
Rhône-Poulenc: 1994, 1996	14	Good discussion of what sustainable development means for Rhône-Poulenc. Examines impacts of atmospheric release on the environment.
Kunert: 1994, 1994/95	13	Small improvements in many sections, especially stakeholder relations.
Dow Canada: 1994, 1996	12	Improvement in performance data.
British Airways: 1995, 1997	11	Scaled down in size, but increased comprehensiveness of reporting. Good overview of significant environmental issues of company operations and use of indicators (EPIs).
BP: 1994, 1996	10	More information on sustainable development, plus improvements on management systems and input–output data.

Table 2: GOING UP IN SCORE

Roger Adams (ACCA), Professor Rob Gray (CSEAR) and Nancy Bennet (UNEP) provided valuable inputs into the process of selecting the 100 CERs for the 1997 survey. In particular, the benchmarking team wanted to include a range of new CERs in the survey, in addition to achieving a good spread across sectors and nations.

The rankings that follow are based on scoring each of the 100 CERs against the SustainAbility/UNEP 50 reporting criteria. The criteria cover five main areas of reporting: Management Policies and Systems; Input and Output Inventory; Finance; Stakeholder Relations and Partnerships; and Sustainable Development. It is worth remembering that the top score possible is 194, which leaves even the top-scoring company 63 points of headroom still to play for.

Company and year of CERs	Move downwards	Why?
DuPont: 1994, 1996	30	Scaled down report from 25-page CER to 8-page leaflet. Reader is signposted to website instead.
Monsanto: 1995, 1996	23	Main focus of CER (10 pages of 29) on stakeholder roundtable, youth survey. Lower score on input–output.
Ontario Hydro: 1994, 1996	22	Cut heavily (from 60 pages to 24 pages), possibly due to internal management changes?
Phillips Petroleum: 1994, 1996	16	Lower score on input–output section
Union Carbide: 1994, 1995	14	Lower scores on input–output data and stakeholder relations

Table 3: GOING DOWN IN SCORE

◢ *The Top 11*

So which companies head the 1997 rankings? Once again, The Body Shop is first—and even nudged up its score by a few points compared to 1996. Next in line was the US company Baxter, only the second company to break the '100 barrier' of all the CERs benchmarked to date by SustainAbility. Alphabetically, as shown in Table 1, the other high-scoring companies were: British Airways (UK), Bristol Myers Squibb (USA), General Motors (USA), Neste (Finland), Novo Nordisk (Denmark), Polaroid (USA), Sun Company (USA), Tokyo Electric Power (Japan) and Volvo (Sweden).

In terms of the five different elements of reporting, the highest average scores were achieved in the three longer-established areas: 'Management Policies and Systems'; 'Input and Output Inventory'; and 'Stakeholder Relations and Partnerships'. The average scores in relation to coverage of 'Sustainable Development' and 'Finance' were much lower and indicate a real need for further investment of time and effort in these areas.

◢ *Biggest Jumps; Biggest Falls*

Of the 100 1997 survey companies, 24 were also covered in our 1996 *Engaging Stakeholders* survey (SustainAbility/UNEP 1996a). The biggest upward movement between the 1996 and 1997 surveys was achieved by Norske Skog of Norway (33 points), followed by Landesgirokasse (Germany; 27) and then by ICI (UK; 23) (see

Table 2). The biggest drops were recorded for DuPont (USA; 30), Monsanto (USA; 23) and Ontario Hydro (Canada; 22) (See Table 3). Those CERs moving down the ratings were usually cut fairly dramatically in terms of page length.[1] DuPont's CER, for example, shrank from a 25-page 'medium-quality' CER to an eight-page leaflet, while Ontario Hydro's shrivelled from a state-of-the-art 60-page CER to a 24-page report which no longer even mentions the topic it helped to pioneer, full-cost accounting. An even more dramatic example is BSO/Origin (The Netherlands), an early pioneer in environmental reporting and accounting, which no longer produces its *Environmental Result Statement*.

◢ *Report Design and Accessibility*

'Report Design and Accessibility' is a new reporting criterion, added at the request of stakeholders, report users and report makers alike. Since CERs are designed to communicate to people who may not be desperately keen to read such documents from cover to cover, the design dimension is becoming more important, not less. Some CERs that caught the benchmarking team's attention in this area were as follows:

- ▼ J. Sainsbury (UK) shows how good design can be used to make data accessible, while—from another hemisphere entirely—Umgeni Water (South Africa) made excellent use of lively, colourful design.

- ▼ It is tough to produce a good, comprehensive environmental report for a large international company that is less than 30 pages. Indeed, the average length of the 100 CERs in the survey is 38 pages. However, Statoil (Norway) managed to score 86 points with a 28-page report. Another highly accessible, pleasant-to-pick-up-and-read CER was the 1996 offering from Nortel (Canada).

- ▼ Companies are now using different channels of communication (for example, annual reports, the Internet, diskettes, CD-ROMs) to disseminate information on social and environmental issues. Since this can add to the complexity of reporting, clear links between the different ways of communication are crucial. Novo Nordisk (Denmark), British Telecom (UK), British Petroleum (UK) and Bristol Myers Squibb (USA) are good examples of CERs giving clear references to additional publications and signposting readers to further information on the Internet.[2]

---

1   See Chapter 20 (page 404) for discussion of a 'focus index' which relates a report's SustainAbility/ UNEP points to its length.
2   See Chapter 21 for a fuller review of Internet-based environmental reporting.

◢ Sectoral Scores

Currently, the SustainAbility work consists 'simply' of comparing and rating reports. But our main aim as we move into the 21st century must be to work out how to compare and rate company *performance* towards reducing impacts. Initially, the focus will be on corporate performance in relation to environmental, health and safety standards and benchmarks, but longer term we are also likely to see a growing interest in benchmarking against 'triple bottom line' indicators (that is, indicators that measure economic prosperity, environmental quality and social equity).

'Benchmarking' is one of those words that is easy to use, but which can be very difficult to put into practice. If we are to make sense of a given company's performance data, the first step is to understand what other companies operating in the same industry sector are doing and aiming to do. This will demand much greater effort at the sectoral level, often involving the active co-operation of industry associations and federations.

Figure 1 shows the 1997 sectoral breakdown of benchmarked CERs, ranked by the average score for each sector. The international pharmaceutical sector leads, followed by the transport and retail sectors.

The 1997 *Benchmark Survey*, we believe, has taken an important step forward by focusing on best reporting practice in five main sectors. These are:

- ▼ The **automobile** sector, with the 'star' companies being Volvo (Sweden) and General Motors (USA)

- ▼ The **chemical** sector—'star' companies being BASF (Germany) and DSM (Netherlands)

- ▼ The **oil** sector—'star' companies being Neste (Finland) and the Sun Company (USA)

- ▼ The **pharmaceutical** sector—'star' companies being Baxter (USA) and Novo Nordisk (Denmark)

- ▼ The **retail** sector—'star' companies being The Body Shop (UK) and J. Sainsbury (UK)

◢ Regional and Country Scores

Readers may wonder whether there are biases in our sample. For example, is there a nationality bias? In terms of the numbers of CERs in the survey, the USA contributed 19, closely followed by the UK with 18. Definitely a skew, but also perhaps a reflection of the fact that the voluntary reporting movement has evolved faster and further to date in these countries, providing a larger pool of reports upon which to draw.

But other countries also figured strongly in the 1997 rankings (see Fig. 2): Germany and Sweden (both contributing eight CERs), Canada, Japan and Norway (each contributing six), the Netherlands and South Africa (five each), Finland and

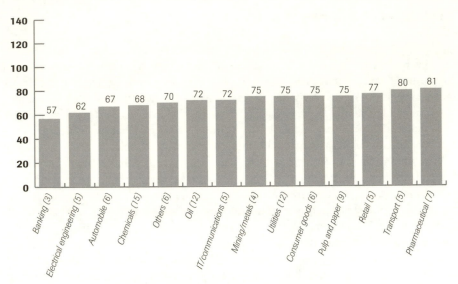

Figure 1: AVERAGE CER SCORES BY INDUSTRY SECTOR

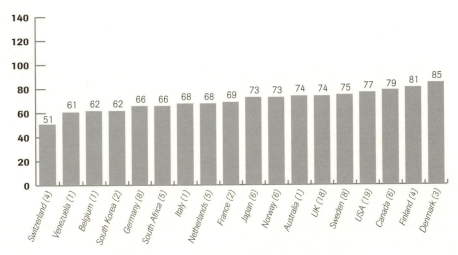

Figure 2: AVERAGE CER SCORES BY COUNTRY

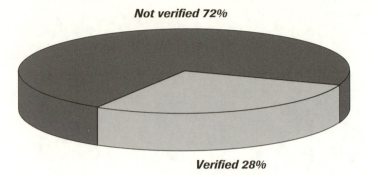

Figure 3: THE PROPORTION OF CERs WITH VERIFICATION STATEMENTS

Switzerland (four each), Denmark (three), France and South Korea (two each) and Australia, Belgium, Italy and Venezuela (one each). The highest average CER scores were for the Americas (26 CERs covered), while the next highest were for Europe (60 CERs covered).

◢ Verification

> The primary purpose of verification is to underpin the credibility of the report. Verification also provides BT's management with a level of comfort that its reporting systems are adequate and that it has addressed all key environmental impacts and risks.
>
> *A Report on BT's Environmental Performance 1996/7*

In our 1993–94 100-CER survey, just four CERs had been verified in some way. The intervening three years saw marked change in this area. As Figure 3 shows, 28 of the latest crop of 100 CERs had been verified—representing a seven-fold increase. Of the ten top-scoring companies in the 1997 survey, five had their reports verified. The scope of the verification varied widely. Some verification statements merely provide a sign-off on the report, whereas others are far more challenging and highlight areas for improvement. Clearly, verification has arrived, but there is still a fair way to go before it is accepted in the same way that it is in relation to corporate financial accounting and reporting.

Looking at the survey results through a different lens, we thought it would be interesting to see if there was any connection between the quality of the CERs that companies produced and the sort of industry-level company they kept. We focused on companies that support one or more of the following: the Coalition for Environmentally Responsible Economies (CERES) (the US-based coalition that evolved from the Valdez Principles); the International Chamber of Commerce (ICC), with its Business Charter for Sustainable Development; or the US-based Global Climate

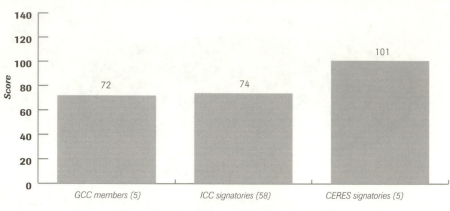

Figure 4: ICC SIGNATORIES VERSUS CERES SUPPORTERS VERSUS GCC MEMBERS

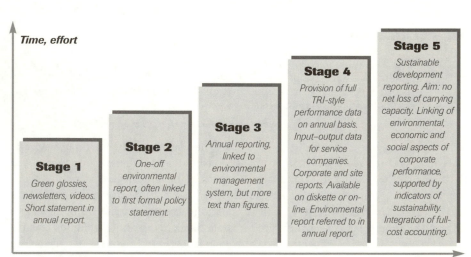

Figure 5: THE ORIGINAL FIVE-STAGE MODEL

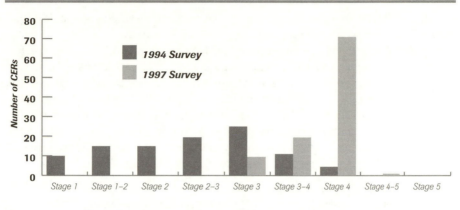

Figure 6: 1994 AND 1997 FIVE-STAGE MODEL SURVEY RESULTS

Coalition (GCC) established in 1989 to co-ordinate business participation in the debate on climate change. These organisations, as most readers will know, are very different.

- CERES is the 'greenest'. Among CERES companies are Baxter, The Body Shop, General Motors, Polaroid and Sun Company.

- The ICC is more towards the conservative end of the spectrum. Some 58% of the companies in the 1997 Survey are signatories (but very few announce the fact in their CER).

- The GCC, on the other hand, is sharply skewed towards the cause of reaction—given that its mission is to slow down progress on setting reduction targets for CO_2 emissions. These companies do not seem over-keen to identify their GCC memberships in public. Their number includes Dow Chemical (Dow Canada are in the survey), General Motors, Shell Oil (the US end of Shell), Texaco and Union Carbide.

The results in Figure 4 speak for themselves. The GCC members score lowest on average. The ICC Charter signatories do better, but are only a couple of points up on the all-company score. The real winners, by contrast, are the companies involved in CERES.

◢ The Five-Stage Model

One of the most widely used outputs of the SustainAbility/UNEP partnership has been the five-stage reporting model, first introduced in *Company Environment Reporting* in 1994 (UNEP 1994a). This distinguished different levels of reporting, from Stage 1, 'green glossies', through to Stage 5, 'sustainability reporting', as shown in Figure 5. The shift in quality of reporting is dramatically illustrated in Figure 6, which shows the results of the 1997 survey against those of the 1994 survey. The model has been used for all three of our *Benchmark Surveys*, but—following subsequent stakeholder inputs—was revised for the 1996 *Engaging Stakeholders* survey.

Paradoxically, the problem that necessitated the revision was caused by a surfeit of (relative) excellence: too many companies were reaching Stage 4. So we subdivided Stage 4 into three sub-stages, measuring the level of quantification (Stage 4.1), the quality of reporting (Stage 4.2) and the comparability of the reported data (Stage 4.3). The real dearth in the CERs reaching Stage 4.3 underscores a key conclusion of the 1997 survey: that most companies are still failing to address the central issue of performance benchmarking—of how the outside world can compare the performance of reporting companies. One of the rare exceptions is Anglian Water.[3]

> We believe that comparison with water industry averages allows users of this report to benchmark our performance. This policy is shared by the other water companies and the Water Services Association (WSA). Therefore, we are supporting a WSA-funded project to develop a 'set' of sustainable performance indicators that could be used by the whole water industry.
>
> *Anglian Water Environmental Activity Report 1997*

Of the CERs benchmarked in 1997, only The Body Shop's 1995 and 1997 *Values Reports* rank as making the transition from Stages 4 to 5. Stage 5 represents sustainability reporting or, to put it another way, reporting against the 'triple bottom line' (economic prosperity, environmental quality and social equity) of sustainable development. The focus here is not only on economic, social and environmental impacts but also on economic, social and environmental 'value added'.

> Sustainable development has been described in terms of the triple bottom line: economic prosperity, environmental protection and social equity, and the need for a balance between these objectives. We report each year on our performance in these areas through the *Annual Report and Accounts*, *HSE Facts* and *BP in the Community*.
>
> British Petroleum, *Health, Safety and the Environment Facts 1996*

The Benchmarking Tools

The benchmarking tools developed during the 1995–97 *Engaging Stakeholders* programme have:

- Won widespread favourable comment.
- Been used by a growing number of verifiers as part of their assessment framework (e.g. the DSM verification by Deloitte & Touche and Neste verification by SustainAbility reference the fifty reporting criteria).
- Helped influence the structure, format and content of a considerable number of CERs (e.g. see acknowledgement in latest Danish Steel Works CER).

3 See the review in Chapter 20 of environmental reporting across the UK water industry.

But, like all such tools, these benchmarking tools have their weaknesses. In earlier stakeholder and practitioner roundtables, we identified and addressed some of these. But, as reporting becomes more sophisticated, both in terms of content and of the communication channels used, the challenge for the benchmarker grows. Here are some of the limitations and issues that the benchmarking team identified during the 1997 benchmarking round:

- The tools focus on reporting, not performance or impacts.

- The fifty-criteria approach scores CERs on the basis of their comprehensiveness, whereas some companies may decide—quite properly—to adopt a narrower, more focused approach.

- The focus is also on the CER, a printed corporate environmental performance report. As other environmental reports are published in parallel by the same company, and as the Internet is increasingly used, surely this is too restrictive? What do we do about companies that produce group reports, business reports and/or site reports?

- Despite the fact that a retailer has come top of the rankings two years running, the fifty reporting criteria are biased towards global manufacturing companies. They are also less appropriate for the service sector and for small and medium-sized enterprises (SMEs). How can this problem be addressed?

- The survey compares 'apples and oranges'. Is it right to compare the reports produced by companies in the manufacturing and service sectors, for example, or in the USA and South Korea?

- As the triple bottom line approach becomes more common, some companies will opt for parallel accounting and reporting. How can we do justice to their work?

- We do not reward companies for any environmental reporting in their annual reports. Is this fair? If not, what can we do about it?

- There are no negative scores. For example, should we be penalising companies when they fail to cover key issues related to their mainstream business activities in their reports?

No doubt, others will identify their own concerns. But to address several of those listed above, we are planning to take a number of parallel paths in the future *Engaging Stakeholders* programme. For example, we plan to:

- Tackle the 'apples and oranges' issue by focusing more effort on sectoral analyses.

- Take a sample of major companies and investigate in depth their total package of information products across the triple-bottom-line spectrum.

▼ Take a sample of leading CERs and compare the differences between the fifty-criteria approach and a new approach based on the triple bottom line.

◤ Recommendations for Future CERs

Some companies will continue to find all of this upsetting, even threatening. But for those who can overcome their fear of snoops and spies, the race for ever-greater—and more useful—disclosure continues. In the full report on the 1997 survey (SustainAbility/UNEP 1997), we offer 12 key recommendations. Here are five of them.

◻ *Account for the Triple Bottom Line*

No company pursuing sustainability—or operating in value chains where key actors have decided to move in this direction—will be able to ignore the triple bottom line (environmental, financial and social). But remember that integration means more than putting financial, environmental and community reports in a shiny cardboard presentation case (the BAA approach) or even on a CD-ROM (the BP approach). Companies will increasingly need to account for and report on their economic, environmental and social commitments, targets and performance. The lead provided by companies such as The Body Shop, BP, Shared Earth and BT will be built upon.

◻ *Spotlight the Real Issues, Impacts and Priorities*

Usually, the critical issues are linked directly to the company's core business, which may be why they are so often ignored. So a biotechnology-based company (Monsanto, for instance) fails to tackle the real genetic engineering issues, or an auto or oil industry CER chooses to ignore the global warming agenda. The banks are also a prime example of this problem: they are increasingly happy to discuss green housekeeping measures, but most provide little or no information on the social and environmental issues associated with their mainstream financial activities. Make sure that, as a minimum, that you focus on the essentials.

◻ *Think SMART—and Verify*

Whatever the indicators, be sure to develop and publish SMART (specific, measurable, attainable, relevant and trackable) targets. And, in measuring and tracking, recognise the value of verification. Given the growing interest in verification, any company thinking of producing non-verified CERs really ought to think again. The number of CERs being verified increased seven-fold between our 1994 and 1997 surveys, and half of the top 10 CERs are verified this time around.

◻ *Focus on Financial Market Users*

Increasingly, reporting will need to be targeted at financial institutions. Insurers woke up first and are now being followed by the lenders, particularly the banks. The Swiss banks, for example, are trying to standardise the environmental indicators used to track company risk and performance. The equity markets will be next. But if the financial markets are to pay real attention to environmental—and, eventually, triple bottom line—performance, they will need very different types of data and information from the companies they insure, lend to or invest in. By the early years of the 21st century, this will be a priority area for chief financial officers (CFOs).

⌑ *Link your CER with your Annual Report*

As the metrics evolve, it is likely that leading companies will start to include more—and more relevant—information on environmental and broader triple bottom line targets and performance in their annual reports. Reporting companies will also need to explain how they are accounting for the net economic, environmental and social value added. New guidelines are constantly emerging: be aware of them and review the longer-term implications.

◢ *Appendix: UNEP Programme Corporate Sponsors*

The latest stage of the SustainAbility/UNEP CER programme is supported by the following companies:

- Anglian Water
- Astra
- BAA
- Bayer
- BHP
- Bristol Myers Squibb
- British Petroleum
- Danish Steelworks

- DSM
- Eastern Group
- General Motors
- Imperial Chemical Industries
- Intel
- Neste
- Norsk Hydro

- Norvatis
- Novo Nordisk
- Rohm and Haas
- Rhône-Poulenc
- Royal Dutch/Shell
- Saga Petroleum
- Statoil

16
Statutory Environmental Reporting in Denmark

Status and Challenges

Pall M. Rikhardsson*

THE PUBLICATION of corporate environmental reports is rapidly gaining acceptance as a means of communicating corporate environmental performance to company stakeholders. Studies estimate that 7,000–10,000 environmental reports are being published worldwide, ranging from voluntary reports, Eco-Management and Auditing Scheme environmental statements, the Danish Green Accounts and significant environmental sections in annual reports (Rikhardsson 1998).

Several countries have made environmental reporting into a statutory requirement. One is Denmark, where, in 1996, an act requiring approximately 1,300 Danish companies[1] to publish stand-alone environmental reports came into effect. Such statutory environmental reports have been designated 'Green Accounts' by the Danish authorities and the act will be referred to here as the Danish Environmental Reporting Act, or DERA for short. The rest of this chapter will briefly explore the development of Danish environmental reporting, describe the contents of and requirements made by the DERA, report some results of studies of Green Accounts, and address important development issues.

---

* The views expressed in this chapter are the author's own and should not necessarily be associated with the institutions he represents.

1 As the obligation to publish Green Accounts is production site-based, corporations are required to publish Green Accounts for each of their production sites. So the actual number of *corporate* legal entities producing Green Accounts is smaller than 1,300. However, the following will refer to the DERA as encompassing 1,300 companies, thus counting each production site as one company.

◢ Developments in Danish Environmental Reporting

Environmental reporting was an almost unknown phenomenon in Denmark until the beginning of the 1990s. There are no surveys of environmental disclosures before 1991, but one may assume, based on later survey findings, that there were no major initiatives in this field before that time.

During 1992, the Danish Steel Works published what were referred to as 'Green Accounts' as a separate part of their Annual Financial Report, which included a mass balance and a description of the company's environmental impacts. According to a survey of 92 Danish annual reports made by Deloitte & Touche in 1993 (Deloitte & Touche 1993), approximately half of the respondents included environmental information, mostly concerning environmental legislation and product development. Rikhardsson *et al.* (1996) analysed 156 Danish annual reports from 1993, presenting findings similar to those of the Deloitte & Touche report. Additionally, Rikhardsson also attempted to measure the quality of the information disclosed, his main conclusion being that the information was generally disclosed in qualitative and non-verifiable terms. The characteristics of Danish environmental reporting in the period from 1991 to 1994 were that only a few companies included limited environmental information in their annual reports and no stand-alone environmental reports were published.

During 1994, the first separate environmental report appeared when the pharmaceutical company Novo Nordisk published a 36-page report focusing on its products and their life-cycles. Later, in 1994, several other companies followed suit. A total of 12 Danish environmental reports or significant environmental sections in annual reports competed for the annual 'Green Information' prize awarded by the Danish Institute of State-Authorised Public Accountants and the business newspaper *Børsen* in October 1995.

In light of the above, it is safe to conclude that before year-end 1995 and the introduction of the DERA, environmental reporting, whether in the annual report or in a stand-alone environmental report, was not a widespread activity in corporate Denmark—despite there being more than 7,000 Danish companies that are required to obtain environmental approvals from local or regional authorities.

◢ Statutory Environmental Reporting in Denmark

Setting a precedent, in 1996 Denmark introduced an act requiring certain Danish companies to publish separate annual environmental reports. Such environmental reports were designated 'Green Accounts' by the Danish authorities. Until then, there had been no specific requirements for the publication of environmental information except when required by accounting law and standards in relation to, for example, liabilities and the valuation of assets (Price Waterhouse 1995b). In one sweep, environmental reporting was made statutory for a large number of Danish companies. The DERA caused quite a stir among corporate Denmark, which argued that the cost of producing the Green Accounts would exceed by far the benefits to the users. However, the DERA discussions in 1995 were overshadowed by discussions about the introduction of taxes on emissions of CO_2 and SO_2, as well as other environmental taxes; the DERA was therefore voted through the Danish parliament with less controversy than might have been expected.

The actual name of the act is 'Act no. 403 of 14 June 1995 on the publication of Green Accounts' and it is an addition to the Danish Environmental Protection Act. The specifying rules of the act are laid out in the Ministry of Environment and Energy's regulation no. 975 of 13 December 1995 on the duty of firms subject to environmental approval to publish Green Accounts. Both the act and the regulation came into force on 1 January 1996. According to the Danish Ministry of Environment and Energy, the stated aim of the DERA is to inform the public, in non-technical terms, through the Green Accounts, of companies with significant environmental impacts (Thy 1997). This is intended, according to the Ministry, to improve the ability of 'ordinary people' to participate actively in protecting the environment by giving them access to information about corporate environmental impacts. Statutory environmental reporting should therefore be seen as a natural element of the effort of the Danish government to encourage citizens to participate in initiatives to protect the environment—at local, regional, national and global levels (Thy 1997).

◻ *Which businesses are required to publish Green Accounts?*

In order for the DERA to apply, the company must be subject to environmental approval under the Danish Environmental Protection Act. Approximately 7,000 Danish companies must obtain environmental approval by local or regional authorities before they can operate or expand.

The actual number of businesses required to publish Green Accounts is much smaller, however. The DERA includes a complete list of environmentally intensive industry categories: only if a company belongs to one of these categories (as would be indicated in its environmental approval), is it required to publish Green Accounts. The Danish Ministry has further limited this number by making companies with fewer than 20 employees exempt from the law. It should be noted that the act is site-based, meaning that, if a company has more than one production site falling within such industry categories, it has to publish one set of Green Accounts for every site. Currently, approximately 1,300 Danish companies are under a requirement to publish annual Green Accounts.

◻ *What is to be disclosed?*

DERA requirements relating to the contents of annual Green Accounts may be divided into three categories. First, there are requirements on what company information should be published. The information required includes company name, industry, location, regulatory authority and environmental approvals. Second, the Green Accounts must contain a management report. The management report must explain the relevance and significance of the environmental information disclosed in the Green Accounts. According to the DERA, this is to give the reader of the Green

Accounts an understanding of what significant environmental impacts are involved, and of why the company has chosen to inform about them in the format that they have adopted in the Green Accounts. Furthermore, the management report must explain any significant changes from the previous year's Green Accounts. The report must also address whether toxic substances used in the production process pose a threat to employees' health and safety, and describe the extent of employee involvement in preparing the Green Accounts. If the Green Accounts have been verified by an external third party, this has also to be included in the management report. Third, there are requirements on which quantitative environmental data have to be disclosed. Information requirements include:

- Consumption of raw materials
- Consumption of energy
- Consumption of water
- Emissions and description of significant pollutants used in production processes
- Emissions and description of significant pollutants discharged into soil, water or air
- Emissions and description of significant pollutants that end up in solid waste
- Emissions and description of significant pollutants that end up in the company's products

The data must be disclosed in absolute terms, i.e. tons, litres, joules, etc., though a company may of course supplement with other reporting forms such as figures in relative terms, or compare absolute figures between years. Companies are allowed to use indices[2] instead of absolute values when the latter might disclose information that is sensitive for competitive reasons. However, this requires that the information is classified as sensitive according to various legal rules governing public access to information in Denmark.

As yet, companies are not required to have their Green Accounts examined by an auditor or other independent third party, but have the option of doing so if the company feels this adds value to its Green Accounts.

◻ How are the Green Accounts to be published?

Generally, the Green Accounts must reflect the same financial period as that covered by the company's financial statement. Companies are then required to send the Green Accounts to the Danish Commerce and Companies Agency (CCA) in the same manner as annual financial statements. Accordingly, external stakeholders may obtain the Green Accounts from the CCA. Companies are under no obligation to send the

---

2   Meaning simple indices where the current value is related to some standard value selected by the company. This might, e.g., be the value for last year's performance.

Green Accounts to any stakeholders other than the CCA. Potential users may search for companies publishing Green Accounts by using the CCA's search engine.[3]

It should be noted that companies that have adopted, or are in the process of introducing, the Eco-Management and Auditing Scheme (EMAS) do not have to publish Green Accounts. Instead, such companies must send the required EMAS annual environmental statement to the CCA.

◻ *Governmental Verification of Green Accounts*

The CCA is formally in charge of the publication of Green Accounts. It is therefore the CCA's responsibility to check whether the accounts actually contain the information described in the regulations. Not later than six months after the end of the company's financial year, or with the company's financial statement if this has to be submitted sooner, the Green Accounts must be submitted to the CCA. Upon receiving the Green Accounts, the CCA will send them to the local environmental regulatory authority of the company (i.e. production site). The local regulatory authority can submit comments on the Green Accounts to the CCA up until four weeks after the regulatory authority has received the accounts. Any comments by the regulatory authority will be published with the Green Accounts.

Checking the quality of the environmental information disclosed in a company's Green Accounts is the responsibility of the environmental authorities, who are, in this case, represented by the Danish Environmental Protection Agency. After possibly obtaining more information from the company and the local environmental regulatory authority concerned, this agency will forward its conclusions to the CCA. On the basis of this information, the CCA draws its own conclusions on the company's Green Accounts. It may either reject the accounts altogether, or direct the company's attention to matters that must be corrected in the next Green Accounts if these are to be accepted for publication (Thy 1997). However, it has been stated by Danish environmental authorities that a company's Green Accounts will be rejected only if they give a grossly misleading overall picture of its environmental situation (Thy 1997). Rejections may be appealed to an environmental appeals board.

◢ *Green Accounts in Denmark: Some Results*

Danish companies are now well into their third Green Accounting period. Although the act has been in effect for three years and this period covers two full Green Accounting periods, there have been remarkably few studies of the Green Accounts themselves and even fewer of the use of Green Accounts by external stakeholders. Although there have been a number of piecemeal studies looking at the reporting practices of different industries or for other purposes, no comprehensive studies of the status and practice of environmental reporting in Denmark have yet been conducted—neither on environmental reporting practice of companies nor the use

---

3   At *http://www.publi-com.dk/GroenneRegnskaber/hside.htm* (regrettably in Danish only).

of environmental information by stakeholders. A possible explanation for this apparent lack of interest could be that few research institutions in Denmark have focused on environmental reporting as a field of study. And with 1,300 environmental reports to evaluate, some theoretical and methodological experience is called for. There has certainly been widespread interest in the Green Accounts among companies, accountants, environmental organisations, local authorities and the media.

In 1997 Rikhardsson and Bojsen (Rikhardsson and Bojsen 1998) interviewed 19 environmental managers of companies that had published environmental reports in 1996 and were working on their first Green Accounts. The respondents found the main benefits of their work with environmental reporting and the Green Accounts to be internal. None had received any response from external stakeholders regarding previous environmental reports. All of the companies therefore approached their Green Accounts as an environmental management system tool to increase employees' environmental awareness, quantify environmental performance, increase awareness of external stakeholders and, in some cases, help identify potential cost savings in, for example, energy consumption and waste generation.

The general cost of publishing a set of Green Accounts ranged from an estimated €10,000–100,000 for the respondent companies. This included company time and, in some cases, external consultants' efforts associated with environmental data collection, data processing and publishing the accounts. The variations in cost were mostly due to different levels of ambition, company size and prior experiences with environmental management and reporting. The time needed to produce a set of Green Accounts (planning, data collection and data verification) was equivalent to an average three months' full-time work by one person, ranging, however, from one month to one year among the respondents.

The main conclusion of the Rikhardsson and Bojsen survey was, first, that there was a lack of internal structure among the respondent companies for the purpose of collecting, processing and reporting environmental data, for example, in the Green Accounts. Few companies used information technology for this purpose although this might be changing (see Chapter 21). Second, most of the companies expressed disappointment with the lack of active interest from their stakeholders in the company Green Accounts. Few of the companies, however, had attempted to measure what their stakeholders expected or how they received the environmental report. This is important if the Green Accounts of the company are to be actively used as an external environmental communication tool. Third, some of the companies had engaged an external third party to review their Green Accounts. However, few had included a third-party statement in the Green Accounts. Accordingly, the credibility of the Green Accounts was not necessarily linked to the presence of such a statement and the work underlying it.

In 1998 Holgaard *et al.* (1999) performed a contents analysis of 108 Green Accounts from industries such as electronics, textiles, plastics, metal and consumables. The survey was a continuation of a similar survey carried out in 1997 of 43 different Green Accounts (Rasmussen and Remmen 1997). The main findings were that 81 (75%) of the companies complied with the requirements of the DERA. However, 27 Green Accounts (25%) did not comply with the DERA requirements and, in Holgaard *et al.*'s opinion, should have been rejected by the authorities. The authors further report that 27 (25%) companies do not state any targets or objectives in their Green Accounts. According to the authors, the omission of targets and objectives is a problem as systematic environmental management is, to a certain degree, based on setting targets and achieving them. However, it should be noted that, although targets have not been disclosed in the Green Accounts, it cannot necessarily be concluded from this that companies do not practise environmental target-setting.

Another interesting finding regards the frame of reference adopted by the Green Accounts, or what the authors call environmental understanding. All 108 Green Accounts view corporate environmental impacts through input–output 'spectacles'— i.e. as consumption of resources and emission of pollutants. Or, in the terminology of ISO 14031, as operational environmental performance. However, 46 companies (43%) also disclose information about systematic environmental activities focused on continuous improvement of environmental performance (i.e. management performance), thus exhibiting, in the authors' view, a broader frame of reference. Only eight companies (7%) see the company as part of a product life-cycle and address impacts during that life-cycle. Holgaard *et al.* do not note any reference to environmental condition-type performance measurements. None of the 108 Green Accounts includes any reference to stated political aims of sustainable development or even addresses this concept.

Finally, the authors looked at the environmental performance evaluation criteria used in the Green Accounts. Sixty-five (60%) of the Green Accounts surveyed use the previous year as a reference value for evaluating environmental performance; 43 (46%) companies relate environmental data to governmental consent limits to illustrate environmental compliance. No other types of performance evaluation benchmark, such as industry averages or household equivalents, are used.

◢ Issues for the Future

Does DERA live up to its stated aim of providing external stakeholders with non-technical information about corporate environmental performance? Not yet. Although the above surveys come nowhere near covering all of the approximately 1,300 Green Accounts currently being published, the results are interesting and are used here to identify three general issues that need to be addressed if the DERA is to fully live up to its aim.

The first issue is that Green Accounts are often viewed as internal environmental management tools (Rikhardsson and Bojsen 1998). Even Holgaard *et al.* also seem to regard the Green Accounts as purely an internal exercise, in that they see the Green Accounts '. . . as a tool in the preventive environmental work of companies' (Holgaard *et al.* 1999). However, the *raison d'être* of environmental reporting, including Green Accounts, is surely to provide external stakeholders with reliable environmental performance information. Internal environmental reporting is important but has a different purpose, target group and reporting format (Schaltegger *et al.* 1996). But very few of the Danish companies governed by the DERA have actively questioned their stakeholders about, for example, performance evaluations, credibility, usefulness, presentation of data and so on. Unlike financial annual reporting, it is often difficult to discern who is the actual target group of many Green Accounts, and in this respect the DERA does not provide much guidance. A clear definition of the target groups of the Green Accounts, their information requirements, and presentation format, has to be addressed in the future if Green Accounts are to develop into an efficient external communication tool.

The Holgaard *et al.* study (1999) points out that 27 out of 108 Green Accounts contained serious errors and omissions which should have led to the rejection of the accounts. This would mean (taking the risk of generalising on such insubstantial data) that approximately 380 out of 1,300 Green Accounts might not comply with the requirements of the DERA.[4] This obviously poses a threat to the credibility and serviceability of Green Accounts as a reliable information source for external stakeholders. If external users cannot rest assured that the data they are looking at are, at the very least, accurate and complete, the potential serviceability diminishes drastically. There seems to be a trend in Danish environmental reporting towards increased use of third-party verification of the Green Accounts, which includes large companies such as Shell, DiverseyLever and TeleDanmark. However, this is done on a voluntary basis. Statutory third-party verification and qualified governmental control of submitted Green Accounts is thus a very important issue to be addressed.

The third issue is the need to develop the DERA reporting framework further as an environmental reporting standard. At present, the DERA merely provides an overall framework within which there is much room for variation in, for example, contents valuations, evaluations, presentation and comparisons. Much is left to the discretion of management in selecting environmental information content and reporting form. This current lack of standardisation might be one explanation for the apparent lack of broad stakeholder use of the Green Accounts as a decision-support tool. Anecdotal evidence suggests that currently the primary users of Green Accounts are students, consultants and academics. If the external communication aspect of Green Accounts is to be developed further, issues such as environmental data disclosures and environmental data presentation have to be clarified. An example could be the choice of environmental performance evaluation criteria. How can an external user of Green Accounts be sure that an improvement in environmental performance in relative terms compared to the previous year reflects a real environmental performance improvement, rather than being attributable to cutbacks and closure of production lines? As also pointed out by Holgaard *et al.* (1999), certain requirements regarding the selection and presentation of environmental performance indicators as well as environmental performance evaluation criteria are therefore very important—in short, environmental book-keeping law along the same lines as the law governing financial accounting.

---

4   However, the CCA has not to date actually rejected any reports, as it is entitled to do, although it has returned several to the companies with requirements for further information, or for changes in presentation to be made.

◢ *Conclusion*

It may be argued that simply by introducing environmental reporting as part of the external reporting obligations of companies, the DERA has done much to institutionalise environmental reporting in Denmark compared to other countries. And the introduction of statutory environmental reporting certainly has increased the amount of environmental information disclosed by Danish companies. However, there are some indications that Green Accounts have yet some way to go before they can be considered a 'reliable source of environmental performance information for external stakeholders', as the stated aim of the DERA implies.

Other countries that might be considering introducing statutory environmental reporting could very well benefit from the Danish experience as well as progress in environmental reporting research and corporate practice. Law-makers might thus want to consider:

1. Whose information needs does the environmental reporting law aim to satisfy? Target groups such as 'society', 'the informed reader' or 'the concerned citizen' are too broad. Experience shows that a single environmental report cannot possibly satisfy all information needs in all stakeholder groups. Different stakeholder groups can be classified differently regarding, for example, information needs, environmental understanding, business understanding, technical knowledge, etc. Therefore, attempting to address all stakeholder needs might lead to none of these being fulfilled. Target group clarification is thus an important part of any proposed obligatory environmental reporting act.

2. How can comparability and transparency be assured? The legal requirement of certain high-level environmental information content, while the actual presentation is left to the companies themselves, results in each company adopting its own reporting style, indicators, evaluation criteria, reporting level, etc. An environmental reporting law has to be more specific, given the current knowledge of environmental reporting practice. Only by defining the environmental reporting framework to include issues such as types of performance indicator, types of performance evaluation criterion, acceptable information detail, allowable use of indices, etc. will the obligatory environmental reports become more than general information brochures.

3. How can information quality be assured? Lack of assurance that environmental data are complete, accurate, valid, reliable, etc. can seriously hinder stakeholder use and acceptance of environmental reports. And this means that some sort of independent third-party verification of environmental reports, leading to a verification statement in the report itself, is needed to ensure future credibility.

It should be noted that the Danish authorities are performing an overall review of the DERA during the first six months of 1999, which may include some of the above issues.

17

Reaching Consensus on the Implementation of Good Practice in Environmental Reporting

A Dutch NGO's Perspective

Jan Willem Biekart and Karin Ree

'PILES OF PAPER that nobody reads.' For many years, this has been the standard reaction by VNO/NCW, the general Dutch Confederation of Industry and Employers, to proposals for a statutory corporate environmental report (CER). Companies in the Netherlands, however, are being influenced by growing national and international pressures to report—pressures such as current reporting practices in Scandinavia, the US and the UK, the reporting requirement of the Environmental Management and Auditing Scheme (EMAS) in Europe, and the chemical industry's Responsible Care programme. Their understanding of the merits of reporting is increasing slowly but steadily, as shown by KPMG's annual reviews of Dutch environmental reports (KPMG 1998; see also Van Dalen 1997). Well over a hundred environmental reports were published by companies in 1996, at both site and corporate level. Reporting companies can be found in a wide range of economic sectors, although the chemical industry is still leading the way. The total number is still low, however, as a proportion of medium-sized and large companies in the relevant sectors. Many Dutch companies listed on the Amsterdam stock market do not report.

◢ Public Policy Motives for Environmental Reporting

Since the 1980s, Dutch environmental organisations have been arguing for annual environmental reports to be compulsory for industrial organisations, with limited public access to industrial emission data initially being the major argument. At the same time, industries have begun to feel an increasing need to demonstrate their environmental responsibility. A public discussion on the function of environmental management systems (EMSs) and auditing was initiated in 1986 by the general Dutch employers' organisations VNO and NCW (then separate), and this also stimulated a debate on environmental reporting. In 1989, the Dutch government introduced an official policy on EMSs, largely consisting of an extensive programme of subsidies for industry sector-specific activities, which ran until 1996. Environmental organisations argued for three essential elements of an EMS: an environmental programme, an annual environmental report, and the opportunity for the regulatory authorities to order an independent audit of any EMS. They were partly successful: following a request from Parliament in 1989, the Minister of the Environment agreed to make reporting compulsory for a limited number of industrial production sites.

In the early 1990s, the Dutch government also instituted its 'target group' approach to setting long-term environmental targets in national policy plans, and implementing them through covenants (or environmental agreements) between government and sectors of industry (Ministry of Housing, Spatial Planning and the Environment 1996). These agreements require company environmental plans (CEPs), at site level, to be made by the larger companies in industry sectors such as chemicals, base metals, oil/gas, paper and dairy. These CEPs are a type of environmental programme in which companies are required to describe the environmental measures that they plan to implement in the next four years and the resulting expected reduction in environmental impacts. CEPs are public information and under certain conditions are formalised in environmental permits. This element of the target group policy has stimulated progress in the implementation of environmental management systems, in the certification of these systems (ISO 14001, EMAS), and particularly in improving the quality of companies' environmental data.

Despite industry opposition, the new law on environmental reporting was finally accepted by Parliament in spring 1997 (Ministry of Housing, Spatial Planning and the Environment 1997). It requires two site environmental reports (SERs), one for the regulatory authorities and one for the general public, from about 330 of the largest Dutch industrial sites, covering all production sectors with major environmental emissions. Both SERs must cover one calendar year, and must be published before 1 May and 1 July respectively in the following year. The first year on which sites must report is 1999, so that the first reports are due to be published in 2000. The parliamentary debate led to the adoption of two amendments which created the possibility in law that (at a later stage) information on the environmental aspects of products and on verification may be required.

In 1997, less than a third of all companies in the Netherlands that publish a report (i.e. some 35 companies) belonged to this group of 330. This means that several hundreds of production sites will have to prepare a public report for the first time.

As stated, the law requires two SERs: one for the regulatory authorities and one for the general public. Both versions are publicly available, aiming for a high level of transparency, reliability and consistency of data on the continuous improvement of environmental performance. The obligation to produce two SERs may appear to be a burden on industry, but in fact it could be an advantage. Until recently, companies have complained about their many legal obligations (often laid down in permits) to report on various environmental issues to separate regulatory authorities in different formats and following different time schedules. The introduction of one integrated report for all regulatory authorities harmonises these procedures and fits well with common EMS practice in most larger companies. The SER for the general public and/or specific user groups can be at least partly based on the data from the integrated SER for the regulatory authorities. Obviously, the report for the regulatory authorities is much more quantitative, detailed and emission-focused, while the public report summarises these data and can also emphasise other issues that are not addressed in the legal permits, such as the number and treatment of complaints, product impacts, etc. An outline for an annual SER for regulatory authorities, integrating the permit-based legal obligations for reporting, was designed by the regulatory authorities and enforcement organisations together, ensuring the continuous provision of data for accurate control on industrial performance and compliance. The task of checking the data for accuracy and reliability remains with the regulatory authorities. The requirements on the format and contents of the report for the regulatory authorities are elaborated in a special Order in Council (Ministry of Housing, Spatial Planning and the Environment 1998). Legal requirements for public reports are minimal.

◢ The Quality of Dutch Environmental Reports from the NGOs' Perspective

Dutch environmental groups have put considerable effort into stimulating the quality of environmental reporting. Reliability of the information in environmental reports is their primary interest, and misleading images and glossy public-relations publications elicit sharp reactions from them. In 1992, a well-known environmental organisation active in the industrialised Rotterdam region had already made explicit its expectations of environmental reports in the chemical industry (Muilerman *et al.* 1992). This booklet was followed by a report on the quality of the environmental reports of nine large industries in this province (Boer *et al.* 1996). On a national scale, 11 provincial and national environmental organisations jointly published an evaluation of 30 reports published in 1995 (Robesin 1997).

In summary, these evaluations demonstrate that the topics best described in environmental reports are: actual emissions, the organisation, and the comprehensive goals of environmental management. Generally, reports mention the companies' orientation on the environment, but this is restricted to rather general commitments and usually has no direct relation to the companies' products and production processes. Even less information is presented on future emission targets and concrete plans for environmental measures and research. Information is seldom put into the perspective of the companies' own environmental targets in the reporting year, permit requirements, possible achievements of best available techniques and/or the performance of comparable companies. Financial information on planned investments and on the costs and benefits of realised measures are dealt with in a perfunctory manner. There is room for considerable improvement in the reports' readability. Finally, in general, it is not possible to ascertain whether the reports provide a true and fair picture of companies' environmental performance.

The results of the evaluation were discussed with the companies involved and, in spite of the fact that a considerable number of reports failed to elicit a favourable response, the reaction of most companies was enthusiastic. They took public reaction in any form as at least an indication of public interest in the reports.

◢ *A Unique Initiative*

Convergence of various stakeholders' opinions on the desired content and quality of an environmental report can contribute greatly to the status and value of this instrument, both for its producers and its users. For this convergence of opinion to occur, relevant user groups need to be identified and encouraged to express their information needs. This point has been recognised quite clearly by environmental organisations, and the formation of coalitions with relevant influential organisations, not excluding opponents, can help in this. Already in 1996, before the law was passed in parliament, the Netherlands Society for Nature and Environment (SNM), an influential national lobbying organisation, had invited the general Dutch employers' confederation VNO/NCW to rethink current reporting practice (VNO/NCW 1996) with a view to making it a valuable instrument of communication. This invitation met with a cautious reaction.

Because legal requirements for a public SER are minimal, the explanatory memorandum to the legislation refers to a ministerial proposal addressed to 'the most interested parties', i.e. VNO/NCW and the environmental organisations, inviting them to come to an agreement on the desired contents and format of a public SER. Both SNM and VNO/NCW accepted this proposal and agreed to compile a (non-binding) guideline based on their shared opinions to elaborate on the basic legal requirements. The Ministry of the Environment guided the process and made available the necessary funds. After a year of negotiation and consultation with the respective supporters, a brochure was published (VNO/NCW and Stichting Natuur en Milieu 1998).

An interesting aspect of this negotiating process was the set of preconditions of both parties. Most of these were expressed at the first meeting, though some turned up only later. The primary concerns of the VNO/NCW were:

▼ To explain the general requirements of the law, without extensions

▼ To provide basic and generally accepted content requirements, illustrated by a number of good examples taken from existing reports. Detailed and ambitious content requirements would hamper companies with little or no experience in reporting.

▼ To find an approach with which companies can identify, avoiding utopian statements

- To elaborate SERs as an instrument of communication, not as an isolated tool for environmental progress

The primary concerns of SNM were:

- To ascertain companies' awareness of the existence of different user groups of SERs

- To specify the information needs of the different user groups

- To position reporting as an important, though not the only, instrument of corporate environmental communication

- To specify criteria for 'true and fair' information

- To report on more than just the environmental performance of the primary production process, i.e. to involve also future emissions targets, environmental aspects of products, transport and raw materials, the use of dangerous substances, etc.

These concerns clearly reflect the position of both organisations in Dutch society. In spite of the mutual understanding of concerns and positions, however, the negotiations turned out to be rather difficult, due to differences in culture and modes of communication. Several drafts were made alternately by SNM and VNO/NCW; but they were either too controversial and explicit in the eyes of VNO/NCW, or too vague and non-committal in the eyes of SNM. On several occasions, it became clear that it was also difficult for one party to admit to the other's success, even in an instance where it was outside the scope of its immediate concerns. Finally these problems were solved with the help of a professional copywriter and an independent consultant, who also assisted in the process of reaching consensus on the content and structure of the brochure.

Major recurrent items of discussion were:

- The specification of different user groups and their information needs

- How far one must go in explaining the very general requirements of the law

- The relevance of international developments in environmental reporting, in particular in the English-speaking West

- The substantiation of the 'true and fair' requirement of the law

The two major drivers to overcoming differences in opinion were:

- The awareness that failing negotiations would lead to a guidance document from the Ministry of the Environment

- The challenge of showing that co-operation between environmental and employers' organisations is possible, at least in the field of environmental reporting

Finally, both parties agreed on a guideline which was pre-tested at a number of companies (those liable under the law to produce an SER) and user groups. The brochure was presented to the Minister of the Environment by the chairmen of both organisations at a press conference in May 1998, and distributed widely.

◢ The Contents of the Guideline

The structure and contents of the guideline were partly inspired by the World Industry Council for the Environment publication on environmental reporting (WICE 1994). For example, one element that was adopted was a list of preliminary questions that should always be answered before attempting to write an environmental report. Specific stakeholder groups and their information needs are addressed in a box, based on empirical studies carried out in the Netherlands. Box 1 presents a translation of the text of this box.

The main body of this consists of an explanation of the statutory requirements for a public environmental report, as listed below, followed by a number of recommendations about how to fulfil them. Most requirements are illustrated by examples of good practice drawn from actual Dutch environmental reports. The guideline suggests that a report of 10–30 pages will usually be appropriate.

A company may combine several SERs into a single corporate environmental report, or integrate environmental reporting with reporting on finance or on safety and health, provided that the legal requirements are met. Some of the guidelines refer to the (minimum) contents of SERs (nos. 1–4), while others refer to their presentation (5–7), reliability (8) and publication (9–10) of the reports.

1. **The production site.** This item includes the layout of the site, the position of the site within the company, the nature of the activities, the production capacity, the number of employees, major incoming raw materials, production processes and products/services, as well as markets. Examples are taken from the reports of Hoogovens Steel 1996 and DSM corporate 1997.

2. **The environmental consequences of the site's activities, with particular attention to changes since the previous year.** Quantitative environmental data can be compared to permitted levels, other legal requirements, or other relevant environmental standards. This item also includes a brief explanation of the direct and indirect environmental effects of raw materials use, emissions, substances and products. Topical issues need special attention. Examples are taken from the reports of BASF Netherlands 1996, AVR Chemical 1996, DSM corporate 1997 and Electrolux corporate Sweden 1996 (see Box 2).

3. **The environmental policy (principles, goals and targets) and the actual system of environmental management.** This requirement refers to the policy statement and a description of the environmental management system at a technical, organisational and administrative level. This

Employees. Many companies consider their own employees to be an important user group of the environmental report. Management is informed in a simple and well-organised way, while other staff will be motivated by a good and clear report. Employees often hear about the environmental performance of their company from acquaintances; in the report they can read what has been achieved. They can also find out about the plans and policies of their company for the coming period. It can be expected that will they take special interest in the relationship between the environmental situation and working conditions, including accidents and crises and the way in which these are dealt with, and plans and potential for internal training in environmental matters. It is compulsory for a company to present the environmental report for discussion at its works council, and Dutch trade unions have developed a checklist for this purpose.*

Local residents. Local residents experience some of the direct consequences of a company's environmental behaviour. Because they are often unaware of the company's actions to lessen its impacts, the environmental report provides an excellent opportunity to explain measures achieved and its future plans. Special attention can be expected to be paid to the environmental and health aspects of substances produced and emitted. Local residents will also be interested in external risks and how the company prevents or deals with them. This also holds true for information about the content, the location and the number of complaints and the way in which complaints are answered. Furthermore, information about non-compliances with permitted emissions and preventative measures will be useful.

Financial relations. A growing group of investors is interested in companies' environmental strategy and performance, with a number of private investors preferring environmental front-runners. Institutional investors may focus on the long-term environmental risks (and opportunities) of companies. Special interest is to be expected in the environmental strategy and performance of a company at a corporate level. Investors are not particularly interested in the format of the information, as long as it is reliable, complete, clear and relevant. The relationship between environmental and financial information is relevant, as well as the comparability of this information with other companies. Insurance companies and lenders will also be interested in the compliance behaviour of the company and the quality of its environmental management. Issues will be soil pollution and the presence of high-risk substances such as asbestos in buildings, and the possibility of environmental risks related to new production processes, products or services.[†]

Other commercial relationships. The relationships between a company and its suppliers and customers are usually long-term and, in such relationships, mutual trust is highly desirable. Customers are especially influential in making environmental demands on their suppliers (procurement policies), relating to products, processes or management. Close contact and co-operation is needed to meet customers' specific needs for information and improvements.[‡]

Other parties. Consumers and consumer organisations, as well as environmental NGOs, are often interested in companies' environmental policies and performance, related to processes and products. Issues that are topical in the political domain or in the media are relevant: for example, recycling efforts in the electronics industry; elimination of toxic substances in paints and glues; sourcing of wood in the timber and furniture industry, etc. A company should realise that it is wise to clarify its position, efforts and results on these issues. Environmental NGOs are also interested in the development of environmental performance over time on a local as well as on a corporate level. They want to be able to put this information into a clear context, so that comparisons can be made with legal requirements, best available technologies, and the performance of other, comparable, companies. Information on concrete goals and targets for the shorter and longer term is essential, not only with regard to emissions, but also concerning the use of raw materials and energy, products and transport.**

---

* Empirical research on this can be found in Boer *et al.* 1996.
† Empirical research on this can be found in Schrama and Schelleman 1996;
  VBDO 1996; Hollandse Koopmansbank 1997.
‡ Empirical research in this area can be found in Biekart 1996.
** Environmental NGOs have expressed their information needs in Robesin 1997.

Box 1: USER GROUPS AND THEIR INFORMATION NEEDS AS DESCRIBED IN THE GUIDELINE

includes certification ambitions, results of internal and external audits, and corrective actions, as well as insights into environmental costs and investments. Recommended issues also include legal compliance, incidents and complaints, training of staff and contractors, procurement policies, etc. Examples are taken from the reports of Rockwool 1996, Hoogovens Steel 1996 (see Box 3) and Dow Benelux 1996.

4. **Developments to be expected in the coming year(s) with regard to the items previously mentioned.** It is emphasised that the company should look further ahead than one year only. Plans for research and development can incorporate environmental considerations and should be part of this item. Examples are taken from the reports of Parenco 1996 (see Box 4) and NAM 1996.

5. **The SER should be published in Dutch.**

6. **The text should be concise.** Examples are taken from the reports of Hoechst 1996 and Crosfield 1996.

7. **The text should be comprehensible.** An example is taken from the report of Crown Van Gelder 1997.

Commercial Refrigeration Equipment

Key environmental issues:

- Cooling agents
- Energy
- Noise
- Work environment
- Resource efficiency

Eliminating the use of ozone-depleting substances and reducing energy consumption are the primary areas of concern in our environmental work with commercial refrigeration and cooling equipment.

The phase-out of chlorofluorocarbons (CFCs) in our products was completed in 1995 and, in 1996, we also completed the phase-out of the less harmful hydrochlorofluorocarbons (HCFCs) in Europe. A supermarket cooling system may contain up to 600 kilograms of ozone-depleting substances—with an annual leakage of up to 10%. This illustrates how important the phase-out is. Electrolux now offers a unique system of natural refrigerants. In an indirect system, the refrigerant—ammonia or propane—circulates only in the refrigeration unit itself, and only in small amounts. The only thing pumped out to the refrigerator or freezer is the carrier. In previous product generations, the carrier could be a saline solution or propylene glycol. The new pressurised CO_2 systems reduce environmental impact and improve performance.

Natural refrigerants have no impact on the ozone layer and only negligible greenhouse effect. The new systems offer opportunities to improve the energy efficiency of the equipment. It also reduces maintenance costs. Consequently, the life cost of refrigeration equipment, of which energy consumption accounts for up to 75%, is considerably reduced.*

---

* Illustrated by a graph demonstrating that the energy consumption per year and per metres of refrigeration unit has decreased between 1989 and 1996 from c. 4,500 kWh to less than 2,000 kWh.

Box 2: THE ELECTROLUX EXAMPLE: THE 1996 CORPORATE REPORT (PRODUCTS)

Environmental Policy Statement

Hoogovens Steel considers environmental care to be a societal duty and of great importance for the continuity of its operations.

Hoogovens Steel focuses its environmental policy on:

- Compliance with legal requirements and commitments laid down in environmental agreements
- The environmental aspects of its products covering the whole of the life-cycle
- The optimal use of environmental facilities
- Lowering of the use of energy and raw materials
- Attention to the environmental impacts of investments
- The encouragement of each employee's responsible behaviour with regard to the environment
- Providing for external information concerning environmental matters

The realisation of this policy also depends on the financial possibilities within business economic boundaries.

Hoogovens Steel operationalises this environmental policy as follows:

- Compliance with legal requirements and commitments laid down in environmental agreements is assured through a well-functioning system of environmental management following ISO 14001. Every year the operational units formulate—as part of their yearly operational plans—an environmental programme, in which all the activities in the environmental area are specified.
- Through its pursuit of closing of the loop, the recycling of materials and application of life-cycle assessment, Hoogovens Steel gives form and substance to sustainable development with regard to its products.
- Hoogovens Steel strives towards a further lowering of the environmental impacts of its processes: for example, by the optimal use of environmental facilities. This includes people, management and materials, available methods and installations.
- Environmental care is completely integrated into daily operations. Hoogovens Steel holds every employee responsible for environmental care at their place of work and provides them with the means of fulfilling this responsibility.
- Hoogovens Steel actively seeks to adapt and refocus the working methods throughout the whole organisation towards continuous care for the environment. Relevant environmental subjects are part of education and training programmes.
- The goal of lowering energy use is realised on the one hand by a more efficient use of materials, and on the other hand by the application of technologies the energy use of which is as low as possible.
- Apart from providing information about the company in general, Hoogovens Steel considers it its task to provide information about its environmental policies.

Box 3: THE HOOGOVENS STEEL EXAMPLE:
THE 1996 REPORT (ENVIRONMENTAL POLICY STATEMENT)

Translated by the authors

Future

The production capacity of Parenco will be increased in 1998 from 410,000 to 460,000 tonnes of paper per year, by the alteration of paper machine PM1 and an extension of the de-inking capacity for used paper.

The most important part of the alteration of PM1 is the renewal of the cloths; the drying part and the calendars will also be adapted. With regard to the de-inking of used paper, the oldest lines (nos. 1 and 3) will be taken out of production and replaced by a larger line, no. 5.

The floating bed oven will be adapted to a higher sludge supply; the increasing need for steam will be met by a temporary steam boiler, anticipating the construction of a new co-generation plant. Environmental emissions will increase proportionately to the production increase, with the exception of noise levels, groundwater use and waste-water emissions, which will stay within the present levels of the permits.

Environmental measures for the coming years are laid down in the Company Environmental Plan 1996–2000. The measures implemented in 1996 are described in Chapter 3. The measures planned for 1997–2000 are summarised in the table below.

AIR	completion of co-generation plant study (1997)
	biological NO_X reduction (1997)
	drafting of Company Energy Plan (1997)
	construction plan floating bed oven (1998)
WASTE-WATER	start-up of micro-flotation (1997)
	optimisation of nutrients (1997)
	monitoring chlorinated phenols (1998)
SOIL	removal of oil tank (1997)
	soil risk analysis (1998)
	reconstruction of storage of chemicals (1998)
WASTE	reduction of fibre losses (1998)
ODOUR	covering of selector (1997)
	inventory (1998)
GROUNDWATER	research on possibilities of stream water infiltration (1997)
	re-use of effluent (1999)
	Green Paper project (1999)
MANAGEMENT	audit (1997)
	certification of environmental management system ISO 14001/EMAS

After the year 2000, depending on actual developments, the following items may arise:

- Adaptation of the energy supply (new co-generation plant)
- Renewal of the sludge-burning technology
- Reduction of groundwater use (via closed-loop systems and/or a shift to surface-water supply)
- Reduction of the emission of heavy metals

Box 4: THE PARENCO EXAMPLE: THE 1996 REPORT (FUTURE PLANS)

Translated by the authors

8. **The SER should be reliable.** This means that the report is complete (all relevant environmental subjects, no selective account) and that the information is objective and representative (that the picture presented is realistic; information is presented in context; there are no value judgements). Reliability is essential, because the reader cannot verify the information. Tips for enhancing the report's reliability are:

   ▼ Seek independent verification.

   ▼ Be cautious about dubious data.

   ▼ Be sure that data and information in the public report correspond to data reported to the permitting authorities.

   ▼ Be sure that the data and information in the public report correspond to those mentioned in other reports of the company;

   ▼ Present actual environmental performance in comparison with standards in permit requirements and in company targets, while explaining all differences.

   ▼ Be explicit and constant in the basic methods of the collection of data and explain the reason for any changes in methods.

   ▼ Disclose the annual environmental operational costs, and the environmental investments of actual or planned measures.

   Examples are taken from the reports of Hoogovens Steel 1996, NAM 1996, DSM corporate 1997 (see Box 5) and Unilever corporate 1998.

9. **The SER should be published before 1 July of the following year.**

10. **Publication of the report must be publicly announced in an adequate manner, and the report made available to anyone at cost-price or less.**

Supervision and inspection

Every (sub)division of DSM is screened periodically, not only by their own HSE experts, but also by corporate experts. Attention is focused mainly on the question of how the implementation of the HSE management system is carried out and what the results are. Every factory is audited once every three years and receives an assessment. Following the assessment, an improvement programme is agreed. In order to guarantee the quality of the audits, the working method is periodically reviewed by external experts.

In 1997 a HSE audit was carried out by the central audit group of DSM at 32 (sub)divisions of DSM. In 81% of these, the final score was 'more than satisfactory' or 'good'. The target is for this percentage to be at least 90%.*

---

* A graph follows with the internal audit results divided into four classes of excellence over the years 1991 to 1997, related to the 90% target.

Box 5: THE DSM EXAMPLE:
THE 1997 CORPORATE RESPONSIBLE CARE PROGRESS REPORT (RELIABILITY)

Translated by the authors

◢ Directions for the Future

Both the employers' organisation and the environmental organisation realise that the guideline is not a final product, but rather the starting point of a continuing process. Hopefully, this will lead to a further consensus in the near future with a higher level of ambition. Environmental reporting is a dynamic area; VNO/NCW and SNM have agreed to evaluate and adapt their brochure within two to three years' time. In the meantime, the Ministry of the Environment will arrange an arbitration board (consisting of representatives of producers and user groups of the reports), as well as an information bureau and an interactive website, in order to:

- Settle disputes about published reports failing to meet legislative requirements
- Answer questions about the law
- Answer questions about both environmental reports for the public and environmental reports for the authorities
- Collect and distribute up-to-date information about national and international developments in environmental reporting
- Evaluate the information needs of various user groups of environmental reports
- Assist the continuing process of reaching consensus about environmental reporting, involving a growing number of stakeholders

The focus remains on the Netherlands, and both VNO/NCW and SNM will continue to participate in the process. The environmental NGOs have some explicit priorities for the coming period:

- First, representatives of other relevant user groups should be encouraged to participate in the process and to make their information needs explicit in terms of desired SER content and quality. Accurate and harmonised performance indicators, not currently in the guideline, will obviously help to address their demands.

- Second, the requirements for SER content should be more explicit in encouraging companies to go beyond emissions from their primary production processes. Sustainable production must somehow be put into practice, addressing issues such as products, services, transport, raw materials, supplier certification, etc.

- Third, environmental reporting should be encouraged in other organisations, both industrial and non-industrial. This broadening is also encouraged in the proposal of the European Commission for a revised EMAS regulation, which will become effective by 2000.

In the light of these ambitions, it is a major challenge to keep SERs comprehensible, concise, complete and true. Environmental organisations therefore expect that, in the near future, other means of disseminating company environmental information will be introduced into the public realm for distribution on a wider scale—in particular on the Internet.

18
Environmental Reporting in Japan

Current Status and Implications of ISO 14001 and a Pollutant Release Inventory

Takehiko Murayama

FOLLOWING A SERIES of well-publicised pollution incidents in the 1960s and 1970s, environmental awareness and related action within Japanese society and among Japanese businesses has increased.[1] However, there is only a limited amount of English-language literature on environmental performance measurement and reporting in Japan, and many Western discussions on the topic assume that progress on this is negligible. This chapter examines the truth of this assumption by examining the recent history and current status of corporate environmental reporting in Japan, and the implications of ISO 14001 and the development of pollutant release inventories for future progress.

◢ Corporate Environmental Reporting in Japan

There is no tradition of Japanese companies providing information of any kind to the public. Environmental disclosure is a particularly sensitive issue because of controversial incidents such as the cases of organic mercury poisoning from chemical factories in Minamata and Niigata, and asthma caused by emissions from an industrial complex in Yokkaichi City (JEA 1969). While such experiences have

---

1 According to a public opinion poll in 1995 (Japan Prime Minister's Office 1995), the proportion of people who consider that Japan should implement environmental protection measures in advance of other countries is gradually increasing, compared to 1988 and 1990.

ultimately led to positive action from companies on environmental protection, they may well have had a negative impact on attitudes about releasing information. Unlike other countries, Japan, until recently, has not witnessed significant pressure from public agencies for greater disclosure (see below).

◻ **Surveys of Reporting Practice**

The first detailed survey on the nature and extent of environmental disclosure in Japan was conducted by the Valdez Society in 1993. The Society, which was founded in 1991 to publicise the CERES (Coalition for Environmentally Responsible Economies) Principles in Japan, collected and analysed 73 companies' published action plans based on a proposal made by the Japanese Ministry of International Trade and Industry (MITI) in 1992 (Tsunoda 1994). One finding was that more manufacturing industries published environmental reports than did service industries. And, of all manufacturing industries, industries producing goods for end-consumers published more detailed reports than did raw materials industries. The closer their products are to the public, the more positive are industries about environmental reporting. Generally speaking, industries that deal with toxic chemicals, medical supplies, or pesticides, or that release toxic materials, such as in paper manufacturing, and that are expanding their business in European and North American countries, are positive about environmental auditing. A survey on similar issues in SMEs in the same year found that very few had published environmental reports (Maruyama 1993).

The Valdez Society produced a second survey on disclosure in 1997, when they analysed the reports and other published materials of 55 companies (Tsunoda and Kawaguchi 1997). A much higher number of corporations, including electricity-generating plants and the electrical appliance industry, were producing full environmental reports than was the case in the earlier study. The proportion of companies with full reports reached around 60%, and there was also greater emphasis on quantitative targets. However, companies published more realistic targets regarding the environmental impacts caused by their activities and products. Some companies' reports supplied specific information on the use of chemical materials as well as on the generation and disposal of industrial waste, whereas other companies did not provide any such detail. Although this analysis found that the content of reports had improved in general, it also pointed out that attitudes to environmental management varied between different industry sectors. Electricity-generating plants and the electric utility industry were the most enthusiastic about reporting, routinely publishing annual environmental reports publicising their environmentally sound activities. For example, one of the largest electricity utilities, Tokyo Electric Power Co. Ltd, publishes detailed material amounting to over 100 pages (Tokyo Electric Power Co. 1998). This report came joint ninth in the 1997 *Engaging Stakeholders* survey (SustainAbility/UNEP 1997; and Chapter 15).

Electrical appliance, automobile and automobile parts manufacturing industries demonstrated the greatest achievements in terms of previous targets. Environmental reports published by the electrical appliance industry—for example, that of NEC (1998)—appeared to offer the most effective format from the viewpoint of publica-

	Total mailed	Respondents	Publishing a public report	Publishing an internal report	Considering publishing a report	Others
Distribution	99	18	8	2	4	4
Co-op	29	13	7	0	6	0
Manufacturing	315	62	22	7	23	10
Electric and gas	12	8	8	0	0	0
Construction	10	7	6	0	1	0
Housing	10	0	0	–	–	–
Hotel	36	0	0	–	–	–
Total	511	108	51	9	34	14

Table 1: PUBLICATION OF ENVIRONMENTAL REPORTS BY INDUSTRY SECTOR

Source: GCS and GRF 1998

tion of targets and results on quantitative reductions in environmental loads. The Valdez Society analysis also found that, in contrast, reports by the steel industry were mostly characterised by conceptual descriptions without precise targets. Chemical and textile industries also had no plans to make public the results of their environmental management activities. While some chemical corporations had implemented 'Responsible Care' projects, it was notable that these reports were not made available to the public.

The Green Consumer Society (GCS) and Green Reporting Forum (GRF) also conducted a questionnaire survey on environmental reports in 1997 (GCS and GRF 1998). Table 1 summarises the results. According to this survey, 60 companies had already produced independent environmental reports (external and internal). The ratio of companies publishing environmental reports as a proportion of total respondents is over 90% in the electricity, gas and construction industries, whereas in manufacturing and distribution it is less than 40%. The main items that respondents regard as important in environmental reports were found to be explanations of management and reporting policy, and summaries of environmental impact reductions. Many respondents were still finding difficulties in deciding the range and depth of the report's content, how to make it easy to understand, and effective data collection. When asked about the benefits of reporting, 92% of respondents cited increasing understanding inside corporations; improvement of dialogue with stakeholders was supported by 51%. Table 2 presents the publication of information on each facility. While 20% have published information on all facilities, 77% have not, citing mainly reasons of expense and time, and the fact that publishing on every site would be too narrow an operation.

	Publishing	Not publishing	n/a
Distribution	0	9	1
Co-op	2	5	0
Manufacturing	7	21	1
Electric and gas	2	6	0
Construction	1	5	0
Total	12	46	2

Table 2: PUBLICATION OF ENVIRONMENTAL REPORT FOR EACH FACILITY

Source: GCS and GRF 1998

◁ *Detailed Analysis of the Electrical Appliance Industry*

In 1997, the Valdez Society also conducted an in-depth analysis of reports from the electrical appliance and automobile industries (Tsunoda and Kawaguchi 1997). Table 3 summarises their results for six reporting companies in the electrical appliance sector. The study found that, in comparison to their previous survey, issues were more easily defined and targets set were more likely to be achieved. Past experience of environmental reporting may also have provided a learning experience for these companies. The priority in implementation of environmental measures had shifted, from substitution of CFCs, to certification to ISO 14001. Energy saving was the area in which self-appointed targets were least likely to be achieved, mainly because much effort had already been spent in this area since the energy crisis of 1978. Four of the six companies had met or exceeded their waste targets and three their packaging targets.

One new item in the environmental reports was the management of chemical releases. The introduction of a PRTR (Pollutant Release and Transfer Register) system in the near future (see below) may encourage further initiatives in this area.

Although no company summarised the results of its materials recycling, many described their ability rate (the period required to break appliances down into recyclable parts). This is mainly because Japan currently has no collection system for used electrical appliances. To address this situation, Fujitsu and NEC have formed their own recycling systems.

One of the companies analysed, NEC, also provides a good example of state-of-the-art environmental reporting in Japan. Their report contains the following elements: company profile; outline of the EMS; environmental impacts and counter-measures; target-setting and results; charitable activities; and environmental charter. Within each element, annual targets and results are given for each environmental perfor-

	Energy saving	Industrial waste	Recycling	Environ-mental impacts of products	Packaging materials	EMS (ISO 14001)	Management of chemical releases
NEC	○	○	◉	○	○	◉	–
Hitachi	○	◉	○	○	◉	○	–
Toshiba	○	◉	○	○	◉	◉	◉
Fujitsu	◉	◉	◉	○	◉	◉	◉
Panasonic	○	○	–	○	○	◉	–
Sony	○	○	○	○	○	◉	○
Mitsubishi	○	◉	○	○	○	◉	○

Legend
- ◉ Good (as regards savings, reduction and progress)
- ○ Fair
- – Not mentioned

Notes
- Each evaluation refers to the quality of environmental performance itself.
- Evaluation criteria are as follows:
  Energy saving: reduction level of the ratio of CO_2 volume per sales quantities in fiscal 1995
  Industrial waste reduction: the ratio of the result compared to the target in fiscal 1995
  Recycling: implementation rate of recycling
  Environmental impact of products: reduction of pollutants caused during production
  Packaging materials: reduction of more than 50% by fiscal 1995
  EMS: willingness to be ISO 14001 certified not only in domestic but also in foreign factories
  Management of chemical releases: level of target-setting

Table 3: EVALUATION OF ITEMS IN ENVIRONMENTAL REPORTS
(ELECTRICAL APPLIANCE INDUSTRY)

Source: Tsunoda and Kawaguchi 1997

mance category, which include: development of environmentally sound products; green purchasing; energy saving; recycling; waste reduction; improvement of air quality; and environmental management system. There are 19 of these sub-categories in total, and for each of these the report evaluates the result for that year. In its latest report, while targets in 16 categories were accomplished, those in the other three were not. NEC set a target for the recycling rate of waste plastic at 48% for fiscal 1997. As the result was 51%, the report presented a positive evaluation. While the company met its targets for recycling, waste reduction and green purchasing, it failed in its energy-saving goals. In 1996, it tried to reduce factories' energy consumption by 10.5% from 1990 levels, but the result was only 5.2%.

Overall, the report appears to reach the fourth of the five stages of environmental reporting identified by UNEP (UNEP 1994a) and to be at least as good as those of other electrical appliance companies in developed countries. This would be supported by the fact that NEC's environmental activities have received several awards: for example, from the California Environmental Protection Agency in the US and from the Energy Supply Board of Ireland.

◻ Further Impetus for Environmental Reporting

The pressures for environmental reporting felt by Japanese companies will be further increased by several recent developments. A new Japanese Environmental Impact Assessment law requires a more transparent environmental decision-making process (Harashina 1998). In 1998, GRF and Toyo Keizai Inc., one of Japan's largest publishers, established an environmental reporting award, which should generate considerable publicity when the first winners are announced. Most significantly, Japan is also seeing a burgeoning of interest in ISO 14001 and a new initiative on pollutant releases. The next sections discuss the implications of these developments for corporate environmental reporting.

◢ ISO 14001 and Environmental Performance Measurement and Reporting in Japan

ISO 14001 was adopted in Japan in October 1996,[2] and the total number of certified facilities reached 730 by the end of March 1998. Figure 1 shows the numbers of various certified facilities; Figure 2 shows the proportions of certified corporations. One of the notable characteristics of the Japanese situation is that electrical appliance manufacturers now make up more than 50% of all certified facilities. A number of non-commercial organisations, including local governments and universities, have also been certified (JEA 1998a; Nakagawa 1998). In addition, environmental audits are gradually spreading through Japanese companies (JEA 1998a).

These changes have led to a much greater emphasis on environmental performance measurement in larger companies. For instance, Hitachi Ltd introduced a new environmental measurement system in April 1997 which collects and regularly reports data on 249 parameters including energy, materials and water flows through facilities (Kaneko and Sawada 1998). This system allowed Hitachi to measure new indicators including pH and volume of oil film in waste-water in real time. As yet there is no evidence that this has translated into increased environmental reporting, but this has certainly been made easier by the more systemised measurement procedures that ISO 14001 has introduced.

---

2   MITI announced in a White Paper that international standardisation, including environmental management systems, was becoming steadily more important (MITI 1994). A state-of-the-environment report (JEA 1998a) also shows that all kinds of corporation are increasingly eager to be certified. In addition, Yabe (1998), Nakagawa (1998), Terada (1998) and Yoshizawa (1998) have described recent examples of positive attitudes towards ISO 14001 certification.

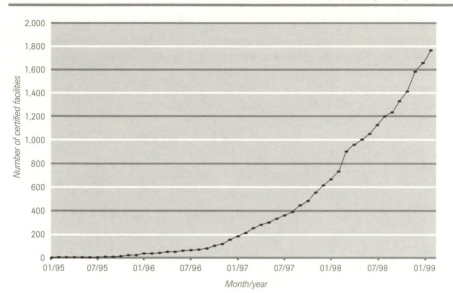

Figure 1: PROGRESS OF CERTIFIED FACILITIES IN BS 7750 AND ISO 14001

Source: Japanese Industrial Standards Committee

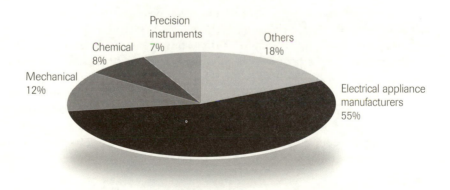

Figure 2: FACILITIES CERTIFIED TO ISO 14001 BY INDUSTRY TYPE

However, it is uncertain how much influence the standard is having on small and medium-sized enterprises (SMEs). In order to gain a better understanding of this question—and of the general impact of ISO 14001—the author conducted a questionnaire survey on environmental management systems in 150 electrical appliance companies in Fukushima Prefecture[3] (Murayama and Nonaka 1997). In summary, the findings were that 7% of all respondent companies already refer to environmental protection in their corporation management philosophy or policy and a further 24% are planning to do so, but the rest (69%) had no such reference.[4] Of all respondents, only 7% had made specific action plans for the above activities. One out of every five corporations had established a section in its organisation with responsibility for environmental protection, or was considering doing so. Approximately half of all corporations had installed technology for environmental protection. On the other hand, life-cycle assessment (LCA) had already been implemented in 15% of respondent companies, while 10% had a plan to conduct LCAs. Although it was clear that respondents took a long-term view of LCA development for recyclable products, the result showed a positive attitude towards new types of environmental protection. With respect to measures for worker education on environmental protection, about half the corporations had already been implementing such measures or were planning them. The rate of implementation was relatively higher for this than for other activities described above.

The rate of implementation for periodic examination or audit was relatively higher, although 60% had no plan. However, few companies then go on to report the results to executive boards: only 25% of the respondents reported internally, and only two respondents reported publicly. Such a negative situation towards reporting, whereby the outcome is not reported even within the organisation, renders any exhaustive audit useless for improving environmental protection. In terms of ISO 14001, three companies had already been certified and seven were planning to register for such certification.

These responses were mostly related to company size. Generally speaking, the larger the size of the corporation, the more likely it is that it has already implemented, or plans to implement, specific measures. Large corporations, however, are not always positive in all items. Environmental equipment, workers' education and internal reporting are implemented more often in medium-sized corporations. In particular, no large corporation has yet implemented full internal reporting, while there are a few small and medium-sized corporations that have. This suggests that only a small number of corporations implement advanced environmental protection measures,

---

3 Japan has three levels of administrative government: national, prefectural and municipal. Although prefectures correspond to states in the USA, their powers and rights are not as strong.

4 Companies with under 49 employees made up the largest group of respondents (48%) and large companies with over 200 workers made up 20%. Despite the sampling method, which was designed to extract data from each size range equally, the result showed that smaller companies were more likely to respond to this kind of survey than are larger companies. Of the respondents, 45% had under ¥1.2 million in capital, and comparatively larger companies (over ¥100 million) made up around 22%. As companies with fewer employees will generally have lower amounts of capital, either attribute can be used as a measure of size.

irrespective of their sizes. Those that do are often suppliers to larger companies. This was certainly true for the Adatara Electric and Takahashi Electric case studies, which were conducted as part of the research.

Perhaps the most significant finding for performance measurement was that many companies conduct environmental protection activities without a coherent philosophy or detailed plan and, in particular, do not set measurable targets. There was also no evidence that any of the companies were considering introducing external environmental reporting.

All in all, therefore, it seems that ISO 14001 will, to a certain extent, raise the general level of environmental performance measurement in Japanese business, but will have only a limited impact in driving more environmental reporting.

◢ Standardised Pollutant Release Inventories in Japan

Work in this area began in 1992, when the Japanese Chemical Manufacturers' Association (JCMA) conducted a survey of emissions for 13 chemical substances and also conducted a similar survey on 28 substances in the following year (JCMA 1998). After producing a guideline of survey procedures, based on its experience of those surveys, the Association conducted surveys on other chemicals: 55 in 1995 and 152 in 1996. Although these surveys were only preliminary trials to estimate volumes of chemical releases, the companies that participated were all members of JCMA, and release information on each facility was not made available to the public.

◻ The Pilot Project of the Japanese Environment Agency (JEA)

Government action commenced in February 1996 when, following an OECD recommendation (OECD 1996), the JEA established a review panel for a Pollutant Release and Transfer Register (PRTR) pilot project in October that year (JEA 1998b). The panel had four subcommittees: a comprehensive task force; a committee for editing a manual on estimating pollution release and transfer volumes; a committee for information processing and dissemination; and a committee on chemical use surveys. Each subcommittee consisted of about a dozen people, drawn from local government, industries, NGOs and academia.

The purpose of the pilot project was to identify the technical problems in implementing actual systems as well as to foster a common understanding among related parties. Information relating to accidental releases was outside the brief of the pilot project. Specific items to be addressed were covered mainly by the following questions:

▼ Were industries and related chemical substances appropriately matched?

▼ Was the minimum facility size appropriate?

▼ Did target companies have sufficient abilities to conduct a pilot project?

▼ What kinds of steps are required to obtain information about chemical release and transfer?

▼ What are the deficiencies of the guidance manual with respect to release and transfer estimation?

▼ How should technical training be improved?

▼ Is information processing and dissemination appropriately implemented?

As a pilot area, certain jurisdictions in Kanagawa and Aichi Prefectures were selected where advanced management on chemical safety had been implemented by local governments. Many chemical facilities are established in these areas. Chemicals were selected not only on the basis of being regulated materials, but also in view of their toxicity with respect to carcinogenicity, mutagenicity, reproductive toxicity and chronic toxicity. In addition, possible levels of exposure as estimated by domestic environmental surveys and past amounts of chemical use were taken into account. Chemicals that were unregulated were divided into four levels. As a result, 191 materials were initially selected, but reduced to 178 at the implementation stage, due to difficulties encountered in the survey.

For these substances, the following sources of release and transfer were surveyed: exhaust and release into the air; discharge to public water zones and waste-water facilities; permeation into the soil inside facilities; land reclamation; transfer of industrial wastes to disposal facilities; and materials newly produced by waste disposal. This project was aimed at industries across the board, regardless of the amount of chemical usage, because chemicals can be used in a diverse range of human activities. While smaller facilities have greater difficulty managing chemicals appropriately, they also have less ability in correcting estimates of chemical release and transfer. Taking this into account, the project selected comparatively large facilities, but assessed the amount of each substance used by target facilities in over 75% of cases. Target facilities were divided into two categories: those with over 30 employees and those with over 100. Wide differences in average sizes among industries made such a classification feasible, and, using these criteria, about 700 facilities in Kanagawa and about 1,000 in Aichi were selected. In addition to the above, volumes from non-point sources,[5] including waste generated by final consumers and transporters, were estimated by local governments. Each facility was asked to supply the following: name of CEO; name and address of facility; type of business; annual release volume of each material into various media; and annual transfer volume of each material.

The results of this pilot project—the first to be implemented in Japan by the national government—were published in May 1998. The review panel decided in principle that data for each facility should not be made publicly available, but that area-wide data would. This was mainly justified in three ways: (1) each company took part in this project on the condition that JEA did not publish specific information on each facility; (2) Japan is currently developing a national information disclosure

---

5 Those sources that are too small and too numerous to be identified individually.

act, and, because this act is yet to be formulated, information disclosure was not considered in great detail; (3) the panel was concerned that there would be an excessive public response to the PRTR data, being the first to collect and publish such kinds of data for general consumption in Japan. This principle mostly does not allow detailed mapping of impacts but, in Kawasaki City—which experienced serious pollution incidents in the 1960s and therefore has a high degree of environmental awareness today—data was released for three relatively small zones, which gave Kawasaki citizens access to more detailed information than was the case in other cities.

◻ *Evaluation*

Based on his experience as a member of the JEA PRTR initiative review panel, the author has identified three strengths of the approach adopted. First, the project dealt with a broad range of chemical-using industries, including not only manufacturers but also the steel, mining, electricity and gas utilities, construction and waste disposal industries and medical institutions. This contrasts with other advanced PRTR systems in the US and the UK, where manufacturers are the main target. Second, the project collected data on chemical releases from non-point sources. Again, this contrasts with the UK and US, although a similar approach has been adopted in the Collective Emission Inventory System (CEIS) of the Netherlands. Third, the definition of pollutants is relatively broad, including, for example, NO_x and SO_x emissions and pesticide release data.

However, there are some matters still to be addressed. The lack of access to facility data contrasts with the situation in other countries such as Canada, the Netherlands, the UK and the US (JEA 1997). However, it is unlikely that this situation will change through voluntary action. According to interviews with industries conducted by local governments, the unique situation in Japan, where each company tends to follow similar reporting behaviour to other companies in its industry, may make it difficult for all companies to publish data from each of their facilities (Abe and Takahashi 1998). One solution would be mandatory disclosure but, although the Japanese government is preparing legislation, it is likely to allow considerable discretion for each company to decide how much information it can withhold from local government or the general public. This situation is unfortunate because it makes it difficult for local authorities to develop comprehensive risk management plans.

Another problem is the methods used to estimate chemical release volumes. Non-manufacturing industries, which were a major target of the Japanese pilot project, generally do not have sufficient knowledge about the chemical substances that they use in their own products and services. Although a guidance manual may help such industries in their estimations of release and transfer volumes, no one knows how accurate these might turn out to be.

Finally, Japan has not yet established a credible database with which to assess the toxicity of each chemical substance, unlike the Integrated Risk Information System (IRIS) in the US and International Uniform Chemical Information Database (IUCLID) in the EU. Accurate and up-to-date information on toxicity is crucial in analysing release and transfer data. Without such data, published information may cause undue concern to the Japanese public, which has no sophisticated consensual risk communication rules.

◢ *Conclusion*

This chapter has shown that there is considerable activity with regard to environmental management, performance measurement and reporting in Japan. However, as in Europe and North America, this tends to be focused on larger companies in specific sectors. Generally speaking, electricity-generating plants and electrical appliance, distribution and automobile industries publish reports that provide detailed information. Industries that provide services or products directly for the end-consumer are also more likely than others to make their reports available to the public. In contrast, steel, chemical and textile industries tend to have negative attitudes towards information dissemination, although, when they do report publicly, the quality of their environmental reports is often quite high.

Two developments that could potentially create pressure for increased disclosure are: introduction by companies of environmental management systems (which may or may not be certified to ISO 14001); and the adoption of a PRTR system. However, research suggests that many companies, especially in the SME sector, are unlikely to adopt environmental management systems in the near future and, even if they do, may not do a lot more in terms of environmental performance measurement or, still less, environmental reporting. The PRTR system is also unlikely to be a driver because access to facility data will be restricted and/or it is unlikely that many Japanese companies will be willing to do this voluntarily. Hence, while environmental performance measurement and reporting will continue to develop in Japan, there are unlikely to be any radical changes from the current situation.

19

South African Corporate Environmental Reporting

Contrasts with the Experience in Developed Countries

Charl de Villiers

CORPORATE DISCLOSURES of information regarding the natural environment are undertaken largely on a voluntary basis in South Africa,[1] as in most other countries. There has been an increase over time in this type of disclosure by corporations. However, the pressures on South African corporations in this regard may be different from those experienced by their counterparts in developed countries. This fact can perhaps best be illustrated by way of a quotation from the environmental report of South Africa's only electricity utility, Eskom. Eskom employs approximately 39,000 staff and has featured prominently in the WWF (SA) (World Wide Fund for Nature South Africa) Environmental Annual Report Award, being placed third for their 1996 report. In the 1997 report (Eskom 1998: 1), the chairman, Reuel Khoza, states that:

> Social pressures for economic growth are real and pressing. Short-term solutions are necessary, but must not contribute to the long-term deterioration of the environment to the point where quality of life can no longer be sustained. Success is finding the desired equilibrium between these opposing requirements.

---

1 The national environmental management bill was promulgated in the *Government Gazette* on 29 January 1999. According to the act, any person shall have access to environment-related information held by any organ of state. Organs of state, in turn, shall have access to any environment related information held by any person that is necessary to enable them to carry out their duties. Their duties include environment implementation and management plans that have to be produced by a wide range of government departments within one year. At the time of writing, one can only speculate how the various plans will eventually impact on corporate environmental disclosure.

> The challenge remains: how to raise awareness of broader environmental issues at grass-roots level and at the same time achieve better living standards for the poorer communities.

These statements reveal a strong commitment to social improvement and indeed an attitude of considering the environment only if the long-term effect of activities may be to detrimentally affect the 'quality of life' of society. There is no sense of responsibility for passing on the environment to our children in at least the same state as it was received from our parents. The emphasis seems to be on economic growth to the maximum extent that can be achieved. It is to be assumed that public and environmental groups in developed countries would not accept this kind of statement.

In South Africa, a larger amount of the social reporting found in annual reports can be classified as employee reporting (reporting for and about employees) rather than as environmental reporting. For example, 39% of listed companies in South Africa reported an employment policy in their 1996 annual reports (De Villiers 1997a: 9), whereas only 23% disclosed an environmental objective (De Villiers 1997b: 20).[2] Erasmus (1998: 268) also concluded that employee matters enjoy more emphasis than environmental matters in the annual reports of companies listed on the Johannesburg Stock Exchange (JSE). The trade union movement is well developed in South Africa and the pressure they put on companies may well outweigh the pressure currently applied by environmentally concerned individuals and groups. However, the discussion here will be confined to environmental reporting.

In this chapter, the evidence is presented that South African environmental reporting is increasing, both in annual reports and in stand-alone reports. However, environmental reporting in South African annual reports is still not at the same level of disclosure as in developed countries. The reason for this may be the differing social priorities already referred to.

The fact that environmental reporting is voluntary begs the question of why there has been an increase in disclosure. An attempt is made to answer this question. Some of the reasons relate to stakeholder requirements and, therefore, the question of what should be reported is answered from the perspective of stakeholders as well as from the perspective of organisations that have produced standards or recommendations. Finally the question of importance or materiality of environmental information to the decision-making process of corporate stakeholders is addressed. It is concluded that environmental information is material to stakeholders and will, therefore, be used by them if it is disclosed.

2　Employment policies and environmental objectives are not directly comparable, but these two items represent the highest incidence of a specific type of disclosure in each of the two surveys.

◢ South African Corporate Environmental Reporting in the Annual Report

Many regard the legally required corporate annual report as the most important vehicle for the disclosure of information about an organisation. It has the major advantage of being accessible to many and containing information regarding every aspect of the organisation's activities. Gray *et al.* (1995b: 82) also believe it to be a way for the corporation to create and manage its own image:

> . . . in keeping with the majority of the literature, the annual report is used as the principal focus of reporting. There is some justification for this. The annual report not only is a statutory document, produced regularly, but it also represents what is probably the most important document in terms of the organization's construction of its own social imagery.

Many (and increasing numbers of) organisations, therefore, choose to address, among other issues, the environment in their annual reports.

Konar (1989: 270) investigated corporate social responsibility disclosures made by large companies listed on the JSE and found that 9.1% of the companies disclosed pollution control in manufacturing, and 9.1% disclosed protecting, restoring and improving the environment.[3] Other categories were disclosed by a considerably smaller percentage of the companies in the sample. In assessing these percentages, it should be remembered that larger companies are generally more likely to disclose information of a social and an environmental nature than are smaller companies.

De Villiers (1997a: 20-29) carried out a survey of the 1994, 1995 and 1996 annual reports of all companies listed on the JSE (559, 596 and 606 companies respectively) and found, among other disclosures about the environment, the items presented in Table 1. The information for the top 100 companies (measured in terms of disclosed turnover, and therefore excluding companies that did not disclose turnover) for 1996 was also extracted in order to obtain an idea of the impact of firm size on the results. Finally, the results for companies in the top 100 for 1996 in the extractive, chemical, oil and steel industries (i.e. heavy industry) were summarised in order to obtain an idea of the influence of industry sector on the results (15 companies in these industries were in the top 100).

Although there is a definite increase in the number of companies reporting environmental information, the results of the survey do not compare favourably with similar surveys in developed countries. A comparison in general terms for the same years reveals that the natural environment is mentioned in 70% of corporate annual reports worldwide (KPMG 1997; Gray *et al.* 1995a), whereas this is the case for only 23% of the South African companies included in the survey. This can be explained

---

3   These percentages were calculated as follows: The top 100 companies listed on the JSE (according to the *Financial Mail* survey, which is based on net asset value) were included in the survey. Only 66 companies made any form of corporate social disclosure. The percentages are calculated based on these 66 companies; therefore, 9.1% indicates that six companies included a certain type of reporting.

	All listed companies, 1996			Top 100 companies, 1996	Heavy-impact companies in top 100, 1996
	1994	**1995**	**1996**	**1996**	**1996**
1. Does the annual report mention the natural environment?	17%	19%	23%	41%	87%
2. Does the corporate policy/mission statement mention a policy/mission regarding the environment?	8%	9%	11%	22%	40%
3. Are the company's environmental objectives disclosed?	16%	19%	23%	36%	87%
4. If the environmental objectives are disclosed, do they set measurable standards, enabling environmental performance achieved to be compared with the objectives?	10%	10%	17%	26%	73%
5. Has the company disclosed whether it has achieved its objectives in respect of the environment?	8%	12%	13%	19%	67%
6. Is mention made of the environmental impacts and risks of the business?	6%	6%	14%	18%	67%
7. Is mention made of negative aspects of environmental activities?	6%	8%	11%	19%	73%
8. If mention is made of compliance with a standard, what standard is mentioned?					
Legal standard	5%	6%	8%	8%	40%
Industry standard	1%	4%	3%	3%	7%
Company standard	7%	6%	13%	25%	73%
Other	1%	2%	3%	8%	20%
9. Is mention made of an environmental audit?	3%	4%	5%	12%	20%
10. If an environmental audit is conducted, is it attested independently (externally)?	0.3%	1%	2%	3%	7%
11. If financial information is provided in respect of environmental expenditure, are details of the following given?					
Operating expenditure	2%	2%	6%	9%	53%
Capital expenditure	1%	4%	2%	4%	7%

Percentages represent number of respondents who answered 'yes'.

Table 1: DISCLOSURES ABOUT THE ENVIRONMENT IN 1994, 1995 AND 1996
ANNUAL REPORTS OF SOUTH AFRICAN COMPANIES

Source: De Villiers 1997a: 20-29

in two ways. First, the companies included in the South African survey are on average smaller than those included in most international surveys. Whereas other surveys normally include only the largest corporations, this survey included all listed companies. The incidence of environmental reporting is much higher for the top 100 listed companies in South Africa than for listed companies as a whole (see Bogiages and Vorster 1993; Steyn and Vorster 1994). Using the 1996 database, it was established that 41 of the 100 largest companies by turnover disclosed environmental objectives, i.e. 41%, compared with 23% for all listed companies.

This is still below the level typically found in international surveys. One can argue that the top 100 South African companies are still, on average, smaller than, for example, the top 100 in the UK. This may explain the difference, but there is arguably a second reason, namely the fact that South Africa is a developing country and, therefore, companies do not experience the same level of environmental awareness and militancy from environmental pressure groups as do their counterparts in the developed world. The increase in environmental reporting in South Africa should continue at its current slow pace until the social priorities change. This type of change occurred quite rapidly in Australia where a dramatic increase in membership of environmental groups went hand in hand with an equally dramatic increase in disclosure between 1988 and 1991 (Deegan and Gordon 1996: 193).

It is clear from the results given above that the percentage of companies that report under each category is very low. Companies disclose environmental information voluntarily. Should they choose to disclose environmental information, they have a further choice, namely what type of information to disclose and in what format to disclose. Environmental disclosure in its current form, therefore, does not lend itself to comparisons between companies. Even companies of similar size in the same industry may have vastly differing environmental disclosure policies.

The last column of the research results given above confirm previous international findings, that companies in environmentally sensitive industries tend to disclose more environmental information than do companies in other industries. In this case, it is clear that companies in these industries (extractive, chemicals, oil and steel) are much more likely to report environmental information. Indeed, in most of the instances cited, the percentage of companies in these industries in the top 100 that reported certain types of environmental information is more than double the percentage for the entire top 100. Doppegieter and De Villiers (1996: 37) also conclude that companies in the South African energy sector disclose more environmental information than does the average company. Erasmus (1998: 268) found that companies in the mining sector published the highest quality of environmental information. This is further evidence that environmental disclosures differ from industry to industry in South Africa.

◢ Corporate Environmental Reporting in Separate Environmental Reports

An increasing number of organisations, including companies, are also disclosing environmental information in separate reports. WWF (SA) had 13 entries for their 1996 Environmental Annual Report Award and 14 entries for the 1997 version. This compares with 44 entries for a similar award scheme, run by ACCA, in the UK in 1995. The WWF Environmental Report Award is a relatively low-key event and organisations are grateful for the honour of receiving an award, but it is probably safe to say that it is not regarded as a key issue by general managers.

These separate reports are wholly devoted to the disclosure of environmental information and therefore the reporting is more substantial in both breadth and depth than that found in annual reports. In annual reports, environmental issues are weighed against other social issues, as well as against financial information, to decide whether they should be included or not. Issues of cost–benefit and information overload may sometimes lead to the exclusion of environmental information. Separate reports have more scope for expanding the range of environmental issues dealt with as well as the level of detail of the information.

The language used and the explanations given in the separate environmental reports give an insight into the motivations of organisations to disclose environmental information. In the introduction to Eskom's 1996 report, Allen Morgan, chief executive says:

> We have endeavoured once again to meet the expectations of our stakeholders and our customers in reporting honestly and openly about the impact of our business on the environment. We are grateful for the many contacts that we have had with our various publics and the many letters we have received commenting on the way in which we manage our environmental affairs. These help us to shape the overall approach and style of our environmental reporting.
>
> Awareness about environmental matters both inside and outside of the organisation is increasing along with expectations. I am pleased that consultation with our customers and the public at large on how best to solve environmental problems is steadily becoming common practice (Eskom 1997: 3).

Note the references to stakeholders, various publics and the public at large. It is also clear from the quotation above that external pressure as well as pressure from employees plays a large part in the decision to disclose and also in the decision about exactly what to disclose.

In order to be accountable, companies have to report on (i.e. to give an account of) their management of everything under their control. This includes capital, but also natural resources such as clean air, waterways, etc. In the introduction to the 1996 Environmental Report by Sasol—an oil company employing approximately 25,000—chief executive officer Pieter Cox claims:

> As a leading player in the South African economy and due to our core business being traditionally associated with environmental consequences,

> we support pro-active environmental management and clear accountabil-
> ity. Sasol strongly favours responsible self-regulation of industry, especially
> in the absence of integrated legislation and enforcement (Sasol 1996: 2).

In two short sentences, he gives two possible reasons why Sasol reports environmental information. One is to discharge its accountability to the public and the other is
to forestall legislation and enforcement by demonstrating self-regulation. Cox further
says, 'This, our first external environmental report, has been aimed specifically at
providing answers to our stakeholders . . .' (Sasol 1996: 3), which is further confirmation that pressure from stakeholders often plays an important part in the reporting
decision.

The foreword of the environmental report of Umgeni Water (1997), South Africa's
largest water utility, contains the following statement:

> [The way in which we conduct our business] is done in a climate of
> environmental, social and financial accountability.

Reference is again made to accountability, and this time it is stated explicitly that
'accountability' refers to environmental, social and financial issues: in other words
to all the resources under the control or influence of the organisation.

The separate environmental reports include a wide range of information in order
to demonstrate accountability to the relevant publics, which includes narrative and
quantitative information. The reports tend to be between 20 and 40 pages in length
and they include colour photographs, charts, figures, etc. Separate environmental
reports typically include the following general sections:

1. Foreword and/or introduction by the chairman/managing director

2. Environmental policy

3. Management processes

4. Targets

5. Performance against targets

6. Response form

Information is often given on a site-by-site basis and the better reports tend to be
candid about negative information or failures. External verification is mentioned in
very few cases and, when it is, usually fails to cover the entire organisation or the
entire process of environmental management.

The 1997 separate environmental report of Umgeni Water won the 1997 WWF
Environmental Annual Report Award (see Box 1 for an overview of the report). The
judges' report (WWF [SA] 1997) states that:

> . . . Umgeni Water is very target driven, has comprehensive progress report-
> ing and an all-embracing environmental management programme. They
> are one of the few entrants using a systems approach. The report covered
> a vast area of responsibility, complied with all six main criteria and pro-
> vided financial figures spent in order to ensure environmental compliance.

THE REPORT consists of 22 pages and contains a foreword by the chief executive. The foreword explains the importance of environmental management for a water utility and its customers. Environmental, social and financial accountability are mentioned as important issues for Umgeni Water. The chief executive shows his understanding of environmental issues when he acknowledges that environmental sustainability 'remains a challenge'.

A brief history and overview of Umgeni Water's activities follows the foreword. The utility is responsible for the storage, treatment and distribution of water in a 24,000 km^2 area. A review of the environmental performance during the past year is provided on the next two pages, which is presented in four columns. The issue is described in the first column, the relevant target in the next column, followed by a description of the progress, and the last column presents an indication of whether the target was achieved, partially achieved or not achieved. Fifteen issues are identified in this way, which translates into 34 targets. Thirteen of the targets have been achieved, 17 have been partially achieved and four have not been achieved. Unfortunately, none of the targets is quantified or quantifiable. They are essentially a 'to do' list, such as 'Finalise the existing Environmental Procedure Manual'.

The environmental policy of Umgeni Water is published as well as their environmental management system. Umgeni's environmental impacts are explained over the next nine pages in a section that contains many graphs and tables with information on water quality.

The next seven pages are devoted to Umgeni's 'environmental outreach', which deals with their non-core environmental activities, such as conservation, environmental education and recycling programmes. On the back page, the contact details of a number of individuals are given in case additional information is sought. Umgeni's sponsorship of environmental charities and its membership of organisations of an environmental nature are also presented on this page.

Box 1: 1997 ENVIRONMENTAL REPORT: UMGENI WATER

The six main criteria referred to in the judges' report are: completeness; credibility and clarity; commitment; continual improvement; accountability to the community; and employee awareness and involvement.

◢ *Innovative Approaches to Environmental Reporting*

Being part of a developing country, South Africans tend to follow approaches developed elsewhere instead of developing their own. The area of environmental reporting is no exception to the rule. South African environmental reporting tends to be conservative and to stay within known boundaries. The well-documented innovations of companies such as Norsk Hydro and BSO/Origin, the ecobalance (*Ökobilanz*) used commonly in Germany, and the innovative valuation of wildlife by Earth Sanctuaries in Australia are some examples of some leading-edge methods being developed elsewhere. In South Africa, attempts are only seldom, if ever, made to convert physical measures into financial equivalents and no significant innovations could be found.

◢ Reasons for Corporations to Report

The reasons for organisations to report may be varied, and two possible factors have already been highlighted in the previous section. These were, first, accountability of management to their various stakeholders or publics, and pressure from these sources; and, second, to forestall legislation. The first reason can be interpreted as a response to external pressure: the reason for environmental disclosure may be an attempt by management to legitimise its operations and procedures in the eyes of its stake-holders, to ensure the continued and uninterrupted existence of the organisation.

According to Tsotsi (1996), Eskom's Corporate Environmental Affairs Manager at the time, stakeholder pressure and the introduction of environmental standards are the strongest reasons for environmental reporting in South Africa. He mentions pressure from investors as another (less important) reason. He subscribes to the notion of corporate accountability and regards this as the basis of stakeholder information rights.

Eskom's current Corporate Environmental Affairs Manager, Vanida Govender, believes that:

> . . . Eskom started to disclose environmental information because of three main reasons:
>
> 1. the examples of similar organisations elsewhere in the world
>
> 2. pressure from international financial institutions, and
>
> 3. public attacks on environmental grounds based on incomplete information. In other words Eskom wanted to set the record straight.
>
> The lack of environmental performance measurement is not a reason for not reporting.[4] The Eskom experience was that the need for reporting dictated the amendment of existing measurement systems and in some cases the implementation of new ones.[5]

Both these reasons for reporting (legitimacy and accountability) imply that the information required by stakeholders or relevant publics should be addressed. This leads into the next question to be answered, namely: what kind of environmental information to report.

◢ What should be reported?

Many influential organisations and researchers have made recommendations regarding the content of environmental disclosures. However, none of these recommenda-

---

4 Erasmus (1998: 262) conducted an empirical study and found that only 24% of South African listed companies that indicated that they performed certain environmental activities provided any information regarding those activities in their annual reports. This provides additional evidence that many companies manage (and thus presumably measure) environmental activities, yet do not report it. So the lack of reporting in South Africa is not necessarily because of a lack of measurement.

5 Interview with the author on 4 September 1998.

tions or standards enjoys universal acceptance. A different approach to the question of what should be reported is to ask stakeholders. A South African perspective on stakeholders is presented in the next section, followed by a section exploring the recommendations/standards and a section describing previous research into stakeholder requirements.

◁ South African Stakeholders

More than 50% of South Africans live in urban areas. These urban citizens can, as the rest of the population, be divided between a first world and a third world component. Although the country is classified as a developing country, a large proportion of the population, of all its ethnic groups, enjoys the lifestyle of the developed world. This is made possible by, among other things, a well-developed banking, road and energy supply system. Merchant bankers, stockbrokers, lawyers, doctors and other professionals abound and their value system and perceptions of issues such as the environment is very similar to those of their counterparts in the developed world.

It is the third world component of South Africa that may have different views. This component can again be distinguished between traditional rural black people and 'others', such as farm labourers and urban residents with little or no income. The 'others' tend not to be vociferous regarding environmental matters. One can argue that they concentrate their efforts on more basic issues such as survival. Traditional rural black people, however, enjoy a much closer relationship with the environment and their thinking is not so tainted by the Western emphasis on economic measures. There have been several instances, for example, where objections have been made to a proposed new development that would improve economic conditions on the grounds that this might cause disturbance to ancestral spirits—though these objections may also be motivated (consciously or unconsciously) by a desire to defend traditional social customs and methods of subsistence.

In dealing with matters such as corporate environmental accounting, there is a tendency in South Africa to address only the concerns of the first world component of the population. They represent informed opinion and they have the potential to procure the support of the media. They can be communicated with through annual reports, newspapers, the Internet, etc. The third world component of the population sometimes gets involved in localised issues, such as pollution caused by a plant in a certain township, but they may not be users of financial statements or even read the local paper, so their concerns have to be dealt with in different ways.

Eskom, for example, communicates environmental information in various ways, such as:

1. A 32-page environmental report
2. Environmental information that is included in their annual report
3. A shortened environmental report (1 page)
4. Environmental information on their Internet site

5. Environmental education for employees

6. Environmental education for other stakeholders

7. Media campaigns

8. Community campaigns

Although South Africa has 11 official languages, the printed material used by Eskom is mostly in English. This is understandable, as English is either the first or the second language of most citizens. Eskom does not have a simplified environmental report other than the shortened version. A shortened report that includes complicated language can be as inaccessible to some individuals as a full report. Govender[6] believes the important issue is not mother-tongue communication or simplified communication but rather how to communicate with the illiterate. Eskom has solved this problem by employing a 'community practitioner' at each site, basically a public relations officer, whose function is to communicate verbally with the local community in their own language. Complaints and two-way communication are encouraged by Eskom and are dealt with immediately.

Individuals and groups in South Africa who are interested in the environment usually concentrate their efforts on local issues, such as air pollution by a nearby plant. The individuals that comprise these groups tend to become more interested when emotive issues come to the fore, and to disappear when these issues are addressed. In other words, there is very little continuity in the pressure groups and they tend to focus on local issues. The 'Greenpeace' type of activity, where a specific company is targeted and their activities placed under the spotlight, appears to be absent in South Africa.

◻ *Recommendations*

Some of the organisations that have recommended the types of environmental disclosure that corporations should make are the Institute of Chartered Accountants in England and Wales (ICAEW 1992), the Canadian Institute of Chartered Accountants (CICA 1994), the United Nations (1991, 1998) and the International Organization for Standardisation (ISO 1996). From these and many other guidelines (but excluding the UN 1998 position paper and the ISO 14000 guidelines), De Villiers (1996) produced a recommended minimum requirement for corporate environmental reporting. The list was compiled after taking into account the responses by South African users of annual reports to a survey to determine the types of environmental reporting they would find most valuable. This recommendation is contained in Table 2.

More recently, and not included in the De Villiers study mentioned above, the South African Institute of Chartered Accountants (SAICA) published a guideline called *Stakeholder Communication in the Annual Report,* which contains, among others, recommendations concerning the environment. Although these recommendations have many shortcomings compared with others in terms of the types of environ-

---

6 Interview with the author on 4 September 1998.

- A descriptive overview of the major environmental risks and impacts of the organisation
- The environmental policy of the organisation
- Measurable targets in physical units and monetary amounts, where applicable, based on the environmental policy, e.g. emissions
- Performance against environmental targets and comparative figures (previous year)
- Accounting policies for recording liabilities, provisions, contingent liabilities and catastrophe reserves
- Environmental costs (energy; waste handling; treatment and disposal; legal compliance; packaging; fines; rehabilitation; recycling; etc.) by category, charged to operating expenses during the period
- Monetary amounts of environmental liabilities, contingent liabilities and reserves established in the current period
- Government environmental grants received
- Likely effect of environmental policy on future capital investment and earnings
- Environmental litigation in which the organisation is currently involved
- Independent third-party attestation of all environmental reporting

Table 2: RECOMMENDED MINIMUM REQUIREMENTS
FOR CORPORATE ENVIRONMENTAL REPORTING

Source: De Villiers 1996: 202

mental reporting required (De Villiers 1997c), it is an important initiative, as SAICA enjoys considerable stature and influence in matters concerning disclosure; it produces the accounting standards for South Africa. These disclosure rules have to be followed by companies to ensure that they comply with the requirement of 'generally accepted accounting practice' as required by the Companies' Act. Therefore, the guideline sends out the important message that the premier standard-setting body in South Africa is in favour of, among other things, the disclosure of environmental information in the annual report. A summary of the guidelines is reproduced in Box 2.

The SAICA guideline has been criticised for theoretical incoherence, on the grounds that it clings to a concept of decision-usefulness for financial decision-making while also attempting to address the information needs of non-financial stakeholders, such as environmental groups (De Villiers 1997c); further, that SAICA did not establish the information needs of users of financial statements, and that its recommendations failed to address important issues which independent empirical studies indicate that users need. De Villiers (1997c) argues that the types of environmental disclosure that users want, but which SAICA fails to recommend, are:

1. Overview of environmental impacts

2. Measurable targets

3. Environmental costs

IN THE Introduction, under the heading Scope, it is stated that the guide is intended for listed companies, large public entities, banks, financial and insurance entities, large unlisted dependent companies and large quasi-state entities. It is also stated that:

> *Compliance is not mandatory but is considered best practice. The guidance set out in this document will contribute towards compliance with the King Report* (IOD 1994) as regards stakeholder communication.*

In the Introduction, under the heading Background it is stated that:

> *Formerly, directors addressed their efforts towards communicating with the shareholders but, as society is increasingly expecting greater transparency and accountability from enterprises with regard to financial and non-financial matters, directors' communication should be directed at all stakeholders.*

The Introduction, under the heading Style, states that:

> *The essential qualities of any stakeholder communication are that it should:*
> * *be objective, unbiased and balanced, dealing fairly with both positive and negative aspects,*
> * *deal with comments made in previous communications not borne out by events, as well as those that were,*
> * *be forward looking, as well as a review of historic events, and*
> * *be prompt, relevant, open, transparent (with substance ruling over legal form), and fairly set out the position.†*

The section on Detailed Guidance, under the heading Dynamics of the Business (Risks and Uncertainties), states the following:

> *Examples of factors and influences, which may be incorporated, are:*
> * *health and safety issues,*
> * *environmental issues (protection and restoration costs, potential liability)†*

The section on Detailed Guidance,‡ under the heading Environmental Issues, states the following:

> *The enterprise should see itself as a resident in the broad community, and should act in a spirit of social consciousness and awareness. It should be sensitive to the needs of the local community. With this in mind, the annual report should contain a full and separate commentary of relevance to the community at large, which should address matters such as:*
> * *environmental protection policies and goals,*
> * *compliance with consumer protection standards and consequences of violation,*
> * *compliance with environmental laws and regulations and consequences of violation,*
> * *existing and planned pollution control,*
> * *protection costs,*
> * *restoration costs, and*
> * *potential liability and any current or pending investigations or proceedings by regulators.*

---

* The King Report was commissioned by the Institute of Directors in Southern Africa in response to growing concern that proper corporate governance was lacking in many public companies and other public entities. The report was published in 1994 and contained recommendations similar to those of the Cadbury Report in the UK, including improved communication with stakeholders other than shareholders.

† Not all the content is reproduced here.

‡ This subheading is reproduced in full.

Box 2: EXTRACTS FROM THE SAICA GUIDE ON STAKEHOLDER COMMUNICATION IN THE ANNUAL REPORT

Source: SAICA 1997

4. Environmental audit (third-party attestation) of reporting

5. Waste management

6. The extent of land contamination

There is now a growing literature on the needs of financial stakeholders (for example, Bennett and James 1998c; Deegan and Rankin 1997; Rankin 1996)). De Villiers and Vorster (1995) and De Villiers (1998) have investigated this topic within South Africa. They found that corporate environmental disclosure was a popular concept among users of financial statements as well as among company directors and auditors. A study by De Vries and De Villiers (1997) revealed a similar positive stance among portfolio managers of unit trusts. The results of the three studies are shown in Table 3. According to De Villiers (1998: 162), the fact that his survey's percentages were apparently higher (although not significantly so) could be explained by the fact that his survey questionnaire was only a fifth of the length of the De Villiers and Vorster questionnaire. Respondents seem to be inclined to choose only a few types of environmental disclosure if faced with a long list; however, they may also choose the same number of types from a shorter list.

De Villiers and Vorster (1995: 57)	Managers	Auditors	Users/others*
Positive re more environmental disclosure (voluntary)	63%	65%	66%
Positive re more environmental disclosure (compulsory)	49%	48%	62%
Environmental disclosure should be part of annual statements	69%	71%	81%
Specific environmental disclosures			
Average of responses to all specific disclosures	56%	57%	75%
De Villiers (1998: 159)	Managers	Auditors	Users[†]
Positive re more environmental disclosure (voluntary)	89%	78%	84%
Positive re more environmental disclosure (compulsory)	58%	57%	90%
Environmental disclosure should be part of annual statements	84%	70%	89%
Specific environmental disclosures			
Average of responses to all specific disclosures	71%	76%	83%
De Vries and de Villiers (1997: 41): Survey of unit trust portfolio managers			
More social (including environmental) disclosure required in financial statements by	90% of portfolio managers		
This additional information will influence my investment decisions	75% of portfolio managers		

* Users/others included chartered accountants not in public practice (32%), chartered management accountants (48%), chartered certified accountants (4%), internal auditors (13%) and stockbrokers (3%).

[†] Users included chartered accountants who were shareholders and/or company employees (21%), stockbrokers (26%), bank managers (corporate accounts) (26%) and assurance company portfolio managers (27%).

Table 3: RESULTS OF THREE STUDIES ON ENVIRONMENTAL REPORTING IN SOUTH AFRICA

South Africans seem to be very positive about increased environmental disclosures in the annual statements of companies. In addition, 75% of portfolio managers thought that additional environmental information would influence their decision-making. This indicates that they regard environmental information as material to their decision-making regarding investments in companies. In other words, environmental information is not only sought as a 'nice to have', but as an essential part of the business of portfolio management.

This matches the findings of an Australian study by Deegan and Rankin (1997) which concludes that 'shareholders consider that environmental information is material to the particular decisions they undertake'.

◢ Conclusion

South African corporate environmental reporting is on the increase, but lags behind the level of disclosure found in developed countries. This is probably because environmental reporting is currently undertaken on a voluntary basis and companies do not experience the same level of pressure from either external (environmental) or internal (employee) groups. In a developing country, one would expect less pressure from environmentally aware groups and individuals, which would explain the fact that South African companies provide less environmental information.

South African environmental reporting is unsystematic (as it is internationally), and this makes comparisons between different companies difficult. Larger companies tend to provide more environmental information, as do companies in industries with a major environmental impact, such as mining, chemical, oil and steel companies.

A list of recommended minimum environmental reporting for companies is presented in Table 2, which may be used as a starting point for legislation or rules regarding environmental reporting.

South African corporate stakeholders require more environmental information than they are getting. One could argue that they are entitled to such information, because managers are accountable for their management of free goods, such as water and air. Stakeholders have also indicated that environmental information would have an impact on the various decisions they make regarding corporations.

If corporate environmental disclosures are to be used as the basis for decision-making by stakeholders, then legislation will have to be enacted to ensure that comparable information in all the required categories is available.

20

The Relationship between Company Environmental Reports and their Environmental Performance

A Study of the UK Water Industry

Peter Hopkinson and Michael Whitaker

A RECURRING THEME in the literature on business environmental performance measurement and reporting is how to evaluate and compare the actual environmental performance of individual companies and how this compares to the material presented in environmental reports (Bennett and James 1998a). A related theme is whether, as many have argued (for example, Ditz and Ranganathan 1998), the key to effective environmental performance measurement and evaluation should be the development of a small number of standardised, comparable environmental performance indicators.

These questions are of particular interest to the UK water industry, whose environmental performance has been under considerable scrutiny by government, regulators and environmental groups. This is a consequence both of the industry's major impact on river and bathing water quality as a result of its sewage treatment activities, and of the high levels of leakage from water mains. The latter exacerbates summertime shortages of water in the UK and also creates environmental problems through the additional abstraction and construction of new reservoirs, which are needed to compensate for the leakage.

The UK water industry is also unusual in environmental performance measurement terms in that the regulators have required the creation of considerable amounts of standardised data, and all the main companies in the sector produce corporate environmental reports (CERs). This is interesting both in its own right, and also because it allows comparison both of real performance in companies and of the relationship between this real performance and the information presented in their CERs. This chapter attempts to make these comparisons.

Section 1 provides some background to this comparison by providing contextual information on the UK water industry and describing the standardised data that is currently available, or will be in future. Section 2 scores water industry CERs using the SustainAbility/UNEP benchmarking criteria and then evaluates the results. Section 3 analyses the extent to which standardised environmental performance data is utilised in water company CERs. Section 4 provides a case study of the relationship between performance and reporting at one specific water company, Yorkshire Water. Section 5 provides overall conclusions.

1. *Environmental Issues and Performance of the Water Industry in England and Wales*

⌑ *Industry Context*

The provision of water and sewerage services in England and Wales was privatised in 1989. Ten publicly listed companies now provide approximately 21 million households and 550,000 industrial and commercial customers with unmetered water, and approximately 2,500,000 household and industrial customers with metered water. There is a similar scale of activity for sewage services.

The water industry is profoundly linked to the 'environment' and through its business activities generates a large number of environmental impacts. These include:

- River water quality and levels

- Groundwater quality and levels

- Bathing water quality

- Drinking water quality

- Emissions to air from incineration of sewage sludge and various categories of solid waste

- Land take for water storage, e.g. reservoirs

However, there is considerable regional variation in the precise nature and extent of these impacts.

The industry is also heavily regulated. In England and Wales, the core business areas of supplying clean water to customers, and treating and disposing of dirty water and its by-products, are overseen by (1) an Office of Water Services (OFWAT), which is responsible for economic and financial issues, e.g. price capping formulae, leakage control; and (2) environmentally through the Environment Agency and Drinking Water Inspectorate (although some environmental performance data is also reported to OFWAT; see below). The non-core business activities, such as environmental consultancy and waste management, are not regulated in the same way (but are, of course, subject to normal environmental legislation).

This regulation—and the environmental legislation that underpins it—is a major driver of investment within the sector. As an illustration, the UK government, through the Department of Environment, Transport and Regions (DETR), has recently published *Raising the Quality*, a document that provides guidance to the Director-General of the Office of Water Services on the environmental and quality objectives to be achieved by the water industry in England and Wales 2000–2005 (DETR 1998a). The recommended improvements include:

- Meeting drinking water standards, especially for lead, specified in the European Commission Drinking Water Directive

- Ensuring that adverse effects of discharges and abstractions do not damage protected habitats

- Achieving a significant increase in bathing water standards (under the Bathing Waters Directive)

- Accelerating the programme to improve unsatisfactory sewer outflows

- Accelerating progress in meeting river quality objectives

- Improving sewage treatment and ensuring compliance with the Urban Waste Water Treatment Directive (91/276/EEC)

The full set of guidance and recommendations set out in *Raising the Quality* is costed at between £8.0 and £8.5 billion. Water UK, an industry body, has disputed these figures and suggested that the real cost may be closer to £10 billion.

However, one problem with assessing the commercial significance of environmental legislation and standards using data from individual companies is that it is difficult to separate out environmental expenditure from other classes of expenditure. For example, in the 1998 CER published by Yorkshire Water plc, its operating company, Yorkshire Water Services, classifies its core business capital programme as environmental expenditure. How much of the reported £400 million expenditure on the waste-water treatment improvement programme is capital renewal (i.e. would have been needed regardless of new environmental legislation), rather than investment to meet or anticipate future environmental standards, is not explained. Figures reported as environmental expenditure, in the absence of industry-wide criteria, should therefore be interpreted with caution.

◻ Disclosure of Environmental Information

The water companies are subject to several requirements for mandatory disclosure of environmental performance data.

First, they must publish an annual report detailing their activities relating to Sections 8 and 9 of the 1989 Water Act. In essence, these relate to the conservation and recreational activities associated with the water and land holdings of the companies, such as fishing, sailing and water sports, informal recreation, and species and habitat protection. Second, the conditions of their operating licences require them to disclose certain environmental information to the water industry regulator, the Director-General of OFWAT. This includes environment-related data required under the conditions of their operating licence such as effects of pollution on bathing beaches, sewage works discharges, emissions from sewage sludge incinerators, and water leakages. As described below, considerable attention has been, and continues to be, paid to ensuring that this data is measured and reported in a standardised way across the industry. Finally, the industry is required to provide information to the relevant national registers of environmental information established by the 1990 Environmental Protection Act (EPA). These include: Drinking Water; Water Quality and Water Pollution; Water Resources; Bathing Waters; Deposits at Sea; Integrated Pollution Control; Flood Defence; Sewerage and Waterworks; and Nitrate-Sensitive Areas; and are all available for public scrutiny (DoE 1995).

The industry also has several voluntary initiatives. All of the ten major water and sewerage companies have published CERs (see Section 2). The industry has generically, under the auspices of the Water Services Association (WSA, renamed 'Water UK' in 1998) also published a Code of Practice (WSA 1997a). This is titled *Access to Environmental and Water Quality Information in the Water Industry*, and details a set of principles that the water sector has adopted, as well as defining the information that the industry produces. The WSA also released a document bearing the title *Water: Meeting the Challenge* (WSA 1997b). Here, the association states that the sector 'will be the most environmentally conscious industry in Britain'.

◻ *Standardised Pollution Data in the Water Industry*

OFWAT and the Environment Agency publish a number of reports, which include comparative data on the environmental performance of individual companies within the water industry (OFWAT 1998a, 1998b; Environment Agency 1996). These two regulators have drawn together regulatory information for a number of years to provide an overview of water company performance and to provide input into the regulatory price-setting formulae for individual companies. The key environmental performance indicators published are:

a Unsatisfactory combined sewer overflows

b Bathing waters non-compliance

c Equivalent population served by unsatisfactory sea outfalls

d Successful prosecutions

e Category 1 and 2 pollution incidents (as defined by the Environment Agency)

Section 3 examines how many of these standardised indicators are to be found within CERs of individual water companies. The latest tables of environmental performance compare the ten water and sewerage companies for the years 1994–98 (OFWAT 1998a). More detailed information on some of the indicators (e.g. bathing waters) can be found in other published reports. OFWAT report that the Environment Agency is very concerned about the continuing high level of pollution incidents.

◻ Standardised Leakage Data in the Water Industry

The water industry in England and Wales has been the subject of intense scrutiny over leakage of water from the supply system since the drought conditions of 1995, which brought supplies in many parts of the country to crisis levels. This has many environmental implications, notably actual ecological damage due to high levels of water abstraction from water courses and lakes, and potential damage from construction of new reservoirs and pipelines to deal with these and other problems, the need for which could often be avoided if there were less leakage.

OFWAT have been severe in their criticism of water companies for the methods they use to calculate leakage levels and the voluntary approach to target-setting which was in place up to 1997 (OFWAT 1998b). Their main criticisms are of an over-reliance on outdated national data, and a failure to assess leakage control strategies based on sound economic analysis (the 'economic level of leakage', i.e. where the long-run marginal costs of leakage control are equal to the long-run marginal benefits of the water saved, including environmental and social considerations). This analysis is carried out and justified by each company. The aim is to reduce leakage levels to the point where to make further reductions would be more costly than to augment supplies in other ways. OFWAT recognises that the 'economic level of leakage' is a dynamic concept and will vary between companies and the various options available for balancing supply and demand. The economic level may therefore vary not only over time but also between zones within a company. OFWAT therefore expects companies to demonstrate a good grasp of company-specific economic levels of leakage on a zonal basis.

OFWAT have therefore begun to require more thorough and detailed analysis of leakage rates and economic levels of leakage, but stop short of demanding a specific methodology. OFWAT uses the comparative leakage data to investigate companies with higher-than-industry-average losses (e.g. Dwr Cymru), and also to review progress against targets and examples of good practice for wider dissemination.

Up to 1997/98, all companies set themselves voluntary leakage targets. These were specified in terms of million litres per day (Ml/d), cubic meters per km of water mains per day, and litres per property per day (l/prop/day). In that year, OFWAT set mandatory leakage targets for the first time for each company up to 2000. These targets mean that companies will, overall, need to reduce leakage levels by approximately 8% from their 1998/99 targets (OFWAT 1998b). A summary of these targets is shown in Table 1. These targets were set on a pragmatic basis, because only one company (Yorkshire Water) had provided OFWAT with a satisfactory assessment of 'economic levels of leakage'. It is the view of OFWAT that, due to deficiencies in the methodology used for assessing 'economic levels of leakage' (essentially how costs and benefits are derived and measured and the robustness of the data), companies are not yet operating at an economic level of leakage and that further tightening of targets will be set for 2001.

Company	1997/98 target	1997/98 actual	1998/99 target	1999/2000 target
Anglian	211	235	205	195
Dwr Cymru	354	336	308	292
North West	705	578	515	489
Northumbrian	187	184	173	168
Severn Trent	410	399	348	342
Southern	100	99	95	93
South West	110	101	96	84
Thames	962	905	781	665
Wessex	124	109	103	89
Yorkshire	434	368	363	329

Table 1: LEAKAGE TARGETS FOR THE TEN WATER AND SEWERAGE COMPANIES FOR 1998/99 AND 1999/2000 (MEGALITRE/DAY)

In the absence of robust economic data, the target-setting was approached by applying a percentage reduction to each company's distribution losses taking account of the resource supply position (tight, marginal, adequate) and the estimated leakage level (high, medium, low) (see Table 1). It would be too simplistic to use the data in isolation to judge performance, as there may be mitigating circumstances or valid reasons for regional variations. This said, however, the table provides an overview of what is actually happening for leakage control within each company using reliable, consistent data. A later section examines the extent to which this data is published in CERs.

◻ *Further Developments in Standardising Environmental Performance Indicators*

As a result of pressure from stakeholders, and a desire by some companies to benchmark their performance, a Water Industry Group on Sustainable Development (with which one of the authors of this chapter has been involved) is currently seeking to achieve further standardisation of indicators and measurement protocols. It has been proposed that these will be published in the form of comparative tables, though until the final report is published this remains uncertain.

The development of the indicators has three phases. Phase 1 involved workshops in which representatives from the UK water industry were consulted to ensure a common understanding of key issues within the industry. Next, a workshop was held for external stakeholders, involving approximately 35 key opinion-formers (including representatives from UK government environment and agricultural departments, the Environment Agency, the CBI, and NGOs such as Friends of the Earth, Greenpeace, and Surfers against Sewage). This identified a list of key issues that the participants felt should be covered by the indicators. The third workshop involved the representatives from the UK water industry again, to focus on the intended audience for the indicators and trim down the list to no more than 30 that are capable of being presented either as an aggregate for the industry as a whole, or on a company-by-company basis. Further workshops are planned to review progress.

The five performance areas that the indicators will cover are:

1. The provision of water services

2. Good environmental management

3. Energy management

4. Use of materials and resources

5. Local environments, biodiversity and communities

The specific indicators within each performance area are likely to consist of a mix of regulatory and voluntary measures. The regulatory indicators are likely to be driven by compliance standards and targets, and include a number that are already supplied to OFWAT (see above). Indicators under discussion relate to water quality, bathing water failures, consent breaches for waste-water treatment works, sewer flooding, leakage and prosecution.

Many other indicators will, however, be new, including those relating to water resource balance, rivers with low flows, biodiversity and indirect CO_2 emissions. The indicators are being designed to ensure that they will remain consistent over time. They will include a mixture of indicators: some will be the direct responsibility of the water sector (e.g. leakage and compliance), and for others there will be a shared responsibility (e.g. domestic and non-domestic water consumption, river water quality flows, etc.). The full list of indicators will be published in 1999, although no specific date has yet been set. The indicators under discussion for biodiversity and habitat, rivers with low flows, and materials purchased, have been noted as potentially requiring new data collection, although until the final list of indicators has been presented the implications cannot be assessed. As an illustration, however, Table 2 shows the indicators under consideration for the area of energy management. The indicators, as can be seen, are a mix of relative and absolute measures.

2. Benchmarking Environmental Reporting

◻ Introduction

Much of the literature on environmental performance measurement and benchmarking has been in the context of external environmental reporting. This is now a well-

Performance area	Unit	Indicator
Electrical energy from external sources consumed at fixed sites	kWh	kWh per megalitre of water or waste-water treated
Renewable energy exported from fixed sites	kWh	As percentage of total energy consumption
CO_2 emissions from energy used at fixed sites	Total UK emissions (in tonnes)	Total water sector emissions (in tonnes)
CO_2 emissions from energy use in transport	Fuel consumption (total litres of petrol/diesel/LPG)	Total water sector emissions (in tonnes)

Table 2: EXAMPLE OF PROPOSED INDICATORS FOR ENERGY MANAGEMENT

established practice, with many companies preparing reports and several schemas available for their evaluation. The best known of these is that developed by the consultancy SustainAbility in collaboration with the United Nations Environment Programme (hereafter referred to as the SustainAbility/UNEP approach) (Sustain-Ability/UNEP 1997 and Chapter 15).

However, a number of concerns have been expressed about reporting, for example that:

- Published data may be unreliable.

- Many companies are selective about the material they include in their reports.

- Data is not comparable (either within a report, between reports of differing years, or between reports from different companies even within the same sector).

As previously noted, it is often said that standardisation of reporting formats and/or of performance measures is an important part of the solution to such problems. In this and the following two sections we examine several aspects of this topic as it relates to the water industry in England and Wales. This section examines the value of the SustainAbility/UNEP approach as a standardised template for developing and comparing water company environmental reports. The next two sections examine the relationship between these reports and the standardised performance data that is already available within the water industry in England and Wales, both for the industry as a whole and for a representative company, Yorkshire Water.

⌂ *Benchmarking Corporate Environmental Reports*

The SustainAbility/UNEP benchmarking template was first developed in *Engaging Stakeholders: The Benchmark Survey* (SustainAbility/UNEP 1996a), where it was used to assess 100 CERs. SustainAbility/UNEP have responded to some of the criticisms of the original method and have made revisions, although the principles of the method of analysis and the majority of the scoring elements remain the same as reported below (see also Chapter 15). They identify best practice through the use of a scoring system for 50 reporting elements, and, in qualitative terms, through the use of a five-stage model.

Fifty 'reporting elements' were identified, based on extensive stakeholder discussion and review. They are collated into five separate categories, shown below, together with the maximum possible score for the elements making up each category, the scores running from 0 (poorest) to 4 (best) for most individual elements.

1. Management Policies and Systems (45)

2. Input–Output Inventory (72)

3. Finance (17)

4. Stakeholder Relations and Partnerships (40)

5. Sustainable Development (20)

This framework was used by the authors to assess the ten water company environmental reports, utilising one of the authors' long experience in environmental management within the industry (including preparation of CERs). The analysis was carried out in 1997 and examined the reports for the business year 1995/96, with the exception of Northumbrian Water, which covered the period 1994/95.

A simple spreadsheet was created allowing a score for each of the 50 elements to be tabulated. The scoring system awards a score of one point for 'shallow' reporting and up to a maximum of 4 points for detailed reporting. Detailed comments were made for each report against each score to justify and support the points score awarded and to highlight problems in interpretation. Each report required between 14 and 20 hours to complete the scoring. Given the detail of the scoring system and length and complexity of some of the individual CERs, it was necessary to read each report more than once, and then to re-read a final time to check against the scoring criteria. A full explanation of the method and results can be found in Hopkinson and Whitaker 1998.

The scores for each water company against the 50 elements are shown in Table 3 (aggregated into category scores). The classification system devised for 'characterising' the individual CERs is shown in Table 4.

The analysis of the reports revealed a number of common points. One, which has already been discussed, is the absence of much of the standardised data that is required by regulators. All but two of the reports included an environmental policy, although generally the reports are weak in the area of management responsibility and accountability (Element 4). Conversely, as would be expected from a highly regulated industry, all the reports score highly under legal compliance (Element 7). None of

	Total (max. 194)	Category 1 (max. 45)	Category 2 (max. 72)	Category 3 (max. 17)	Category 4 (max. 40)	Category 5 (max. 20)
Northumbrian	57	23	14	5	11	4
Severn Trent	56	24	12	5	11	4
South West	51	20	20	2	8	1
Anglian	49	20	18	5	6	0
Thames	37	16	14	3	4	0
Wessex	34	9	15	3	7	0
Yorkshire	32	13	11	2	6	0
Southern	26	9	8	1	8	0
Welsh	26	9	11	1	5	0
North West	25	6	10	3	6	0

Table 3: THE FIFTY REPORTING ELEMENTS: POINTS AND RANKING

Scores	UNEP description
00–20	'bottom crawlers'
21–40	'ultra narrow'
41–60	'not so hot'
61–80	'pressing hard'
81–100	'state of the art'
101–120	'new benchmarks'
121–140	'trailblazers'
141–194	'over the horizon'

Table 4: UNEP/SUSTAINABILITY BANDING SYSTEM FOR CHARACTERISING
THE TOTAL SCORES OF THE REPORTS

the reports made any reference to internal water consumption (Element 15) and only three reports had any mention of health and safety (Element 17) even though all water companies have a long history of involvement and are tightly regulated in this area.

All the reports were very weak in reference to accidents and emergencies (Element 18) and land contamination and remediation. Severn Trent was the only company to score a zero for 'stewardship: local habitats and ecosystems' (ironically, the title of their report was 'Stewardship'), although they do also produce a separate report on this topic (which was excluded from this analysis). All the reports scored only zero or one for life-cycle design, environmental liabilities and environmental cost accounting. The 'sustainable development' category was the weakest area of all the reports, with the entire sector achieving a total score of only nine for the four elements included. It should be recalled that the reports being analysed were from 1995/96, a time when sustainable development was a less fashionable concept than it is today, and that ideas and the content of reporting have moved on considerably.

One striking feature of the score is the discrepancy between the 57 points we awarded to Northumbrian Water and the 92 awarded by SustainAbility/UNEP for the same report. Although the latter's detailed scorings are not available, the figures for each of the five sections are reproduced in Table 5. As can be seen, the main discrepancies are in Categories 2 (input–output inventory) and 4 (stakeholder relationships and partnerships). Some possible reasons for this discrepancy include:

1. The sensitivity of the scoring system does not allow differences in reporting content to be differentiated. The narrowness of the rating scale (1–4), and the guidance on applying the scale, meant that even where there were noticeable differences in the level of detail reported, it was not possible to increase the score for that element to reflect the difference.

2. Subjectivity in the scoring system. The person scoring the ten reports in our study has over 30 years' experience in the water industry, and in many instances deemed it essential to apply a subjective or personal interpretation to the scoring system. This unavoidable subjectivity will inevitably lead to discrepancies in scores when assessed by different individuals. In the absence of clear protocols for defining elements, or the units of measurement, such subjectivity will always present problems in interpretation and call into question the reliability of the scores produced.

3. Reports that focus on specific target audiences appear to have an inbuilt penalty. Due to the comprehensive 'all things to all people' approach of the SustainAbility/UNEP scoring system, there is an inherent bias to reward comprehensiveness regardless of whether the reports meet the needs of the specific target audiences for individual companies. We regard this as a real weakness which could lead to a 'report everything that the SustainAbility/ UNEP tool deems important' syndrome, regardless of the needs of particular audiences.

4. The scoring system builds in some counter-productive or potentially ambiguous measures. For example, a company would score highly for having

Category	Category title	Hopkinson and Whitaker score	SustainAbility/ UNEP score
1	Management Policies and Systems	23	22
2	Input–Output Inventory	14	37
3	Finance	5	9
4	Stakeholder Relations and Partnerships	11	21
5	Sustainable Development	4	3
	Grand total	**57**	**92**

Table 5: COMPARISON OF SUSTAINABILITY STUDY VERSUS HOPKINSON AND WHITAKER SCORE FOR NORTHUMBRIAN WATER

Water company	Total (max. 194)	No. pages	Focus index	Rank-order
Northumbrian	57	48	1.19	6
Severn Trent	56	37	1.51	2
South West	51	37	1.38	4
Anglian	49	25	1.96	1
Thames	37	25	1.48	3
Wessex	34	56	0.61	10
Yorkshire	32	40	0.8	9
Southern	26	29	0.9	8
Welsh	26	20	1.3	5
North West	25	27	0.93	7

Table 6: A FOCUS INDEX FOR THE TEN WATER AND SEWERAGE CERs

provisions against existing and future liabilities but, against the wording of the scoring system set out for Element 32, 'environmental liabilities', past actions to 'manage out' such liabilities would not register a score. Clearly, a company that had managed out such liabilities or taken action to reduce exposure should be regarded as having performed well in this area.

5. The measurement system does not specify the units for quantitative data, so that information being compared between different reports may have been measured in different units. Although SustainAbility/UNEP make no claims in this respect, it should nevertheless be noted that, in the absence of consistent or uniform quantitative measures, their tool does not necessarily help users to compare the effectiveness of environmental performance between different companies.

6. The benchmarking tool takes no account of the length of the report. ACCA (1997b) commented that the ever-increasing size (of reports) was tending to lessen their effectiveness as a means of communication with major stakeholder groups. The ten reports in our study varied between 20 and 56 pages in length. Interestingly, when a focus index was calculated by dividing each report's SustainAbility/UNEP points by the number of pages in the report, the two shortest reports score two of the three highest focus index scores while the longest report, of 56 pages, was ranked lowest (see Table 6). The companies with the highest total scores from the SustainAbility/UNEP study were ranked 6, 3 and 4 respectively under the focus index. While there is no consistent relationship between number of points scored and length of report, a focus index does provide an incentive to produce shorter reports.

7. Finally, the template does not really take into account any differences between CERs that are a company's sole form of communication with its stakeholders, and CERs that form part of an overall communications mix. Several of the water companies examined produce a variety of reports, leaflets and bulletins on specific topics which are often targeted at individual audiences. Examination of those produced by one water company, Yorkshire Water, revealed that much of this was not reproduced in their CER. Some of the reports themselves also target specific audiences. For instance, the Welsh Water (now Dwr Cymru) report is titled a 'Customer and Environment Report', the Southern Water report is called a 'Conservation and Environment Report', and the North West Water report has the title 'Drinking Water and Environmental Quality Report'. This difference in emphasis results in a not insignificant proportion of the report being dedicated to one particular topic area, leaving a smaller proportion to provide detail on all other issues. Hence, when using the benchmarking tool in these and other similar cases, it would almost seem that these reports are in fact being penalised for focusing on a particular issue, to the detriment of others.

Indicator: Company	A	B	C	D	E	F	G	H	I	J	K
Anglian	Y	N	Y	Y	N	Y	Y	Y	Y	Y	Y
Dwr Cymru	N	N	N	Y	N	Y	N	N	N	N	N
Northumbrian	N	N	N	Y	N	Y	N	N	N	N	N
North West	N	N	Y	Y	N	Y	Y	Y	Y	Y	Y
Severn Trent	N	Y	Y	n/a	n/a	Y	N	N	Y	Y	Y
South West	N	N	Y	Y	N	Y	N	N	Y	Y	Y
Southern	Y	N	N	Y	N	Y	Y	Y	Y	Y	Y
Thames	N	N	N	n/a	n/a	Y	N	N	Y	Y	Y
Wessex	Y	N	Y	Y	N	Y	Y	Y	Y	Y	Y
Yorkshire	N	N	Y	Y	N	Y	N	N	Y	Y	N
Total Yes	2	1	6	7	0	10	4	4	8	8	7

Key

A: Equivalent population served by sewage treatment works (millions residents)
B: Equivalent population served by sewage treatment works (%) in breach of consent
C: Unsatisfactory combined sewer overflows (%)
D: Bathing water non-compliant
E: Equivalent population served by unsatisfactory sea outfalls (thousands)
F: Successful prosecutions
G: Category 1 pollution incidents (major incidents as defined by Environment Agency)
H: Category 2 pollution incidents (significant incidents as defined by Environment Agency)
I: 1997/8 total leakage target (megalitre/day); as set by OFWAT
J: 1997/98 leakage performance (megalitre/day); as set by OFWAT
K: 1998/99 and 1999/2000 leakage targets (megalitre/day); as set by OFWAT

Y: disclosed
N: not disclosed
n/a: not applicable. Thames and Severn Trent are classified as having no discharges to bathing waters or sea.

Note: Dwr Cymru, South West and Southern Water data taken from Hyder Utilities, Pennon Group and Scottish Power environment reports respectively.

Table 7: INCLUSION OF STANDARDISED ENVIRONMENTAL PERFORMANCE INDICATORS DISCLOSED TO OFWAT AND ENVIRONMENT AGENCY WITHIN ENVIRONMENTAL REPORTS OF INDIVIDUAL COMPANIES

Our analysis demonstrates that, at the very least, considerable care is needed in applying or interpreting the results of CER benchmarking exercises. It also suggests that there is no direct relationship between CERs and real environmental performance. The following sections examine this issue further.

3. *Standardised Data in Environmental Reports*

This section analyses how many of the standardised indicators described in Section 1 were actually published in water company CERs. Table 7 sets out the key standardised environmental performance indicators that are reported by each water company to OFWAT and the Environment Agency. The indicators are of two types. Those relating to waste-water treatment and disposal (indicators A–H) include sewage treatment works in breach of consent, non-compliant bathing waters, unsatisfactory combined sewer overflows, unsatisfactory sea outfalls, pollution incidents (defined in terms of severity based on a number of criteria) and successful prosecutions. It is interesting to note that two of the indicators are expressed in terms of population equivalent, which enables the number of people potentially affected by breaches of consent of pollution incidents to be highlighted. OFWAT publishes these key environmental performance indicators (indicators A–H) in the form of a comparative table (titled 'Environmental Impact: Company Performance') which enables the relative performance of each company to be viewed at a glance (OFWAT 1998a). OFWAT also publishes a large number of comparative statistics on leakage. Indicators I–K were selected for illustrative purposes but were also felt to be particularly important for environmental performance evaluation. The latest CERs (1997/98) for the ten water plcs were obtained to identify whether the standardised environmental performance indicators are published by the companies themselves, and also whether the companies make comparisons between themselves.

It is evident that there is considerable variability in the reporting of standardised environmental performance indicators, and that it is currently impossible to reconstruct the comparative table published by OFWAT based on the data found within the CERs. Very few presented data in the form of population equivalents, and, while most of the companies indicated where they had been prosecuted, few mentioned or defined Category 1 and 2 pollution incidents, even though this is an area of concern expressed by OFWAT. Most of the companies presented leakage data, although several presented data as percentages, which (as discussed in Section 1) is not recommended through OFWAT. What was surprising was the difficulty of identifying whether the standardised data was present or not (or could be constructed from the data present), and the huge variation in the level of detail and explanation given to each indicator. Data on combined sewer overflows and sea outfalls was particularly limited in most cases. Some of the reports provide targets and explanations of how and why they might have failed to reach a target, or of how they plan to improve performance further in future years.

Several reports present some of the indicators (A–K) very simply and clearly in a format very similar to that published by OFWAT, whereas others present data in ways

Environmental performance measurement area	Indicator or measurement method	Progress against 1997 targets
Environmental audit for operational sites	Number of audits and resulting scores	11 operational sites to be audited by March 1999
Environmental assessment for new abstraction schemes	Full environmental assessment method agreed with Environment Agency	All new schemes assessed since April 1997
Supplier environmental performance	Environmental Vendor Evaluation System (EVES)	33 contractors to be evaluated during 1998/99
Employee awareness	Information pack for employee use	Currently being distributed
Vehicle emissions	Biannual emission check on all vehicles	Achieved
Emission to air (incineration)	Zero non-compliance prosecution	One non-compliance, not prosecuted
Operational failures	Zero non-compliance prosecutions	Prosecuted twice for one sewer overflow
Waste-water treatment compliance	No more than 12 failures with compliance standards	4 failures
Groundwater abstraction	Zero prosecutions	Achieved for exceeding licence
Water use internally	Reduce water use by 10%	Probably achieved (lack of historical data)
Photocopying	Sheets and tonnage of paper reduced or recycled	Reductions described

Performance indicator	Target/(timescale)	Unit	Progress
Chemical: water supply	Chemical use at clean water works held constant (96/97 baseline) (98/00)	kg/megalitre* treated water	First year completed. 9% above target.
Substitute less toxic chemicals	None stated (97/00)	Percentage substitution	40% substitution chlorine gas in first year
Chemicals: sewage incineration plant	Polymer dosage reduction 5.6 to 5.5 (97/00)	kg/tonne dry solids	No reduction in first 6 months
Chemicals: sewage incineration plant	Sodium hydroxide 42 to 41 (97/00)	kg/tonne dry solid	First 6 months' data: 44.99 kg/tonne dry solid. Redefining target against new data.
Chemical: waste-water	Reduce fly control chemical from 160,000 (97/99)	litres/annum	First year data: 32,780 litres
Chemical: waste-water	Reduce odour control chemicals (98/99)	none specified	No progress
Accommodation	Environmental best practice	none specified	Out to tender

* Megalitre = million litres

Table 8: SUMMARY OF KEY ENVIRONMENTAL PERFORMANCE MEASUREMENT INDICATORS AND PROGRESS AGAINST TARGETS FOR YWS NON-CORE BUSINESS

Source: Yorkshire Water 1998

that were difficult both to find and to interpret. Only one report indicated what Category 1 and 2 pollution incidents are. Only two companies made any explicit reference to their performance against the rest of the sector and in each case, not surprisingly, it was to show that they were above average. No company attempted to provide a comparative performance table for the sector as a whole for any indicator.

The overall conclusion from the analysis is that, despite the existence and external publication of standardised environmental performance indicator data, the inclusion of such data within individual CERs is very patchy and inconsistent.

4. Standardised Data in the Yorkshire Water CER

In order to provide further light on this question of how water companies use standardised performance data in their reports we examined the CER of Yorkshire Water Services (YWS), the main subsidiary of Yorkshire Water plc. It provides water for 4.5 million people and collects and treats waste-water from 4.3 million people and 130,000 businesses in the Yorkshire region of the UK.

YW plc first published a Corporate Environmental Report in 1994 and has done so annually since then. The report covers all of its businesses, although this chapter focuses only on the sections relating to YWS. The most recent CER (1998) contains two separate sections. One of these focuses on environmental performance issues and targets relating to the company's internal environmental management activities; the other deals with the areas that are subject to regulation. There is considerable overlap between the two in terms of content, but considerable differences in terms of style and comprehensiveness.

Table 8 summarises the targets, and progress towards them, for the key environmental performance indicators (KEPIs) identified in the internal management section of the report. These KEPIs were the output of an initiative during 1996/97 to rationalise and quantify environmental performance measurement in a consistent way. The business areas responsible for the individual environmental impacts were asked to develop specific, measurable, achievable and relevant targets with a clear deadline. Performance measures for each indicator are reported monthly to the main Board through the 'Management Book' alongside traditional business performance measures. The data in Table 8 is derived from an aggregation of these monthly reports.

One noteworthy feature of Table 8 is that the language and detail of the targets and performance data are taken almost directly from the CER, as this is the form in which they were originally developed. In the authors' experience, their precision has been an important factor in generating commitment and action in the company to their achievement.

The inclusion of EPIs, KEPIs and performance against targets in a standardised format also makes it much easier to digest the environmental performance data. Reducing environmental performance into key indicators enables both internal management and external audiences to judge progress at a glance. From this, attention can be focused on critical questions about the choice of indicator (are the right indicators and performance areas included?); the targets set (e.g. are they

Activity	Indicator(s)	Targets	Comments
Drinking water supply	None specified	None specified	Narrative on current actions: current abstraction practices, automated metering and monitoring
Drinking water quality	Percentage water non-compliant supply zones (9 chemical or biological indicators included)	None specified. Data for 1994–97.	
	Percentage samples meeting standard	None specified. Data for 1994–97.	
Leakage control	Total leakage megalitre/day	363 megalitre/day x 1998/99	Target set by OFWAT. Currently in discussion with OFWAT and Environment Agency over targets.
Water conservation	None specified	None specified	Narrative on household metering, small-scale water conservation projects and working with stakeholders
Waste-water treatment	Compliance with consent standards: domestic and trade effluent releases	Full compliance	Four trade discharges did not meet standard
Designated bathing waters	EU/UK standards	Full compliance	
Sewer overflows	Compliance with consent standards		Targets agreed with OFWAT and Environment Agency in 1994 but cumulative performance against target not reported
Sewage sludge disposal	Tonnages disposed by different means	None specified	Narrative and tonnage data on some current practices and actions
Releases to air	Emissions of range of compounds in kg/year	Authorisation limits shown	Tabular data for 4 incinerators shown
Energy use	Electricity consumption kWh for main business units	None specified	General plans for efficiency improvements discussed. Description of new wood-burning electricity plant.
Transport	Emission levels	None specified	Narrative on current actions and proposals
Accommodation	Water and electricity consumption	None specified	
Paper use	Number of sheets, tonnage recycled	6,200 kg recycling target	Targets exceeded for recycling by factor of 8
Conservation and land access			Narrative on some current issues and actions

Table 9: SUMMARY OF KEY ENVIRONMENTAL PERFORMANCE AREAS, INDICATORS AND TARGETS FOR YWS CORE BUSINESS

Source: Yorkshire Water 1998

internally or externally set? are they challenging?); and progress (is the company being effective?).

In contrast, constructing Table 9 as a summary of the section of the CER dealing with regulated environmental data was much less straightforward, since the data was presented in widely different ways and to different levels of detail. Some of the performance areas, e.g. drinking water quality, set out a number of chemical and biological indicators and compliance against external standards, although these are not discussed as KEPIs. Other activity areas, e.g. sewage sludge disposal, are presented through a narrative and have no discussion or presentation of indicators or targets. This section of the CER also lacks explicit targets. It is not clear which of the performance areas are considered most important. For example, the section on leakage, one of the more contentious and strategically significant issues facing the water industry at the current time (see Section 1), is a short paragraph compared to two pages on energy use and consumption—a topic that, although important, is of much less strategic importance. All of this hinders comparison between Yorkshire Water and other water companies.

The comparison confirms the evidence from Section 3 that, although standardised data is available, it is either not being published at all or, if so, is sometimes published in a selective manner. Nor are any comparisons made with other water companies. For example, the report from OFWAT on levels of service for the water industry in England and Wales includes comparative tables that show Yorkshire Water to have 30% unsatisfactory combined sewer overflows (ranked fourth worst in the list of ten companies); 14% bathing water non-compliance (ranked second worst); and 37 Category 2 pollution incidents (ranked worst). While there may be good reasons and explanations for these figures (for example, not all companies have sea outfalls or bathing waters), it is noteworthy that the Category 2 pollution incidents are not included in the 1998 CER, further emphasising the weakness of the CER as a comprehensive representation of environmental performance.

The purpose of this analysis is not to castigate Yorkshire Water: similar points could be made from the CERs from other water companies (see Table 7). The overall conclusion is that a CER remains a voluntary activity under the control of the individual company. Even where there is mandatory disclosure of standardised data, which is published in the public domain in a comparative way, there is no guarantee that this will then also appear in a CER. This raises a host of questions about the extent to which CERs as an activity, even with strong regulatory pressures, can provide the basis for benchmarking performance.

5. Conclusion

A CER is currently a voluntary activity, which can be prepared and published by a company for many different reasons. One function it serves is to provide internal and external audiences with a snapshot of environmental performance activities, achievements and progress. In the absence of agreed protocols of what to report, and how to report, each company is free to present and report environmental performance data as it sees fit. This freedom can be viewed as both a strength and a weakness. One strength is that it encourages diversity and permits each company to define its own reporting style and to shape the report to the particular interests of its own target audience(s). From an internal perspective, it is also likely that a major benefit of a CER is that it requires the drawing together of disparate data from within the company, and requires management to take an overview of environmental performance across the full range of activities. If a reporting system is too rigid or prescriptive in the early stages, then some of the value of the process of putting together a report may be lost.

From an external perspective, the weakness of self-assessment through a CER is that the data presented is only a snapshot and is likely to comprise a wide range of data and activities in different styles to try to meet different audiences' requirements. This problem is likely to be compounded where the target audience for the report is ill defined, or the report tries to meet the needs of many different target audiences. Moreover, as we have shown, the content of a CER is controlled entirely by the company, which is likely to be selective.

Our conclusion—that great care is needed in interpreting CERs and the information contained in them—is, of course, not original. However, the degree of variation and selection in what was reported between ten apparently similar companies did surprise us. So too did the degree of subjectivity that is possible when assessing reports against the SustainAbility/UNEP model.

Our research also suggests that creation of standardised data in itself will not necessarily lead to improved comparability or better reporting. The patchy reporting of mandatory standardised environmental performance indicators and the absence of any sectoral comparisons within individual CERs, even though such data is published and publicly available, was a source of concern, especially as it would be very easy to overcome. The fact that improved comparability and reporting in the US appears to be in large part attributable to the disclosure of Toxic Release Inventory (TRI) data may be a consequence of the high degree of environmentalist and public interest there in the information. Where this interest is absent or weak— as is the case with much of the UK water data—the same results may not occur. Indeed, companies appear to have a bias against reporting comparative data because it will often put them in a poor light. However, environmental performance measurement in the water industry is still evolving and it may be that the current initiatives to take standardisation further—initiated and managed by the water companies themselves—may improve the situation. If so, it would suggest that the best way forward towards standardised data and better reporting in future may lie in strong external pressures driving sectoral initiatives by companies themselves, rather than in mandatory data stipulated by regulators, or generic cross-industry benchmarking schemes such as those of SustainAbility/UNEP.[1]

---

1   The SustainAbility/UNEP approach appears to have reached similar conclusions, with recent publications emphasising the importance of sectoral benchmarking schemes.

21
Internet-Based Environmental Reporting

Key Components*

Kathryn Jones and Julia Walton

THE BENEFITS of reporting corporate environmental performance are already widely documented (Palmer and van der Vorst 1997: 58; Davis-Walling and Batterman 1997: 865, and references therein) and environmental reporting award schemes are now creating additional incentives for companies to produce environmental reports and thus gain from a heightened positive profile (Menon and Menon 1997: 51-67; Prothero *et al.* 1997: 74-75; KPMG 1997: 2; Wehrmeyer 1996: 12; SustainAbility/UNEP 1997: 26).

Companies from many sectors have already committed themselves to producing environmental reports on an annual basis and therefore require new information and data each year that can be used to demonstrate progress (Palmer and Cooper 1997: 1). Not only are the number of companies producing environmental reports increasing, but also the range of countries and sectors in which they operate is becoming ever more diverse (SustainAbility/UNEP 1997: 3). Indeed, environmental reporting is becoming more sophisticated as well as more widespread (KPMG 1997: 2), as demonstrated by the fact that environmental reports are now appearing in different formats as companies experiment with different communication methods. Daimler-Benz, for example, produced its 1997 environmental report in the form of a newspaper; EPCOR Group produced its 1996 environmental report as a poster; and several companies, including Hoechst (1996), British Petroleum (1996), ENI (1995 and 1996) and Swiss Air (*Third Environmental Audit*) have produced their environmental reports on CD-ROMs. However, the reporting medium fast becoming popular with

---

*   This chapter is an updated version of K. Jones, T. Alabaster and J. Walton, 'Virtual Environments for Environmental Reporting', *Greener Management International* 21 (Spring 1998): 121-37.
    The website addresses listed throughout this chapter were correct at the time of publication, but may have changed subsequently.

many companies is the Internet, and it is expected that, over the next four years, there will be a large migration of paper CERs to the World Wide Web (Centre for Sustainable Design 1998: 13; SustainAbility/UNEP 1998b).

However in their recent *The Non-Reporting Report*, SustainAbility said that, according to their definition of reporting, the following type of company would be considered as a non-reporter: 'a company that does not produce a stand-alone, printed report, but makes information available via other channels' (SustainAbility/UNEP 1998b: 6). Therefore, companies who disclose their environmental report only via the Internet—for example, Sun[1] and Texas Instruments[2] —in the eyes of SustainAbility do not produce an environmental report. In addition to this, companies can be placed at a disadvantage in the SustainAbility ranking system if they reduce the volume of information in their hard-copy report and increase the amount on the Internet. For example, in the SustainAbility *1997 Benchmark Survey*, DuPont was penalised for a 'scaled-down report from 25-page CER to 8-page leaflet. Reader is signposted to website instead' (SustainAbility/UNEP 1997; and Chapter 15, page 334).

Although the concept of corporate environmental reporting via the Internet is mentioned in a variety of articles, there has been little in the way of in-depth analysis of how this new information and communication technology (ICT) is being used for the benefit of environmental reporting (Lober *et al.* 1997: 63-64; Lober 1997: 17-18; Butner 1996: 1-3; C21 1997: 4; Davis-Walling and Batterman 1997: 857; Elkington 1997: 180; SustainAbility/ UNEP 1996a: 45-47; KPMG 1997: 23; Walton *et al.* 1997: 201). The aim of this chapter is therefore to examine the Internet as an environmental communications and information management tool and discuss the key criteria for creating and maintaining an effective environmental reporting website.[3]

◢ The Internet as a Communications Tool

Communicating with stakeholders is a major challenge for companies (Prothero *et al.* 1997: 75), a point also noted by the European Environmental Agency itself who indicate that many data sources remain under-used and insufficiently exposed to a greater audience, and that it is possible to make data more relevant and improve existing data by 'putting information to work' (UNEP 1995: 3). Table 1 shows various media through which this can be achieved and clearly reveals that the communications medium that embraces all of the beneficial characteristics that are displayed only selectively by more traditional media is the Internet. One method of using the Internet is the World Wide Web (WWW), and the number of corporate websites is escalating. Professionals are increasingly turning to them to locate information rather than relying on seasonal or annual distribution of printed materials.

---

1 *http://www.sun.com/corporateoverview/ehs/*
2 *http://www.ti.com/corp/docs/esh/commitment.htm*
3 The data were gathered in March 1998 and updated in February 1999; for a more updated list of references and corporate environmental reporting websites, visit *http://cei.sund.ac.uk/envrep/index.htm*.

	Print	Fax	Audio/Tape	Phone	Video	Video conferencing	PC disk	CD-ROM	Internet
Text	✓	✓					✓	✓	✓
Still image	✓	✓			✓	✓	✓	✓	✓
Moving image					✓	✓		✓	✓
Sound			✓	✓	✓	✓		✓	✓
Interaction	Sim	Sim	Sim	✓	Sim	✓	Sim	Sim	✓

Sim = Simulated

Table 1: MEDIA FOR COMMUNICATION

The Internet is flexible in that it can be accessed 24 hours a day from any networked terminal anywhere in the world, and search engines such as InfoSeek, Excite, Yahoo, etc. assist users in locating relevant documents from the mass of information available (Ollier 1996: 1). This flexibility satisfies users' demands for 'high quality, timely information that is easy to obtain' (Foy 1996: 1) and also allows documents, audio, video, animated graphics and 3D simulations to be connected via hyperlinks. These types of multimedia function can all be incorporated into sites by using freely available specialised software known as 'plug-ins'.[4] The Internet thus allows for interaction with users, engaging them in many types of communication cheaply and effectively (Ritzenthaler and Ostroff 1996: 1).

When information is put 'on-line', it can be rapidly accessed by users, thus potentially freeing companies from the 'constraints of time and space associated with traditional forms of corporate communications' (Ritzenthaler and Ostroff 1996: 16), and may also reduce printing and distribution costs as companies cut down on the number of hard-copy documents they produce (Lober 1997: 18). Indeed, Sun Microsystems are just one of the companies that have realised the benefits and opportunities this affords them.[5] An additional feature of the Internet is the capability to gather information automatically on how many people have visited the site, who they are, where they are from and which pages they have read (Lober 1997). This information can be analysed, using specialised software, to gain valuable information about who an organisation's stakeholders are, user trends, ease of site navigation, etc.[6]

Notwithstanding the above, there are concerns that the Internet will result in a divide between the information-rich and the information-poor, or those who have access to the Internet and those that do not. Regulation is needed to ensure that access is widely available. The paramount issue regarding the Internet is that,

---

4   For example, RealAudio, *http://www.real.com/index.html*, Shockwave, *http://www.macromedia.com/shockwave*, and QuickTime, *http://www.apple.com/quicktime*.

5   See Sun Microsystems, *http://www.sun.com/corporateoverview/corpaffairs/ehs-about_this_site.html*.

6   See Microsoft Usage Analyst, *http://www.microsoft.com/siteserver/default.asp*, or WebTracker, *http://www.fxweb.com/tracker*.

paradoxically, its downfall might be realised as a result of its own success; conservative projections have suggested that 120 million computers are currently connected, and users are expected to double every year, leading to concern that the Internet cannot sustain this volume of traffic.There are predictions that there will be an increase in computer bugs and incompatibilities, longer waits for access, and servers crashing. In the long term, these issues will be addressed as the industry evolves.

Although the Internet is considered to be a cheap method of communicating information, maintaining an up-to-date, lively website does represent a significant commitment in time, attention, energy and, in many cases, bottom-line costs. 'While start-up costs and risks are low, there's a growing investment in expensive management time as you gradually get round to properly exploiting the technology' (Ring 1999). By purchasing its own server, a company can expect a large initial outlay, but long-term costs will be minimised, especially if an employee is provided with suitable software and trained to an adequate level to manage the site. In-house experts, which avoid the middleman, can provide a polished web service with updating of the web pages being almost effortless, as well as providing informed replies to feedback and monitoring the use of the website.

◢ Environmental Reporting on the Internet

Although guidelines exist for hard-copy-based environmental reporting (see e.g. Chapter 23), as yet, there are no clear guidelines for web-based environmental reporting that take into account the unique design and content capabilities of the Internet. The Internet can reduce the cost for companies moving towards producing a series of audience-specific documents to address all stakeholder groups (KPMG 1997) and companies may prefer to use the Internet to produce environmental information in more diverse formats on their websites.

Azzone *et al.* (1997) identified eight core stakeholder groups for environmental reports and analysed each for their preferred content requirements and preferred media for receiving environmental information (see Table 2). Interestingly, each of these requirements can be met by using the Internet. For example, one method of producing comparative reports is to create hyperlinks between relevant sections from previous years' reports, thus avoiding the practical difficulties commonly associated with creating standardised hard-copy reports (Azzone *et al.* 1997: 702). Additional information, including non-technical, informal information required by some of the stakeholder groups, can be accommodated by creating separate web pages or creating links to existing pages. Information on the website can also be updated as frequently as each of the stakeholder groups requires without much additional cost or effort and stakeholders can gain access to the Internet through terminals at work or in local libraries or community centres. While the Internet can embrace the eight core stakeholders' requirements, it can also encourage a broader spectrum of stakeholders to read, learn and understand what specific environmental measures a company is undertaking by using the interactive and multimedia capabilities of the Internet.

Format	Academia	Local community	NGOs	Financial community and shareholders	Trade and industry	Employees
Standardisation of reports for comparison	✓		✓		✓	
Additional detailed information	✓		✓			
Frequent reports at least annually			✓		✓	✓
Access to report at work or home		✓				✓
Linked to annual report				✓		
Non-technical informal information		✓				✓
Brief leaflet or fact sheet		✓			✓	

Notes:

- Trade and industry require annual fact sheets alongside full-scale reports every 3–5 years.
- Regulators and policy-makers only require that the report is of 'appropriate style or format to meet the information requirements of other target groups' (Azzone et al. 1997: 705).

Table 2: ENVIRONMENTAL REPORTING FORMAT REQUIREMENTS OF KEY STAKEHOLDERS

Source: Adapted from Azzone *et al.* 1997: 702-706

At present, hard-copy documents still represent perhaps the predominant communications medium, with the Internet being viewed as a complementary supplement. Hard-copy environmental reports are frequently directly translated by external Internet design companies into HyperText Mark-up Language (HTML), the formatting language used by the WWW, and then directly transferred to the Internet.[7] This approach often results in the design and content capabilities that can be facilitated by the Internet being overlooked. So a key question is: is it still sufficient for corporate environmental reports to be directly translated and then transferred to the Internet? People are no longer satisfied with hard-copy documentation or mere electronic reproduction of it. Instead, they want an electronic version of the information that exploits the capabilities of the medium, giving them the ability to access, navigate and search for what they need (Rauch *et al.* 1997: 115). Companies need to provide structured, interactive documents which are defined by Rauch *et al.* (1997) as 'documents that accommodate HyperText linking, graphics, multimedia, linking to external URL's from within the document, and complex searches'. Therefore, the question should perhaps not be how to translate the hard-copy report for the Internet, but how to create an integrated environmental communications strategy that develops environmental disclosures in a holistic manner in all media.

Whatever the nature of the current debate, it is evident that the Internet is becoming an increasingly popular medium for companies to communicate their

---

7   See Chapter 12 for a similar development over time of Internet reporting by Baxter International.

Content	**1.**	Environmental reports on-line
	2.	Environmental reports in Portable Document Format (PDF)
	3.	Additional environmental documents on-line and PDF
	4.	Interactive and multimedia environmental information
	5.	Environmental education
	6.	Information about the environmental team and contact details
	7.	Automatic order forms
	8.	Automatic feedback forms
	9.	Environmental forums
Design	**1.**	Internal hyperlinks
	2.	External hyperlinks
	3.	Site design
	4.	Graphics and backgrounds
	5.	Navigation
	6.	Regular updates
	7.	Site promotion

Table 3: KEY COMPONENTS OF AN ENVIRONMENTAL REPORTING WEBSITE

environmental reports (Ollier 1996). It is already starting to transform the task of corporate environmental reporting as more consideration is beginning to be given to some of the design and content capabilities of the Internet as identified in Table 3. Each of the key components under the headings of 'Content' and 'Design' in Table 3 will now be addressed, analysing why they are important and how they can be accommodated within an environmental reporting website.

◁ *Content*

1. **Environmental reports on-line.** Many companies have directly translated and transferred their hard-copy environmental report onto their website. However, in some situations (at the time of writing), sections of text are missing (Ryder Company),[8] or only a summary of each chapter appears (SwissAir),[9] or vital graphs and diagrams are missing (British Steel).[10] It is therefore not made clear to the user that the information provided constitutes only excerpts from the full environmental report and, as yet, the various companies have not produced transparent reasons on why their full report has not been included on their website. Furthermore, when new environmental reports are produced, it is not necessary to remove the previous year's report (see Unilever, who removed its 1996 environmental report when the

---

8   *http://www.ryder.com/enviroenvrpt01.shtml*
9   *http://www.swissair.com/aboutus/swissair/environment.htm*
10 *http://www.britishsteel.co.uk/enviro.htm*

1997 report was issued, which in turn was replaced by the 1998 report[11]). Noranda, on the other hand, includes three consecutive environmental reports on its website, which play a valuable role in allowing users to compare their reports year on year.[12] 'Users are no longer satisfied with hardcopy documentation or with a mere electronic reproduction of it. Instead they want an electronic version of the information that exploits the capabilities of the medium, giving them the ability to access, navigate and search for what they need' (Rauch *et al.* 1997).

2. **Environmental reports in Portable Document Format (PDF).** Portable Document Format (PDF) is a tool for reproducing hard-copy reports and documents on the Internet. PDF files are downloaded to the hard drive and freely available specialised software, such as Adobe Acrobat Reader, can be used to view them.[13] When viewed in such software, the reports retain the same design and formatting features as the hard-copy report. This has made PDF a popular option with traditional designers, as this level of control over the design cannot be achieved with HTML because the browsers that are used to interpret it, such as Netscape Navigator and Microsoft Explorer, do so in different ways. Moreover, on an individual level, users can change the settings on their browsers specifying the font and style of the page, even turning off graphics (Ritzenthaler and Ostroff 1996: 17).

The primary concern regarding PDF files is that, because it is so easy to translate files into PDF, companies frequently make their environmental report available only by PDF and not on-line. For example, the 1995 Body Shop *Values Report*[14] is available on-line, but its 1997 *Values Report*[15] is available only in PDF. As PDF files are often very large due to all the graphics they contain, this can present a barrier to users with only a small hard drive, little spare computer memory, or slow modems, as the files can take time to download. Several companies are avoiding this by creating PDF files for each chapter of the report (e.g. Texaco[16]) or sometimes in conjunction with a PDF of the whole report to allow users to choose which format to download (e.g. Petrofina[17]). But many users find it difficult to know which chapter contains the information they require and so have to download the whole report anyway. It is therefore recommended that companies should provide the report on-line, as a single PDF file, and with individual PDF files for each chapter (e.g. Sony[18]).

3. **Additional environmental documents on-line and PDF.** Some companies produce additional environmentally related documents which may include fact sheets (for example, Sulzer Management Ltd's environmental report 1996 contains individ-

---

11   *http://www.unilever.com/public/env/review/env_revi.htm*

12   See Noranda, *http://www.noranda.com/english/environment/environment.cfm?subsect_id= 34&environment=yes*

13   See *http://www.adobe.com/prodindex/acrobat/main.html*.

14   *http://www.think-act-change.com*

15   *http://www.the-body-shop.com/values/valuesrep.html*

16   *http://www.texaco.com/compinfo/ehs/ehs.htm*

17   *http://www.fina.com/en/ch11/4.htm*

18   *http://www.sony.co.jp/soj/CorporateInfo/EnvironmentalReport97/pdf.html*

ual fact sheets), environmental magazines (for example, *Hoechst's Environmental Magazine*), issue papers (American Electric Power, *Beyond Environmental Compliance*) and environmental awards brochures (Jefferson Smurfit, *Innovation Environmental Awards*). These can also be translated into HTML (see NEC Eco Action Plan 21[19]), PDF (see ICI environmental burden approach[20]) or, preferably, both (see North Environment safety and health management system[21]) and incorporated into the environmental reporting website. Thus, with a little effort, the documents can acquire more diverse and dynamic characteristics than can be achieved by paper alone. If a company wishes to provide more detailed background information, for example on the PERI environmental reporting guidelines (see Nortel[22]), this can be linked from the environmental report for the benefit of those who want to know more. Corporate press releases are often put onto the Internet to keep users up to date with the company's activities. However, environmentally related press releases are rarely linked from the environmental website, although a few companies are experimenting with this (see IBM[23]).

4. Interactive and multimedia environmental information. Internet technology has advanced greatly over the last few years. Virtual reality is already starting to make an appearance on the Internet in the form of 3D imagery but, as yet, few companies have experimented with this new technology. Nevertheless, some companies have made use of multimedia in their attempts to engage more stakeholders, and examples of this include:

▼ Video clips (e.g. General Motors[24])

▼ Audio clips (e.g. American Electric Power[25])

▼ Quizzes (e.g. SC Johnson Wax[26])

▼ Environmental training manuals (e.g. Electrolux[27])

▼ Adventure stories (e.g. AT&T[28])

▼ Interactive games (e.g. BC Hydro[29])

5. Environmental education. Environmental education plays an important role in helping to ensure that future generations can become environmentally responsible citizens (UNESCO 1998; UNCED 1992; Alabaster and Hawthorne 1999). Companies

---

19 *http://www.nec.co.jp/english/profile/Icon/ecoac/ecoac.html),*
20 *http://www.ici.com/downloads/index.htm)*
21 *http://www.north.com.au/esh-management/*
22 *http://www1.nortelnetworks.com/cool/Habitat/CommSol/peri.html*
23 *http://www.ibm.com/ibm/Environment*
24 *http://www.gm.com/about/info/news/speech/index.htm*
25 *http://www.aep.com/environment/gore/index1.html*
26 *http://www.scjohnsonwax.com/htdocs/we-are/teenGPA1.html*
27 *http://www.electrolux.se/show.asp?id=59*
28 *http://www.att.com/ehs*
29 *http://eww.bchydro.bc.ca/environment/html/game.html*

already produce hard-copy educational materials which are frequently targeted at the local community. However, the Internet now allows companies to disseminate this information to a much wider audience. Although some companies merely passively describe their involvement in environmental education in the local area (see National Grid[30]), a few proactive companies such as BC Hydro devote a whole section of their website to interactive education.[31] Companies also recognise that they can have an environmental impact on their local community, and that the Internet can be an important medium through which to communicate local environmental activities. Yorkshire Electricity, for example, entitles a section of its website 'Community Matters', and this includes community sponsorship policy, community projects in which it has been involved, and community press releases;[32] Scottish Power provides a PDF version of its community report;[33] and General Motors includes several mini-websites for each of its community awareness activities.[34]

6. Information about the environmental team and contact details. Stakeholders generally have an inherent interest in precisely who is providing information on the Internet, and therefore companies can find it beneficial to incorporate a web page explaining who the environmental team are, their position relative to the company, why they have created their website and what they hope to achieve from it (Walton and Alabaster 1996: 33). Sun Microsystems is one of the few companies already providing this background information.[35] Furthermore, Internet users generally do not spend much time searching for contact details, so companies may wish to encourage interaction by making it as easy as possible to contact the relevant person within the company. The index page is the most prominent page within the environmental reporting website and provides an excellent opportunity for providing contact details of the environmental department, and ideally these should also be available on, or linked from, every page within the site. Some users of the Internet do not have an e-mail account, and thus postal addresses as well as e-mail addresses should be provided (see PPG[36]).

7. Automatic order forms. Although environmental reports are available on-line, some users prefer a hard-copy report to refer to. Specific forms can be created on-line to collect the users' addresses, to ascertain which documents they require and in what quantity (see WMC[37]). As the Internet becomes an inherent part of everyday life, and as technology improves its capabilities, this function may become extinct as people become used to viewing information on-line and downloading PDF files.

---

30   *http://www.ngc.co.uk/whatwedo/education.html*

31   See *http://eww.bchydro.bc.ca/education/index.html*.

32   See Yorkshire Electricity, *http://www.yeg.co.uk/community/*.

33   See Scottish Power, *http://www.scottishpower.co.uk/aboutus/commrep/*.

34   See General Motors, *http://www.gm.com/about/community/index.html*.

35   See Sun Microsystems, *http://www.sun.com/corporateoverview/corpaffairs/ehs-about_this_site.html*.

36   *http://www.ppg.com/frames/environ.htm*

37   *http://www.wmc.com.au/order.htm*

Sun Microsystems,[38] for example, does not produce a hard-copy environmental report but supplies information only via the Internet. Furthermore, the company claims, 'we've created a reporting tool which provides faster, more up-to-date, and more intuitive access to our information than a paper report could provide'.[39]

8. Automatic feedback forms. Companies have already identified that they require feedback on their environmental reports to assess the needs and requirements of their stakeholders (e.g. WMC 1996; Novo Nordisk 1996). Specific feedback cards designed to gather, *inter alia*, information about who has read the report, what they thought of it, what additional information they require, and which areas can be improved, are frequently included in hard-copy reports—for example, BHP 1997, Eastern Group 1996–97, Roche 1996, Severn Trent 1997 (Walton *et al.* 1997: 201). However, they are rarely completed and returned to the companies (Beecham 1993: 2). By using the Internet, similar feedback cards can be created as forms and sent with the touch of a button (see Atlantic Richfield Company[40]), encouraging more users to respond and thus providing greater, more timely and unique audience feedback (Lober 1997: 18). Companies should, however, be aware that users will be discouraged from completing a feedback form if is too long (see Philips[41]) and perhaps should aim to gather more responses on a few specific questions rather than only a few responses on numerous detailed questions.

9. Environmental forums. Environmental forums are interactive discussion groups similar to face-to-face seminars or briefings. They can either be moderated by the Webmaster or unmoderated, and conducted publicly or privately (with the use of a password). Companies can designate a member of their environmental team to act as a spokesperson to participate directly in these forums, allowing users to participate actively and thus go beyond simply accessing information (Alabaster and Walton 1997: 13). Forums can be utilised in many ways: for example, to discuss a topical issue relating to the environment, for environmental education or training sessions, or to gather experts to discuss best-practice ideas, all of which 'allow you to poll the opinions of invited persons on selected topics. In other words, you can have your own public consultation process with virtually no overhead' (Communicopia 1998).

◁ *Design*

1. Internal hyperlinks. Hard-copy environmental reports are separate entities that rarely refer to other corporate documents; companies would benefit from creating a cohesive set of documents by using their environmental reports as signposts to other information (SustainAbility/UNEP 1997: 29). Also, some stakeholders and first-time users may require significant details on various areas; however, it may not be

---

38   *http://www.sun.com/corporateoverview/corpaffairs/enviro.html*
39   See Sun Microsystems, *http://www.sun.com/corporateoverview/corpaffairs/ehs-about_this_site.html*.
40   *http://www.arco.com/Corporate/ehs/form.htm*
41   *http://www.philips.com/cgi-bin/tb?s=ceeo*

necessary to reproduce this information year after year, as subsequent reports need only refer to the original publication (Azzone *et al.* 1997: 702). Both of these can be achieved on the Internet by creating a simple hyperlink to the relevant section in the previous year's report, or to an additional web page containing the relevant information, thereby bringing 'background and consistency to corporate documents' (Ritzenthaler and Ostroff: 16). Kodak's 1995 report contained hyperlinks within the text of the report, not only to further environmental information but also to product and corporate information. However, this report has now been removed and no other examples can be found that demonstrate this level of internal link, although Exxon and BHP provide examples of internal hyperlinks to further information in the environmental report.[42] Novo Nordisk's 1996 report contains a hyperlink on every page back to the index of its 1995 report which allows users to compare the quality and quantity of information provided in the two documents, although their 1997 report does not provide this feature.[43] J. Sainsbury went further in its 1997 report; for example, under 'waste management' in its 1997 report is a link to waste management information contained in its 1996 report.[44] However, of its 1998 report, only a review is available on-line and it appears that it has not continued with this leading-edge navigational feature. Furthermore, if hyperlinks are not kept up to date, then, instead of accessing the information requested, users are faced with a blank page, which can become very frustrating. It is therefore important to check the hyperlinks within a website regularly and, to aid this process, specialised website management software is available: for example, Microsoft Front Page,[45] which incorporates a hyperlink verifier that automatically checks every link, internal and external, in a website.

2. **External hyperlinks.** The Internet also allows hyperlinks to be made to other websites. Traditionally, though, companies mainly provide information about themselves and therefore environmental reports on the Internet have tended not to contain external hyperlinks. Some companies are now experimenting by creating external hyperlinks to environmental organisations with which they are associated, either from within the text of their environmental report (for example, Sulzer link to the World Business Council for Sustainable Development and the International Chamber of Commerce[46]) or on a links page (see Bristol Myers Squibb[47]).

3. **Site design.** It is generally accepted that there are three generations of website, categorised according to design and style. First-generation sites are described as text-based, linear and monochrome in style, designed for text-only terminals, black-and-white monitors and low-resolution colour displays. Second-generation sites are

---

42   See Exxon, *http://www.exxon.com/exxoncorp/news/publications/safety_report/risk/index.html* and BHP, *http://www.bhp.com.au/environment/env98/*.
43   See Novo Nordisk, *http://www.novo.dk/environm/er96/index.html*.
44   See J. Sainsbury, *http://www.j-sainsbury.co.uk/environment/97/hi-fi/index.html*.
45   *http://www.microsoft.com/frontpage*
46   See Sulzer, *http://www.sulzer.com/environment/env_involvement.html*.
47   *http://www.bms.com/EHS/Links/index.htm*

described as menu-, icon- and technology-driven, designed when Netscape announced its new set of HTML extensions. Although more colourful than first-generation sites, technology has in some cases overtaken legibility with noisy backgrounds distracting from the content of the page. Third-generation sites are shaped by design rather than by technological competence, creating a complete experience within a website from entrance to exit (Siegal 1996: 26-29).

Companies can benefit from creating third-generation environmental reporting websites that not only effectively convey their environmental message but also provide experiences that keep users interested. 'Most information based sites present endless pages of text and bulleted lists' (Siegal 1996: 39), which can be overcome by splitting information into smaller sections and placing it on separate interlinked web pages presenting users with the opportunity to take unexpected turns or see new sections. A company must be able to engage its users and convey its message almost effortlessly.

4. Graphics and backgrounds. When producing a website, it is tempting to use all the latest technologies and software available, which can include creating complex graphics and backgrounds, fancy buttons and elaborate logos, etc. However, if a site is cluttered and confusing, or takes too long to download, it distracts users from the content of the site. Some users have now taken to navigating with graphics switched off to increase the speed at which they 'surf' the Internet (*Internet Business* 1997), in which case alternative text tags or 'alt tags' can be used to notify users of what the graphics represent.

To introduce an environmental report within their websites, companies frequently transform the cover of the hard-copy report into a graphic (see American Electric Power[48]). These graphics are generally large and, as a result, the web page can take a long time to load, especially for users with slow modems. The same problem can occur with large graphics contained within the report, and some companies have avoided this by putting large graphics onto separate web pages, e.g. ARCO.[49] Another option is to reduce the size of graphics by using specialised software.[50]

5. Navigation. A website benefits from having a clear structure and links that prevent the user from getting lost within it (Walton *et al.* 1997: 201). 'Good design lets the user focus on accomplishing the task rather than figuring out how to accomplish the task' (Rauch *et al.* 1997: 115). Specialised software is now available to allow users to search for relevant web pages within a site: for example, the large search engines, such as EXCITE and Infoseek, freely provide small search engines for individual websites (see 3M[51]).

Hard-copy environmental reports allow readers to flick through the pages and dip in and out if they do not wish to read the report from cover to cover. If print designers

---

48   *http://www.aep.com/environment/report/index.html*
49   See Atlantic Richfield Company, *http://www.arco.com/Corporate/ehs/contents.htm*.
50   See GIF SmartSaver, *http://www.ulead.com*.
51   *http://www.mmm.com/search*

are given the task of transforming the environmental report for the Internet, they may include an index page with forward and backward buttons on every web page within the report (see Compaq[52]). This, however, restricts the ability of the user to flick through web pages in order to see relevant sections. Instead, the user must return to the index page to view the contents of the report. Site navigation can be improved if a menu is available on every web page, allowing users to flick through the report; one popular method of achieving this is to use frames (see Monsanto[53]). This method can in itself lead to difficulties with such basic functions as bookmarking, printing and locating URLs (Rauch *et al.* 1997: 117), and therefore companies that currently use frames may find it beneficial to experiment creating a menu without them (see Northern Ireland Electricity[54]).

6. **Regular updates.** A well-designed website enables developments on environmental progress to be seen to occur continuously, whereas a hard-copy report makes the progress appear more static than is necessary (Walton *et al.* 1997: 206). Companies can benefit from keeping their website fresh by updating 'perishable' information and adding new items, thus helping to keep users interested and ensure that they return regularly to view new developments. New information can be added to the website by creating new files or revising existing files when necessary: for example, whenever environmental press releases are issued or new environmental initiatives are started (Azzone *et al.* 1997: 702; Walton *et al.* 1997). Therefore, when the deadline for the annual hard-copy environmental report arrives, some information should already have been available and feedback on it may have been obtained. Users like to know the age of the information they are reading and therefore companies should consider including throughout the website the date that the site was last updated, assuring users that the information is relevant and topical.

7. **Site promotion.** Investment in a high-quality website is pointless unless the site is visible and well advertised. Companies need to promote their website by including their environmental web address on hard-copy documents (see IBM 1996; Solvay Group 1996), business cards and on any e-mails they send out. Companies can also promote their website on-line by asking relevant sites to signpost them, buying an advertising banner on another site and, perhaps most importantly, registering their sites with the major search engines.

Companies that consider the website criteria detailed above and implement relevant aspects when creating or updating their websites may find that they have a significant increase in the number of users and that these users are also able to gather more information from the environmental reporting website. Moreover, this could lead to further dialogue with stakeholders, thus providing more constructive feedback about their environmental activities and operations. Organisations and universities

52   *http://www.compaq.com/corporate/ehss/97-98rpt*
53   *http://www.monsanto.com/Monsanto/Sustainability/default.htm*
54   *http://www.nie.co.uk/Environment/index.htm*

can also play an important role in empowering stakeholders to compare companies on an individual basis and enabling benchmarking: for example, by commenting on companies' environmental reports[55] or by signposting environmental reporting websites.[56]

◢ *Conclusions*

There is little doubt that the Internet is a valuable medium through which companies can communicate their environmental reports, but it is likely that, for the foreseeable future, traditional methods of communication will remain prominent (Sustain-Ability/UNEP 1996a: 47). Nevertheless, if the number of companies producing environmental reporting websites is to increase, environmental information must meet the objectives of the website itself. Companies create websites to promote their business, and, as the environment is increasingly becoming an integral business function, there is no real reason for not including and using the unique advantages of the WWW to present environmental information.

Environmental reporting and the Internet are, however, both relatively new concepts and the responsibility for them often falls into different corporate departments, so even innovative companies may experience difficulties combining these areas. The guidelines presented in this chapter may assist companies in clarifying their position, but, although the Internet can offer many advantages over hard copy if the technology is properly exploited, the actual quality of the environmental report remains paramount. Having said that, there is little point in creating an environmental reporting website if users are not aware of its existence, or if it is hidden within the site, or if information is not presented in an attractive and interesting manner.

Analysis of environmental reporting websites is clearly at an embryonic stage, although a recent study examined 275 environmental reporting websites and informally surveyed 100 environmental managers (Jones *et al.* 1999); and further assessment of how effectively companies are using the Internet is an important task, especially as there continue to be wide perceived variations in the quality and accessibility of environmental information (Elkington 1997: 180). However, the future rating, ranking and benchmarking of corporate environmental websites will have to be considered carefully, as scoring systems used to rate, rank and benchmark hard-copy environmental reports are frequently flawed and contain skewed or misleading results (Jones and Alabaster 1999).

Finally, many discussions continue on what the Internet will look like beyond 2000, who will have access to it, what kind of information is demanded, and how it is presented (Randall 1997: 157-68; Perugini 1996: 4-15). Therefore, the guidelines presented here, like the websites to which they refer, need to be flexible enough to reflect the continuing dynamic evolution of the Internet itself.

---

55   See *http://www.dundee.ac.uk/accountancy/csear/corporat.htm*.
56   See *http://cei.sund.ac.uk/envrep/*.

22
Sustainable Industrial Development

Benchmarking Environmental Policies and Reports*

Riva Krut and Ken Munis

THERE HAS BEEN much discussion about the part industry could play if it used its considerable economic and technological resources to pursue creative solutions towards sustainable development (i.e. an integrated strategy of economic, social and environmental development). Increasingly, we hear reports of firms that are rising to this challenge and embarking on activities associated with sustainable development. For example, voluntary 'beyond-compliance' corporate environmental management is a dynamic new field that could offer a foundation for a new public–private performance-based partnership. Such a partnership could give businesses incentives to improve their environmental performance and increase their flexibility for doing this.

In practice, however, this opens a series of questions: How do we define and measure good environmental performance? How are targets set to encourage continuous improvement towards sustainable industrial development? For the partnership to work, regulators must support this voluntary momentum by finding ways of tracking and evaluating it against the objectives of environmental performance, compliance and sustainable development.

---

*   This chapter expresses the views of the authors and not necessarily those of the US Environmental Protection Agency.
    It is based on work completed under contract for the US Environmental Protection Agency by Benchmark Environmental Consulting. Complete reports may be requested from Ken Munis, US Environmental Protection Agency, 401 M Street, SW (MC 2128), Washington, DC 20460, USA.

A new partnership will require both a vision of industrial 'sustainability' and a pragmatic dose of reality. We need some idea of what sustainable industrial development 'looks like', so that targets can be set and industry environmental management can focus on sustainable development objectives. At the same time, we need a sense of what is practical (e.g. what leading firms are already doing) so that our expectations can be realistic.

Developing both this vision and reality is not easy. Much of voluntary environmental management is just that—voluntary. In contrast to financial reporting, there is no pro forma, or even generally accepted formula, for measuring or reporting 'sustainable' performance. This makes evaluations, particularly comparative evaluations, quite difficult. This chapter responds to this challenge by:

- Creating a set of benchmark criteria for a 'sustainable firm'

- Looking at the public environmental policies and reports of a handful of leaders in the electronics and photographic sectors

- Evaluating the public commitments of these firms against the benchmark criteria.

We believe that this framework is an important contribution for firms and governments struggling to apply the concept of sustainable development to industry performance.

◢ Why Look at Sustainable Industrial Development?

There were three goals of this research. The first was to understand what a sustainable company might look like. There is broad agreement that the concept of sustainable development requires an integrated approach to economic, environmental and social development needs. There has been too little work on what a sustainable firm might look like in principle. To contribute to this debate, we synthesised a range of recommendations for sustainable industrial development called for by various stakeholder groups. The second goal was to sketch a sense of what is currently practicable for firms. To do this, we looked at what industry leaders in two industry sectors are saying and doing. The third goal was to facilitate voluntary industry initiatives towards environmental performance improvement and sustainable industrial development.

The intention here was twofold. For firms, evaluating what leading companies say on critical sustainability themes provides working models of sustainability. Firms without public policies and reports, or those that wish to benchmark and improve their public materials, can see what leading practice is and make choices for their own company policies and reporting. Second, for regulators and the public, this research is offered as part of the emerging literature on tools for evaluating corporate voluntary environmental management.

◢ Defining Sustainable Industrial Development

A common external reference point or benchmark sets a qualitative standard that allows us to see how far a particular firm or a group of firms is moving towards sustainable development. Creating such a benchmark could be highly normative. However, this report took a different approach. It sought a consensus definition by synthesising the guidelines and recommendations of a number of major policy sources on sustainable industrial development. As this research was primarily focused on the US, the most important reference source was the US President's Council on Sustainable Development (1996). Others included the Chemical Manufacturers' Association's 'Responsible Care' programme, the Public Environmental Reporting Initiative, the International Chamber of Commerce Business Charter on Sustainable Development, the CERES (Coalition for Environmentally Responsible Economies) Principles, and Agenda 21. Although the original research was US-based, our sense is that the template has application beyond the United States.

From these sources, we derived four themes:

- ◢ Environmentally sound products, processes and services
- ◢ Integration of sustainable development and economic growth
- ◢ Reducing risks and hazards to human health and the ecosystem
- ◢ Community/stakeholder participation in sustainable development.

Environmentally sound products, processes and services covers mostly conventional environmental management and requires that sustainable firms take responsibility for the environmental impact of their products and processes through their life-cycle. **Integration of sustainable development and economic growth** is fundamental to discussions of sustainable development. Particular activities in this group include technological innovation and social issues such as job creation. **Reducing risks and hazards to human health and to the ecosystem** stresses environmental impact evaluation and reporting, including adopting a global rather than a national perspective. Finally, **community and stakeholder participation** addresses the issue of public credibility and accountability. These four themes were broken down into nineteen benchmark criteria. This was used as a template against which a firm's publicly available corporate environmental management materials can be evaluated. The complete set of criteria is provided in Box 1.

◢ Evaluating Corporate Efforts: What is Practicable?

To see if firms are 'operationalising' the concepts of sustainable development, a small group of leading firms in two sectors was selected. These firms have voluntary environmental policies and, in most cases, publish environmental reports. The firms selected are among the leaders in this field, as demonstrated by their public policy commitments to environmental management and their publication of public materials and reports on their environmental records.

Environmentally sound products, processes and services

1. Accept responsibility for environmental effects throughout all phases of a product's life.
2. Commit to the ideal of a zero-waste society through more efficient use and recycling of natural resources in the economy.
3. Commit to materials, energy and water conservation throughout the organisation.
4. Specify product stewardship targets and goals and explain procedures to monitor and measure company performance toward these targets and goals.

Integration of sustainable development and economic growth

5. Encourage economic development that creates jobs and renews our cities while reducing risks to human health and harm to the environment.
6. Pursue technological innovation that will result in superior environmental protection at far lower costs.
7. Have in place supplier programmes designed to reduce environmental impacts or add environmental value to the design or redesign of products and services provided to the company by the supplier.
8. Introduce policies and commitments to adopt equivalent or not less stringent standards of operation abroad where existing environmental management systems are weak or ineffective.
9. Participate in moving toward a greater reliance on pricing systems that internalise environmental costs.

Reducing risks and hazards to human health and to the ecosystem

10. Provide environmental release information—emissions, effluents, or wastes—based on the global activity of the organisation, with details provided for smaller geographic regions.
11. Provide baseline quantified emission data against which the organisation measures itself each year to determine its progress in reducing its environmental impact.
12. Undertake research into the phase-out of the firm's processes and chemicals that pose the greatest environmental risk.
13. Modify procedures, including among affiliates and suppliers, in order to reflect local ecological conditions.
14. Phase out, where appropriate, and dispose of any banned chemicals that are still in stock or in use, in an environmentally sound manner.
15. Voluntarily provide environmental information for the public in excess of governmental regulations, particularly information that would help in the assessment of potential risks to human and environmental health.

Community/stakeholder participation in sustainable development

16. Strategies and activities should integrate economic development, environmental quality and social policy-making.
17. Identify any beyond-compliance recommendations or voluntary standards developed by other organisations (EPA, PCSD, ICC, CMA, etc.) that have changed the operations of the business.
18. Collaborate on research and development of environmentally sound technologies and environmental management systems with non-industrial stakeholders such as academics, community groups, minorities, local authorities, Federal government and/or international organisations.
19. Show a commitment to sustainable development and ecosystem approaches, including the relationship between human and natural systems, human health issues, and emerging global problems such as global climate change and the loss of biodiversity.

Box 1: ENVIRONMENTALLY SOUND PRODUCTS, PROCESSES AND SERVICES

By exploring the contours of environmental management as defined by leading firms, we can set new standards of expectations for the sector. At the same time, the benchmark template allows readers to see what issues still need to be addressed. The results give us both individual firm reporting against a range of 'sustainable development' goals and a practical sense of what is being addressed among major firms in this sector. Our view is that, although the environmental impact of firms within an industry sector will vary, there are enough common elements to allow a more useful assessment of policies and practices than is possible across sectors. For example, although there is wide variation in the financial and technological dimensions of firms within the electronics sector, there is less than there would be in comparing electronics with chemical companies.

△ Evaluation Methodology

Each company's publicly available materials were then evaluated against each of the benchmark criteria, using typographic symbols to show the degree of commitment. A numeric evaluation was rejected because this would encourage readers to create averages and rankings, which would be inappropriate. Firstly, the nineteen categories may not have equivalent value. A commitment to global emissions reporting (criterion 10) is not equivalent to a commitment to collaborative research (criterion 18). Secondly, it would be unfair to rank companies with different activities associated with different environmental impacts. It is important to note that we did not evaluate what a firm is actually doing, but what it is committed to do in policy, and what it says it is doing in its public information. We recognise that public materials may not provide a complete picture of environmental performance. For example, some argue that public material probably inflates the real performance of firms. On the other hand, most of the firms evaluated point out that they are doing far more than they report in their public material and that evaluating their practice would show more achievement against the benchmark criteria. For all its limitations, this research confines itself to the publicly available material. These provide a consistent data set and we assume that, if firms say in public that they are committed to a particular policy or that they are working at a specific issue, they can be held to their commitments or claims.

Figure 1 presents an illustration of the evaluation approach for the benchmark criterion 'commit to the "ideal" of a zero-waste society through more efficient use and recycling of natural resources in the community'.[1] The information contained in this figure comes from the evaluation of electronic firms and illustrates the qualitative 'scoring' approach. Each of the symbols in the table was supported by the text indicated. The text was extracted or generalised from the corporate environmental policies and/or the environmental reports of the firms evaluated. All the firms were then given an opportunity to review and comment on the qualitative scores. As indicated here, substantial commitments are being made to this benchmark criterion by the firms evaluated.

---

1   Each of the graphical scores in the evaluation reports is supported by documentation such as that illustrated in Figure 2.

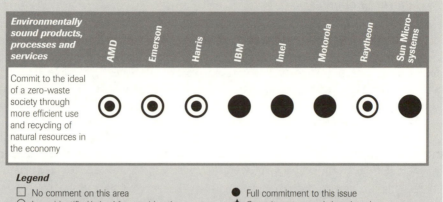

Environmentally sound products, processes and services	AMD	Emerson	Harris	IBM	Intel	Motorola	Raytheon	Sun Micro-systems
Commit to the ideal of a zero-waste society through more efficient use and recycling of natural resources in the economy	◉	◉	◉	●	●	●	◉	●

Legend

- ☐ No comment on this area
- ○ Issue identified/raised for consideration
- ◉ Partial commitment
- ● Full commitment to this issue
- ★ Commitment exceeds benchmark

AMD, partial commitment: 'Review manufacturing processes that generate hazardous waste and identify opportunities for waste reduction, combining environmental improvements with effective manufacturing methods'. The evaluation is 'partial' because of the commitment to reduction of waste, not the ideal of zero waste.

Emerson Electric, partial commitment: 'The policy of the Company is to . . . reduce and, where possible, eliminate hazardous waste through source reduction and recycling.' 'Partial commitment' because it commits only to hazardous waste reduction and recycling.

Harris, partial commitment: Strong efforts across environmental media emphasise reductions, not zero-waste.

IBM, full commitment: 'The best solution is not to have it in the first place . . . The war on waste—hazardous and non-hazardous—goes on . . . IBM [has a] hierarchical strategy of reducing, reusing, recycling or, only as a last resort, safe treatment and disposal . . . Make the product green, keep the process clean and reuse at end of life.'

Intel, full commitment: 'We are committed to conserving natural resources and reducing the environmental burden of waste generation and emissions to the air, water and land . . . Our Design for Environment model applies the hierarchy from the US Pollution Prevention Act of 1990, which priorities the reduction of pollutants at the source over "end-of-the-pipe" solutions.'

Motorola, full commitment: Motorola is committed to a closed-loop manufacturing system.

Raytheon, partial commitment: Strong efforts across environmental media emphasise reductions and recycling, including recycling of all electronic scrap, but there is no mention of an ideal of zero waste. The evaluation is 'partial' because the emphasis on recycling is an end-of-pipe activity rather than front-of-pipe.

Sun Microsystems, full commitment: Sun shows strong policies and practices in the areas of recycling and product take-back and re-use.

Figure 1: BENCHMARKING THE ELECTRONICS INDUSTRY COMMITMENTS TO THE IDEAL OF ZERO WASTE

Source: Compiled from Krut 1997

◻ *General Findings*

Eight companies from the electronics sector and eight firms from the photographic sector were selected for the benchmarking exercise. The firms were primarily US-based companies, usually with global operations, although a few relatively smaller companies were selected as well. Evaluations were qualitative and range from 'no comment on this area' to 'commitment exceeds benchmark criteria'. The full summary evaluation of the electronics firms is provided here in Figure 2. Text supporting the complete evaluation is found in Appendix A of the full report.

In both sectors, considerable commitments are being made to benchmark activities related to developing 'environmentally sound products, processes and services'. In particular, electronic-sector firms were very active in the area of extended product responsibility. This is consistent with some of the leadership initiatives in the electronics sector such as design for the environment and product stewardship. Among the photographic firms, commitments to the 'ideal of zero waste' through more efficient use and recycling of natural resources in the economy were particularly strong.

Substantial commitments are also being made to activities related to the category 'reduce risks and hazards to human health and to the ecosystem'. In the electronics sector, international environmental agreements appear to be influencing leading firms to report globally—particularly commitments and reports of efforts to phase out CFCs. There was more variation among photographic firms in the overall commitments to this category of benchmark criterion, although the majority of these firms were, at a minimum, discussing efforts aimed at reducing the chemicals and processes that present the greatest risk.

In both sectors, far more variation is seen in commitments made related to the other two benchmark themes—'integration of sustainable development and economic growth' and 'community/stakeholder participation in sustainable development'. Not surprisingly, firms in both sectors talked about their commitments to technological innovation. However, much less discussion and commitment is seen related to internalising environmental costs and promoting social goals such as job creation and urban renewal. Efforts to work more closely with suppliers were particularly strong among electronic firms. Interestingly, six of the eight photographic firms evaluated address goals such as job creation and urban renewal.

Overall, the activities related to community and stakeholder participation received the least attention. However, many firms are addressing these issues in their published materials. Some firms have efforts under way that target particular stakeholders such as employees and key customers. Firms are more likely to identify trade associations, principal customers and suppliers as their 'first-tier' set of stakeholders, rather than the broader public. Other firms are participating in research or contributing to global environmental programmes such as those of the World Wide Fund for Nature, or participating in voluntary environmental programmes sponsored by the US Environmental Protection Agency or other groups.

Environmentally sound products, processes and services	AMD	Emerson	Harris	IBM	Intel	Motorola	Raytheon	Sun Micro-systems
1. Accept responsibility for environmental effects throughout all phases of a product's life.	●	□	●	★	●	●	◉	●
2. Commit to the ideal of a zero-waste society through more efficient use and recycling of natural resources in the economy.	◉	◉	◉	●	●	●	◉	●
3. Commit to materials, energy and water conservation throughout the organisation.	●	●	●	★	●	●	◉	●
4. Specify product stewardship targets and goals and explain procedures to monitor and measure company performance toward these targets and goals.	●	●	●	★	★	◉	●	●

Integration of sustainable development and economic growth	AMD	Emerson	Harris	IBM	Intel	Motorola	Raytheon	Sun Micro-systems
5. Encourage economic development that creates jobs and renews our cities while reducing risks to human health and harm to the environment.	●	□	□	□	●	□	◉	●
6. Pursue technological innovation that will result in superior environmental protection at far lower costs.	●	●	●	●	●	●	●	●
7. Have in place supplier programmes designed to reduce environmental impacts or add environmental value to the design or redesign of products and services provided to the company by the supplier.	●	□	●	★	◉	●	★	★
8. Introduce policies and commitments to adopt equivalent or not less stringent standards of operation abroad where existing environmental management systems are weak or ineffective.	●	□	●	★	●	●	◉	◉
9. Participate in moving toward a greater reliance on pricing systems that internalise environmental costs.	□	□	○	●	□	□	□	□

Figure 2: BENCHMARKING SUSTAINABLE INDUSTRIAL DEVELOPMENT: SUMMARY OF THE FINDINGS
(*continued over*)

Reducing risks and hazards to human health and to the ecosystem	AMD	Emerson	Harris	IBM	Intel	Motorola	Raytheon	Sun Micro-systems
10. Provide environmental release information—emissions, effluents or wastes—based on the global activity of the organisation, with details provided for smaller geographic regions.	◉	☐	●	★	★	●	☐	◉
11. Provide baseline quantified emission data against which the organisation measures itself each year to determine its progress in reducing its environmental impact.	◉	☐	◉	●	★	☐	●	★
12. Undertake research into the phase-out of the firm's processes and chemicals that pose the greatest environmental risk.	●	☐	●	●	●	●	◉	●
13. Expand the use of ecosystem approaches by using collaborative partnerships . . . Encourage affiliates and suppliers to modify procedures in order to reflect local ecological conditions.	●	☐	◉	●	●	●	◉	●
14. Phase out, where appropriate, and dispose of any banned chemicals that are still in stock or in use, in an environmentally sound manner.	●	●	●	●	◉	●	○	●
15. Voluntarily provide environmental information for the public in excess of governmental regulations, particularly information that would help in the assessment of potential risks to human and environmental health.	◉	☐	○	●	●	☐	◉	●

Community/stakeholder participation in sustainable development	AMD	Emerson	Harris	IBM	Intel	Motorola	Raytheon	Sun Micro-systems
16. Strategies and activities should integrate economic development, environmental quality and social policy-making.	●	☐	☐	●	●	●	☐	◉
17. Identify any beyond-compliance recommendations or voluntary standards developed by other organisations (EPA, PCSD, ICC, CMA, etc.) that have changed the operations of the business.	●	◉	●	●	●	☐	◉	●

Figure 2: BENCHMARKING SUSTAINABLE INDUSTRIAL DEVELOPMENT: SUMMARY OF THE FINDINGS
(*from previous page; continued opposite*)

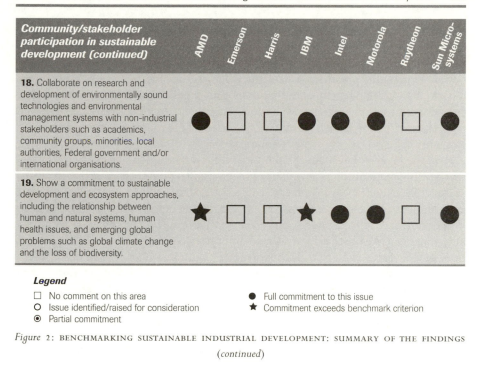

Community/stakeholder participation in sustainable development (continued)	AMD	Emerson	Harris	IBM	Intel	Motorola	Raytheon	Sun Microsystems
18. Collaborate on research and development of environmentally sound technologies and environmental management systems with non-industrial stakeholders such as academics, community groups, minorities, local authorities, Federal government and/or international organisations.	●	☐	☐	●	●	●	☐	●
19. Show a commitment to sustainable development and ecosystem approaches, including the relationship between human and natural systems, human health issues, and emerging global problems such as global climate change and the loss of biodiversity.	★	☐	☐	★	●	●	☐	●

Legend

☐ No comment on this area
○ Issue identified/raised for consideration
◉ Partial commitment

● Full commitment to this issue
★ Commitment exceeds benchmark criterion

Figure 2: BENCHMARKING SUSTAINABLE INDUSTRIAL DEVELOPMENT: SUMMARY OF THE FINDINGS
(continued)

◁ *Opportunities for Improvement*

The greatest opportunity for improvement exists in the integration of the more social aspects of sustainable development. While there was some activity in this area in both sectors, this was the area where commitments of policy and reporting were the least robust. One partial explanation for this may be that, although firms are trying to be good neighbours, they are not including this information in their corporate environmental policies and reports. To the extent this is true, the fairly recent effort by some companies to develop 'sustainability reports' rather than environmental reports (e.g. Shell and Monsanto) may overcome this shortcoming. There is reason for hope, however. For example, the photographic company CPI 'believes it has a responsibility to contribute to society's quality of life however it can' (CPI *Environmental Policy*). The 'CPI Corporate Philanthropic Programs Policy, Structure and Guidelines' was attached to their *Policy and Annual Report* in response to a request for the Annual Report and environmental policy and materials. The opening statement reads as follows:

> The CPI Corporate Philanthropic Programs represent the charitable arm of the CPI Corporation. The Company recognises that as a free-enterprise corporation operating in and at the sufferance of a free society, it has important responsibilities to help build and strengthen that free society.

CPI donates 2% of the previous year's pre-tax income to charitable programmes.

◢ Implications and Usefulness of this Report

A benchmark tool of corporate policies and reports has value for corporate practitioners or potential practitioners. Benchmarking these reports is useful for environmental managers and companies that do not have policies or reports, or those that do and want to improve them. Many companies benchmark their own policies and reports against competitors and industry leaders. This chapter presents a methodology for doing so quickly and systematically.

A methodology for evaluating voluntary public environmental reporting is crucial to the development of a new paradigm of public–private partnership towards sustainable industrial development. Most companies still do not produce public environmental policies or reports. But environmental report-writing should be seen in the context of growing public expectations that firms become more environmentally conscious. Within this debate, the clamour from corporate environmental leaders to be given greater discretion and opportunity to innovate can only be heard if self-regulation demonstrates that it brings continuous improvement of human and ecosystem health. The emergence of environmental reporting was in direct response to this need (i.e. voluntarily to demonstrate corporate environmental accountability). Over the years, this original reason may have become blurred, and environmental reporting has taken on its own momentum. Environmental reports are vastly different from each other in terms of their commitments, their scope and their degree of detail, numerical or descriptive.

But for regulators and firms seeking tools to develop the much-vaunted new paradigm of public–private partnership, environmental reports are potentially part of a solution. In their current form, however, their very creativity and diversity cause complications. It is not the existence of a policy or report, or the number of charts and graphs, that will provide a basis for this partnership. It is content. In other words, there need to be continuously improved standards or frameworks set for voluntary corporate environmental management that encourage companies to move towards sustainable industrial development.

Standards for corporate environmental reporting could have enormous value for firms and for the public. For firms, they could differentiate reporting categories and processes with public value from those without. For the public, they could provide the basis for co-regulation of corporate environmental management. Such standards cannot be developed without putting voluntary environmental management under the microscope, taking into consideration both the public objectives of sustainable industrial development, and the reality of what firms can be expected to achieve in their 'beyond-compliance' activities.

◢ Conclusion

The field of voluntary environmental policy and report-making is growing exponentially. As these policies and reports are voluntary, they are diverse and offer a rich source of material for the understanding of 'beyond-compliance' environmental management. It is not an easy area to research. Policies and reports are not standardised. An external template such as the one described here can force comparisons between apparently similar practices that actually come out of quite different contexts. Published materials capture only a part of a dynamic set of environmental management practices, and cannot tell us what the firm is actually doing in all areas.

Nevertheless, tools are needed to evaluate beyond-compliance environmental management, and benchmarking against indicators for sustainable industrial development will be extremely useful. Firms can use this methodology to look at leading standards for policy and reporting already in place. This work will have practical value for environmental managers seeking to produce or improve their environmental policies and practices. For the public, benchmarking provides a systematic method for exploring where industry is committed to the principles of sustainable industrial development, where it is ahead of the debate, and where it is lagging. This benchmark information will be a vital starting point for firms, regulators and the public as they seek to explore new ways of working towards a co-regulation partnership.

◢ *Sources for the Benchmark Criteria*

Caux Roundtable (1986) *Principles for Business, 1986* (Drawn from the Minnesota Principles, a statement of business behaviour developed by the Minnesota Center for Corporate Responsibility).

Chemical Manufacturers' Association, *Responsible Care Codes of Conduct*.

Coalition of Environmentally Responsible Economies and Societies (CERES) (1989) *CERES Principles, 1989.*

President's Council on Sustainable Development (PCSD) (1996) *Sustainable America: A New Consensus for Prosperity, Opportunity, and a Healthy Environment for the Future* (President's Council on Sustainable Development).

Public Environmental Reporting Initiative (PERI) (1993) *Guidelines, 1993.*

United Nations Conference on Environment and Development (UNCED) (1992) *Agenda 21* (United Nations).

United Nations (1993) *Report of the Secretary-General to the Commissions on Transnational Corporations* (E/C 10/1993/14; Follow-up to the UNCED as it related to Transnational Corporations; United Nations, April 1993).

3 SOCIAL AND SUSTAINABILITY PERFORMANCE EVALUATION AND REPORTING

23

Sustainability Reporting Guidelines

Exposure Draft for
Public Comment and Pilot-Testing

The Global Reporting Initiative

◢ Introduction

◨ About the GRI

The Global Reporting Initiative (GRI) was established in late 1997 with the mission of designing globally applicable guidelines for preparing enterprise-level sustainability reports. These Guidelines, presented as an Exposure Draft for comment and pilot testing, are the GRI's first major product.[1]

The GRI is convened by CERES (Coalition for Environmentally Responsible Economies)[2] and incorporates the active participation of corporations, non-governmental organisations (NGOs), consultants, accountancy organisations, business associations, universities and other stakeholders from around the world. The GRI seeks to establish a common framework for enterprise-level reporting on the linked aspects of sustainability: the environmental, the economic and the social. It seeks

---

1   This Exposure Draft was published in March 1999, and there will be a consultative period until approximately 31 December 1999, during which GRI will welcome any comments (see also pages 453-54).
    See also Chapters 1, 4 and 24 for discussion of the GRI guidelines.
2   The Coalition for Environmentally Responsible Economies (CERES) is a non-profit, non-governmental organisation based in Boston, USA, comprising environmental organisations, socially responsible investment professionals, institutional investors, labour and religious organisations. It is the author of the CERES Principles, formerly the Valdez Principles, a ten-point code of conduct on environmentally responsible corporate behaviour.

Environmental aspects. Environmental aspects include impacts through processes, products or services. These may include air, water, land, natural resources, flora, fauna and human health.

Social aspects include, for example, treatment of minorities and women, involvement in shaping local, national and international public policy, and child labour, and labour union issues.

Economic aspects include, but extend beyond, financial performance. They include activities related to shaping demand for products and services, employee compensation, community contributions, and local procurement policies.

Box 1: SUSTAINABILITY AT THE ENTERPRISE LEVEL

to elevate enterprise-level sustainable development reporting to the level of general acceptance and practice now accorded financial reporting. To ensure the long-term value of these reporting practices, the GRI also seeks to develop and advocate greater stakeholder awareness and use of such reports.

This Exposure Draft embodies the contributions of a diverse range of individuals. Efforts were made to include in the GRI as many different perspectives as possible by convening meetings in various locations, maintaining openness and transparency at meetings, inviting all interested to take part in Working Group activities, and posting of documents on the Internet.

These Guidelines have been developed for public comment and testing through to the end of 1999. This test period will serve as a laboratory for assembling examples and experiences in this early stage of developing sustainability reporting guidelines. GRI seeks to advance the relevance of these Guidelines to critical stakeholders, including corporations, the developing world and prominent standards-setting organisations. This comment and testing period is essential for increasing the global applicability of these Guidelines and building consensus among interested parties, who inevitably represent a range of views, countries and cultures.

GRI seeks to encourage reporting enterprises and other stakeholders alike to review and pilot-test the Guidelines and to bring feedback and experiences to the attention of GRI. As a result of this information, the Guidelines will be revised and re-released in early 2000. Thereafter, GRI intends that ongoing stewardship of the process will be the role of a new permanent, independent, international body, governed by a range of stakeholders including, but not limited to, those currently involved in GRI.

◁ Sustainability Reporting

The GRI Guidelines are designed to encourage both accountability and learning. The intent of the Guidelines is to provide a sustainability reporting framework that stresses the linkages between the environmental, social and economic aspects of enterprise performance. Environmental measurement and reporting is becoming a relatively well-established practice among leading enterprises. But integrating the environmental with the social and economic is at a very early stage. Applying these linkages to decision-making within the enterprise is also just beginning.

The GRI Sustainability Reporting Guidelines comprise three sections:

The **Preamble** describes the rationale and underpinnings of the Guidelines, their value and applicability, general reporting principles, and other information on their continuing evolution.

The **Guidelines** recommend specific data related to sustainability performance, along with explanatory notes to assist in interpreting and compiling the recommended information. The Guidelines are divided into nine parts:

- CEO Statement
- Key Indicators
- Profile of Reporting Entity
- Policies, Organisation and Management Systems
- Stakeholder Relationships
- Management Performance
- Operational Performance
- Product Performance
- Sustainability Overview

Several **Appendices** provide additional explanation and illustrations pertaining to various parts of the Guidelines.

BOX 2: GENERAL OVERVIEW OF THE GUIDELINES

Some enterprises already view sustainability as the linkages and interface in environmental, social and economic performance. Thus, enterprises wishing to improve their sustainability performance would strive to improve all three areas, understanding that environmental, social and economic goals are not always in harmony. The notion that these three aspects of sustainability work together suggests that actions in any one area must be carefully reviewed for their effects on the other two.

While there have been recent efforts by various enterprises to measure and report on environmental, social and economic performance, they have tended to involve compilation of information without integration. That is, they lack an explicit methodology for understanding the linkages between the environmental, social and economic. Yet managers increasingly are asked to make decisions that account for these linkages. They need information that enables effects to be forecast, competing goals to be balanced, and stakeholders' interests to be heard. What is needed is a comprehensive and systematic methodology for integrating the major aspects of sustainability. While these Guidelines offer a step in that direction, much work remains to improve the methods for integration.

The Exposure Draft of the Guidelines addresses with greatest specificity the environmental aspects of sustainability. Indicators of social and economic performance are, by nature, generally more specific to location and culture than their environmental counterparts. While future strengthening of the social and economic indicators in the Guidelines is planned, the site- and culture-specific nature of such indicators places limits on their standardisation. Further development of social and economic indicators will be informed by the feedback received by GRI during the pilot phase.

◻ *Future Agenda*

In the immediate future, GRI will work to address a number of critical areas such as verification, North–South implications, implications for small and medium-sized enterprises, and potential sector-specific reporting activities. Over the longer term, GRI seeks to advance the usefulness of sustainability reporting by enterprises around the world. At the same time, the value to stakeholders of reports prepared according to GRI Guidelines as tools for benchmarking, investment, purchasing and advocacy is substantial and growing. The many participants in the GRI will jointly determine the course of the programme in the future. In addition to monitoring the pilot test and revising the Guidelines, this may include dissemination of information about corporate sustainability performance, reporting awards, or further exploration of the role of sustainability measurement and reporting in various governmental and quasi-governmental initiatives. GRI welcomes all interested parties to participate actively in the continuing process.

PREAMBLE

1. *Why these Guidelines have been Developed*

In increasing numbers, enterprises around the world are choosing to publish reports pertaining to their environmental, social and economic policies, practices and performance. These reports serve multiple purposes. They provide enterprises with a management tool to enhance the quality of their operations through continuous improvement while strengthening public accountability. At the same time, the reports address the needs and expectations of external stakeholders—e.g. investors, customers, NGOs, communities, academics—for environmental, social and economic information.

The Global Reporting Initiative (GRI) Sustainability Reporting Guidelines seek to assist those enterprises and other organisations that choose to publish reports about their performance and progress toward the environmental, social and economic aspects of sustainable development. GRI seeks to do this:

- In a way that provides stakeholders with reliable information relevant to their needs and interests, and that invites further stakeholder dialogue and enquiry

- In accordance with well-established, widely accepted external reporting principles, applied consistently from one reporting period to the next, to promote transparency and credibility

- In a uniform format that facilitates reader understanding and comparison with similar reports by other enterprises

- In a way that illuminates the relationship between an enterprise's financial performance and its performance on the three aspects of sustainability: environmental, social and economic

These Guidelines, presented at this time as an Exposure Draft for public comment and pilot testing by volunteer enterprises, are a primary vehicle for fulfilling the first two of the three elements of the GRI mission:

- To elevate sustainability reporting practices worldwide to a level equivalent to, and as routine as, financial reporting in terms of comparability, auditability and generally accepted practices

- To design, disseminate and promote standardised reporting, core measurements applicable to all enterprises, and customised, sector-specific measurements, all reflecting the environmental, economic and social dimensions of sustainability

The third element of the GRI mission follows from the first two:

- To ensure a permanent and effective institutional host to support such reporting practices

The GRI Guidelines and process are dynamic while moving steadily toward full sustainability reporting. The first version of the Guidelines presented in this chapter reflects the longer history and greater consensus on environmental reporting practices compared to that achieved to date regarding social and economic reporting. Over time, GRI will strengthen the latter two elements while working to fully mesh all three elements into a framework that stresses the interdependencies of the environmental, social and economic aspects of sustainability.

From the outset, GRI has been conceived as a voluntary, multi-stakeholder process involving business, NGOs, accounting societies, consultancy groups and others. Participants share the view that the dozens of reporting initiatives worldwide, while valuable in their own right, will all benefit from a harmonised approach to help shape the future of sustainability reporting. The structure and content—and ultimately the legitimacy and credibility—of these Guidelines is a result of merging the viewpoints of these diverse stakeholders into a common framework for sustainability reporting (see Appendix C for a list of the GRI Steering Committee members and other participants).

2. *What these Guidelines Provide*

These Guidelines aim to provide guidance to enterprises preparing sustainability reports. For purposes of the Guidelines, 'guidance' signifies a structured yet flexible framework for reporting that follows a uniform format, with due consideration to the practical considerations of collecting and presenting information in a way that effectively tells the sustainability 'story' of the reporting entity. The Guidelines are built on a number of principles that seek to ensure the integrity of the reported information. These principles are discussed in Sections 6 and 7 of this Preamble and in Chapter 14.[3]

These Guidelines do not provide guidance for implementing data collection, information and reporting systems and organisational procedures for preparing sustainability reports. These are matters left to the discretion of enterprises, and appropriate guidance is available through the efforts of parallel initiatives that focus on protocols and procedures for data development and auditability (e.g. ISO and EMAS).

These Guidelines also do not present standards for rating sustainability management and performance, although enterprises publishing such reports are often evaluated by benchmarking organisations of various kinds.

3. *Who is Encouraged to Use these Guidelines*

General statement of applicability. These Guidelines are intended to be applicable to any size and any type of enterprise that chooses to prepare a sustainability report. The Guidelines are not specific to any industry or business sector. That is, they are designed to incorporate information common to most enterprises regardless of business sector. Indeed, while the focus is on corporate sustainability reports in the business sector, the Guidelines might also be applied to other entities such as government agencies and non-profit organisations.

The Guidelines are designed with enterprise-level information in mind. As in financial reporting, full coverage of all enterprise activities is the goal for a comprehensive sustainability report. Initially, an enterprise may not be in a position to cover all such operations, and may choose to move in that direction gradually by covering a portion of its activities: e.g. a business unit, a facility, a region. If this approach is chosen, care should be taken to develop information in a form that is readily aggregated across sub-entities such that an enterprise-wide report becomes possible in the future. Of course, in addition to the enterprise-wide sustainability report, complementary facility, regional or other disaggregated sub-reports may well be appropriate for different stakeholders.

The GRI Guidelines are intended for voluntary use to advance the quality and consistency of sustainability reporting. Where enterprises already are subject to reporting requirements regarding one or more aspects of sustainability, such as under national laws and regulations, these Guidelines in no way aim to override or contradict such other reporting requirements. In the future, business groups, NGOs, accounting societies, governments and other entities may choose to refer to the Guidelines in their own programmes. Such convergence is supportive of the goal of fostering worldwide uniform sustainability reporting practices.

---

3   Appendix A of the original *Sustainable Reporting Guidelines* contains a summary of the European Federation of Accountants (FEE) Discussion Paper, 'Towards a Generally Accepted Framework for Environmental Reporting'. Since this report is summarised (in more detail) in Chapter 14 of this book, it has been omitted from this version of the Guidelines.

To assist in the process of continuously improving these Guidelines, the decision by an enterprise to use the GRI Guidelines should be explicitly stated in the published report.

Reporting by smaller enterprises. It is unrealistic to expect many smaller enterprises to prepare and issue full sustainability reports. Nonetheless, some may wish to report in some way on their commitment to sustainability. The Guidelines provide a starting point for considering possible topics, as well as an overall reporting framework, for such smaller enterprises. During the 1999 pilot period, GRI will assess approaches to making the Guidelines most useful to such enterprises.

Scope. While some enterprises may have information systems in place for immediate coverage of all operations, others will choose to phase in coverage of operations gradually, beginning with only portions of their operations, business units or regions. Though GRI seeks to encourage eventual global coverage for all reporting entities, it recognises this will evolve gradually for many—perhaps most—GRI adopters. For this reason, it is essential for a reporting entity to state precisely in the Profile Section what is included and what is excluded in a report, and what its intention is regarding expanding future coverage.

4. *Value of these Guidelines*

Within reporting entities, the Guidelines are intended to be a valuable tool for decision-making at three levels.

- At the level of board of directors and senior management, the Guidelines provide an internal vehicle for evaluating the consistency between corporate sustainability policy and strategy on the one hand, and actual performance on the other. Increased uniformity in reporting facilitated by the Guidelines will help leaders more readily distinguish themselves from laggards, and be recognised for improved performance.

- At the operational level, the Guidelines provide a logical structure for applying sustainability concepts to enterprise operations, for guiding data development for tracking progress toward sustainability goals and targets, and for benchmarking performance among comparable enterprises.

- From a communications standpoint, the Guidelines provide a framework for effectively sharing and promoting dialogue with internal and external stakeholders regarding the enterprise's accomplishments and challenges in achieving its sustainability goals.

Users of sustainability reports may also find the Guidelines helpful in a number of ways in gaining a better understanding of:

- What is reported and why, including relationships between different aspects of sustainability on the one hand, and different sets of information and performance indicators on the other

▼ How performance information is compiled from underlying data

▼ Issues related to the precision, scope and reliability in reported information

As more enterprises choose to adopt the GRI Guidelines, the opportunities for comparing performance within and across sectors and nations will strengthen stakeholders' capacity to advocate continuous progress toward business practices compatible with sustainable development.

5. *Structure of these Guidelines*

These Guidelines comprise three sections.

The Preamble sets out overarching aims, general reporting principles, specific issues to consider in reporting, and other general matters about the application, implementation and development of the Guidelines.

The Guidelines present recommendations for reporting information about enterprises and aspects of their performance that is relevant to understanding and assessing their progress towards sustainability. The Guidelines attempt to balance flexibility within an overall uniform structure, recognising that, while each reporting entity is unique, sustainability reporting is best served by adherence to certain common elements.

The recommended disclosures are organised into major sections and are seen as a minimum, not a maximum. Enterprises are encouraged to go beyond the recommended disclosures if that would communicate a more complete and balanced picture of their operations and performance.

Enterprises adopting the GRI Guidelines are asked to use the sections in the order in which they appear. This will be of benefit to report users for tracking performance over time, as well as making comparisons between entities at one point in time. However, flexibility is expected and encouraged *within* sections with respect to the order in which information appears and the emphasis assigned to each information item. The emphasis accorded various items in the Guidelines should reflect the nature of the enterprise—the environmental, social and economic aspects of its operations. This balance of uniformity and flexibility will enable GRI reports to achieve the overarching goals of consistency and comparability discussed above while attending to enterprise and sectoral differences.

In this Exposure Draft of the GRI Guidelines, the performance portions of the Guidelines (Parts 6, 7 and 8) address with greatest specificity the environmental aspects of sustainability. Future versions of the Guidelines will be strengthened in social and economic content which in the present version is limited to categories and aspects of reported information. Indicators of social and economic (beyond financial) performance are, by nature, generally more specific to location and culture than their environmental counterparts. While future strengthening of the social and economic indicators in the Guidelines is anticipated, the site- and culture-specific nature of such indicators currently places limits on their standardisation (see Section 6 of this Preamble for definitions). Informed by the experiences of the enterprises during the pilot phase, further development of social and economic indicators will occur.

Part 9 of the Guidelines is the 'Sustainability Overview'. This section of an enterprise's report is designed to provide a discussion of how the enterprise addresses the linkages between environmental, social and economic aspects of its operations, and how these linkages are manifested in the enterprise's decision-making and operations. GRI anticipates valuable feedback on Part 9 from enterprises pilot testing the Guidelines.

The Appendices provide additional information, including explanatory notes for the Guidelines in Appendix B. Additional guidance for preparing the Sustainability Overview appears in Appendix B. A thematic approach is recommended to explore how the environmental–social–economic linkages and balance occur in the real world. The guidance provided in this Appendix is suggestive only; reporters should prepare the Overview in the form most suitable to their enterprise. In addition to further guidance on the Sustainability Overview, Appendix B provides a placeholder for future explanatory notes for other parts of the Guidelines. Draft examples of such notes are currently provided for Parts 7 and 8. Revisions to the Explanatory Notes will benefit from experimentation and feedback during the pilot phase of GRI. Over time, and with benefit of experience of reporting enterprises, these appendices will assist in continuously improving the clarity, consistency and comparability of GRI-based sustainability reports.

6. *General Reporting Principles*

This section of the Preamble identifies those underlying reporting principles that are crucial to the objectives of usefulness, comparability and verifiability. These principles are explained further in Chapter 14.[4] GRI gratefully acknowledges the work of the Environmental Task Force of the European Federation of Accountants (FEE) in formulating these draft reporting principles. Note that material contained in Chapter 14[5] has not yet been subject to full discussion by GRI.

Qualitative characteristics. Over time, financial reporting has identified a number of qualitative characteristics that enhance the credibility of reported financial data. The GRI Guidelines incorporate and reflect these same qualitative characteristics, appropriately modified for sustainability reporting purposes:

▼ Relevance—to user groups with diverse expectations and needs

---

4   See Note 3 on page 445.
5   See Note 3 on page 445.

- ✔ Reliability—free from bias and material error
  - – Valid description
  - – Substance
  - – Neutrality
  - – Completeness
  - – Prudence

- ✔ Understandability—to informed users

- ✔ Comparability—to enable monitoring and benchmarking

- ✔ Timeliness—to identify outcomes and trends in an expeditious fashion

- ✔ Verifiability—to enhance credibility of reported information

These qualitative characteristics are discussed in more detail in Chapter 14.[6]

Underlying assumptions. Financial reporting has also adopted a set of under-pinning assumptions. These have, with some necessary modifications, been adopted by the GRI as underlying assumptions for sustainability reporting. These are:

- ✔ The entity assumption: a clear definition of boundaries of the reporting entity

- ✔ The accruals basis of accounting: events and activities are disclosed within the reporting period in which they occur

- ✔ The 'going-concern' assumption: the entity is expected to continue operations into the foreseeable future

- ✔ The conservatism or precautionary principle: minimisation and avoidance of risk is core to policy and practices

- ✔ The concept of materiality or significance: consideration is given to how information may influence the behaviour of the user (or the reporter)

The underlying assumptions are discussed in more detail in Chapter 14.[7]

Hierarchy of performance reporting elements. GRI has adopted the following hierarchy for organising and presenting information in sustainability reports:

- ✔ **Category**: i.e. general class or grouping of issues of concern to stakeholders (e.g. air, energy, labour practices, local economic impacts)

- ✔ **Aspect**: i.e. specific issue about which information is to be reported (e.g. smog precursors, greenhouse gas emissions, energy consumed by source, energy efficiency, child labour practices, corporate giving to host communities)

---

6   See Note 3 on page 445.
7   See Note 3 on page 445.

▼ **Indicator:** i.e. the most precise (and usually quantitative) measures of performance during a reporting period (e.g. metric tons of emissions, joules used from a specific energy source, water consumption per unit of product, adherence to a specific international standard on child labour, net joules used per ton of product, monetary contributions per year to host communities)

This hierarchy, which is consistent with the approach adopted by both the ISO 14000 series and the World Business Council for Sustainable Development (WBCSD), informed the development of performance information elements in Section B of these Guidelines. Enterprises that choose to go beyond GRI information elements and provide supplementary information may benefit from applying this structure to such additional information.

7. Specific Issues to Consider when Using these Guidelines

Disclosure of reporting principles. Users of sustainability reports need to be informed as to the principles applied in preparing and presenting the reports. This is essential to building integrity and credibility in the reported information, and can be achieved by stating in reports, at a minimum:

▼ That they have been prepared and presented in accordance with the GRI Sustainability Reporting Guidelines (except as otherwise indicated)

▼ The nature and effect of any re-statements of information reported previously, and the reason for such re-statement (e.g. significant changes in composition of enterprise, change of base years/periods, nature of business, measurement methods)

▼ The basis for any conversions of, for example, mass, volume, energy or currencies

▼ Any precision or measurement rules applied to data compilation and how the materiality or significance principle has been applied in deciding what to report or to omit

▼ The basis for reporting on joint ventures, operations of partially owned subsidiaries, leased facilities, outsourced operations and other situations that can significantly affect comparability from period to period and/or between enterprises

Frequency and medium of reporting. Enterprises need to decide how frequently they will prepare sustainability reports in accordance with these Guidelines, and what medium/media to use in communicating such reports. This will require consideration of the timing and integration with other external reporting, such as annual reports and financial statements.

The costs of preparing the information in accordance with the GRI Guidelines will vary from entity to entity. For those already preparing environmental or sustainability reports, the incremental cost may be minimal. For those new to such reporting, initial costs may be substantial to put in place data compilation, analysis and reporting systems. The costs of various reporting media and frequencies—e.g. paper copy of full report, shorter versions of selected sections, electronic/Internet versions of full report with regular updates—need to be weighed against the stakeholder needs and resource requirements to meet such needs. Preferences for and practical implications concerning independent verification also need to be considered when deciding frequency and medium of reporting.

Normalisation and units of measure. Reporting enterprises should use the generally accepted international metrics, e.g. kilograms, tons, litres.

It is recommended that, where appropriate, enterprises report values for the identified reporting year and the two previous years, as well as target values and years. To ensure responsiveness to various stakeholders, enterprises should express indicators not only in terms of absolute values, but also in terms of normalised values that will be meaningful to users, using normalising factors from Part 1, 'Profile of Reporting Entity'. Report users will thereby be in a position to accept the company's choice of normalisation factor or, should they choose, select different factors suitable to their needs.

For example, in order to illuminate the relationship between financial performance and environmental performance, an enterprise may wish to use eco-efficiency indicators. One way to express eco-efficiency is the ratio of unit of value provided per unit of environmental burden. Unit of value provided can be expressed by monetary indicators such as net sales or value added, by unit of enterprise activity level, such as mass or number of products sold, or by the functional value a product finally delivers to its user. Unit of environmental burden, such as energy, material consumption, or air or water pollutants, may be derived from values reported under Guidelines Part 7, operational performance (for production) or Part 8, product performance (for product use) respectively.

Enterprise-specific and sector-specific reporting. These Guidelines are intended to be applicable to all reporting entities. In places where the recommended disclosures are not applicable, preparers are encouraged to note this in their reports, with appropriate explanations. Providing additional information, either quantitative or qualitative, relevant to particular sectors not adequately covered in these Guidelines, is encouraged. Enterprises should report such supplemental information in the appropriate section within the Guidelines. Where detailed information is of interest to only a limited number of readers, appendices may be used. This may be the case, for example, with facility-specific information or detailed lists of many individual chemical releases. Enterprises that have previously published environmental or sustainability reports may find this approach helpful in adapting earlier reporting formats to the GRI Guidelines.

It is part of the long-range workplan of GRI to develop sector-specific guidelines to complement these core Guidelines. Throughout the 1999 pilot-test period, enterprise feedback will inform the extent to which such sector-specific customisation is desirable and feasible.

Use of graphics. The use of graphics can enhance the quality of reporting. However, research shows that graphics used in operational and financial reporting may unintentionally lead readers to reach incorrect conclusions and interpretations of data and results, or may confuse readers when inconsistent with data and explanations provided in text. It is thus essential that care be taken in the selection of axes, scales and data (including conversion of raw data to ratios and indices for graphic purposes), and use of colours and different types of graphs and charts. Therefore, graphics use should be a supplement to—not a substitute for—text and narrative disclosure of information. As a general rule, raw data should accompany all graphical presentations, either alongside or in appendices.

Independent review/verification of sustainability reports. Methodologies for the independent examination (either by way of a limited review or a full verification) of non-financial reports are being developed. At the same time, an increasing number of enterprises, recognising the additional credibility conferred by some form of independent attestation, have included reports by independent experts.

GRI is in the process of considering alternatives for independent report review and verification. An effective approach should strengthen the reliability of information in a sustainability report, without relieving the management of the enterprise of responsibility for the accuracy, completeness, and—in particular—balance and fairness of the representations it makes. Independent assurance that the report is in accordance with the GRI Guidelines will *in itself* be useful for readers to know, regardless of any particular reader's subjective interpretation and assessment of the performance of the reporting entity.

There is, as yet, no generally accepted approach to the review or verification of sustainability reports. However, GRI believes that experimentation and innovation in this area are vital. Consequently, GRI encourages enterprises to consider independent review or verification of sustainability reports, taking into account the costs and benefits of such an exercise, as well as the possible limitations inherent in such a new field. Until such time as a generally accepted methodology does emerge, GRI views the following as important, minimum elements of an independent reviewer's report:

▼ The scope and purpose of any review/verification exercise, indicating the level of assurance provided for various types of subject matter in reports

▼ The nature of stakeholder input in shaping the objectives of the report

▼ The procedures employed by the independent expert and the qualifications and relevant expertise of the independent expert

▼ The professional standards governing the conduct of the work of the independent expert

▼ The extent of application of the GRI Guidelines on Sustainability Reporting

When making arrangements for independent review or verification, enterprises will need to consider all the above issues as well as the form and wording of the report the independent expert will provide, and the proposed timing of that report.[8]

9. *Relationship with Other Reporting Guidelines*

The GRI seeks to foster a generally accepted framework for sustainability reporting. The GRI Guidelines were developed through consultation with a broad group of stakeholders in an effort to harmonise disparate reporting initiatives worldwide. In the course of developing the Guidelines, GRI participants reviewed and synthesised an extensive range of existing guidance, requirements and studies of one or more aspects of sustainability reporting. There is no intention on the part of GRI to displace or modify existing financial reporting standards and practices.

Today, there continue to be various international, national and sectoral sources of guidance (e.g. the WBCSD eco-efficiency metrics and reporting programme) and, in some cases, governmental requirements for certain aspects of sustainability reporting (e.g. environmental reporting requirements in the Netherlands and Denmark; see Chapters 16 and 17). To the maximum extent possible, these Guidelines have attempted to accommodate other sources while remaining faithful to GRI's overarching mission and reporting principles. While, in the short term, enterprises may see some benefit in maintaining their existing commitments to other reporting programmes, the GRI process intends in due course to accommodate and incorporate such initiatives into a single, globally accepted reporting framework.

GRI is aware of the potential for linkages to the ISO 14000 series environmental management standards. At least for GRI's environmental component, the menu of management and operational indicators contained in ISO 14031 (Environmental Performance Evaluation) provides a starting point for such a linkage. As discussions proceed regarding revisions to ISO 14001, and as ISO 14031 advances to approval and implementation, the GRI Guidelines may provide a valuable framework to accommodate needs for guidance about external reporting on environmental performance and management, and to complement these and other ISO 14000 series standards and guidelines.

10. *Continuing Evolution of these Guidelines*

These Guidelines are subject to continuous improvement over time. GRI intends to establish a new, independent multi-stakeholder organisation to monitor the implementation and usefulness of the Guidelines, to identify needs for change and enhancements, and to take steps in consultation with stakeholders and enterprises to modify and communicate such changes as are needed.

Users of these Guidelines are encouraged both to seek and collect feedback on their sustainability reports, and to communicate with GRI from time to time as needs arise for changes and enhancements in all aspects of the Guidelines.

---

8 During 1999, GRI will establish a working group to explore and develop the possibilities for achieving generally accepted sustainability report review/verification methodologies.

Following the publication of these Guidelines in March 1999, there will be a consultative period extending until approximately 31 December 1999. During this period:

▶ The Guidelines will be 'pilot-tested' by a number of enterprises worldwide. GRI will work actively with these volunteer enterprises to elicit feedback on their experience in applying the Guidelines.

▶ All interested parties are encouraged to review the Guidelines and send their comments to the GRI Secretariat. Unless otherwise indicated, GRI will assume that all comments will be a matter of public record.

GUIDELINES

General notes:

▶ Unless otherwise specified, all information throughout report pertains to the 'reporting entity' defined in item 3.1 and circumscribed by item 3.10.

▶ Appendix B contains additional detail clarifying information for those items marked with an asterisk.

▶ Report values for the current reporting period (e.g. year) and the two previous periods, as well as target periods.

▶ Report both absolute data and normalised data using appropriate normalising factor(s) from item 3.8 and/or item 3.9.

▶ Report the nature and effect of any re-statements of information reported previously, and the reason for such re-statement (e.g. significant changes in composition of enterprise, change of base years/periods, nature of business, measurement methods).

▶ Report the basis for any conversions of, for example, mass, volume, energy or currencies.

▶ Report any precision or measurement rules applied to data compilation and how the materiality or significance principle has been applied in deciding what to report or to omit.

▶ Report the basis for reporting on joint ventures, operations of partially owned subsidiaries, leased facilities, outsourced operations and other situations that can significantly affect comparability from period to period and/or between enterprises.

Part 1: *CEO Statement*

Statement of the CEO, or equivalent officer for reporting entity, describing key elements of the report.

Including, at minimum, the following:

- ▼ Explicit statement of the decision to apply the GRI Guidelines to the report

- ▼ Highlights of report content and commitment to targets

- ▼ Acknowledgement of successes and failures

- ▼ Performance on benchmarks versus previous years and industry norms

- ▼ Major sustainability challenges for the enterprise and its business sector as a whole

Part 2: *Key Indicators*

The following selected items, drawn directly from subsequent parts of the Guidelines, provide an overview of aspects and indicators for the reporting entity.

Concise presentation of the following items including appropriate ratios (e.g. eco-efficiency indicators) extracted from Parts 3–8 of the Guidelines (contained in the following pages):

Item   Description

3.7   Key environmental, social and economic issues and impacts ('aspects' per ISO 14001) associated with operations, products and/or services

5.1   Major stakeholder groups

6.2   Number, volume and nature of accidental or non-routine releases to land, air and water, including chemical spills, oil spills, emissions resulting from upset combustion conditions

7.1   Indicators of occupational health and safety

7.2   Total energy use

7.7   Total materials use other than fuel

7.10   Total water use

7.13   Quantity of non-product output (NPO) returned to process or market by recycling or re-use by material type and by on- and off-site management type

7.15   Quantity of NPO to land by material type and by on- and off-site management type

7.17   Emissions to air, by type

7.19 Discharges to water, by type

7.21 Indicators of social and economic aspects of operational performance

8.1 Major environmental, social and economic impacts associated with the life-cycle of products and services, with quantitative estimates of such impacts

Part 3: *Profile of Reporting Entity*

An overview of the reporting entity and scope of the report to provide a context for understanding and evaluating information in subsequent sections.

3.1 Name of enterprise or other reporting entity

3.2 Major products and/or services

3.3 Nature of ownership; legal form; stock exchange listings

3.4 Nature of markets or customers served (e.g. retail, wholesale, governments)

3.5 Principal industry and business association memberships

3.6 Contact person(s) regarding report

3.7 Key environmental, social and economic issues and impacts ('aspects' per ISO 14001) associated with operations, products and/or services

3.8 Financial information:

Net sales	Debt/equity ratio	Employee wages/salaries/benefits
Total taxes	Total assets	Other(s) (e.g. gross margin, value added, net profit)

Breakdown of sales/revenues by country for those countries that comprise 5% or more of total revenues, as well as by major products and/or services identified in item 3.2

3.9 Other relevant information regarding enterprise activity level, including measures that may be used for normalisation of absolute values provided in the report:

Number of employees	Product (mass/amount/quantity)
Total floor space	Other(s) as appropriate

3.10 Coverage of report (countries, products/services, divisions/facilities/joint ventures/subsidiaries). If coverage is not complete, projected time-line for complete coverage.

3.11 Items 3.8 and 3.9 revised to reflect report coverage specified in item 3.10

3.12 Reporting period (e.g. fiscal/calendar year) for information provided (unless otherwise noted)

3.13 Date of most recent previous report, if any

3.14 Significant changes in size, structure, ownership, products/services, that have occurred in the reporting period

3.15 Public accessibility of information or reports about environmental, social, economic or similar performance, including how to obtain copies of such reports

Part 4: *Policies, Organisation and Management Systems*

A statement of the reporting entity's public commitment to the elements of sustainable development and how the entity has implemented organisational structures and management processes intended to fulfil that commitment.

4.1 Publicly available missions and values statement(s), and statements of economic, social and environmental policy, including date of adoption and countries of applicability[9]

4.2 Environmental, social, economic or similar charters, codes or voluntary initiatives subscribed to, including date of adoption and countries of applicability

4.3 Organisational structure and responsibilities (e.g. board, senior management, special staff, operating staff, committees and councils) for oversight and implementation of environmental, social, economic and related policies

4.4 Management systems pertaining to social and environmental performance (e.g. ISO 14001, EMAS), such as: employee orientation and awareness programmes, social auditing and reporting, environmental risk assessment, environmental accounting, performance evaluation, internal communications, linkages between management performance and compensation, with countries of applicability

4.5 Status and date, by country, of environmental, social, economic or similar external certification (e.g. EMAS, ISO 14001, SA 8000)

4.6 Management systems for supplier and supply chain (including outsourcing), including selection criteria, training, monitoring and other procedures and practices, and countries of applicability

Part 5: *Stakeholder Relationships*

Information on the process and methods by which stakeholders—both internal and external to the enterprise—are engaged.

5.1 Basis for selection, definition and profile of major stakeholders (e.g. employees, investors, suppliers, customers, local authorities, public interest groups, non-governmental organisations)

---

9   See Appendix B for guidance on economic and social categories and aspects.

5.2 Approaches to consultation with each stakeholder (e.g. surveys, focus groups, community panels, written communications). Number of such consultations by type.

5.3 Type of information generated by such consultations

5.4 Use of such information (e.g. performance benchmarks and indicators), including applications in this report

5.5 Plans for strengthening stakeholder consultation

Part 6: *Management Performance*

Indicators of the reporting entity's performance regarding compliance with applicable mandatory standards, and adherence to internal policies and standards reported in Part 4.

▼ **Pertaining to laws, conventions and other mandatory standards**

6.1 Magnitude and nature of penalties for non-compliance with all applicable international declarations, conventions and treaties, and national, sub-national and local regulations associated with environmental (e.g. air quality, water quality), workplace (e.g. worker health and safety, harassment, discrimination), community (e.g. human rights, noise, odour) and other similar issues. Explain based on countries of operations.

6.2 Number, volume and nature of accidental or non-routine releases to land, air and water, including chemical spills, oil spills, emissions resulting from upset combustion conditions

6.3 Response of management to improve performance noted in items 6.1 and 6.2

6.4 Costs associated with environmental compliance: environmental operating costs (e.g. training, licensing, legal monitoring, permitting, waste management) and environmental capital costs (e.g. waste-water treatment plants, emissions control equipment)

6.5 Environmental liabilities under applicable laws and regulations

6.6 Site remediation costs under applicable laws and regulations

▼ **Pertaining to internal policies and standards and voluntary initiatives**

6.7 Performance regarding internal environmental, social and economic policies and standards, and voluntary initiatives discussed in Part 4 (excluding supplier issues)

6.8 Response of management to improve performance noted in item 6.7

▼ External recognition and activities

6.9 Major awards received in the reporting period regarding environmental, social, economic or similar performance and activities. Reasons for such awards.

6.10 Other external activities

▼ Suppliers

6.11 Supplier performance per item 4.6

▼ Additional indicators

6.12 Additional indicators of core relevance to the enterprise's management performance, including those arising from stakeholder engagement or other sources (e.g. ISO 14031)

Part 7: *Operational Performance*

Indicators of the reporting entity's operational performance regarding key aspects of sustainability.

Notes

▼ Additional guidance for those items marked with an asterisk is contained in Appendix B.

▼ Include definitions and calculation methods where appropriate.

▼ Health and safety

*7.1 Indicators of occupational health and safety

▼ Environmental performance

Energy—values in Joules

7.2 Total energy use (sum of 7.3 to 7.5)

*7.3 Total electricity use. Amount purchased, by primary fuel source, where known. Amount self-generated (describe source).

*7.4 Total fuel use. Vehicle and non-vehicle fuel, by type.

7.5 Other energy use (e.g. district heat)

7.6 Objectives, programmes and targets regarding energy use and progress toward same

Materials—values in metric tons

*7.7 Total materials use other than fuel, including definition and how calculated

7.8   Objectives, programmes and targets regarding materials use and progress toward same

7.9   Objectives, programmes and targets regarding procurement and use of virgin and reclaimed materials and progress toward same

Water—values in litres

7.10   Total water use

7.11   Objectives, programmes and targets regarding water use and progress toward same

Land

7.12   Habitat improvements and damages due to enterprise operations

Non-Product Output—values in metric tons
Non-product output (NPO) is defined as waste prior to treatment, off-site recycling or disposal.

Non-Product Output returned to process or market

7.13   Quantity of NPO returned to process or market by recycling or re-use by material type (hazardous or not hazardous under applicable national, sub-national or local laws or regulation) and by on- and off-site management type (e.g. recycled, re-used, remanufactured)

7.14   Objectives, programs and targets regarding non-product output returned to process or market and progress toward same.

Non-Product Output to land

7.15   Quantity of NPO to land by material type (hazardous or not hazardous under applicable national, sub-national or local laws or regulation) and by on- and off-site management type (e.g. incinerated with energy recovery, landfilled, deep-well injected)

7.16   Objectives, programmes and targets regarding Non-Product Output to land and progress toward same

Non-Product Output to air

*7.17   Emissions to air, by type

7.18   Objectives, programmes and targets regarding routine air emissions and progress toward same

Non-Product Output to water

*7.19   Discharges to water, by type

7.20   Objectives, programmes and targets regarding routine discharges to water and progress toward same

▾ Social and economic indicators

7.21   Indicators of social and economic aspects of operational performance within the following categories and aspects:

- Corporate (e.g. ethical standards, bribery/corruption)
- Employees (e.g. freedom of association, workforce diversity [gender, race, age])
- Local and global community (e.g. community involvement, skills transfer)
- Suppliers (e.g. procurement standards, partnership screens and standards)
- Customers (e.g. labelling standards, advertising standards)[10]

▾ Additional indicators

7.22   Additional indicators of core relevance to the enterprise's operational performance, including those arising from stakeholder engagement or other sources (e.g. ISO 14031)

Part 8: *Product Performance*

Indicators of the performance of the reporting entity's product(s) regarding environmental, social and economic aspects of sustainability.

Notes

- ▾ Additional information for those items marked with an asterisk is contained in Appendix B.
- ▾ See Appendix B for guidance on economic and social categories and aspects.

*8.1   Major environmental, social and economic impacts associated with the life-cycle of products and services, with quantitative estimates of such impacts

8.2   Formal, written commitments requiring an evaluation of life-cycle impacts associated with the use of new and existing products and services offered, and procedures in place to monitor this commitment

8.3   Programmes or procedures to prevent or minimise potentially adverse impacts of products and services, including product stewardship initiatives

8.4   Procedures to assist product and service designers to create products or services with reduced adverse life-cycle impact

8.5   Additional indicators of core relevance to the environmental, social and economic performance of the enterprise's product(s), including those arising from stakeholder engagement or other sources (e.g. ISO 14031)

---

10   Appendix B contains additional illustrative aspects of these categories.

Part 9: *Sustainability Overview*

A discussion of the reporting entity's efforts and progress towards integrating sustainability into its decision-making and performance measurement.

A discussion of how environmental, economic and social goals and values intersect and are balanced in the organisation, and how such linkages and balancing shape the enterprise's decision-making. The overview seeks to assist the enterprise in articulating a long-term vision of sustainability, including obstacles and time-scales, and communicating this vision to stakeholders.

The Sustainability Overview is an evolving tool. Reporters should use maximum flexibility and creativity in preparing the overview. Appendix B offers an illustrative approach which may be of value.

APPENDICES

◢ *Appendix A: General Reporting Principles*

Appendix A of the original *Sustainable Reporting Guidelines* contains a summary of the European Federation of Accountants (FEE) Discussion Paper, 'Towards a Generally Accepted Framework for Environmental Reporting'. Since this report is summarised (in more detail) in Chapter 14 of this book, it has been omitted from this version of the Guidelines.

◢ *Appendix B: Explanatory Notes*

This appendix is the seed of what GRI intends to become a robust set of explanatory notes to the Guidelines. In this exposure draft, explanatory notes for many of the items are absent or incomplete. Comments, contributions and recommendations GRI receives from enterprises that volunteer to pilot-test the Guidelines, as well as from other reviewers, will be critical for developing this appendix. **We encourage your contributions.**

◿ *Guidance on Social and Economic Categories and Aspects*

Below are illustrative categories and aspects of the social and economic areas of sustainability beyond conventional EHS that the reporting entity might consider in its report. This list is not intended to be comprehensive—the items are provided as a starting point for reporting enterprises.

GRI recognises that established indicators/metrics may not exist for many of the aspects listed. **GRI actively seeks your input in the pilot phase as it refines this information.** In particular, GRI seeks input on defining and developing indicators for the various aspects listed below.

Corporate

- Ethical standards
- Bribery/corruption
- Transparency
- Human rights
- Political activities

Employees

- Workforce diversity (gender, race, age)
- Freedom of association
- Child labour
- Turnover rate (recruitment and retention)
- Absenteeism
- Compensation and benefits: standards and equity
- Wages, salaries, benefits
- Flexibility in work arrangements
- Assistance for displaced workers

Community (local and global)

- Community involvement
- Skills transfer
- Technology transfer
- Site selection
- Complaints (noise/odour)
- Community reinvestment
- Activities in developing countries
- Philanthropy
- Taxes

Suppliers

- Procurement standards
- Partnership screens and standards
- Outsourcing

Customers

- ◗ Product labelling standards

- ◗ Advertising standards

- ◗ Training in product use

- ◗ Monitoring for proper use of product[11]

◁ *Guidance for Part 7: Operational Performance*

GRI recognises that established definitions may not exist for many of the indicators/metrics listed. **GRI seeks your input in the pilot phase as it refines this information.** In particular, GRI seeks input on further developing indicators that allow maximum consistency across reporting enterprises.

In addition to the item components listed here, please include regional or sector-specific components as appropriate (e.g. nutrient enrichment for discharges to water).

7.1 Indicators of occupational health and safety should include:

Counts and, if meaningful, rates of occupational injuries and illnesses and lost workdays

Include definition and method of calculation

7.3 Fuel sources for electricity should include:

Fossil carbon-based (oil, gas, coal)

Hydro power

Nuclear

Solar, wind, biomass

Other (specify)

Unknown

7.4 Vehicle fuel types should include:

Leaded gasoline (including diesel)

Unleaded gasoline (including diesel)

Other (specify)

Unknown

Non-vehicle fuel types should include:

Fossil carbon-based (oil, gas, coal)

Biomass

Other (specify)

Unknown

---

11   Product performance is covered in Part 8.

7.7   Total materials use: select materials and categories of materials significant for reporting entity. **GRI actively seeks your input in the pilot phase as it refines this item.**

Sample materials categories include:

>   Renewable/non-renewable
>
>   Virgin/recycled
>
>   Natural/man-made
>
>   Hazardous/non-hazardous (using equivalency numbers)

7.17   Emissions to air should include:

>   Greenhouse gases (GHGs), per Kyoto Protocol, in CO_2 equivalent, per IPCC GWP 100 Factors
>
>   Ozone-depleting substances (ODSs)—per Montreal Protocol, in CFC-11 equivalent
>
>   Sulphur dioxide
>
> NO_x
>
>   Volatile organic compounds (VOCs)
>
>   Priority heavy metals
>
>   Persistent organic pollutants (POPs)

7.19   Discharges to water should include:

>   Chemical oxygen demand (COD)
>
>   Biological oxygen demand (BOD)
>
>   Priority heavy metals
>
>   Persistent organic pollutants (POPs)

◻ *Guidance for Part 8: Product Performance*

8.1   *Major environmental, social and economic impacts associated with the life-cycle of products and services, with quantitative estimates of such impacts*

Sample product/service impacts at selected life-cycle stages

Use stage

- Hazardous nature to user
- Hazardous nature to non-user
- Addictiveness
- Durability or expected lifetime
- Expected energy consumption

- Emissions of NPO during use

- Non-NPO emissions (e.g. microwave radiation)

- Noise generation

Post-use stage (disposal or resource recovery)

- Packaging content

- Material content per unit of production

- Recyclability

- Emissions during disposal or recovery

- Product reparability

Items 8.2–8.4. Refer to ISO 14000 series standards and guidelines pertaining to life-cycle assessment and product labelling for further guidance.

⌑ *Guidance for Part 9: Sustainability Overview*

Introduction. Understanding and addressing sustainability issues is important for enterprises wishing to plan their future progress in contributing to wider sustainability. Additionally, it can help them to reconcile their many different, and frequently conflicting, responsibilities—maximising shareholder returns while creating environmental, social and economic value.

In order to build a complete sustainability report, an enterprise will need to understand and assess its decision-making processes and performance across all three dimensions of sustainability: environmental, social and economic. A sustainability report, however, is more than the sum of environmental, social and economic information. It must also seek to integrate this information to allow readers to understand the interrelations and balance between the three dimensions from the standpoint of both process (how decisions are made) and outcome (the results of decisions). Enterprises are just beginning to explore the implications of this for their public reporting programmes.

The Guidelines present recommendations for reporting indicators of performance. This explanatory note seeks to assist reporters in preparing Part 9 of the Guidelines: the Sustainability Overview. This explanatory note does not specify environmental, social and economic information as the Guidelines do. Rather, its goal is to provide guidance on how a reporting entity can present its thinking, decision-making and practices with respect to operationalising sustainability.

GRI views the Sustainability Overview as a key component for reporting an enterprise's commitment to integrating sustainability into its decision-making. It is, however, experimental in nature. Thus, this explanatory note should be viewed as part of an evolving process—it has been a challenge for GRI to design, and the experiences of pilot-testers and others will be crucial in building the methods for this key component of the Guidelines.

11. **Overall approach.** Sustainability reporting at the enterprise level provides an important contribution to the goals of sustainability. In order to make systematic progress towards global sustainability, the work by individual enterprises will need to be complemented by a range of other players and sectors (e.g. governments, communities, markets and investors). Within GRI, the focus is on enterprise reporting as a contributor to overall progress toward sustainability.

Sustainability reporting is evolving through experimentation and learning as enterprises try different methods to communicate their 'sustainability story'. Most, however, are just beginning to consider their approach to sustainability reporting, and may be initially prepared to provide only a trial overview in their public reports. A few enterprises are already able to provide more sophisticated overviews based on their greater experience with integrating sustainability concepts into their operations. Many participants in the GRI share the belief that reports produced by entities using the Guidelines will represent a range of stages along a continuum of practice, although it is not yet possible to define that continuum.

In order to make progress towards sustainability, enterprises will need relevant and reliable information on which to make decisions. The Guidelines present recommendations for reporting on operational and management performance, as well as product performance and stakeholder relationships. Sustainability reporting demands that performance be understood and measured across each of these areas. This is because decisions about sustainability arise not simply from technical issues of operational performance, but encompass an evolving set of views and priorities among those involved and affected, that is, relevant stakeholders. The implication of this is that sustainability reporting should continue to evolve in a manner that demonstrates learning and represents continuous engagement.

12. **Styles of reporting.** An enterprise may use several different reporting styles to construct a Sustainability Overview:

- **Systematic Accounting and Reporting.** A total approach comprising economic, social and environmental accounts, including flows and accumulated balances of value. Systematic Accounting and Reporting requires a sophisticated knowledge of causes and effects within and between the environmental, economic and social dimensions, and, though not yet well developed, presents a model for future sustainability reporting.

- **Thematic Statement.** The enterprise's interpretation of a conceptual theme—a core issue or challenge—that relates in some way to all dimensions of sustainability.

- **Case Studies.** An exploration of the enterprise's decision-making in a particular situation, treating the interrelations of environmental, economic and social aspects in terms of how it manages specific situations in the past, present or future.

These complementary reporting styles all have a role in developing a Sustainability Overview. They are further described below.

Systematic Accounting and Reporting. Systematic Accounting and Reporting would involve production of integrated accounts of performance across environmental, social and economic dimensions. In theory, such reporting would resemble standard financial accounting in many ways. Although standards are as yet not defined, this style of reporting offers an integrated view of performance and reveals whether or not performance in the reporting period represents an improvement over time. Some of the components of Systematic Accounting and Reporting are contained in Parts 3–8 of the Guidelines.

In Systematic Accounting and Reporting, an enterprise will need to define both stocks and flows of various forms of value into and out of environmental, social and economic accounts. In other words, in order to understand sustainability, there is a need to report not only on the 'bottom line' (i.e. the sustainability equivalent of the profit and loss statement), but also on the accumulated effects of various activities (similar to capital balances or asset–liability balances). So-called 'ecobalance' methods of environmental accounting provide an example of a limited form of this practice. In sustainability reporting, this requires accounting for each dimension of sustainability, which in turn will help advance an understanding of the interrelationships and balance between environmental, social and economic impacts. Guidance on approaches for Systematic Accounting and Reporting will be further developed as the Guidelines are updated and revised.

Thematic Statements. Themes are significant issues or concepts faced by an enterprise that address the linkages between the environmental, economic and social aspects of business operations. Relating the information collected in the Guidelines to such themes helps illuminate the complex relationships between key aspects of sustainability. By considering one or more of these themes in a sustainability overview, enterprises can begin to develop an effective sustainability message. A 'thematic statement' is a description of the way the enterprise understands and is addressing a given issue. The thematic statement as part of a sustainability report may deal with more than one theme.

Suggestions for broad themes are provided at the end of this note; however, an enterprise may prefer to refine a theme further to provide a more specific focus for its statement, such as:

- Maintaining ethical integrity in a global context
- The health impact of enterprise activities
- Use of transportation
- Total product impact
- Use of new technology
- Investment strategy
- Use of natural resources
- Use of human resources

- Dematerialisation

- Transition from product- to service-based enterprise

Any selected theme should be especially relevant to a reporting enterprise, in light of its products, services and aspects. It is helpful to bear the following points in mind:

- Will the thematic statement help to show how the enterprise is thinking about and working towards sustainability?

- Will the choice of theme be useful to report users in their understanding of the reporting enterprise's impact on sustainability?

- Are appropriate indicators available to describe the issue sufficiently?

- What policies are in place which bear on the theme?

Reporting enterprises should determine the structure of the thematic overview so as to be suitable to the theme selected. The following questions may help determine which aspects could usefully be included:

- What are the environmental aspects of the issue?

- What are the social aspects of the issue?

- What are the financial, and broader economic, aspects of the issue?

- How are the environmental, social and economic aspects of the issue reconciled or balanced among each other?

- To what extent is the reporting enterprise willing to take responsibility for the issue?

- How are decisions made in relation to the issue?

- Which indicators has the enterprise used to describe the issue?

- How are stakeholders involved in dealing with the issue and in making decisions about it?

- What knowledge and resources are needed to deal with the issue? How much are these currently available internally?

- How can addressing the issue add value to the enterprise?

- How can innovation be harnessed to addressing the issue?

- What positive changes have been, or could be, made that move the enterprise further towards sustainability?

- To what extent has a long-term perspective been adopted in exploring the issue?

- How is the enterprise learning from dealing with the issue?

- How can what has been learned be applied to other issues?

IT MAY BE POSSIBLE to use a case study as a part of a thematic statement, but thematic statements and case studies should not be confused. Whereas case studies describe specific situations or achievements, themes are broader issues or challenges faced by an enterprise. Certain aspects of themes may be illustrated by case studies, but the complexity and depth of a theme cannot be presented simply as a series of case studies.

Box 3: CASE STUDIES AND THEMES: WHAT'S THE DIFFERENCE?

It is intended that experience gained during the pilot test period will contribute more concrete examples of themes and their use in sustainability reports.

Case Studies. Case studies provide a powerful mechanism to explore and communicate how decisions are made by organisations and what outcomes have been achieved. Case studies focus on specific situations such as a facility opening or closure, an accidental release of a dangerous substance or a community project. Case studies do not provide a comprehensive measure of performance or a system-wide overview. But they do serve as a valuable complement to themes by illustrating enterprise behaviour under real conditions.

Reporters may choose to consider and prepare multiple case studies. One way to enrich case study material is to set out the perspectives of different stakeholders so that the interrelationships between different views may be analysed. Case studies may also be written by external stakeholders.

There are three broad categories of case study:

- Historical case studies that record past actions in particular situations

- Real-time case studies that require an enterprise to 'think out loud' through observation of actions in particular current situations

- Future case studies (often referred to as 'scenarios') that set out what an enterprise plans to do in particular situations in the future

Historical and real time case studies may be preferred by stakeholders, as results are more transparent. In examples to date, virtually all case studies that appear in published social or environmental reports are historical, but real-time and future case studies will allow considerably greater insight to emerge. New communications technologies (e.g. electronic reporting) strengthen the ability of enterprises both to share their thinking and to benefit from stakeholder input as decisions unfold.

13. **Further guidance on the thematic approach.** GRI has developed a set of illustrative themes as one basis for exploring sustainability and for presentation as part of a Sustainability Overview. These sample themes are offered as a conceptual framework, not a guide to sustainable corporate behaviour. They can provide the basis for developing a Sustainability Overview should an enterprise choose to make such use of them.

Sample themes	Sample economic dimensions	Sample social dimensions	Sample environmental dimensions
Diversity *An enterprise's mix and balance of activities and human, ecological and economic resources*	• Business diversification	• Employee diversity, including employment of minorities and disabled people and empowerment of women	• Resource use diversity • Consumption of non-renewable natural resources • Consumption of renewable resources
Added value *Increasing of relative worth, utility or importance as a result of enterprise activities*	• Return on capital employed • Shareholder value • Economic value added • Investor satisfaction	• Intangible value (e.g. goodwill) • Information or knowledge held by employees • Employee satisfaction • Customer satisfaction	• Conversion of waste to usable or saleable product • Activities to offset negative effects of other activities (e.g. carbon sinks for CO_2 emissions) • Local impacts such as landscaping
Productivity *Effectiveness in creating results, benefits, profits or other forms of value*	• Profit margins • Stability of economic impacts on communities	• Rate of employee turnover • Customer retention rate • Involvement in civic activities	• Resource efficiency • Material efficiency
Integrity *Adherence to principles and ideals*	• Bribery • Political contributions • Lawsuits • Qualified accounts; exceptions to auditors'/ verifiers' statements • Information disclosure policies and practices	• Complaints • Lawsuits • Public opinion • Membership in social responsibility fora • Information disclosure policies and practices	• Lawsuits • Environmental management systems • Membership in environmental responsibility fora • Information disclosure policies and practices
Health *Soundness and resilience*	• Profitability • Demand for products or services • Solvency/liquidity • Rating by investment agencies	• Health of workforce (e.g. employee injury rate, lost time days) • Healthcare entitlements/benefits • Health of community • Local health risk of manufacture or service	• Health risk of product or service • Consumption of critical natural capital • Remediation • Contribution to ecological problems or changes (such as climate change contribution)
Development *Evolution, growth, progression*	• Innovation programmes • Investments or capital expenditures	• Employee training and development • Contribution to or impact on local infrastructure or services • Socially or ethically targeted investments	• Investment in environmental technologies • Product line substitution • Environmentally targeted investments

Table 1: ILLUSTRATIVE APPLICATION OF THEMES TO MAJOR DIMENSIONS OF SUSTAINABILITY

It is neither possible nor desirable to provide a definitive set of themes; the chosen approach must reflect an enterprise's particular situation. The set of themes in Table 1 is not prescriptive, but illustrative of how various aspects of business operations intersect for the purposes of preparing a Sustainability Overview. Choosing one or more such themes for discussion may be helpful to enterprises in this process.

Indicators provided to illustrate themes in many cases may be drawn directly from process and performance information recommended in the Guidelines. In other cases, the examples suggest a further development of performance indicators, or even wholly new indicators. For these reasons, themes and their indicators should not be viewed as questions to be answered or boxes to be ticked in developing a sustainability report. They are intended to motivate creative thinking in developing a Sustainability Overview.

◢ Appendix C: GRI Participants

◁ Steering Committee Members

Roger Adams, Association of Chartered Certified Accountants
Anil Agarwal, Centre for Science and Environment
Mark Bateman, Investor Responsibility Research Center
Nancy Bennet, United Nations Environment Programme
Maria Emilia Correa, CECODES (Colombian Business Council for Sustainable
    Development)
John Elkington, SustainAbility
Magnus Enell, ITT Flygt
Toshihiko Goto, Environmental Auditing Research Group
Kristin Haldeman, Investor Responsibility Research Center (through December 1998)
Heinrich Hugenschmidt, UBS AG
Franz Knecht, E2 Management Consulting
Markus Lehni, World Business Council for Sustainable Development
Robert Kinloch Massie, Coalition for Environmentally Responsible Economies
Judith Mullins, General Motors
Amy Muska, Council on Economic Priorities
Janet Ranganathan, World Resources Institute
Allen White, Stockholm Environment Institute/Tellus Institute
Alan Willis, Canadian Institute of Chartered Accountants
Simon Zadek, New Economics Foundation

◁ Other GRI Participants

In addition to Steering Committee members, the following people have participated in one or more GRI meetings. Institutional affiliations are provided for identification purposes. We regret any omission from this list.

In addition, GRI has benefited from contributions by many people not on this list, generally in the form of comments on earlier draft versions of these Guidelines.

Jacqueline Aloisi de Larderel	United Nations Environment Programme, Industry and Environment
Stephen Barg	International Institute for Sustainable Development
Andreas Barkman	TetraPak Carton Packaging Division

Matteo Bartolomeo	Fondazione Eni Enrico Mattei
Jan Bebbington	University of Dundee
Uwe Bergmann	Institut für Ökologie und Unternehmensführung
Andrew J. Blaza	Imperial College Centre for Environmental Technology
Frank Bosshardt	Anova
Chandra Bushan	Centre for Science and Environment
Colin Chellman	Council on Economic Priorities
David F. Cockburn	TetraPak Carton Packaging Division
David Constable	SmithKline Beecham
Deborah Cornland	Stockholm Environment Institute
Owen Cylke	Winrock International
Sophie Depraz	IPIECA
Linda Descano	Salomon Smith Barney.
Daryl Ditz	Environmental Law Institute
Harry Fatkin	Polaroid Corporation
Ira Feldman	United Nations Association of USA
Daniel J Fiorino	US Environmental Protection Agency
Thomas Gameson	European Commission, Institute for Prospective Technological Studies
Colin Gomm	British Petroleum Company
Claudia Gonella	New Economics Foundation
Anne Grafe-Buckens	Imperial College of Science, Technology & Medicine
Robert Graff	Stockholm Environment Institute/Tellus Institute
Marianne Gramstrup	Novo Nordisk A/S
Kristin M Haldeman	Investor Responsibility Research Center (IRRC)
Gilbert S Hedstrom	Arthur D Little, Inc.
Adrian Henriques	New Economics Foundation
Ruth Hillary	Imperial College of Science, Technology and Medicine
Filip Jonckheere	CEFIC
Tomoko Kurasaka	Environmental Auditing Research Group
Judith Kuszewski	CERES
Lars-Olle Larsson	KPMG
Jonathan Lash	World Resources Institute
Mark Lee	Business for Social Responsibility
Lars Lundahl	TetraPak Carton Packaging Division
Andrea Marsanich	Fondazione Eni Enrico Mattei
Madeleine Marteng	Electrolux
Malcolm McIntosh	Council on Economic Priorities
Joyce Miller	Sustainable Business Associates
Kaspar Müller	Ellipson AG
Tell Münzing	SustainAbility
Thomas Ruddy	RuddyConsult
Lorraine T Ruffing	UNCTAD, Division on Investment, Technology and Enterprise Development
Thomas Scheiwiller	PricewaterhouseCoopers
Eberhard K Seifert	Wuppertal Institute for Climate, Environment and Energy
Jonathan Shopley	Arthur D Little International Inc.
Preben J Sørensen	Deloitte & Touche
W. Ross Stevens	Stevens Associates
Helen Stibbard	SustainAbility
Björn Stigson	World Business Council for Sustainable Development
Tessa Tennant	NPI Global Care Investments
Kimie Tsunoda	Green Reporting Forum
Chris Tuppen	British Telecom
Kurt Urquhart	ITT Industries
Ariane van Buren	Interfaith Center on Corporate Responsibility (ICCR)
Paula J Van Lare	US Environmental Protection Agency

Simone Vollmer	Opel
Iain Watt	CERES
Anne Weiss	PricewaterhouseCoopers
Ulrika Wennberg	IIIEE at Lund University
Jan-Olaf Willums	Storebrand
Mike Wright	World Business Council for Sustainable Development

◻ *Support*

Initial funding for the Global Reporting Initiative was provided in 1997 by the following charitable foundations:

John D. and Catherine T. MacArthur Foundation
Charles Stewart Mott Foundation
Spencer T. and Ann W. Olin Foundation

24

Signs of Sustainability

Measuring Corporate Environmental and Social Performance

Janet Ranganathan

WE ARE BEGINNING to witness the emergence of a new era in corporate reporting and accountability. In the not too distant future, a new global framework will govern the measurement and reporting of corporate social, environmental and economic performance—the three dimensions of business sustainability. Companies will routinely report on key aspects of their social and environmental performance, just as they currently report their financial performance. Standardised metrics will emerge and be adopted by both business and others outside firms. Public disclosure of key aspects of a firm's social and environmental performance will foster greater competition towards sustainability, and enable regulators to focus attention on laggards. New information and monitoring technologies will provide the necessary infrastructure and tools to collect, analyse and disseminate information worldwide.

Is this a romantic illusion or a realistic projection of current trends? To answer this question, the World Resources Institute (WRI) reviewed over 50 initiatives that are developing measures of business sustainability. These included efforts to devise indicators of corporate environmental or social performance, as well as a handful of recent attempts to produce measures of sustainability that incorporate social and environmental performance. A summary of these initiatives is included in the appendix at the end of this chapter. The remainder of the chapter is structured as follows: Section 1 discusses the case for sustainability measurement and reporting and provides a conceptual framework for sustainability measurement; Sections 2–4 discuss, respectively, economic, environmental and social performance measurement and reporting; Section 5 considers integrated measurement and reporting of sustainability; Section 6 comments on the Global Reporting Initiative; and Section 7 provides conclusions.

1. *Articulating the Need for Sustainability Measurement and Reporting*

Clearly businesses' economic power is expanding in our increasingly global economy. However, with power comes responsibility, and with responsibility there must also be accountability—not only to shareholders, but also to the many other stakeholders impacted by business activities. Yet the nearest we have to a uniform accountability standard is the mechanisms that govern how a company measures and reports its financial performance, though even this falls short of a global standard and at best provides only a partial snapshot of a company's activities. Social and environmental performance—dimensions that companies are increasingly recognising as necessary for long-term sustainability and stakeholder relations—are emerging as of equal importance to financial performance in the eyes of many stakeholders.

To date there is no universally accepted accountability tool for companies and other organisations to report on their impacts across the three dimensions of sustainable development: social, environmental and economic performance. Instead, they and we must rely on a confusing patchwork of overlapping, incomplete and non-comparable voluntary reporting guidelines and other accountability measures that address specific aspects of business sustainability, cover specific geographical areas, or relate to particular business sectors. This is confusing, not only for business but also for the many stakeholders—customers, communities, employees, regulators and the financial community—that seek information on the overall performance of business.

To serve these multiple needs, sustainability indicators must be comparable, complete, and credible—the 'three Cs' of measurement. Comparability makes it possible to track performance over time and across firms; completeness is required both in the scope of the indicators and their application across firms, sectors and countries; and credibility means that businesses and others trust the indicators and make reliable decisions based on the information reported. The evolution of a standardised reporting structure, resembling today's financial reporting system, will address the comparability and credibility issues and simplify the task of measuring and reporting—especially for businesses operating globally. It will also allow leaders to distinguish themselves more readily from laggards in their industry.

Figure 1 proposes a simple schematic for conceptualising the measurement of sustainability which emphasises its three dimensions, as well as their interlinkages. Some may contest this separation of sustainability into three elements: corporate social performance, for example, is sometimes broadly interpreted to encompass both environmental and financial performance. However, this framework does help to map the focus of current sustainability measurement and reporting efforts and to identify critical elements and interconnections; for example:

- **Socio-environmental:** equity in access to natural resources, land tenure and siting of high-environmental-impact industrial facilities

- **Socioeconomic:** employment creation, equitable distribution of wealth, business markets serving social needs, investment in employee education, minority supplier access, and corporate donations

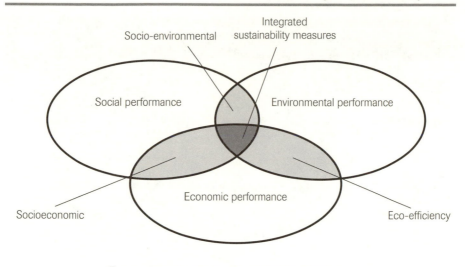

Figure 1: SUSTAINABILITY MEASUREMENT SCHEMATIC

▼ **Environmental-economic (eco-efficiency):** materials efficiency, energy efficiency, and economic value-added per environmental footprint

In the future, as our understanding of measuring social performance develops, it is likely that the broad category of social performance in Figure 1 will separate into several other circles—each representing different stakeholder groups such as employees, customers, communities, regulators and suppliers.

The following sections discuss each of the three areas of economic, environmental and social performance, with Table 1 providing a summary.

2. Economic Performance

In view of its more mature status, economic and financial performance measurement is examined only in regard to how it can be linked to social and environmental performance. But financial measurement and reporting is still evolving and there is no universally accepted measurement framework—only generally accepted accounting practices. Some argue that, because not all the costs of doing business are borne by firms, current financial accounting practices are flawed and partially responsible for creating the unsustainable businesses of today. Clearly, business financial performance does not always equate to economic performance. However, if it is successful, business sustainability reporting should aid efforts to change the current rules of the game for measuring financial performance.

	Economic performance	Environmental performance	Social performance	Integrated sustainability
Number of initiatives	Accounting standards	Many	Few	Handful
Developmental stages	Mature	Moving toward standardisation	Infancy	Embryonic
Business penetration	Mainstream	Moving toward mainstream	Limited (niche)	Very limited
Public reporting	Mandatory	Mandatory and voluntary	Mostly voluntary	Voluntary
Linkages to other sustainability dimensions	None	Eco-efficiency	None	Multiple
Utility of information outside firms	Universal	Multiple	Narrow	Potentially large
Current focus	Company	Company, facility, product	Company, project	Company, product

Table 1: SUSTAINABILITY MEASUREMENT: AN OVERVIEW OF CURRENT PRACTICE

3. *Environmental Performance*

In the US and Europe, there are numerous initiatives by business and others to develop measures of corporate environmental performance. For many leading firms, the issue is no longer *whether* to measure, but rather *what* to measure. However, after two decades of experimentation, particularly as part of voluntary environmental reporting efforts, there is a profusion of different indicators in use. Unfortunately, while advancing our understanding of measurement, the vital attribute of comparability has been lost. Without any agreement on the fundamentals of what to measure, by whom, and how, we are becoming awash in a sea of confusing, contradictory, incomplete and incomparable information.

With the exception of mandatory reporting requirements that typically focus on pollutant releases, spills and other end-of-pipe measures, it is virtually impossible to make comparisons between firms on the basis of environmental performance. This is not in the interests of customers, the financial community, regulators or anyone else who has a stake in corporate environmental performance—nor is it in the interests of those firms who have made genuine commitments to improvement.

The next critical step in environmental performance measurement is therefore to forge agreement on the key elements of performance and to move toward greater comparability, completeness and credibility. Of course, firms should continue to construct customised measures to capture the specific issues of their business—as a complement to, not instead of, a common set of indicators that enable business and others to draw meaningful comparisons across facilities, products, companies and countries.

◻ The Standardisation Movement

The good news is that several standardisation efforts are beginning to emerge from the plethora of voluntary metrics efforts. The Global Reporting Initiative (GRI), the World Business Council for Sustainable Development (WBCSD), and the Canadian National Round Table on Environment and the Economy (NRTEE) have independently undertaken to develop and bring about broad agreement on a core set of environmental performance indicators. What should this core set of indicators look like? An earlier World Resources Institute study (Ditz and Ranganathan 1997) identified the following four key categories of environmental performance that emphasise resource efficiency and pollution prevention:

- **Materials use.** Quantities and types of materials used. This indicator tracks resource inputs, distinguishing their composition and source.

- **Energy consumption.** Quantities and types of energy used or generated. This indicator, the energy analogue to materials use, also differentiates between types.

- **Non-product output.** Quantities and types of waste created before recycling, treatment or disposal. This indicator distinguishes production efficiency from end-of-pipe pollution control.

- **Pollutant releases.** Quantities and types of pollutant released to air, water and land. This indicator includes toxic chemicals, as well as greenhouse gases, solid wastes and other pollutants.

NRTEE, WBCSD and GRI have subsequently proposed similar generic categories of performance. However, unless these efforts are co-ordinated and ultimately converge on a single common set of metrics, businesses will find themselves having to report to several different standards, depending on their location, affiliations and sector. Clearly, the evolution of several different frameworks does not equate to standardisation. The immediate challenge for these separate efforts is to find ways of uniting and leveraging their different constituencies and skills. Collectively, these efforts could represent a powerful and positive force for change.

In addition to voluntary reporting initiatives, public disclosure and comparability also are being driven by regulations. The Organisation for Economic Co-operation and Development (OECD) initiative on Pollutant Release and Transfer Registers has built on experience in countries such as Canada, the Netherlands, the UK and the US to establish reporting requirements similar to the US Toxic Release Inventory (TRI).

The TRI, a mandatory information tool, requires annual reporting on specific amounts and types of several hundred chemicals released or otherwise managed by certain industrial facilities. All of the information contained in the TRI database is publicly available through public libraries, electronic channels[1] and other means. Typically, these inventories cover waste generation and pollutant releases at the facility level. The Netherlands has also included some non-point sources. Leaving aside the criticisms that have been levied at TRI, such as the two-year lag in information disclosure and its limited coverage from both the business and chemicals perspectives, it remains an unequivocal testament to the power of publicly disclosed standardised information in driving business improvement. It has also been instrumental in educating business and others about the quantities and sources of industrial waste—both economic and environmental.

State laws in New Jersey and Massachusetts already address the measurement of pollution prevention. The proposed national expansion of TRI would broaden the current regulatory focus to include information on pollution prevention and resource efficiency. While business has become more comfortable in reporting on outputs, such as waste and pollutant releases, the new focus on inputs, such as materials and energy consumption, has many business opponents. TRI, the prototype in standardisation, has been a bitter-sweet experience for business. Those companies that once headed the top of the list will not easily forget the ensuing public wrath. Yet it is TRI that allows companies to take credit for dramatic reductions in pollutant releases. The protection of confidential business information is another key business concern when moving beyond end-of-pipe measurement. But evidence from New Jersey and Massachusetts indicates that few companies ever claim chemical use data as a trade secret. Nonetheless, public disclosure remains a cultural barrier and legitimate business concerns must be addressed, while fulfilling stakeholders' information needs.

◻ *Level of Focus and Linkages*

On what scale do firms typically measure and report corporate environmental performance? Until recently, the answer would have been at the facility or corporate level, with most efforts focusing on improvements in manufacturing processes. In the US, this can be traced, in part, to the facility-based TRI reporting requirements. In addition, firms typically find it easier to manage those aspects of environmental performance that reside within their factory gates. However, the next wave of environmental performance improvements will probably come from efforts to reduce the environmental impacts of products during use and disposition. For example, in the case of energy consumption in electrical appliances, 80%–90% of life-cycle environmental impact can occur during product use. This translates into higher operating costs for consumers, what some firms call the 'invisible second price tag'. The implication for future measurement development is clear: there will be greater attention paid to measures of product life-cycle performance, particularly in regard to creating competitive market advantage through improved product design.

---

1   *http://rtk.net*

Environmental performance measures are increasingly being linked with economic measures to create eco-efficiency metrics. The economic–environmental linkage is a key driver in mainstreaming environmental performance within the business community. The prefix 'eco' stands for both ecological and economic. Eco-efficiency measures typically express environmental impact per unit of value added, for example, materials or energy use per dollar of economic value added. In addition to standardising the numerator, agreement needs to be reached on the appropriate normalisation method. At present, a variety of approaches are used, including unit of product, sales dollars and economic value added. If it is standardised, economic value added has the advantage of permitting comparisons of environmental impact per dollar of economic value added across different industries.

4. Social Performance

After a brief surge of interest in the 1970s, corporate social performance all but disappeared from business radar screens. This may soon change. The recent spate of high-profile corporate social crises (e.g. Shell and human rights issues in Nigeria, Nike and 'sweatshops' in Asia, and charges of racism against Texaco), combined with growing interest in the social element of business sustainability, is resurrecting interest in corporate social performance. If Bhopal was the precursor for corporate environmental performance reporting, Shell's Brent Spar fiasco could well signal the re-emergence of corporate social citizenship. Global businesses are finding that their overseas operations and upstream activities are increasingly coming under public scrutiny. As Cor Herkstroter, Managing Director of Shell International, recently stated, 'Companies operate in an increasingly CNN world.' This increasing transparency means that businesses will be expected to assume greater social responsibility than hitherto. With the human population set to reach nearly 10 billion by 2050 and persistent North–South economic disparities, how can social issues not be key business issues?

The number of initiatives by both business and others to measure corporate social performance—although still few in comparison to environmental performance—is growing. While most activity still comes from firms such as The Body Shop, Ben & Jerry's, and Patagonia, which have an overriding corporate social culture, there are signs that corporate social reporting may soon make the leap to mainstream business. Shell, GrandMet, Denmark's Sbn Bank and General Motors have already published a corporate social or ethical report. Honeywell, Citizens' Bank of Canada, and Nike have established Vice-Presidents of Corporate Social Responsibility. Perhaps there is a growing recognition by these companies that social issues are rapidly becoming a business opportunity and source of competitive advantage.

However, there still remains considerable confusion about definitions and terminology. Terms such as corporate citizenship, eco-justice, business ethics and stakeholder relationships abound. Simply stated, business social performance measures the relationship of business with its different stakeholder groups. This definition makes social performance more readily understandable, since most businesses already have measures and accountability mechanisms for certain key stakeholder groups, such as shareholders and customers. The new social performance measurement challenge is to define business performance in relation to its impact on other stakeholders: communities, employees, developing countries, suppliers, etc. This discussion must include issues of business ethics, such as participatory decision-making, community commitment, bribery, honesty and corruption.

◻ *Towards Standardised Measures*

A consensus needs to be developed that defines what should be measured and how. In this respect, the current state of development of corporate social performance indicators is running at least a decade behind that of environmental performance. Many of the organisations working on social performance are only just beginning to turn their attention to the development of measures. Those that are doing so are typically working in isolation.

Is it realistic to think that a common set of corporate social performance indicators could be developed with universal application? To date, there is no driving force similar to that provided by the need to develop toxic release measures in the early days of environmental performance measurement. Sceptics also argue that evaluation of social performance depends on values, which differ from country to country, and even from person to person. They also point out that the choice of measures depends both on the stakeholders and specific issues of the firms. Similar arguments have been articulated for environmental performance measurement, yet the standardisation vision is gaining support. Of course, social issues and stakeholder groups differ from company to company, but it is likely that there will be a core set of social issues that have broad utility across stakeholders and firms. These might include:

- ▾ **Employment practices.** The provision of a safe working environment; financial and job security; freedom from discrimination on race, gender, colour or creed; and opportunity for professional development.

- ▾ **Community relations.** The contribution of a firm to community development, including: job creation; taxes paid/tax breaks received; philanthropy; and employee volunteerism.

- ▾ **Ethical sourcing.** Engage in fair trading practices with suppliers, distributors and partners; ensure that suppliers do not use child or forced labour, and that they provide safe working conditions and fair wages.

- ▾ **Social impact of product.** The contribution of products and services to: social welfare; equity; and the meeting of basic human needs, such as food, shelter, water and healthcare.

One potential approach for measuring the key elements of social performance is the evolving social audit process. Simon Zadek of the UK-based New Economics Foundation defines social auditing as 'a means of assessing social impact and ethical behaviour of an organisation in relation to its aims and those of its stakeholders' (Zadek *et al.* 1997). Both the Body Shop and Ben & Jerry's have used social auditing as a framework for measuring and reporting their social performance (see Chapter 26). The 1997 Body Shop *Values Report*, for example, dedicates a chapter to each stakeholder group, including: employees, franchises, suppliers, communities, shareholders and customers. For each stakeholder group, two types of indicator are used. The first involves 'quantitative' indicators and benchmarks that compare performance across similar companies (e.g. staff turnover). However, The Body Shop's efforts to benchmark externally were for the most part thwarted because of the dearth of external information on corporate social performance. The second type of indicator involves the use of 'qualitative' indicators, derived from stakeholder opinion surveys (e.g. staff perception on job security). Although helpful, stakeholder attitudes are typically difficult to gauge and need to be supplemented by external benchmarks. In the near term, focusing efforts on the standardisation of process indicators that relate to issues such as stakeholder engagement, ethical sourcing and community relations seems the most promising course of action. Not only is this likely to be more feasible, but it will also be of use to those firms that are beginning to integrate social considerations into their decision-making.

⌐ *Level of Focus and Linkages*

What about the level of focus for social performance metrics? For the most part, measurement and reporting has been at the level of the firm. The advent of *Social Accountability 8000*, a new international and inter-industry standard on workplace conditions championed by the Council on Economic Priorities Accreditation Agency (CEPAA), is likely to train measurement focus on supply chain activities, particularly in relation to the use of child and slave labour.[2] But the actual process of social reporting will probably continue at the corporate level for the foreseeable future. Exceptions might include the preparation of reports for particularly socially sensitive projects, such as mineral extraction and dam constructions which entail human resettlement issues.

Robust linkages between a firm's social performance and its economic and environmental performance have not yet been established; the link between corporate social and economic performance is especially ripe for further work. There have been efforts in the world of social and ethical investment funds to link social and financial performance, but much of this work is based on exclusions of socially objectionable businesses, such as tobacco, alcohol and weapons, rather than focusing on firms with superior social performance. While certain aspects of corporate environmental performance, such as pollution prevention and resource efficiency, can be more readily linked to the economic bottom line, social performance appears to be more top-line-sensitive. As firms such as Shell, Nestlé and Nike can attest, the

---

2   Launched in 1998, SA 8000 is a uniform auditable standard for a third-party verification system. It sets out specific requirements on child and forced labour, health and safety, union matters, discrimination, compensation, working hours and management systems. The standard was developed by a coalition led by the New York-based Council on Economic Priorities and CEPAA and is based on various conventions of the International Labour Organisation, the Universal Declaration of Human Rights, and the United Nations Convention on the Rights of the Child.

perception of a poor social record can translate into customer boycotts and reduced sales and revenues. Although attention is mostly focused on these top-line effects of negative performance, such as a fall in sales or share price, it is possible that the real business opportunities will be found in the benefits of positive social performance on both the top and bottom lines.

5. *Sustainability Performance*

In the state-of-play summary presented at the end of this chapter, the six initiatives that include measurement of both social and environmental performance are listed under the 'sustainability measures' category. In most of these initiatives, the primary focus is the environmental dimension of sustainability. Social performance is typically assessed using more qualitative metrics. To date, none of these efforts has succeeded in developing measures of business sustainability that are a true integration of social, environmental and economic performance. The current fragmented approach is partly attributable to the fact that both students and practitioners of measurement have traditionally maintained a single-sustainability-element focus. New integrated sustainability measurement tools are needed to help business and others understand how decisions translate into impacts across three dimensions of sustainability—a challenge that will need time and experimentation to move forward successfully.

One approach to integrated measurement is the use of indices that calculate a single sustainability score, based on a number of weighted individual parameters.[3] This approach trades off metric complexity for the simplicity of a single overall score. The key design issues are the numbers and types of parameter included and how they are weighted. Such indices have limited value beyond the company in which they are developed, unless the disaggregated data also is made available to permit comparisons, otherwise they risk being condemned to the 'black box' category. However, it can be a useful internal tool and the very process of assigning weights helps improve awareness of the relative importance of individual parameters.

An alternative method is a 'balanced scorecard' approach, whereby companies measure and report on their performance using a range of financial and non-financial measures. This reduces the risk of becoming too focused on a few measures, at the expense of the broader picture of overall performance. Dow Chemical, for example, is combining this approach with the use of key performance indicators to develop a sustainability measurement system that covers four broad categories of performance: economic, environment, social and health. The advantage of a balanced scorecard approach is that it trains business attention on a range of different performance measures. The challenge is in the choice and number of metrics to include, and the resulting difficulties in comprehending a broad range of indicators.

---

3   See Chapters 10 and 11 for a description and analysis of such indices at Niagara Mohawk Power Company and Unox, albeit focusing on environmental issues only.

The predominant focus of integrated sustainability measurement efforts is at the product level. In terms of reducing a firm's environmental impact, this product focus makes sense, since most business impacts stem from the manufacture and use of products. But in terms of transforming the strategic course of business towards more sustainable practices, a product-by-product focus falls short. Businesses must also develop measures at the corporate and business unit levels. A firm must ask not only 'how' it makes a product, but also ask, more fundamentally, what business it is actually in—such as whether it is exists to manufacture cars or to provide transportation services. This will help to create an overarching sustainability framework to guide both new product development and the evaluation of existing product portfolios.

As Chapter 23 demonstrates, the GRI exposure draft guidelines proposes three complementary reporting styles to help understand the interrelations and balance between the three dimensions of sustainability:

- **Systematic accounting and reporting**: a total approach comprising economic, social and environmental accounts, including both flows and accumulated balances of values. Systematic accounting and reporting requires a sophisticated knowledge of causes and effects within and between the environmental, economic and social dimensions, and, though not yet well developed, presents a model for future sustainability reporting.

- **Thematic statement**: the enterprise's interpretation of a conceptual theme—a core issue or challenge—that relates in some way to all dimensions of sustainability.

- **Case studies**: an exploration of an enterprise's decision-making in a particular situation, treating the interrelations of environmental, economic and social aspects in terms of how it manages specific situations in the past, present or future.

Integrated approaches to measuring business sustainability represent an important step forward. They help provide a better understanding of business impacts across the three dimensions of sustainability. They also act as a 'sustainability compass'—helping business and others to see more readily whether they are moving in a more sustainable direction. However, they tell us very little about the 'sustainability gap'—the distance between current performance levels and those required to achieve sustainability. In order to develop a better understanding of this gap, business must examine its relationship both with its immediate community (employees, customers, suppliers, local communities) and with broader society. After all, business does not operate in a vacuum and its ultimate sustainability depends on many external factors, such as the existence of a healthy economy and environment, access to customers who have the freedom to choose, and global markets that are not ravaged by the effects of war. New approaches to business sustainability measurement must address this gap, by developing indicators of business impact (positive–negative, direct–indirect), on broader sustainability issues, such as: quality of life; equity; human health; and ecological carrying capacity.

6. *The Global Reporting Initiative*

Both standardisation and integrated sustainability measurement may be given a boost by the launch of the GRI exposure draft guidelines in March 1999, which are reproduced in Chapter 23. One important strength of GRI is its collaborative process, involving many players. It was convened by the Coalition for Environmentally Responsible Economies (CERES) and overseen by an international Steering Group which comprises experts from corporations, professional accounting bodies, consultancies, NGOs and the United Nations. The GRI's core mission is to establish, through a global, voluntary and multi-stakeholder process, the foundation for uniform corporate sustainability reporting worldwide. It differs from existing initiatives in the scope of its membership, the breadth of its content and the framework it provides both for communication and for detailed auditing and verification. The GRI is also unique among existing reporting efforts in providing guidance on how to integrate performance information across the three dimensions of sustainability.

The GRI released a pilot version of its guidelines at an international symposium in London in March 1999,[4] which will be tested by approximately two dozen companies, and the GRI will invite feedback from a much wider range of stakeholders. In parallel with this pilot testing and feedback, the GRI will develop a strategy to shift ownership of the GRI process and products to an independent, permanent host organisation capable of monitoring, refining and promoting standardised sustainability reporting in the future. Imagine that the GRI is successful in its mission to establish through a process of consensus a set of reporting guidelines that are used globally by business. Next, consider the possible implications for a range of different stakeholders—business, communities, customers, financial institutions, governments and other reporting initiatives:sustainability reporting

Business

The business constituency, both as a user and reporter of information, represents the single most important audience for the GRI. Over the past decade, business has encountered a growing list of demands for information on its environmental and social performance, from a range of stakeholders, including customers, governments, NGOs, communities and the financial and investment sector. Typically, each request is framed in a different way, which imposes a significant reporting burden on the targeted company—especially if it has global operations. Furthermore, the resulting information constitutes a jumble of different indicators that generally cannot be compared over time, even for the same company. In fact it is virtually impossible, at this time, for a company to benchmark its performance against other companies using existing publicly available information. The adoption of a global sustainability reporting standard should lighten the reporting burden for companies, increase the value of reported information, and enable corporate leaders to distinguish

4 See *www.ceres.org* for further information.

themselves from lagging competitors and thereby to take credit for their achievements. A global measurement and reporting standard could also provide a credible tool to enable novel regulatory approaches that broker regulatory flexibility in exchange for public accountability of improved environmental performance. And, even if a company decides not to report publicly on its sustainability performance, it will still need a powerful instrument with which to measure its performance and manage its affairs internally.

Communities

Communities typically seek access to information on the environmental performance of local facilities. They also have an interest in the employment and social policies of firms: Will the company provide jobs for local people? Will the firm be a good neighbour to the community? How will a company manage closures of plants to minimise the social impacts on the surrounding community? Although the GRI's initial focus is on providing information at the level of a company, rather than a facility, communities are likely to find broad utility from being able to benchmark companies' performance across a range of social, environmental and economic criteria.

Customers

Currently, it is impossible either for business, as commercial customers, or for the public, as consumers, to distinguish between products and providers based on social and environmental performance during production, use and disposal. Championing the role of discerning consumers is ultimately central to the success of market-based solutions to environmental and social problems. For this demand-led approach to work, however, there must be a credible and transparent comparison mechanism to permit customers to distinguish both products and providers on the basis of performance. A global measurement and reporting standard, while not replacing the need for existing certification schemes, will nonetheless facilitate access to some of the critical information on which these schemes are based.

Financial Institutions

Harnessing the power of the financial community's investment, lending and insurance decisions both to reward and to promote corporate sustainability remains an elusive goal. Two prerequisites are necessary to make corporate sustainability a routine part of financial decisions. First, a clear quantifiable link must be made between corporate sustainability performance and financial performance. Second, information gaps on corporate sustainability must be filled, and a standardised method must emerge that governs the measurement and reporting of corporate sustainability. The GRI clearly addresses the information gap. It may also help to establish a link between sustainability and financial performance. In other words, if a global measurement and reporting tool emerges that has widespread buy-in, different stakeholders will increasingly be able to factor corporate sustainability performance into a broad array of decisions, such as purchasing, recruitment, permitting and investment. The effect of this collective action will be to financially reward companies with superior performance, while penalising those with poor performance.

◻ *Employees*

A number of studies about audiences for corporate environmental reports (Bennett and James 1998a; SustainAbility/UNEP 1996a) suggest that a company's own employees are considered an important target group. Just how much employees take advantage of the opportunity afforded by the GRI to make comparisons between their own firm's performance on both social and environmental issues remains to be seen. It is also not clear how useful highly aggregated information at the level of a company will be to the internal audience. The aggregated information contained in the GRI report might be thought of as the tip of the iceberg—supported by more detailed, but publicly unavailable, information below the surface. Environmental performance information at the level of a facility or product is likely to be more useful and relevant to internal audiences. However, for certain aspects of sustainability reporting, such as information on employment practices, employees might well be interested in comparing their own company's practices with those of other firms, and, where appropriate, using the information to leverage improvements in their own workplace. Reports using GRI-style information will support this aspect of benchmarking.

◻ *Governments*

Corporate sustainability reporting is not being driven by voluntary efforts alone: as mentioned above, a number of countries have established mandatory reporting requirements for certain elements of business sustainability.[5] In order to reduce the reporting burden on companies, and avoid a plethora of different reporting formats across borders, national governments might consider incorporating GRI reporting formats into their national reporting requirements. Governments could also use GRI-style reporting as a mechanism for tracking corporate progress on implementing national commitments under international conventions, such as the Kyoto Protocol. The GRI will also enable governments to benchmark the performance of their country's industrial sectors with those in other countries. As an example, the Netherlands government is developing an Energy Efficiency Covenant with energy-intensive companies which will not impose any additional energy efficiency requirements, providing that companies involved can demonstrate, through international benchmarking, that they are the best in the world for their specific sector.[6]

---

5   See Chapters 16 and 17 for reviews of the environmental reporting that has recently become required by law of companies in Denmark and the Netherlands respectively.

6   Personal communication with Wilfred Albias, Dutch Ministry of Housing, Spatial Planning and the Environment, November 1998.

◻ *Other Reporting Initiatives*

What are the implications of the GRI for the many other voluntary reporting initiatives? Whether or not the GRI is ultimately successful in its bold mission, there will always be a need for diversity in voluntary reporting initiatives. Corporate sustainability is a relatively new and evolving concept, and much effort is still needed to address the various complexities and cultural differences of interpreting what corporate sustainability means, and how it should be measured and reported. Indeed, it would be arrogant for an initiative to assume that it could be everything to everyone. The challenge is to find a balance between the need for standardisation and the importance of encouraging experimentation and specialisation in regard to this multifaceted issue. However, some convergence on the definition of basic reference elements of reporting, such as defining the boundaries of a company for reporting purposes, common identifiers and reporting time-frames, would help to reduce confusion and overlap between different voluntary reporting initiatives. This would help clarify the difference between schemes that provide reporting guidance, such as the GRI's guidelines, and those that certify conformance to practice or systems standards, such as SA 8000 and ISO 14001.

7. Conclusions

Clever businesses are starting to recognise that there are many benefits in measuring and reporting on sustainability. It heightens internal awareness of its various dimensions and stimulates management action. It can also enhance their reputation and stakeholder relations, and ultimately maintain the company's licence to operate, and its bottom line.

However, the current fragmented approach to corporate sustainability measurement and reporting does not serve the purpose of helping companies describe and disclose their accountability for the social, environmental and economic impacts of their operations around the globe. Nor does it meet the needs of a growing number of stakeholders who seek information on business performance in relation to sustainability. A uniform global framework will ultimately serve the interests and needs of both business and other stakeholders.

It is inevitable that such a framework will eventually emerge. At present, the GRI seems to be the best seed to begin its growth. But the framework will be built from more than one component and is likely to be assembled from some of the pieces available today: financial reporting schemes, voluntary environmental reporting initiatives, and the emerging social performance measurement movement. In a world with nearly twice the current human population, there will be little room for businesses that fail to demonstrate progress toward sustainability based on the 'three Cs' principles—comparability, credibility and completeness.

◢ Appendix
The State of Play: A Summary of Initiatives[7]

◻ Environmental Performance Measurement

American Institute of Chemical Engineers Sustainability Metrics Project
A collaborative project aimed at developing a group of core and optional metrics for each of the seven areas of eco-efficiency promulgated by the WBCSD. *Contact Dana Ponciroli on +1 212 705 7462 or at danap@aiche.org*

Association of Chartered Certified Accountants
A 1998 report, *Environment under the Spotlight: Current Practices and Future Trends in Environment-Related Performance Measurement for Business* (Bennett and James 1998a), reviews current practice and future trends in environmental performance measurement, together with the results of a practitioners survey. *Contact Roger Adams on +44 171 396 5971, or at roger.adams@acca.co.uk*

Business in the Community
BitC has developed an index of environmental management. *Contact Peter Davis on +44 171 224 1600, or at pdavies@bitc.org.uk*

Consolidated Uniform Report for the Environment (CURE)
An EPA-initiated effort, the Consolidated Uniform Report for the Environment (CURE) was created in order to simplify and clarify both the reporting of and accessibility to environmental performance information in the electronics sector. *Contact Daphne McMurrer on +1 512 239 5920, or visit http://www.epa.gov/ooaujeag/csi/computer/cure/htm*

Council on Economic Priorities
CEP publishes a quarterly SCREEN report on business environmental performance and conducts an annual Campaign for Cleaner Corporations. *Contact CEP on +1 212 420 1133 or at CEP@echonyc.com*

Dow Eco-Compass
A product assessment tool that measures life-cycle impact along six 'poles': energy intensity; mass intensity; environmental and health risk; sustainability of resource usage; extent of revalorisation; and service intensity. *Contact Claude Fussler on +41 172 82 403, or visit http://www.dow.com/cgi-bin/frameup.cgi?/environment/ehs.html*

Eco-Efficiency Assessment Per Unit of Service (ECOPUS)
The ECOPUS metric calculates the utility of a product in relation to the burden it imposes on the environment during its life-cycle. *Contact Ir. N. van Nes at Delft University of Technology on +31 15 278 4521 or at N.vanNes@IO.TUDelft.nl*

Environmental Defense Fund Chemical Scorecard
EDF's Chemical Scorecard provides a free World Wide Web service that allows users to rank US facilities by TRI data. *Visit http://www.scorecard.org*

The European Chemical Industry Council (CEFIC)
CEFIC has introduced new health, safety and environmental reporting guidelines. *Contact J. Busson on +32 2 676 7302 or at jbs@cefic.be, or visit http://www.cefic.be/*

---

7   Readers interested in a more detailed description of the initiatives are referred to the WRI website, *http://www.wri.org/wri/meb/*

European Eco-Management and Auditing Scheme (EMAS)
Europe's alternative to ISO 14000 requires participants to publish an independently verified site-specific public environmental statement containing information on environmental performance. Currently undergoing review by the EU. *Contact EMAS on +32 2 502 04 72 or at emas@dg11.cec.be*

Global Environmental Management Initiative
GEMI, a partnership of 21 leading US companies, published a 1997 primer that examines the design of an EMS through the use of performance indicators. *Contact GEMI on +1 202 296 7449 or at mgemi@worldweb.net*

International Standards Organisation: ISO 14031
The draft ISO standard on environmental performance evaluation provides guidance on the selection, use and reporting of corporate environmental performance. *Contact Steve Cornish on +1 212 642 4969, or visit http://www.iso.ch*

Investor Responsibility Research Center
IRRC calculates three indices of business environmental performance: an emissions efficiency index, a spill index, and a compliance index. *Contact Mark Bateman on +1 202 833 0700*

National Academy of Engineering: Industrial Environmental Performance Metrics
A forthcoming NAE report identifies factors that have contributed to industrial environmental performance improvements and recommends ways in which better approaches of measuring performance may be incorporated into business strategies and governmental policies. *Contact Deanna Richards on +1 202 334 1679 or at metrics@nae.edu*

NPI Global Warming Indicator
A generic framework that calculates both an aggregate and normalised measure of a firm's carbon dioxide equivalent emissions by summing emissions from transport use, energy use, and process related emissions and normalising by unit turnover. *Contact Toby Belsom on +44 171 665 3458*

National Round Table on the Environment and the Economy
The Canadian-based NRTEE's Eco-efficiency Program is developing a measurement system for eco-efficiency, including methods of assessing the eco-efficiency concept, in order to develop wide acceptance of those indicators and to build commitment to their routine inclusion in corporate annual reports. *Contact Elizabeth Atkinson on +1 613 943 0394 or at admin@nrtee-trnee.ca, or visit http://www.nrtee-trnee.ca*

OECD Pollutant Release and Transfer Registers
Through a series of international workshops, the OECD developed and published a 1996 guidance document to aid governments developing facility reporting on releases to air, land and water, and transfers to waste facilities. *Contact OECD at ehscont@oecd.org, or visit http://www.oecd.org/ehs/prtr/index.htm*

Storebrand Scudder Environmental Value Fund
Storebrand Scudder uses a proprietary sustainability index to assess business environmental performance in regard to: global warming, ozone depletion, material efficiency, toxic release, energy intensity, water use, environmental liabilities and environmental management quality. *Contact Storebrand on +47 22 31 29 31, or visit www.storebrand.no/web/enelsk.nsf=20*

SustainAbility/UNEP Environmental Reporting Framework

A five-stage model for environmental performance reporting, covering management policies and systems; inputs and outputs; finance; stakeholder relations; and sustainable development. *Contact SustainAbility on +44 171 937 9996 or at info@sustainability.co.uk*

UNCTAD

The United Nations Conference on Trade and Development's Intergovernmental Working Group of Experts on International Standards of Accounting and Reporting is developing a global standard on environmental accounting that focuses on the reporting of environmental costs and liabilities that affect financial performance. *Visit www.unctad.org*

Verein für Umweltmanagement in Banken, Sparkassen und Versicherungen (VfU)

VfU, the German Association for Environmental Management in Banks, Savings Banks and Insurance Companies, has published a guidance document for environmental reporting that defines 11 metrics: two for energy consumption, one for water consumption, three for paper consumption, three for waste generation, two for business traffic (measured in km/yr/employee) and one for carbon dioxide emissions. *Contact Gabriella Urban on +49 228 766 8494 or at 101330.3112@compuserve.com*

WBCSD Eco-efficiency Metrics Project

The project intends to define a standardised set of eco-efficiency metrics. *Contact Marcus Lehni on +41 22 839 31 84 or at Lehni@wbcsd.ch*

World Resources Institute

The WRI is convening a collaborative multi-stakeholder effort to develop a standardised protocol for measuring and reporting an organisation's greenhouse gas emissions. *Contact Janet Ranganathan on +1 202 729 7656 or at Janetr@wri.org, or visit http://www.wri.org/wri/meb/*

Wuppertal Materials Intensity Per Unit of Service

The German-based Wuppertal Institute has proposed a product life-cycle-based metric that quantifies environmental burden per unit of service in terms of all the direct and indirect material inputs associated with the manufacture and use of a product. *Contact F. Hinterberger on +49 202 2492 0, or visit http://www.wupperinst.org*

◿ Social Performance Measurement

Ben & Jerry's

Ben & Jerry's, a Vermont-based ice cream company, publishes an annual independently audited social report constructed around key stakeholders. *Contact Ben & Jerry's on +1 802 651 9600, or visit http://www.benjerry.com*

The Body Shop International

Kirk Hanson, at Stanford Business School, conducted an independent evaluation of the social performance and impact of The Body Shop using 39 dimensions of social performance, organised primarily by stakeholder group. *Contact Kirk Hanson on +1 650 723 2270 or at hanson.kirk@GSB.stanford.edu; contact The Body Shop on +44 181 202 9426, or visit http://www.the-body-shop.com*

Business in the Community

BitC's principles of corporate community investment include a set of indicators to measure investment impact in a community. *Contact Peter Davis on +44 171 224 1600 or at pdavies@bitc.org.uk*

Business for Social Responsibility
In 1998 BSR launched a Global Business Responsibility Resource Center and programmes in the areas of governance and accountability. *Contact Nik Haas-Dehejia on +1 415 537 0890 ext. 122 or at ndehejia@bsr.org*

Conference Board
In 1996 the Conference Board undertook a survey to assess the extent to which companies measure and benchmark their contributions and community relations programmes. *Contact Myra Alperson on +1 212 339 0435, or visit http://www.conference-board.org*

Corporate Citizenship Company
A UK-based research consultancy that has developed models to help companies assess their community involvement activities, social responsibility and supply chain management. *Contact Michael Tuffrey on +44 171 287 6676 or at mtuffrey@cix.co.uk*

Council on Economic Priorities
CEP undertakes many activities on corporate social performance, including an annual Corporate Conscience Award and a new project to develop methods for assessing transnational corporate responsibility. *Contact cep on +1 212 420 1133 or at CEP@echonyc.com*

EthicScan Canada
EthicScan reports on corporate metrics through publications such as: *Shopping with a Conscience*, *Lemon-Aid: The Consumer Guide* (1998) and a newsletter, *The Corporate Ethics Monitor*. *Contact Paul Pellizzari on +1 416 783 6776 or at ethic@concentric.net, or visit http://www.ethicscan.on.ca*

Ethical Trading Initiative
A UK-based initiative that aims to develop and promote the use of standards, codes of conduct and monitoring and auditing methods, to enable companies to work with organisations outside the corporate sector to improve labour conditions around the world. *Visit www.EthicalTrade.org*

Institute of Social and Ethical AccountAbility
AccountAbility, a UK-based professional body, is developing standards for social and ethical accounting, auditing and reporting. *Contact AccountAbility at http://www.accountability.org.uk*

Interfaith Center on Corporate Responsibility
In 1998 ICCR's Principles Project published *Principles for Global Corporate Responsibility: Bench Marks for Measuring Business Performance* to help forward the dialogue on corporate social responsibility and investing. *Contact David Schilling on +1 212 870 2928 or at david@iccr.org*

International Labour Organisation Human Development Enterprise Index
The ILO has developed an index to measure the orientation of enterprises toward human development which is an amalgam of three individual indexes, covering: enterprise skill formation; work security and social equity (non-discriminatory labour practices); and economic equity or earning differentials between employees. *Contact Guy Standing at ILO, or visit http://www.ilo.org*

Investor Responsibility Research Center
The IRRC's Social Issues Service publishes an independent newsletter, *Corporate Social Issues Reporter*, which provides data on corporate social responsibility. *Contact IRRC on +1 202 833 0700*

New Economics Foundation
The UK-based New Economics Foundation, an independent research charity, has an indicators programme that focuses on developing indicators of quality of life and sustainable development. *Contact Peter Raynard on +44 171 377 5696 or at neweconomics@gn.apc.org*

Social Accountability Standard (SA 8000)
The Center for Economics Priorities Accreditation Agency launched a social accountability standard, SA 8000, which focuses on ethical sourcing, including: child and forced labour, health and safety, union matters, discrimination, compensation, working hours and management systems. *Contact CEPAA on +44 171 831 9420 or at SA8000@aol.com*

Social Equity Funds
There are numerous social investment or equity funds that screen firms on the basis of social performance. For example, the Domini Social Equity Fund assesses performance in four areas: safe and useful products, employee relations, corporate citizenship, and the environment. *Contact Steve Lydenburg on +1 800 762 6814*

Social Venture Network
SVN's Social Performance Project is using their ten global principles for corporate social responsibility to develop a business implementation model of corporate social responsibility. *Contact Edward Goodell on +1 973 744 6464 or at Goodell@Concentric.net*

The Stakeholder Alliance
The Stakeholder Alliance has developed the Sunshine Standards for corporate reporting to stakeholders as an alternative to general accepted accounting standards. *Contact Ralph Estes on +1 202 797 0600 or at stakeholder@essential.org, or visit http://www.essential.org/capp/sa.html*

WBCSD Corporate Social Responsibility Project
This project is examining corporate social responsibility on three tiers: scoping/mapping the boundaries; practice; and measuring, assessing and reporting. *Contact Margaret Flaherty on +41 22 839 3100 or at Flaherty@WBCSD.ch, or visit http://www.wbcsd.ch/*

⌑ Sustainability Measures

The Colombian Business Council for Sustainable Development
CECODES, a regional arm of the WBCSD, publishes an annual report that includes indicators of economic performance, eco-efficiency and social responsibility. *Contact María Emilia Correa at cecodes@colomsat.net.com*

Global Reporting Initiative
The CERES-led GRI seeks to standardise corporate environmental and social performance reporting worldwide. *Contact Judith Kuszewski on +1 617 247 0700, or visit http://www.ceres.org*

McDonough Braungart Design Chemistry: Product Sustainability Index
MBDC, a Virginia-based product development and design firm, is developing a proprietary product-based Index of Sustainability based on three interdependent performance categories (ecology, social equity and economy). *Contact Joe Rinkevich on +1 804 295 1111, or visit http://www.mbdc.com*

Öko-Institut Product Sustainability Assessment Tool
In a 1997 study produced for Hoechst chemical company, the German non-profit Öko-Institut developed a product sustainability assessment tool (PROSA) for rating the sustainability of new product design and business development efforts. *Contact Christian Hochfeld on +49 61 518 19133 or at hochfeld@oeko.de, or visit http://www.oeko.de*

The Sustainability Product Wheel
Building on Dow's Eco-Compass, Peter James of UK-based Sustainable Business has developed a framework for assessing the sustainability of products, utilising a generic performance assessment model (see appendix of Chapter 13). *Contact Peter James on +44 1260 290472 or at sustainablebusiness@compuserve.com*

Wuppertal Sustainability Indicators
Joachim Spangenberg and Odile Bonniot from the German-based Wuppertal Institute have published a draft set of business sustainability indicators in a February 1998 paper from Wuppertal's Sustainable Societies Programme. *Contact Joachim Spangenberg at Spangenberg@wupperinst.org*

25
Socially Challenged

Trends in Social Reporting

John Elkington and Franceska van Dijk

CORPORATE SOCIAL ACCOUNTABILITY and reporting is becoming increasingly relevant for business. This chapter reviews the wide spectrum of work under way in this area, and its relationship to environmental accountability and reporting. It is based on SustainAbility's recently published *Social Reporting Report*, which was produced in partnership with the United Nations Environment Programme and Royal Dutch/Shell Group (SustainAbility/UNEP 1999a).

The 1990s have seen an explosion in the number of companies reporting on their environmental performance and targets. The process started in 1990, with pioneering companies such as Norsk Hydro in Norway and Monsanto in the USA, but the trend has widened out rapidly to embrace most sectors, including even financial services companies such as banks.

Even though many of these reporting companies had signed *sustainable development* charters such as that launched by the International Chamber of Commerce (ICC) in 1991, they saw the challenge as *environmental performance and reporting*. This approach was challenged in the mid-1990s by the introduction of the concept of the 'triple bottom line' of sustainable development (Elkington 1997). This focuses companies and other organisations not only on their environmental performance but also on their economic and social impacts (SustainAbility/UNEP 1998a).

Although international government organisations, among them the International Labour Organisation (ILO) and the United Nations Environment Programme (UNEP), have long been active in this area, business is now starting to engage. Business organisations and companies are doing so because they increasingly see corporate social responsibility and accountability as a strategic business issue. Some are also now beginning to explore the links with the triple bottom line of sustainable development. And recent turmoil in world financial markets has further increased the pressures for greater transparency by business.

The corporate accountability challenge is now greatest in two areas: first, in social and ethical accounting and reporting; and, second, in the integration of the three different streams of information into management accounts and decision-making.

◣ From 'Trust Me' to 'Show Me'

In the past, business leaders—and, to a degree, politicians—could rely on a culture where there was a greater degree of trust in the 'Establishment'. In its *Profits and Principles* report, Shell International notes that the world is moving from a 'Trust Me' culture (where companies can rely on society's broad acceptance that they act in good faith), through a 'Tell Me' culture (where society wants to be told what is going on) to a 'Show Me' culture (in which companies have to demonstrate their serious intent to change for the better).

Different parts of the world still operate on different lines, clearly. Until the recent focus on 'crony capitalism' in countries such as Indonesia and Malaysia, for example, most of Asia was still very much in 'Trust Me' mode. But the globalisation of the media, leading to the creation of what some dub a 'CNN World', means that all major international companies will increasingly be exposed to 'Tell Me' and 'Show Me' requirements.

So what does this greater accountability imply? For many companies, it means turning the concept of a 'Show Me' world into a reality—and a starting point is to listen to stakeholders and respond to their views. The result will be a seismic shift. The implications for corporate governance, strategy, management, auditing and reporting are profound. And we see social accountability and reporting as central drivers in the process.

◣ What is corporate social reporting?

There are a number of definitions of corporate social reporting, but one of the best known comes from the Institute of Social and Ethical Accountability (ISEA), whose concept of social and ethical accounting, auditing and reporting (SEAAR) is becoming increasingly influential. It is important, however, to distinguish between the *process* of corporate social accounting and the *end-product*, the corporate social report.

As in other areas of corporate disclosure, diversity rules here, too. To date, there is no such thing as a 'standard' social report, because the nature of each report depends on: the range of stakeholders for whom it is intended; what the reporting organisation is trying to achieve; and the variety of issues covered. Some people debate whether aspects of social reporting—for example, community relations—are properly part of a corporate environmental report (CER), or whether environmental reporting should be seen as part of wider corporate social reporting. It is our view that corporate social accounting and reporting represent one of three (social, environmental and economic) dimensions of triple-bottom-line accounting and reporting, and that these three bottom lines will become increasingly integrated as we move towards 'sustainability reporting': the focus of SustainAbility's forthcoming 1999 benchmark survey.

◢ An Emerging Toolkit

Today, environmental management and reporting is treated by a growing number of companies as a core business activity, and SEAAR is fast following suit. Why? In terms of business benefits, social accounting and reporting can be seen as an emerging set of management tools that can:

- ◢ Reinforce and communicate the company's core values and visions

- ◢ Identify 'blind spots' and areas of weakness, pinpointing high-risk activities requiring sound management

- ◢ Promote stability and protect organisations from unexpected shocks

- ◢ Create windows on the world, helping companies explore and understand stakeholder concerns and interests

- ◢ Help all organisations, including NGOs, understand how to manage 'intangibles', such as reputation and trust

- ◢ Provide a credible means of communicating with stakeholders

- ◢ Help companies attract, understand, motivate and retain employees in an economy that is increasingly reliant on knowledge, not just products

But with no agreement as to what a social report should look like, and no common language or agreed approach to social reporting, the need for convergence is pressing. Setting up a framework for the process of social accounting and reporting is one of the key challenges now facing organisations committed to the sustainability transition. And there is no better time than a global economic downturn in which to think or rethink.

◢ Areas of Diversity

Anyone looking at social reports for the first time may have problems finding many similarities between them. There is common ground, but practitioners in SEAAR inevitably approach the subject from different angles. Below we explore four ways in which such reports can differ.

Philanthropy versus Social Value Added. Many companies bring out community reports which are little more than a description of their philanthropic activities. Although this is a form of social reporting (and communities are indeed an important stakeholder group), there is a stark and growing differentiation between those companies that see the strategic business value of their social activities, and those who treat these as an 'add-on'. Companies such as Tata Iron and Steel, United Utilities, Diageo and British Petroleum go to great lengths to measure, evaluate and benchmark their social activities, viewing their standing in the community as key to their future business potential.

Ethical versus Social. Some experts, such as Sheena Carmichael of Ethos, argue that getting the internal ethics of an organisation straight has to be the main priority. Everything else, she believes, will follow, including reporting. Others advocate a broader approach, in which stakeholders are widely consulted. This is typical, for example, of the methodology used by the New Economics Foundation (NEF), adopted by companies such as The Body Shop and VanCity Credit Union.

Company Voice versus Stakeholders' Voices. There is a school of thought, represented by Professor Rob Gray at the Centre for Social and Environmental Accounting Research (CSEAR), that social accounting can be modelled on conventional accounting thinking—in which the sole reporting entity is the company itself. Most of us are familiar with the financial accounts laid out in company annual reports, but few are probably aware that, in the UK at least, annual reports are required by law to include social information on, among other things: charitable donations, pension fund adequacy, employment data and employee share ownership schemes.

Gray calls this type of disclosure 'silent accounting', and believes that the practice could form a template for truly benchmarkable corporate social reporting. This approach, however, is very different from that adopted by NEF, which tends to combine internal and external participant inputs, focusing on the 'voices' of stakeholders, rather than that of the company.

Verified versus Unverified. There is also some disagreement about external verification. In the traditionally 'high-trust' countries of Scandinavia, there is often little or no perceived social need for a third party to verify reports or the methodologies used. The assumption is that an organisation will be honest. Thus, the Ethical Accounts produced by Denmark's Sbn Bank are not externally verified. In the UK and North American context, by contrast, readers' scepticism means that many consider an unverified report to be little more than a PR document. As a result, there is a growing trend towards third-party verification.

◢ A Strong Convergence

We should not over-stress the areas of divergence, however. Indeed, Professor Peter Pruzan of the Copenhagen Business School, a pioneer in 'ethical accounting' in Scandinavia, is distinctly upbeat. He notes that there is 'a strong convergence in terminology, methodology and practice'. And ISEA, in which many of the key actors are now involved, is tackling the task of drawing together mainstream approaches to SEAAR. If one looks at who is undertaking SEAAR work, the companies and organisations are increasingly mainstream. Where once values-led organisations such as Traidcraft, VanCity and The Body Shop blazed the trail, we now see mainstream organisations such as BP, BT, IKEA, Novo Nordisk, Rio Tinto and Shell joining in. And where pioneers such as Ethos and NEF once worked in isolation, mainstream management accountancy groups are now beginning to pile in. Hopefully, these trends will help spread the new thinking to a much larger universe of companies and other organisations as we move into the 21st century. Some key questions are:

What are the implications for corporate environmental reporting? In social reporting, the environment is often considered to be a 'stakeholder' like any other. So will social reports replace environmental reports, simply including some environmental data? No. Instead, here are some clues to the future. NEF has developed a set of assessment criteria for social reports called the 'Quality Scoring Framework'. Building on the SustainAbility/UNEP environmental reporting criteria and 'Five-Stage Model', the NEF 'Five-Stage Ladder' of social reporting will help benchmark future social reports.

As far as integrated triple-bottom-line reporting is concerned, The Centre for Tomorrow's Company (1998) proposes a new format for company annual reports in its *Prototype plc* report. The CERES Global Reporting Initiative (GRI) aims to integrate the three dimensions of sustainability reporting (see Chapter 23). And the forthcoming 1999 SustainAbility/UNEP benchmark survey will focus on sustainability or 'triple-bottom-line' reporting.

Is this a Trojan Horse? This is a real worry for some companies, particularly those based in the USA. They fear that sustainable development and social reporting potentially represent Trojan Horses—through which socialism (or even communism) might be wheeled in through the back door. Anything is possible in human affairs, but it is far more likely that social reporting—and the social dimension of sustainability reporting—will provide business with channels through which to re-engage key stakeholders.

Will social reporting become mandatory? In some parts of the world, yes. France already has a legal requirement for companies with over 300 employees to produce a *Bilan Social*, and it looks as if Brazil will be following suit. But elsewhere this is going to remain an uphill struggle.

What is the link with sustainable development? Sustainable development will be most likely—and will be achieved at the lowest overall cost to the economy—in societies enjoying the highest levels of trust and other forms of 'social capital'. Broadly, social reporting can bring clarity to the ways in which social capital is created, conserved, effectively invested or eroded in any given society.

What's the best way to address stakeholders? Most fully fledged social reports address the interests of many of their key stakeholders simultaneously. On the other hand, some approaches focus on just one stakeholder. The appendix examines the needs of five core stakeholder groups—employees, communities, suppliers, clients/customers and investors—and examines the indicators that are most commonly reported against and the ways in which the information is reported. For each stakeholder group we also 'spotlight' the activities of a company that is undertaking active dialogue with that particular group.

◢ Conclusions and Recommendations

We conclude that social accounting, auditing and reporting will be a central business agenda item in the early years of the 21st century. In terms of advice to would-be reporters, we offer six recommendations. Here they are in summary:

First, build the business case. Think early on about institutional barriers, cost and budgets. Pioneering SEAAR companies report costs ranging from C$100,000 (VanCity) through US$750,000 (The Body Shop) per cycle. In the case of companies the size of BP or Shell, however, the costs can be significantly greater when international verification processes are taken into account.

Second, spotlight the financial risks and opportunities. In preparing your business case, include the financial risks linked to key aspects of your organisation's actual or perceived performance against the social bottom line. Among the risks that may surface are: alienated stakeholders; a damaged reputation; an impaired or lost licence to operate; and disillusioned financial analysts and shareholders. At the same time, ponder potential business opportunities in this area. These might include: better employee morale; greater community tolerance for any occasional mistakes; more loyal customers and new contracts and business relationships.

Third, understand the changing role of governments. There are some world regions where government is weak or virtually non-existent. The SEAAR approach will be almost impossible in such places. In some countries, governments are struggling. One example is South Africa, but the country is producing some very interesting company reports, including the *Corporate Citizenship Review* by South African Breweries. In some such countries, business is having to fill something of an accountability vacuum.

Fourth, focus on benchmarkability—and benchmark. Ensure that the indicators and metrics in your social reporting are appropriate and benchmarkable. And consider including benchmark survey information in your reports.

Fifth, don't fall into the local/global divide. Globalisation will continue, despite current difficulties in countries such as Indonesia, Malaysia, Thailand and Russia. But there will be political environments in which social reporting will not work— for example, in countries: where there are gross abuses of human rights or civil insecurity (e.g. Myanmar, Rwanda, Sri Lanka); where there is endemic corruption (e.g. Nigeria, Russia); or where transparency is seen as a negative virtue (e.g. Japan). Recognise the differences between emerging global standards and local values and expectations. As Ann Leikersfeldt, Director of Compensation and Labour Relations at Novo Nordisk, points out, there are 'huge difficulties facing companies who want global operating standards, but for whom local social indicators are very important. For example, human rights concerns are very different in South Africa, China and Denmark'(SustainAbility/UNEP 1999a).

Sixth, fasten your safety belt. As the recession bites and competition intensifies, expect growing pressure to downgrade the importance of social and environmental priorities. But also expect these same trends to intensify social pressures on capitalism in general and on exposed corporations in particular. New sectors are now coming under pressure, among them gambling. The Australian industry is under fire, for example, and the battered UK lottery company Camelot says it will spend £250,000 on a social audit to restore its reputation before bidding for a new licence.

The number of social reports rolling into the office is growing steadily. We are also hearing a significant number of international companies pledging themselves to produce their first sustainability or triple-bottom-line reports in the near future. These, by definition, will report against a range of social and ethical indicators.

Even longer term, some early pioneers in this area expect to see major changes. 'In ten years, we won't have social reports—we're going to move towards not simply web-delivered reports but also to real-time reporting', according to Simon Zadek, development director at NEF. 'Audiences will become users of information, rather than just receivers. Software will enable each user to access and assemble customised information from the original accounts'(SustainAbility/UNEP 1999a). There is a lot still to do, clearly.

◢ *Appendix: Stakeholder Approaches to Social Reporting*

◻ *Employees*

Why? Time and again, organisations putting together social reports stress that the real value to their company had been in the process of auditing, rather than in the existence of the final product, or audit report. Ethical auditing, explained Sheena Carmichael of the UK consultancy Ethos, 'is crucially about the values of a company and how they are implemented first internally, then externally. Change always comes from within—get things right internally', she argued, 'then these basic values will expand outwardly to the relationship between the company and its stakeholders' (Elkington and Stibbard 1997). In other words, the most crucial stakeholders of all in the SEAAR process are employees.

What? It is no surprise that most companies producing full-blooded social reports talk in some detail about employees. Typically, areas covered include gender and ethnic ratios, pay rates, benefits, holidays, training and qualitative comments about various aspects of job satisfaction.

How? Social reports such as The Body Shop's 1997 *Values Report* and the Co-operative Bank's 1997 *Partnership Report* include detailed qualitative and quantitative sections on employment issues, in which employees' views are highlighted. In contrast, Italy's UNIPOL Assicurazioni's 1995 *Rapporto Sociale* is more objective in tone, concentrating on quantitative employment data.

Investors in People (IIP). 'Getting things right internally' may not necessarily mean developing a report for public consumption. In the UK, the prestigious IIP standard requires companies to develop rolling staff training programmes and demonstrate to assessors how they relate to business strategy. The report is not published publicly, but the IIP award is usually enough to convince most people that this is a company that takes its staff and their potential at work seriously.

Sozialbericht and Sozialbilanz. Like the *Bilan Social* (see 'Spotlight on Renault', below), the German *Sozialbericht* grew out of labour concerns stemming from strike action in the 1960s and 1970s. Despite its declining popularity, some companies are still committed to *Sozialbericht*, and some of the documents make impressive reading. ABB Switzerland and the communications giant Bertelsmann produce comprehensive reports, while Saarbergwerke, the mining company, publishes a *Sozialbilanz*—which includes a financial analysis of funds spent on employees, society and the environment and national, state and local governments (i.e. taxes and other contributions).

Are these reports credible? The answer is yes: each carries a wealth of factual and qualitative data and, although not verified, includes a statement from either a trade union member or an elected employee representative.

Spotlight on Renault, France. In common with all French companies with over 300 employees, Renault is required by law to produce an annual *Bilan Social*: an employee report that includes information under a variety of category headings, including:

- Gender/age

- Levels of remuneration

- Hygiene and security

- Hours of work

- Noise and night work

- Staff development and training

- Indications of internal social climate

- Initiatives such as employer subsidies to staff facilities.

The resulting quantitative and financial report is factual and detailed, and is used internally to benchmark progress over time. Prepared for employees, shareholders and government inspectors (who check the data), the *Bilan Social* is not intended for the general public, although some companies such as Renault will make them available on request.

⌐ *Communities*

Why? For many years, corporate community involvement (CCI) was regarded as essentially a charitable activity, operating in the margins of mainstream business life. Perhaps it is worth pointing out, however, that the CCI concept is predominantly British and North American.

On the European continent, where the state is more active than in the UK or the USA, many companies emphasise that their most important role in social cohesion is as the providers of employment. And in smaller countries, such as Denmark, companies are often viewed as an integral part of society, rather than as separate entities.

Increasingly, however, leading companies are recognising that it is smart to track, measure, benchmark and report on their community activities—for some, or all, of the following reasons:

1. Companies need to know how much they are spending, what they are spending it on, and with what results.

2. A 1997 MORI survey in the UK revealed that 81% of people feel that knowing about a company's activities in society and the community is important when judging that company (MORI 1997).

3. Tracking and reporting on community projects gives the recipients of funding a chance to provide feedback, and to suggest ways of improving on projects in the future.

What? There are still many companies that talk warmly but vaguely about community activities in their PR literature, but some business leaders are helping to set new standards for quantitative and qualitative measurement and reporting. In the UK, for example, the members of the London Benchmarking Group have devised an increasingly accepted framework for classifying CCI activities. The aim is to help companies account for the inputs they make to society—over and above cash donations.

How? There are many approaches to reporting on CCI. Most companies still choose their own path, but increasingly we are seeing the emergence of recognised—if still embryonic— frameworks for the gathering and disclosure of information.

So which reporting models make the link to 'mainstream' business activities? One model is proposed by the European Foundation for Quality Management (EFQM). Their 'model for business excellence' places the 'Impact on Society' category in the context of Leadership, People Management, Policy and Strategy, Resources, Processes, Customer Satisfaction, People Satisfaction and Business Results. British Telecommunications (BT) has used this approach with great success, and Business in the Community's *Principles of Corporate Community Investment* are closely aligned to the EFQM model.

And which types of CCI reporting aid comparison between companies? The main answer here is the London Benchmarking Group, a group of 18 companies, which has developed a model to classify the value and leverage of corporate contributions to the community, permitting comparisons between companies.

Spotlight on Tata Iron and Steel, India. Tata Iron and Steel, one of India's leading companies, is known throughout the country for its visionary social welfare programme, spanning almost 100 years. The company has a long commitment to social auditing and reporting. In 1979, the then chairman invited an audit committee to report on 'whether, and the extent to which the company has fulfilled the objectives . . . regarding the social and moral responsibilities to consumers, employees, shareholders society and the local community' (Subbaraman 1997). A second and more detailed audit was commissioned in 1990. The audit committee made an assessment of the company's Community Development Schemes and of the work done by the Tata Steel Rural Development Society and the Tata Relief Centre. Contributions to schools, hospitals and sports activities were also discussed.

◻ *Suppliers*

Why? Supply chains are increasingly in the spotlight. Consumer concerns, fuelled by media stories about poor labour standards associated with well-known brands such as Nike and Reebok, are forcing companies to look again at their supplier relationships. Traditionally, global outsourcing has enabled companies to order products from overseas manufacturers without ownership of—or involvement in—the running of these factories. And the trend is becoming even more prevalent as many large companies are centralised and downsized, so that managers often simply do not know what subcontractors are doing.

Business has responded to consumer concerns with codes of conduct, but it has been hard to tell to what extent these written commitments are backed up by action. Simultaneously, the NGO community has been working in partnership with industry to develop initiatives such as the Clean Clothes Campaign in Europe and the Apparel Industry Partnership in the United States. In the UK, the government-backed Ethical Trading Initiative (ETI) is a coalition of NGOs, companies and trades unions which aims to develop a shared approach and a set of tools to improve the working lives of people worldwide.

Meanwhile in the United States, the Council on Economic Priorities Accreditation Agency (CEPAA) has worked with an international group of business, NGOs and other professional certification organisations to produce a standard, SA 8000, which can be audited.

What? While companies with mainly Northern suppliers may address in their codes of conduct such issues as the number of products bought locally, the length of supplier relationships and payment on time, those with Southern suppliers usually face additional concerns such as freedom of association, child labour and working hours. These have been highlighted in agreements such as the UN Declaration of Human Rights and the Convention on the Rights of the Child.

How? Finding the best way to communicate about decent labour conditions is proving tricky. The American Apparel Industry Partnership plans to allow companies that adhere to its code and undergo external verification to sew a 'No Sweat' label onto their clothes. On the other hand, SA 8000 is systems-based and site-specific standard, and companies may not communicate their certification on individual products. Certified factories will be posted on the Internet. Meanwhile, at the ETI the jury is still out in terms of the best way forward on communication. But Raj Thamotheram, the ETI's manager, expects that companies will report to the ETI on their progress on policy, process and corrective action. How much of this reporting will be available to the public is still open to discussion.

Spotlight on Traidcraft, UK. Traidcraft plc was the first business in the UK to develop voluntary social accounts and to publish independently audited social reports. It was set up in the UK in 1979 with the aim of paying fair prices to producers in the South, and to give them access to affluent consumers in the North.

Traidcraft works with its suppliers to develop performance indicators and targets to which all parties can work. All stakeholders agree that the most important ethical aim is to pay a fair price for the products. But the excellent 1997 Social Accounts provide much richer information, including Traidcraft's progress on:

1. Increasing the percentage of 'third world-sourced' products

2. Providing financial advances to suppliers

3. Developing long-term business relationships with suppliers

What's more, suppliers are encouraged to voice their opinions through questionnaires and general comments, also published in the accounts.

◻ *Clients/Customers*

Why? Waves of 'green consumers', 'ethical consumers' and even 'vigilante consumers' have demonstrated that it is no longer enough for high-profile companies to claim that they are environmentally, socially and ethically aware; they may be called upon to prove it. But, like all forms of reporting, information needs usually operate in two directions. Not only do customers want information about companies and their products, but increasingly businesses are also seeing the benefit of exploring customer perceptions so that they can build long-term relationships based on trust and shared values.

Not-for-profit organisations, such as the UK's Black Country Housing Association, often place a strong emphasis on relationships with their clients. Alison Pilling, social auditor with NEF, explained: 'Housing associations have always focused primarily on their clients because they have a mission to provide quality housing and service to their tenants' (SustainAbility/UNEP 1999a).

What? Since the US Council on Economic Priorities' pioneering work on disclosing company information in the early 1970s, others have joined the fray, including EthicScan in Canada and Ethical Consumer in the UK. EthicScan's recent book, *Shopping with a Conscience*, takes 114 major Canadian corporations and provides information on a range of issues from gender and family issues to sourcing and trading practices.

The kinds of information gained in the SEAAR process by companies about their customers and their views depend very much on the type of organisation involved. A bank such as the Sbn Bank in Denmark asks customers to evaluate the organisation on issues ranging from the speed and friendliness of the service to whether or not the bank expresses its opinion on important local and societal matters.

In Italy, meanwhile, the Consumer Co-operative sees its social balance as an important communication instrument that informs members, consumers and other stakeholders about the extent to which the organisation is performing against its mission. The Co-op also uses its report to encourage stakeholders to participate in its social and environmental initiatives.

How? Organisations, among them EthicScan, that disclose information about companies' practices, typically use a rigorous and lengthy research process to gather their data. The information collected is normally sent to the company in question, to give them a chance to verify, add information or query findings. Companies seeking information about their customers' views use a variety of methods to collect this qualitative and quantitative data, including round tables, focus groups, questionnaires and telephone interviews.

Spotlight on The Body Shop, UK. Until 1992, The Body Shop conducted almost no market research to explore customer opinions on the company, its stores or its products. But customer research for the 1995 and 1997 *Values Reports* offered the company a welcome opportunity to fully integrate values-based questions about how customers consider it performs against its mission statement with business-focused questions about the quality of products.

Maria Sillanpää, then team leader of the company's ethical audit group, highlighted three benefits of this integrated approach to customer research:

1. It enhances credibility and buy-in to the social audit process from key internal decision-makers.

2. It transmits integrated values/business agenda deep inside the business.

3. It also takes this agenda to customers, demonstrating that The Body Shop is serious about both the quality of its products as well as its message.

◻ *Investors*

Why? Investors count. They wield huge potential influence over the fortunes of publicly quoted companies. Unfortunately, many pursue short-term profits at the expense of sustainability. As Dee Hock, Visa founder and president put it: 'Institutions that operate so as to capitalise all gain in the interests of a few, while socialising all loss to the detriment of many, are ethically, socially and operationally unsound. Yet that is precisely what far too many corporations demand and far too many societies tolerate. It must change.'[1]

There are two main reasons for reporting social information to current or potential investors. First, growing numbers of investors want to 'win without sin'. They require information about a company's social, ethical and environmental performance. Second, once they have bought shares, such investors are increasingly interested in receiving more information about its activities than is available in the annual report.

What? Supply is responding to demand. Funds that set specific social, ethical or environmental criteria for investment are growing rapidly, both in number and value. According to the US Social Investment Forum, more than $1 trillion are held in socially and environmentally responsible portfolios under professional management in the USA. Although growing fast in Europe, the figure under ethical management is substantially lower here.

The Domini Social Equity Fund (DSEF) was the first socially responsible index fund in the USA. The DSEF practises positive discrimination, investing in companies demonstrating corporate citizenship, gender and ethnic diversity, good employee relations, a respect for the environment, an equitable approach to suppliers in less developed countries, and safe and useful products.

While such funds aim to address the information needs of potential investors, more must be done to fill the information gap for company boards, individual shareholders and financial markets. The UK Centre for Tomorrow's Company argues that current annual reports are backward-looking and fail to fulfil their full potential. The Centre suggests the core annual report should cover the following:

1. What the company is for (purpose)

2. What the company stands for (values)

3. Where success comes from (success model)

4. Comparison with past performance and with forecast

5. Comparison with other companies, where relevant

6. How indicators used are verified (Centre for Tomorrow's Company 1998)

How? Companies can report their social policies, targets and performance to investors in many ways. They can be proactive, using press releases, annual reports, quarterly reports, or briefings. Or they can respond to external pressures, including shareholder resolutions. The key thing, however, is to avoid unpleasant surprises. Explain risks as they evolve. Explain, too, how programmes and expenditures will convert into longer-term shareholder value.

Spotlight on VanCity, Canada. Vancouver City Savings & Credit Union, known locally as VanCity, is Canada's largest credit union. It has over C$4 billion in assets and nearly 240,000

---

1   Personal communication to Stephen Viederman, President, Jessie Smith Noyes Foundation, 13 January 1998.

members or customers. Competing with banks, it provides a complete range of financial products and services.

VanCity has been working to improve the depth and credibility of its non-financial reporting since 1992. In October 1998 it published its first stand-alone, externally verified social report, relating to the year 1997. Taking a stakeholder approach, the report charts VanCity's progress against its policies and principles, highlights key indicators for each stakeholder group and outlines its future commitments. Wherever possible, the report also benchmarks VanCity's activities against those of other Canadian credit unions and banks.

26

Social Reporting

Developing Theory and Current Practice

Andrew Wilson

MANAGING, measuring and reporting on social performance is currently rising up the corporate agenda as more and more business leaders appreciate its relevance and value. Despite this, the area remains one that is clouded with confusion and contradictions. Different organisations practise very different approaches to exercises that seem to bear similar names.

Some talk about social assessment, social audit, social accounting or social reporting. Others replace the word 'social' with the word 'ethical'—sometimes without changing the meaning, but on other occasions referring to a completely different concept. The Body Shop, for example, talks of its approach to 'integrated ethical auditing, which takes into account social, animal protection and environmental protection issues' (The Body Shop *Values Report* 1997). This underlines the fact that approaches to social audit vary from organisation to organisation: monitoring and reporting on animal protection, for example, would appear to be of little or no relevance to companies operating in most other sectors.

The Body Shop approach does, however, emphasise an important element of social accounting and reporting: that it is based on assessing the degree to which corporate performance matches the stated values of the organisation. As such, it is not simply a case of reporting the hard facts about equal opportunities, employment policies, or support for education programmes. Rather, social accounting and reporting attempts to assess how far stakeholders (customers, employees, shareholders, suppliers, the community and others) feel that the organisation lives up to its promises in the way it operates. In particular, the process of social accounting takes as its starting point what an individual organisation says it wants to achieve through its 'public face': its statements of mission and vision, its advertising and promotions, its involvement in the community, etc.

There is now an extensive literature on this topic (Gonella *et al.* 1998; Wheeler 1996; Zadek *et al.* 1997), which includes several other chapters in this volume and the report, for the UK telecommunications company, British Telecom (BT), on which this particular chapter is based (Wilson 1998).

Rather than rehearse this discourse, the purpose of this chapter is to examine some practical approaches that have been adopted by companies in measuring and reporting their social (rather than environmental or financial) performance. Section 1 provides a framework for considering such approaches, while Sections 2–4 analyse three leading examples of corporate social reports: The Co-operative, The Body Shop and Ben & Jerry's. Section 5 provides some conclusions.

1. *What is Social Accounting and Reporting?*

◻ *Developing a Framework for Social Accounting and Reporting*

There is a whole host of activities currently undertaken by business organisations to increase the degree to which they measure and report on non-financial aspects of their corporate performance. Some of these are internally driven (e.g. measures of employee or customer satisfaction), while others are being forced on them by external demands (perhaps through legislation, regulatory control or pressure from lobbying groups). Many activities are conducted whose sole purpose is to improve management decision-making; others are intended to inform a much wider audience and are published for distribution outside the organisation.

In discussing different approaches to social accounting and reporting, two key issues seem to be of great importance in differentiating particular activities in this field.

1. *The degree to which different stakeholders get access to the information that is collected and analysed.* Is the data purely an aid to internal decision-making (e.g. market research reports on customer satisfaction levels) or is it shared among all employees (e.g. results of staff attitude surveys)? How are other stakeholders involved and informed? What information is published and distributed to shareholders, customers, suppliers, the local community, etc.?

2. *The degree to which the exercise is comprehensive and inclusive.* This parameter has two closely related elements. The first concerns *what* information is gathered. Does the data refer exclusively to one small aspect of the organisation's activities (e.g. the company's support and involvement in community initiatives) or does it try to capture the totality of the organisation's social impact? The second concerns *who* is involved in the information-gathering process. Does the data refer simply to one stakeholder group or to several? By combining these two parameters in a simple two-by-two matrix, it is possible to map out a range of different activities that contribute in some way to accounting for and reporting the social impact of business (see Fig. 1). It is important to recognise that both parameters represent a continuum of possible approaches, with the boundaries between them being somewhat blurred. In the following pages, this matrix is used to consider a number of activities that capture certain aspects of the social impact of business.

Complete/inclusive

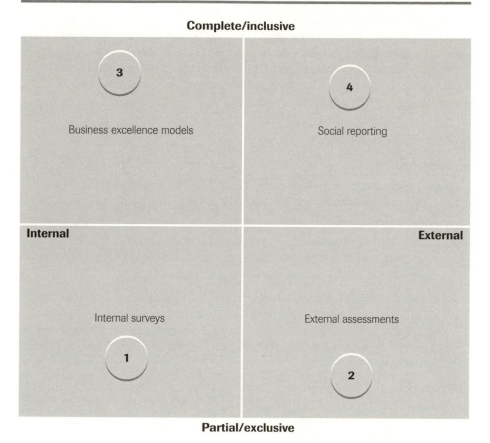

Figure 1: A FRAMEWORK FOR SOCIAL ACCOUNTING AND REPORTING

1. Quadrant 1: Internal surveys

Examples

- Staff attitude surveys
- Surveys and focus group discussions with customers

Key features

- Such approaches tend to consider single stakeholder groups in isolation.
- The results of these exercises are not widely reported. Indeed, in some cases the results are not made available even to those participating in the data collection process.

2. Quadrant 2: External assessments

External assessments of corporate social performance can encompass two distinctly different approaches. The first, which might be termed 'stakeholder reporting', is carried out by the organisation itself. The second type of assessment is conducted by external third parties and can be described as 'corporate benchmarking'. Each of these two approaches is discussed in turn below.

a. Stakeholder reporting

Examples

▼ BT's reports, such as the *Community Partnership Programme Review* and *Building Corporate Reputation through Community Involvement*, are good examples of this type of stakeholder reporting.

▼ Other organisations reporting on their social activities include *BP in the Community*, NatWest Group's *Investing in the Community*, and the *Report on Corporate Citizenship* by Grand Metropolitan (now Diageo).

▼ North West Water (part of United Utilities) has recently produced its second *Community Voice* report. This review of its community activities includes the results of independent research among customers, suppliers, employees, community leaders and opinion-formers about the company's strategy and performance in this area.

▼ Skandia, the Swedish financial services company, has produced a report *Visualizing Intellectual Capital*. This defines intellectual capital as 'the knowledge, skill and capacity of individual employees' (Skandia 1994).

Key features

▼ This type of stakeholder reporting tends to consider particular aspects of the organisation's activities in isolation.

▼ The information gathered is usually widely reported.

▼ The data is almost exclusively internally collected, compiled and presented, with little or no attempt to seek external verification or validation.

▼ That said, there might be an attempt at ongoing consultation with those participating in the data collection process.

b. Corporate benchmarking

Examples

▼ The Council on Economic Priorities is a research organisation (founded in the USA) that analyses and reports on the social and environmental records of companies.

- In the UK, New Consumer conducts similar work and in 1991 published a book, *Changing Corporate Values* (Adams *et al.* 1991), described as 'a guide to social and environmental policy and practice in Britain's top companies'.

- Both organisations combine published data (produced by companies themselves, press cuttings, information from public interest bodies and trade associations, etc.) supplemented with a self-completion questionnaire sent out to participating companies.

Key features

- This approach differs from stakeholder reporting (described above) because the data are externally compiled.

- Typically, this type of external benchmarking includes measures on a large number of indices (e.g. disclosure, equal opportunity policies, community involvement, environmental impact, policies covering overseas trade, animal welfare and human rights).

- However, the results of this type of reporting remain incomplete because they are usually confined to information that is already in the public domain, especially if a particular company chooses not to participate in the survey process.

- There is no real way for this information to be externally verified in any meaningful sense.

3. Quadrant 3: Business excellence models

Examples

- The European Quality Award (EQA) based on the European Foundation for Quality Management business excellence model
- The Baldridge Award in the USA.

Key features

- The entry requirements of both these awards require a company to provide data on a wide range of its activities, including its impact on society.

- Organisations need to look at the impact of the business from the perspective of a number of stakeholders.

- Although the data is compiled and collected internally, it is subject to external scrutiny and assessment.

- For the EQA, there is no obligation on the part of the company to publish any detailed data (apart from making it available to the assessors). Interestingly, in the United States, the Baldridge Award requires award-winners to publish their submissions to encourage the spread of best practice.

▼ Finally, by the very nature of an award scheme, what a company chooses to include in its submission is likely to be selective—reporting on only the positive aspects of its performance.

4. Quadrant 4: Social reporting

Examples

▼ The Body Shop International plc

▼ Ben & Jerry's Homemade, Inc.

▼ The Co-operative

▼ BP (now BP Amoco)

▼ Shell International

▼ Shell UK

▼ The Co-operative Bank

▼ Traidcraft

▼ Sbn Bank

The first three of these examples (The Body Shop, Ben & Jerry's and The Co-operative) are considered in some detail in sections 2–4.

Key features

▼ The process of social reporting requires a company to provide data on a wide range of its activities.

▼ The social report will include the views of a number of stakeholder groups.

▼ Data can be compiled and collected internally and externally.

▼ Both the results of the report and the process by which data are collected are subject to external scrutiny and verification.

▼ Disclosure—the full and frank publication of the results—is a key concept of the social report.

◻ The Essential Elements of Social Reporting

The purpose of developing this simple matrix of social accounting and reporting has been to illustrate three key points.

First, there is a wide variety of activity that most large companies are already carrying out in collecting and collating information about the social impact of business. Whether driven by statutory requirement or by a desire to achieve a better understanding of the 'nature of the business', most large companies already have a number of systems that can provide the type of information described in the preceding sections.

Second, despite the level of current activity, it requires a great effort on behalf of an organisation to meet fully the demands of a social report. In particular, in moving through the matrix from Quadrant 1 to Quadrant 4, a company must demonstrate its willingness to be more open in the key areas identified earlier:

- Allowing wider access to information

- Being more comprehensive by reporting on a wider range of issues

- Being more inclusive in giving a voice to a wider range of stakeholders

Finally, it is important to note one further element of the process of social accounting and reporting that is not adequately captured in the four-quadrant model presented above. This concerns the degree to which the information gathered is used as part of a process of dialogue and continuous improvement—which implies an extension of the notion of inclusivity referred to above. Clearly, at one level, it is possible to consult with a range of stakeholder groups without offering any commitment to respond to their concerns and aspirations. At another level, this process of consultation can be made much more inclusive by engaging stakeholders in a dialogue that helps to shape and define the process for future social reports. So, for example, stakeholders might be invited to offer suggestions for defining social indicators, presenting data, or even reporting on performance measures. It is also possible to conceive of a third level of inclusivity that allows stakeholders some say in influencing and forming the values by which the organisation operates. This implies a need to balance the expectations of different stakeholder groups and to allow each some influence over setting priorities for the future direction of the organisation.

Many would argue that a fundamental principle of the social report is to encourage this notion of inclusivity through stakeholder dialogue. However, the degree to which it is practical and desirable to pay heed to different stakeholder voices in this way will vary from organisation to organisation.

◻ *Conclusions*

This section has attempted to shed some light on theoretical perspectives under-pinning the process of social accounting and reporting. It is clear that the phrase 'social accounting' is often used as a generic term to describe a wide variety of different activities and processes.

Despite much debate on the subject and frequent calls for the establishment of standard measures, we are still a very long way from reaching agreement about what constitutes best practice in this area. In many respects, this debate is likely to continue. Companies operating in different industries, which articulate different value systems, and seek to meet the aspirations of different stakeholder groups, will almost inevitably wish to monitor, measure and report on their social impact in different ways. As such, it is legitimate to argue that there remains a need for continuing experimentation in this field. It is counter-productive to impose rigid processes or systems of social accounting that are impractical or irrelevant to any particular organisation. However, the preceding discussion has identified a number of key elements that need to be considered in designing and developing mechanisms for social accounting and reporting. The next section will consider how these elements have been put into practice by examining the social reports of three different organisations.

2. *The Co-operative* Social Audit *Report*

The Co-operative is one of the UK's largest independent retailers with a range of food and department stores, funeral services and car dealerships. As a co-operative society, the organisation is owned and run by its members. It operates some 500 retail outlets throughout England and Wales, with net sales in 1997 of £1.54 billion, employing about 25,000 people.

Since 1988, the Co-operative has published, every two years, a *Social Report* outlining the organisation's 'community and ethical activities'. However, in 1997, the Co-operative published its first *Social Audit*, which reports on a process of consultation with its members and employees, together with a survey of charities. Recognising that there are other stakeholder groups connected with the business, the Co-operative has committed itself to 'consult with other groups in the future as part of an on-going programme'. Customers (who are not necessarily also members of the Co-operative) and suppliers will be included in later cycles of the social audit process. It is interesting to turn to the glossary at the end of the report to see that the organisation defines a social audit in the following terms:

> An exercise similar to market research examining stakeholder perceptions
> of an organisation's performance against core values and specific stake-
> holder needs.

This statement very much captures the tone, style and content of their report.

The external verifier of the social audit was the organisation, New Economics Foundation (NEF). Their role involved monitoring the different stages of the audit process, comprising: the scope and design of the exercise; focus groups; survey sampling frameworks; quantitative survey outputs; qualitative results; and the content and form of the report itself.

◁ The Methodology

The Co-operative *Social Audit* report gives some detail about how the audit was carried out. Six focus group discussions (comprising 8–10 people) were held with randomly selected representatives of the members around the country. These discussions informed the design of a postal questionnaire that was sent to 10,000 members. (The total membership base numbers some 1.5 million.) This survey generated 2,171 responses.

For employees, a number (unspecified) of face-to-face interviews with staff around the country took place. Staff were chosen to reflect the variety of job types, length of service, and business units within the Co-operative. Again, these discussions informed the design of a questionnaire that was distributed to 10,000 employees, of whom 1,744 responded.

Perhaps not surprisingly, given the methodology described above, the bulk of the report reads much like a typical market research or employee attitude survey. It is biased towards attitudes and opinions and contains relatively little objective or comparative data. Most of the 90-plus pages of the *Social Audit* are devoted to presenting the results of the consultation exercise, rather than reporting on the activities of the Co-operative itself.

◻ The Members' Survey

Apart from some factual information about the composition of respondent members—in terms of age, gender, working status, ethnic origin, etc.—the members' survey reports views on the following broad topic areas:

▼ Reasons for joining the Co-op

▼ Awareness and importance of its social objectives

▼ Knowledge and attitudes towards rights of membership

▼ Receipt and rating of information

▼ Awareness of and participation in activities

▼ Importance of and satisfaction with membership

Each of the above issues is related to the Co-operative's stated social objectives for the members. As such, the audit can be seen to be testing attitudes towards the organisation's performance against its mission. Only in a number of limited instances is this subjective data supplemented with normative measures of actual achievements. One example illustrates this point.

One of the social objectives of the Co-operative is as follows: 'By the efficient management of the Society's resources to provide a fair return, with maximum security, on members' investment.' The *Social Audit* reports in some detail respondents' attitudes towards saving and investing with the Co-operative. However, this attitudinal data is supplemented only with the rather narrow comparison of the interest rates offered by the Co-operative against those offered by Sainsbury's Bank over the period in question.

◻ The Employee Survey

In the section that considers employee attitudes, there is slightly more of this type of external benchmarking. So, for example, union membership in the Co-operative is compared with that of other retailers; so too is the percentage of staff in a pension scheme and the pension fund contributions required. The ethnic origin of employees is contrasted with data from the Labour Force Survey, while national figures on reportable accidents are used to benchmark the Co-operative's performance in health and safety.

Beyond such measures, employees were questioned about the following issues:

- Training and education

- Rating the place of work

- Job satisfaction

- Pay and benefits

- The level of support offered by the Co-operative (e.g. management and communications, working atmosphere)

- Appraisal systems

- Equal opportunities

- Charity and local events.

Again, with a number of notable exceptions (including relative pay levels in retail organisations and the amount of staff discount offered to employees), much of the data report employee attitudes towards the issues identified, rather than actual performance.

The final short section of the Co-operative *Social Audit* gives some limited information about the organisation's support to voluntary-sector organisations, and reports on a survey that received 88 responses from charitable and community groups in the North of England which had sought financial support from the Co-operative in 1995.

◻ *Conclusion*

The results of the Co-operative *Social Audit* report must be taken in context and seen as the first stage in a developmental process. This said (as the verifier's report recognises), a major weakness of the report is the lack of quantitative indicators of performance. The report concentrates too heavily on stakeholder perceptions of the organisation, rather than seeking to quantify significant measures of their experience of how well the Co-operative is actually performing.

3. *The Body Shop* Values Report

The Body Shop's 1997 *Values Report* is the second major milestone in the organisation's pioneering work in the field of social accounting and reporting, building on their first *Values Report* which appeared in 1995. The very fact that this latest document has taken two years to compile gives some indication of the depth and scope of the project.

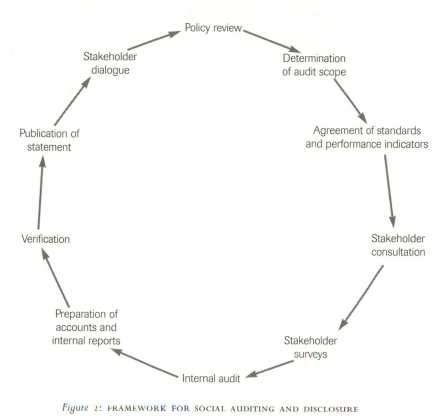

Figure 2: FRAMEWORK FOR SOCIAL AUDITING AND DISCLOSURE

Source: The Body Shop *Values Report*

An essential feature of the latest *Values Report* is the way in which it integrates three themes: social, environmental and animal protection. In contrast to the 1995 report, which comprised three separate volumes on each of these issues, the results of the 1997 audit present the views of various stakeholder groups on each theme. The following analysis will concentrate on the social impact of the business.

In a document of over 200 pages, the *Values Report* looks at the results of a series of consultation exercises with the following stakeholders: employees, international franchisees, UK franchisees, customers, suppliers, shareholders, local communities, the environment and the animal protection campaign. It is worth noting that the media, regulators and the ethical investment community have been identified as potential stakeholder groups for future inclusion in the audit process.

The Body Shop's approach to social audit is clearly predicated on the principal tenet of the company's mission statement: 'to dedicate our business to the pursuit of social and environmental change'. The framework they use is illustrated in Figure 2.[1] A key

---

1   For a more complete description of this cycle, see Body Shop International 1996 and Chapter 27.

characteristic of this approach is the balance it attempts to strike between two complementary elements. The first is a process of consultation with stakeholders, which generally involves focus group discussions followed by wide-scale opinion surveys. These questionnaire surveys are intended to capture perceptions about issues of interest to stakeholders, and the values articulated by the organisation. The second element consists of tracking the impact of the organisation's operations through a range of quantitative and qualitative performance indicators. This involves the ongoing internal measurement of a wide range of metrics. Where applicable, the data generated by this process are compared to internal targets and external benchmarks.

The Body Shop describes their methodology for the process in the following terms:

- The development of qualitative and quantitative performance indicators for social, environmental and animal protection impacts in order to track progress towards more sustainable operations

- The engagement of stakeholder representatives in dialogue to identify salient issues for each group

- The conducting of wide-scale confidential surveys of stakeholder opinion

- The setting of strategic targets and 'Next Steps' for continuous improvement

- The facilitation of feedback and follow-up dialogue with stakeholders following publication of the social audit results, which help to shape future audit cycles and to set priorities for future action.[2]

This work is largely undertaken by the Ethical Audit department of the company, and concentrates on its UK operations. The process and results of the audit are subject to external verification by a number of different organisations, including:

- Environmental content: the British Standards Institution

- Social content: New Economics Foundation

- Animal protection content: SGS Yarsley International

The following paragraphs consider in more detail those sections of the 1997 *Values Report* that relate to the social impact of the business on employees, customers, suppliers, shareholders and the community. It is worth noting that each chapter of the *Values Audit* includes a summary of the organisation's aims prior to describing the consultation process undertaken with each particular stakeholder group. The results of this consultation process, focusing on perceptions of corporate behaviour, together with measures of actual performance where these exist, comprise the main body of each chapter. At the end of each chapter, the report includes targets for environmental, animal protection and social issues (where appropriate). Finally, there is a company response in the form of a quote from a board member or senior manager setting out the 'Next Steps' for the organisation in terms of progress made and areas for improvement.

---

2   Source: The Body Shop website, *www.the-body-shop.com*

⌐ *Employees*

In February 1997, The Body Shop directly employed 2,426 staff in the UK. The process for consulting with employees began in June 1995 with a survey, designed after a series of focus groups. Following a series of consultation sessions, where the results of the 1995 survey were discussed, further focus groups and seminars were held to refine the design of the 1997 audit. As a result of this process, a questionnaire survey (which was anonymous and confidential) was sent to every employee. The survey was administered externally by the Centre for Stakeholding and Sustainable Enterprise at Kingston University. In total, 1,721 employees returned the questionnaire for analysis.

The report of the results of this survey includes measures of opinion on the following:

- The mission and values of the organisation

- Learning and development (which includes data on the number of days spent on work-based and course-based learning)

- Career development

- Diversity and equal opportunities (which includes data on the breakdown of staff by age, gender and ethnic background)

- Communication

- Work satisfaction (including comparative data drawn from a range of sources, including the IPD *Labour Turnover Survey* and the IFF Research Ltd report, *Skills Needs in Britain 1995*)

- Views on working for The Body Shop

- Pay and benefits. (This section measures pay levels against an internal benchmark of the company's target to reward employees between the median and upper quartile of market rates. It also provides comparative data drawn from market salary surveys.)

- Views of the company's action in response to the 1995 social audit

- Quantitative and qualitative data on attitudes towards, and actual performance in relation to, health and safety issues

This section also includes information on environmental performance standards and animal protection standards that are of particular relevance to employees.

⌐ *Customers*

Indications of the relative size of this stakeholder group are given only in terms of customer transactions and retail sales by each of the international regions in which The Body Shop operates. In absolute terms, the figures show that in 1996/97 the company's revenue totalled £655.5 million.

For the 1995 social audit, the company undertook a series of ten focus group discussions, followed by an omnibus survey of 1,000 individuals, both customers and non-customers. Since that time, The Body Shop has consulted extensively with customers and the public in all the countries in which it operates.

Further independent research was carried out in the UK through a general survey of 1,000 adults, and more in-depth interviews with 300 women aged between 18 and 45. This work, which is reported in the 1997 *Values Report*, looks at the following issues:

- Views on the company's mission and values
- Awareness of The Body Shop's campaigns
- Concerns and issues of importance to respondents
- Factors affecting brand choice
- The products sold by The Body Shop
- Promotion
- The social and environmental performance of the company

Suppliers

At the beginning of 1997, The Body Shop had 1,281 suppliers on the company's main database. Suppliers were invited to participate in the social audit process carried out in 1995, through focus group discussions and a postal survey (sent to 285 suppliers). The organisation is committed to a three-year social audit cycle of suppliers. During the latter half of 1996, a team at Oxford Brookes University carried out a limited research exercise among 20 supplier organisations. The results of this research, reported in the 1997 *Values Report*, offer the following recommendations to The Body Shop:

- Help to classify the environmental policies and management systems used by suppliers
- Identify suppliers' perceptions of the main facilitators for, and blocks to, improved environmental performance
- Determine the clarity of The Body Shop's own environmental approach
- Test how far the suppliers' values on environmental performance match those of the company

Shareholders

At the end of the 1997 financial year, The Body Shop had 5,464 entries in its shareholder register, broken down as follows:

- Individual shareholders: 7%
- Institutions: 41%

- Directors (principally Anita and Gordon Roddick): 25%

- Significant individual shareholder: 24%

- Significant single company holding: 3%

As with suppliers, the process of shareholder consultation for the 1995 audit took the form of focus group discussions (with separate focus groups held for individual and institutional shareholders) and a postal survey sent to just over one-fifth of the shareholders. Only four institutional investors responded to this survey. Shareholders were contacted again during 1997/98 and the results of this consultation will be reported in future audits.

In the 1997 *Values Report*, apart from a financial summary, information is given on The Body Shop's compliance with the codes of practice issued by the Cadbury and Greenbury committees. The report also gives fluctuations in the company's share price over the preceding two years, relative to the FTSE all-share index.

△ Community Involvement

The 1997 *Values Report* contains sub-sections on each of the following: local communities; campaigns for human rights, animal protection and the environment; and company giving.

The Body Shop's head office is located in Littlehampton, West Sussex. This site includes the company's main manufacturing, production and warehousing facilities (although, recently, plans have been announced to outsource manufacturing). In 1996, a street survey was carried out in the town and received 589 responses, with people questioned about a range of issues to do with their awareness of The Body Shop and their thoughts on the company. Almost two-thirds of respondents thought that the organisation plays an active role in the local community, and one-third were aware that the company encourages employees to do voluntary work in the community. In relation to its community involvement and investment, the *Values Report* gives details of company giving from both The Body Shop and its charitable foundation. These figures are recorded in terms of:

- Financial donations

- In-kind donations

- Administration costs of public campaigns

- The administration costs of the company's volunteering programme

△ Conclusions

The Body Shop's *Values Report* is clearly a very comprehensive document that contains a wealth of data. The preceding summary cannot hope to cover all of the issues it raises. However, it is possible to make some general observations about the style and content of The Body Shop's approach to social accounting and reporting.

▶ The *Values Report* demonstrates a clear commitment to the process of stakeholder dialogue. The company is prepared to be challenged on the parameters of this dialogue and is seeking to update and improve the process of social reporting at each stage of the cycle.

▶ A fundamental aim of this process of dialogue is to narrow the gap between principle and practice. Each stakeholder group is invited to challenge the organisation on its performance against stated aims and objectives contained within its mission statement, formal policies, guidelines and procedures.

▶ Stakeholder perceptions are supplemented by documentary information on particular aspects of the company's performance provided by internal management systems.

▶ These elements are combined to set targets, in response to the audit results, for future performance. Indeed, the *Values Report* contains a specific section (running to 23 pages) detailing targets to 2000 and beyond 'in pursuit of social and ecological change'.

4. *Ben & Jerry's* Social Report

Of the three organisations considered in this chapter, Ben & Jerry's has the longest track record of activity in the field of social accounting and reporting, having published social performance reports since 1988.

A fundamental feature of the approach previously adopted by the company was to engage an independent expert to provide an impartial perspective on the organisation's social performance. The external assessor was invited to investigate, without limitations, any aspect of the company's operations. The organisation agreed in advance to publish the conclusions of the assessor, editing only factually incorrect material. This approach (which the organisation describes as 'social assessment') relied largely on the particular perspectives of the assessor and did not involve the systematic collection or analysis of data on corporate performance.

The company is now moving from social assessment to social auditing and is introducing a more systematic and comprehensive approach to measuring and reporting its social performance. The company's stated aim, in this respect, is as follows:

> Our goal is to seek information from stakeholders regularly, to make specific measurements of social performance, to state them consistently over the years, to make our method of deriving measurements stand up to independent scrutiny, and to disclose the substantive results of our assessment in a manner that is relevant and accessible to our stakeholders.[3]

---

3   Source: Ben & Jerry's website, *www.benjerry.com*

◻ *Current Audit Process*

Ben & Jerry's has identified seven stakeholder groups: employees, franchisees, the community, suppliers, customers, shareholders and the environment. The company recognises that as the process of social reporting evolves, it is possible that new stakeholder groups might emerge.

At the time of writing, the latest available report was the *1995 Social Report*, published in April 1996. In this *Social Report*, franchisees and employees were the primary focus of the survey process. The key elements of the organisation's approach to conducting their social report are set out below.

- **Dialogue with stakeholders.** This is done by means of surveys of each group over a cycle of years, with more informal dialogue, such as focus groups, in alternate years.

- **Performance indicators.** The company has tried to establish specific measurements of performance relative to each stakeholder group. These measures are derived from internal sources and are largely numerical.

- **External benchmarks.** Where possible, internal performance measurements are set against external benchmarks.

- **Management commitments.** Each *Social Report* contains a review by management of the key issues raised in the audit process, together with commitments against which to assess future performance.

- **Audit verifier's report.** This is the statement by the external auditors (NEF in the case of the *1995 Social Report*) that describes the auditor's role, details the extent of the review process, and comments on the accuracy and completeness of the audit.

Ben & Jerry's *1995 Social Report* follows a similar format to that adopted by the Body Shop's *Values Report 1997*. The following describe the main features.

- A separate section is devoted to each of the different stakeholder groups.

- Within each section, the report details the organisation's 'intentions with respect to' the stakeholders in terms of the company's mission statements, policies and procedures.

- There is a description of the scope of the consultation process (although, as has been made clear, not all stakeholder groups are consulted every year).

- The results of the audit's findings are reported.

- There is a section on management comments and commitments that sets goals and targets for future performance.

◻ *Conclusions*

Ben & Jerry's *Social Report* differs in tone and style from the two previous examples in the amount of quantifiable information that it contains. For example, the section that deals with employees details staff profiles, provides expenditure on staff training, and reports on compensation levels including the ratio between highest and lowest salaries. The section on customers provides data on sales volumes, changes in market share, and the number and nature of customer contacts (complaints and positive feedback). Finally, the section dealing with suppliers provides information on the retention rate of suppliers and the performance of suppliers in respect of the company's social goals.

This list is meant to be indicative rather than exhaustive. The point is simply to demonstrate the range of potential performance indices that can be reported in the social accounting process.

5. Conclusions

◻ Three Levels of Measurement

This examination of the three reports shows that it is possible to measure an organisation's impact on society at three different levels. Each is closely interrelated and it is desirable for all of them to feature in a comprehensive social reporting process.

The first level measures an organisation's performance against its stated objectives, usually in terms of its mission, vision or values. Typically, adopting this approach will involve a process of consultation with different stakeholder groups, the purpose of which is to question people about their perceptions of the organisation's performance in relation to its stated values. At this level, the process of social accounting draws heavily on existing approaches, such as market research or attitude surveys. As discussed, the Co-operative social report concentrates largely on this level of analysis.

At the second level, stakeholders can be questioned on their views about what the organisation should be doing—both in terms of its social performance and in relation to the values it espouses. At this level, the organisation is seeking to understand better stakeholders' expectations. The purpose is to gather data on the needs and desires of important stakeholder groups. A legitimate aspect of this dialogue is to allow stakeholders to comment on the suitability and applicability of the organisation's values. In certain respects, this process can be seen as akin to consumer research exercises (perhaps through focus group work) that seek to understand customers' current, and as yet unmet, needs.

The third level of analysis seeks to measure stakeholders' actual experience of how an organisation is performing. Sometimes, these measures are set internally by the organisation. Preferably, they should reflect the views and concerns of the stakeholders as described in the consultation process. At this level, the process moves beyond the previous two measures to encapsulate the real social impact of an organisation's operations. When reporting performance against these measures, it is desirable to offer some type of comparative benchmark. Again, these benchmarks might be internal (e.g. targets for customer satisfaction levels) or they might be compared with external 'norms' (e.g. industry standard measures of staff turnover rates[4]). Finally, while performance measures will be collated at a particular point in time, it is also desirable that they are reported on a longitudinal basis, allowing comparisons of corporate performance year on year.

It is important to recognise that these three levels of inquiry are not mutually exclusive. It is possible and desirable to incorporate all three measures (of perceptions, expectations and experience) in a social report. Indeed, to a certain extent, the examples of current practice reported in previous sections reflect this—although there were marked differences in the emphasis of each organisation.

◻ *Publishing Reports*

Another point demonstrated by the three cases is that the results of the audit process can be presented in different ways. Clearly, there is a need to balance a desire for comprehensive documentation while allowing the report to be understood by a wide range of stakeholders. Some might argue, for example, that The Body Shop's 1997 *Values Report* is simply too long to be accessible to all but the most determined reader (although a summary of the full report is available).

It is also important to consider the medium used for publication. Is a written document the best method, or is new technology (the Internet, CD-ROMs) more appropriate? In this respect, it is perhaps worth noting that The Body Shop charge £10 for a paper copy of their *Values Report*. However the results of the audit are published and distributed, some sort of response mechanism (allowing stakeholders to comment on the social audit) is crucial to the ongoing process of dialogue.

◻ *The Key Elements of the Process*

It is easy to dismiss the pioneers of social auditing, such as the three companies described in previous sections, as business 'eccentrics'. As mentioned, The Body Shop's mission states that the principal objective of the company is 'to dedicate our business to the pursuit of social and environmental change'. Ben & Jerry's define their corporate goals in terms of a triple mission: economic, social and product-focused. Although a successful retailer, the Co-operative is also a membership-based organisation with explicit social goals. However, the experience of these organisations is useful for the burgeoning numbers of larger, mainstream companies following in their footsteps. It allows the development of a template that embraces all the major components of the audit process:

- ▼ Define the company's stakeholders. Which groups are important for the organisation? (These are likely to include employees, customers, suppliers, shareholders and the community; but might also embrace the media, non-governmental organisations, local and national government.)

---

4   Indeed, the external benchmark might be prescribed by regulatory or legislative pressures (e.g. the percentage of employees who are registered disabled).

▼ Define the company's approach and aims for each stakeholder group. What does the organisation stand for?

▼ Conduct a process of consultation with a representative sample of stakeholder groups.

▼ Analyse the results of this consultation exercise.

▼ Collect data on internal measures (both quantitative and qualitative) of standards of performance that are relevant to the concerns and aspirations of stakeholders. Provide internal and external benchmarks to place data in context.

▼ Ensure that the whole process is open to the scrutiny of an external verifier or auditor. They should be free to monitor, advise on and participate in every stage of the audit process.

▼ Develop a corporate response to the social accounting process. This should include specific targets for future performance improvements and a commitment to repeat the cycle of social accounting and reporting.

▼ Publish a report detailing the results of the consultation exercise, the measures of performance and targets for the future. This report should be widely available and incorporate a response mechanism allowing stakeholders to comment on the social report, thereby encouraging an ongoing process of dialogue.

While there remains some scepticism about the value of social accounting, there is growing evidence of the business benefits of assessing corporate performance in an inclusive manner against a wide range of parameters. Companies that are doing this effectively are likely to strengthen both their relationships with stakeholders and their bottom line.

27

A New Deal for Sustainable Development in Business

Taking the Social Dimension Seriously at The Body Shop

Maria Sillanpää

IN 1987, The World Commission on Environment and Development (the 'Brundt-land Commission') published a report entitled *Our Common Future*. The report breathed life into a definition of sustainable development that has since achieved widespread if not universal acceptance: 'sustainable development meets the needs of the present without compromising the ability of future generations to meet their own needs' (WCED 1987).

The Brundtland Commission definition embraces the notion that sustainable development is not simply about environmental protection, conservation of finite resources or maintenance of biodiversity. It recognises a wider set of challenges for attaining genuine sustainable development: for instance, the questions of poverty alleviation, population stabilisation, female empowerment, employment creation, human rights observance and opportunity redistribution. Need, futurity and equity are socioeconomic and political issues; they are only relevant to the extent that they can be delivered to present and future generations through human endeavour. So, if the Brundtland definition is accepted, then environmental and social progress together with economic sufficiency must all form part of the agenda for sustainable development.

In 1992, representatives of around 175 nations met at the United Nations Conference on Environment and Development (UNCED) in Rio de Janeiro. The conference had particular difficulty in uniting environmental and social agendas. Governments, international agencies and even non-governmental organisations were simply not sufficiently organised in the run-up to the conference to establish the complementarity of environmental and social progress, still less resolve potential conflicts between environmental and social goals.

Of course, Western countries especially have had several hundred years of practice in separating all things material, conceptual and ideological (e.g. Porritt 1984; Zohar and Marshall 1993). So perhaps it is not surprising that, in the five years that elapsed between the Brundtland Commission and the UNCED conference, the transition to a more holistic agenda had not quite been made. Indeed, the philosophical forces that have kept these issues and agendas separate for so long are still very dominant. In contrast, the forces of holism, integration and interdependence are still relatively weak.

◢ Philosophical Traditions: Friends or Foes of Sustainable Development?

In considering the philosophical basis for ecological and social ethics, three broad traditions may be identified which illustrate the diverse starting points influencing different constituents partaking in the debate about sustainable development: liberal individualism, communitarianism and ecocentrism (see e.g. Capra 1996; Gladwin *et al.* 1995; Gray *et al.* 1996; Hobsbawm 1996; Merchant 1992; Zohar and Marshall 1993).

The origins of **liberal individualism**[1] can be traced back to the Scientific Revolution of the 17th century, the emergence of liberal political and economic theories, and the bias toward human dominion over nature some see embedded in the Judaeo-Christian tradition and in Cartesian dualism. Liberalism took its inspiration from the mechanistic vision of Isaac Newton, who developed a theory of the universe as a celestial machine.

Where Newton formulated the fundamental laws of physical reality, philosophers, early economists and social scientists (such as Hobbes, Mill, Locke and Bentham) following in his wake hoped to discover the basic axioms and principles of social reality. Newton's universal clockwork machine became their model for describing society as a precise, law-abiding mechanism and for portraying human beings as living machines.

Liberal individualism advocated a rigorously rationalist and secular world-view; and was convinced of human ability to solve all questions by the use of reason. Its ideal society consisted of self-contained individuals, all of them seeking primarily to maximise their own satisfactions. Society was a sum of individuals, and its aims the arithmetical sum of individual aims. Happiness was each individual's supreme object; the greatest happiness of the greatest number was the aim of society.

---

1   Different authors have referred to the paradigm by different names: e.g. 'technocentrism' by Gladwin *et al.* (1995); 'egocentrism' by Merchant (1992); 'mechanism' by Capra (1996) and Zohar and Marshall (1993). 'Liberal individualism' is used here to reflect the 'root' philosophy underpinning the paradigm. It should be noted that liberalism in this context does not refer to the modem political liberalism, but rather to the classical liberalism articulated in the 17th and 18th centuries. All the many forms that liberalism has taken since then preserve the basic features discussed here, though specific political and economic ends sought have varied considerably.

The ethical foundations of liberalism were articulated by the utilitarian school of moral philosophy that treats pleasure and desire satisfaction as the sole element of human good, or utility.[2] Pure utilitarianism reduces *all* human relations entirely to this pattern. These assumptions were to be taken to their extreme by the classical economists, together with John Locke's assertion that private property was to be considered as the most basic of 'natural rights'. The publication of Adam Smith's *An Inquiry into the Nature and Causes of Wealth of Nations* in 1776 marked the beginning of the development of classical economic theory.

Smith envisaged a world of equal and sovereign individuals pursuing their own self-interests via their actions in markets or in the political arena. According to Smith, it could be shown that these activities, when left to operate so far as possible unchecked, produced the most rapid possible increase in the 'wealth of nations'—and therefore the happiness of all men. The basis of such social order was the division of labour.

The sum total of all these self-interested actions would produce maximum economic efficiency. The self-interested pursuit of efficiency seeks out the 'best' economic choices and ensures that resources are put to the 'best' economic uses. As a result, this generates maximum profits. Thus, it is concluded, an economy that is generating more wealth must also make society and everyone in it better off.

For the last 200 years, liberal individualism has dominated much of the development of social sciences in the Western world: sociology, psychology and evolutionary and management theories, to name but a few. Its most dominant influence can be perceived in the development of economic and organisational theories. The paradigm continues to exert its influence in mainstream elements of business practice, research and teaching (see e.g. Gray *et al.* 1996; Morgan 1997; Zohar 1997). It is typically taken for granted in conventional academic journals and textbooks, and expressed most forcefully by the neoclassical school of free-market economists headed by Milton Friedman (e.g. Friedman 1962). More recent free-market champions include, for example, Lowell and Farrell (1996) and Reisman (1997).

In the early 19th century, the classical economist theory came under attack mostly because the actual economic and social results of capitalism proved to be less happy than had been forecast. Of course, it could still be held that the misery of the poor was part of the process of the greatest happiness being conferred on the greatest number, which happened to be much lower than first expected. But optimism was dampened and critical enquiry provoked, especially into *distribution* of wealth as against its *production,* which had preoccupied Smith's generation.

A new ideology—**communitarianism**[3] —started to reformulate the old liberal verities. It shared the same foundation as liberalism: reason, science and progress.

---

2   In the liberal economy of recent history, this utility is to be measured by cash flows, profit and gross national product and, thus, the consequences (and therefore the 'rightness') of an action are captured in profit. A profitable action is a good action.

3   Communitarianism is used here in a similar way to 'liberalism': i.e. to capture a wide variety of views (such as anthropocentrism, socialism, communism, democratic socialism, utopian socialism, communal anarchism) that share basic tenets on concepts such as individuals and society.

The early socialists especially shared a belief in the Industrial Revolution, albeit for different reasons. Claude de Saint-Simon, the father of 'utopian socialism', was first and foremost the apostle of industrialism. Robert Owen, one of the early radical pioneers of the movement in Britain, was also a highly successful pioneer of the cotton industry.

However, communitarianism broke radically away from the liberal assumption that society was a mere aggregate of its individual atoms, that its motive force was their self-interest and competition. Instead, they argued that human beings have always lived in groups and in fact need to do so. Society was not a necessary but regrettable diminution of man's unlimited natural rights, but the setting of his life, happiness and individuality. As Owen (1813) put it: 'The primary and necessary object of all existence is to be happy, but happiness cannot be obtained individually; it is useless to expect isolated happiness; all must partake of it or the few will never enjoy it.'

During the first part of the 19th century, depression, falling wages, heavy unemployment and doubts about future expansive prospects of the economy were endemic. Critics could therefore fix not merely on the injustice of the economy, but on the defects of its operation, its 'internal contradictions'. The cyclical market fluctuations were detected and the increasingly uneven distribution of national incomes noted. The conclusion was that these were not accidents but built-in products of a defective system. The Smithian idea, that the exchange of equivalents in the market somehow assured social justice, struck communitarians as either incomprehensible or immoral.

The major historical philosophers representing this tradition include, for instance, Hegel and, following in his wake, Marx and Engels, including this century such postmodern philosophers as Wittgenstein and interventionist economist John Maynard Keynes.

Ecocentrism is a more recent phenomenon than the previous two, although its philosophical and spiritual antecedents are as old as Buddhism and Taoism. Ecocentrism asserts that everything on the planet is interconnected and interdependent, that stability comes from maintaining the diversity and harmony of living and non-living things. In addition to Eastern philosophies, supporters of the ecocentric worldview draw inspiration from indigenous reverence for life-giving earth, or the Gaia hypothesis (e.g. Lovelock 1988), the deep ecology (e.g. Merchant 1992; Sessions 1995), green or 'steady-state' economics (e.g. Schumacher 1973), and from new science systems thinking (e.g. Capra 1996).

Unlike liberalism and communitarianism, where humans are assumed to be 'the measure of all things' and in a dominant position over nature, ecocentrism places humanity alongside other species within and dependent upon natural systems. Non-human nature has intrinsic value, independent of human values and consciousness. This places limits to the extent of human prerogatives to use and alter it. Non-interference is considered to be the primary moral duty: 'a thing is right when it tends to preserve the integrity, stability and beauty of the biotic community' (Leopold 1949).

In stark contrast to the previous two paradigms, ecocentrism believes that humanity and the natural world are on a collision course that will result in global decay and chaos in the absence of urgent and radical reform (e.g. Kaplan 1994). The earth's life-supporting systems are viewed as fragile and its resources limited. Therefore, a minimalist development strategy is needed and human welfare understood as secondary to the wellbeing of the earth. Small-scale community-based economies defined by regional boundaries (bioregionalism) are advocated as the most appropriate way of organising production.

The great political struggles of the last two hundred years have been between liberalism and communitarianism: individualism versus collectivism, capitalism versus socialism, right against left. In contrast, ecocentrism is barely on the starting blocks. There are a few texts describing how difficult it is for socialists and ecologists to work together because of their different world-views. But there are entire libraries devoted to the struggles between capitalism and socialism. However, it is not likely that this 'either/or' struggle between different traditions will advance our understanding of how to establish a framework that embraces sustainable development in a holistic and integrated way. A reintegration of our understanding of individuals, communities and the biosphere is needed—clearly all of the traditions discussed here have something to contribute to such a paradigm. However, such a reintegration requires a shift in our mind-sets; it requires that we go beyond 'either/or' towards 'both/and' thinking. We need to open rather than close the dialogue between different stakeholders to sustainable development.

◢ Economic Barriers to the Advancement of an Integrated Sustainable Development Agenda

It has been estimated that the world's top 500 companies control 70% of global trade (Worldwatch Institute 1994). This type of monopolistic, or oligarchical, control is absolutely consistent with the development of Western corporate enterprise, even if it is not compatible with the original free-market theories of Adam Smith. The implications of oligarchical capitalism include distortion of trade and inequality of resource distribution. This is not an academic matter; the side-effects for people and environments are sometimes catastrophic (Jacobs 1991).

Accelerating global trade based on over-exploitation of people and natural resources will lead, if not checked, to numerous highly undesirable outcomes. The Wuppertal Institute has calculated that, if today's rate of consumption of resources in the industrialised countries is applied evenly to the entire population of the planet, and if the global population doubles by the year 2050, energy and material resource flows would have to increase tenfold (Weaver with Schmidt-Bleek 1999).

The implications of such calculations are dire indeed. If the newly industrialised countries of the Pacific Rim and the less developed countries of Africa and Latin America strive for levels of material consumption equal to that of industrialised countries in the next half-century, eco-efficiency will have to improve by nearly 90%. If such gains in eco-efficiency do not materialise, the kind of outcome predicted by the Worldwatch Institute will inevitably follow. The world in 2050 will not be an especially pleasant place: declining life expectancy, declining food resources and plummeting availability of goods and services.

Paradoxically, the scenario predicted above is still more of a barrier rather than a spur to integrative considerations of economic, ecological and social agendas. Those who currently hold economic power are not yet able quite to grasp the type of radical shift in economic relationships that would have to occur to avert the scenario described above. Economic self-interest argues for strengthening control over dwindling resources, further globalisation and monopolisation of markets, and further exploitation of people and environments in less developed countries. If there is going to be suffering, it had better be as far away as possible. So, debt in the majority world continues to rise, poverty increases and political conflict becomes more common— not necessarily in Western Europe and North America, but in Asia, Africa, Eastern Europe, the Middle East and Latin America.

◢ Business Ethics and Sustainable Development

These days it is not very fashionable to talk about the rights of workers, the rights of consumers or the rights of the community. Instead, we talk about opportunities for partnership, for consensus and for win–win solutions. But there can be no true partnerships in business or in any walk of life without a framework of basic rights. There can be no consensus without democratic decision-making and there can be no win–win situations in business when basic regulations on working conditions and the environment are being eroded. And, if this happens in mature democracies, no one should be too surprised if standards are flouted in countries where democratic governance structures are lagging behind or yet to emerge.

Franklin D. Roosevelt once said, 'Goods produced under conditions which do not meet a rudimentary standard of decency should be regarded as contraband and ought not to be allowed to pollute the channels of interstate trade.' It would be interesting to hear what he would have to say today. What would he make of the phenomenal acceleration of global trade, spurred on by the GATT and NAFTA and paid for in the sweatshops of South-East Asia and in the plantations of South America? What would Roosevelt say today about the control of global trade by transnational corporations more powerful than sovereign states? Or about the trillions of dollars that slosh around the international money markets chasing the fastest profits and (as often as not) the lowest costs?

Whether one is in business, in politics or simply an ordinary worker or consumer, like it or not, one is linked directly or indirectly the world's most distressing and depressing problems. Switching on a domestic appliance makes one a consumer of electricity and therefore a contributor to pollution, climate change and the depletion of non-renewable natural resources. Driving a car links one to all of the above plus urban smog and hence respiratory diseases. A cup of coffee (unless the brand is carefully chosen) links one to exploitation of coffee pickers in developing countries. Even wearing cotton (unless it is organic) links one to the routine pesticide poisoning of tens of thousands of plantation workers.

So where does one start with problems as immense and as depressing as these? How can individuals and corporations change their behaviours so that they become part of the solution, rather than part of an accelerating problem? In short, how do we all become more economically, ecologically and socially sustainable?

If Roosevelt were alive today, perhaps he would successfully diagnose the depression and prescribe a New Deal. But what would such a new deal for sustainable development in business look like? The rest of this chapter aims to explore this and to propose some practical ways forward.

◢ The Renewal of Business

The Body Shop approach to socially and ecologically responsible business is driven by three simple and straightforward concepts.

1. Compliance

First, the company aims to take into account the responsibility of business never to abuse people, the environment or animals. This means adhering to defined standards of human rights, social responsibility and safety. It means a commitment to environmental protection and, where relevant, wider ethical issues such as animal welfare.

2. Accountability and Transparency

As the next step, the company aims to go beyond compliance with standards and be open about the company's record on social, environmental and ethical issues. The premise here is that transparency develops relationships of trust and facilitates constructive dialogue between the company and its stakeholders.

3. Active Engagement and Dialogue

The Body Shop believes that a truly socially engaged company will take the third step after compliance and disclosure. This is actively to engage in dialogue and advocate positive change in the way the business world—and, ultimately, the wider society—works. The Body Shop's mission statement dedicates the company to the pursuit of social and environmental change.

The company acknowledges that advocacy requires a political outlook. This does not mean party politics, but it does require that the company's stakeholders are prepared to join a common platform; without this no constructive dialogue or mutual learning can take place.

These ideas are not new. There is a long record of philosophical thinking and entrepreneurial initiatives that have been driven by motives other than maximisation of profit. In the 18th century Robert Owen developed a new model for worker-friendly capitalism in New Lanark; the Rochdale Pioneers followed by establishing the co-operative movement in 1844 (Cannon 1992); while various Quaker-run enterprises developed new models for consumer-friendly commerce (Galbraith 1977). A century ago William Morris showed how an enterprise could produce aesthetically pleasing and commercially successful products without excessively damaging the environment or human dignity in the process (MacCarthy 1994).

In the 20th century we have seen the emergence of municipal and state enterprises aimed at delivering integrated public services and prioritising health and wellbeing before profits. For the best part of a century Britain did not need share options and fabulous salaries to run the sewers and water supplies of its major cities efficiently.

Today, more and more evidence is surfacing that some companies have for a long time taken Roosevelt's notion of 'rudimentary standards of decency' and inclusion of stakeholders very seriously and, in doing so, have gained significant competitive advantages.

In their best-selling book, *Built to Last*, Collins and Porras (1995) demonstrated that the key to success for 18 US corporations with successful 100-year track records was a strong commitment to developing people and an unfailing ability to capture and share knowledge. The 18 companies also outperformed US stock markets by a factor of 70.

In a study conducted by two Harvard researchers, the performance of businesses that balanced stakeholder interests was compared with that of companies following a 'shareholder first' philosophy. Over an 11-year period, companies that gave equal priority to employees, customers and shareholders enjoyed sales growth of four times and employment growth of eight times that of the 'shareholder first' companies (Kotter and Heskett 1992).

In a study of British firms following stakeholder-inclusive principles, Kleinwort Benson—a merchant banker—found that 32 'stakeholder-inclusive' stocks rose 90% over a 3½-year period compared with an all-share average rise of 38% (Phillips *et al.* 1997).

So, the lesson to draw from 200 years of European and North American enterprise is that in the long term it is most efficient when it is in closest harmony with producers, consumers and the wider community of stakeholders. Private or public ownership does not seem to matter so much as stakeholder inclusion and support. This is where a systematic approach to accountability and transparency fits in. It is also where the opportunities for sustainable development and enlightened enterprise coincide.

◢ Accounting for Sustainable Development?

In recent years European and North American companies have been at the vanguard of corporate accountability with respect to disclosure of environmental information (SustainAbility *et al.* 1993; SustainAbility/UNEP 1996a, 1997). Leading companies are now producing regular environmental reports that present comprehensive profiles, increasingly verified by independent agencies and freely distributed to stakeholders.

The Body Shop has produced five such statements in line with the European Union Eco-Management and Auditing Scheme (EMAS).

In 1992 the Rio Conference produced a blueprint for a more sustainable planet entitled *Agenda 21*. That document made clear the desire of world leaders that corporations should be held accountable for their environmental impacts. The chapter on business and industry stated: 'Business and industry, including transnational corporations, should be encouraged to report annually on their environmental records, as well as on their use of energy and natural resources.'

The Fifth Environmental Action Programme of the European Community, entitled *Towards Sustainability*, also included an exhortation to transparency on environmental performance: 'The public must have access to environmentally relevant data to enable them to monitor the performance of industry and regulators alike.'

But, while it is laudable and impressive that *environmental* accountability has arrived—at least for a handful of large corporations—there are other dimensions that need to be considered in order to facilitate the move towards a more holistic understanding of accountability. Without an acceptance on the part of business of a wider notion of accountability and its underpinning concepts of auditing, accounting and public reporting, the advancement of the holistic sustainable development agenda will suffer. Environmental accountability is clearly necessary but not a sufficient condition for discharging accountability within the domain of sustainable development.

As noted earlier, sustainable development is not just about the environment, it is also about socially and economically sustainable development in their own right. And social and economic justice is needed if sustainable development in any of the three dimensions is to be achieved. Sustainable development needs to embrace the rights of people living in the impoverished, debt-laden majority world as well as the rights of generations as yet unborn. We cannot ignore the fact that 80% of the world's resources are consumed by 20% of the people on the planet. We cannot ignore the likely implications of a doubling of the world's population in the next few decades set against increasing inequality of access to natural resources. And we cannot ignore the accelerating fragmentation of social cohesion in the industrialised world, where a 'culture of contentment' for some means dispossession and depression for so many (Galbraith 1992). These are some of the reasons why the social dimension of sustainable development needs to be taken seriously.

◻ *The Body Shop Approach to Social Auditing*

In the early 1990s The Body Shop recognised that environmental auditing and public reporting was not enough to discharge accountability on the wider obligations and responsibilities the company had to society and its stakeholders (The Body Shop 1996). A wider approach was needed in order to help the company improve its ethical performance more systematically over time and assess its other than environmental impacts. The company needed an approach that would enable it to assess its performance: first of all against the aspirations it had set itself in its mission statement; secondly against the specific aspirations and needs of its stakeholders;

and thirdly against the established statutory and non-statutory norms relating to its social performance.

So in 1993 The Body Shop started looking for ways to answer these questions in a systematic, comprehensive and public way. The first task was to review existing methods of social auditing. Immediately it emerged that it was not going to be a simple task. Unlike environmental auditing and reporting where there were clear regulations and best-practice frameworks to follow, there was no equivalent for social auditing.

The development of social auditing can be traced back at least to the 1960s. The first attempts were largely concerned with expanding conventional financial reporting to include information on 'corporate social expenditure' in response to intensifying criticism from the general public. By the late 1970s the majority of the US *Fortune 500* companies included a page or two in their annual reports to inform readers of their social expenditure or to provide information on such issues as equal opportunities or community relations.

In the 1980s a second 'wave' of social auditing emerged, essentially driven by the consumer movement and the ethical investment community who were keen to build up and publish profiles of corporate social performance. Although not necessarily referred to as 'social audits', that was very much what they were trying to do—to measure and communicate how companies rated against certain sets of ethical criteria. A number of these investigations became instant bestsellers in the late 1980s and early 1990s: for instance, *Shopping for a Better World* (Council on Economic Priorities *et al.* 1994) and *The 100 Best Companies to Work for in America* (Levering and Moskowitz 1993).

The 1990s have seen the beginning of a third wave in social auditing driven mostly by companies from within the progressive social responsibility movement. This time social auditing was to be driven by the organisations themselves, no longer imposed from the outside.

In 1991 Traidcraft plc, a UK-based fair-trading organisation, joined forces with the not-for-profit think-tank, the New Economics Foundation (NEF), to develop an internally driven, systematic approach to social auditing based on a mix of participative research and organisational development techniques. This initiative was a pioneering effort in advancing a more rigorous approach to social auditing driven by the 'stakeholder' philosophy (Zadek and Evans 1993).

The early 1990s also saw the emergence of the 'ethical accounting' approach adopted by Sbn Bank, a regional Danish bank. A number of Scandinavian organisations, ranging from small companies to hospitals and schools, have now adopted this method. Like the NEF/Traidcraft method, ethical accounting involves a consultation process with the organisation's key stakeholders. Beyond this, the approach encourages stakeholders to propose practical changes to the organisation's operational practices: e.g. customer services or product development. Unlike the NEF/ Traidcraft approach, however, the published statement is not externally verified (Pruzan 1997).

Another example is the approach adopted by the American ice cream manufacturer, Ben & Jerry's Homemade. The main feature of the Ben & Jerry's approach was to invite a high-profile advocate of corporate social responsibility to spend time each year exploring any aspect of the company's activities that he or she might deem important. The idea is that the external commentator has free access to the company's internal records and freedom to consult the company's stakeholders. Based on this process, the investigator then wrote a personal evaluation or 'social statement' (Parker 1997).

As Zadek *et al.* (1997) point out, a comparison of the various emerging approaches is not straightforward, since the circumstances of different processes have often been critical in determining the design. However, they suggest that there are clear signs of a convergence of standards and emergence of consensus about what constitutes good practice. In particular, the establishment of the Institute of Social and Ethical AccountAbility in 1996 encouraged the emergence of a professional approach with agreed standards not only in the method but also in the quality of practice (Gonella *et al.* 1998).

The key principles of social auditing advocated by the Institute are shown in Box 1. These have been adopted by The Body Shop as drivers for the continuous development of its own methodology and process of implementation.

As mentioned earlier, the development of the social audit methodology used by The Body Shop commenced in 1993 and was formalised for the first audit cycle of 1994/95. The methodology was developed collaboratively with NEF with the aim of synthesising aspects of environmental auditing, total quality management and the

Completeness: the unbiased inclusion, over time, of all appropriate areas of activity in the accounting process.

Comparability: the extent to which it is possible to compare an organisation's performance with (1) that of previous periods; or (2) external benchmarks drawn from the experience of other organisations, statutory regulations or non-statutory norms.

Inclusivity: the conduct of an audit with appropriate dialogue with all its stakeholders on terms that allow them to voice their interests and concerns without fear or any other basis for restriction.

Regularity and evolution: the periodic preparation of accounts and conduct of an audit; the conduct of audits at appropriate times.

Embeddedness: the appropriate incorporation of accounting processes, consultation and audit findings within the strategic, managerial practice and policy, and operational levels of the organisation.

Disclosure: the appropriate and effective communication to one or more of an organisation's stakeholders of (1) the statements or reports produced by an organisation; (2) the audit process (e.g. stakeholder consultation records); (3) related externally produced verification statements.

External verification: the verification of the records, process, reports or statements of an organisation by an independent third party.

Continuous improvement: recognised and verified steps taken to improve performance in relation to values and objectives of stakeholders (including management) and broader social norms.

Box 1: THE KEY PRINCIPLES OF SOCIAL AUDIT

Source: Gonella *et al.* 1998: iii

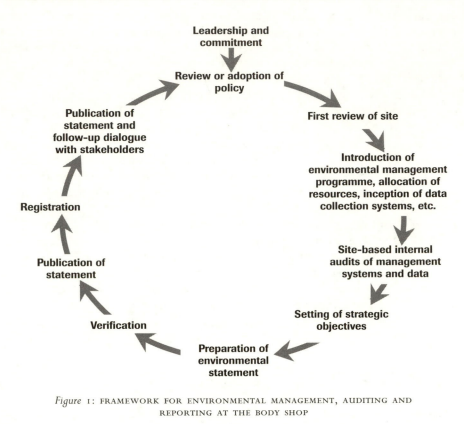

Figure 1: FRAMEWORK FOR ENVIRONMENTAL MANAGEMENT, AUDITING AND
REPORTING AT THE BODY SHOP

Source: The Body Shop 1996: 12

existing tradition of academic and practical work in social auditing. The ideas behind stakeholder inclusion and learning organisations were also key sources of inspiration for the development work.

The framework presented in Fig. 1 depicts a generalised cycle of stakeholder inclusion which may be used for auditing and improving relationships with employees, customers, investors and indeed any social stakeholder group.

Readers familiar with processes of continuous improvement for quality, environmental or safety will be familiar with the cyclical nature of such processes. Broadly speaking, they all follow the mantra 'think–plan–do–check'. They also fit neatly within systems that may be externally certified by bodies accredited under national, European or international (ISO) standards.

It is worth noting that, by the time The Body Shop started the development of its social audit methodology, the company was in the midst of its third environmental audit cycle. In 1991 The Body Shop adopted the (then draft) European Community Eco-Audit Regulation as the principle framework for the company's environmental

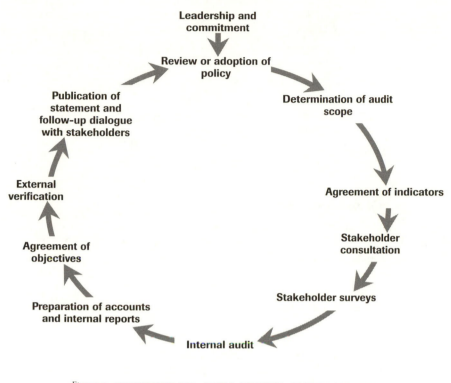

Figure 2: FRAMEWORK FOR SOCIAL AUDITING AT THE BODY SHOP

Source: The Body Shop 1996: 17

management, auditing and public reporting. During 1992/93, the draft regulation underwent further negotiation and development, eventually emerging as the European Union Eco-Management and Auditing Scheme (EMAS). The scheme retained its voluntary nature, but several essential components—most notably continuous improvement of performance, a commitment to best practice and independently verified public disclosure—ensured that the measure retained credibility. The Body Shop's experience of EMAS has been very positive. Despite the parallel emergence of British (BS 7750) and international (ISO 14001) standards, the company believes that EMAS represents the most exacting framework for ensuring best environmental practice in industry.

The experience gained in conducting environmental audits provided significant guidance for the systematisation of the emerging social audit approach. This can easily be seen by comparing the audit frameworks in use by the company as depicted in Figures 1 and 2.

However, the driving philosophy behind social audit development work has been that all continuous improvement standards, whether for environment, safety or quality, must be linked to cycles of dialogue and inclusion for stakeholders. Thus a product quality standard means very little if there is no active dialogue between suppliers, business partners, employees and customers. An occupational safety and health management system necessarily needs to link with processes of dialogue with employees, enforcing authorities and relevant professionals. The added value of a social audit methodology, as depicted in Figure 2, is the systematisation of such dialogue and inclusion into the overall audit framework.

The following describes each of the key components of the social audit cycle briefly; more guidance and case studies can be found in *The Stakeholder Corporation* (Wheeler and Sillanpää 1997).

⌀ Leadership and Commitment

The Body Shop's commitment to social auditing followed the publication of Anita Roddick's autobiography in 1991 in which she wrote: 'I would love it if every shareholder of every company wrote a letter every time they received a company's annual report and accounts. I would like them to say something like, "OK, that's fine, very good. But where are the details of your environmental audit? Where are the details of your accounting to the community? Where is your social audit?"' (Roddick 1991).

There is no doubt that, had it not been for the commitment of the company founders and the development of an 'accountability ethos' within The Body Shop in the early 1990s, the company would not have been in a position to publish a statement of its social performance in 1996. As with environmental auditing, clear leadership is probably the most important single factor in driving a process of social auditing to a successful conclusion.

⌀ Review or Adoption of Policy

In every company there will be a variety of formal and non-formal policies that prescribe the organisation's intentions with respect to its stakeholders or its social performance in general. These may include occupational safety and health, remuneration and benefits policies, and terms and conditions for suppliers. There may be dividend policies for shareholders, codes of ethics for company representatives working overseas, product development guidelines and so on.

Clear policies help provide a framework for assessing the quality of a company's relationships with and impact on its stakeholders. Before any assessment or audit of social relationships, a company should be aware of its explicit and implicit intentions with respect to each stakeholder group and its overall social aspirations.

For The Body Shop's first social audit, the main policies against which performance was assessed were the company's mission statement and trading charter. More specific policies and guidelines existed, for instance, for human resources and fair trade.

◻ *Determination of Audit Scope*

Because parallel systems existed at The Body Shop for auditing performance with respect to animal protection and the environment, the subject area of the social audit was restricted to people: human stakeholders who may affect or be affected by the company. The number of individual stakeholder groups could theoretically be quite large and a decision had to be taken as to which groups should be included in the first and subsequent audit cycles. The Body Shop took the view that, in the first cycle, the net should be cast as wide and as deep as possible. But inevitably some groups and sub-groups could not be reached for practical reasons.

Another important factor in the scoping of a social audit is geography. Where a company has wholly or majority-owned operations in different countries, a decision has to be taken as to whether one or all countries are to be covered in each cycle. For The Body Shop this meant choosing to concentrate mostly on UK-based groups in the first cycle.

The last factor to be taken into account in scoping is the degree to which indirect stakeholders may be embraced. For The Body Shop this required a decision about whether, for example, staff of franchisees or non-governmental organisations in franchised markets should be included. It was decided that such stakeholders were better consulted directly at such a time when franchisees were able to conduct their own audit processes.

The stakeholder groups for The Body Shop's first social audit included:

- Staff employed directly by The Body Shop International
- International head franchisees
- UK and US local franchisees
- UK and US customers
- Suppliers
- Community Trade suppliers
- Shareholders
- Local community (Littlehampton)
- UK non-governmental organisations
- The Body Shop Foundation applicants

◻ *Agreement of Benchmarks and Performance Indicators*

There are two types of measure for assessing the quality of human relationships: those based on quantifiable norms and standards and those based on perceptions.

Quantitative measures in business are frequently described as benchmarks or performance indicators. For a shareholder it might be earnings per share or dividend cover; for a supplier it might be average speed of payments; for an employee from an ethnic minority group it might be statistics on promotion rates for minorities.

There are three types of performance measurement in The Body Shop's approach to social auditing.

Performance against standards (performance indicators). These should reflect information on activities and policies relevant to the organisation's social performance. Measures may be both quantitative and qualitative. The internal audit team agrees standards with relevant departments which then have the responsibility for collecting data, which in turn are validated by the audit and verification processes.

Where appropriate, departments are encouraged to set internal benchmarks/targets relating to individual standards, and to collate information on external benchmarks. Therefore, the ideal set of information relating to individual standards should evolve towards the format shown in Table 1. Where data are available, historical data on performance indicators should be reported at least for the preceding audit cycle.

Stakeholder perception of performance against core values. These core values are essentially defined by the organisation itself (e.g., in The Body Shop's case, its mission statement). Each stakeholder group is consulted to establish their perception of how closely the organisation's performance matches its stated aspirations.

Stakeholder perception of performance against specific needs of stakeholders. These needs are particular to individual stakeholder groups. They are identified as salient through consultation with stakeholders in focus groups and measured in anonymous and confidential surveys of opinion.

◁ *Stakeholder Consultation and Surveys*

Qualitative measures are arguably the most important barometer of human relationships. For effective stakeholder inclusion, *perceptions are reality*. Engaging stakeholders in direct dialogue is one of the most important and sensitive processes in social auditing. It is especially important that the process engages stakeholder groups in face-to-face dialogue to explore specific stakeholder needs and to allow stakeholder views and concerns to be expressed.

Standard	Performance indicator	Internal benchmark/target	External benchmark
e.g. employee turnover	Based on ongoing internal monitoring; data and monitoring process subject to internal audit and verification	Based on target-setting by relevant department or company	Based on publicly available data on, e.g., industry performance

Table 1: IDEAL FORMAT FOR REPORTING PERFORMANCE INDICATORS

After specific issues have been identified as salient or of particular interest to stakeholders, questionnaires are designed to measure more wide-scale opinion. These questionnaires are intended to capture perceptions of the company's performance against both stakeholder-specific needs and core values articulated by the company.

The Body Shop uses professional assistance in the final design of the questionnaires in order to avoid inadvertent introduction of bias. Space is allowed on the questionnaires themselves for open-ended commentary on the company's performance. Respondents complete the questionnaires anonymously and return them to an independent organisation for confidential analysis. Only summary information and lists of comments are submitted to The Body Shop for inclusion in the audit process.

In The Body Shop's experience, large-scale confidential surveys of opinion where the questionnaires themselves are co-designed with stakeholder representatives can be applied to almost any relationship.

◻ *Internal Audits, Preparation of Accounts and Internal Reports*

Management audits are sometimes based on professional codes and standards; this is especially true of financial audits. They may be based on checklists and document inspection, or they may be interview-based. Audits may include a mix of all of these approaches in order to check that systems of quality control and continuous improvement are in place and working effectively.

With stakeholder relationships and social performance, all of the above applies, but formal audit procedures have developed only recently. There are as yet no professional or accredited international standards, although the Institute for Social and Ethical AccountAbility is working towards them (ISEA 1997).

There are three main sources of information for The Body Shop's social audit process: (1) the results of the stakeholder consultation described above; (2) data on agreed quantitative and qualitative indicators; and (3) the output from confidential internal audit interviews with staff and managers. Checklists have been developed specifically for the purpose of the interviews and results used to build up a dynamic picture of departmental handling and knowledge of issues and company policies relevant to social performance.

In recent years, the internal management systems audit has been further developed toward an integrated methodology whereby individual departments were audited on systems relating to policies on environment, animal protection, human resources, communications, occupational health and safety, information management and other relevant ethical issues.

The audits result in timetabled action plans prioritising recommendations for proposed improvements. The audit reports together with procedural documentation are made available to external verifiers. The management systems audits are conducted by a semi-independent audit team which reports directly to the executive committee of the company.

◻ *Agreement of Objectives*

Target-setting provides perhaps the key leverage for continuous improvement in any auditing and public reporting context. Strategic objectives help clarify the future priorities of the company and give practical meaning to its long-term vision. Thus an organisation committed to the long-term environmental dimension of sustainable development might set a medium-term objective of achieving an environmental management systems standard such as EMAS—or ISO 14001, its less demanding international equivalent.

Setting strategic objectives and placing these in the public domain requires a significant amount of internal discussion, management commitment and senior 'sign-off'. Objectives should be consistent with both organisational direction and stakeholder aspirations. Obviously, a balance must be maintained between the various needs or aspirations and the available resources. But the overall direction should be one of continuous improvement and progress in all relationships.

Each objective relating to specific stakeholder relationships should be visibly 'owned' by individual senior executives, who may then be held accountable for delivering within agreed time-scales. It is a prerequisite, therefore, that all executives should feel comfortable with their commitments and that they have adequate resources to execute them. In The Body Shop's experience, an important point is that target-setting within the social audit process tends to embrace a wider set of senior decision-makers within the company, compared to target-setting within the environmental audit process. This is one of the reasons why social auditing is perceived to have significant governance implications.

The Body Shop has had a formal target-setting programme within its environmental management system since 1992. Similar target-setting programmes were established for animal protection and stakeholder-related performance when audit methodologies were established for these during 1994/95.

The Body Shop's first Social Statement, published in January 1996, included a response from the relevant board member or senior executive to each stakeholder section. In all, 89 specific 'Next Step' commitments were made together with seven company-wide strategic targets. The *Values Report 1997* reports on progress towards these targets. The external verifiers assessed the company's claims towards these targets. The 1997 statement included 99 new targets relating to the company's social performance as well as 11 integrated targets where social performance forms a component part (in addition, 38 environmental and seven animal protection related targets were set). Table 2 gives some examples of the targets set in response to the 1997 social audit results.

◻ *Verification and Certification*

As noted earlier, independent verification or certification is now accepted practice in financial accounting, environmental management and quality. In The Body Shop's experience, it is also of enormous value in assessing and improving the quality of relationships with stakeholders. Organisations such as the New Economics Founda-

Stakeholder group	Target
Employees	**Disability.** We will introduce and communicate a new Disability Policy in 1998 following a review of current working practices through a 'disability lens'.

Advocacy. An Employee Advocacy system will have been launched in September 1997 following selection and training of 12 employees to advise, support and, if appropriate, represent employees facing disciplinary interviews and taking out grievances against the company. |
| International head franchisees | **Clarification of roles and responsibilities of The Body Shop International and head franchisees.** Roles and responsibilities will be drafted for discussion and agreement with head franchisees by the end of 1997.

Accessory supplier auditing. From 1998 all suppliers of accessories purchased directly by head franchisees will be screened via an ethical audit process.* |
| Customers | **Genetically modified ingredients.** From 1998 we will request information from our suppliers on whether ingredients have been genetically modified and, if so, provide information to our customers.* |
| Suppliers | **Improved forecasting.** By August 1998 we will have established mechanisms to improve forecasting information provided to suppliers.

Human rights policy and evaluation. By the end of 1997 we will have implemented a company-wide human rights policy and appropriate processes for monitoring our external (e.g. supplier) relationships. We will also involve our franchisees in implementing equivalent policies in their markets. |
Shareholders	**Employee investors.** During 1998 we will implement a system to monitor the proportion of employees holding shares in the company.
Local community	**Local community regeneration.** We will set an annual budget for 1998 and 1999 in support of Littlehampton 2000 regeneration initiatives.
Campaigning partners	**Guidelines for lobbying.** By 1999 we will have formalised guidelines on our approach to lobbying for the benefit of The Body Shop International employees, franchisees and franchisee employees.

* Targets marked with an asterisk denote 'integrated' targets: i.e. targets that have relevance to social, environmental and/or animal protection performance.

Table 2: SOME EXAMPLES OF 1997 SOCIAL AUDIT TARGETS

tion have pioneered techniques of social audit verification with some success. It involves, for instance, documentation review, testing the veracity of numerical accounts, examining the integrity of internal management and audit systems and ultimately signing off on the accuracy of published reports as 'true and fair' accounts. Such panels also provide an additional level of civic-society 'verification' or appropriation of the audit process.

◯ *Publication of Statement and Dialogue with Stakeholders*

In order to make the cycle of inclusion complete, it is important that effective communication of results occurs. Stakeholders who have been consulted need to know (1) what was the output of that consultation; and (2) what is the company's response. How else can they judge the benefits (or otherwise) of their continued participation in the process itself? Follow-up dialogue helps shape future audit cycles, enables indicators and data presentation to be fine-tuned for future cycles and helps set priorities for future action by the company. In effect, the true process of dialogue begins to take shape after the first report has been published. In this way, transparency facilitates genuine dialogue between well-informed parties. True dialogue is only possible where all parties have access to adequate information.

◢ *Sustainable Development and the Future of Social Auditing*

Sustainability and sustainable development remain elusive concepts. They have variously been referred to as, for instance, 'vision expression', 'value change', 'moral development', 'social reorganisation', or 'transformational process' (see e.g. Gladwin *et al.* 1995). As noted in the introduction to this chapter, the core idea has been defined most influentially by the Brundtland Commission. However, the definition remains abstract and difficult to operationalise. Some observers predict that the concept will remain fuzzy, elusive, contestable and controversial for some time to come. This hardly comes as a surprise bearing in mind the ideological juxtapositions briefly discussed earlier in this chapter.

Yet definitional diversity is to be expected when dealing with an emerging 'big idea'. Sustainable development has been likened to concepts such as democracy, liberty and equality—which have all taken considerable time to evolve. However, rather than lament the difficult task ahead, we may find some solace in Kuhn's (1970) observations about the nature of scientific revolutions: the development of new paradigms requires that we accept initial ambiguity and at the same time proactively participate in the debate between competing and conflicting views.

This is where stakeholder-inclusive social auditing fits in. It offers two avenues for further exploration: (1) helping to establish the substantive meaning of the social dimension of sustainable development in its own right; and (2) facilitating the development of integrated auditing tools across the different dimensions of sustainable development.

So far the social audit process as implemented by The Body Shop and other companies using similar methods has chiefly addressed issues that fall within the realm of assessing the sustainability of the company's relationships with its human stakeholders. The existing methodology does not as yet enable any objective assessments of whether or not an organisation is more or less socially sustainable (either over time or compared to other organisations), or whether or not its actions have contributed to socially sustainable development. Such substantive assessments are not possible in the absence of agreed criteria defining socially sustainable outcomes.[4]

The stakeholder-inclusive techniques utilised by the social audit process may provide useful starting points for establishing such criteria. It is unlikely—and indeed undesirable—that any organisation on its own will be able to define sustainable development and redirect its operations accordingly without engaging its external and internal stakeholders in the process. Understanding sustainable development requires mediation (Blauert and Zadek 1998).

The second inroad into deeper understanding of sustainable development is related to the above. Ultimately there must be an integration of economic, ecological and social accounting methodologies if our aim is to establish a holistic methodology for assessing progress or contributions toward sustainable development. Towards this aim, it would be relatively easy to widen the scope of the social audit consultation process to solicit stakeholder views relating to the ecological and economic dimensions of sustainable development in addition to the social dimension. This development could provide useful insights into perceived development priorities as well as levels of tolerance in regard to different trade-offs. Understanding trade-offs and the interfaces across different dimensions potentially presents the most challenging area for sustainability accounting (e.g. Elkington 1997). Stakeholder consultation and dialogue may provide the pragmatic springboard for approaching this challenge.

◢ *Conclusion*

In recent years business leaders have been forced to take seriously the demands of stakeholders for safer and more environmentally responsible operations (Schmidheiny *et al.* 1992; Taylor *et al.* 1994). This has been manifested in the adoption of diverse technical management solutions (WBCSD 1995) and an increase in environmental accountability on the part of larger corporations who have elected to publish reports of their environmental performance (SustainAbility *et al.* 1993; SustainAbility/UNEP 1996a, 1997).

These developments, though welcome, cannot deliver sustainable development for business and industry on their own. New paradigms are needed, together with complementary management theories and practices (Gladwin *et al.* 1995; Shrivastava 1996). New economic models, new measures of performance as well as measurement techniques are required in order to facilitate sustainable development that embraces a more holistic agenda covering the economic, ecological and social dimensions (Elkington 1997; Daly and Cobb 1994; Welford and Jones 1994). This chapter has focused on social accountability as one of the essential arenas where new methodologies and techniques need to be developed. The Body Shop experience in social auditing has been offered as one possible model for advancing transparency of corporate social performance.

---

4   The situation is similar within the realm of ecological sustainability. However, the Natural Step initiative has had some success in defining criteria for sustainability-enhancing decision-making (Robèrt 1994).

Genuine progress towards sustainable development will require willingness on the part of business to be held accountable for its performance across the spectrum of stakeholders' ethical concerns. This in turn presents a challenge to the development of sustainability accounting. Economic, ecological and social accounting methodologies are clearly at very different evolutionary stages and their development and implementation is often underpinned by incongruent world-views. Ultimately, however, there must be an integration of accounting methodologies if our aim is to establish a holistic tool for assessing progress or contributions toward sustainable development. This chapter concludes that the social audit methodology provides some useful avenues for exploring the meaning of the social dimension of sustainable development in its own right as well as providing a stakeholder-inclusive model for exploring the meaning of the wider sustainable development agenda.

Bibliography

Abe, A., and M. Takahashi (1998) 'The Actual Situation regarding Use and Release of Chemical Substances in Facilities of the Kanagawa Prefecture', *Management of Environmental Resources* 34.1: 27-37.

ACBE (Advisory Council on Business and the Environment) (1996) *Environmental Reporting and the Financial Sector: An Approach to Good Practice* (London: Department of Environment).

ACCA (Association of Chartered Certified Accountants) (1997a) *The First European Environmental Reporting Award Scheme: Criteria Used by Judges* (London: ACCA).

ACCA (Association of Chartered Certified Accountants) in association with Aspinwall & Co. and BRECSU (1997b) *Guide to Environment and Energy Reporting and Accounting* (London: ACCA).

Accounting Standards Board (UK) (1996) *Draft Statement of Principles* (London: Accounting Standards Board).

Adams, C., W. Hill and C. Roberts (1995) *Environmental, Employee and Ethical Reporting in Europe* (London: Association of Chartered Certified Accountants [ACCA]).

Adams, R. (1997) 'Are Financial and Environmental Performance Related?', *Environmental Accounting and Auditing Reporter*, May 1997: 4-7.

Adams, R., J. Carruthers and S. Hamil (1991) *Changing Corporate Values* (London: New Consumer/ Kogan Page).

Adams, R., and A. Willis (1998) *Sustainability Reporting: Frameworks, Concepts and Credibility* (Prepared for the Global Reporting Initiative; Boston, MA: CERES, August 1998).

Adriaanse, A. (1994) *Environmental Policy Indicators: A Study on the Development of Indicators for Environmental Policy in the Netherlands* (The Hague: VROM [Dutch Ministry of Housing, Spatial Planning and Environment]).

Alabaster, T., and M. Hawthorne (1999) 'Information for Environmental Citizenship', *Sustainable Development* 8 (in press).

Alabaster, T., and J. Walton (1997) 'Practising what they Teach: Universities, Industry and Environmental Reporting', *Environmental Information Bulletin* 64 (February 1997): 11-15.

American Petroleum Institute (1998) *Petroleum Industry Environmental Performance* (Washington, DC: American Petroleum Institute).

Arnold, M., and R. Day (1998) *The Next Bottom Line: Making Sustainable Development Tangible* (Washington, DC: World Resources Institute).

Ashford, N.A., and R. Meima (1993) 'Designing the Sustainable Enterprise', *Summary Report, Second International Research Conference, The Greening of Industry Network* (Cambridge, MA, November 1993).

Aucott, M. (1995) 'Release versus Throughput', *Pollution Prevention Review*, Winter 1994/95: 3-16.

Axelrod, R. (1998) 'Ten Years Later: The State of Environmental Performance Reports Today', *Environmental Quality Management*, Winter 1998: 1-13.

Azzone, G., M. Brophy, G. Noci, R. Welford and W. Young (1997) 'A Stakeholder's View of Environmental Reporting', *Long Range Planning* 30.5 (October 1997): 699-709.

Azzone, G., and R. Manzini (1994) 'Measuring Strategic Environmental Performance', *Business Strategy and the Environment* 3.1 (Spring 1994): 1-4.

Azzone, G., R. Manzini, G. Noci, R. Welford and C.W. Young (1996) 'Defining Environmental Performance Indicators: An Integrated Framework', *Business Strategy and the Environment* 5.2: 69-80.

Barrett, R. (1998) *Liberating the Corporate Soul* (London: Butterworth–Heinemann).

Barry, N. (1998) *Business Ethics* (London: Macmillan).

Bartolomeo, M. (1995) *Environmental Performance Indicators in Industry* (Milan: Fondazione ENI Enrico Mattei).

Bartolomeo, M., M. Bennett, J. Bouma, P. Heydkamp, P. James and T. Wolters (1999) *Eco-Management Accounting* (Dordrecht: Kluwer).

Bartolomeo, M., and F. Ranghieri (1998) *The Ceramic Tiles Association HSE Report* (Milan: Fonadazione ENI Enrico Mattei).

Bebbington, J., and I. Thompson (1996) *Business Concepts of Sustainability and the Implications for Accountancy* (London: Association of Chartered Certified Accountants [ACCA]).

Beecham, K. (1993) 'Corporate Environmental Reporting: The Theory and Practice', *The Green Alliance Practitioners' Conference* (17 December 1993), at *http://www.gn.apc.org/gralliance/tross.html*.

Behmanesh, N., J. Roque and D. Allen (1993) 'An Analysis of Normalised Measures of Pollution Prevention', *Pollution Prevention Review*, Spring 1993: 161-66.

Benchmark Environmental Consulting (1995) *ISO 14000: An Uncommon Perspective* (Brussels: European Environmental Bureau).

Bennett, M., and P. James (1997) 'Environment-Related Management Accounting: Current Practice and Future Trends', *Greener Management International* 17 (Spring 1997): 32-51; also in M. Bennett and P. James (eds.), *The Green Bottom Line. Environmental Accounting for Management: Current Practice and Future Trends* (Sheffield, UK: Greenleaf Publishing, 1998).

Bennett, M., and P. James (1998a) *Environment under the Spotlight: Current Practices and Future Trends in Environment-Related Performance Measurement for Business* (Research Report 55; London: Association of Chartered Certified Accountants [ACCA]).

Bennett, M., and P. James (1998b) *The Green Bottom Line. Environmental Accounting for Management: Current Practice and Future Trends* (Sheffield, UK: Greenleaf Publishing).

Bennett, M., and P. James (1998c) 'Views of Financial Stakeholders on Environmental Accounting and Performance Measurement in Business: Report on a Consultation Project', Proceedings of *Continuity, Credibility and Comparability: Key Challenges for Corporate Environmental Performance Measurement and Communication*, Invitational Expert Seminar, Eze, France, 13–16 June 1998, International Institute for Industrial Environmental Economics, Lund University, Sweden.

Biekart, J.W. (1996) *Verslag van de workshop toeleveranciers/afnemers (Report on the Suppliers/Customers Workshop)* (internal report; Utrecht: Stichting Natuur en Milieu).

Binney, G., and C. Williams (1992) *Making Quality Work: Lessons from Europe's Leading Companies* (London: Economist Intelligence Unit).

Birchard, B. (1999) 'Green management lurches ahead', *Tomorrow*, January/February 1999: 32-33.

Birkin, F., and D. Woodward (1997) 'Management Accounting for Sustainable Development', *Management Accounting* (UK), June 1997: 24-26.

Blauert, J., and S. Zadek (1998) (eds.) *Mediating Sustainability: Growing Policy from the Grassroots* (West Hartford, CT: Kumarian Press).

Blum, G., J. Blumberg and A. Korsvold (1997) *Environmental Performance and Shareholder Value* (Geneva: World Business Council for Sustainable Development).

BMU (Bundesumweltministerium; German Federal Ministry of the Environment) and UBA (Umweltbundesamt; German Federal Environment Agency) (eds.) (1997) *Leitfaden betriebliche Umweltkennzahlen (Basic Guide to Environmental Indicators for Companies)* (Bonn: BMU; Berlin: UBA).

Body Shop International (1996) *The Body Shop Approach to Ethical Auditing* (Littlehampton, UK: The Body Shop International).

Boer, M., B. Bakker and H. Muilerman (1996) *Kwaliteit van milieuverslagen: Welke eisen stellen de doelgroepen (Quality of Environmental Reports: What demands do the target groups have?)* (Rotterdam: Zuid-Hollandse Milieufederatie).

Bogiages, G.H., and Q. Vorster (1993) *Green Reporting in the Republic of South Africa* (Pretoria: University of Pretoria School of Accounting Sciences).

Bouma, J.J. (1996) *Management Accounting and Environmental Management: A Survey among German and Dutch Companies* (Rotterdam: Erasmus Centre for Environmental Studies).

Bragg, S., P. Knapp and R. McLean (1993) *Improving Environmental Performance: A Guide to a Proven and Effective Approach* (Letchworth, UK: Technical Communications).

Brophy, M. (1995) 'Review of UK Environmental Policies 1994–1995', *Business and Environment Abstracts* 2.1: 1-5.

Brophy, M., and R. Starkey (1996) 'Environmental Reporting', in R. Welford (ed.), *Corporate Environmental Management: Systems and Strategies* (London: Earthscan).

Brouwers, W., and A. Stevels (1997) 'A Cost Model for the End-of-Life Stage of Electronic Consumer Goods', *Greener Management International* 17 (Spring 1997): 129-39.

Brown, H., and T. Larson (1997) 'Demystifying the EMIS Purchasing Process and Decisions', *Environmental Quality Management*, Winter 1997: 21-27.

Brown, L., R. Ward and E. Titus (1996) 'Using New LCA Performance Metrics: Getting the Most out of your EMS', *Environmental Quality Management*, Autumn 1996: 3-10.

Bruck, M., C. Jasch and P. Tuschl (1996) *Handbuch für ökologische Bilanzierung in der Stein- und Keramischen Industrie* (Vienna: Austrian Chamber of Commerce).

BSI (British Standards Institute) (1994) *BS 7750: Specification for Environmental Management Systems* (London: BSI).

BTI (1997) *Benchmarking Environmental Management Performance* (Boston, MA: BTI Consulting Group).

Business and the Environment (1999) 'KPMG partners with The Body Shop to offer social auditing and reporting services', *Business and the Environment*, February 1999: 10.

Business in the Community (1998) *Business in Society: Assessing the Impact* (London: Business in the Community).

Business in the Environment (1992) *A Measure of Commitment: Guidelines for Measuring Environmental Performance* (London: Business in the Environment and KPMG Peat Marwick).

Business in the Environment (1994) *City Analysts and the Environment* (London: Business in the Environment and Extel Financial).

Business in the Environment (1996) *Index of Corporate Environmental Engagement* (London: Business in the Environment).

Business in the Environment (1998) *Index of Corporate Environmental Engagement* (London: Business in the Environment).

Business Roundtable (1993) *Facility-Level Pollution Prevention Benchmarking Report* (Washington, DC: The Business Roundtable).

Butner, S. (1996) 'Using the Internet for Environmental Benchmarking', *Seattle Daily Journal of Commerce: Environmental Supplement*, 3 August 1996.

BUWAL (Bundesamt für Umwelt, Wald und Landschaft) (1991) *Ökobilanzen von Packstoffen* (Schriftenreihe, 133; Bern: BUWAL).

C21 (1997) 'Environmental Reports: Worth the paper they're printed on?', at *http://www.activemultimedia.co.uk/c21* (17 September 1997).

Callens, I., and D. Tyteca (1995) 'Towards Indicators of Sustainable Development for Firms: Concepts and Definitions', *Fourth International Research Conference of the Greening of Industry Network* (Toronto, November 1995).

Canadian National Round Table on the Environment and the Economy (1997) *Measuring Eco-efficiency in Business* (Ottawa: Canadian National Round Table).

Cannon, T. (1992) *Corporate Responsibility* (London: FT/Pitman Publishing).

Capra, F. (1996) *The Web of Life: A New Synthesis of Mind and Matter* (London: HarperCollins).

Carter, C. (1997) *The Green Stream: Managing the Flow of Corporate Environmental Information* (Cambridge, UK: UK Centre for Environment and Economic Development).

CBI (Confederation of British Industry) (1996) *CONTOUR: Mapping Environmental, Health and Safety Performance* (London: CBI).

Centre for Sustainable Design (1997) *Environmental Reporting: A Video Guide for Environmental Managers and Designers* (Farnham, UK: Centre for Sustainable Design).

Centre for Sustainable Design (1998) *Corporate Environmental Reports: A Guide for Environmental Managers* (Farnham, UK: Centre for Sustainable Design).

Centre for the Study of Financial Innovation (1995) *An Environmental Risk Rating for Scottish Nuclear* (London: Centre for the Study of Financial Innovation).

Centre for the Study of Financial Innovation (1998) 'Rating Environmental Risk: The Eastern Experience', London, *www.csfi.demon.co.uk*.

Centre for Tomorrow's Company (1997) *The Inclusive Approach and Business Success* (London: Centre for Tomorrow's Company)μ

Centre for Tomorrow's Company (1998) *Sooner, Sharper, Simpler: A Lean Vision of an Inclusive Annual Report* (London: Centre for Tomorrow's Company).

Charkham, J. (1994) *Keeping Good Company: A Study of Corporate Governance in Five Countries* (Oxford: Oxford University Press).

Chemical Industries Association (CIA) (1996) *Responsible Care: The UK Indicators of Performance 1990–1995* (London: CIA).

CICA (Canadian Institute of Chartered Accountants) (1994) *Reporting on Environmental Performance* (Toronto: Canadian Institute of Chartered Accountants).

Clausen, J., and K. Fichter (1998) *Environmental Reports, Environmental Statements: Guidelines on Preparation and Dissemination* (Berlin: International Network for Environmental Management [INIM]).

Collins, J.C., and J.I. Porras (1995) *Built to Last: Successful Habits of Visionary Companies* (London: Century/Random House).

Communicopia (1998) 'Corporate Environmental Communications', at *http://www.communicopia.bc.ca/service/corprep.html*.

Company Reporting (1996) *Corporate Environmental Reporting in the UK* (Edinburgh: Company Reporting).

Company Reporting (1997) *The 1996 Environmental Reporting Scorecard* (Edinburgh: Company Reporting).

Confederation of Indian Industry (1995) *India: An Emerging Environmental Market. A Handbook for Trade and Business Opportunities* (New Delhi: Confederation of Indian Industry).

Conway-Schempf, N., and L. Lave (1996) 'Pollution Prevention through Green Design', *Pollution Prevention Review*, Winter 1995/96: 11-20.

Costanza, R., R. d'Arge, R. de Groot, S. Farber, M. Grasso, B. Hannon, K. Limburg, S. Naeem, R. O'Neill, J. Paruelo, R. Raskin, P. Sutton and M. van den Belt (1997) 'The Value of the World's Ecosystem Services and Natural Capital', *Nature* 387 (15 May 1997): 253-60.

Costaras, N.E. (1996) 'Environmental Risk Rating for the Financial Sector', *Journal for Cleaner Production* 4.1: 17-20.

Council on Economic Priorities and B. Hollister, R. Will, A. Tepper-Marlin, S. Dyott, S. Kovacs and L. Richardson (1994) *Shopping for a Better World* (San Francisco: Sierra Club Books).

Daly, H.E., and J.B. Cobb (1994) *For the Common Good: Redirecting the Economy toward Community, the Environment and a Sustainable Future* (Boston, MA: Beacon Press).

Danish Steelworks (1996) *Green Accounts 1996* (Denmark: Danish Steelworks).

Davis, J. (1994) *Greening Business: Managing for Sustainable Development* (Oxford: Blackwell).

Davis-Walling, P., and S. Batterman (1997) 'Environmental Reporting by Fortune 50 Firms', *Environmental Management* 21.6: 865-75.

Day, R. (1998) *Green Shareholder Value: Hype or Hit?* (Washington, DC: World Resources Institute).

De Villiers, C.J. (1996) 'Towards a Corporate Environmental Reporting Standard', *Meditari* 1996: 39-60.

De Villiers, C.J. (1997a) *Employee Reporting in South Africa* (Pretoria: University of Pretoria Department of Accounting, 4th edn).

De Villiers, C.J. (1997b) *Green Reporting in South Africa* (Pretoria: University of Pretoria Department of Accounting, 4th edn).

De Villiers, C.J. (1997c) 'Corporate Environmental Reporting: A Critical Analysis of the SAICA Recommendations', *Meditari* 1997: 1-16.

De Villiers, C.J. (1998) 'The Willingness of South Africans to Support More Green Reporting', *South African Journal of Economic and Management Sciences* NS 1.1: 145-67.

De Villiers, C.J., and Q. Vorster (1995) 'More Corporate Environmental Reporting in South Africa?', *Meditari* 1995: 44-66.

De Vries, I., and De Villiers, C.J. (1997) 'Ethical Investing by South African Unit Trust Managers', *Meditari* 1997: 34-47.

Deegan, C., and B. Gordon (1996) 'A Study of the Environmental Disclosure Practices of Australian Corporations', *Accounting and Business Research* 26.3: 187-99.

Deegan, C., and M. Rankin (1997) 'The Materiality of Environmental Information to Users of Annual Reports', *Accounting, Auditing and Accountability Journal* 10.4: 562-83.

Deloitte & Touche (1993) *Corporate Environmental Reporting 1993* (Copenhagen: Deloitte & Touche).

Deloitte & Touche (1996) *Corporate Environmental Reporting 1995* (Copenhagen: Deloitte & Touche).

Deloitte & Touche Miljo (1997) *Assessor's Manual* (Copenhagen: Deloitte & Touche Miljo).

DeSimone, L., and F. Popoff with the WBCSD (World Business Council for Sustainable Development) (1997) *Eco-efficiency: The Business Link to Sustainable Development* (Cambridge, MA: MIT Press).

DETR (Department of Environment, Transport and the Regions) (1998a) *Raising the Quality: Guidance to Director-General of Water Services on the Environmental and Quality Objectives to be Achieved by the Water Industry in England and Wales, 2000–2005* (London: DETR).

DETR (Department of Environment, Transport and the Regions) (1998b) *Opportunities for Change* (London: DETR).

Ditz, D., and J. Ranganathan (1997) *Measuring Up: Toward a Common Framework for Tracking Corporate Environmental Performance* (Washington, DC: World Resources Institute).

DoE (Department of Environment) (1995) *Environmental Facts: A Guide to Using Public Registers of Environmental Information* (London: HMSO).

Donley Technology (1996) *Environmental Management Information System Report* (Colonial Beach, VA: Donley Technology).

Doppegieter, J.J., and C.J. de Villiers (1996) 'Environmental Reporting Practices in the South African Energy Sector', *Management Dynamics* 5.1: 15-42.

Dow Chemical (1996) *1996 Progress Report on Environmental Health and Safety* (Midland, MI: Dow Chemical).

Doyle, P. (1994) 'Setting Business Objectives and Measuring Performance', *Journal of General Management,* Winter 1994: 1-19.

EAG Environ (1998) *Solving the Costs Puzzle* (Corsham, UK: EAG Environ).

Earth Resources Research (1993) *Costing the Benefits: The Value of Cycling* (a report for the Cyclists' Touring Club; London: Earth Resources Research).

Eberstadt, N. (1996) *The Tyranny of Numbers: Mismeasurement and Misrule* (London: Eurospan).

Eccles, R.G. (1991) 'The Performance Measurement Manifesto', *Harvard Business Review* January/February 1991: 131-37.

EHSSDG (Environmental Health and Safety Software Development Group) (1996) 'Functional Requirements Outline', presented at the 1996 *Environmental Health and Safety and Management Information Systems Conference*, Washington, DC.

Elkington, J. (1997) *Cannibals with Forks: The Triple Bottom Line of 21st Century Business* (Oxford: Capstone Publishing).

Elkington, J., and A. Spencer-Cooke (1997) 'How do we measure up?', *Tomorrow,* March/April 1997: 42-47.

Elkington, J., and H. Stibbard (1997) 'Socially Challenged', *Tomorrow,* March/April 1997: 54-59.

Elkington, J., and S. Fennell (1996) 'Verification: Can credibility be bought?', *Tomorrow,* September/October 1996: 58-61.

ENDS (1993) 'Improving the Chemical Industry's Performance: Lessons from the USA and Netherlands', *ENDS Report,* August 1993: 16-19.

ENDS (1996) 'ISO under fire over environmental standards', *ENDS Report,* September 1996: 3-4

ENDS (1997a) 'Environmental benchmarking project gets under way', *ENDS Report* 267 (April 1997): 6.

ENDS (1997b) 'CBI revamps environment forum with benchmarking scheme', *ENDS Report* 272 (September 1997): 8.

ENDS (1997c) 'Chemical Release Inventory at the Crossroads', *ENDS Report,* June 1997:19-21.

ENDS (1997d) 'Paper firm examines impact of transporting its products', *ENDS Report,* December 1997: 12.

ENDS (1998a) 'Benchmark studies confirm poor progress on stakeholder reporting', *ENDS Report,* February 1998: 8-9.

ENDS (1998b) 'Stakeholders drive reporting, but businesses discover other benefits', *ENDS Report,* October 1998: 9.

ENDS (1998c) 'Meacher asks top firms to report on greenhouse gases', *ENDS Report,* October 1998: 6.

ENDS (1999a) 'Loose ISO Framework on Measuring Environmental Performance', *ENDS Report,* January 1999: 10.

ENDS (1999b) 'Volvo issues externally verified product profile based on LCA', *ENDS Report,* January 1999: 26-27.

Engel, C.P., and A.K. Miedema (1998) *1997 Environmental Benchmarking Program* (unpublished, confidential report; Research Triangle Park, NC: Research Triangle Institute, Center for Economics Research, March 1998).

Environment Agency (1996) *Water Pollution Incidents in England and Wales 1996* (Bristol, UK: Environment Agency).

Environmental Accounting (1997) 'German Standard on Public Environmental Reports', *Environmental Accounting and Auditing Reporter,* June 1997: 3.

Environmental Accounting (1998a) 'Sustainability reporting is the new rock'n'roll', *Environmental Accounting and Auditing Reporter,* September 1998: 4-6.

Environmental Accounting (1998b) 'Verification Statements', *Environmental Accounting and Auditing Reporter,* September 1998: 6-7.

Environmental Accounting (1998c) 'Environmental Reporting: Europe', *Environmental Accounting and Auditing Reporter,* July/August 1998: 4-6.

Environmental Information Services, Inc. (1998) *Niagara Mohawk 1998 Environmental Research Project* (New York: Environmental Information Services, Inc.).

EPA (US Environmental Protection Agency) (1997a) *TRI Phase 3: Expansion of EPA Community Right-to-Know Program to Increase the Information Available to the Public on Chemical Use* (Office of Pollution Prevention and Toxics; Issues Paper, 3; Washington, DC: EPA).

EPA (US Environmental Protection Agency) (1997b) 'Sector Facility Indexing Project', *http://es.epa.gov/oeca/sfi/index.html*.

Epstein, M.J. (1996) *Measuring Corporate Environmental Performance: Best Practices for Costing and Managing an Effective Environmental Strategy* (New York: Irwin).

Erasmus, J.C. (1998) *Werknemers- en omgewingsverantwoording deur Suid-Afrikaanse genoteerde maatskappye* (unpublished DCom thesis; Pretoria: University of Pretoria).

Eskom (1997) *Continual Improvement Environmental Report 1996* (Johannesburg: Eskom).

Eskom (1998) *Environmental Report 1997: Managing Eskom's Impact on the Environment* (Johannesburg: Eskom).

European Commission (1993) 'Council Regulation (EEC) No 1836/93 of 19 June 1993 Allowing Voluntary Participation by Companies in the Industrial Sector in a Community Eco-Management and Audit Scheme', *Official Journal of the European Communities* L 168/1-18.

European Commission (1995) JOULE ExternE: Externalities of Energy (6 vols.; DG XII; Luxembourg: European Commission).

European Federation for Transport and Environment (1993) *Getting the Prices Right* (Brussels: European Federation for Transport and Environment).

European Green Table (1993) *Environmental Performance Indicators in Industry: A System for Corporate Environmental Performance Evaluation. Report 3: Draft Handbook* (Oslo: European Green Table).

European Green Table (1997) *Environmental Performance Indicators in Industry. Report 5: Practical Experiences with Developing EPIs in 12 Companies* (Oslo: Norwegian Confederation of Business and Industry).

Federal Environment Ministry and Federal Environment Agency (1997) *A Guide to Corporate Environmental Indicators* (Bonn: Federal Environment Ministry and Federal Environment Agency).

Feldman, S., and P. Soyka (1997) 'Capturing the Business Value of EH&S Excellence', *Journal of Corporate Environmental Strategy*, Winter 1997.

FASB (Financial Accounting Standards Board) (1998) 'Business Reporting Research Project', Washington DC, *www.fasb.org*.

FEE (Fédération des Experts Comptables Européens) (1996) *Research Paper on Expert Statements in Environmental Reports* (Brussels: FEE).

Fiksel, J. (1994) 'Quality Metrics in Design for Environment', *Total Quality Environmental Management* Winter: 181-92.

Fiksel, J., J. McDaniel and D. Spitzley (1998) 'Measuring Product Sustainability', *Journal of Sustainable Product Design*, July 1998: 7-18.

Financial Times Management (1998) *Visions of Ethical Business* (London: Financial Times Management).

Fitzgerald, C. (1995) 'Environmental Management Information Systems', *Total Quality Environmental Management*, Winter 1994/95: 21-33.

Fitzgerald, C. (1997) 'Systems vs Metasystems: EMS at the Crossroads', *Environmental Quality Management*, Winter 1997: 71-80.

Fomburn, C. (1996) *Reputation: Realizing Value from the Corporate Image* (Cambridge, MA: Harvard Business School Press).

Fondazione ENI Enrico Mattei (1995) *Company Environmental Reports* (Milan: Fondazione ENI Enrico Mattei).

Foundation of Performance Measurement (1998) 'The Well Rounded Company Report', Surbiton, UK, *www.fpm.com*.

Foy, P. (1996) 'The Re-invention of the Corporate Information Model', *IEEE Transactions on Professional Communications* 39.1 (March 1996): 23-29.

Frankel, C. (1998) *In Earth's Company: Business, Environment and the Challenge of Sustainability* (Gabriola Island, Canada: New Society Publishers).

Freedman, M. (1993), 'Accounting and the Reporting of Pollution Information', *Advances in Public Interest Accounting* 5: 31-43.

Freeman, H., T. Harten, J. Springer, M.A. Curran and K. Stone (1992) 'Industrial Pollution Prevention: A Critical Review', *Journal of Air and Waste Management Association* 42.5 (May 1992): 618-65.

Friedman, F. (1992) *A Practical Guide to Environmental Management* (Washington, DC: Environmental Law Institute).

Friedman, M. (1962) *Capitalism and Freedom* (Chicago: University of Chicago Press).

Fukuyama, F. (1995) *Trust: The Social Virtues and the Creation of Prosperity* (London: Hamish Hamilton).

Fussler, C., with P. James (1996) *Driving Eco-Innovation: A Breakthrough Discipline for Innovation and Sustainability* (London: FT/Pitman).

Galbraith, J.K. (1977) *The Age of Uncertainty* (London: BBC/André Deutsch).

Galbraith, J.K. (1992) *The Culture of Contentment* (London: Sinclair–Stevenson).

Gamble, G.O., K. Hsu, D. Kite and R.R. Radtke (1995) 'Environmental Disclosures in Annual Reports and 10Ks: An Examination', *Accounting Horizons* 9.3: 34-54.

Gameson, T. (1998) *Private Sector Methods for Weighting Environmental Indicators* (EUR 18655 EN; Brussels: Joint Research Centre, European Commission).

GCS (Green Consumer Society) and GRS (Green Reporting Forum) (1998) *The Current Situation of Environmental Reports: Towards the Evaluation of Environmental Performance in View of Green Consumption* (Kanagawa, Japan: GCS/GRS, 30 August 1998).

Geanuracos, J. (1997) *Performance Measurement: The New Agenda* (London: Business Intelligence).

GEMI (Global Environmental Management Initiative) (1992) *Environmental Self Assessment Program* (Washington, DC: GEMI).

GEMI (Global Environmental Management Initiative) (1994a) *Benchmarking: The Primer* (Washington, DC: GEMI).

GEMI (Global Environmental Management Initiative) (1994b) *Environmental Reporting in a Total Quality Management Framework* (Washington, DC: GEMI).

GEMI (Global Environmental Management Initiative) (1997) Measuring Environmental Performance: A Primer and Survey of Metrics in Use (Washington, DC: GEMI).

Gladwin, T.N., J.J. Kennelly and T.S. Krause (1995) 'Shifting Paradigms for Sustainable Development: Implications for Management Theory and Research', *Academy of Management Review* 20.4.

Glaxo Wellcome (1996) *Stakeholder Survey for Environmental Performance Report* (Oxford: Environmental Resources Management).

Gonella, C., A. Pilling and S. Zadek (1998) *Making Values Count: Contemporary Experience in Social and Ethical Accounting, Auditing and Reporting* (Research Report 57; London: Association of Chartered Certified Accountants/The New Economics Foundation).

Görtz, S. (1998) 'Environmental Debt', presentation to *Continuity, Credibility and Comparability* international expert seminar, Eze, France, 13–16 June 1998 (Malmø, Sweden: Sydkraft Konsult).

Grafe-Buckens, A. (1998) 'Environmental Statements: Meeting the User's Needs', paper presented to *Continuity, Credibility and Comparability* Invitational Expert Seminar, Eze, France, 13–16 June 1998, International Institute for Industrial Environmental Economics, Lund University, Sweden.

Grant, R., R. Shani and R. Krishnan (1994) 'TQM's Challenge to Management Theory and Practice', *Sloan Management Review*, Winter 1994: 25-35.

Gray, R. (1997) 'The Silent Practice of Corporate Social Reporting in Companies', in S. Zadek, P. Pruzan and R. Evans (eds.), *Building Corporate Accountability: Emerging Practice in Social and Ethical Accounting, Auditing and Reporting* (London: Earthscan).

Gray, R., J. Bebbington and D. Walters (1993) *Accounting for the Environment* (London: Paul Chapman/ Institute of Chartered Certified Accountants).

Gray, R., R. Kouhy and S. Lavers (1995a) 'Corporate Social and Environmental Reporting: A Review of the Literature and a Longitudinal Study of UK Disclosure', *Accounting, Auditing and Accountability Journal* 8.2: 47-77.

Gray, R., R. Kouhy, and S. Lavers (1995b) 'Methodological Themes: Constructing a Research Database of Social and Environmental Reporting by UK Companies', *Accounting, Auditing and Accountability Journal* 8.2: 78-101.

Gray, R., D. Owen and C. Adams (1996) *Accounting and Accountability: Changes and Challenges in Corporate Social and Environmental Reporting* (Hemel Hempstead, UK: Prentice–Hall).

Green Alliance (1996) *Corporate Environmental Reporting: Matching Stakeholder Needs for Reporting Methods* (London: Green Alliance).

Greenberg, R., and C. Unger (1992) 'Improving the Environmental Process', *Total Quality Environmental Management*, Spring 1992: 269-76.

Greiner, T. (1995) 'Normalizing P2 Data for TRI Reports', *Pollution Prevention Review*, Winter 1994/95: 65-75.

Grimshaw, C., M. Howard and M. Wilmott (1998) *The Responsible Organisation* (London: Future Foundation and BT).

Griss, P. (1999) 'The Mother of all Environmental Problems', *Tomorrow*, January/February 1999: 18-19.

Hammond, A., A. Adriaanse, E. Rodenburg, D. Bryand and R. Woodward (1995) *Environmental Indicators: A Systematic Approach to Measuring and Reporting on Environmental Policy Performance in the Context of Sustainable Development* (Washington, DC: World Resources Institute).

Hanssen, O.J. (1996) 'General Experiences from the EPI Project (Test Phase): Proposal for a Nordic EPI Network Project', *International Conference on Experiences with EPI* (Stockholm: Federation of Swedish Industries, 18 November 1996).

Harashina, S. (1998) 'EIA in Japan: Creating a More Transparent Society?', *Environmental Impact Assessment Review* 18.4: 309-11.

Hauschild, M., and H. Wenzel (1998) *Environmental Assessment of Products* (London: Chapman Hall).

Hearne, S. (1996) 'Tracking Toxics: Chemical Use and the Public's Right-to-Know', *Environment* 38.6 (July/August 1996).

Hibbitt, C., and H. Blokdijk (eds.) (1997) *Environmental Accounting and Sustainable Development* (Leiden: Limpberg Institute).

HMIP (Her Majesty's Inspectorate of Pollution) (1995) *Operator and Pollution Risk Appraisal (OPRA)* (London: HMIP).

Hobsbawm, E. (1996) *The Age of Capital* (London: Weidenfeld & Nicolson).

Hockerts, K. (1999) 'Innovation of Eco-Efficient Services: Increasing the Efficiency of Products and Services', in M. Charter and M.J. Polonsky (eds.), *Greener Marketing: A Global Perspective on Greening Marketing Practice* (Sheffield, UK: Greenleaf Publishing): 94-107.

Holgaard, J.E., H. Kirkegaard and A. Remmen (1999) 'Grønne Regnskaber' ('Green Accounts'), *Ugebladet Ingeniøren (The Engineer)*, 18.1–24.1 (Copenhagen, see e.g. *http://www.ing.dk/arkiv/0399/regnskab01.html*).

Hollandse Koopmansbank (1997) *Milieu als element in de beleggingsstrategie (Environment as an Element of the Investment Strategy)* (Utrecht: Hollandse Koopmansbank).

Hopkinson, P., and M. Whitaker (1998) *Corporate Environmental Reporting and the UNEP/SustainAbility Benchmarking Tool* (Bradford, UK: Sustainable Business Initiative. University of Bradford).

Horngren, C., and G.L. Sundem (1993) *Introduction to Management Accounting* (Englewood Cliffs, NJ: Prentice–Hall).

IASC (International Accounting Standards Committee) (1998) *IAS 37: Provisions, Contingent Liabilities and Contingent Assets* (London: IASC, September 1998).

IBM (1995) *Consulting the Stakeholder* (Portsmouth: IBM UK).

ICAA (Institute of Chartered Accountants in Australia) (1998) *The Impact of Environmental Matters on the Accountancy Profession* (Sydney: ICAA).

ICAEW (Institute of Chartered Accountants in England and Wales) (1992) *Business, Accountancy and the Environment: A Policy and Research Agenda* (London: ICAEW).

ICAEW (Institute of Chartered Accountants in England and Wales) (1996) *Environmental Issues in Financial Reporting* (London: Institute of Chartered Accountants in England and Wales).

ICAEW (Institute of Chartered Accountants in England and Wales) (1998) *The 21st Century Annual Report* (London: ICAEW).

ICI (1996) *Environmental Performance 1990/1995* (London: ICI).

ICI (1997) *Environmental Burden: The ICI Approach* (London: ICI).

IIIEE (International Institute for Industrial Environmental Economics) and VTT Non-Waste Technology (1997) *Challenges and Approaches to Incorporating the Environment into Business Decisions: International Expert Seminar* (Lund, Sweden: IIIEE; Helsinki: VTT).

Internet Business (1997) 'Web Design Stepping through the Minefield', *Internet Business* 8 (September): 86-87.

IOD (Institute of Directors in Southern Africa) (1994) *The King Report on Corporate Governance* (Johannesburg: IOD).

IÖW (Institut für Ökologische Wirtschaftsforschung) (1989) *Die Ökobilanz: Ein betriebliches Informationssystem* (Berlin: IÖW).

IRRC (Investor Responsibility Research Centre) (1996) *Environmental Reporting and Third Party Statements* (Washington, DC: Investor Responsibility Research Centre/Global Environmental Management Institute).

Irwin, F., T. Natan, W. Muir, E. Howard, L. Lobo and S. Martin (1995) *A Benchmark for Reporting on Chemicals at Industrial Facilities* (Washington, DC: World Wildlife Fund).

ISEA (Institute of Social and Ethical AccountAbility) (1997) *Towards Standards in Social and Ethical Accounting, Auditing and Reporting* (London: ISEA).

ISO (International Organization for Standardisation) (1996) *ISO 14001: Environmental Management Systems: Specifications with Guidance for Use* (Geneva: ISO).

ISO (International Organization for Standardisation) (1997) *ISO 14031 (Draft): Environmental Performance Evaluation* (Geneva: ISO).

ISO (International Organization for Standardisation) (1998a) *ISO 14040, Life-Cycle Assessment: Principles and Frameworks* (Geneva: ISO).

ISO (International Organization for Standardisation) (1998b) *ISO/DIS 14031, Environmental Performance Evaluation* (Geneva: ISO).

Jacobs, M. (1991) *The Green Economy* (London: Pluto).

James, P. (1993) 'Environmental Performance Measurement: The State of the Art', *EM & EARN Seminar: Environmental Performance Measurement and Reporting*, University of Wolverhampton, UK, 25 August 1993.

James, P. (1994a) 'Business Environmental Performance Measurement', *Business Strategy and the Environment* 3.2: 59-67.

James, P. (1994b) 'Quality and the Environment: From Total Quality Management to Sustainable Quality Management', *Greener Management International* 6 (Spring 1994): 62-71.

James, P. (1994c) 'Best Practice Benchmarking Guidelines', *Environmental Excellence*, December 1994: 25-27.

James, P. (1997) 'The Sustainability Cycle: A New Tool for Product Evaluation and Design', *Journal of Sustainable Product Design*, July 1997: 52-57.

James, P., and M. Bennett (1994) *Environmental-Related Performance Measurement in Business: From Emissions to Profit and Sustainability?* (Berkhamsted, UK: Ashridge Management Group).

James, P., M. Prehn and U. Steger (1997) *Corporate Environmental Management in Britain and Germany* (London: Anglo-German Foundation).

Japan Prime Minister's Office (1995) 'Attitude on Environmental Protection and Way of Life', *Opinion Poll* 27.9: 2-39.

Jasch, C. (1992) *Ökobilanzen in der Konservenindustrie: Veröffentlichung des Methodenteils zum Forschungs-projekt* (Schriftenreihe des IÖW, 13/1992; Vienna: IÖW).

Jasch, C. (1997) *Praxishandbuch Umweltmanagement und Öko-Audit: Wegweiser durch die ISO 14000 Normenserie in Verbindung mit der EMAS-Verordnung* (Vienna: WEKA-Verlag).

Jasch, C. (1998) *MEPI: Measuring Environmental Performance of Industry* (Informationsdienst, 4/1998; Vienna: IÖW).

Jasch, C., and R. Gyallay-Pap (1998) Environmental Statements and Environmental Performance indicators in Austria and Germany (Informationsdienst, 4/1998; Vienna: IÖW).

Jasch, C., and R. Rauberger (1998) *Leitfaden Umweltkennzahlen zur Messung der betrieblichen Umwelt-leistung* (Vienna: Bundesministerium für Umwelt, Jugend und Familie).

JCMA (Japan Chemical Manufacturers' Association) (1998) *Survey Report of Chemical Substances Release in 1996* (Tokyo: JCMA, 23 January 1998).

JEA (Japan Environmental Agency) (1969) *White Paper on Environmental Disruption in Japan* (Tokyo: Government Printing Office, May 1969).

JEA (Japan Environmental Agency) (1997) *Report of the Second International Symposium on the Reduction of Environmental Risks by Chemicals* (Tokyo: Government Printing Office, 1 July 1997).

JEA (Japan Environmental Agency) (1998a) *White Paper on the Environment in Japan* (Tokyo: Government Printing Office, June 1998): 107-27.

JEA (Japan Environmental Agency) (1998b) *Survey Report on PRTR Pilot Project* (Tokyo: Government Printing Office, April 1998).

Jebsen, I., and I.S. Schlumberger (1997) 'Auditing and Benchmarking Environmental Management: A Pioneer in the Off-Shore Service Industry', *Eco-Management and Auditing Conference*, Manchester, 3-4 July 1997.

Johnson, H., and R. Kaplan (1987) *Relevance Lost: The Rise and Fall of Management Accounting* (Cambridge, MA: Harvard Business School Press).

Johnson, S. (1996) 'Environmental Performance Evaluation: Prioritising Environmental Performance Objectives', *Corporate Environmental Strategy*, Autumn 1996: 17-28.

Jones, D.R. (1996) 'The Sustainable Enterprise: Leaning into the Future', *Fifth Greening of Industry Network Conference*, Heidelberg, Germany.

Jones, K., and T. Alabaster (1999) 'Critical Analysis of Environmental Reporting Scoring Systems', *Journal of Environmental Policy Assessment and Management* (in press).

Jones, K., T. Alabaster and K. Hetherington (1999) 'Internet-Based Environmental Reporting: Current Trends', (unpublished paper).

Kamp-Roelands, N. (1999) *Audits of Environmental Reports* (Amsterdam: NIVRA [Koninklijk Nederlands Institut van Registeraccountants]).

Kaneko, Y., and T. Sawada (1998) 'The Environment Measurement and Management System of Hitachi Ltd', *Instrument and Automation* 26.7 (June 1998): 16-19.

Kaplan, R. (1994) 'The Coming Anarchy', *The Atlantic Monthly* 273.2: 43-76.

Kaplan, R., and D. Norton (1992a) 'The Balanced Scorecard: Measures that Drive Performance', *Harvard Business Review*, January/February 1992: 71-79.

Kaplan, R., and D. Norton (1992b) 'Putting the Balanced Scorecard to Work', *Harvard Business Review,* September/October 1992: 134-42.

Kaplan, R., and D. Norton (1996a) *The Balanced Scorecard* (Cambridge, MA: Harvard Business School Press).

Kaplan, R., and D. Norton (1996b) 'Using the Balanced Scorecard as a Strategic Management System', *Harvard Business Review,* January/February 1996: 75-85.

Kelly, J. (1996) 'Could Try Harder', *Financial Times,* 17 April 1996.

Kingo, L. (1999) 'Challenges of Sustainability and the Role of Corporations', presentation to *Global Reporting Initiative Launch Conference,* Imperial College, London, 4–5 March 1999.

Klafter, B. (1992) 'Pollution Prevention Benchmarking: AT&T and Intel work together with the best', *Total Quality Environmental Management,* Autumn 1992: 27-34.

Klovning, J., and E. Nilsen (1995) 'Quantitative Environmental Risk Analysis', paper presented to *Society of Petroleum Engineers Annual Technical Conference,* Dallas, TX, 22–25 October 1995.

Kokubu, K., K. Tsunoda and T. Mizuguchi (1998) 'Environmental Reporting: Japan', *Environmental Accounting and Auditing Reporter,* July/August 1998: 6-9.

Konar, D. (1989) *An Empirical Investigation of the Informational Content of Corporate Social Responsibility Disclosure in S.A.* (unpublished DCom dissertation; Pretoria: University of South Africa).

Kotter, J., and J. Heskett (1992) *Corporate Culture and Performance* (New York: The Free Press).

KPMG (1997) *UK Environmental Reporting Survey 1997* (London: KPMG).

KPMG (1998) *Environmental Reporting in the Netherlands in 1996* (The Hague: KPMG).

Krut, R. (1997) *Sustainable Industrial Development: A Benchmark Evaluation of Policies and Reporting in the Electronics Industry* (Benchmark Environmental Consulting under contract to US Environmental Protection Agency, Office of Policy, Planning and Evaluation, November 1997).

Kuhn, T.S. (1970) *The Structure of Scientific Revolutions* (Chicago: University of Chicago Press).

Kuhre, W. (1998) *ISO 14031: Environmental Performance Evaluation* (Toronto: Prentice–Hall Canada).

Kunert AG (1996) *Environmental Report 1994/95* (Immenstadt, Germany: Kunert AG).

Kunert AG (1997) *Umweltbericht 1995/96* (Immenstadt, Germany: Kunert AG).

Larson, T., and H. Brown (1997) 'Designing Metrics that Fit', *Environmental Quality Management,* Winter 1997: 81-88.

LBG (London Benchmarking Group) (1997) *Companies in Communities: Getting the Measure* (London: LBG).

Leopold, A. (1949) *A Sand County Almanac* (New York: Oxford University Press).

Levering, R., and M. Moskowitz (1993) *The 100 Best Companies to Work for in America* (New York: Currency).

Levinson, J. (1997) 'Benchmarking Compliance Performance', *Environmental Quality Management,* Spring 1997: 1-12.

Levinson, J. (1998) 'Highlights from a New Chemical Industry Report Benchmarking Performance, Policies, and Expenditures', *Environmental Quality Management,* Summer 1998: 97-110.

Lober, D. (1996) 'Evaluating the Environmental Performance of Corporations', *Journal of Managerial Issues* 8.2 (Summer 1996): 184-205.

Lober, D. (1997) 'What makes environmental reports effective? Current Trends in Corporate Reporting', *Corporate Environmental Strategy* 4.2: 15-24.

Lober, D., D. Bynum, E. Campbell and M. Jacques (1997) 'The 100+ Corporate Environmental Report Study: A Survey of an Evolving Management Tool', *Business Strategy and the Environment* 6: 57-73.

Long, L. (1989) *Management Information Systems* (New York: Prentice–Hall).

Loughran, K. (1998) 'Kingo: The Queen of Reporting', *Tomorrow,* September/October 1998: 24-26.

Lovelock, J. (1988) *The Ages of Gaia* (New York: W.W. Norton).

Lowell, B., and D. Farrell (1996) *Market Unbound: Unleashing the Global Capitalism* (New York: John Wiley).

MacCarthy, F. (1994) *William Morris* (London: Faber & Faber).

Maddison, D., *et al.* (1996) *Blueprint 5: The True Costs of Transport* (London: Earthscan).

Marlin, A. (1998) 'Visions of Social Accountability: SA 8000', in Financial Times Management, *Visions of Ethical Business* (London: Financial Times Management).

Marsanich, A. (1997) *Environmental Indicators in EMAS Environmental Statements* (Milan: Fondazione ENI Enrico Mattei).

Martin, P. (1999) 'Real-Time Accounts', *Financial Times,* 2 March 1999.

Maruyama, T. (1993) 'Environmental activities of corporations progressing even under depression', *Shukan Toyo Keizai,* 25 December 1993: 122-24.

Maxwell, J., S. Rothenburg, F. Briscoe and A. Marcus (1997) 'Green Schemes: Corporate Environmental Strategies and their Implementation', *California Management Review*, Spring 1997: 118-34.

Mayhew, N. (1998) 'Trouble with the Triple Bottom Line', *Financial Times*, 10 August 1998.

McCarthy, M. (1998) 'Quality of Life Index will test national happiness', *The Independent*, 24 November 1998.

Menon, A., and A. Menon (1997) 'Enviropreneurial Marketing Strategy: The Emergence of Corporate Environmentalism as Market Strategy', *Journal of Marketing* 61 (January 1997): 51-67.

Merchant, C. (1992) *Radical Ecology* (London: Routledge).

Metcalf, K.R., P.L. Williams, J.R. Minter and C.M. Hobson (1996) 'Environmental Performance Indicators for Enhancing Environmental Management', *Total Quality Environmental Management* 5.4: 7-11.

Miakisz, J.A. (1994) 'Measuring Environmental Performance at Niagara Mohawk Power', *Total Quality Environmental Management*, Autumn 1994: 51-53.

Miakisz, J.A., and A.K. Miedema (1998) 'Environmental Performance Benchmarking for Electric Utilities', *Environmental Quality Management*, Summer 1998: 54-57.

Miljoeko (1997) *EMAS Environmental Statements: Analysis, Conclusions, Recommendations: A Survey of 465 EMAS Environmental Statements* (Stockholm: Miljoeko).

Mining Association of Canada (1998) *Environmental Progress Report* (Ottawa: Mining Association of Canada).

Ministry of Housing, Spatial Planning and the Environment (VROM) (Netherlands) (1996) *Industry and the Environment: Target Group Environmental and Industrial Policy in the Netherlands* (Video; Den Haag: Ministerie van VROM).

Ministry of Housing, Spatial Planning and the Environment (VROM) (Netherlands) (1997) *Act of 10 April 1997 Extending the Environmental Management Act to Provide for Environmental Reporting* (Bulletin of the Acts and Decrees of the Kingdom of the Netherlands, 1997/170).

Ministry of Housing, Spatial Planning and the Environment (VROM) (Netherlands) (1998) *Environmental Reporting Decree* (Bulletin of the Acts and Decrees of the Kingdom of the Netherlands, 1998/655).

MITI (Japanese Ministry of International Trading and Industry) (1994) *White Paper on International Trading and Industry* (Tokyo: Government Printing Office, May 1994): 76-88.

Monsanto (1996) *Environmental Annual Review 1996* (St Louis, MO: Monsanto).

Moody, G.H. (1977) *The Valuation of Human Life* (London: Macmillan).

Morgan, G. (1997) *Images of Organisation* (Thousand Oaks, CA: Sage).

MORI (1997) *Corporate Social Responsibility Study* (London: MORI).

Morris, J. (1998) *Climate Change: Challenging the Conventional Wisdom* (London: Institute for Economic Affairs).

Morris, V., J. Shopley and E. Turner (1998) ''The Role of Metrics in Sustainable Development: A Progress Report', *Prism*, 4th quarter 1998: 63-80.

Muilerman, H., B. Bakker and W. Berends (1992) *Naar een compleet en inzichtelijk milieuverslag (Towards a Complete and Transparent Environmental Report)* (Rotterdam: Zuid-Hollandse Milieufederatie).

Müller, K., J. de Frutos, K. Schussler and H. Haarbosch (1994) *Environmental Reporting and Disclosures* (Basel: European Federation of Financial Analysts' Societies).

Müller, K., J. de Frutos, K. Schüssler, H. Haarbosch and M. Randel (1996) *Eco-efficiency and Financial Analysis* (Basel: European Federation of Financial Analysts' Societies).

Müller-Wenk, R. (1978) *Die ökologische Buchhaltung* (Frankfurt/New York: Campus).

Murayama, T., and F. Nonaka (1997) 'Environment Management Activities and Response to Standardisation of ISO 14000s: The Case of Manufacturing Industries of Electric Appliances and Devices in Fukushima', *Fukushima University Regional Studies* 9.2 (October 1997): 51-66.

Naimon, J.S. (1994) 'Benchmarking and Environmental Trend Indicators', *Total Quality Environmental Management* Spring 1994: 269-81.

Nakagawa, M. (1998) 'Diffusion and Issues on ISO 14001', *JMA Management Review* 4.8 (August 1998): 5-7.

Nash, J., K. Nutt, J. Maxwell and J. Ehrenfeld (1992) 'Polaroid's Environmental Accounting and Reporting System', *Total Quality Environmental Management*, Autumn 1992: 3-15.

NEC Corporation (1998) *Annual Report on Environmental Management* (Tokyo: NEC, June 1998).

Neely, A. (1999) *Measuring Business Performance* (London: Economist Books).

NEF (New Economics Foundation) (1997) *More isn't always better* (London: NEF).

Nelson, J. (1998) *Building Competitiveness and Communities: How World Class Companies are Creating Shareholder Value and Societal Value* (London: The Prince of Wales Business Leader's Forum).

NEPP (National Environmental Policy Plans) (1989) *National Environmental Policy Plan 1* (The Hague: VROM [Dutch Ministry of Housing, Spatial Planning and Environment]).

NEPP (National Environmental Policy Plans) (1990) *National Environmental Policy Plan +* (The Hague: VROM [Dutch Ministry of Housing, Spatial Planning and Environment]).

NEPP (National Environmental Policy Plans) (1994) *National Environmental Policy Plan 2* (The Hague: VROM [Dutch Ministry of Housing, Spatial Planning and Environment]).

NEPP (National Environmental Policy Plans) (1998) *National Environmental Policy Plan 3* (The Hague: VROM [Dutch Ministry of Housing, Spatial Planning and Environment]).

Newall, S. (1996) *The Healthy Organisation: Fairness, Ethics and Effective Management* (London: Routledge).

NMPC (Niagara Mohawk Power Corporation) (1991) *Report on the Feasibility and Value of Establishing Environmental Performance Index* (Syracuse, NY: NMPC, December 1991).

Nortel (1997) *Fulfilling Our Commitments: A Progress Report on Environment, Health and Safety* (Brampton, Canada: Nortel; see also *http://www.nortel.com/cool/environ*).

O'Riordan, T. (1995) *Environmental Science for Environmental Management* (Harlow: Longman).

Obermurtaler Brauereigenossenschaft (1996) *Environmental Statement 1996* (Murau, Austria: Obermurtaler Brauereigenossenschaft GmbH).

OECD (Organisation for Economic Co-operation and Development) (1993) *OECD Core Set of Indicators for Environmental Performance Reviews* (Paris: OECD).

OECD (Organisation for Economic Co-operation and Development) (1996) *Pollutant Release and Transfer Registers (PRTRs): A Tool for Environmental Policy and Sustainable Development. Guideline Manual for Governments* (Paris: OECD).

OECD (Organisation for Economic Co-operation and Development) (1998) *Eco-efficiency* (Paris: OECD).

OFWAT (Office of Water Services) (1998a) *1997–8 Report on Levels of Service for the Water Industry in England and Wales* (Birmingham, UK: OFWAT).

OFWAT (Office of Water Services) (1998b) *1997–98 Report on Leakage and Water Efficiency* (Birmingham, UK: OFWAT).

Ollier, A. (1996) 'Corporate Environmental Reporting on the Internet', *Environmental Issues in Visual Communications Design Seminar and Workshops Proceedings*, 27 March 1996.

Orlin, J., P. Swalwell and C. Fitzgerald, 'How to Integrate Information Strategy Planning with Environmental Management Information Systems', *Total Quality Environmental Management*, Winter 1993/94: 193-202.

Owen, D. (ed.) (1992) *Green Reporting: Accountancy and the Challenge of the Nineties* (London: Chapman & Hall).

Owen, D., R. Gray and R. Adams (1997) *Corporate Environmental Disclosure: Encouraging Trends* (London: Association of Chartered Certified Accountants [ACCA]).

Owen, R. (1813). *A New Vision of Society: Or Essays on the Principle of the Formation of the Human Character.*

PACE University Center for Environmental Legal Studies (1990) *Environmental Costs of Electricity* (Debbs Ferry, NY: Oceana Publications).

Pachauri, R.K., and P.V. Sridharan (eds.) (1998) *Looking Back to Think Ahead: GREEN India 2047* (New Delhi: Tata Energy Research Institute [TERI]).

Palmer, J., and I. Cooper (1997) 'The Unsustainable Charm of Environmental Reporting: Lessons from Current UK Practice', at *http://www.pangea.org/events/sostenible/doc/palmer.html* (7 April 1997).

Palmer, J., and R. van der Vorst (1997) 'New Recipe Green Reporting for Small and Medium-Size Enterprises', *Eco-Management and Auditing* 4: 57-67.

Parker, A. (1997) 'The Expert View: Ben & Jerry's Homemade Inc., USA', in S. Zadek, P. Pruzan and R. Evans (eds.), *Building Corporate Accountability: Emerging Practice in Social and Ethical Accounting, Auditing and Reporting* (London: Earthscan): 129-42.

Pearce, D.W. (1991) *Blueprint 2: Greening The World Economy* (London: Earthscan).

Pearce, D.W., and E.B. Barbier (eds.) (1994) *Blueprint 4: Sustaining the Earth, Capturing Global Value* (London: Earthscan).

Pearce, D.W., A. Markandya and E.B. Barbier (1989) *Blueprint for a Green Economy* (London: Earthscan).

Pearce, D.W., *et al.* (1993) *Blueprint 3: Measuring Sustainable Development* (London: Earthscan).

Perugini, V. (1996) 'Anytime, Anywhere: The Social Impact of Emerging Communication Technology', *IEEE Transactions on Professional Communications* 39.1 (March 1996): 4-15.

Phillips, M., P. Sadler and D. Edington (1997) *The Inclusive Approach and Business Success: The Research Evidence* (London: Centre for Tomorrow's Company).

Plender, J. (1997) *A Stake in the Future* (London: Nicholas Brealey).

Porritt, J. (1984) *Seeing Green* (Oxford: Blackwell).

Power, M. (1997) *The Audit Society* (Oxford: Oxford University Press).

President's Commission on Environmental Quality (1993) *Total Quality Management: A Framework for Pollution Prevention* (Washington, DC: President's Commission on Environmental Quality).

President's Council on Sustainable Development (1996) *Sustainable America: A New Consensus* (Washington, DC: President's Council on Sustainable Development).

Price Waterhouse (1995a) *Better Change* (New York: Irwin).

Price Waterhouse (1995b) *The Annual Environmental Report: Measuring and Reporting Environmental Performance* (Copenhagen: Price Waterhouse).

Prothero, A., K. Peattie and P. McDonagh (1997) 'Communicating Greener Strategies: A Study of On-Pack Communication', *Business Strategy and the Environment* 6: 74-82.

Pruzan, P. (1997) 'The Ethical Dimensions of Banking: Sbn Bank, Denmark', in S. Zadek, P. Pruzan and R. Evans (eds.), *Building Corporate Accountability: Emerging Practice in Social and Ethical Accounting, Auditing and Reporting* (London: Earthscan): 63-83.

Randall, D. (1997) 'Consumer Strategies for the Internet: Four Scenarios', *Long Range Planning* 30.2 (April 1997): 157-68.

Rankin, M. (1996) *Corporate Reporting: The Green Gap* (Sydney: The Environmental Accounting Task Force of The Institute of Chartered Accountants in Australia).

Rappaport, A. (1998) *Creating Shareholder Value* (New York: Free Press).

Rasmussen, B.D., and A. Remmen (1997) 'Grønne Regnskaber: De første erfaringer' ('Green Accounts: The First Experience'), *Ugebladet Ingeniøren (The Engineer)* (Copenhagen), available in Danish only from *http://www.ing.dk/arkiv/regnskab.html*.

Rauberger, R. (1994) *Does environmental management help reduce costs? Case study of Kunert AG* (London: Imperial College of Science, Technology and Medicine, Centre for Environmental Technology).

Rauberger, R. (1995) 'Produktionsanlagen', in BMU/UBA (eds.), *Handbuch Umweltcontrolling* (Munich: Vahlen): 343-58.

Rauberger, R. (1996) 'Measuring and Reporting Environmental Performance', in J. Ulhøi and H. Madsen (eds.), *Industry and the Environment: Proceedings from the Third Conference of the Nordic Business Network* (Aarhus, Denmark: The Aarhus School of Business).

Rauberger, R. (1998) 'Environmental Reporting: The VfU Case of Benchmarking with Environmental Indicators in the Banking Sector', *Continuity, Credibility and Comparability* international expert seminar, Eze, France, 13–16 June 1998 (Augsburg: Institut für Management and Umwelt).

Rauberger, R., and B. Wagner (1996) *Environmental Reporting of Financial Service Providers: A Guide to Content, Structure and Performance Ratios of Environmental Reports for Banks and Savings Banks* (Berlin: Verein für Umweltmanagement in Banken, Sparkassen und Versicherungen [VfU] [Association for Environmental Management in Banks, Savings Banks, and Insurance Companies]).

Rauch, T., P. Leone and D. Gillhan (1997) 'Enabling the Book Metaphor for the World Wide Web: Disseminating On-line Information as Dynamic Web Documents', *IEEE Transactions on Professional Communications* 40.2 (June 1997): 111-27.

Reisman, G. (1997) *Capitalism: A Complete and Integrated Understanding of the Nature and Value of Human Economic Life* (New York: Jameson Books).

Rice, F. (1993) 'Who scores best on the environment?', *Fortune*, 26 July 1993: 104-11.

Rikhardsson, P.M. (1998) *Corporate Environmental Performance Measurement: Systems and Strategies* (Aarhus School of Business PhD thesis series; Aarhus, Denmark: The Aarhus School of Business).

Rikhardsson, P.M., and I. Bojsen (1998) 'Erfaringer med Miljøregnskaber i Danmark' ('Danish Environmental Reporting Experience'), in *Virksomhedens Økonomistyring (Corporate Accounting and Control Handbook)* (Copenhagen: Børsen, December 1998).

Rikhardsson, P.M., J.P. Ulhøi and H. Madsen (1996) 'Danish Environmental Reporting: An Empirical Study', *Eco-Management and Auditing Journal* 3.2: 63-68.

Ring, T. (1999) 'Net Profit', *Information Age*, January 1999: 17-20.

Ritzenthaler, G., and D. Ostroff (1996) 'The Web and Corporate Communication: Potential and Pitfalls', *IEEE Transactions on Professional Communications* 39.1 (March 1996): 16-22.

RIVM (1997) *Environmental Balance 96 and National Environmental Monitoring 1997–2020* (Alphen aan de Rijn: RIVM).

Robèrt, K.H. (1994) *Den Naturliga Utmaningen* (Falun, Sweden: Ekerlids Förlag).

Roberts, P. (1994) 'Environmental Sustainability and Business: Recognising the Problem and Taking Positive Action', in C.C. Williams and G. Haughton (eds.), *Perspectives towards Sustainable Environmental Development* (Aldershot, UK: Avebury Studies).

Robertson, D.C., and N. Nicholson (1996) 'Expressions of Corporate Social Responsibility in UK Firms', *Journal of Business Ethics* 15: 1095-1106.

Robesin, M. (1997) *Milieujaarverslagen beoordeeld: Milieujaarverslagen over 1995 langs de meetlat van milieu-organisaties (Environmental Reports Evaluated: Environmental Reports of 1995 alongside the Benchmark of Environmental Organisations)* (Utrecht: Stichting Natuur en Milieu).

Robson, C. (1994) *Real World Research* (Oxford: Blackwell).

Roddick, A. (1991) *Body and Soul* (London: Ebury Press).

Roome, N. (ed.) (1998) *Sustainable Strategies for Industry* (Washington, DC: Island Press).

Royal Commission on Environmental Pollution (1994) *Eighteenth Report: Transport and the Environment* (London: HMSO).

RSA (Royal Society of Arts) (1996) *Tomorrow's Company: The Role of Business in a Changing World* (London: RSA).

Rubik, F., and T. Baumgartner (1992) 'Technological Innovation in the Plastics Industry and its Influence on the Environmental Problems of Plastic Waste: Evaluation of Eco-Balances', *MONITOR: Strategic Analysis in Science and Technology (SAST) Activity* (SAST Project, 7; Brussels: Commission of the European Communities).

SAICA (South African Institute of Chartered Accountants) (1997) *Stakeholder Communication in the Annual Report* (Johannesburg: SAICA).

Sasol (1996) *Sasol Environmental Report 1996* (Johannesburg: Sasol).

Schaltegger, S., with K. Müller and H. Hindrichsen (1996) *Corporate Environmental Accounting* (Chichester, UK: John Wiley).

Schmidheiny, S., with the Business Council for Sustainable Development (1992) *Changing Course: A Global Perspective on Development and the Environment* (Cambridge, MA: MIT Press).

Schrama, G.J.I., and F. Schelleman (1996) 'Banks as External Stakeholders to Corporate Environmental Management: Trends in The Netherlands', paper presented at the *Fifth International Conference of the Greening of Industry Network*, Heidelberg, Germany.

Schulz, W., and E. Schulz (1995) *Ökomanagement* (Munich: dtv).

Schumacher, E.F. (1973) *Small is Beautiful* (London: Abacus).

Sessions, G. (ed.) (1995) *Deep Ecology for the 21st Century* (Boston, MA: Shambhala).

Seifert, E. (1996) *Linking Micro-Macro Information Systems of Integrated Economic and Environmental Accounting* (Wuppertal: Wuppertal Institute).

SETAC (Society for Environmental Toxicology and Chemistry) (1992) *Product Life Cycle Assessment* (Paris: SETAC).

Shapiro, K., E. Harriman and A. Dierks (1995) 'Measuring Toxic Use Reduction', *Pollution Prevention Review*, Summer 1995: 47-55.

Shell (1998a) *Profits and Principles: Does there have to be a choice?* (London: Shell International).

Shell (1998b) 'The Triple Bottom Line in Action', briefing paper at *www.shell.com/values/content/ 1,1240,1042-1175,00.html*.

Shrivastava, P. (1996) *Greening Business: Profiting the Corporation and the Environment* (Cincinnati: Thomson Executive Press).

Siegal, D. (1996) *Creating Killer Web Sites: The Art of Third Generation Site Design* (Indianapolis: Hatden Books).

Siegenthaler, C.P., C. Noppeney and F. Pagliari (1995) *Ökobilanz-software: Marktübersicht 1995* (Aldiswill, Switzerland: Schweizerische Vereinigung für ökologisch bewußte Unternehmungsführung).

Simon, J. (1996) *The State of Humanity* (Oxford: Blackwell).

Simon, J. (1997) *The Ultimate Resource 2* (London: Princeton University Press).

Simon, M., S. Evan, T. McAlone, A. Sweatman, T. Bhamra and S. Poole (1998) *Ecodesign Navigator: A Key Resource in the Drive Towards Environmentally Efficient Product Design* (Manchester: Manchester Metropolitan University and Cranfield University).

Skandia (1994) *Visualising Intellectual Capital in Skandia: Supplement to Skandia's 1994 Annual Report* (Stockholm: Skandia).

Skillius, A., and U. Wennberg (1998) *Continuity, Credibility and Comparability: Key Challenges for Corporate Environmental Performance Measurement and Communication* (report for the European Environment Agency; Lund, Sweden: International Institute for Industrial Environmental Economics).

Spannenberg, J. (1998) *Sustainability Indicators: A Compass on the Road towards Sustainability* (Wuppertal, Germany: Wuppertal Institute).

Spencer-Cooke, A. (1998) 'The True Asset of the Social Bottom Line', *The Tomorrow Exchange* (interactive video conference programme; Stockholm: Tomorrow Publishing, *www.tomorrow-web.com/exchange*).

Steyn, J.O., and Q. Vorster (1994) *Green Reporting in the Republic of South Africa* (Pretoria: University of Pretoria Department of Accounting, 2nd edn).

Stray, S. (1998) 'Corporate Environmental Reporting in Six Industrial Sectors', paper to the *Continuity, Credibility and Comparability* international expert seminar, Eze, France, 13–16 June 1998 (Warwick, UK: University of Warwick).

Subbaraman, S.R. (1997) *Sixth Environment Foundation Consultation on Corporate Social and Ethical Accounting, Auditing and Reporting: Summary of Proceedings* (London: Environment Foundation, April 1997).

SustainAbility (1999) 'Integrity at Work', *Sustainability Headlines*, March 1999: 3.

SustainAbility and UNEP (United Nations Environment Programme) (1996a) *Engaging Stakeholders. I. The Benchmark Survey: The Second International Progress Report on Company Environmental Reporting* (Paris: UNEP; London: SustainAbility).

SustainAbility and UNEP (United Nations Environment Programme) (1996b) *Engaging Stakeholders. II. The Case Studies* (London: SustainAbility/UNEP).

SustainAbility and UNEP (United Nations Environment Programme) (1997) *Engaging Stakeholders: The 1997 Benchmark Survey* (London: SustainAbility/UNEP).

SustainAbility and UNEP (United Nations Environment Programme) (1998a) *Engaging Stakeholders. The CEO Agenda: Can business leaders satisfy the triple bottom line?* (London: SustainAbility/UNEP).

SustainAbility and UNEP (United Nations Environment Programme) (1998b) *Engaging Stakeholders. The Non-Reporting Report* (London: SustainAbility/UNEP).

SustainAbility and UNEP (United Nations Environment Programme) (1999a) *Engaging Stakeholders. The Social Reporting Report* (in association with Royal Dutch/Shell Group; London: SustainAbility/UNEP).

SustainAbility and UNEP (United Nations Environment Programme) (1999b) *Engaging Stakeholders. The Internet Reporting Report* (London: SustainAbility/UNEP).

SustainAbility, Deloitte Touche Tohmatsu International (DTTI) and International Institute for Sustainable Development (IISD) (1993) *Coming Clean: Corporate Environmental Reporting* (London: DTTI).

Szekely, F., T. Vollman and A. Ebbinghaus (1997) *Environmental Benchmarking* (Cheltenham, UK: Stanley Thornes).

Taylor, B., C. Hutchinson, S. Pollack and R. Tapper (1994) *Environmental Management Handbook* (London: Pitman).

Ten Brink, P., R. Haines, S. Owen, D. Smith and B. Whitaker (1996) 'Consulting the Stakeholder: A New Approach to Environmental Reporting for IBM (UK) Ltd', in *Greener Management International* 13 (January 1996): 108-20.

Terada, H. (1998) 'ISO 14001 (Environmental Management System) in Japan', *Environmental Conservation Engineering* 27.2 (February 1998): 3-9.

Thy, C. (1997) 'Den danske lov om grønt regnskab: Elementer og implikationer' ('The Danish Act on Green Accounts: Elements and Implications'), in J. Ulhøi and P.M. Rikhardsson (eds.), *Virksomhedens Miljøregnskab: Måling, Rapportering og Revision* (*Corporate Environmental Reports: Measuring, Reporting and Audit*) (Copenhagen: Børsen).

Tokyo Electric Power Co. (1998) *Annual Report on Environmental Management* (Tokyo: Tokyo Electric Power Co.).

Tsotsi, Z. (1996), 'The Significance of Environmental Reporting for Industry', paper presented at *Ecoworld Conference*, Midrand, South Africa.

Tsunoda, K. (1994) 'A List and Outline of Corporations Implementing Environmental Audit', *Risaikuru Bunka* 46 (October 1994): 55-84.

Tsunoda, K., and M. Kawaguchi (1997) 'Follow-up Analysis of Environmental Protection Action Plans of Corporations', *Environmental Management* 33.11 (November 1997): 53-60.

Tulenheimo, V., R. Thun and M. Backman (eds.) (1996) *Tools and Methods for Environmental Decision-Making in Energy Production Companies* (Helsinki: VTT Non-Waste Technology; Lund, Sweden: International Institute for Industrial Environmental Economics).μ¤

Tuppen, C. (ed.) (1996) *Environmental Accounting in Industry: A Practical Review* (London: British Telecom).

Tyteca, D. (1994a) *DEA Models for the Measurement of Environmental Performance of Firms: Concepts and Empirical Results* (unpublished; Université Catholique de Louvain).

Tyteca, D. (1994b) *On the Measurement of Environmental Performance in Firms; Literature Review and Productive Efficiency Approach* (unpublished; Université Catholique de Louvain).

Tyteca, D. (1996) ''On the Measurement of the Environmental Performance of Firms: A Literature Review and a Productive Efficiency Perspective', *Journal of Environmental Management* 46: 281-308.

Ulhøi, J., and P.M. Rikhardsson (eds.) (1997) *Virksomhedens Miljøregnskab* (*The Corporate Environmental Account*) (Copenhagen: Børsen).

Umgeni Water (1997) *Environmental Report 1996-1997* (Durban, South Africa: Umgeni Water).

UNCED (United Nations Conference on Environment and Development) (1992) *Agenda 21* (Rio de Janeiro, 3–14 June 1992; Geneva: United Nations).

UNDP (United Nations Development Programme) (1997) *Valuing the Environment: How Fortune 500 Companies and Analysts Measure Corporate Performance* (New York: UNDP).

UNEP (United Nations Environment Programme) (1994a) *The UNEP Corporate Reporting Guide. Company Environmental Reporting: A Measure of Progress in Business and Industry towards Sustainable Development* (The UNEP Industry and Environment Activity Centre; Nairobi: UNEP).

UNEP (United Nations Environment Programme) (1994b) *Corporate Environmental Reporting* (Technical Report, 24; Paris: UNEP).

UNEP (United Nations Environment Programme) (1995) 'The Role of the Electronic Highway in the Preparation of Environmental Information for Decision-Making', *UNEP Seminar*, Arendal, Norway, 1 September 1995, at *http://www.eea.dk/frames/agency/mission/speeches/ARENDEL.htm*.

UNESCO (United Nations Educational, Scientific and Cultural Organisation) (1978) *Intergovernmental Conference on Environmental Education, Tibilisi (1997): Final Report* (Paris: UNESCO).

Unison (1995) *The Right Stuff: Using the Toxics Release Inventory* (Washington, DC: Unison Institute/ OMB Watch).

United Nations (1991) *Accounting for Environmental Protection Measures* (Paper E/C.10/AC.3/1991/5; New York: United Nations CTC ISAR).

United Nations (1998) *Position Paper: Accounting and Financial Reporting for Environmental Costs and Liabilities* (Geneva: United Nations Conference on Trade and Development, Commission on Investment, Technology and Related Financial Matters, Intergovernmental Working Group of Experts on International Standards of Accounting and Reporting).

Van Dalen, M. (1997) *Company Environmental Reporting: Conditions for the Optimal Information Structure of Environmental Reports* (Publicatiereeks milieubeheer 1997/6; Den Haag: Ministerie van Volkshuisvesting, Ruimtelijke Ordening en Milieubeheer).

Van Epps, R., and S. Walters (1996) 'Evaluating Environmental Performance with Tact and Insight', *Journal of Corporate Environmental Strategy*, Autumn 1996: 41-48.

Van Luijk, H., S. Carmichael, G. Hummels and A. ten Klooster (1995) *The Technology of Ethical Auditing* (Breukelen, Netherlands: Nijenrode University, Netherlands Business School and European Institute of Business Ethics).

Van Riemsdijk, P. (1997), 'The Yardstick of Sustainable Development: Getting Started with Self-Assessment', *AccountAbility*, Winter 1996/97: 3.

Van Soest, J.P., H. Sas and G. de Wit (1997) *Appels, peren en milieumaatregelen, Afweging van milieumaatregelen op basis van kosten effectiviteit* (Delft, Netherlands: Centrum voor energy besparing en schone technologie).

VBDO (Vereniging van Beleggers voor Duurzame Ontwikkeling) (1996) *Verslag symposium beleggers en duurzame ontwikkeling* (*Report on the Symposium on Shareholders and Sustainable Development*) (Culemborg, Netherlands: VBDO).

VNO/NCW (1996) *Milieuverslaglegging in perspectief: Stand van zaken* (*Environmental Reporting in Perspective: Current Status*) (Den Haag: VNO/NCW).

VNO/NCW and Stichting Natuur en Milieu (1998) *Het publieksmilieuverslag* (Den Haag/Utrecht: VNO/NCW, SNM [abridged English language version available: *The Public Environmental Report*]).

Von Weizsäcker, E.U., A.B. Lovins and L.H. Lovins (1997) *Factor Four: Doubling Wealth, Halving Resource Use* (London: Earthscan).

Wagner, B., and M. White (1994) 'Lessons from Germany: The Eco-balance as a Tool for Pollution Prevention', Proceedings of *Environment Virginia '94*, 7–8 April 1994, VM Institute, Lexington, VA: 48-52.

Walton, J., and T. Alabaster (1996) 'Institutional Environmental Reporting using the World Wide Web', *Industry and the Environment: Practical Applications of Environmental Management Approaches in Business: Proceedings of the 3rd Conference of the Nordic Business Environmental Management Network, 28–30 March 1996* (Aarhus, Denmark: Narayana Press).

Walton, J., T. Alabaster, S. Richardson and B. Harrison (1997) 'Environmental Reporting for Global Higher Education Institutions using the World Wide Web', *The Environmentalist* 17 (September 1997): 197-208.

WBCSD (World Business Council for Sustainable Development) (1995) *Achieving Eco-efficiency in Business* (Conches, Switzerland: WBCSD).

WBCSD (World Business Council for Sustainable Development) (1996a) *Environmental Performance and Shareholder Value*, (Geneva: WBCSD).

WBCSD (World Business Council for Sustainable Development) (1998) *How Companies Measure and Report their Eco-Efficiency* (Geneva: WBCSD).

WBCSD (World Business Council for Sustainable Development) (1999) *Eco-efficiency: Bulletin, January 1999* (Geneva: WBCSD).

WCED (World Commission on Environment and Development) (1987) *Our Common Future* (Oxford: Oxford University Press).

Weaver, P., with F. Schmidt-Bleek (1999) *Factor 10: Manifesto for a Sustainable Planet* (Sheffield, UK: Greenleaf Publishing).

Wehrmeyer, W. (1993) 'The Scientific Measurement of Environmental Performance', *EM and EARN Seminar, Environmental Performance Measurement and Reporting*, University of Wolverhampton, UK, 25 August 1993.

Wehrmeyer, W. (1995) *Measuring Environmental Business Performance: A Comprehensive Guide* (Business and the Environment Practitioner Series; Cheltenham, UK: Stanley Thornes).

Wehrmeyer, W. (ed.) (1996) *Greening People: Human Resources and Environmental Management* (Sheffield, UK: Greenleaf Publishing).

Welford, R. (1996a) 'Hijacking Environmentalism', in J. Ulhøi and H. Madsen (eds.), *Industry and the Environment* (Aarhus, Denmark: University of Aarhus).

Welford, R. (1996b) *Corporate Environmental Management: Systems and Strategies* (London: Earthscan).

Welford, R., and A. Gouldson (1993) *Environmental Management and Business Strategy* (London: Pitman).

Welford, R., and D. Jones (1994) *Measures of Sustainability in Business* (Huddersfield, UK: University of Huddersfield).

Welford, R., and R. Starkey (1996) *Reader in Business and the Environment* (London: Earthscan).

Wells, R.P., M.N. Hochman, S.D. Hochman and P.A. O'Connell (1993) 'Measuring Environmental Success', in Executive Enterprises Publications, *Measuring Environmental Performance: Selecting Measures, Setting Standards and Establishing Benchmarks* (New York: Executive Enterprises Publications): 1-13; also in *Total Quality Environmental Management*, Summer 1992: 315-27.

Wenzel, H., M. Hauschild and L. Alting (1997) *Environmental Assessment of Products* (2 vols.; London: Chapman & Hall).

Wheeler, D. (1996) 'Auditing for Sustainability: Philosophy and Practice of The Body Shop International', in L.L. Harrison (ed.), *The McGraw–Hill Environmental Auditing Handbook: A Guide to Corporate and Environmental Risk Management* (New York: McGraw-Hill).

Wheeler, D., and M. Sillanpää (1997) *The Stakeholder Corporation: A Blueprint for Maximising Stakeholder Value* (London: Pitman).

White, A., and D. Zinkl (1997) *Corporate Environmental Performance Indicators: A Benchmark Survey of Business Decision Makers* (Boston, MA: Tellus Institute).

White, A., and D. Zinkl (1998a) 'Raising Standardization', *The Environmental Forum*, 15.1 (January/February 1998): 28-37.

White, A., and D. Zinkl (1998b) *Green Metrics: A Global Status Report on Standardized Corporate Environmental Reporting* (Boston, MA: Tellus Institute, April 1998).

White, A., and D. Zinkl (1998c) *Touchstone: Issues in Sustainability Reporting. Volume 1* (Boston, MA: CERES, July 1998).

White, A., S. Helms and A. Dierks (1997) *Chemical Use Information Disclosure: Seeking Common Ground among Business and Environmental Stakeholders* (Boston, MA: Tellus Institute, October 1997).

White, M.A., and B. Wagner (1994) 'Lessons from Germany: The "Ecobalance" as a Tool for Pollution Prevention', *Proceedings of Environment Virginia '94* (Lexington, VA: Virginia Military Institute, 7–8 April 1994): 48-52.

WICE (World Industry Council for the Environment) (1994) *Environmental Reporting: A Manager's Guide* (Paris: WICE/ICC).

Wiebke, S. (1998) 'ISO 14001 in Developing Countries: The Indian Experience', *Tech Monitor*, September/October 1998: 30-37.

Willums, J.-O., with the World Business Council for Sustainable Development (1998) *The Sustainable Business Challenge: A Briefing for Tomorrow's Business Leaders* (Sheffield, UK: Greenleaf Publishing).

Wilson, A. (1998) *Social Reporting: An Executive Overview* (Berkhamsted, UK: Ashridge Centre for Business and Society).

Wolfe, A., and H.A. Howes (1993) 'Measuring Environmental Performance: Theory and Practice at Ontario Hydro', *Total Quality Environmental Management* Summer 1993: 355-66.

Worldwatch Institute (1994) *Vital Signs* (London: Earthscan).

Wright, M., R. Allen, R. Clift and H. Sas (1998) 'Measuring Corporate Environmental Performance: The ICI Environmental Burden System', *Journal of Industrial Ecology* 1.4: 117-27.

WSA (Water Services Association) (1997a) *Codes of Practice: Access to Environmental and Water Quality Information in the Water Industry* (London: Water Services Association of England and Wales).

WSA (Water Services Association) (1997b) *Water: Meeting the Challenge. The Vision of the Water and Sewerage Companies of England and Wales* (London: Water Services Association of England and Wales).

Wucherer, C., M. Kreeb and R. Rauberger (1997) 'Kostensenkung und Umweltentlastung bei der Kunert AG', in H. Fischer, C. Wucherer, B. Wagner and C. Burschel (eds.), *Umweltkostenmanagement: Kosten senken durch praxiserprobtes Umweltmanagement* (Munich: Hanser).

WWF (SA) (World Wide Fund for Nature South Africa) (1997) *1997 WWF Environmental Annual Report Award: Judges' Report* (Stellenbosch, South Africa: WWF [SA]).

WWF (World Wide Fund for Nature) (1996) *ISO Inside Out: ISO and Environmental Management* (Gland, Switzerland: WWF).

Yabe, H. (1998) 'ISO 14000 and the Environmental Strategy of Corporations: Comparative Analysis between EU and Japan', *Environment and Pollution* 27.3: 44-51.

Yorkshire Water plc (1998) *Environmental Protection and Stewardship 1998: Corporate Environmental Report* (Leeds, UK: Yorkshire Water).

Yoshizawa, T. (1998) 'Corporate Measures on Environmental Management System', *Standardization and Quality Control* 51.6 (June 1998): 4-8.

Young, C.W. (1996) 'Measuring Environmental Performance', in R. Welford (ed.), *Corporate Environmental Management: Systems and Strategies* (London: Earthscan).

Young, C.W., and P.M. Rikhardsson (1996) 'Environmental Performance Indicators for Business', *Eco-Management and Auditing* 3.3: 113-25.

Zadek, S., and R. Evans (eds.) (1993) *Auditing the Market: A Practical Approach to Social Auditing* (Gateshead, UK: Traidcraft/ New Economics Foundation).

Zadek, S., P. Pruzan and R. Evans (eds.) (1997) *Building Corporate Accountability: Emerging Practice in Social and Ethical Accounting, Auditing and Reporting* (London: Earthscan).

Zohar, D. (1997) *ReWiring the Corporate Brain: Using the New Science to Rethink how we Structure and Lead Organisations* (San Francisco: Barrett– Koehler).

Zohar, D., and I. Marshall (1993) The Quantum Society: Mind, Physics and a New Social Vision (London: Bloomsbury).

Biographies

Roger Adams is the Head of Technical Services and research at the Association of Chartered Certified Accountants (ACCA) in London. He is a member of the Environmental Task Force of the European Federation of Accountants (FEE) and is on the Steering Committee of the CERES Global Reporting Initiative (GRI). *roger.adams@acca.co.uk*

Shakeb Afsah is Senior Manager at the International Resources Group Ltd in Washington, DC. He has served as technical advisor for the PROPER programme in the Environmental Impact and Management Agency (BAPEDAL), Government of Indonesia, since 1994. *safsah@irgltd.com*

Martin Bennett is Principal Lecturer in Financial Management at Gloucestershire Business School, Cheltenham and Gloucester College of Higher Education, UK, where he recently moved after leading the Environmental Management Accounting Group at the University of Wolverhampton. He previously worked in the accountancy profession with BDO Binder Hamlyn and KPMG, in industry with Great Universal Stores, and in education with Nottingham Trent University and Ashridge Management College. His research interests include environmental accounting, environmental performance measurement and reporting, and the relevance of environmental performance in industry to financial stakeholders, on which he has run seminars and courses at Carnegie Mellon, Ghent and Brunel Universities. *MartinDBennett@compuserve.com*

Vandana Bhatnagar works with the Tata Energy Research Institute (TERI), New Delhi, India, as a research associate, in the field of corporate environmental management. Prior to that, she worked for over five years (1991–96) in Standard Chartered Bank, in areas including corporate lending, credit evaluation and marketing. She joined TERI at the end of 1996, to develop and implement the Eco-Rating programme—currently under implementation and dissemination. Other work areas include environmental management and strategy in Indian industry, barriers to financing of photovoltaic technologies, strategies for overcoming the same, and environmental indicator frameworks for municipal bodies. Her academic background is in the field of business management. *vbhat@teri.res.in*

Jan Willem Biekart has, since 1990, worked for the Dutch environmental NGO Stichting Natuur en Milieu (Netherlands Society for Nature and Environment), currently on the theme of Industry and Environment. His main areas of work are management systems, reporting, industry coalitions and new policy instruments. His educational background is in geology and environmental sciences. *j.w.biekart@snm.nl*

Charl de Villiers is Professor at the Department of Accounting, University of Pretoria, South Africa. He has authored and co-authored in excess of 30 refereed articles, research reports and popular-scientific articles, and presented 15 conference papers, including seven to international audiences outside South Africa. He is the editor, co-editor or referee of six journals, and the co-ordinator of the Department of Accounting at the University of Pretoria's ongoing research and tracking of all social reporting (including environmental reporting and employee reporting). He is an adjudicator of the annual WWF(SA) environmental report awards. His qualifications are Chartered Accountant (SA), MBA (University of Stellenbosch), Doctor of Commerce (Environmental Accounting) (University of Pretoria). *cdeville@hakuna.up.ac.za*

John Elkington is Chairman and founder of strategy consultants SustainAbility, Chairman of The Environment Foundation, author of *Cannibals with Forks: The Triple Bottom Line of 21st Century Business* (Oxford: Capstone Publishing, 1997), and a member of the Council of the Institute of Social and Ethical Accountability (ISEA) and of the Steering Group of the Global Reporting Initiative (GRI). *elkington@sustainability.co.uk*

Dr **Peter Hopkinson** is a lecturer in environmental economics and management at the University of Bradford and co-director of the Sustainable Business Initiative. He runs the UK's only postgraduate programme in Business Strategy and Environmental Management, which seeks to integrate environmental thinking into mainstream business processes. He is currently involved in an EU project investigating the development of eco-innovation, service developments, and a UK Skills Challenge Project to develop IT-based environmental management training for SMEs. *p.g.hopkinson@bradford.ac.uk*

Martin Houldin is a management accountant turned environmental management systems accreditation expert. Formerly part of KPMG's environmental team, he is now a director of EMAG Ltd, a specialist environmental consultancy. Martin has been deeply involved in the implementation of ISO 14000 systems in various multinational companies and in environmental management training and education. He is the chairman of the Institute of Environmental Management Standards and Accreditation Panel and sits on various environmental committees. He works in Europe, the Far East, Africa and North America. *martinhouldin_emag@compuserve.com*

Andy Hughes manages an open learning programme in Business Strategy and Environmental Management at the University of Bradford, UK. His recent research includes environmental impacts on corporate distribution strategy, eco-innovation and product development, environmental accounting, and environmental influences on institutional investors' analyses and stock market performance. His recent background is in environmental management consultancy, and corporate environmental management with the NatWest Group, where he implemented the IT Division's environmental management and performance measurement systems. Prior to becoming involved in environmental management, Andy managed consumer credit marketing, also at NatWest. *a.r.hughes3@bradford.ac.uk*

Peter James has worked as a consultant; business school researcher, teacher and professor; and manager and journalist in the areas of management of technology and environmental management. This has included positions with BBC Television Science Features department and as senior research fellow at the University of Warwick Business School, Professor of Management and MBA director at the University of Limerick and Assistant Director, Research, at Ashridge Management College. He is currently Visiting Professor of Environmental Management at the University of Bradford and a research associate of Ashridge and the UK Centre for Environment and Economic Development. His publications, with co-authors, include *The Green Bottom Line: Environmental Accounting for Management* (Greenleaf Publishing, 1998), *Driving Eco-*

Innovation (FT Pitman, 1996), *Corporate Environmental Management in Britain and Germany* (Anglo-German Foundation, 1997) and *Environment under the Spotlight: Current Practice and Future Trends in Environment-Related Performance Measurement in Business* (ACCA, 1998), as well as many articles on environmental management, environmental accounting, performance evaluation and product evaluation for environmental and business journals.
sustainablebusiness@compuserve.com

Christine Jasch is founder and manager of the Vienna Institut für Ökologische Wirtschafts-forschung (IÖW) (Institute for Environmental Management and Economics). She studied political economy, business administration and agriculture, and works as an independent tax advisor and chartered public accountant in Vienna. Her scientific emphasis at the Institute lies in the linkage of business and economic instruments with environmentally relevant criteria, as well as their further development as a decision tool for environmental policy. Further working areas include environmental performance evaluation and indicators, ecobalances and product life-cycle assessment, environmental management and eco-auditing, green accounting and ecotaxes, ecological product design and eco-services. She is Austrian delegate to ISO TC207 Environmental Management SC 1, 2 and 4 and chairperson at the equivalent Austrian Standardisation Body. She is Austrian delegate to the Environmental Task Force of the Fédération des Experts Comptables Européens (FEE) in Brussels and founder of the Austrian Institute for verifiers, auditors and environmental consultants. She was registered as Principal Environmental Auditor at the Environmental Auditor Registration Association (EARA) in the UK and accredited as lead verifier under the EMAS regulation in December 1995. *info@ioew.at*

Kathryn Jones is a Research Assistant at the Centre for Environmental Informatics (CEI), University of Sunderland, UK. She has been employed on two European Projects, the latest of which involves an analysis of the environmental disclosures in corporate annual/financial reports. She has also published papers in relation to environmental reporting via the Internet and has developed the free on-line environmental reporting clearing house (*http://cei.sund.ac.uk/envrep/index.htm*). *kathryn.jones@sunderland.ac.uk*

Leon Klinkers has worked at several universities, researching the role of internal communication as a critical success factor in implementing an environmental management system and was jointly responsible for developing an international postgraduate course in environmental management. He currently works for PricewaterhouseCoopers and advises companies on strategic environmental management, integrated supply chain management, EMS and environmental marketing. He also advises the Netherlands Ministry of Housing, Spatial Planning and Environment on the initiation, implementation and evaluation of their policies. *leon.klinkers@nl.pwcglobal.com*

Niklas Kreander is co-author of the SustainAbility/UNEP 1997 *Benchmark Survey*. He has also worked for Deloitte & Touche Environmental Services and was part of the team responsible for *Environmental Reporting: A Nordic Survey* and the Finnish survey of environmental reporting.

Riva Krut, President of Benchmark Environmental Consulting, is an organisational and management development consultant who works on sustainable development and corporate environmental management. *benchmark@mindspring.com*

Joseph A. Miakisz has 23 years of experience in the environmental field and currently serves as Director, Environmental Regulatory Affairs for Niagara Mohawk Power Corporation (an investor-owned electric and gas company) in Syracuse, New York. He has authored several papers on the subject of environmental performance measurement and the integration of environmental factors into mainstream business planning activities. *cardm@nimo.com*

Ken Munis is an analyst in the US Environmental Protection Agency, Office of Policy Development, working on issues of corporate sustainability. *munis.ken@epamail.epa.gov*

Takehiko Murayama is an Associate Professor at the Faculty of Administration and Social Sciences, Fukushima University, Japan. He received his PhD in Engineering (Environmental Policy and Planning) in 1989 from the Tokyo Institute of Technology. His major field of research is the decision-making process in risk assessment and management. He is a member of several national and local government committees, including those concerned with the development of the Pollutant Release and Transfer Register (PRTR) system, a remedial system for hazardous waste sites and a research project on risk communication. He is a member of the Editorial Board of the US journal, *Risk: Health, Safety and Environment*. *tmurayam@ads.fukushima-u.ac.jp*

Janet Ranganathan is a Senior Associate in the Management Institute for Environment and Business at the World Resources Institute in Washington, DC, where she works on business sustainability issues. She is co-author and editor of the WRI publications: *Green Ledgers: Case Studies in Corporate Environmental Accounting*, with Daryl Ditz and Darryl Banks, and *Measuring Up: Toward a Common Framework for Tracking Corporate Environmental Performance*, which she co-authored with Daryl Ditz. Prior to joining WRI, she worked on business and environmental issues in the UK both as a Senior Lecturer at the University of Hertfordshire and in a regulatory capacity with Hertfordshire Waste Regulatory Authority. *janetr@wri.org*

Damayanti Ratunanda is the lead analyst of the PROPER Team at the Environmental Impact and Management Agency (BAPEDAL), Government of Indonesia.

Rainer Rauberger studied Applied Economics at the Universities of Augsburg, Germany, and Mons, Belgium, and holds a Master's degree in Environmental Technology from Imperial College, London. He worked for Kunert AG in 1992–93 on an in-house project on ecobalancing, and from then as an external consultant. Since 1994 he has worked as an environmental consultant at the Institut für Management und Umwelt (Institute for Management and Environment) in Augsburg. He has consultancy experience in various industry and service sectors, and has participated in various research projects. Since 1996, he has been a member of the German Standardisation Board for Environment and a German delegate to ISO TC207 SC4, 'Environmental Performance Evaluation'. He lectures in Environmental Management at Augsburg University and at Augsburg Polytechnic. *imu.rauberger@augsburg.baynet.de*

Karin Ree has been Co-ordinator of the Chemistry Shop (Science Shop) at the University of Groningen since 1986. The Chemistry Shop is a department for research and advice on behalf of non-commercial organisations and individuals; its main topics are in the fields of environmental chemistry and industrial health and safety. Karin Ree is an environmental chemist by training. *c.m.ree@chem.rug.nl*

Pall M. Rikhardsson holds a PhD from the Aarhus School of Business in corporate environmental management. He is a senior consultant with Corporate Accountability Services of PricewaterhouseCoopers in Denmark. The main types of client service undertaken by Dr Rikhardsson are design and implementation of environmental management information systems, assistance in the selection of environmental reporting strategies, and environmental reporting assurance services. Dr Rikhardsson is also an external lecturer on environmental reporting and environmental information systems at the Aarhus School of Business in Denmark. *pall.m.rikhardsson@dk.pwcglobal.com*

Prior to joining KPMG's Sustainability Advisory Services team in January 1999, **Maria Sillanpää** was responsible for The Body Shop's auditing and public reporting on environmental, animal protection and social performance. An acknowledged expert on social auditing, Maria has an academic track record in corporate social responsibility, business ethics and stakeholder management. Published in a variety of academic and management journals and co-author of *The Stakeholder Corporation*, she is an Industrial Fellow at Kingston University Centre for Stakeholding and Sustainable Enterprise and a Council member of the Institute of Social and Ethical Accountability. *maria.sillanpaa@kpmg.co.uk*

Saskia Slomp is Technical Director for the Brussels-based European Federation of Accountants (FEE). A member of Royal NIVRA, the leading Dutch accountancy body, she spent eight years as an auditor with KPMG before joining FEE where she has responsibility for a wide range of technical topics, including the FEE Environmental Task Force. *secretariat@fee.be*

Helen Stibbard is a co-author of the SustainAbility/UNEP 1997 Benchmark Survey. She was also part of the 1996 company environmental reporting team that produced *Engaging Stakeholders. Volume 1: The Benchmark Survey* and *Volume 2: The Case Studies* which focused on 12 different report users.

At the time of writing the paper for this volume, **Willem van der Werf** worked as an environmental engineer for the Unilever companies of Van den Bergh Nederland, which has six companies operating in the food sector.

Franceska van Dijk heads SustainAbility's social reporting programme and is co-author of *The Social Reporting Report*. *vandijk@sustainability.co.uk*

Bernd Wagner is Professor in Economics and Programme Director at Augsburg University Management Centre, Germany. He initiated the Kunert ecobalance project in 1990 and is co-founder of the Institute für Management und Umwelt (Institute for Management and Environment) in Augsburg. He has had much consultancy and research experience in various fields of environmental management. In the 1980s, he held short-term lectureships in Freetown, Sierra Leone, and Beijing. *bernd.wagner@ksm.uni-augsburg.de*

Dr **Julia Walton** is a researcher at the Centre for Environmental Informatics (CEI), University of Sunderland, UK. She has co-ordinated two European Projects incorporating environmental reporting; co-produced two environmental reports for the University via hard copy and the World Wide Web; and recently published in *The Environmentalist*. Her current research areas include international environmental voluntary agreements and environmental and sustainability reporting strategies. *julia.walton@sunderland.ac.uk*

Richard J. Welford is Professor of Corporate Environmental Management and Director of the Centre for Corporate Environmental Management at Huddersfield University Business School and Visiting Professor at the Norwegian School of Management. He has published widely on corporate environmental management and sustainable development and is editor of *Business Strategy and the Environment* and *Sustainable Development* journals.

Mick Whitaker worked for Yorkshire Water for nearly 30 years both in waste and in clean water treatment services. Latterly, he as worked for the Environment Unit, with responsibility for publishing the corporate environmental report and for developing greener purchasing policies. He was the Yorkshire Water plc representative in the Water Industry Group to develop key environmental performance indicators for the water industry. He is now a freelance environmental consultant specialising in water-related project work.

Allen L. White, PhD, is Vice-President of Tellus Institute in Boston, MA, a non-profit, independent research and consulting organisation. He is also affiliated with the Stockholm Environment Institute, Boston. Dr White is the principal technical advisor to the Global Reporting Initiative, an international effort to develop uniform corporate sustainability reporting guidelines worldwide. *awhite@tellus.org*

Andrew Wilson is Director of the Centre for Business and Society at Ashridge, a leading international business school in the UK. He is responsible for a series of major research programmes investigating issues of global business ethics; social auditing and reporting; and the convergence of values across public, private and voluntary sectors. As well as conducting research and consultancy, Andrew is the programme director of the Ashridge/Business in the Community executive development programme, Managing Corporate Community Investment. He has presented papers to a large number of international conferences including those organised by the American Academy of Management and the British Academy of Management. *andrew.wilson@ashridge.org.uk*

Dr **C. William Young** is a Research Associate at the Manchester School of Management at the University of Manchester Institute of Science and Technology. His current research includes sustainable households, environmental performance indicators and sustainable development indicators. He is also a UK expert sitting on the ISO 14031 Environmental Performance Evaluation standard guidelines drafting committee.

Diana M. Zinkl is a former research analyst at Tellus Institute in Boston, MA, a non-profit, independent research and consulting organisation. *william.young@umist.ac.uk*

Index